'This book provides excellent coverage of the s[...]
be widely used . . . I am especially struck by the very good balan[...]
rial pertaining to the state of the discipline and material bearing on particular
issues. I only wish I had written for it!'
Paul Heelas, Professor of Sociology of Religion, Lancaster University

'This is an exciting and interesting book which I will certainly enjoy reading.'
Eileen Barker, Professor of Sociology, London School of Economics and
Political Science

'I will jump at the chance to use this book . . . Fenn does good work, typically
innovative.'
Phillip E. Hammond, D. Mackenzie Brown, Professor of Religious Studies,
University of California, Santa Barbara

'This is a book to savour and return to.'
Mark D. Chapman, Ripon College, Cuddesdon

Blackwell Companions to Religion

The Blackwell Companions to Religion series presents a collection of the most recent scholarship and knowledge about world religions. Each volume draws together newly-commissioned essays by distinguished authors in the field, and is presented in a style which is accessible to undergraduate students, as well as scholars and the interested general reader. These volumes approach the subject in a creative and forward-thinking style, providing a forum in which leading scholars in the field can make their views and research available to a wider audience.

Published

The Blackwell Companion to Judaism
Edited by Jacob Neusner and Alan J. Avery-Peck

The Blackwell Companion to Sociology of Religion
Edited by Richard K. Fenn

The Blackwell Companion to the Hebrew Bible
Edited by Leo G. Perdue

The Blackwell Companion to Postmodern Theology
Edited by Graham Ward

The Blackwell Companion to Hinduism
Edited by Gavin Flood

The Blackwell Companion to Political Theology
Edited by Peter Scott and William T. Cavanaugh

The Blackwell Companion to Protestantism
Edited by Alister E. McGrath and Darren C. Marks

The Blackwell Companion to Modern Theology
Edited by Gareth Jones

The Blackwell Companion to Christian Ethics
Edited by Stanley Hauerwas and Samuel Wells

The Blackwell Companion to Religious Ethics
Edited by William Schweiker

Forthcoming

The Blackwell Companion to the Study of Religion
Edited by Robert A. Segal

The Blackwell Companion to Eastern Christianity
Edited by Ken Parry

The Blackwell Companion to Christian Spirituality
Edited by Arthur Holder

The Blackwell Companion to the New Testament
Edited by David Aune

The Blackwell Companion to Sociology of Religion

Edited by

Richard K. Fenn

Princeton Theological Seminary

© 2001, 2003 by Blackwell Publishing Ltd
except for editorial material and organization © 2001, 2003 by Richard K. Fenn

350 Main Street, Malden, MA 02148-5020, USA
108 Cowley Road, Oxford OX4 1JF, UK
550 Swanston Street, Carlton, Victoria 3053, Australia

First published 2001
First published in paperback 2003 by Blackwell Publishing Ltd
Reprinted 2004

Library of Congress Cataloging-in-Publication Data

The Blackwell companion to sociology of religion / edited by Richard K. Fenn.
    p.   cm. — (Blackwell companions to religion)
  Includes bibliographical references and index.
  ISBN 0–631–21240–X (hardcover : alk. paper) — ISBN 0–631–21241–8 (pbk. : alk.
paper)
  1. Religion and sociology.   I. Series.

  BL60 .B53   2000
  306.6—dc21   00-060791

A catalogue record for this title is available from the British Library.

Set in 10½ on 12½ pt Photina
by Best-set Typesetter Ltd, Hong Kong
Printed and bound in the United Kingdom
by TJ International Ltd, Padstow, Cornwall

For further information on
Blackwell Publishing, visit our website:
http://www.blackwellpublishing.com

Contents

List of contributors   viii
Acknowledgments   xii
Preface   xiv

Part I Classical and Contemporary Theory: Recycling, Continuity, Progress, or New Departures?

Editorial Commentary: Religion and the Secular; the Sacred
and the Profane: The Scope of the Argument   3

1 Personal Reflections in the Mirror of Halévy and Weber
   David Martin   23

2 Salvation, Secularization, and De-moralization
   Bryan Wilson   39

3 The Pentecostal Gender Paradox: A Cautionary Tale for
   the Sociology of Religion
   Bernice Martin   52

4 Feminism and the Sociology of Religion: From
   Gender-blindness to Gendered Difference
   Linda Woodhead   67

5 Melancholia, Utopia, and the Psychoanalysis of Dreams
   Donald Capps   85

6 Georg Simmel: American Sociology Chooses the Stone
   the Builders Refused
   Victoria Lee Erickson   105

7   Transformations of Society and the Sacred in Durkheim's
    Religious Sociology
    Donald A. Nielsen   120

8   Classics in the Sociology of Religion: An Ambiguous
    Legacy
    Roger O'Toole   133

9   Individualism, the Validation of Faith, and the Social
    Nature of Religion in Modernity
    Danièle Hervieu-Léger   161

10 The Origins of Religion
    Richard K. Fenn   176

Part II   Contemporary Trends in the Relation of
            Religion to Society

    Editorial Commentary: Whose Problem is it? The Question of
    Prediction versus Projection   197

11 Secularization Extended: From Religious "Myth" to
    Cultural Commonplace
    Nicholas J. Demerath III   211

12 Social Movements as Free-floating Religious Phenomena
    James A. Beckford   229

13 The Social Process of Secularization
    Steve Bruce   249

14 Patterns of Religion in Western Europe: An Exceptional
    Case
    Grace Davie   264

15 The Future of Religious Participation and Belief in Britain
    and Beyond
    Robin Gill   279

16 Religion as Diffusion of Values. "Diffused Religion" in the
    Context of a Dominant Religious Institution: The Italian
    Case
    Roberto Cipriani   292

17 Spirituality and Spiritual Practice
    Robert Wuthnow   306

18 The Renaissance of Community Economic Development
    among African-American Churches in the 1990s
    Katherine Day   321

19   Hell as a Residual Category: Possibilities Excluded from the
      Social System
      Richard K. Fenn and Marianne Delaporte   336

**Part III   The Sociology of Religion and Related Areas
             of Inquiry**

      Editorial Commentary: Looking for the Boundaries of the
      Field: Social Anthropology, Theology, and Ethnography   363

20   Acting Ritually: Evidence from the Social Life of Chinese
      Rites
      Catherine Bell   371

21   Moralizing Sermons, Then and Now
      Thomas Luckmann   388

22   Health, Morality and Sacrifice: The Sociology of
      Disasters
      Douglas J. Davies   404

23   Contemporary Social Theory as it Applies to the
      Understanding of Religion in Cross-cultural
      Perspective
      Peter Beyer   418

24   The Return of Theology: Sociology's Distant Relative
      Kieran Flanagan   432

25   Epilogue: Toward a Secular View of the Individual
      Richard K. Fenn   445

Index   469

Contributors

James A. Beckford is Professor of Sociology at the University of Warwick. His main publications in the sociology of religion include *Religious Organization* (1973), *Cult Controversies. The Societal Response to New Religious Movements* (1985), and *Religion in Prison. Equal Rites in a Multi-Faith Society* (with Sophie Gilliat, 1998). He is the editor of *New Religious Movements and Rapid Social Change* (1986), and coeditor of *The Changing Face of Religion* (with Thomas Luckmann, 1989), and *Secularization, Rationalism and Sectarianism* (1993).

Catherine Bell is Bernard J. Hanley Professor of Religious Studies at Santa Clara University, CA. Recent publications include: *Ritual: Dimensions and Perspectives* (1997), "Performance," in *Critical Terms for Religious Studies* (1998), "Pragmatic Theory" in *Secular Theories on Religion* (2000), and articles for *The Encyclopedia of Taoism* (2001).

Peter Beyer is associate professor in religious studies at the University of Ottawa in Canada. His publications are *Religion and Globalization* (1994), and numerous articles including "The Modern Emergence of Religions and a Global Social System for Religion," in *International Sociology* 13 (1998), "The City and Beyond as Dialogue: Negotiating Religious Authenticity in Global Society," in *Social Compass* 45 (1998) and "Religious Vitality in Canada: The Complementarity of Religious Market and Secularization Perspectives," in *Journal for the Scientific Study of Religion* 36 (1997).

Steve Bruce is Professor of Sociology at the University of Aberdeen. His most recent works are *Religion in the Modern World: From Cathedrals to Cults* (1996), *Conservative Protestant Politics* (1998) and *Choice and Religion: A Critique of Rational Choice Theory* (1999).

Donald Capps is William Harte Felmeth Professor of Pastoral Theology at Princeton Theological Seminary. His most recent books include *Men, Religion, and Melancholia: James, Otto, Jung, and Erikson* (1997), *Social Phobia: Alleviating*

Anxiety in an Age of Self-promotion (1999), and *Jesus: A Psychological Biography* (2000).

Roberto Cipriani is Full Professor of Sociology at the University of Rome 3. He is also past president of the ISA Research Committee for the Sociology of Religion. He has been editor in chief of *International Sociology*. His publications include *Sociology of Religion. An Historical Introduction* (2000).

Grace Davie is a Reader in the Sociology of Religion, University of Exeter. Her recent publications include *Religion in Britain since 1945* (Blackwell, 1994), *Identités religieuses en Europe* (coeditor with Danièle Hervieu-Léger, 1996), *Modern France: Society in Transition* (coeditor with Malcolm Cook, 1999), and *European Religion: A Memory Mutates* (2000). She has also contributed to *The Impact of Religious Conviction on the Politics of the Twenty-first Century* (1999), and *Sociology* (special millennial edition, 2000/1).

Douglas J. Davies is Professor in the Study of Religion at the University of Durham. His most recent publications are *Reusing Old Graves* (with Alastair Shaw, 1995), *Mormon Identities in Transition* (ed., 1996), *Death, Ritual and Belief* (1997), and *The Mormon Culture of Salvation* (2000).

Katherine Day is Professor of Church and Society at the Lutheran Theological Seminary at Philadelphia. Her primary areas of research have been African American churches and social movements. She has published a number of articles in this area as well as two books, *Modern Work and Human Meaning* (1986) and *Prelude to Struggle* (forthcoming). Currently she is engaged in research on the phenomenon of racially motivated church burnings and the volunteer rebuilding movement.

Marianne Delaporte is a Ph.D. student in Medieval History at Princeton Theological Seminary. She is currently working on her dissertation: "The Headless Holy Man: Hilduin's Lives of Saint Denis."

Nicholas J. Demerath III is Professor of Sociology at the University of Massachusetts, Amherst and immediate past president of the Society for the Scientific Study of Religion. His recent books include *A Bridging of Faiths: Religion and Politics in a New England City*, (with R. Williams, 1992), *Sacred Companies: Organizational Aspects of Religion and Religious Aspects of Organizations* (coedited with P.D. Hall, T. Schmitt, and R. Williams, 1998), and the forthcoming *Crossing the Gods: Religion, Violence, Politics, and the State Across the World*.

Victoria Lee Erickson is Associated Professor of the Sociology of Religion, Drew University, Madison, NJ. She has written *Where Silence Speaks: Feminism, Social Theory and Religion* (1993), and the forthcoming *Terror: A Witness to Human Community* (with Michelle Lim Jones).

Richard K. Fenn is currently the Maxwell Upson Professor of Christianity and Society at Princeton Theological Seminary. His recent works include *The Persistence of Purgatory* (1995), *The End of Time* (1997) and *Time Exposure* (in press).

Kieran Flanagan is a Reader in Sociology at the University of Bristol. His main publications are: *Sociology and Liturgy: Re-presentations of the Holy* (1991), and

The Enchantment of Sociology: A Study of Theology and Culture (1996). He has coedited *Postmodernity, Sociology and Religion* (1996), and *Virtue, Ethics and Sociology: Issues of Modernity and Religion* (with Peter C. Jupp, 2000). He is completing a book, *Seen and Unseen: A Sociology in Theology* and is working on a study of virtue and vocation.

Robin Gill is the Michael Ramsey Professor of Modern Theology at the University of Kent at Canterbury. He has postgraduate degrees in both sociology and theology and has written widely on both. Among his recent books are *The Myth of the Empty Church* (1993) and *Churchgoing and Christian Ethics* (1999).

Danièle Hervieu-Léger is a Professor at the Ecole des Hautes Etudes en Sciences Sociales in Paris, is director of the Centre Interdisciplinaire d'Etudes des Faits Religieux, and chief editor of the journal *Archives de Sciences Sociales des Religions.* Among her publications are *Le Féminisme en France* (1982), *De l'Emotion en Religion* (coeditor with F. Champion, 1990), *La religion au lycée* (ed. 1991) *Religion et Ecologie* (ed. 1993), *La religion pour mémoire* (1993), *Identités religieuses en Europe* (coeditor with G. Davie, 1996), *Le Pèlerin et le converti. La religion en mouvement* (1999).

Thomas Luckmann is Professor of Sociology at the University of Constance, Germany. His publications include *Life-World and Social Realities* (1983), *The Changing Face of Religion* (with James A. Beckford, 1989), *Religion* (1991), and *Modernity, Pluralism and the Crisis of Meaning. The Orientation of Modern Man* (with Peter Berger, 1995).

Bernice Martin is Emeritus Reader in Sociology at London University. She has recently written *Betterment on High: Life Worlds of Pentecostals in Chile and Brazil* (with David Martin).

David Martin is Emeritus Professor of Sociology at London University (LSE) and Honorary Professor in the Department of Religious Studies at Lancaster University. His most recent books include *Does Christianity Cause War?* (1997), and he is currently writing *The World Their Parish: Pentecostalism as Cultural Revolution and Global Option* for Blackwell.

Donald A. Nielsen is Professor of Sociology, State University of New York. Included among his publications is *Three Faces of God: Society, Religion and the Categories of Totality in the Philosophy of Emile Durkheim* (1999), as well as essays on Philo of Alexandria, Thucydides, churches and sects in Russia, the Medieval Inquisition, Georg Simmel and Biblical exegesis, Max Weber, and other topics in the history of social theory and the sociology of religion.

Roger O'Toole is Professor of Sociology at the University of Toronto, Canada and is cross-appointed to the university's interdisciplinary postgraduate Centre for the Study of Religion. His articles and reviews have appeared in various journals and many edited volumes. He is a former editor-in-chief of *Sociology of Religion*, a former associated editor of *Studies in Religion* and is currently a member of the editorial board of the new journal *Implicit Religion*. He is the author of *Religion: Classic Sociological Approaches* and *The Precipitous Path: Studies In Political Sects.*

Bryan Wilson is Reader Emeritus in the University of Oxford and Emeritus Fellow of All Souls. His recent publications include *The Social Dimensions of Sectarianism* (1990), *A Time To Chant: The Soka Gakkai Buddhists in Britain* (with K. Dobbelaere, 1994), and *New Religious Movements: Challenge and Response* (coeditor with J. Cresswell, 1999).

Linda Woodhead is Senior Lecturer in Christian Studies at Lancaster University. She is coauthor of *Religion in Modern Times: An Interpretive Anthology* (with Paul Heelas, Blackwell 2000) and coeditor of *Diana: The Making of a Media Saint* (with Scott Wilson and Jeffrey Richards, 2000). She is currently writing an *Introduction to Christianity.*

Robert Wuthnow is the Gerhard R. Andlinger Professor of Sociology and Director of the Center for the Study of Religion at Princeton University. His recent books include *After Heaven: Spirituality in America Since the 1950s* (1998), *Loose Connections: Joining Together in America's Fragmented Communities* (1998), and *Growing Up Religious: Christians and Jews and Their Journeys of Faith* (1999).

Acknowledgments

To all the contributors I wish to express my gratitude for their participation, their willingness to consult and revise, and their patience with editorial correspondence. Reading their work has reminded me of the breadth and depth they bring to this field and of their commitment to understanding what is beyond us all.

To my editorial assistant, Marianne Delaporte, I wish to express my thanks for her intelligent, tough-minded grasp of the work at hand. Not only was she willing to check and recheck, call and correspond, edit and revise; she kept her good humor. Ms. Delaporte also helped me to see the kinship among the essays and to order the volume as a whole. Quite literally, this work would not have been finished had it not been for her repeated efforts and her willingness to make her daughter Emma wait while we put the pieces together.

The Dean and the Computer Services Department of Princeton Theological Seminary were essential from the beginning of this project. James Armstrong advised me, provided financial support for editorial assistance and the work of translation, and gave me good-humored advice. Rodney Hillsman and Chris Carpenter of Computer Services, under the guidance of Adrian Backus, made it possible for us to access the seminary's computer from various locations over the course of many months, and they made it seem easy. Michael Davis, as faculty secretary, handled multiple letters and phone calls – for which I am very grateful – as well as the work of translation.

It was Alex Wright, editor and colleague of long standing, formerly of Blackwell's, who invited and encouraged me to undertake this project, helped me to think through the nature of this volume, and corrected my errors and oversights. Clare Woodford and Joanna Pyke have been kind and sustaining as the work progressed. I would also like to thank Jenny Roberts, who edited this manuscript with skill, flexibility, and patience in the face of several cross-Atlantic complications. Any remaining infelicities of expression are mine alone.

There are two generations of sociologists at work together in these pages, and they provide a foundation for more to come. How long the world will last as they have described it here is anybody's guess. That they have given us a striking picture of the sociological landscape and of some of its very personal heights and depths, I have no doubt at all.

In editing a book of this length there are inevitable differences in style among the authors. As editor I have sought to impose as little uniformity as possible in this regard, and where authors have disagreed with the advice of the publisher I have tended to support the author. No one but myself is therefore responsible for variations in the use of inclusive language or for some authors' references, for instance, to places and times that will resonate with some readers but not all. Having asked authors to make sure that their own viewpoints are clearly visible even in fairly abstract or complex discussions, as editor I was in no position and had no desire to smooth out the differences in their usage. The reader, I trust, will gain an appreciation of the extraordinary differences among authors that nonetheless contribute to what is a remarkable consensus on the shape and direction of religious and social change.

Of course I have regrets that some sociologists who might have appeared in these pages are not represented. There are therefore also some topics that we have not covered as well as we might. I bear sole responsibility for the final shape of this volume.

Richard K. Fenn

The editor and publishers are grateful to the following for permission to reproduce copyright material:

Excerpts from *The Cloud of Unknowing and Other Works*, translated by Clifton Wolters (Penguin Classics, 1961); © Clifton Wolters, 1961. By permission of the publishers.
Excerpts from *Goethe: The Collected Works*, Volume 2, translated by Stuart Atkins (Princeton University Press, 1984).

The publishers apologize for any errors or omissions in the above list and would be grateful to be notified of any corrections that should be incorporated in the next edition or reprint of this book.

Preface

Sociologists' ideas about the causes and consequences of religion are scattered in a variety of studies, each of which focuses on a particular development in the relation of religion to social systems. Some, like Bernice Martin in her chapter on Pentecostals and on women, focus on various groups and their claims to the sacred, while others, like Grace Davie in her chapter for this volume, focus on established institutions and their struggles to keep and expand their clientele. Still others focus on the way professional groups seek to answer the questions and meet the needs of their clients, in a way that seeks, often unsuccessfully, to maintain the status and authority of the professional providers of consolation and advice. See, for example, the chapter on the viability of the churches by Robin Gill for a sober assessment of their prospects for the future. See also the interesting argument, put forward by James Beckford, that religion increasingly resembles a social movement rather than an institution. Still others focus on the way that whole societies attract and seek to hold the loyalty and allegiance of their members through the adept use of sacred symbol. Roberto Cipriani's chapter, for instance, argues that there is a religious culture in Italy that does enhance the value and legitimacy of the public sphere: a civic culture that is profoundly religious in origin and sacred in the sentiments of allegiance that it attracts and sustains. There is a wealth of detail and no small amount of theory involved in these accounts, but there is also no single overriding theory that places each of them in a larger perspective.

The resulting literature thus generates a number of claims that appear to be competing and sometimes contradictory. Take, for example, the sociological discussion of the process of secularization. Some argue that Christianity is subject to that process, and that Christianity itself is therefore headed for various changes and even a slow but inevitable decline. Steve Bruce's chapter is a particularly good case in point. Others claim that Christianity is a secularizing force in Western societies. So far from being a victim of the process of secularization, it has set it in motion and continued to secularize the more resistant and communal forms of magic and piety. That has long been one of the arguments of Bryan Wilson, whose contribution to this volume reminds us that the result is a moral wasteland. Some sociologists claim that societies inevitably generate their own forms of religious identity and symbolism; religion is thus going to be a continuing factor wherever societies are to be found. This is a Durkheimian viewpoint, and it is well worth reading Donald Nielsen's chapter to encounter a nuanced and somewhat modernized version of that position. Others claim that these forms of religion are secondary and derivative from the interactions and endeavors of individuals. On this view the societal forms of religion are at best a halo effect, a residue of the past and thus vulnerable to being undermined by the innovations and struggles of individuals themselves. Steve Bruce and Danièle Hervieu-Léger, in their contributions to this volume, make it clear that individuals are taking responsibility for an increasingly broad range of decisions, activities, and concerns; in the future institutionalized forms of religion cannot provide an obligatory framework for individual piety and allegiance but merely a set of resources and options for individual devotion. It is a view consistent with the methodological individualism of Max Weber and at odds with a Durkheimian perspective that makes individual religiosity the by-product of social facts and forces. Of sociological debates and apparent differences there appears to be no end.

What, then, is to be done? In this Preface I would like to suggest that there is less to these differences than meets the eye. They are largely the result of selective attention to different parts of the sociological landscape. It matters a great deal whether sociologists are looking at an entire society, a nation perhaps, or whether they are looking at an institution, a community, a professional group, or merely at two or three gathered together in the desperate hope of gaining some freedom from the social forces that are keeping them dependent and helpless. It also matters a great deal whether sociologists are looking at societies that are relatively immune to the forces of nature or the intrusion of other societies and can substitute social for natural laws, or whether they are looking at vulnerable societies whose boundaries against outside influences and unpredictable threats are relatively weak and who must therefore live more by the Spirit. For the same reason it matters a lot whether sociologists are looking at societies in which the division of labor is not very complicated, and many individuals can thus aspire to many roles, or whether in fact the division of labor is fairly specialized and is arranged in hierarchies, such that many are called but very few are chosen for particular duties. Linda Woodhead, in her contribution to this volume, makes the telling point that the advent of women in the workforce is indeed changing the degree to which roles can be not only specialized but segregated, so that the separation of work from family life and the concerns of the community is less pronounced today than it has been even in the recent past. It is no wonder that sociologists of religion disagree about the relation of religion to social life; they are looking at something like a cross between a mosaic and a mobile.

Nonetheless, there are some very simple propositions that one can cull from the literature of the last century: very simple indeed. The first is that religious beliefs and practices are born in the separation of social systems from their natural surroundings. It is not just Freudians who would argue that the illusion of a presence in the world of supernatural beings is the result of living in a social order that has just begun to distinguish itself from nature itself. Among the first islands of social life the world beyond its shores was indeed huge, mysterious, inviting, threatening, and supremely powerful. No wonder that it was personified in the social imagination with the same figures who to a child seemed necessary for one's survival and yet dangerous to one's desires and aspirations.

Later sociologists who do not drink from the well of psychoanalysis nonetheless have carried forward the same argument: that religion emerges as social systems seek to distance themselves from the natural world around them. Societies need time to react to threats from their environments: at first to threats from the wind and the rain, as Freud pointed out, but also later on from the threat of subversion and invasion. Some, like Israel, can count the time in which they have to react to attack from neighbors in a matter of minutes and seconds; others have more time in which to muster their forces. Time is always, however, of the essence of a society's survival. It is not only danger but opportunity that lies outside the borders of a social system: herds of buffalo moving across the plains, or shifts in international capital. Here, too, societies need time in order to react, to safeguard their currencies, and seize opportunities for investment. For many societies, as Peter Beyer points out, this distance from a complex environment is increasingly difficult to obtain.

It is not surprising, then, that societies have used religious symbols and beliefs to imagine their relationship to their natural and social environments. It is also no accident that societies have used religious practices to manage their relationships to their environments. Societies must have ways to reduce the terror of the unknown and to imagine the opportunities for new life and vitality that lie beyond the borders of their immediate and customary knowledge. They have needed access to gods that bring terror and mercy, whose favor spells the difference between life and death, and whose domains extend beyond the borders of the community or the nation. Societies have needed seers who can see beyond those borders, who can tell them who and what is coming, and who can point the way to new freedoms, new land, new sources of milk and honey. These are the gods of space, and they are the more essential, the more a society begins to have distance from its environment. Now, however, it is increasingly clear, as Nicholas Demerath and Peter Beyer argue, that religion itself is subject to forces from outside any particular society, and that we may need therefore to redefine or imagine religion in entirely new ways that take into account the cross-cultural influences that are shaping religion in any particular social system. How can religion be a secondary line of cultural defense for any nation when it is subject to precisely the same transnational forces that are eroding the identity and autonomy of the nation itself?

It is also not surprising that as a society can buy time by strengthening its borders with nature or with other societies, it begins to feel dependent on divine sources of time. No wonder that gods have been those who can warn of coming floods or who can avert disastrous plagues, visiting them on a society's neighbors in the nick of time. No wonder that the gods have been those who could promise a forthcoming day of relief and liberation, or who are remembered as having signaled and provided a decisive event at the formation of the community itself. Since timing is essential to maintaining a society's boundaries with nature, it has had to use divine sources of authority to know when to plant and when to harvest, when to store up against periods of famine and when to provide relief. Take away from religion the knowledge of the times, of better days, and days of wrath, and one has a god of space alone.

Of course, boundaries between nature and social systems are seldom perfect. As transplants of organs from animals to humans become more commonplace, so does the recognition that chimpanzees, for instance, not only employ rituals to pacify their communities but also can be relatively human in their use of symbols, lies, deception, and humor to trick their captors. It is not surprising, therefore, that modern fears focus on immigrants who bring microbes and the wrong genes, or on terrorists who bring germ warfare or explosives into the world of the familiar and the ordinary. Neither is it surprising that popular entertainment focuses on aliens from other planets who bring various forms of wisdom, terror, or captivation from other worlds beyond our ken and imagination.

That is why it is particularly important that David Martin, Bryan Wilson, Bernice Martin, and Nicholas Jay Demerath have provided us with several models for understanding processes of secularization that originate outside the social system as well as come from within. The Martins have made us aware that in many societies the impetus to change and development is coming from within. In her chapter on the community development that is emanating from the African-American churches, Katie Day also calls our attention to similar processes of innovation and social change: some of these, from quarters insufficiently studied by sociologists, some of whom have had a very limited notion of the capacity of individuals to find their own sources of regeneration and to make their own declarations of relative freedom. They are quite capable of standing outside their social systems and of facing both life and death on their own terms.

The very inventiveness and openness of individuals to new sources of inspiration and authority make it difficult for any society to know where nature ends and social life begins or to decide where its moral and cultural or even demographic boundaries are drawn. That is why some societies have used religion not only to symbolize and imagine the unknown elements of their environments but to purify themselves of unwanted, alien influences. In turn, it is not surprising that religion has treated some enemies as though they were forces of nature. The unruly young or the merely seditious have been thought subject to animal spirits, from which they must be liberated. Neighboring peoples of an inferior and unreliable nature have been typified as monkeys, pigs, or worse, in the lexicon of natural epithets. Religion has offered a panoply of demonic symbols for humans that are overtly animal in nature; their horns and hoofs are especially revealing. Religion has also offered a set of practices for exorcising the animal-demonic and restoring a harmonious relationship with nature, as though nature were indeed a person. That was precisely Freud's point in *The Future of An Illusion*.

Thus, even when boundaries between nature and society are relatively clear, the boundaries between one social system and another are notoriously difficult to specify and maintain. Outside influences creep in and internal resources go astray. This has been especially true of peoples, like Israel, who have been subject to other kingdoms and empires. Wherever currency and language, marriages and worship, have been double-coded, so to speak, it has been hard for the members of these societies to know to whom they truly belong. Loyalty becomes a perennial issue, as do purity and openness to exchange with outsiders. What does the use of a foreign currency say about one's primary allegiance? What is the proper language or register for speaking in public or in private, among fellow believers and among dissidents, and in the privacy of one's own devotions? What is one to do with a foreign wife or an Arab suitor, when love and loyalty conflict with social obligation and cultic obedience? What is one to do with prayers for the emperor or with gentiles in the courtyard? Religion has helped to say which of these issues is serious and which is of no account.

Religious beliefs have reassured a people that they are divinely chosen, even if their own choices must remain ambiguous and conflicting. Sometimes religion has imposed the harshest of penalties on foreign spouses and alien devotion, but at other times it has merely provided a language for a society to express its awareness that alien and seditious forces are at work in its midst. Inevitably, when boundaries are at issue the question of time is raised to the boiling point. Religion then instructs a society whether to wait for a time of purification and renewed independence or to mobilize for a day of final accounting. Otherwise its edicts would only be about space, keeping a safe distance, and digging below the surface, whereas it is time that is running out on any society whose boundaries are more like the Maginot Line than the Chinese Wall.

Now, if we look back at these fairly simple statements, we find that they have one thing in common. Individuals and communities, institutions and whole societies, live in a world that is beyond their knowledge but not beyond their imagination. In fact, imagination is absolutely necessary to personal and communal survival. One has to rely on dreams or visions, seers or prophets, futurists or sociologists, in order to sense the possibilities for fulfillment and satisfaction that the world might in fact have to offer. David Martin's chapter in this volume makes it clear that the religious vision and the sociological imagination have much in common; both face empirical tests and are subject to the passage of time. However, those whom sociologists may overlook or despise, religious enthusiasts especially of a Pentecostal variety, may in fact have a vision of the future and of the possibilities that a social system has yet to offer that is far more accurate, in the long run, than sociologists' prognostications. Hope and faith are sometimes right, if only because they may be self-fulfilling. Conversely, the threats to human life often beggar the imagination; one has to conceive imaginatively of mortal threats that range from microbes to jealous siblings, from angry fathers to rival peoples, and from these more familiar dangers to those that come from distant warlords and natural eruptions from the tops of mountains or the bottom of the sea. One does not need to have been Sigmund Freud to realize that conscious life is something of a conspiracy against reality, so loathsome and fearful are the dangers or so forbidden are the objects of human desire. One could be a Malinowski or even a Talcott Parsons, both of whom understood that the sacred was a vast reduction of the very real uncertainty with which individuals and societies have had to cope over time.

Reductions of the sort that make up sacred beliefs and practices, then, take some of the mystery out of the unknown. The first steps toward demystification have always been taken under the auspices of groups and individuals who claimed to be able to spare ordinary mortals a full and devastating encounter with what was in any case beyond their knowledge and control. The reduction might take the form of ten laws carved in tablets of stone, or a veil in the temple separating all but the highest and purest of priests from a devastating and mortally dangerous encounter with the truly Sacred. Let Sacred with a capital S, then, stand for the sum total of the unknown that lies beyond human imagination, knowledge, and control. That leaves the sacred as the sphere of beliefs and practices that reduce uncertainty to something that can be depicted or seen or stated and which can be approached by those select groups and practitioners who have acquired the proper, prescribed actions and states of mind. In studies of ritual we find examples of this professionalized approach to the sacred: this vast reduction of ambiguity and uncertainty. Nonetheless, as Catherine Bell argues, it would be a mistake to find in rituals merely a group of individuals being prompted and put through their paces by professionalized seers or magicians, clergy or officials of various sorts. Even in the more formal rituals there are elements of play and subversion, in which individual and groups lay claim to invisible and unspoken aspects of the Sacred that lie behind the more or less authorized forms of the sacred.

Steps toward demystification, then, appear to initiate the process that sociologists have long called "secularization." Looking only at that aspect of the process that reduces hitherto unimaginable uncertainty to what might be grasped figuratively by the mind or spirit, the process is just what one would expect of a social system: a reduction of the range of possible events, relationships, encounters, and choices to a range that can be symbolized. It is in that sense a conscious conspiracy against reality. Looked at, however, as a cultural innovation, the first step constitutes the original manufacture of the sacred out of the apparently ordinary or trivial matter of everyday life. Thus feathers and stones, syllables and intonations, take on a level of meaning and mystery that they had hitherto lacked until they were set aside for that purpose. It all depends on where one is standing whether one is able to focus primarily on the process of secularization or the manufacture of the sacred. They are twin aspects of the same moment. Be sure to note Thomas Luckmann's chapter on moral communication in Germany, in which the sacred lives in and under the more secular forms of communication, and in which secular offices, like that of the President, are the vehicle for communication about the sacred.

I have been suggesting that secularization is a process in which lesser mysteries are substituted for greater ones. I have also been arguing that the process initially occurs as social systems slowly separate themselves from their natural and social environments. Further, I am arguing that to grasp what is going on at any given time sociologists need to develop a conception of "the times" or the moment in which they live or which they are intent on describing. At any point it is safe to say that the past is present in the very acts by which those in the present are seeking to separate the present from the past. It is also safe to say that every attempt to reduce mystery creates a lesser mystery that takes the place of what was once transcendent and obscure, threatening or filled with elusive promise. In turn these monuments to the sacred become themselves the objects of further attempts to reduce mystery, to make it available, to turn it from silence or suggestion into discourse, and to appropriate it for the proximate world of tasks in hand. Note Danièle Hervieu-Léger's dialectical argument about the process of secularization at various levels of society.

PART I

Classical and Contemporary Theory: Recycling, Continuity, Progress, or New Departures?

Editorial Commentary: Religion and the Secular; the Sacred
and the Profane: The Scope of the Argument   3

1   Personal Reflections in the Mirror of Halévy and Weber   23

2   Salvation, Secularization, and De-moralization   39

3   The Pentecostal Gender Paradox: A Cautionary Tale for
the Sociology of Religion   52

4   Feminism and the Sociology of Religion: From Gender-
blindness to Gendered Difference   67

5   Melancholia, Utopia, and the Psychoanalysis of Dreams   85

6   Georg Simmel: American Sociology Chooses the Stone
the Builders Refused   105

7   Transformations of Society and the Sacred in Durkheim's
Religious Sociology   120

8   Classics in the Sociology of Religion: An Ambiguous
Legacy   133

9   Individualism, the Validation of Faith, and the Social
Nature of Religion in Modernity   161

10   The Origins of Religion   176

Editorial Commentary: Religion and the Secular; the Sacred and the Profane: The Scope of the Argument

Richard K. Fenn

There is a startling degree of unanimity in this book. Certainly there is a tendency among these contributors to agree that institutionalized religion has lost its monopoly on the sacred and that other sectors of modern societies have taken over many of the functions and some of the meaning formerly invested in religious institutions. The secular world, so to speak, has therefore developed its own sources of inspiration and authority. Religion may therefore be no longer able to bind together the manifestations of the sacred that typify complex societies, especially because the sacred is now strewn across a wide range. Furthermore, individuals and communities now claim direct access to the sacred, without mediation by religious professionals or a clerical elite. This new immediacy allows individuals and communities to construct the sacred in ways that are more democratic, egalitarian, playful, inventive, and potentially subversive than in the recent past.

This increased spiritual inventiveness, along with the dispersion and diffusion of the sacred outside of major institutions like the church or the state, has opened up a wide range of possibilities for mutuality and interaction. Some of these possibilities are as risky as they are ambiguous. In China the spread of a well-organized religious group devoted to traditional shamanic and meditative practices, Falun Gong, is seen to pose a threat to the state and is vilified as fomenting superstition, "evil thinking," and social instability. Its leader's use of the Internet to communicate with tens of millions of followers compounds the appearance of a cohesive and disciplined body capable of instant mobilization. Other religious groups, with an international leadership and with followers in a variety of nations may also pose a threat to the cohesiveness of particular societies, whether they support paramilitary and terrorist organizations or declare the independence of their members from traditional sources of discrimination and oppression. The international Pentecostal movement is a prime example of such liberation from below.

The sacred is the institution by which individuals and groups, communities and societies attempt to transcend the passage of time. The sacred reduces multiple possibilities both for life and death to times and occasions that can be marked and solemnized, celebrated and remembered. Thus the seasons of an individual's life are sacralized in rites of passage that mark the coming of adulthood, marriage, and death itself. The sacred thus links the passage of time for the individual to the observances of the larger society. That linkage assures the individual that the rhythms and seasons of life are part of a larger temporal order, the tides of which will continue to ebb and flow according to the sacred calendar. The momentous occasions in the life of the society such as war and peace are similarly celebrated in memorials that assure its citizens that no sacrifice for the nation or the people will go unremembered and prove therefore to have been in vain. The anniversaries of the death of Malcolm X, of the holocaust of the Branch Davidians, of the death of Princess Diana, of the bombing of the federal building in Oklahoma City, of the Easter uprising, of massacres in Vietnam, North Korea, or Beijing are remembered and honored locally or in private among those whose lives were most deeply affected. Some indeed are mentioned on the national media in brief segments of reporting on what happened "on this day" in years past. As the sacred becomes dispersed and unfocused, however, the nation's ceremonies can no longer collect, as it were, the woes and aspirations, the griefs and hopes of all the people.

What passes for the sacred vastly reduces the wide range of possibility that in fact exists within society: possibilities for cruelty and the destruction of the spirit as well as possibilities for the resuscitation of the crushed soul and the rejuvenation of moribund communities. When societies become integrated, however, these various possibilities no longer stay within the range of professional understanding and common sense. They may sometimes come back, moreover, with a vengeance. In the meantime, eschatologies and millennial religious enthusiasm are expressions of the desire of some members of a society for a final accounting and for a settlement of all grievances. It is part of the sociological task to look under the surface of the familiar for what has long been concealed there in the way of patient longing and forceful anticipation.

Of course, sociologists seldom agree on everything, and those who have contributed to this book are no exception. Some, for instance, would argue that secularization consists of the process in which religion loses its influence on politics and economics as well as its monopoly over the sacred. The worlds of work and government become increasingly autonomous, follow their own rules, and regard religious groups and institutions as one among many interests to be brokered. Just as religion loses its control over how people raise children, make their living, or govern themselves, it also loses its control over the sacred itself. Thus the sacred is less often to be found at times or in places owned and controlled by professionals like the clergy. Instead, the sacred is increasingly to be found in a wide diversity of locales, among groups that had previously enjoyed very little in the way of spiritual gifts or charisma, and among individuals who find their own sources of inspiration and authority. Others, however, find in this same process a resacralizing of the world, in which areas of social life formerly considered to be under the domain of rationality come under spiritual influence, and what was once profane and lacked any mystery becomes enchanted once again. From their viewpoint, for instance, women who bring spiritual and moral concerns back into the workplace and gain new freedom for themselves under the auspices of the Holy Spirit are signs that secularization is hardly as widespread or inevitable a social process as some sociologists have thought it to be. While many of the sociologists represented in this volume might therefore agree that the sacred genie, so to speak, is out of the bottle of institutionalized religion, they might not agree as to whether that Great Escape represents or undermines the process of secularization.

The more complex and diverse a society becomes, moreover, and the more varied become the expressions of the sacred, the more abstract and formulaic become the beliefs and values of religion, and the more distant they are from the decisions and contexts that constitute everyday life. Activities or functions, rites and other symbolic acts, that were once owned and controlled by a single institution are transferred to other contexts. Shoes that were once produced within the household economy were later produced under the central control of a manager who monopolized the means of production, provided capital and machinery, set schedules and quotas, and provided sole access to the larger market. Religious instruction on marriage and child raising, churchly prohibitions on sexual or economic activity, and the prescriptions for government that were once produced by religious officials and intellectuals, are now produced under secular auspices. Note that these changes are often discussed as aspects of "differentiation."

With regard to the process of differentiation, secularization usually represents a narrowing of the scope of institutionalized religion's authoritative control over the sacred. Other institutions then lay claim to the sacred, as in the "sacred" doctor–patient relationship or attorney–client communication. These operate under the seal of a secular confessional, except where insurance companies and public prosecutors assert their interests and authority. Similarly, the arts and crafts of teaching, healing, judging, predicting the future, and pastoral care have been transferred from the church to educators, doctors, an independent judiciary, social scientists and social workers and therapists.

Secularization thus makes it difficult for individuals to act as if their allegiances to this world and the next could be played out on a single stage. There is no religious framework to guarantee that they could be both faithful sons and daughters of their families and natural communities, on the one hand, and citizens of a larger society on the other. The loyalty of the child to the home and family, to the place of birth and the familiarity of old surroundings comes inevitably into conflict with the demands of the larger society for tribute, for the development of skills, the performance of duties, and possibly for the sacrifice of one's very life. Early loves become untenable or embarrassing. Secularization exposes the conflict between personal inspiration and allegiance to a higher social authority or the contradiction embedded in dying that others may live.

The more secularized a society, the more it will therefore have to articulate and control its perennial and endemic sources of conflict and cleavage. The world of the small community comes more visibly into conflict with the opportunities and threats represented by the larger society. The family and all ties based on kinship are threatened by the possibilities for association and satisfaction represented by commerce, work, politics, and the military. However, secularization limits the capacity of religion to integrate conflicting ways of life and to place sectional loyalties and class divisions within a larger context of adherence and belief.

It may therefore now be necessary for sociologists to redefine religion or at least imagine it in new ways. It may help, for the sake of threading one's way through the discussions in this volume, to think of *religion as a way of tying together multiple experiences and memories of the sacred into a single system of belief and practice*. That is, after all, what major religions do; they integrate a vast repertoire of insights into the sacred, of memories and experience, of revelations and pronouncements. Thus integrated, these forms of the sacred represent a more or less comprehensive and authoritative view of the world: of things to be hoped for and dreaded, of persons to be feared and loved, of ways of life to be honored and despised, of times and places to be approached freely or with careful circumspection.

However, to study religion from a sociological viewpoint opens us not only to the world that has emerged from a welter of sacred moments and peoples, times and places, but also to forms of the sacred that have been lost. That missing world may be an imaginary social order remembered as harmonious and egalitarian, organic and cooperative, or it may be the original matrix from which all humans have come: a maternal world where there was a peace that passed all understanding. In either event, religion expresses the awareness that we live in a world whose foundations are known only by the signs of their former presence. Indeed, religion is as much about absence as it is about presence.

That is why there is so often a touch of nostalgia or even melancholy in religion, and an awareness of loss often typifies studies of the sacred. Indeed, several of the sociologists represented in this volume know the world to be a place where the sacred is distinguished more by its absence than its presence: empty cathedrals, collective amnesia, the ghosts of dead beliefs, and the emptiness of a cultural wasteland. For instance, Bryan Wilson's contribution to this volume notes the tragic passing of a world that was once essential to the formation of modern societies and still remains necessary in its absence. He argues that the world of face-to-face relations was once the basis of all social obligations. In the family and the local community one learned the disciplines of self-restraint and acquired a self-regard that dignified others as well as the self. The disciplines of reliability and work so essential to industrial societies were acquired in the very contexts that industrial societies are so effective in destroying: the home, the community, and indeed all the other stable matrices of personal identity. In Part 2, moreover, we will find Grace Davie suggesting that there are still public places in Europe that enshrine sacred memory, but they are increasingly becoming empty of any direct expression of piety and are more like museums than shrines. Participation in the sacred is thus optional, temporary, vicarious, and derivative: a state that may well be one of transition toward a final extension of the profane into the sanctuary itself. The sense of a holding environment, a maternal space that encompasses all profane activities, may finally yield to the recognition that sacred space is empty after all. Disenchantment continues, though somewhat less intensely and more abated than previously may have been thought to be true of European societies.

Wilson notes that, whereas roles were once clusters of social obligation, they are now largely impersonal, empty of moral instruction, and governed by rational standards of technique and performance. Whereas government once embodied a moral order, it is now based on incentives and relies on surveillance. Indeed government itself is a source of the very cynicism and "de-moralization" that make modern societies conducive to skepticism and silent protest. The economy itself, once reliant on moral standards for work and credit, relies heavily on surveillance and offers a meaningless array of artificial choices. It is consumption, he argues, no longer production, that provides the currency for personal identity in a market of rival selves.

Wilson's chapter on the de-moralization of Western societies is nicely in tension with the emphasis of Bernice Martin on what might be called the re-moralization of Latin America, Africa, Asia, and parts of Eastern Europe and the remains of the Soviet Union. Bernice Martin notes that women are using traditional, even patriarchal, forms of Christianity to negotiate for themselves a social order that recognizes their gifts, gives them renewed authority and a real, however limited, social status, and that opens up to them positions of leadership not only in the home but in the community. There is, in the Pentecostal movement worldwide, a creative adaptation of religious dissent for the purpose of creating new forms of solidarity between men and women, new havens in a heartless world, and new opportunities for personal growth and for upward social mobility. These opportunities come to those who refuse to become ciphers or victims, however much they have been abused by authoritarian regimes or left out of the mainstream of technological development.

Bernice Martin's chapter particularly addresses the cultured despisers of religious enthusiasm who have notably failed either to see or, if they saw, to understand the significance of the Pentecostal revolution worldwide. Feminists appear to have noticed women taking leadership roles in Pentecostal communities, but they focused instead primarily on the patriarchal forms and ideology and failed to analize the actual renegotiation of the roles and authority of women in the community. Marxists appear to have failed to see the significance of the Pentecostal movement for the liberation of women and the empowerment of an oppressed class. Some saw in Pentecostalism the fruits of American colonialism or a new extension of capitalist-induced desires for consumption; others were more interested in liberation theology and ecclesial base communities that had a more direct connection with Western Marxist ideology but enjoyed far less popularity among the poor than Pentecostalism itself. Sociologists who were insistent on the notion of secularization failed to see Pentecostalism as any thing more than a regression or a movement that, by instilling the Protestant ethic, would create worldly success and religious disinterest. From Bernice Martin's chapter we gain a picture of a religious movement that is not likely to defeat itself by its own successes; rather it is one that calls into question the hitherto successful paradigms of Western sociology. Certainly it provides new forms of self-discipline, arouses long-term commitments to self-improvement, defends the family from external pressure, releases the energies and recruits the talents of women and men alike, and opens up new futures for a generation of children who otherwise would have been trapped in traditional gender roles and in the poverty that these roles perpetuate.

Bernice Martin's comments on the narrowness of disciplinary or ideological viewpoints tells us that the sociology of religion needs to be open to insights and methods from other fields of inquiry. Crossing disciplinary borders is particularly fruitful when sociologists are candid and articulate about their commitments and make clear how the field looks from the place where they have chosen to stand. For instance, another contributor, David Martin, combines sociological with theological insight into the modern city. Indeed he sees in cities not only a pattern for the larger society, in which some groups or communities are rendered relatively marginal, but also a pattern that evokes certain cities of antiquity. With his historically oriented sociological vision, furthermore, Martin can perceive the city as being both maternal and heavenly, as in the case of Jerusalem itself. Unless one understands cities as embodying reminiscence, therefore, as well as referring to the future, one will not understand either the innovations of the modern world or its continuity with the past. Indeed, David Martin's chapter suggests that the city embodies the sacred in all its contemporary complexity, ambiguity, risk, and possibility.

Over and beyond the aspects of the sacred that are institutionalized in religious beliefs and practices or located either in the city or in landscape, the Sacred is the sum total of a society's potential. It is the realm of what is unknown: the partially realized potentiality for new forms of social life or for division and destruction. Thus the Sacred contains knowledge that is unimaginable until it is discovered or revealed, and this knowledge can upset the premises on which a society or community is based. The Sacred also contains motives and ambitions, intentions and impulses, that have the potential either to generate new recruits for parenting and soldiering or for rebellion and revolution. It is therefore no wonder that societies take considerable pains to orchestrate and regulate the Sacred so that individuals are exposed to its power in limited and socially acceptable forms and on stated occasions.

The Sacred is always full of an uncanny potency. Where that force comes from, of course, is a matter on which not all sociologists can yet agree. Some find it reflected in the potent symbols of a faith that itself has origins outside society and nature. Others see it reflecting only society itself. Even if social in origin, however, the Sacred nonetheless can be socially disruptive. Emile Durkheim spoke of *mana*; Weber spoke of charisma. Georg Simmel spoke, as Victoria Erickson reminds us in this volume, of the soul as having the capacity to create communities and to imagine wholeness emerging from chaos. In each case the sacred is both psychological and social, and potentially either divisive or conducive to the formation of new communities. One might say, following Freud, that the Sacred emanates from and reflects individual longings and frustrations, imaginatively projected onto the community or society.

Once embedded in social life, the sacred loses its ecstatic character and becomes external, superior, constraining, and larger than life. When the sacred is given shape, definition, plausibility, coherence, and authority by religion, it becomes the arbiter of reality itself. Religion then sets limits on human aspiration and freedom by defining the range of the individual's obligation to the larger society. When religion loses its capacity to arbitrate the sacred, new demands for satisfaction, autonomy, and vengeance may threaten the social order. Indeed, religion is failing to define and control the sacred.

Religion, in binding together the various forms of the sacred, is thus having difficulty in reducing the sacred to what can be known and managed at least by shamans or a professionally elite. As Nielsen points out, religion for Durkheim was the way in which a society sensed the world around it, probed and imagined its environment, and symbolized whatever might nourish or threaten it. Taken together, these hidden potentials could spell the life or death of a society and were thus considered sacred. Now, however, religion is less able than in the past to symbolize and control, to orchestrate and distribute the sacred in ways that guarantee the survival of the society itself.

Religion has lost the capacity to synthesize the vast and varied array of encounters with the sacred into a moral universe that unites the worlds of work and politics with the more intimate worlds of family, friendship, and of the inner self. Modernization requires the division of the world into compartments and expels the spirit of caring from formal organizations. These processes are taken up in Nielsen's discussion of Durkheim. There he investigates the extent to which a secular society is viable, in which the sacred takes on a variety of forms over which the larger society has little oversight or control. Nielsen points out that for Durkheim, and now for us, such transformations of the sacred pose historic challenges to religion. If the Sacred is the sum total of a society's potential, the area of possible surprise, new opportunity, or threat, it is the task of religion to provide an adequate array of symbols and concepts for constructing the sacred in its many forms and messages. This task religion now shares with a wide range of other cultural systems, from science to cryptography, politics to economics, but the challenge posed to religious thought and institutions by the transformation of the sacred still remains. A number of our contributors in Part 2 will focus on how religion is responding to this threat to its capacity to conceptualize the environment of a society, to warn of dangers, to foresee new opportunities, to imagine new forms of solidarity, and to expose a wide range of influences that may prove formative or disruptive.

The discussion of Durkheim also takes up the question of what constitutes the individual. The individual, as an institution with rights and responsibilities, freedoms of choice and of movement, is constituted by religion, which confers on the individual a measure of the sacred. However, the fully constituted individual makes it impossible for religion ever again to reassert its own control over the sacred. Thus the sacred in the future will be what individuals say it is, not what the clergy pronounce it to be or the prophets proclaim. It may be that the institution of the individual is itself the harbinger of a new form of the sacred in modern societies.

The question is then whether the institution of the individual is itself sacred or profane. Is the modern individual a form of the sacred, a source of the sacred, or merely an object for sociological study that poses no inherent mystery? It would appear from Nielsen's account that Durkheim's legacy is ambivalent on this issue. Is the modern individual, burdened with high levels of responsibility and authority, the embodiment of the larger society's central religious beliefs, or is that individual an anomaly, even a new thing under the sun, unprecedented in his or her authority and control? Again, Nielsen honestly and helpfully explores Durkheim's ambiguity in this regard as well.

The more a society has forms of the sacred that are outside the authority of the state or of traditional religious institutions, the more appropriate it is to consider such a society secular. If secularizing societies are therefore more open than in the past to outside influences, and if the range of social possibility is therefore being expanded to unprecedented levels, it is because so many individuals represent not only insiders but also outsiders. They are what Simmel called "strangers": people who are close, who challenge us with "dangerous possibilities," and who are therefore both attractive and the object of considerable suspicion. They embody the sacred in our midst: the slightly inaccessible, not entirely visible, and yet proximate source of an extraordinary potential both for happiness and destruction. Essential to a social order's adaptability, they are also threatening to its pervasive institutions and illusions of security. The sacred may proliferate, disperse, and diversify in ways that make it very difficult for any single or central authority to monitor or control.

If the term "sacred" applies to areas of social life that are relatively unknowable and inaccessible, beyond the immediate control of the larger society, and filled with the potential either to strengthen or undermine the society's institutions and vitality, the profane is just the opposite. It is, as the name applies, before the temple, out in front and open, therefore, to public inspection. Lacking mystery, and separated from hidden sources of inspiration and authority, its potential for surprise is limited indeed. The more transparent are a society's institutions and practices, that is, the more open is the social system to public inspection and control, the less there is need for religion to conceptualize, coordinate and control the sacred.

As O'Toole points out in his discussion of debates in the sociology of religion, there is no agreement on the key terms of reference. No one can agree on what religion means or what it refers to. This ambiguity may be due, however, not only to the ambiguity of the classical texts but to the diverse and ambiguous shape of the sacred in contemporary societies. In a world where the sacred has thoroughly escaped institutional controls, is proliferating and diversifying, and is taking on a variety of new forms, the subject matter of the sociology of religion will similarly become difficult to define. In a world in which the sacred not only becomes dispersed but diffuses, so that it is difficult to know whether or not a particular event, group, community, or movement is or is not "sacred," the subject matter of the sociology of religion becomes more problematical.

As Linda Woodhead tellingly argues, the process of secularization itself is being offset by a renewed emphasis on the connection between one part of life and another. As women enter the labor force in increasing numbers, the very relatedness of people to one another will make it increasingly difficult even for corporations and bureaucracies to separate domains such as education and the family, the neighborhood and the community, from the spheres of work and politics. In fact, the increased presence of women in the areas formerly dominated by men may intensify pressures to put back together areas of social life that the Western world has torn apart. Caring for children goes on in the workplace while work is taken into the home. As the world of work becomes feminized, relationships on the job will become connected to wider possibilities, networks of relationships, and universes of meaning.

As Woodhead points out, the increasing entry of women into spheres from which they have previously been excluded will also affect another aspect of the process of secularization: one that has often been called the demystification or the disenchantment of the universe. Thus, what Woodhead calls "spiritualities of life" are replacing the old "religions of difference" as women leave the "private" world of domesticity for the worlds that were formerly dominated by men and therefore considered to be "public." It may thus be as a direct result of women entering the workplace that so many employers have made room for groups to explore their religious traditions in small groups that meet on the job. If this process simply means that individuals are free to bring their spiritual life to work, that is entirely compatible with the process of differentiation by which religion loses its capacity to create a system out of the sacred. If, however, the world of work is itself being transformed by these new forms of the sacred, the process of secularization may in fact be suffering a reversal.

For years sociologists have agreed on little else than that the process of differentiation dominates modern societies. It is the process that separates industrial production from the family, or religion from the economy. The more differentiated a society becomes, the less possible is it for religion to turn the disparate and varied experiences of the sacred into a single system of belief and practice. The process of differentiation thus allows each separate sphere to become relatively autonomous of the others in setting its own internal standards, setting its goals and policies, and determining its own identity and belief system. If differentiation is the term for the process by which areas of social life become separated from each other and operate under their own, independent auspices, it is essential to the process of secularization.

Discussions that take their point of departure from the classical literature of Weber and Durkheim may take it for granted that the dominant processes in the modern – at least in the Western – world are those that tend to pull religion apart from the rest of the society, relegate it to an increasingly diminished and voluntary sphere, and free individuals to find the sacred wherever they can. It has been assumed that the predominant processes are those governed by the value of rationality, in which each sphere, work or politics, the economy or religion, is governed by its own principles and controls its own operations without deference to external authorities other than the state itself. However, Linda Woodhead calls into question the discussions that take these processes for granted as the most important features of Western society. Instead of increasing differentiation, for instance, she sees modern societies beginning to put back together the pieces that have been torn apart under the auspices of a predominantly masculine set of values.

Thus, as some institutions and practices are becoming more separate from each other, others are losing their boundaries. For instance, the practice of medicine is becoming increasingly subject to controls from insurance and pharmaceutical companies; what appear to be decisions made on medical grounds by medical practitioners may be made for quite other reasons: to facilitate pharmaceutical research or satisfy the protocols for care managed by an insurance company. The close association of lobbyists with legislators is a similar case in point. The process of dedifferentiation makes it increasingly difficult for sociologists to know where to draw the line between the sacred and the profane.

What Woodhead and others are calling the sacralization of everyday life is the result of the process of dedifferentiation, which opens up specialized roles and institutions to a wider range of social and psychological possibilities. Woodhead attacks the notion that some roles are diffuse while others are quite narrowly specific. It was the American sociologist Talcott Parsons who initially distinguished roles that were diffuse, in the sense of incorporating many aspects of the individual's personality and relationships, from roles that were specifically related to a particular place in the division of labor. That distinction, Woodhead notes, is the result of a gender-blind picture of the way that roles are defined, organized, and distributed. As women increasingly enter the labor force, roles in general are becoming more complex and diffuse. Gender roles in particular are becoming more difficult to define.

It is in just such a complex and ambiguous world that possibilities for social change and personal transformation acquire not only political and economic but also sacred significance. As the process of dedifferentiation enriches the composition of roles, specific responsibilities, whether in work or politics, education or the family become open to a wider range of responsibilities, opportunities, and possibilities. If the sacred is difficult to define or contain, it is therefore because the significance of locale has been diminished by the flow of people and ideas across traditional boundaries and in disregard of status distinctions, job descriptions, by-laws and constitutions. Wherever the sacred manifests itself, lives are interrupted, characters changed, institutions shaken, and sometimes whole societies are brought to the point of crisis. The sacred is therefore more likely to appear not according to the schedules of institutionalized religion, nor on specific days and at certain seasons, but in more obscure, diffuse, and unpredictable forms. As everyday life has become open and permeable to outside influences, specialized roles and mundane routines may become increasingly responsive to the demands of the individual for personal satisfaction, meaning, and transcendental significance.

Not only is the Western world, at least, becoming less differentiated in the way people relate to one another at home and on the job; the sacred is also gathering new strength in unlikely places. Even when religious groups lack any political agenda or military capabilities, alien sources of inspiration and authority may threaten traditional values and undermine the elites that seek to impose them. The dissemination of American popular culture, for instance, has had just such a subversive effect on more than one traditional society. Although it is clearly not a religious phenomenon, popular culture does embody elements of the sacred that can attract the loyalty of a mass following and shape individual identities and aspirations for a lifetime. Certainly the use of the computer and the expansion of information to include whatever is offered on the Internet has been instrumental in enabling more than one religious movement to achieve high levels of organization. Paradoxically, without the process of differentiation and a complex division of labor, the Internet could not have been built. However, once the Internet becomes a mode of communication for members of a religious community, the sacred and the profane become tightly intermingled and are no longer sharply differentiated from each other.

In the future we will be more likely to see public figures like Princess Diana who combine power with caring. Diana in particular is a good example of the tendencies described by Woodhead, since Diana herself played with otherwise rigid social forms and formulae. She allowed direct access to royalty, broke silence on what had been hitherto regarded as unfit for public discussion, and pointed to an alternative society in which caring and intimacy were as appropriate in the public sphere as were formality and self-control. Thatcherism has been replaced by a third way in which the UK Prime Minister, Tony Blair, can weep publicly for the refugees in Kosovo and inject an intensity and seriousness of moral concern about the obligation of NATO to redress the refugees' grievances. Both Linda Woodhead and Bernice Martin make it clear that the modern world is increasingly open to the infusion of emotional intensity, personal caring, social transformation, and a network of new relationships in which self-discipline replaces machismo and commitment replaces professional indifference. The question is whether the genie of the sacred can ever be restored to the lamp of religion.

That is, it remains an open question whether religion can yet unite the varied forms and experiences of the sacred within any society into various systems of adherence and devotion. As Nielsen points out in his discussion of Durkheim, religion in the past has often succeeded in containing the sacred in moments of high collective enthusiasm and festival. There it can generate new forms of solidarity, heighten social commitments, and generate energies for the hard work of production and reproduction. Thus, as an institution, religion gives definition to the sacred, gives the sacred shape and form, and finds ways of containing the sacred so that its power to transform and unify an entire community or society outweighs its potential for division and disruption. Erickson finds a similar understanding of religion in Simmel, for whom religion "is the meeting ground where differences are blended in the search for something higher: truth, justice, perfection, God."

What would happen, however, if the sacred, like the proverbial genie, should escape the confines of the churches and rites, national days of solemn observance, and ceremonies that celebrate the saints and heroes of the communal past? What would happen if people should call their souls their own? As Erickson points out in her discussion of Simmel, the soul is the ultimate source of the sacred. If, therefore, the soul withdraws its trust, its faith, from the community or from the nation, those social systems will become fragile and moribund.

It is precisely such a development that Danièle Hervieu-Léger describes in theoretical detail in her chapter on individualism and modern religion. Drawing primarily on the work of Max Weber and Ernst Troeltsch, she demonstrates their continuing relevance to the sociology of modern religion in a world in which traditional or communal forms of religiosity have increasingly been replaced by those of the small group or autonomous individual. Just as Weber was concerned with the ways that charisma, or grace, becomes part of everyday life or institutionalized into authoritative beliefs and practices, Hervieu-Léger concerns herself with the ways that faith is validated in modern societies. The problem, as Weber put it, was with the forms and the fate of authority in a world in which the traditional and the communal increasingly gives way to the rational or the purely personal. So it is with Hervieu-Léger, who gives us four forms of the validation of faith in the modern world.

In every institution, of course, there is some tension between the forms of authority. Thus Hervieu-Léger notes the perennial conflict between institutional or prescribed patterns of belief and practice, guaranteed by tradition, and the more communal types of faith whose authority comes from the adherence of the members of the religious community to its basic values and attitudes toward the world. Replacing authority based on conformity and community self-discipline, however, are two more contemporary manifestations of religious commitment: one based on the ability of individuals to convince one another of the value and authenticity of their spiritual journeys; the other based on a principle of authority that is entirely personal and seeks no validation from others. The former type is inherently mystical and individualistic, but it seeks the sort of solidarity that comes from the mutual self-understanding of those whose spiritual journeys have allowed them to share with one another their experience and their visions. It is the sort of mysticism that is typical, Hervieu-Léger argues, of modern societies. The latter type represents something of a limit toward which the others eventually tend, and it is fluid, ephemeral, and perhaps dangerous both to society and the individual.

As a limiting condition for religious authority, the purely personal, self-validating form of faith represents a threat to any and all forms of solidarity. The institutional, the communal, and the group-based sources of social life give way to the dispositions of the individual. The specter of such a total dissolution of social life long has haunted that strand of French sociology associated primarily with the name and work of Emile Durkheim.

Modern individualism of the religious sort emphasizes the autonomy of the individual: not the individual's surrender to a higher reality external and superior to the self. Unlike its mystical predecessors, furthermore, modern individualism, as Hervieu-Léger describes it, puts a high value on the goods of this world, on achievements and satisfactions, as opposed to an ethic or spirituality of responsible self-renunciation. It is as if individuals were suffering from a form of spiritual amnesia in which they forget not only their traditions but, despite their self-concern, who they truly are. Their souls are thus in perennial danger because they lack a spiritual and social context in which to thrive and against which to discover their own limitations. Narcissism replaces spirituality.

How, then, can a society survive in which the sacred escapes the confines of religion? A society in which individuals own and control the means of manufacturing the sacred gives them the authority once reserved to priests and kings. That is just what one would expect, of course, in societies that are highly democratized and that have been informed by a Protestant ethic in which all believers are indeed priests. Individuals can now enchant the universe in their own terms without the permission or control of the clergy, and the society as a whole has lost the religious framework for deciding what is legitimately sacred and what should be kept in the profane world outside the Temple. As Nielsen notes in his discussion of Durkheim, "the ambiguous qualities of the unbound sacred as a social force provide a dynamic element which "religion" alone lacks."

It is no wonder, then, that the nature of the sacred and of its relationship to religion remain problematical even in the classic works of sociology. However, it is these issues' very ambiguity, O'Toole reminds us, that is responsible for their continuing influence in the sociology of religion. In part the classics' ambiguity is due to their own internal inconsistencies and their refusal to be bound even by their own definitions. On the other hand, some of their ambiguity is due, O'Toole rightly notes, to the fruitful suggestiveness of their interpretations and to the broad range of their observations and insights. Whether for positive or negative reasons, then, the seminal works of Marx, Weber, Durkheim, Simmel, and Troeltsch continue to provide a basis for contemporary discussions, arguments, and discoveries in the sociology of religion.

What is confusing in the world around us will no doubt therefore remain at least ambiguous despite the efforts of sociologists to describe, interpret, and explain it. However, we trust that our readers, like our contributors, will go back into the foundational works of sociology on their own to reformulate them for their own entirely contemporaneous reasons. It is our conviction that these classical texts can still provide guidance for the study of religion in a world where the sacred itself is difficult not only to confine but to identify. However, as O'Toole warns us, some writers may reinvent the classical texts in order to come to terms with developments that were neither adequately understood nor foreseen by writers such as Durkheim and Weber. Did Durkheim, as Nielsen argues, fully understand how difficult it is in modern societies entirely to distinguish the sacred from the profane?

In his discussion of the classics O'Toole therefore suggests that contemporary sociologists remain in a critical as well as appreciative dialogue with Durkheim and Weber. To show that conversation at work is one of the purposes of this volume, particularly in Part 1. Indeed, religion, as Flanagan and Erickson note in their discussion of Simmel, has been the institution that not only expresses and transcends the conflicts endemic within societies but also adjudicates those conflicts that threaten to disintegrate the soul. We should therefore expect to find religious movements that are heavily defensive of authentic selfhood, and others that seek to entice the soul to sacrifice some of its spontaneity and autonomy for the sake of the larger society. Indeed the religious battlefield exhibits this contest between the self and society. What antagonizes the Chinese government, for instance, about the Falun Gong may be precisely that individuals have found in it ways of preserving their selfhood, the experience of their inner selves, without the blessing of the state or the control of its functionaries. The same thought may concern sociologists who study movements such as Pentecostalism. From a Durkheimian perspective, the individual is entirely derivative from the social order and can only be deluded or dangerous if he or she claims to have found the sources of selfhood outside the social system. For David Martin, however, who traces his sociological lineage back to Max Weber, religion has long been the source of an authoritative personal vision, but it is a vision that is socially responsible, self-disciplined, and altruistic. A similar legacy of responsible individualism is now being carried out by evangelical communities throughout Latin America, Africa, and Eastern Europe, and Martin's work has done much to bring it to light.

Moreover, in the contemporary and very complex societies that increasingly dominate the global system, the sacred is proliferating; it is showing up in new and more diverse forms in places where the sacred was once more firmly under communal or institutional control. Proliferation, diversification, and dispersion, dissension, and disruption: these are some of the forms taken by the sacred in societies undergoing the sort of social changes that are associated with the growth of cities, the spread of industry, the movement of people and capital, and the interchange of ideas and symbols across the borders of communities and nations.

As is often noted, the root meaning of the term "religion" refers to tying together. The very suggestion of religion as a binding element has often been translated into a simple-minded suggestion that religion unites societies. Of course, everyone knows that in fact religion can be quite divisive, especially when it provides the basis for a society's identity and self-understanding. Certainly those on the periphery or who have been marginalized in various ways often seek to define themselves in terms of opposition to whatever the center represents. Thus, when the sacred is difficult to distinguish from the profane, religion may be unable to confine the sacred within a framework that makes it available and attractive to all sectors of the larger society.

No wonder, then, that many sociologists therefore see the sacred as a source of perennially subversive interest, enthusiasm, aspiration, and authority. For Max Weber, charisma was often disruptive, but it was also the source of continuing relationships, stable routines, and eventually of solid institutions. We owe to Simmel, moreover, the sociological conviction that societies depend on the striving of the individual for a relation to the sacred. Social life itself depends, in his view, on the striving for access to a form of being that is unconditional, beyond the self, and yet accessible and responsive. That is why, as Erickson notes, for Simmel sociability and society itself are the product of the spiritual strivings of the individual. Allow those strivings to be defeated or deflected onto objects that confine or destroy sociability, and the social order itself becomes vulnerable.

The sacred is thus a two-edged sword. It can divide people from their natural communities, upset established forms of leadership, and make people hungry for the sort of rewards and satisfactions, justice and peace, that the world as it is organized for them fails to give. On the other hand the sacred can be a primitive and perennial source of sociability. Thus the future of social systems depends precisely on the sort of spiritual openness and freedom that Martin has located among Pentecostals and evangelicals in Central and Latin America and in Southern and Eastern Europe. On the other hand, in these same movements one can see how the sacred can also be the inspiration behind movements for liberation and reform.

Of course, the sacred is often bottled up and packaged in ways that make it seem entirely within the knowledge and control of those few who are licensed to inquire into its mysteries. Wherever a professional elite is entitled to investigate the secrets of the heart or to acquire esoteric knowledge of the universe, for instance, that same elite will seek to own and control access to the sacred. The usual justification for such a monopoly is that such knowledge is too dangerous for the uninitiated and requires someone with the advantages of special training and personal capacity in order to protect the larger society from unpleasant surprises. The same knowledge is also essential if the society is to take full advantage of the opportunities that the world has yet to offer.

However, there are always communities that probe the sacred on their own without professional guidance, that acquire extraordinary amounts of literacy and information, and that therefore can let the future begin in ways that are often not prescribed by those in authority. They live by the spirit, so to speak. They usually live on the social periphery, where they preserve their vision of a better society and wait for an opportune moment to make a move toward the center. In the meantime they pose a continuous threat to any attempt to monopolize the sacred. The Martins' research on Pentecostalism in Latin America makes both points exactly.

In Christianity the long tradition of eschatological hope has placed a question mark over everything and everyone that in the mean time lays claim to sacred status. David Martin's chapter is a reminder that the avant garde of history may be found in unlikely places, and especially among those who seem to sociologists as hopelessly out of date. Indeed, his early upbringing in a home that was familiar with expectations of the end introduced Martin to the hope for a divine kingdom that would upset the ordinary course of events and institute a realm based on peace and justice rather than violence. That same hope, tempered by the experience of World War II and later repression, animates a wide range of Christian communities, from Pentecostal cells in Latin America to the Protestant congregations that sparked the final resistance to Romanian dictatorship. Martin has made it clear in his work that the future is always beginning in the communities for whom the end is a present reality.

Seers have long known that access to the sacred gives foreknowledge of the future. The sacred is, after all, that which lies beyond the present range of social order and beyond what is normally considered the limit of human potential. The sacred dwells in the bush outside the village or in the future that is known only to the shaman and the seer. In ritual the future can be discerned and either anticipated or forestalled, depending on the omens or the liturgy. However, there is no guarantee that the future will begin in the places where it is expected. Religion is thus not only the friend of the sacred but its worst enemy.

In seeking to domesticate the sacred, religion often confines and controls it, substituting the letter of belief for the spirit of faith itself. Ironically, therefore, those in the Church and the theological schools who are most hostile toward the process of secularization are themselves often the carriers of a very secularized version of religion that substitutes formal belief systems for the promptings of faith. The heart goes out of any religion that substitutes the letter of doctrine or the routine of office for the spirit. That is why David Martin is not entirely happy with the experience of those Pentecostals who are no longer suspicious of theology. It would be well, he suggests, to be very wary of any discipline of the spirit that seeks to reduce faith to a set of objective propositions. Thus David Martin writes in the tradition of Max Weber, who notably argued that aspects of Protestantism are the bearers and causes of secularization.

As a sociologist who finds in the sacred the sources of a subversive social imagination, David Martin directs our attention to the sacred as the source of dissent against the abstract formulae of theology and the law. Religion, Weber noted, may find itself in tension with the world for a variety of reasons, and some forms of religion tend to reject the world as a place that inhibits or subverts the practice of genuine piety. Other forms of religious faith, however, see the world as a place that is to be overcome: an arena in which faith is to be tested and applied with more or less consistency and rigor. The world in that sense becomes what faith has made it. Read David Martin, then, as a way of seeing for yourself what an active sociological imagination and rigorous research can make of contemporary religious rejections of the world.

Of course, every society oversimplifies the world in order to limit the range of social imagination. Otherwise everything would be negotiable and dependent on circumstances and mutual consent. However, there are always individuals who are in touch with a wider range of possibility and who see the danger to human sociability in every form of social order. This sense of the "beyond" is indeed the primary source of conflict in any society. No wonder, then, that societies have often turned to religion in order to soften, if not overcome, the most fundamental and dangerous sources of cleavage and opposition between the sacred and the world, between charisma, as Weber put it, and its institutionalized forms. In psychoanalytic terms, then, religion has provided a reality principle that expresses but limits the hopes for social and personal transformation. The "beyond" is the Sacred, and it is always in tension with what a society wants to teach its members or call 'sacred'.

In reading the various contributions in this volume, then, it would be well to keep in mind a set of paradoxes. Religion is the collective expression of the sacred, but religion also deprives the sacred of its primitive capacity to create a new world. Without the help of religious institutions, the sacred disappears as easily and quickly as it appears; however, with the benefits of institutionalization the sacred loses its capacity for transcendence. Left to its own devices, the sacred provides multiple epiphanies in a wide range of contexts, whereas religion has the capacity to collect these many and varied sources of inspiration and authority into a more or less unified framework for an entire community or society. Once the sacred is adequately framed, however, religion deprives the individual or the group of the authority of their original vision, and access to the sacred becomes derivative and mediated through religious professionals and elites. Religion, as it seeks to relieve the discontent caused by civilization, is therefore always in tension with the sacred. That is in part because the sacred provides hints of another society that is waiting in the future for someone to pave its streets and build its houses: a new Jerusalem, perhaps, a new Athens or Rome. However, the sacred keeps alive the aspiration for a society that does not depend on the actual or veiled threat of force to keep its citizens in line.

Any sociology of religion that claims to be able to get at what it means to be religious will therefore have to come to terms with paradoxes of the most poignant and existential sort. David Martin gives paradox its due in deciphering the code of Christian belief and practice. He refuses to translate Christian belief into a set of propositions that can stand or fall on their own existential merit without the support of tradition or institutional authority. To attempt such a project would be to lend a hand to the process of secularization. Instead, he leads his readers into the labyrinth of paradoxes, where it is crucial to understand how it is that dying may be a form of living, that death can lead to resurrection, that weakness provides the occasion for uncanny strength, and that what a society rejects as beneath its own dignity may eventually have the last word.

Sociologists have long understood that even for the devout, things never turn out quite the way they are supposed to. That is why a religion that announces a peaceable kingdom can give its blessing and authority to a repressive and militant regime; it is why a religious movement that relies entirely on invisible sources of authority can end up by being a church that justifies its decisions entirely on procedural grounds alone. The sacred always ends up being processed and contained by some bureaucratic agency, just as the cross, David Martin points out, becomes a sword when it is taken up by certain groups with a vested interest in maintaining their power.

It is not only paradox and the tragedy of unintended consequences that perplex sociological inquiry. It is also the chronic and perennial sense of primitive loss that keeps recurring in the sacred. When Martin spoke of a nostalgia evoked by the presence of his mother in an environment as enchanted as that of his native West Country in England, he is speaking of a primitive break in the individual's experience of the world. The other, the transcendent, is present under the sign of its absence. There is indeed something missing, as Capps goes on to say in his discussion of the sense of melancholy. Others, too, have noted that the process of secularization begins with a sense that there is a mystery at the heart of the universe. The world hints that it is no longer organically related to its spiritual sources; on the contrary, the very rocks speak of a deposit, and the holes in the ground speak of an impression, both of which were made by ancestors long gone.

As Donald Capps reminds us in his chapter, the religious imagination and melancholia have much in common: an ambivalent yearning to recover something that is missing but not entirely absent. This missing element reappears in unfamiliar forms, and yet it is also strangely familiar. Toward it individuals may have very conflicting emotions, from yearning and desire to resentment and hatred. They may imagine that it holds the secret of their existence and without it they are lost, but they may also fear that in its presence they will be consumed and suffocated. That object or presence is, of course, the maternal world out of which everyone first was born and toward which many of their later aspirations are unconsciously directed.

Capps's chapter is included here because of the editor's conviction that Freud's work should be included among the classical texts on which the sociology of religion is founded. Sociologists tend to be far more interested and expert in the processes that characterize communities and institutions, peoples and nations than they are in what used to be called "human nature." However, without being open to the insights of psychology and psychoanalysis, sociologists will be never be able to arrive at a satisfactory explanation of phenomena as recurrent as religion. While sociologists may be able to give a partially adequate account of the circumstances and conditions under which religious belief and practice take one form or another, they must look to other disciplines for theories that will account for the persistence and vitality of the experience of the sacred even in societies that are relatively secular.

Capps allows us to understand the sacred as the "other world" from which humans are inevitably separated and which nonetheless seems to hold the secret of their existence. It is a world that was present at our origins and from which all are inevitably separated. In its absence, however, this original matrix still appears in fantasies and dreams, in the imagination of utopias and dystopias, in yearnings for fundamental social change, and in plans to turn the social tables on a wide range of oppressors and tormentors. From Capps's analysis we can infer that the more rebellious Oedipal emotions underlie the grim determination of religious reformers. Similarly, grandiose imaginings that one is entitled to certain infantile satisfactions may underlie the conviction of being chosen for or entitled to a Promised Land. Mystics, however, and those who dream of a reunion with a source of total harmony, beyond rivalry and recompense, may be seeking a more primitive fusion with the maternal source of their being. Their utopias differ, as do their dreams of restoration and return to a heavenly city, from which they were prematurely expelled and which is presumably waiting for their return. The sociologist of religion thus seeks to understand the social processes that tend to thwart perennial aspirations for the sacred and to identify the conditions under which these longings create new harmonies, open up new possibilities for satisfaction and fulfillment, and allow a future to begin that would never have been possible had it not been for these primitive yearnings.

In the sociological study of religion, then, we are examining the disputed territory between the realm of freedom and hoped-for fulfillment and the world of the mundane, of the way-things-are, of necessity and inevitable limitation. For theologians, as Martin points out, this is a familiar territory, where the context is waged between the law and the spirit, between "every jot and tittle of the law and antinomian release from all legalistic impositions," between God's eternal decree and human freedom. For sociology, the task is to probe deeply enough beneath the surfaces of social life to gauge the range of possibility, the intensity of aspiration, and the immanence of threat and opportunity that are normally concealed beneath the surface of the routine and the ordinary.

It is questionable whether in this endeavor sociologists are more helped than hindered by their familiar ways of understanding the perennial tensions in social life. Terms such as "social structure" and individual "action," the "system" and its "environment," or "society," and "personality" may not get at the dynamic tension between aspiration and reality, between the sacred and religion, and between this world and imaginings of the next. That is why, in Part 3, we include Kieran Flanagan's discussion of Simmel and his appeal to sociologists to renew their concepts through close theological readings of their subject matter.

Sociology, like theology, thus comes with a set of formulae that may also limit the range of what the sociologist can envision. This limitation is particularly detrimental when sociologists study something as opaque and problematic as the sacred. It takes a stretch of the sociological imagination to speak of the untold psychological and physical agony that may be embedded in any community or society. Even symbols and events such as the crucifixion may disguise rather than direct public attention to the toll that social life so often takes of the human spirit. A great deal of insight may be lost, David Martin suggests, in this translation of theological into sociological concerns. What is lost are the depths and heights of human discourse, references to good and evil, an ear for the sublime and a fundamental acquaintance with the intractable elements in human suffering.

In Part 2 we will find sociologists who, like Robin Gill, chart signs of decline in institutionalized religion, but who will not convince those who find in modern societies a proliferation of groups and communities that embody the sacred. Other sociologists, like Steve Bruce, find signs of secularization in an irreversible increase in the ability of individuals to think and decide for themselves rather than stay between the lines of orthodox belief and practice. However, he will not deter other sociologists who see in moral conversation, the rituals of everyday life, or the emergence of small groups devoted to study or acts of compassion new signs of the sacred. The debate will not doubt continue well beyond the generations included in this volume.

CHAPTER 1

Personal Reflections in the Mirror of Halévy and Weber

David Martin

A clear remit to place work in life raises problems of relevance, completeness, self-indulgence, and professional exposure. Inevitably the establishing shots of life come long before the work and involve some risk of disjunction as well as personal pain. In so hybrid an enterprise the art of social science is to know how much sociologic must concede to chronology, necessity to contingency, process to personal agency, and broad pattern to unique trajectory. The justification has to be that we hear what people say when we see where they are coming from. Sociology itself suggests there is something to be said for unraveling those secret reasons of the heart which help motivate the reasonings of the public realm.

I was nurtured in a Bible-believing evangelical home between the wars, just at the point where you might hope seriously to better your children's future through public education. Faith was joined to aspiration, and it bred in the bone a sense of difference which never disappeared however much the commitments might appear to mutate. In what follows, for example, I want to show how a domestic atmosphere averse to macho behavior generated a radical political pacifism, and yet the new commitment still remained a rejection of "the world" and an eschatology, however implicit and shorn of mythic support. Being educated, I sought good reasons for what I had already come to believe so that part of the initial fascination of sociology arose because my faith was enquiring of my intellect. That in turn pushed me to make sense of Christianity itself, not as a set of propositions but as a repertoire of transforming signs in historic engagement with the deep structures of power and violence.

In the 1930s my parents were already out of date by half a century, which meant neither I nor they were likely to suppose truth the daughter of time, though I had to traverse much lost cultural time to catch up with my own date. The advantage of being born "out of due time," and having stubborn dissent branded on the soul, is the motive it gives to employ a "hermeneutic of suspicion" against the old masters of suspicion, and, in Peter Berger's phrase, to "relativize the relativizers." Moreover, if a process like secularization is declared inevitable it deserves all the opposition it can get from people steeped in opposition. More recently this built-in refusal of ruling paradigms has combined with childhood experience to provide empathy for the evangelicals now emerging all over the developing world. Theory used to condemn them as nonpeople by refusing them certification as contemporaries and even disallowing their right to be treated as an authentic culture in the postmodern motley. Time and due process should have ensured their secularization and politicization according to approved Western models.

That is where I have to begin, linking the very early with the quite recent. Inner presences can be dormant for decades until aroused by some chance encounter, as when I had opportunity, through the initiative and assistance of Peter Berger, to trace the growth of evangelicalism in Latin America. I compare my family in the 1930s with Latin American evangelicals now. After that I look at the genesis of my pacifism, at pacifist faith enquiring of the intellect through sociology, and at its collapse under pressure into a somber Augustinianism. To lose one faith is understandable but to lose two has certainly not been carelessness.

Evangelicalism at Home (c.1938) and in Latin America (c.1988)

When I was born in 1929 the world slumped spectacularly, but with only short-lived impact in Mortlake, in south-west London. The interwar housing boom which helped my parents buy a house with a mortgage soon picked up. My father was a chauffeur in Kensington before eventually becoming independent with his own taxi, and he was quite uninterested in economics or politics. Apart from the odd outing by Austin 7 "to the country," leisure mattered as little as politics, because all his heroes were evangelists, like D.L. Moody of Chicago, C.H. Spurgeon of the Metropolitan Tabernacle, London, and Gypsy Smith from Epping Forest who converted him. The future he imagined for me through "a good education" was a secure job at £7 a week in the bank, but he also had visions of his son converting thousands at Albert Hall rallies, rather like a faintly doubtful American evangelist called Aimee MacPherson. He himself had left school at 11 and documents show his mother (born 1853) signing her name with a mark.

My father liked Americans, partly because they "always gave a good tip," especially in the war, but also because there were obviously more like himself "over there" than "over here": devout family men with an eye for a bargain. So far as that went he was not at all out-of-date, and like so many millions in today's developing world was halfway to becoming a cultural citizen of the USA. The Continent and Catholics were a different matter, and in that respect we lived in the time warp when anti-Catholicism was quite normal in Britain and the USA. A couple of ladies of Kensitite persuasion poured a kind of "Protestant Truth Society" propaganda into my ears such as today hardly exists outside Ulster. Nor did childhood browsings in Foxe's *Book of Martyrs* and George Borrow's *The Bible in Spain* improve my perspective on the Scarlet Woman. What Linda Colley has to say in *Britons* about England, the Protestant champion against inquisitorial Spain (and wine-imbibing lubricious France), closely approximates our view of the matter. That itself was quite enough to expand the Channel and shrink the Atlantic, and permanently defined for me the crucial cultural affinities. France was "wholly other" and in any case the war ensured that I was 20 before crossing the water and succumbing to the enchantments of Laon, Rheims, and Strasbourg.

My father often left his taxi to preach from a portable pulpit in the open air, usually in Hyde Park, but once he did so outside our house supported by a friend playing on an ocarina. At that my mother prohibited any further attempts to evangelize Ripley Gardens and I've wondered since if maybe she had her reservations. Or was it just that as titular head of the household God was my father's business? At any rate all other business was my mother's, including the little insurances and savings accounts which kept us afloat. Most of the time she was knitting, or reading Dickens and Hardy, or growing and cooking very good Protestant food, and was too busy even to join our Sunday evening hymns and choruses around the piano. It was my father who "fed on the Word," poured out passionate exclamatory prayers at the bedside, and read sermons for which he needed the dictionary, or (later) help from children and grandchildren. Probably the 1932 encyclopedia was my mother's, a slightly problematic acquisition since the entry for "Earth" was altered in my eight-year-old hand to conform to Usher's chronology of Genesis. My mother also bought me, painfully, volume by volume, a *Newnes Pictorial Knowledge*, as well as the papers for "the scholarship" we worked on together in the evenings.

Of course, the Achilles heel of Bible-believing and aspiring people is the breaching of the protective wall of difference by education, and reading beyond the Word. For the moment, however, I rummaged safely in improving Edwardian novels like *The Old Torn Bible*, missionary adventure stories of heroes like David Livingstone, and tales of the imperial frontier by prolific authors like Ballantyne and Henty. The poems I read included Tennyson's "The Charge of the Light Brigade" and "Ode on the Death of the Duke of Wellington," which encouraged me to write a composition for Mr. Gibbs (of Mortlake C. of E. Primary School) about one day becoming another Iron Duke. There were giants and role models in those days.

These dead worlds with their extinct meanings are embarrassing to remember, but I'm sure we believed that so long as "we" (and England) stayed with the Lord we were on the winning side, Protestant and progressive. Though by 1938 there were rumors of wars and trench practice at school with our gas masks on, we kept up our Sunday School "picnics in the sun." Still, the sight of the Fleet lit up off Portland, as well as our evangelical world with its old liberal politics, missionary boxes, and big preachers like Dr. Dinsdale Young, was well into its end time. As for my father, he expected the advent of Jesus rather than the Luftwaffe cruising over our heads.

As the sun set on all this in the summer of 1940, and the two following decades, another version of our world was rising again in the southern hemisphere which now engrosses perhaps a quarter of a billion people from São Paulo to Harare. It really is not so difficult to recognize the similitudes between industrializing England in the 1830s and Latin America under the hammer of global capitalism in the 1960s. Against all the odds put up by social science, Latin America was in train to leave behind its tradition of violent political revolution and go the way of nonviolent religious and cultural pluralism as discussed by Halévy in his classic *A History of the English People*.

This had come about through a cultural explosion in the first decade of the century in Los Angeles and in places as far apart as Korea, Wales, and Chile. To be offered a chance to report on the current progress of that explosion, transporting to new contexts the problematic of Halévy, De Tocqueville, and Weber, was largesse indeed. Globalization had completed John Wesley's vision of "the world as my parish," and the discrete if overlapping revivals of the early nineteenth century were now rolling Pentecostal surges from Rio de Janeiro to Dar-es-Salaam. Though missionaries still had a role to play as initiators or reinforcements, the big picture was of people migrating across all frontiers with a transmigration of souls running in parallel. Messages of transformation were transmitted by people apt for modern technology and keyed in to indigenous culture with amazing facility.

When you think with your life, you have the advantage of insider knowledge; and in this global movement I could easily recognize the open air speaking, the mass singing, the impassioned outbursts, the dictionaries, encyclopedias, concordances, and popular histories, the refusal to blame or complain, the unremitting cleanliness and hard work, the little insurances – and the eye for a bargain.

Family integrity is, of course, central, as Elizabeth Brusco (1995) has persuasively argued. There is a recreation of the family in Latin America round the virtues of nurture, hedged with respect for husbands if faithfully earned. The protective enclave of faith offers just the kind of social clearing my parents inhabited for their own recreation and for the employment of talents not recognized elsewhere. When a Chilean researcher for the Jesuits told us of archaic words properly used but wrongly pronounced, I knew immediately where I was. Reading of millions of labor migrants to the megacity going into domestic service or small business I have the story already.

History doesn't repeat itself exactly, of course, and the spiritual autobiographies we collected (with the help of Paul Freston and Arturo Fontaine) were full of admonitory dreams, healing miracles, and exorcisms more like the Gospels than the Wesleys. That has led a distinguished researcher in the Reformed tradition, J.-P. Bastian (1994), to suspect a recrudescence of a folk Catholicism too casually devalued by the reformers at Vatican II. Perhaps the blessers, healers, and shamans of Latin America have indeed reinvented themselves as potent pastors, but their inventiveness has been comprehensively reframed in an evangelical discourse of the one Holy Spirit.

Unhappily the publication of my *Tongues of Fire* in 1990 exposed me to attack as an agent of American cultural radiation. It was incorrect even to report what theory forbade. The power of the ruling paradigms came home to me most forcibly on a bus full of Western academics in Guatemala. When told that 66 percent of the population was Catholic they asked no questions about where the rest might be, even though the answer shouted at them from texts on huts in remote El Petén, storehouse churches called "Prince of Peace," and buses announcing "Jesus is coming." It took many studies from 1990 on from Stoll (1990), Burdick (1994), Cleary and Stewart-Gambino (1996), Ireland (1992), Lehmann (1996), Chesnut (1997), Bowen (1996), and others – before the paradigm faltered and the obvious was conceded. One difficulty pointed up by David Lehmann is that the supposed rival movement of *basismo* has its proponents in the international intelligentsia, while Pentecostal radicalism lies precisely in not caring whether or not the intelligentsia pronounces you an authentic popular culture.

I have suggested that "we," in Britain, though geographically and socially coming in from the margin, were confident in the care of Providence. Others might gamble on Fortune but we rested in Providence, so even as we declined, the hoped-for end time reversed any seeming secularization. Now in Latin America a similar expectation and reliance on Providence paradoxically sustains hope through secular disaster, and sometimes even helps avert it. Miracles help those who believe in them, as when a garage lay round the corner when my father's car broke down or damaged building materials lay helpfully in the path of a Chilean pastor who needed them for his new church.

I met that pastor, a chunky little Aymara Indian, when I arrived in the Central Valley south of Santiago with colleagues from the Catholic University and the Centro de Estudios Publicos. He was a sometime left-wing union organizer, and told me a tale about the Antichrist of Borges-like complexity. Then he revealed himself as a self-taught renaissance man: headmaster, conductor of the children's choir, architect, teacher, acupuncturist, writer of a book about his son's resurrection, entitled *He didn't die.* Clearly millennial expectation stimulates mundane activity.

It was also clear that the difference between a researcher and an evangelist was not grasped, because I found myself advertised as due to address the evening rally. As villagers processed across the fields towards us strumming their instruments I realized what I had to say. I must tell them that they, like my father and his father, possessed something very special in a "story" to tell which we wanted to hear. So, once assembled, I spoke of my grandfather's conversion from domestic violence and alcohol abuse, and how like them, he played his accordion in the open air as he sang and preached. "He is in Abraham's bosom," one cried as I spoke of his death from the kick of a horse. I said their trucks for collecting wood and spreading the message were like my father's taxi, and Santiago was their "great city" as London had been his. These stories tallied, I said, and in conclusion walked towards them with hands extended quoting Wesley, "If thine heart be as my heart then give me thine hand." This experience was not where I had arrived but where I had begun, and it was neither LSE nor Anglican Evensong.

My question is whether they, too, will enter a secular end time, and the forlorn chapels of North Wales or Cornwall in the 1990s become in 2020 the forlorn chapels of Chile, or Yucatan, or Baja California. How that could happen through mobility and education is not only clear enough from the biographies of my family but also from a story told me by a taxi driver in Mexico City. He was, he said, the "black sheep" of a Methodist clan, and so we went to meet the family patriarch in his spacious home. After migration from Santander in northern Spain, the family had got converted in a kind of chain reaction and our host had made a living as translator for an American evangelist working in the United States and Mexico. He spoke of his youthful belief that Catholicism had held Mexico back and we noted the open Bible in the niche for the Virgin, and the professional diplomas on the wall where a picture of the Sacred Heart might have hung. "My father reads everything now," said our taxi driver, "including Ouspensky." Our own initial conversation had opened with him talking about "L'Albatros" in Baudelaire's *Les Fleurs du Mal*. Under modern conditions everything happens faster: reformations, faith – and apostasy.

Dangerous Transitions: Music and Words

My mother came from a village in the South Dorset downs and her father had moved there to be foreman at the waterworks from the more remote south-west of Exmoor where even today the old alliance of liberalism and nonconformity lingers. In these Dorset villages small ancient churches are faced off by brick chapels, and my grandfather would ring the bells in the parish church before cycling miles to preach in the Methodist circuit or march with the Salvation Army or meet with the Masons. Politically I think he became liberal-labor, but his sons, a railway signalman and a baker, moved left, one into membership of the Communist Party. The countryside around the house had an almost geomantic potency, and it was in this territory that my mother focused my (and her) melancholic sense of Paradise Lost. Here anchors were let down which, refracted by water, lodge out of sight in the Rock.

My mother went up to the megacity of London taking with her a valedictory sermon by her father invoking divine protection. She met my father at the megachurch of the Methodist Central Hall, an Edwardian Baroque structure confronting Westminster Abbey in a magnification of the rural rivalry of church and chapel. This place played a role in English Methodist history analogous to the role now played by the Methodist Pentecostal Cathedral in Santiago. What remains with me is the plangent singing of multitudes who in the same breath praised God and announced their arrival. Today the succession of great preachers there is over and prime ministers like Lloyd George no longer visit. Most of the time I was packed off to a local Methodist Church in Barnes in south-west London, which I could walk to but where they failed to preach the "real gospel."

The myriad hymns and addresses I heard as a child must have been a preparation for music, poetry, and rhetoric. Once in the choir I was introduced to the Victorian cantata market and musical offerings oscillating between Stainer's "Crucifixion" and Chu Chin Chow. This kind of church experience has provided a route into serious music for many singers, and it was foreordained that my developing musical passions would begin with composers of the Protestant north: Mendelssohn and Handel, Bach and Brahms. Indeed, I became (and remain) as passionate about Handel as Samuel Butler in his Notebooks. Opera was then remote, and lieder even more so.

This close partnership of sacred word and music in Anglo-American culture gave me the clue that movements of the spirit acquire a characteristic rhythm and spread as much by singing as by preaching. Nowadays in Latin America rival faiths purloin each other's music and in the latest wave of prosperity gospel in Argentina the popular style of evangelical music counts as much as the healings and exorcisms. The way mass democratic singing has crossed the religious and cultural frontier to Latin America is as sure an index of major change as people moving on to occupy their own religious space. When in Vila Industrial, Campinas, Brazil, I saw many hundreds of mainly black and brown faces at a Pentecostal two-choir festival. I was not surprised when today's popular sacred music came to a climax with the Hallelujah Chorus accompanied by torrential shouts of "Gloria."

In that church I was bombarded by messages of imminent arrival: the best clothes with just a hint of ornament, anticipating an advance out of poverty; the raised voices announcing a presence, as well as securing entrance by the side door into the dangerous house of culture. A female trainee teacher, discreetly made up, claimed "We're not so afraid of theology now," and I wondered how justified such confidence might be.

Of course, there are other routes to follow beside ones familiar to me, particularly if we really are entering into a postmodern fragmentation of the dominant intellectual traditions or an inability to tell high from low culture. In a church in Guadalajara, Mexico, for example, the initial warm up of the grannies, children, and couples grabbing the mike turned into a jamboree with the youth band playing Christian rock. The mansions in the house of culture proliferate.

Years later in Romania I could trace parallel pathways being opened up in the new Baptist megachurch in Oradea, and again felt bombarded by messages of advancement by voluntary religious organization and self-recreation. The power of that creation was generated by prolonged interior prayer during the Ceausescu dictatorship and the effects were more and more visible among country people hounded rather than drawn into the towns and finding a protective enclave in the worshiping community. They had encountered a form of personal address piercing age-old collective impassivities and could envisage a changing future, including the mobile body language of the next generation preparing to be professionals. Though not the effervescent eruption of Latin America, the massed voices raised under the safe conduct of the pastors registered a social presence. A well-trained choir sings Brahms, Schutz, and even Fauré. "Maybe we have reached our cathedral stage," said one of the ministers dubiously. The leaders have spent time at London and Oxford universities and know the dangers; still they press ahead with a college designed to turn the buried talent of centuries into a Christian intelligentsia able to take on the "cultured despisers."

Music has always been religiously ambiguous, handmaid and rival seduction, but it exhibits no trajectory toward unbelieving enlightenment, not even in Beethoven. There is no progressive "Whig" history of music. The "word," however, is different and the tension of minister and musician looks fraternal by comparison with the tension between priest and teacher. Once again the polar oppositions of Latin culture contrast with the modest mutations of the Anglo-American world, even though the Latin polarities may be passing into history; 1789 came to its own end time in 1989.

For me personally to progress from the Word to the expanding universe of words did not need to be a total disorientation, especially since in England poetry and music and the biblical text and music are so closely linked. For anyone prone to fuse the revelation of music and poetry with the music and poetry of revelation, there was a genealogy to follow from the metaphysicals to Blake and Coleridge, and on to Hopkins, Eliot, and Auden. Even in discursive prose my saturation in an imagery and a rhetoric provided immediate access to the resonance found in a writer like Ruskin. (No doubt my revulsion at supposedly modern liturgies and biblical translations had some of its origins here. More has been at stake in terms of identity and continuity than the fumbling banalities of the actual products.)

Naturally such supports would not be available when later reading the literature of the social sciences, though the usual disjunction is found between the revolutionary reversals of Marx and Freud in the continental tradition and the evolutionary progressions of Herbert Spencer, begotten out of dissenting genealogies. Social science literature lacks the personal imagery and narrative character of the Christian story, and in any case you cannot confine yourself to reading the meliorist reformers and moralists of the Anglo-American tradition.

The trouble with evolutionary progressions is that they give less advance notice of their destination than revolutionary reversals. I could recycle the late Victorian and Edwardian experience with its multiple secularizations, still secure in a continuity of image and reference anchored in the long durance of English literature, and of music. This security sustained me even as I, in part, converted faith into politics under the influence of a socialist school friend whose family Methodism had already faltered, and stimulated by discussions at a Methodist youth club. I kept my intermediate way by means of a soft utopianism and a nature mysticism occluding the darker human potentials.

Central to my whole experience was the recovery of Paradise Lost in the ecstatic apprehensions of creation in Traherne and Vaughan ("I dreamed not of poverties, contentions or vices"), and this was supported by reading Evelyn

Underhill's *Mysticism*, by Olive Wyon's *School of Prayer* – and much private *vers libre* of my own in symbolist vein. J.G. Davies's study of Blake even offered a kind of analogue of an evangelical remission of sin. I did not entirely notice the shifting nuances of this "Adamic" ecstasy as I passed from Wordsworth to Richard Jefferies or Rilke or to the mantic celebrant of my childhood paradise, Llewellyn Powys.

Yet the teasing irreverence of Shaw in *Major Barbara* or *The Black Girl in Search of God* struck home in several senses. What sent me into final free fall was Schweitzer's *The Quest of the Historical Jesus*, a disorientation not much relieved by grazing on Loisy or Goguel, or on the wilder shores of Robert Graves. Happily, the theologians made more sense than the critics: Maritain, Gilson, D'Arcy, von Hügel; and (I must say) Chesterton among Catholics; Gore, Quick, Temple, Bevan, and Lewis among Anglicans, as well as Brunner, and my two mentors, Reinhold Niebuhr because he dealt with evil and violence, and Berdyaev because of his free mystical treatment of dogma. I also read the decent scholarly material prescribed for Methodist local preacher's examinations, but it seemed that – Butterfield and Rupp apart – the resources for self-defense nearly all lay elsewhere. My background had been marvelous for generating questions and serious questioning, but it was short on answers, if such existed. So I looked elsewhere, and given that my concerns lay as much in Christian historical practice as in metaphysics I was ready for sociology. After all, Shaw and Spencer were both founders of the London School of Economics.

Résumé: The Emergent Problem

What with bemused imaginings of becoming a writer or poet, and reading off the syllabus, or talking politics into the small hours, I failed to get into a university. That meant immediate conscription and personal crisis since my political translation of Christianity included a liberal socialist pacifism such as was preached by Donald Soper, George MacLeod of the Iona Community, Charles Raven and the Fellowship of Reconciliation. Tolstoy's writing on nonviolence and the Kingdom of God confirmed me in this faith, so I went before a tribunal in Fulham declaring "I refuse to be a state slave of war." I did my national service in the Noncombatant Corps alongside as varied a group of dissidents as any future sociologist of religion could hope for, as well as helping run an orderly room office for "Pioneers" from Moss Side, Tiger Bay, and the Gorbals, and cleaning lavatories for licensed sadists in the Military Police.

That over I went to Westminster College (Methodist) to train as a primary teacher, a good profession for intelligent carers if they can face 40 years of class war, or for failed poets, musicians of moderate talents, disgruntled utopians or aesthetes whose Protestant ethic has fallen on easy times. Clive Bell's writings on civilization appealed to me, and Herbert Read on anarchism and art, which broadly meant I had caught up with the 1930s and would have made a premature recruit for the 1960s – except that I retained a proper deference, and thought universities represented integrity rather than power.

I remained set on justifying and promoting my nonviolent faith in a world resistant to the obvious. I religiously rejected "the world" and the world rejected my solutions. To abridge a longish process, that implied I find out about the structure of international relations as analyzed in writers like Reinhold Niebuhr or Hans Morgenthau. Meanwhile I read books on race in South Africa and on capital punishment (then a public issue) equipping myself with the facts and figures needed for my position. However, I also became interested in problems as problems and it even occurred to me that some were unsolvable. Whereas I had been a connoisseur of altar calls, I now became a connoisseur of political rhetoric and polemic, a good preparation for sociology, though I dismissed all that as mundane concern with social work and community. Better far to feed my imagination on art history and the mysteries of Byzantium or the cloisters of Moissac.

Slowly over the years, the world as it is forced me to construct an implicit model of social relations which took into account the will-to-power and interested character of international politics as worked out in the partial mutualities of everyday society. Here I write proleptically, clarifying in retrospect what was confused in prospect, but the end result was a somber Augustinianism. In due course I would dig a pit under my nonviolence, and also eventually develop a critique of the liberal optimism implicit in sociology outside the acrid realism sometimes promoted on the left. In sociology you are expected to intuit the stance appropriate to a rational liberal person without breaking the taboo against value judgments or introducing inassimilable categories like good and evil. Unfortunately, my background ensured I retained such categories, which meant that even in sociology I was destined for dissidence. I would be seeking cross-references between incompatible discourses, asking whether a sociological analysis of constraints and limits had relevance for a Christian discourse of transformation, or whether the resistance of structures to moralization corresponded to original sin.

The Promise of Sociology

I read sociology only by the accident of teaching alongside a Welsh radical with some remaining affection for the chapels in the valleys, who was taking a correspondence course in it. Once convinced that here was a university subject matching my concerns, I joined him on the course. That way I entered another time warp, because the course had not been newly thought through but assembled from other disciplines like ethics and statistics. Two years later when a perusal of the exam papers revealed what must have happened, I constructed my own course, helped by rummaging in the university library.

In particular I followed up the religious aspects of the subject, occasionally clashing with tutors, for example, on the role of free will in the "criminal career", a notion long disallowed until recently renamed "agency" in relation to "structuration." Why had religion been so central to the classics and yet was now so marginal? As for my fundamental concerns, they were hardly assuaged. On the one hand empirical sociology mainly documented deprivation, while on the other continental theorists were either antimetaphysical or secularist metaphysicians.

Almost the only writer really to connect was Weber, especially his *Religious Rejections of the World and their Direction*. Weber's account of how these rejections worked themselves out in the economic, political, and aesthetic spheres, and in relation to violence, located my problem. I now had a map of where I stood and realized that Christianity was not some array of propositions but a coherent grammar of transcendent signs in tension with mundane reality. Here was a code book of transforming symbols which we decode selectively according to time and social circumstance. Put another way, it is the poetry and the narrative of a Way: a passage by water and wilderness to the goodly city. That viewpoint permeated my own later writing, in particular *The Breaking of the Image* (1980).

Pains of Arrival and the Problematic of Violence

Arriving at the London School of Economics on a postgraduate scholarship meant I could work seriously on why a pacific teaching realized in self-sacrifice at the hands of priest and procurator had itself become integrated into structures of power and violence. I chose the 1930s in Britain as a prime site for studying pacifism of all kinds, religious and secular, and immediately engaged with some major theorists, especially Sorel's (1925) *Reflections on Violence*, which interwove religious and political themes on a large historical canvas, and Mannheim's (1935) *Ideology and Utopia*. Mannheim's analysis of chiliastic religion suggested an alternation between pacific world rejection and the eschatological hope of world renewal, so that pacifist groups encapsulated revolutionary attempts to set up a new Kingdom. Perhaps this dialectic played into the dialectic between disciplined perfectionism, fulfilling every jot and tittle of the law and antinomian release from all legalistic impositions, and between the God infinitely above in heaven and the God immanent within us on earth.

But where to put the meliorist and often conditional pacifism of mainstream voluntary denominations like Methodism and of liberal internationalism? This kind of objection was founded in individual conscience rather than revolutionary consciousness, and it was a seminar paper on this which appeared as my first article, entitled "The Denomination," in *The British Journal of Sociology* for March 1962. Clearly this kind of objection was not apolitical withdrawal and yet it still embodied a more moderate dialectic between reserve about "defense" preparations, national interests, and armaments, and crusades to end wars, establish international law, and enforce liberal solutions. To the absolutist and conditional objections might be added an aesthetic objection such as animated Britten and Tippett. I had in fact put forward all three objections at my tribunal, and in the 1960s found them reappearing in the Campaign for Nuclear Disarmament. Such a secularization of religious themes – usually a moderated eschatology without explicit myth – in both the 1930s and in the 1960s and 1970s showed the remarkable vitality of a major cultural motif in its Anglo-American habitat, with wider echoes in post-Protestant Netherlands and Germany. It also indicated the ambiguity written into secularization, since world rejection may be present even though not couched in religious language.

My linkage of internationalist sentiment on the liberal-labor left with the free churches and their emergence from the collusive embrace of church and state became a key element when I returned to the theme of violence 30 years later in *Does Christianity Cause War?* (Martin 1997a). Though Christianity had begun as a voluntary movement seeking peace and universal reconciliation between man and man, man and God, once adopted by the imperial authorities it developed a double entendre, one shadowing the icons of power and interest and one diffusing contrary images of potent reversal. To understand Christian history it makes no sense to tick off its performance as a religion in terms of a checklist of political virtue. Instead, one needs to enquire how knights and merchants or peasants and artisans will selectively deploy the rich repertoire of signs it carries forward under canonical and ritual protection. The seeds it scatters will fly over the institutional wall and fructify far from the point of origin. No repertoire of signs can be other than ambiguous once adopted into the ineluctable structures of violence, whether we speak of Christianity or the Enlightenment. The cross in knightly hands is bound to be used as a sword.

When I joined the London School of Economics department of sociology in 1962, it was still the epicenter of the subject. For many of its distinguished scholars, some rationalists, some Marxists, my preoccupations were a hangover. They assumed secularization and applauded it, though I soon located an international network of people – disproportionately American – with whom I had some community of interest, such as Daniel Bell, Martin Lipset, Edward Shils and Talcott Parsons. These names suggest there has not only been a major Jewish role in the universal discourse of Enlightenment, challenging a Christian universalism, but a shared concern for the sacred and tradition.

Still I persisted in the pursuit of the sociology of religion, disinclined to suppose that its only appropriate focus was secularization. So when in 1964 I was invited by Julius Gould (as editor) to contribute to the *Penguin Survey of the Social Sciences*, I set about what I believe to be the first critique of secularization, following it up in 1966 with an article in *The British Journal of Sociology* on "The Sociology of Religion: a Case of Status Deprivation?" where I described what it was like to be "an academic deviant living by a non-existent subject."

In the first article I identified three ideological sources of secularization which were as much historical annunciations as empirical observation: the triumph of science and reason over the dark realm of obscurantist superstition and false religious explanation, the Marxist collective liberation through the painful dialectic of class warfare, and the psychological or therapeutic release of a mature humanity from existential dependence. I then went on in various pieces to argue that the concept of secularization was incoherent, encapsulating too many contradictory criteria, utopian hopes, and historical baselines, to be a useful conceptual tool. In *A Sociology of English Religion* (1967) I hoped among other things to show that the decline of religion was followed not by rationality but by subterranean theologies and nonrational sentiments and superstitions. One argument I have not adopted is that the minute take-up of "new religious movements" in any way makes up for the losses of the main religious bodies.

The simplest response to conceptual critique is that *something* has happened since the late Middle Ages, even though one may seek to debate, as I have done, the identification of the crucial episodes (1680–1720? 1870–1914?) or question the role of intellectual movements (Unitarianism, Rationalism) as distinct from social structural change.

My own attempt to cope with the changes melded together under the concept of secularization was accidental and came about because Ernest Gellner as senior academic in charge of a joint seminar asked me to invent a paper when the scheduled speaker failed to turn up. The core of what I devised was as follows. If we delimit the scope of secularization and look at the changes in religious practice over the period covered by modernity, long in Britain, short in Albania, we can identify certain processes like social differentiation and the hiving off of crucial sectors from ecclesiastical control, as well as certain trends, such as the decline of religious practice in relation to size of conurbation. However, these processes and trends pass through historical filters which control their form and direction, above all the difference between organic Catholic patterns, based upon polarization, and more fragmented Protestant patterns based on mutation and privatization. These general trends are in turn affected (a) by whether the national culture is denied statehood, as in Ireland or Poland, Quebec, and Croatia, thus greatly increasing the role of religion; or (b) by the regional presence of a pluralism, as in the Netherlands and Germany, where the south is Catholic; or (c) by the pluralism of competing denominations, initiated in Britain and consummated in North America. I contrasted Anglo-American evolutions with Latin (especially French) revolutions. What was missing was a proper analysis of Latin America, which in a later formulation I divided into a phase of characteristic Latin polarization followed by a switch towards Anglo-American pluralism, so creating a hybrid.

Gellner placed this in The *European Journal of Sociology* for December 1969 and it formed the first chapter and essential framework of my *A General Theory of Secularization* (1978). In that I also incorporated other earlier work on episodes of "reactive organicism" in Greece, Spain, Portugal, and Italy and the variable results of the contest between ethnoreligion and communist overprinting in eastern Europe. I had a particular interest in Bulgaria which I had visited in 1967 as the boasted showcase of communist success, and in the contrast between Bulgaria and what Marxist intellectuals in Sofia called "the retarded case of Poland." The subsequent spread of such retardation in Bulgaria in unpropitious local circumstances is ironic. Romania was another "retarded" case, partly through a collusion between nationalist communist state and ethnic church. There was a certain satisfaction when, in 1994, I set subsequent developments there in the scope of a general review (Martin 1995) of the "General Theory" in Timisoara, given in the University of the city where in 1989 the overthrow of the regime first began. On the other hand the refusal of Poles to replace communist domination by legal imposition of Catholic norms indicates that the process of differentiation indeed is crucial, as José Casanova has brilliantly contended in his *Public Religions in the Modern World* (1995). On other candidates as key components in secularization theory, such as rationalization and privatization, matters remain more ambiguous.

Concluding Sociotheological Postscript

Space must abridge the rest of an academic lifetime, except that the revolution of the late 1960s, at its more furious in the LSE, had both negative and positive consequences. Negatively its romantic propagation of "the naked self," beyond habit and cumulative continuities, struck me as destructive and I used my inaugural lecture at LSE to assert the humane benefits of "Order and Rule" (Martin 1974). Positively it undermined the more crass variants of positivism, allowing the phenomenological reality of religion to be exposed, including the life worlds of believers, how they saw the world and creatively shaped it. New permissions were granted, for which much thanks.

My other concern was with the relation of sociology and theology, for example in *Reflections on Sociology and Theology* (1997b) and how that was worked out in the interaction between the Christian repertoire of signs and social exigency, for example, in *The Breaking of the Image* (1980). The latter used the imagery it analyzed on the ground that demythologized and abstract translations are impossible. I took off from the Weberian analysis of the Christian angle of transcendence and saw this as expressed in a coherent repertoire of transforming images and a redemptive narration. Images and narrative were stored within the protective capsule of the church until released into the cultural bloodstream on the facilitating cues of social circumstance and group interest. The key paradox of the repertoire, combining incarnation and crucifixion, transfiguration and resurrection, turned on abasement and exaltation, desolation and glory, brokenness and wholeness. This paradox was picked up by the polarity of human impoverishment and empowerment: "Blessed are the poor . . . for theirs is the kingdom." The far horizon of this vision is brought "at hand" by the fast-forwarding of God's "good time."

The fundamental grammar of Christian signs decreed a breaking of the boundaries of sacred space: an elimination of the partitions separating God and

Man through the Son of God and Son of Man, and the absorption of the institutional temple into his resurrected and glorified body. A disfigured human face has entered the holy of holies, breaking down its partitions, and through obedience unto death manifesting God's glory. In Revelation 21, the sacrificial Lamb replaces the temple in a new spiritual and universal Jerusalem, and becomes its divine illumination.

Paradoxically this idea came to me as a female Jewish Australian guide took me into the clear open space of the Dome of the Rock. After all, this space witnesses as does no other to the fissures in the monotheistic tradition, and the fragmentation which has beset the global unification it represents. There, on the contentious holy ground of the Jewish temple and Muslim shrine, my guide accidentally quoted the Epistle to the Hebrews 12:22–3: "You are now come to Mount Zion" which my memory immediately completed in the resplendent crescendo of the Authorized Version "and unto the city of the living God, the heavenly Jerusalem . . . to the general assembly and church of the firstborn . . . and to Jesus the mediator of the new covenant."

The object of this exposition is not to give a sermon but to expose a theological and a sociological question. The sociologic makes everyone "in Christ" a priest and a king standing in the holy place and so destroys all hierarchies and spatial partitions. God is "all in all" and the heavenly city is nowhere but "above" and so "the mother of us all." All humanity is peremptorily invited to a wedding feast where life, wholeness, and peace are celebrated by ingesting the broken body of self-giving love and speaking the ecstatic language of heaven promised at Pentecost.

This gives rise to a sociological question because historically this unification has gone into reverse, just as the monotheistic faith has also broken into fragments. The partitions and priestly hierarchies have returned and the coming of the kingdom on earth has been reduced to demarcated holy spaces in physical churches witnessing in a limited way to the potential colonization of earth by heaven. We have to ask, therefore, whether by way of contrast with the viable transcendence of Islamic and Jewish holy communities focused on holy text and holy place, the Christian angle of transcendence has been too acute and too contrary to biological and social nature. It is supposed to be a leaven in the lump, but its brotherhood redeemed by blood is at odds with the blood brotherhoods of the family and of the warrior band. The drastic interpolation whereby Christ and "all in him" are born "of the spirit" outside the reproductive sequence of the generations is sufficiently contrary to nature to run the risk of nullification. Clearly, it threatens an end to our world.

What then is the role of the church? It is to incise the code by ritual repetition and to act as a storehouse of its potentialities. However, it cannot fully realize those potentials within its own boundaries, except in intermittent experiments, because it can only survive socially by incorporating the weights of all those contrary elements which resist transcendent vision – and protect us in our quotidian responsibilities. That means a profoundly feminine character is deposited in the cultural storehouse within a protective patriarchal format, and that the message of peace is carried and maintained through an ecclesiastical institution implicated in state violence. The world upside down is held up before people as a potential (and "held up" in the sense of restrained) by being made complementary to the world the right way up, that is, with authorities, with boundaries, partitions, difference, and power. That means we mostly overhear the Kingdom of Heaven *sotto voce* in the condensed poetic images of liturgy and scripture, or else in the sound of music and singing.

References

Bastian, J.-P. 1994. *Le protestantisme en Amérique Latine*. Geneva: Labor et Fides.

Bowen, K. 1996. *Evangelism and Apostasy*. Montreal: Queens and McGill University Press.

Brusco, E. 1995. *The Reformation of Machismo: Evangelical Conversion and Gender in Colombia*. Austin: University of Texas Press.

Burdick, J. 1994. *Looking for God in Brazil*. Berkeley, University of California Press.

Casanova, J. 1994. *Public Religions in the Modern World*. Chicago: University of Chicago Press.

Chesnut, A. 1997. *Born Again in Brazil*. New Brunswick, NJ: Rutgers University Press.

Cleary, E. and Stewart-Gambino, H. (Eds.) 1996. *Power, Politics, and Pentecostals in Latin America*. Boulder, CO: Westview Press.

Ireland, R. 1992. *Kingdom Come: Religion and Politics in Brazil*. Pittsburgh: Pittsburgh University Press.

Lehmann, D. 1996. *Struggle for the Spirit*. Oxford: Polity.

Mannheim, K. 1935. Ideology and Utopia. London: Routledge.

Martin, D. 1962. "The Denomination," *The British Journal of Sociology* 13(1):1–14.

Martin, D. 1965. "Towards Eliminating the Concept of Secularization," in *The Penguin Survey of the Social Sciences*, Ed. J. Gould.

Martin, D. 1966. "The Sociology of Religion: A Case of Status Deprivation," *The British Journal of Sociology* 17(4):353–9.

Martin, D. 1967. *A Sociology of English Religion*. London: Heinemann.

Martin, D. 1974. "Order and Rule," in *Tracts Against the Times*. London: Lutterworth, pp. 136–55.

Martin, D. 1978. *A General Theory of Secularization*. Oxford: Blackwell.

Martin, D. 1980. *The Breaking of the Image*. Oxford: Blackwell.

Martin, D. 1990. *Tongues of Fire: The Explosion of Protestantism in Latin America*. Oxford: Blackwell.

Martin, D. 1995. "Sociology, Religion and Secularization," *Religion* 25(4):295–303.

Martin, D. 1997a. *Does Christianity Cause War?* Oxford: Oxford University Press.

Martin, D. 1997b. *Reflections on Sociology and Theology*. Oxford: Oxford University Press.

Sorel, G. 1925. *Reflections on Violence*. London: Allen and Unwin.

Stoll, D. 1990. *Is Latin America Turning Protestant*. Berkeley, University of California Press.

CHAPTER 2

Salvation, Secularization, and De-moralization

Bryan Wilson

Secularized Religion

It can readily be contended that all religions have in common the offer of salvation to those who become their votaries. The plausibility of that statement depends of course on how salvation as such is defined, but if we allow that the concept embraces such things as the cure of bodily ills, prevention of witchcraft or protection from its baleful effects, victory over enemies, the acquisition of emotional control, release from existential pain, the attainment of harmony with universal laws, resurrection of the body, transmigration of the soul, ultimate unity with some conception of the infinite – or perhaps other specified goals – then we may say that a given religion is committed to one or more of these ostensible benefits. Furthermore, in projecting its promise, each religion tends to claim that it is uniquely qualified to bring that promise to fulfillment, or that it has a monopoly in doing so at least in a particular set of social circumstances, or at a given point of historical time. To exemplify this contention, one need only recall that for many preliterate tribal societies, witchcraft is a primary concern, and thaumaturgy a saving device. For Theravada Buddhism, release from the cycle of reincarnation, from the suffering experienced in this world, constitutes salvation; for Scientology, "survival" in all eight dynamics of being, amounts to salvation; and for various millenarian Christian sects, which subscribe to what might be called a futuristic, "big bang" theory, apocalypse and resurrection together comprise salvation for some at least of those who believe.

Many of these soteriological claims are made without the possibility of empirical proof of their validity. Salvation is to be realized in another realm or at another time, and thus faith is usually demanded as a prerequisite for salvation to be effected. Or, where faith as such is not in question, recovery from illness or the neutralization of a sorcerer's putative power is attributed, with no further test, to the proclaimed techniques of religious functionaries. In less developed societies and contexts, acceptance of claims that some such salvation was (and in some circumstances still is) available was reinforced by the myths and mores of the community itself. Individuals were not isolated in respect of their hopes for and prospects of salvation. Their salvation was essentially within – and, in some cases, with – the community.

The idea of being "saved" on one's own is alien to all traditional religious systems. An entire people, or a clearly designated section of it, was eligible for salvation. The experience was a communal experience. One's destiny was not only involved in, indeed inextricably mixed with, that of one's family, clan, tribe, community (eventually even nation), but entailed also the survival of the collective way of life, perhaps of the very social structure itself. Even in sophisticated religious systems, such as traditional Christianity, in which strong emphasis was placed on individual belief as a condition for salvation, individuals were encouraged to see themselves as destined for afterlife experience in the company of fellow believers. Individuals were encouraged – whether within the curtilage of the church or the conventicle of the sect – to identify with the community of the faithful and to envisage their soteriological prospects as members "one of another" within that community. Individual faith might be necessary for salvation, but it was less a certificate of achievement than a passport to association.

The global process of secularization, in which the notion of a world order created by some supernatural agency has given considerable place to an understanding of a man-made and man-centered world, has affected, among other aspects of the religious worldview, conceptions of salvation. With the course of scientific and technological advance, life in this world became less arduous, and its depiction as a vale of tears became less plausible. Alternative agencies of salvation, relevant to the here-and-now, or amenable to empirical validation, came to displace the speculative supernaturalism of religious systems. Proximate rather than ultimate devices of reassurance became acceptable. The demand for solace diminished. The experience of everyday life became such that salvation from it by supernatural means or transfer to supernatural spheres lost its erstwhile attraction. Human solutions to humanity's diseases and discontents appeared increasingly adequate, and steadily more plausible than those that had previously been canvassed by established religious systems. There was now a different conception of salvation – not, of course, identified as such by that name (except in some African countries where political parties have been prone to designate themselves as parties of national redemption or salvation). The style and content of what constituted salvation were now changed, and correspondingly, the character of an individual's efforts to achieve it had also undergone transformation. The moral ascetic characteristic of what religions required as a "deposit" towards the cost of salvation was soon to be superseded: moral conduct lost its status as a precondition or even as a predictor of the individual's prospects.

Widespread secularization notwithstanding, the old religious systems did not, of course, suddenly disappear, nor did they immediately lose the endorsement of established political and social authorities. At the highest social levels, lip service continued to be paid in religious terms to traditional communal and national mythologies. Yet the reality was that social systems continued to operate successfully in spite of doing so more and more without the reinforcement of religious nostrums.

Societies as Moral Orders

The social functions of religion, once considered indispensable if social consensus and social cohesion were to be maintained, were now rendered otiose by the rationalization of social organization, in which, even if cohesion could not be claimed, a level of contrived integration was achieved by a variety of rational devices. The declining credibility of communal salvation in another realm to which corporate life would be transferred, and the diminished credence in magical therapies, had the consequence of referring salvation primarily to the individual. Processes of individuation were becoming apparent within the social system generally, and it is not surprising that religion, too, should have reached a stage of development in which the salvation of individuals – now considered independently of their corporate or communal affiliations, such as they now were – should have become a central focus of what remained of religious enterprise.

In communally organized societies (entities, be it noted, of vastly differing size in which, none the less, sociologists often assumed essential similarity of the functions of religion), individuals' prospect of salvation was seen as intimately connected with their participation in the common way of life. It was in their observance of communal mores that individuals were offered the prospect of participating in the common salvation. It was shared values, sentiments, and mores which constituted social consensus and sustained social cohesion. Thus, these orientations were at once the guarantee of individual reassurance (the offer of salvation) and supposedly the bedrock of social unity. In these "moralized" societies (which continued well into our own times, and the residues of which are still in evidence) "good men" contributed to social well-being by acceptance of, and general support for, prevailing moral ideas. Thereby they also helped to sustain the framework of social order, solidarity, and cohesion – itself a type of salvation in the here-and-now – and an earnest promise of a fuller salvation hereafter. Clearly, not all men behaved morally, nor did so all of the time, but they understood the prevailing normative pattern of order. Whether they conducted their own affairs morally or not, they were prepared by and large to endorse the moral code by which affairs were supposed to be conducted, and they expected the comportment of others, and the relationships among them, to conform to these stipulations, even if they were, at times, prepared, or at least tempted, to exempt themselves from the full exactions of the moral order.

Maintenance of the received moral code, realized by men's involvement in observing and judging the behavior of their contemporaries, had the function of social control. In so far as religion prescribed or endorsed the moral code, gradually particularizing the rewards attached to injunctions, and the punishments attributable to infractions, so it became the arbiter of proper moral conduct. Simple social control obtained in relatively undifferentiated societies, where men's lives were lived largely in the sight of others; where, for instance, in the Christian case, "confession" of sin was often no more than the acknowledgment of widely observed dereliction of duty or transgression of the prescribed moral order. But once society had experienced substantial refinement of the division of labor – itself the consequence of the development of new techniques of production and distribution – reliance on such direct devices of social control was no longer sufficient. What then became essential was the internalization of moral dispositions as matters of principle which would carry over into whatever social roles the individual was now expected to perform.

Most significant, and indeed paradigmatic, among the new roles that people were increasingly expected to take on, were roles associated with work. The new work order required a new moral texture, and in the dissemination of the Protestant ethic, and in the subsequent reemphasis of stern moral requirements in Catholicism, one may recognize the golden age of the moralization of Western society. Older patterns of dependence on external communal surveillance to provide social control gave way to reliance on more intense individual socialization, the internalization of moral sense, and the cultivation of encompassing conscience.

It remains an open question whether such a moralization of society could have occurred without the agency of religion to inspire it and probably to sustain it. What may well be contended is that in the history of the modern West, religion was in fact the means by which such a social transformation of popular *mentalité* was effected. It was, paradoxically, the prospect of transmundane salvation as canvassed by religion that facilitated the moralization of society, the acquisition of refinement of personal comportment, and the manifestation of disinterested goodwill. That goodwill eventually inspired a wide variety of moral endeavor and works of charity which, whilst evident enough in medieval times, increasingly manifested disinterestedness of spirit in being unrelated to any direct self-advantage.

Obviously, the process of moralization was not even and equal in all segments of society. It became a significant lay phenomenon in Western Europe following the Reformation. What may have happened in the sixteenth and seventeenth centuries among those in the mercantile classes who espoused Puritanism, appears to have begun among a wider public only in the late eighteenth century during the development of widespread industrialization. Evangelicalism and revivalism inculcated moral dispositions among a broader spectrum of society. This more encompassing moral rectitude was perhaps associated with the theological shift – from a Puritanism which averred a condition that men "could not know but must not doubt" their chance of salvation to the Arminian assertion that "whosoever will may come," and further that those who claimed to be saved could take comfort in a doctrine of assurance. The restrictive conception of salvation and what might be known about it was entirely congruous with the elite position of the mercantile classes, and appealed to them in legitimizing, at least in respect of afterlife prospects, their uncertain claim to social preeminence.

If the masses were to be successfully socialized, however, an altogether less psychologically subtle soteriology was likely to be needed. For the general populace to be considered redeemable morally, the offer of salvation had to be plausible for everyone in general. Arminianism democratically opened the gates of heaven to a self-selected public drawn from the newly industrialized working classes. What the would-be citizens of God's Kingdom need show by way of qualification was not worldly success in the spirit of God "prospering the righteous," but the marks of moral refinement which attested that "by their fruits shall ye know them." Preaching to the masses, the new evangelicalism of necessity canvassed an opportunity open to all. Those who seized that opportunity presented themselves not merely as claimants to be "joint heirs with Christ" in the world to come but as candidates for moral regeneration here and now.

The votaries of evangelical religion were certainly helping themselves, becoming transformed in moral comportment and embodiments of the work ethic in accordance with, for example, Wesley's injunctions that they should earn all they could, and give a fair day's work to their employers. They were, however, even more important as role models for their entire generation, since endorsement of the moral order transcended the confines of evangelical religion. It became crucial to the making of the new culture of industrial society, whether religious or secular. Work, which had once been largely coercive, and which, in early industrialization, was elicited instead by remunerative considerations, had come increasingly to invoke normative commitment. Honesty, diligence, punctuality, willingness, sobriety, responsibility were the canvassed values, combining to evoke the ideal of "pride in one's work." Work was the paradigm case for the demand for moral comportment throughout social organization. The widely embraced assumption was that society could be a good society only as long as men themselves were good, and good not because they were under surveillance, but because of internalized promptings from which were elicited performances which society designated as moral. The model for such comportment rested on the assumptions of direct relationships between known persons, and the responsibility of individuals to their community, which was immediate, visible, and constraining.

Secularization as the Decline of Moral Order

The postindustrial society has seen much of such a moralized social system swept away as the work order has become increasingly impersonalized. Within work activities, role performances as such have superseded dependence on personal qualities. The process of impersonalization went further as technological progress transformed even the intrinsic character of roles by facilitating their mechanization, to a point where role performers were sometimes replaced by actual robots. Whilst the evolution of social roles had raised men above the animals, the depersonalization of work activities threatened to reduce them to the status of the machine. As all this occurred, so work activity became more explicitly part of the rational economic calculus. We talk more of such things as "products" even when we mean services; "customers" or "clients" where we mean passengers, patients, students (and their parents), and litigants; the "work force," "labor units," "redundancy," "rationalizing," "downsizing." The language reflects the impersonality of the system, becoming clinically immune to infection from human and humane values.

A process of *de*-moralization occurs. Human affection and regard persist, of course, but the point is that whereas these qualities – of personal commitment, obligation, loyalty, diligence, willingness, respect, concern for community welfare, compassion – were relied upon for work performances, such is the consequence of mechanization, the electronic revolution, and information technology that these lingering nonrational residues are squeezed out of the complex structure of role performances. The demand is for calculable economic efficiency, which depends on technical competence, not on personal goodwill; it is elicited increasingly solely by remunerative compliance, and less by normative obligation.

Whereas the work order of the industrial past depended in some considerable degree on the general moral commitment of workers who had pride in their jobs, and whose work entailed the mobilization of that sense of pride, the new patterns of work do not engage moral dispositions but only certified technical competencies. Conveyor-belts, electronic controls, automation, and computers effect specific control over the role performance of the individual which renders moral engagement redundant. Good workers need not now be, as they once were, "good men." Their moral quality has become a matter irrelevant to their work. Today's workers do not need to have been socialized for a predominantly moral role.

The postindustrial work order is capable of eliciting from its personnel the performances it requires without those workers having been subjected, as children, to an intense socialization process in which moral orientations were inculcated. Parents are, in any case, less disposed, and have themselves less time, to devote to the moral formation of their offspring. As the modern family is split apart, diurnally as well as organizationally, in consequence of the increased specialization of the social order, and the separation of home from work and home from school, and as television in some measure distances individuals from their home environment, so the interaction of family members diminishes. The elaborate talk about parental role modeling fails to come to terms with the fact that, all too often, the parents are not sufficiently present, not sufficiently engaged in the same pursuits or in the same culture, for the parental model to "take" in the life of the child.

Although intimations of this problem are not infrequently voiced, the postindustrial society espouses its own defensive ideologies which justify the abandonment of the intensive socialization of the past. Contemporary child-rearing ideologies postulate that the individual is in some sense a moral being from birth, whose status and rights are recognized as law at international, indeed virtually at global, level. It is readily assumed that freedom from constraints – from ordered learning, from rules of everyday comportment, from discipline – will in itself be all that is required to bring forth individuals at their best. All this is in stark contrast to traditional attitudes towards moral behavior. Christianity took as its basic premise the assertion that men were born sinners, already indebted to society: their formation, and reformation, depended on a program of threats (about hellfire) and blandishments (the promise and reassurance of salvation in heaven) together with well-established patterns of discipline. The disciplinary code was an imperative element in the creation of moral men from the sinful raw material of mankind.

Secularization, as an inherent part of the process by which industrial society was superseded, allowed society to dispense not only with Christian assumptions about basic human nature, but also with the traditional devices for shaping that nature into durable and responsible moral material. We have noted that the increased specificity of roles, consonant with the enhanced division of labor of advanced society, called for the relinquishment of more generalized moral norms and made more precise demands for technical competence and performance, a process that we have designated the *de*-moralization of the role. Nor were well-defined, specific industrial roles the only ones affected by this development. In advanced societies, even those roles that we might label as diffuse underwent similar processes of de-moralization. Two of the more important diffuse roles in society were those of teacher and clergy. Those were roles that, at least until recent times, were defined primarily in moral terms. Their tasks were socializing tasks. But what is today demanded of these role players has considerably changed. The moral dimension of their roles diminishes. We may see this in the declining concern for pastoral care in schools, and its virtual abandonment in colleges and universities. Moral permissiveness is indignantly justified by teachers, and even by priests, when the charge is made that they should hold themselves responsible for moral waywardness among the young. Parents not infrequently join the same chorus: someone else should take responsibility for the immoral comportment of children and adolescents. Increasingly, teachers and clergy are expected to provide technically competent performances and to display professional attitudes: their basic philosophy has shifted from formulating the moral being to facilitating individuals to discover their own identities, to "be themselves," to "do their own thing." Their concern is no longer to communicate and inculcate virtue, and – like the caring professions that have taken over part of their erstwhile teaching and pastoral roles – instead to cultivate a professionalism that encourages them not to care too much.

Moral socialization has diminished as the nexus of control has shifted. Less and less dependent on generalized attitudes of disinterested goodwill, sympathetic participation, and the cultivated virtues, the social order and social relationships are increasingly characterized by recourse to mechanistic devices. Expertise in such patterns of control and role relationships becomes an autonomous sphere of activity, independent of the substantive concerns of actual organizations: management consultancy instances the emergence of a whole genre of specialists whose specific competence lies in the claim to organize role performances on ever more rational lines by eliminating from such systems any vestiges of human feeling and generalized moral concern. Moral character is no longer regarded as important for the economic well-being of the individual or for the public good: public reputation depends less and less on moral demeanor, more and more on technical expertise.

A part of this evolution may be attributed to the massification of publics; geographic mobility, both in the temporal and spatial sense; to the intensification of casual and transient role-dictated contacts and interactions (perhaps what Durkheim meant by dynamic density?); to the breakdown of local community which has created a cloak of anonymity for the individual who, lacking internalized conscience, also escapes the social control of being a known person with a reputation to lose. In the civic arena, virtue becomes a private predilection. No longer the manifestation within the individual of community values, moral virtue becomes almost a quirk, certainly an eccentricity. Because such developments facilitate a variety of criminal or antisocial behavior, such breakdown of moral control leads inevitably to the threat of more oppressive measures for the maintenance of public order. Modern governments, even in the most liberal states (perhaps especially in the most liberal states), contemplate or institute such devices as data retrieval systems, video monitoring of public space, the electronic tagging of offenders, "three-strikes" convictions, reimposition of visa requirements for migrants, curfews, boot camps, zero tolerance, and the like.

The emergence of anonymous individuals, capable of moving into and through a variety of social situations, undeterred or unaffected by any considerations of what imputations their behavior might have for their "social reputation," relates closely to the breakdown of the sense of civic order. Since work depends less and less on the articulated role structures which control the individual by the intermeshing of the expectations of other role players, so the breakdown of that system of order affects also the civic sphere. Public comportment is "liberated" from the constraints imposed by a role set. The mechanisms of self-control, inculcated in deference to the cumulative expectations of known others, slacken, at times even collapse. Fed on the philosophy of "being oneself," individuals see their highest purpose not in the maintenance of value consensus, public service, community concern, but in realizing their own "potential," in asserting themselves. The traditional conception of what it meant to be saved, was survival within and with one's community. The secularized salvation of modern times surrenders the community: the survivor becomes the self.

As the social system has come to depend less and less on private virtue, and increasingly on technological and rational procedures, so the de-moralization of the public sphere has advanced. In the past, the whole of social life was moralized, from the concerns of "mere manners" to the legitimations for the social structure itself. Dress, adornment, and speech, for example, were moralized, since society was a moralized domain. The way a man dressed carried moral connotations, and those who dressed in even slightly unusual styles risked ridicule if not opprobrium. There may still be moral implications of dress, but these are largely confined to the "undressed" – to the hippies, the punks, and the devotees of grunge, and the moral connotations are emphatically negative. The contrasting social meaning of adornments is unmistakable: on the one hand, wedding rings, which, for those in the married state were virtually mandatory; and, on the other, for the morally permissive, of rings through the pierced lip, nose, and nipple. Styles of dress were morally prescribed as appropriate to particular times and places: one did not work in one's "Sunday clothes." Clothes deserved respect and needed to be cared for. In contrast, modern youth, in expendable jeans, the more esteemed if torn and dirty, squats lightly on any filthy pavement, and reinforces the contemporary message that anything goes: respect for things becomes as alien as respect for persons.

Speech was a moral matter, too, with obligations of honorific usage, courtesy, and style adjusted to the varying claims to status of those who were addressed, as is still the case in Japan and Java. The public domain was a moralized order, which is not to say that everyone was moral, but only to indicate that moralized order was normative, supplying the criteria of judgment. With the displacement by rational, technical, and legal requirements of the demand for moral virtue, all such distinctions have been done away. In the old order, a young man, claiming less public regard, was expected to defer to an older person, or to any person to whom society attached greater social honor: politeness was morally informed. No such subtleties inform the operation of our traffic control systems, our elevators, or our computers. In consequence of the impress of these rational, egalitarian, depersonalizing innovations, we no longer need to be so polite, nor so morally preoccupied in our social intercourse. Morally justified social distinctions are discounted, and we are free to behave, even in our personal relationships, more and more according to rationally calculated self-interest, and with an impersonal indifference that conforms to the principle that we designate as affective neutrality.

The minor decencies of everyday life may in themselves appear to be an almost trivial concern when discussed in the context of economic development, social structural change, and value orientations, yet they are the quotidian manifestation of precisely the moral assumptions on which a society functions. Manners are the diffused operating expression of moral values, and moral values are embedded – at least in the "higher" religions – in the proscriptions and injunctions of religious narratives as guidance towards salvation. Morals are the foundations for manners, and manners ensure recognition of the rights, the dignity, and the feelings of others. They function to sustain social order and to avoid social conflict. Manners are not mere courtesies, rules elaborately evolved in status-bound and elite social contexts: they are rather an expression of care and moral concern for orderly social intercourse. Manners betoken commitment to self-restraint and to self-denial in consideration for the interests of others. It is no accident that the decline of concern for salvation, traditionally conceived as communal well-being – here or hereafter – should occur as a social trend contemporaneous with the abandonment of manners.

If the secularization of religion has been largely attributable to the rationalization of work techniques, that same current of rational process has also been largely responsible for the *de*-moralization of society, and hence for the dissolution of traditional values, and the codes of comportment that were dependent on them. One facet of this process may be perceived in the displacement of moral judgment by causal explanation, conspicuous in the development of a therapeutic orientation. In this process, blame and virtue become obsolescent categories as conduct becomes *de*-moralized. There has been a diminution of culpability, and a corresponding increase in excusability. The formulae are commonplace: "it is not his fault – it's the system"; "he's not responsible, he's sick," added to a willingness to pass off everything from criminality to lack of manners under the rubric of "self-expression" or individuals' need for attention, or their ineffective desire to "tell us something."

Beyond Asceticism and Sacrifice: De-moralization and Hedonism

The secularization of modern societies and the *de*-moralization of social systems, whilst ultimately a consequence of improved technology, are more directly derived from the changing ethos which those improvements have made possible. The burden of the Christian ethic, and in large measure, if in different terms, of all the great religions, has been to reconcile people to suffering. The means of reconciliation have been the promise that present suffering will give place to its abatement at some later (future) time. That relief amounts to reassurance concerning the prospect of salvation – a reassurance which makes suffering endurable. Such salvation was promised without, however, suggesting that humanity's suffering was not deserved. Its release from parlous circumstance was variously ascribed to the improvement of its own comportment, or to the ultimate and conditional mercy of its "savior"; but whatever precise details characterized such conceptions of theodicy, humanity's intrinsic unworthiness remained the premise of the religious ethic. Man was a sinner, and only the mercy of Christ and the proper exercise of ascetic discipline could elevate his condition.

As long as people enjoyed only a low level of technological competence, this ascetic ethic was not only congruous with the social conditions of the masses, but was also a vital agency of social control. Since people were occupied in producing for immediate or early consumption, such control was necessary to avoid waste of resources. In the producer societies of the past, labor was expended for necessities (however, variously conceived). The postponement of gratification, the need to build up incrementally the capital equipment of production, the moral interdiction of self-indulgence, the frequency of communal occasions of penitential fasting, the rigorous self-examination of one's activities and motives, and other items such as these comprised the ascetic ethic which, with some variation over time, Christianity canvassed to its adherents. Whether the idealized role model was the martyred saint of medieval myth or the ascetic Calvinist of the seventeenth-century mercantile classes, self-denial and self-sacrifice, in one form or another were the demands made of the faithful Christian. All of which is not to say that men generally lived up to such models. Clearly they did not. It is rather to emphasize the importance of a given value consensus which set community at a premium, and individual self-interest at a discount. These values were embedded in dominant institutions, and were ceaselessly reiterated by the church – easily the most dominant, and perhaps the only purveyor of value orientations.

The cumulative impact of technological advance has transformed erstwhile producer societies, which used resources primarily for capital accumulation, into consumer societies, in which there is a rising surplus of commodities, and the increasing manufacture of commodities which are, in a strict sense, not needed. Whereas in producer societies, man's focus was on work, in consumer societies increasingly his concern is with leisure. There is necessarily a shift in prevailing values. The old ascetic ethic would be dysfunctional were it to continue to command adherence in the consumer society. That society depends on consumption, hence on an ethic which enjoins indulgence, luxury, extravagance, and pleasure. The values which receive expression and endorsement at all levels – political, social, cultural – are the values of hedonism. Individuals are not only justified in seeking self-gratification, but are positively enjoined to enjoy themselves. Powerful new agencies for the dissemination of values come into being, in the service of consumption. The advertising industry has replaced the church and the school as the source of modern values. People are to be persuaded that they have the right, indeed, almost the duty, to consume. They are told that they have abundant, perhaps unbounded choices and extensive liberty of action, since choice is no longer subject to moral considerations, no longer constrained by values sustained and imposed by the higher spiritual authorities.

The old ascetic ethic lent itself to moral exhortation, and in traditional religions was the very stuff of morality: the new hedonism renders confused the demarcation lines between the moral, the amoral, and the immoral, where it does not relinquish such concepts altogether. The process of secularization, beginning with the remodeling of the state as a secular rather than a religious agency, and continuing in its effects through the polity, the economy, and society's cultural agencies, down to the grass-roots level of declining belief, is thus also a process of *de*-moralization. Society ceases to be held together by shared substantive values. Its unity is no longer to be found in a widely diffused common *mentalité*. Instead of that kind of social cohesion, there is a more mechanical social integration, a framework of technical order, of shared procedures, and a fiscal structure of tax, debt, mortgages, insurance, and remunerative constraints.

The law itself is steadily recast to abandon the purely moral concerns it once enshrined, and to deal with increasingly technical matters. Concepts of fault and blame are gradually eroded in favor of reviewing offenses as purely technical issues. The old values may, in the face of a rational social system, appear arbitrary and increasingly indefensible, sustaining a largely deontological moral code, with "criminal" offenses such as blasphemy, Sabbath-breaking, attempted suicide, abortion, homosexual practices, and treachery (now scaled down to the technical offense of "revealing official secrets").

The old moral prohibitions are now superseded, the community's moral defense which was their latent function must now be mounted on a different front. Whereas the old values were often able to convince men that their salvation lay in cultivating ethically inspired restraint, the new values of hedonism frequently engender only contempt and cynicism. As advertisers, acting in the service of the consumer society, consciously and deliberately oversell consumption goods, so individual consumers need a protective layer of cynicism in order to resist sales talk which is often little removed from confidence trickery. Yet what is clear is that there must be a limit to the extent to which a society can rely on induced cynicism as a collective defense mechanism. The breakdown of civic order, the increase in crime, the diminished safety of the citizen on the streets, the falling standards (despite recurrent legislative attempts to reverse the trend) of honesty and truth-telling in business, and the growing corruption of political and public life, are all in some measure consequences of the cynicism which advertising "hype" has caused to mount among the general public. The society which is *de*-moralized is likely also to be demoralized.

Cynicism is an effect not only of advertising. The ideology of freedom of choice and the canvass of libertarianism and permissiveness stand oddly juxtaposed to the increasing sophistication of state surveillance of citizens, and are a further cause of the alienation of the private individual from the state – marked perhaps most profoundly by the growing distrust of politics and politicians. If the state does not trust the people, the response is that the people do not trust the state. The breakdown epitomizes the collapse of widely diffused, well-defined patterns of moral concern, which were forged in the sphere of interpersonal relations but which shaped and civilized public order. The ideals of comportment in the private sphere informed the need for moral and responsible behavior in the public arena. Conscious of the inadequacy of laws to elicit a level of popular support sufficient to sustain civic decencies, Addison held self-restraint and consideration for the interests of others as the basic private virtue which would sustain public well-being. Burke, describing manners as comparable to the air men breathe, regarded manners as of more importance than laws, since the law itself depended on the manners (morals) of the people. Jefferson sought to devise manners for a new republic by designating, from aristocratic structures of civility and patterns of deference, vital restraints that would serve democracy, and engender moral concern in the publics of his day.

In modern times, governments, too, have endeavored to establish new moral codes, but have done so with the contradictory support of penal sanctions, evident in the attempts to enforce racial and sexual equality, and in the legislation against the expression of sentiments to the contrary. Neither these legislative prescriptions nor the canvass of "political correctness" in its various guises, can offer anything as effective or as spontaneous as what was produced by the inculcation of morals and manners in the process of socializing children. Morality cannot be artificially infused into society by legislative means: it requires that a critical mass of individuals acquire a sense of responsibility, regard for others, the cultivation of virtue, restraint, and self-control. In the past, the development of such a moral sense was intimately associated with humanity's quest for salvation. A modern view might suggest that religions and their votaries made a fundamental mistake in supposing that salvation was necessarily located in some transcendent spiritual sphere, since actual salvation might be said more properly to have been experienced in life in this world. The moral order itself was, indeed, a condition for "saving" grace. Was that mistake in itself necessary for the realization of even that more mundane conception of salvation?

CHAPTER 3

The Pentecostal Gender Paradox: A Cautionary Tale for the Sociology of Religion

Bernice Martin

The Pentecostal Movement

One of the fastest growing and most significant religious developments in the contemporary world is the vast expansion of evangelical, mostly Pentecostal, Christianity. A new wave of evangelical revival is animating the peoples of the developing world as they are drawn irreversibly into global modernity. Indeed the growth of evangelicalism so precisely follows the path of expansion of global capitalism that we must entertain the possibility of a causal link between the two phenomena (Martin 1998). The evidence accumulated over the last decade suggests that the new Protestantism is playing the classic role of modernizing agent in assisting the poor and not-so-poor of the developing world to adapt with some success to the fast and furious economic, social, and cultural changes imposed on them by forces not of their own making. (In the argument below I shall normally use the term "Pentecostalism" as representing the central tendency of the movement, though in particular contexts "evangelical" or "charismatic" is more appropriate.)

In fact it is a repeat-with-variations of an old, familiar story. Methodism performed the same task for the early industrial masses of England and Wales (Halévy 1934, Thompson 1964), and for the pioneer settlers and adventurers who pushed the American frontier steadily westward (Schneider 1994). Religious discipline creates oases of order and meaning within the chaos and dislocation which are inseparable from fast change and extensive mobility; religious hope and spiritual renewal heal bodies and minds, integrate persons and anchor communities; the skills acquired in a do-it-yourself fashion in the religious arena – literacy, organizing, the ability to stand up and speak in public plus the confidence that conversion brings to the newly individualized self (named and claimed for Jesus) – all these are put to good use by people who see possibilities as well as problems in the world turned upside down through which they must make their way.

Something in the order of a quarter of a billion people are currently involved in the movement. They are to be found all over Latin America where they constitute around 10 percent of the population; in the Caribbean; throughout Africa; the Pacific Rim; the Far East including perhaps as many as 40 million on mainland China (Tu Wei Ming, Harvard University, private communication); and on a smaller but increasing scale among the ruins of the old Communist bloc of Russia and Eastern Europe, more particularly along contested borders and in ethnically mixed areas like Transylvania. They are even found among the gypsies of Europe, both East and West, and in a significant proportion of the Hispanic, Korean, and other migrants into North America. They are mostly drawn from the poor, though not usually the very poorest and most hopeless, but a growing sector of Pentecostals can also be found among the small business community and the new middle classes, especially in the high tech information-based areas of economic development. This sector is particularly prominent in the Far East. Overall, the worldwide evangelical movement is second only to the worldwide Islamic revival in sheer magnitude.

One might think that a movement on this scale would have attracted the attention of sociologists of religion, but in fact it has barely even flickered on to the intellectual radar screen of the discipline until very recently, and part of my agenda in this chapter is to ask why. I am more particularly concerned with the aspect of the movement which I have referred to in my title as "the Pentecostal gender paradox." In this respect my chapter is a companion piece to the chapter by Linda Woodhead in this volume. Woodhead argues that towards the end of the 1980s what she terms the "sex-war stance" of "second wave feminism" was superseded by the more nuanced feminist perceptions of a "third wave." She cites a range of studies which showed how the apparently regressive character of certain overtly patriarchal religious movements – notably conservative evangelicalism in the USA, the latest wave of evangelical revival in the developing world, some Islamic revival movements, and conversions to Judaism – masks a very different substantive reality in which women exercise a considerable degree of influence over domestic and family matters, find important arenas of religious expression, and even achieve a surprising measure of individual autonomy.

I shall argue below that, at least in the Pentecostal case, the more nuanced view out of which the documentation of the Pentecostal gender paradox has emerged was not primarily a feminist achievement at all. Certainly the researchers who have described the phenomenon have been aware of feminist ideas but they have not situated themselves, as scholars, within paradigms defined by feminism. In fact, explicitly feminist researchers, even those working among the very populations in which the Pentecostal explosion was occurring, have failed to notice anything of the kind happening. Again, I want to ask why, but before doing so we need to look more closely at that Pentecostal gender paradox which has been so curiously invisible to sociologists of religion, feminists, and sociologists of the family. It is a strange lacuna in the record, a perfect case for Kuhnian concern.

Pentecostalism: A Modernizing Egalitarian Impulse

From Elizabeth Brusco's pioneering study onwards (Brusco 1986, 1995, Cucchiari 1988, 1991, Martin 1990, Burdick 1993, Hackett 1993, Marshall 1993,
Bowen 1996, Austin-Broos 1997, Chesnut 1997, Maxwell 1999), research
on evangelicals/Pentecostals in the developing world has repeatedly found
that women and younger people (the latter particularly in gerontocratic social
systems) are advantaged in new and crucial ways by the movement. It is true that
women are seldom allowed to become pastors and there are usually restrictions
on their participation in the leadership of the ministry of the Word as well as
strict regulations controlling dress and bodily adornment, but women are especially favored with spiritual gifts in a movement which is, after all, expressly constituted around the gifts of the Spirit. Women supply most of the healers and
prophets, they are particularly prone to be "slain in the Spirit," they receive the
gift of tongues and the gift of prayer. Their extensive religious discourse steadily
feminizes the Pentecostal understanding of God. Above all, women have used the
Pentecostal religious discourse to rewrite the moral mandate on which sexual
relations and family life rest. In societies characterized by a tradition of male
dominance they have been enabled to institute a family discipline, sanctioned and
effectively policed by the church community, which puts the collective needs of
the household unit above the freedom and pleasures of men and which has called
an end to the long-tolerated double standard of sexual morality.

In an entirely literal sense, Pentecostal men have been "domesticated,"
returned to the home. An unresolved tension remains between the *de jure* system
of patriarchal authority in church and home and the *de facto* establishment of a
way of life which decisively shifts the domestic and religious priorities in a direction that benefits women and children while morally restraining the traditional
autonomy of the male and the selfish or irresponsible exercise of masculine
power. The implicit deal seems to be that a substantive shift towards greater
gender equality will be tolerated so long as women are not seen to be publicly
exercising formal authority over men.

Traditional cultures of male dominance have usually found it easy to coexist
with religious structures in which hierarchy and the mediation of the sacred are
the institutional norms – Troeltsch's church type, for example. The radical egalitarianism of the Christian doctrine of salvation appears in one of its more naked
forms in Pentecostalism, however. Whatever the organizational hierarchy may
imply about the locus of religious authority, the sacred is not so easily reined in
in the Pentecostal tradition. The Spirit "goeth where it listeth" and lights indis-
criminately upon women, the young, the poor, the unlettered, the marginalized
of every kind, while salvation is proclaimed free to all who accept Jesus as Lord.
These defining features of Pentecostal theology and worship mean that any collusion with surrounding traditions of male dominance will continually stumble
against contradictions, even given the legitimation of Pauline principles of
patriarchal authority in family and church. In short, the Pentecostal doctrine of

salvation, and its liturgical practices based on the gifts of the Spirit, carry a radically modernizing egalitarian impulse, albeit inside a formal patriarchal casing,
just as Methodism did in an earlier phase. (It can even be argued that Christianity
itself is the main source of the egalitarian individualism which characterizes all
modernity, Seligman 2000.)

Nonetheless, it appears to suit both the men and the women in the Pentecostal
populations facing an accelerated transition to modernity that the gender
paradox be sustained rather than resolved. The practical effect has been to give
a new start to gender and family relationships through a transformation of the
moral order which legitimates and sustains them. This moral order seems back-
ward-looking (or "nostalgic" as Cucchiari 1991 terms it), but what it achieves
is an effective limitation on the older forms of male dominance which are not
family-friendly. It shifts in a modernizing direction, not least by constructing the
nuclear family rather than extended kinship obligations as the primary focus of
loyalty and mutual support alongside those that bind together the community
of believers. This moral order both reaffirms old principles that have been routinely ignored (sexual faithfulness in marriage, above all), and insists on the
moral primacy of what in the unregenerate world outside Pentecostalism would
be denigrated as merely women's concerns. It establishes an *experience* of greater
gender equality without destroying what Cucchiari has felicitously called
"gender integrity," that is, the possibility of experiencing the gendered self as
a "good *woman*" or a "good *man*" (Cucchiari 1991). In this way Pentecostalism
acts as a "transformative" mechanism (Cucchiari's term again), nudging a
whole sector of the poor in the direction of modernity.

Within the movement men acquire the dignity of an authority based on the
model of Jesus himself, which requires them to consult those on whose behalf
they exercise responsibility. In exchange for this new dignity – and poor men
have very little hope of dignity or authority in the secular economic or political
sphere – Pentecostal men must put themselves under novel restraint. Much of
what the church expects of them would stigmatize them as unmanly among
their unconverted peers: giving up alcohol, drugs, gambling, sexual adventures,
and the opportunity to sire children in many households, putting the family and
fellow believers before themselves, and so on. As Elizabeth Brusco (1995) has
pointed out it is important not to misunderstand the nature of individualism in
the evangelical Protestantism in the developing world. Each person is redeemed
as an individual soul but the movement does not encourage the atomistic individualism beloved of economic theorists. It morally situates the person within a
household unit constituted through mutual responsibility and interdependence.
The autonomy which men must give up after conversion is a real sacrifice, even
when, as is so often the case, the fruit of that unfettered autonomy has been the
corrosion of individual integrity and family stability. *Any* derogation of the principles of male dominance which prevail in the world beyond the boundaries of
the movement will tend to be experienced as a trial and a loss: even being seen
by his workmates drinking a nonalcoholic soda with lunch – "a young girl's
drink" – can be a daily torment to the recent convert.

Thus, though the Pentecostal gender paradox is one that benefits both women and men, certain indications, such as the predominance of women in the movement (they constitute around two-thirds of all adult evangelicals) and the greater propensity for backsliding among male converts (Bowen 1996), suggest that women stand to gain more and that men find the cost of the benefits they gain higher than they can always sustain. The paradox is therefore always precarious.

For women there are few downsides to conversion other than the regulations imposed to keep them modest, chaste, and sexually unprovocative. Even for those women whose menfolk refuse to follow them into the movement, or those many who lack a stable partner or breadwinner, the church provides the moral and social equivalent of family and offers them a role as guardians of the community's moral heart. A few even find new partners within the community of believers. In fact, many of the women who gravitate to Pentecostalism are casualties of unstable family systems, which have often been put under further strain by war and civil strife as well as dramatic socioeconomic change which frequently entails mass population movement and seasonal work migrations. Kurt Bowen's term for these female household heads, "the independent women of the evangelical community" (Bowen 1996), underlines the positive potential in their situation (even given the usually very unequal, gendered labor market in which they must work to support their families), by refusing to consign them to a simplistic "victim" category as they have declined to consign themselves.

Peru provides an apt illustration of the point. In the seven years since the Shining Path guerilla war has wound down, Pentecostalism has grown dramatically (Krauss 1999). The expansion has been most evident in those areas where the terrorist war claimed the lives of a considerable proportion of male household heads – often a third or more. While in the early stages of the war women in rural and small town areas had often welcomed the Maoist ideas – and even used the Shining Path movement to reform gender and family relations by force (Andreas 1991) – as the toll of the violence intensified it was women who orchestrated the resistance to the terrorists and hid their sons. In the aftermath of the war they have formed Mothers' Clubs which have taken the lead in rebuilding their shattered communities and developing methods of economic cooperation among the many widows. This has been fertile ground for the expansion of the Pentecostal movement. The devastation wrought by AIDS among the men even more than the women in many parts of Africa has posed at least as hard a challenge to the surviving women for whom new partners are a virtual impossibility. Again, Pentecostalism grows fast in such circumstances. (Though so, too, do demands for a return to traditional polygamy in areas where the demographic crisis is worst.)

All of this suggests that, if there is a "women's movement" among the poor of the developing world, Pentecostalism has a good claim to the title. Despite the existence of a discourse of strict gender equality promoted internationally by Western aid agencies, mainstream church organizations, development agencies and the like, it is not Western feminism, even in its Christian variant, which has transformed for the better the lives of millions of poor women in developing societies. They have been "empowered" by a "regressive," "fundamentalist" Christian movement whose theological rawness and lack of intellectual sophistication causes problems and embarrassment to enlightened Western observers, including those in the mainline denominations of the developing world whose young are defecting in droves to this do-it-yourself movement of the vibrant margins or are "Pentecostalizing" parts of those established institutions themselves.

Sociological Blinders

This latest evangelical growth springs from seeds sown all over the globe by the revival which fanned out from Los Angeles in the first decade of the twentieth century. In Latin America the current wave of growth began in the 1940s and 1950s with the major upsurge starting in the 1960s. In Africa the whole sequence took place a decade later with the surge beginning in the 1970s. In the Far East (with the exception of Korea where the roots of the movement are deeper and the pattern is more like that of Latin America), the big spurt occurred mainly in the 1980s. While longstanding historians of Pentecostalism like Walter Hollenweger and Jean-Paul Bastian were routinely keeping track of the movement, and some local scholars were aware of what was happening in their own backyards, the international research community really only began to register the significance of the new Pentecostalism in the late 1980s, beginning with Latin America more than two decades after the major upsurge had begun.

Even then it was neither sociologists of religion nor feminists who noticed it first but anthropologists, especially those in area studies, and missiologists and mission historians. International development specialists missed it and sociologists of the family ignored it. When the existence of this vast global mass movement did finally impress itself upon the scholarly community it was greeted with an extraordinary mixture of denial and hostility. Furthermore, once the phenomenon was deemed worthy of investigation, only a minority of studies either identified or recognized the significance of the gender paradox even though Elisabeth Brusco had described it very lucidly as early as 1986 and Salvatore Cucchiari had produced a sophisticated theoretical analysis in 1991. In fact the focus of so many of the anthropological/area studies was the political or ideological character of this unanticipated and "regressive" movement, that the question of what it meant for the lives of women and children (not the most significant political actors by conventional reckoning) simply never surfaced.

Thus we have a series of problems to address: the long failure of social scientists in general to identify the phenomenal growth of evangelicalism in the developing world as a fact; the hostility it inspired when it could no longer be ignored; the failure of precisely those scholars most concerned with religion to recognize

the movement as a significant social development; and the failure of those scholars most concerned with gender and family, including feminists, to address the
Pentecostal gender paradox.

The first hypothesis to consider is that the whole phenomenon was so unoriginal that it was seen as a nonissue by scholars looking for new problems to
elucidate. After all the Halévy thesis has long been the orthodoxy of the field –
even E.P. Thompson does not so much refute it as put a Marxist spin on it – and
a repeat performance might simply look like old news. On the gender/family
issues the story is also familiar on several levels. The reformation of morals and
manners and the creation of a home-centered family by early Methodism was
an intrinsic part of the Halévy story. On the broader canvas it has long been
accepted that Christianity appeals to those outside the circles of established
power – not only women but slaves, the artisan class, the marginalized of many
sorts – and contains a treasure trove of texts and signs of reversal. For this
reason Christianity has always been a discourse apt for the relatively powerless
to deploy against the powerful.

While the obvious corollary of these characteristics is Christianity's well
attested propensity to give birth to "religions of the oppressed," subtler and more
paradoxical processes also arise out of the fact that both the powerful and the
powerless appeal to the same legitimating and authoritative religious discourse.
This has enabled the relatively powerless to wring concessions, consideration,
even rights, out of the powerful by appealing to the appropriate texts or to signs
of reversal within the common discourse. That women should manage to shape
Christian patriarchy to fit their, and their children's, needs by appealing to a
Christian discourse is nothing new and has its analogues in Jewish, Muslim, and
other religious systems. From the first century onwards Christian women have
appealed to the faith – even to those Pauline elements designed to enforce their
submission to male authority and to the high value placed on celibacy in the
early Christian tradition – to achieve a degree of power and influence within the
family and the church and to achieve a measure of personal autonomy (Brown
1967, 1988, 1995).

Religious history is replete with instances of powerful Christian women, of
families in which partnership cancels out the effects of a formal patriarchy, and
of women who use a Christian discourse to serve their own ends within the
everyday politics of family life. And that, in a sense, is the problem. Contemporary Pentecostalism is a story with more than a family resemblance to what we
already know from earlier times and other places. What caused dismay when
the Pentecostal upsurge forced itself upon the attention of social scientists was
not the unoriginality of the repetition of familiar processes but a sense that the
proper time had passed for such processes of subterfuge and manipulation in the
gender order and for a pre-Enlightenment approach to theology. Pentecostalism
was not a revolutionary religion of the oppressed but to all appearances a conservative throw-back. It should not have happened.

Let us begin with the sociology of religion. Here the problem was not so much
dismay as blinkers. The main factor in its neglect of Pentecostalism is probably

the potency of the secularization paradigm in Western sociological thought. Even David Martin, one of the very few sociologists of religion to take Pentecostalism seriously (Martin 1990, 1995), confesses that despite an academic lifetime spent criticizing the secularization thesis, he very nearly missed the significance of evidence seen first-hand in Central America in the mid-1980s because the European-derived secularization model initially screened out the possibility that Latin Europe and Latin America might have different religious trajectories (see his chapter in this volume). The Western, and perhaps more particularly, the English-language sector of the sociology of religion, whilst unremittingly debating the secularization thesis, has tended to take for granted the decline of the more obvious indices of religious vigor in Western society and to pursue either evidence of "implicit" religion "beyond church and chapel" or signs of the sacred within apparently profane aspects of life. Studies of mainstream religious institutions are certainly no longer the staple fare of the discipline, while the extraordinary proportion of the academic posts and research effort in the sociology of religion in Britain and America especially which has been devoted to the New Religious Movements (NRMs) since the early 1980s is a phenomenon which itself might merit explanation (Arweck 1999).

Distraction by New Religious Movements

The study of NRMs, which has become a largely self-contained subdiscipline of the sociology of religion, has not so much challenged as sidestepped the secularization paradigm. It has taken as the core of its concern the small minority of eclectic, often Eastern-influenced groups which emerged out of the cultural upheavals of the 1960s in the West (though some had links with earlier fringe movements). These developments seemed to promise one remaining island of data for Western sociologists of religion surrounded by a sea of secularity. Ironically, however, when it comes to estimating the scale of the NRM phenomenon – which even the experts agree has only a tiny minority of committed members in any given population though the diffuse penumbra of cultural ideas loosely referred to as New Age may have a wide if shallow penetration among the post-1960s generations (Heelas 1996) – NRM researchers seem curiously willing to include all sorts of developments which more obviously belong in the same tradition as the supposedly moribund mainstream – from evangelical house churches to Independent African Churches (see, for example, Barker 1999 drawing on Melton, Turner and others). Yet conferences and publication on NRMs (including bibliographies such as Arweck and Clarke 1997) seldom if ever include substantive studies of these new evangelical groups and continue to concentrate on the core of accepted NRMs: ISKCON, Scientology, the Unification Church, and so forth (see as an instance Borowik and Babinski 1997, which does not include any of the burgeoning evangelical groups in Eastern Europe).

Something more is involved here than a self-interested talking-up of the size and significance of the NRM constituency. There is a genuine problem over the definition of some of the boundaries in a global religious marketplace where it has become common to find eclectic mixes of elements from the major religious traditions with a variety of local, indigenous religious cultures. It is true, too, that parts of the evangelical/Pentecostal revival have fallen under the scrutiny of NRM researchers because their membership disciplines have attracted the concern of anticult monitors. Nevertheless, it is hard to resist the conclusion that, having assumed the inexorable secularization of the mainstream Christian world, NRM experts have sometimes taken *any* sign of religious vigor as being by definition within their bailiwick and have failed properly to recognize that a movement of mainstream Christianity – albeit one which incorporates local, indigenous religious sensibilities as Christianity so often has done – and on a scale which dwarfs the NRMs, has not only been sweeping the developing world but infiltrating the cities of the West through its migrants and missions. NRM researchers might well have claimed these Western outposts of the new Pentecostal wave as part of their intellectual territory, but they did not (except occasionally for the purpose of counting heads). Anthropologists by contrast have often found in these migrant groups the clue that directed them to the larger movement in the developing world: Brusco first noticed the family revolution among Colombian evangelicals in the USA for example.

The NRM researchers also missed the gender paradox. As Linda Woodhead shows (see her chapter in this volume), the sociology of religion as a whole remained largely blind to the gender issues and conducted little research on the interface of family and religion up to the late 1980s, apart from those second wave feminists in the discipline exclusively concentrating on religion's role as agent of male domination. NRM researchers are no exception to this. Yet we might have expected NRM research to probe gender and family issues. After all, the NRMs had emerged from the cauldron of cultural experimentation of the 1960s and reflected the counterculture's search for alternative patterns of family and sexual relationships, sometimes "regressive" as in ISKCON or the Unification Church, sometimes "progressive" as in The Family or Rajneeshism. Yet these concerns over family and gender have been incidental rather than fundamental in NRM studies. Indeed, in retrospect it is especially intriguing that one obvious hypothesis easily derivable from early sect studies was never seriously pursued in the NRM literature, that is, that joining an NRM is a species of declaration of independence from the family of origin. That this was never taken up is surely attributable to the political context in which the academic study of NRMs arose. As Elisabeth Arweck (1999) has shown, the agenda had already been set by the anticult movement and the moral panic created through the mass media over the defection of young people, largely from educated middle-class families, to these "alien cults."

The sociologists of religion spent over a decade from the late 1970s testing (and usually refuting) the hypotheses generated by the "brainwashing" paradigm which had been promoted by the anticult movement and parents' groups.

Their main efforts went into elucidating the meaning for NRM members of the apparently bizarre beliefs and practices which were causing media-fueled scandals and situating them within the overall worldview of the groups (see for instance Roy Wallis's explanations of "flirty fishing" in Wallis 1978 and Wallis 1979). Although family and gender arrangements have often been described, there has been little focus on the relation between formal and substantive reality in this area (Puttick 1999): we simply do not know whether anything resembling the Pentecostal gender paradox is important within NRMs.

One obvious and honorable exception to the sociology of religion's neglect of family and gender is Nancy Ammerman's pioneering study of conservative evangelical women in America (Ammerman 1987) which was one of the earliest descriptions of the gender paradox. One reason why this major study did not cause more bells to ring within the discipline, more particularly outside the USA, perhaps lies in the effects of a further blinkering paradigm, the concept of "fundamentalism" within which Ammerman's material was filed.

A Confusion with Fundamentalism

The term "fundamentalism" is a coinage of the religious history of the USA. In a society where religion became and remains effectively popularized, all the social divisions are mirrored by religious divisions and built deeply into class, regional, and ethnic identities. A religiously liberal and/or secular elite, largely confined to the cosmopolitan enclaves of the North East and South West, faces a majority of more-or-less conservative and often somewhat anti-intellectual believers within provincial and nonelite milieux. The result has been what James Davidson Hunter calls America's "culture wars" (Hunter 1990) in which the term "fundamentalist" has become the pejorative label describing the authoritarian-populist conservative Protestantism that has most aggressively challenged the liberal position of the cultural elite. The subsumption of a grassroots, *sui generis*, evangelical revival among the peoples of the developing world into a category, "fundamentalism," which has an established and severely negative connotation for North American intellectuals, was both a miscategorization and a cue for hostile academic responses to the new Pentecostalism. In particular the Fundamentalism Project directed by Martin Marty and Scott Appleby in the late 1980s gathered very disparate religious phenomena under the one heading, placing the fissile, essentially voluntaristic Pentecostalism of the developing world incongruously alongside the anti-Western, theocratic Islamic movements, which had posed hard political dilemmas for American and Western governments in the decades since the Iranian Islamic revolution. Indeed it is tempting to speculate that it was these political resonances that largely account for the generous funding of the project.

One consequence, however, was that the analysis of evangelicals and Pentecostals in the developing world became caught up in the local politics of

America's internal culture wars. The approach of the Fundamentalism Project to the whole Christian evangelical movement emphasized, in a notably unnuanced fashion, its patriarchal and authoritarian dimensions and strict boundary maintenance, rather than acknowledging its rich ambiguities and the ease with which it is deployed to solve the problems of daily life in societies undergoing traumatic social and economic modernization (Marty and Appleby 1991, 1995). Moreover, as Linda Woodhead comments, it virtually ignores the gender/family dimensions, and that despite Nancy Ammerman's (1987) input.

The Fundamentalism Project encompassed both sociologists and anthropologists. While most of the fieldwork on the new Pentecostals has come from anthropologists, who are less crippled by the secularization paradigm than sociologists, and more likely directly to encounter Pentecostalism among the populations they study, they too have often suffered from distorted vision, thanks to certain ruling paradigms in their discipline. The two primary culprits collude easily with the category mistake of including the movement under "fundamentalism." The first is an often politicized adherence to a type of Durkheimian thinking which sees the intrusion of Western culture including Christian missions, as a violation of indigenous integrity (see Earle 1992). The second is a Marxist or politically leftist view of development which perceives Western Christian culture as a form of domination imposed initially by colonial regimes and sustained in new guises by global capitalism and more particularly by American geopolitical and military hegemony (see Comaroff and Comaroff 1991, 1997). The assumption that the latest evangelical revival is a species of American cultural imperialism links the two paradigms (see e.g., Deiros 1991).

There is a special irony in the Latin American case since many left-leaning development specialists, both in sociology and anthropology, notwithstanding the colonial nature of Latin American Catholicism, had placed their hopes on the success of liberation theology (which was, after all, the project of Western intellectuals like themselves) as the anticapitalist "option for the poor." The popular success of Pentecostalism and the failure of liberation theology to take off among the masses was not easy to accept. The ideological contortions of a text like that of Manuel A. Vasquez (1998) shows how difficult a pill this can be to swallow.

By the end of the 1980s it had become rare to encounter the crude conspiracy theory version of the thesis of American cultural imperialism, but more sophisticated versions continued to appear throughout the 1990s, partly stimulated by a surge of neo-Pentecostalism from the mid-1980s which promoted an explicit prosperity gospel. There is increasing agreement that notions of salvific healing which unite material, physical, and spiritual well-being derive less from American mission influence than from indigenous pre-Christian religious perspectives (Marshall 1993, Marshall-Fratani 1988, Austin-Broos 1997, Hackett 1998, Martin 1998, Maxwell 1998, Meyer 1998, Stanley 1999). Nevertheless, a number of anthropologists saw these developments as the triumph of American capitalist/consumerist values, notably Brouwer, Gifford, and Rose (1996), who line up the Pentecostals of the developing world alongside the

American Moral Majority and the Unification Church as puppets of capitalism. The heading of chapter 10 gives something of the flavor of their argument: "By Defining Enemies Christian Fundamentalism Defines Itself: Anti-Islamic, Anti-Communist, Anti-Catholic, Anti-Feminist" (1996:279). Ten years after Elizabeth Brusco's analysis these authors had still noticed no fissure or ambiguity in the "patriarchy" of the movement.

Feminism Revised

Feminists, however, have no better record. Here the problem is twofold – religion and the family, both of which are seen as sources of women's oppression. Feminist texts on popular movements concerning women's issues sometimes give a nod in the direction of liberation theology and the base communities but they ignore Pentecostalism (see e.g., Jelin 1990). Even a conscientious and scholarly feminist text like Sylvia Chant's review of the data on mother-headed households in the developing world displays the same blind spots. Indeed Chant's own research data on Costa Rica, the Philippines, and Mexico, all areas of considerable Pentecostal presence, shows that the gender order is such that while men can easily find a woman who fits their ideal, women can never find the kind of partner they want, and men agree this is so and rejoice in the masculinity it demonstrates (Chant 1997). Yet the only movement effectively addressing that problem has not even been noticed by this sympathetic champion of poor women.

Let me finally turn to researchers, all anthropologists, who have done most to make sense of the gender paradox. Elizabeth Brusco's main contribution was to produce the first substantive description of the phenomenon. Ruth Marshall-Fratani and Rosalind Hackett have followed that tradition of empathetic "thick description" in their African research (Marshall 1993, Hackett 1993). The most stimulating theoretical treatments have, however, all come from humanistic Marxists who had to modify or sidestep the paradigm in order to do justice to their observations. Cucchiari (1991) was one of the earliest to make theoretical sense of the meaning of conversion for Pentecostal women in Sicily. His concern with the construction and reconstruction of selfhood and its relation to the gender order is the key to his insights, but one could not describe his work as specifically feminist.

Roger Lancaster, who describes himself as Marxist and gay, has also made a significant contribution to the analysis. His first work in the late 1980s was concerned with religion, including the new Protestants, under the Sandinista regime (Lancaster 1989). He found to his surprise that the evangelicals made deeper inroads into the everyday reality of gender inequality than all the official policies of gender enacted by the government. This led him to write an analysis of Latin American gender culture as a "political economy of the body" in which men are in a chronic and relentless competition with other men for masculine status in which women and *cochones* (passive partners in homosexual acts) are simply counters. It is an indispensable text, suffused with humane empathy and subtle observation, not specifically feminist but certainly informed by the experience of being a North American gay in Latin American culture (Lancaster 1992).

Diane Austin-Broos's later study of Jamaican Pentecostals, which draws on Cucchiari but not Lancaster (Austin-Broos 1997) also offers a subtle theoretical analysis, which displays feminist sympathies but is not much indebted to feminist theory. Austin-Broos situates herself within a Gramscian Marxist tradition but, like Lancaster and Cucchiari, pulls what she needs eclectically from other perspectives, from phenomenology to Clifford Geertz. Here again the key to her insights is empathy and detailed observation and a willingness to take the paradoxes of religious life seriously. Her concept of "a politics of moral orders" is an illuminating approach to what is more usually treated as "cultural struggle." Of particular importance is her interpretation of the way in which Jamaican Pentecostal women take upon themselves the whole "sin" of the female victims of the sexual politics of colonialism and slavery, exorcise it in collusion with the male pastors, and turn the negative burden into positive spiritual energy used on behalf of the whole society. Once she had recognized that Christianity could be used as a resource by poor black women and was not simply a form of domination, she was released from a blinkering paradigm and able to use it, along with other lenses, to see with. There is no magic secret to using paradigms creatively rather than as blinkers which obscure the reality before our eyes, but it is the real stuff of the intellectual excitement which the sociology (and anthropology) of religion is still able to generate. And it often helps if an unanticipated social reality comes and hits academics on the nose, as the rise of Pentecostalism or the fall of Communism have done. Let us hope that this will force us to review our paradigms, rather than simply go through the motions of debating them.

References

Ammerman, N. 1987. *Bible Believers: Fundamentalists in the Modern World*. New Brunswick, NJ: Rutgers University Press.

Andreas, C. 1991. "Women at Work," *North American Congress on Latin America: Report on the Americas* 24(4):19–24.

Arweck, E. 1999. "The Response to New Religious Movements," Unpublished PhD thesis, King's College, University of London.

Arweck, E. and Clarke, P. 1997. *New Religious Movements in Western Europe: An Annotated Bibliography*. Westport: Greenwood.

Austin-Broos, D.J. 1997. *Jamaica Genesis: Religion and the Politics of Moral Orders*. Chicago: University of Chicago Press.

Barker, E. 1999. "New Religious Movements: Their Incidence and Significance," in *New Religious Movements: Challenge and Response*, Eds. B. Wilson and J. Cresswell. London: Routledge, pp. 13–32.

Borowik, I. and Babinski, G., Eds. 1997. *New Religious Phenomena in Central and Eastern Europe*. Kraków: Nomos.

Bowen, K. 1996. *Evangelism and Apostasy*. Montreal, Quebec and Kingston, Ontario: McGill/Queen's University Press.

Brouwer, S., Gifford, P., and Rose, S.D. 1996. *Exporting the American Gospel: Global Christian Fundamentalism*. London: Routledge.

Brown, P.R.L. 1967. *Augustine of Hippo: A Biography*. Berkeley: University of California Press.

Brown, P.R.L. 1988. *The Body and Society: Men, Women and Sexual Renunciation in Early Christianity*. New York: Columbia University Press.

Brown, P.R.L. 1995. *Authority and the Sacred: Aspects of the Christianisation of the Roman World*. Cambridge: Cambridge University Press.

Brusco, E. 1986. "The Household Basis of Evangelical Religion and the Reform of Machismo in Colombia," PhD Dissertation, City University of New York.

Brusco, E. 1995. *The Reformation of Machismo: Evangelical Conversion and Gender in Colombia*. Austin, TX: University of Texas Press.

Burdick, J. 1993. *Looking for God in Brazil*. Los Angeles: University of California Press.

Chant, S. 1997. *Women-Headed Households: Diversity and Dynamics in the Developing World*. New York: St. Martin's Press.

Chesnut, A. 1997. *Born Again in Brazil: The Pentecostal Boom and the Pathogens of Poverty*. New Brunswick, NJ: Rutgers University Press.

Comaroff, J. and Comaroff, J. 1991. *Of Revelation and Revolution: Vol. 1: Christianity, Colonialism and Consciousness in South Africa*. Chicago: University of Chicago Press.

Comaroff, J. and Comaroff, J. 1997. *Vol. 2: The Dialectics of Modernity on a South African Frontier*. Chicago: University of Chicago Press.

Cucchiari, S. 1988. "Adapted for Heaven: Conversion and Culture in Western Sicily," *American Ethnologist* 15:417–41.

Cucchiari, S. 1991. "Between Shame and Sanctification: Patriarchy and its Transformation in Sicilian Pentecostalism," *American Ethnologist* 18:687–707.

Deiros, P.A. 1991, "Protestant Fundamentalism in Latin America," in *Fundamentalisms Observed*, Eds. M.E. Marty and R.S. Appleby. Chicago: University of Chicago Press, pp. 142–96.

Earle, D. 1992. "Authority, Social Conflict and the Rise of Pentecostalism: Religious Conversion in a Mayan Village," *Social Compass* 39(3):377–88.

Hackett, R.I.J. 1993. "The Symbolics of Power Discourse Among Contemporary Religious Groups," in *Religious Transformations of Socio-Economic Change*, Ed. L. Martin. Berlin: Mouton de Gruyter.

Hackett, R.I.J. 1998. "Charismatic/Pentecostal Appropriation of Media Technology in Nigeria and Ghana," *Journal of Religion in Africa* 28(3):258–77.

Halévy, E. 1934. *A History of the English People*. London: Ernest Benn.

Heelas, P. 1996. *The New Age Movement: The Celebration of the Self and the Sacralisation of Modernity*. Oxford: Blackwell.

Hunter, J.D. 1990. *Culture Wars: The Struggle to Define America*. New York: Basic Books.

Jelin, E., Ed. 1990. *Women and Social Change in Latin America*, London and Atlantic Highlands, NJ: UNRISD/Zed Books.

Krauss, C. 1999. "A Revolution Peru's Rebels Didn't Intend," *New York Times*, August 29, pp. 1, 8.

Lancaster, R.N. 1989. *In the Name of God and the Revolution*. Berkeley, CA: University of California Press.

Lancaster, R.N. 1992, *Life is Hard: Machismo, Danger and the Intimacy of Power in Nicaragua.* Berkeley, CA: University of California Press.

Marshall, R. 1993. "'Power in the Name of Jesus': Social Transformation and Pentecostalism in Western Nigeria 'Revisited'," in *Legitimacy and the State in Twentieth Century Africa*, Eds. T. Ranger and O. Vaughan. London: Macmillan.

Marshall-Fratani, R. 1988. "Mediating the Global and Local in Nigerian Pentecostalism," *Journal of Religion in Africa* 28(3):278–315.

Martin, B. 1998. "From Pre- to Post-Modernity in Latin America: The Case of Pentecostalism," in *Religion, Modernity and Postmodernity*, Eds. P. Heelas, with D. Martin and P. Morris. Oxford and Malden, MA: Blackwell, pp. 102–46.

Martin, D.A. 1990. *Tongues of Fire: The Explosion of Protestantism in Latin America.* Oxford: Blackwell.

Martin, D.A. 1995. *Forbidden Revolutions.* London: SPCK.

Marty, M.E. and Appleby, R.S., Eds. 1991. *Fundamentalisms Observed.* Chicago: University of Chicago Press.

Marty, M.E. and Appleby, R.S., Eds. 1995. *Fundamentalisms Comprehended.* Chicago: Chicago University Press.

Maxwell, D. 1998. "Delivered From the Spirit of Poverty?: Pentecostalism, Prosperity, and Modernity in Zimbabwe," *Journal of Religion in Africa* 28(3):350–73.

Maxwell, D. 1999. *Christians and Chiefs in Zimbabwe: A Social History of the Hwesa People.* Edinburgh: University of Edinburgh Press.

Meyer, B. 1998. "Make a Complete Break with the Past: Memory and Post-Colonial Modernity in Ghanaian Pentecostal Discourse," *Journal of Religion in Africa* 28(3): 316–49.

Puttick, E. 1999. "Women in New Religious Movements," in *New Religious Movements: Challenge and Response.* Eds. B. Wilson and J. Cresswell. London: Routledge, pp. 141–62.

Schneider, A.G. 1994. *The War of the Cross Leads Home: The Domestication of American Methodism.* Bloomington, IN/Buckingham, UK: Indiana University Press/Open University Press.

Seligman, A. 2000. *Modernity's Wager: Authority, the Self and Transcendence.* Princeton, NJ: Princeton University Press.

Stanley, B. 1999. "Twentieth Century World Christianity: A Perspective from the History of Missions," Paper delivered at the Oxford Consultation in Christian Expansion on the Twentieth Century Non-Western World, University of Cambridge, 14–17 July.

Thompson, E.P. 1964. *The Making of the English Working Class.* New York: Pantheon.

Vasquez, M.A. 1998. *The Brazilian Popular Church and the Crisis of Modernity.* Cambridge: Cambridge University Press.

Wallis, R. 1978. "Fishing for Men," *The Humanist* 38(1):14–16.

Wallis, R. 1979. "Sex, Marriage and the Children of God," in *Salvation and Protest: Studies of Social and Religious Movements*, Ed. R. Wallis. London and New York: Francis Pinter/St. Martin's Press, pp. 74–90.

CHAPTER 4

Feminism and the Sociology of Religion: From Gender-blindness to Gendered Difference

Linda Woodhead

To begin this chapter with a simple definition of feminism would be to overlook the diversity and fluidity of the movement. Standard studies of feminism tend to distinguish between two waves, the first associated with the struggle for women's rights in the nineteenth and early twentieth century, the second with the explosion of feminism and gender studies since the 1960s (see e.g., Nicholson 1997). Given the continuing development of feminism, however, I believe that it is more helpful to distinguish between *three* phases, which may be differentiated in the following way:

1   First wave feminism, which gathered momentum in the late nineteenth century, tended to be gender-blind in the sense that it wished to claim equality between the sexes and to subsume their differences under a common "humanity."
2   Second wave feminism, which flourished between the 1960s and early 1980s, developed a highly essentialist understanding of men and women, and campaigned for the liberation of women from male oppression or "patriarchy."
3   Third wave feminism, which began to dominate the field in the 1990s, reacts against essentialism and seeks instead to explore gender differences which are now understood as complex, multifaceted, fluid, constructed, and only loosely related to the body.

In terms of their influence in the academy, second wave feminism has been associated with the rise of women's studies, and third wave feminism with the shift to "gender studies." In most cases there is no smooth evolution between these different waves; in some contexts all three continue to coexist, sometimes in conflict.

The sociology of religion is also subject to historical shifts and transformations. One way of conceptualizing its development is in terms of a "classical" period, primarily concerned with theoretical analysis of the development of modern industrial society, and a more recent phase characterized by a turn to microlevel studies of religious life and thought (see e.g., the analyses by Beckford 1989 and Wuthnow 1997). It is interesting to note that this last "wave" of the sociology of religion corresponds not only chronologically but also methodologically with third wave feminism. Coincidence or not, the result has been the possibility of a new creative collaboration between the two disciplines and approaches which, as this chapter will document, has given rise to a crop of important gender-focused studies within the sociology of religion. It will also be noted that the majority of these studies operate at the level of microtheory and analysis. Whilst a great deal of excellent work has now been done in this area, this chapter will go on to document some important lacunae in the study of women and religion. In its closing sections, a plea will be made for the applica-tion of a gendered perspective, not only in microlevel studies, but also at the level of megatheory. To this end, some speculative suggestions will be made about what might be involved in an attempt to reenvision and restate some of the key paradigms and "grand narratives" of the sociology of religion from a feminist perspective.

Areas of Concentration

Using a schema developed by Woodhead and Heelas (1999), and prompted by the work of scholars like Steven Tipton (1982) and Robert Bellah et al. (1985), religion in modern times may be divided into three main varieties: religions of difference, religions of humanity, and spiritualities of life. Religions of difference locate authority in a transcendent reality external to the self, religions of humanity in "the human," and spiritualities of life in the self. In terms of this schema, recent sociological studies of religious communities and congregations have tended to concentrate particularly on religions of difference – ranging from the Jehovah's Witnesses to Orthodox Judaism. Spiritualities of life come second in terms of their ability to command scholarly interest, and religions of human-ity are a definite third (hence the anomaly that liberal mainline Christian con-gregations, despite their great numerical significance in the religious map of the West, are least studied). Far from upsetting this hierarchy of scholarly interest, ethnographic studies in the sociology of religion with a gendered perspective have generally reinforced it.

Religions of Difference

First wave feminism established an early trend by yoking the critique of a male-dominated society to the critique of religion. Christianity and the mainline

Christian churches were its main targets. As Elizabeth Cady Stanton, author of *The Women's Bible* put it, "all the religions of the earth degrade her, and so long as woman accepts the position they assign her, emancipation is impossible" (Stanton 1985:12). There was more than a glimmer of sociological awareness here. Whilst the efforts of Stanton and her collaborators were chiefly focused on a critique of Christian teaching, they also paid some attention to patterns of power and status in the churches, and the ways in which these reinforced other forms of social organization which restricted the sphere of women's choice and action. Even women who remained in the churches and who have subsequently come to be viewed as conservatively Christian were sometimes capable of the most far-reaching criticisms. One thinks of Florence Nightingale, for example, who criticized the church for supporting a suffocating form of family life, resulting in a crucifixion of women which she thought far worse than anything Christ had to suffer. "The two questions of religion and family are so intimately connected," she wrote, "that to ask concerning the higher power or powers acknowledged in heaven and on earth is one" (Nightingale 1991:156).

The critique of religions of difference as collusive with the oppression of women was given new force and fury by second wave feminism, albeit on a somewhat different basis. Whereas first wave feminism had called for a recognition of women's equality with men on the basis of their common humanity, second wave feminism tended to essentialize womanhood and to call for new separatist forms of thought and organization. This call extended into the domain of religion. Thus the erstwhile Catholic nun Mary Daly condemned the church as irredeemably sexist and attempted to create a truly feminist spirituality from which men would be excluded (Daly 1973). Women like Daly – as well as more moderate or "liberal" feminist theologians – worked on a threshold between theology and the study of religion insofar as they engaged in sustained critiques of Christianity and other religions from a gendered perspective. The pioneering collection *Religion and Sexism* edited by Rosemary Radford Ruether (1974) furnishes a good example.

Fired by their anger at religiopatriarchal oppressions, many of these second wave analyses of Christianity were highly incisive. From the point of view of more recent ethnographic and sociological studies of women within religions of difference, however, they were flawed by at least four features: first, a concentration upon Christian symbolism at the expense of the forms of social organization with which it interplays; second, an overreliance upon the notion of "patriarchy," a term central to the discourse of second wave feminism which proved something of a blunt instrument when used to analyze complex forms of social and cultural organization and their interplays with gendered difference; third, a willingness to rely on the explanation that those women who remained within religions of difference were victims suffering from "false consciousness"; and fourth, reliance on an essentialized understanding of the difference between men and women which precluded sensitivity to a continuum of gender orientation not always directly related to biological difference.

The third wave feminists' gradual abandonment of a sex-war stance with its simple dichotomy between "patriarchal" male oppressors and innocent female victims has generally proved fruitful for the study of religions of difference. In particular it has enabled the production of a number of recent studies of women and men in conservative religious communities that have shed light on the ways in which *both* sexes may profit from their involvement, and that has thereby restored some agency to women. One of the earliest studies in this mould was Nancy Ammerman's *Bible Believers* (1987), a study of a North American fundamentalist Christian community with deeply conservative views about the family and the necessary confinement of women to the domestic sphere. What Ammerman discovered in practice, however, was that "most women learn to influence family decision making while still deferring to their husbands' authority, and that both they and their husbands find ways to live with the tension between Fundamentalist norms for family structure and modern norms of individuality and equality" (Ammerman 1987:146).

Ammerman's study has been followed by a number of other illuminating books on women in conservative religious communities in the USA, including the studies of female converts to Orthodox Judaism by Davidman (1991) and Kaufman (1991), and R. Marie Griffith's study of the evangelical Women Aglow movement (1997). (Davidman and Kaufman find that women are attracted to Orthodoxy precisely because it privileges their roles as wives and mothers and gives them a status they would not have in modern "secular" society; Griffith finds that Women Aglow combines evangelical Christianity with a therapeutic culture to enable women to gain some control over difficult domestic roles and situations.) At the same time, a number of studies of women in resurgent Islam and charismatic Christianity worldwide have appeared. Notable amongst the former is Leila Ahmed's *Women and Gender in Islam* (1992), which argues that women's return to the veil is a sign not of subordination but of class and gender assertion. In relation to the Latin American charismatic upsurge, a number of studies including those by David Martin (1990), Burdick (1996), and Bernice Martin (1998) reveal the ways in which charismatic Christianity transforms gender relationships, not only by empowering women, but by domesticating men. Salvatore Cucchiari has expounded the same theme in relation to Sicilian Pentecostalism, maintaining that its "cross-gender God is a crucible in which new models of masculinity/femininity are being forged" (1991:88).

This third wave exposure of the complexities and ambiguities of gender relations within religions of difference has not, however, been entirely at the expense of an emphasis on the patriarchal nature of such religions. Many of the studies just mentioned explicitly acknowledge a continuing patriarchal bias in the communities under investigation, sometimes in explicit reaction to modern ideals of equality and independence. As Griffith comments in relation to her evangelical women, for example, "If, in certain ways, prayer and testimony seem to create possibilities for the liberation and transformation worshipers claim to experience, they may just as readily work to opposite ends, further institutionalizing the roles and boundaries that constrict women's space" (1997:210). Equally, some studies of fundamentalism note its patriarchal dynamics (see e.g., DeBerg 1990, Hawley 1994, but compare the final definition of fundamentalism in Marty and Appleby's "*Fundamentalism Project*", 1995:399–424, which does not make reference to gender). A related theme which emerges in a number of recent studies is the way in which women may act as signs and ciphers of wider social integrities and dislocations: in contemporary Pakistan, for example, the sexual integrity of women comes to symbolize that of the nation-state (van der Veer 1994), whilst in parts of Africa those women identified as witches "embody all the contradictions of the experience of modernity itself, of its inescapable entice-ments, its self-consuming passions, its discriminatory tactics, its devastating social costs" (Comaroff and Comaroff 1993:xxix).

Spiritualities of Life

Some of the more radical first wave feminist critics of religions of difference found refuge in spiritualities of life (the Theosophist Annie Besant who converted from Anglicanism via free thought is a good example). In being drawn to such religiosity these early feminists were following in the footsteps of previous gen-erations of women who had been attracted to the more mystical or experiential wings of established religions, or to some of the new radical Protestant sects and their offshoots (to Unitarian and spiritualist churches, for example). Studies like those by Huber (1979), Burfield (1983), Haywood (1983), and Rendall (1985) suggest that one reason such varieties of spirituality attract women is because they downplay the authority of spheres and offices in which men have tradi-tionally been dominant. Correlatively, their emphasis on the authority of feeling, intuition, and experience in religious matters empowers women to attain a spiritual and institutional power denied them elsewhere. In addition, such spiritualities are sometimes characterized by a strongly feminine symbolic.

Second wave feminists have also been attracted by spiritualities of life. Thus some of the feminist theologians who rejected religions of difference as irre-deemably sexist turned instead to explicitly feminized versions of spiritualities of life, a number of them focused upon worship of the goddess (e.g., Daly 1973, 1979, Christ and Plaskow 1979, Goldenberg 1979). This engaged interest in such spirituality also leaves its mark on many of the studies of spiritualities of life from a feminist perspective which appeared in the 1980s (e.g., Adler 1986, Crowley 1989, Starhawk 1989). Such studies epitomize an approach that has become typical in this field, and that employs techniques typically associated with the scientific study of religion within a framework of commitment and even advocacy of the forms of spirituality described. Like the studies of Christianity made by second wave feminist theologians, these second wave studies of spiri-tualities of life therefore combine a theological – or "theaological," as followers of the goddess prefer to say – agenda with more "scientific" methods of exegesis and interpretation in a way which may leave many sociologists feeling a little uneasy. The distinction between science and theology is blurred too by the fact that the spiritualities of life which are the subject of these studies tend to be highly reflexive and to be shaped in part by an awareness of work in the scientific study of religion. Carol Christ's advocacy of goddess spirituality, for example, draws heavily on Clifford Geertz's definition of religion in order consciously to shape a form of religion which can positively affect women's "long-lasting moods and motivations" (Christ and Plaskow 1979:273–87).

There are now some signs that studies of spiritualities of life may be entering a third phase. Much of the impetus for a shift in methodological focus has come from scholars studying New Religious Movements (NRMs) who, to some degree, now constitute a subdiscipline within the sociology of religion (of course, spiritualities of life constitute just one form of NRM). Janet Jacobs's work on women in NRMs (Jacobs 1989, 1990, 1991) has been influential in this regard. Whilst she acknowledges her debt to second wave scholars like Daly and Ruether and, like them, uses the language of patriarchy, sexism, and androcentrism, she warns against the dangers of "universalizing the experience of all female devotees" (Jacobs 1991:349) and has done much to illuminate the more complex gendered realities of feminist spirituality. Working in the same area as Jacobs, Neitz (Neitz 1990, 1994) offers the interesting argument that feminist spirituality has flourished in the wake of a second wave (secular) feminism whose fragmentation and institutionalization left women with no arenas in which to explore and celebrate their gendered identity. McGuire (1994) also emphasizes women's use of religious and quasi-religious healing as a way of exploring and constructing empowered gender identities, whilst Palmer (1994) moves beyond the simpler schemas of second wave feminism by arguing against the view that NRMs must be seen either as empowering or as oppressing women. Instead, Palmer argues that women temporarily inhabit a range of different stylized gender roles offered by NRMs, thereby preparing themselves to choose a more mature adult mode when they eventually defect. Further examples of third wave scholarship on witchcraft, feminist spirituality, and healing include Eller (1993), Luhrmann (1994), and Griffin (1995).

Lacunae

The fact that the approaches of first and second wave feminism have become influential within some parts of the sociology of religion, and particularly in relation to studies of a more ethnographic nature, should not obscure the fact that large swathes of the discipline remain gender-blind. In exploring this blindness, Ruth Wallace (1991) offers the explanation that religion is itself patriarchal, and that men outnumber women within the sociology of religion – clearly a sociology of the discipline would be needed in order to take these ideas further. Wallace and a handful of other scholars like Jacobs (1991) have also begun to explore particular areas in the discipline where gender-blindness is most apparent (Wallace singles out Talcott Parsons's work for criticism, whilst Jacobs focuses on that of Roy Wallis and Steven Tipton). Here I will attempt to take this enterprise further by singling out two wider areas in the sociology of religion in which disregard of issues of gender appear to leave us with significant gaps in our understanding of religion past, present, and future.

Women in the Churches

In Christianity, the largest of the world's religions, women outnumber men. Yet the reasons for their greater religiosity, and the nature of this religiosity, have attracted little attention or energy within the sociology of religion.

The data proving women's greater religiosity is now overwhelming, and is summarized by Cornwall (1989), Beit-Hallahmi and Argyle (1996), Francis (1997), and Walter and Davie (1998). How is it to be explained? Three main suggestions have been made:

- women are more religious than men because of their structural locations in society (religion, like housework, having become one of the gendered institutions created by the division of labor);
- women are differently socialized;
- women's greater religiosity is a compensatory response to their material and social deprivation.

As yet, however, little empirical work has been undertaken to test these hypotheses. One of the few exceptions, a small-scale survey by Thompson (1991), reached the conclusion that it is not gender *per se* which accounts for religiousness, but a "feminine" orientation (including a greater emphasis on relationality – see below).

In my view, further work is required not just to explain women's greater religiousness in general, but their relationship to Christianity in particular. Which particular features of Christian teaching and community appeal to women? Why do women join or leave the churches? And why do they remain in churches that exclude them from positions of power? One of the few empirical studies to address such questions is that by Ozorak, which found that the majority of women sampled emphasized the centrality of caring and community to their religious experience, and remain in the churches because they find such qualities there. As she says, "Most of the women in this study recognized that by hierarchical social standards, organized religion does not treat them as well as it might . . . but in absolute terms, they do not see themselves as disenfranchised. The power of connection and relationship, most essential to their own views of the faith experience, is available to them in abundance" (1996:27). See also Winter, Lummis, and Stokes (1994), whose national survey of women in the churches found them to be "defecting in place" – deeply dissatisfied with institutional Christianity, often sustained by women's spirituality groups, but working for change within the church communities to which they remain committed.

Failure to study women in the churches, particularly the mainline churches, is clearly related to the sociology of religion's wider lack of concern with liberal religion/religions of humanity noted above (is the feminized nature of such religion one reason for lack of interest?). The few studies of mainline religion that the sociology of religion has produced tend to pay little attention to gender, but more to the family (see e.g., Roof and McKinney 1987). This is symptomatic of the fact that the topic of the family seems to have attracted more attention in the sociology of religion in general than has gender *per se* (see e.g., Lenski 1961 and the critical study by Hargrove 1985). This tangential approach to the issue of gender and religion is also evident in a concentration in the literature on ordained women and women in religious orders. The former in particular tend to take their methodology from the sociology of occupations (Wallace 1975, Lehman 1980, Carroll, Hargrove, and Lummis 1983). More recently, however, a number of studies have considered other questions, including the ways in which gender difference is reflected in ministry style (see e.g., Wallace 1992, Lehman 1980, 1993, Nesbitt 1997).

It is to be hoped that with a wider adoption of a feminist perspective in the sociology of religion, women in the churches may soon become a subject of interest in their own right, rather than an addendum to other sociological agendas.

Secularization

> I would be willing to offer the hypothesis that virtually the entire "decline" of "the churches" in American society can be "explained" by the entrance of women into the workforce, certainly more so than by anything like a "crisis of belief." (Swatos 1994:xi)

This throw-away suggestion by William Swatos is striking precisely because of its novelty. For well over a century the "theory" of secularization has dominated the sociology of religion. A great deal of quantitative data has been collected to demonstrate the reality of secularization, and a large number of theories formulated to explain religious decline. Whilst some of the census data has included gender as a variable, little of the theory it has generated has taken gender into account.

Even in the absence of strong theoretical or empirical support, it is clear that Swatos's suggestion has an obvious plausibility. If women have made up the majority of active churchgoers (and it is with churchgoers that secularization theory is primarily concerned), then their defection from the churches, even at the same rate as men's, will necessarily have greater impact. In addition, if it could be shown that women (or particular cohorts of women) are leaving (or not entering) the churches in greater numbers than their male counterparts, then this would be doubly significant.

There are fragments of research that support something like the latter hypothesis. In his studies of American Catholicism, for example, Andrew Greeley has discovered that one particular cohort of women is disproportionately likely to reject Catholicism, namely college-educated women who had been influenced by feminism and whose Catholic mothers had been confined to domestic roles during the time their daughters were raised (Greeley 1990:230–1). Greeley's conclusion is that such women are deserting Catholicism because they associate it with an image of womanhood belied by their independent lives and occupations. Interesting too in this connection is the gender-focused study of a mainline congregation in the USA by Penny Long Marler (1995). Marler comments on the centrality of the image of the family to this congregation (as to so many similar ones); the church speaks and thinks of itself as a family, and has a particular openness to families. One result, Marler finds, is that two social groups are particularly well represented: young families, and older people who have lost their families and can play other parenting roles in relation to these young families. The implication, Marler notes, is that as the traditional family declines in American society, so the appeal of the churches will decline with it. Singles, single professionals, and professional women are unlikely to be attracted by such religion. In the same volume Hertel finds that the combination of marriage and full-time employment for women is related to a significant decline in their levels of religiosity. His conclusion is that "by far the most significant challenge to organized religion lies in the work-related declines in membership and attendance attributable to full-time employment of married women" (Hertel 1995:116).

On the other hand, the MARC data for England between 1979 and 1990 show that most of the reduction in churchgoing during this period is due to a fall-out among men (Walter and Davie 1998), as it is in Holland (Steggarda 1994). However, Steggarda finds that the differences between men and women fall sharply once employment status and family structure are controlled for, and agrees with Campiche (1993) that the differences between men and women on most indices of religiosity can be explained by an exploration of intermediate variables.

Clearly, a great deal more work needs be done to rescue secularization theory from its gender blindness, and to test Swatos's hypothesis more fully. Equally, as "sacralization" theorists rise up at the end of the twentieth century to challenge secularization theory (Casanova 1994, Woodhead and Heelas 1999), it is to be hoped that their rebellion will include a greater sensitivity to the issue of gender.

Questioning Old Paradigms: Beyond Iron Cage and Anomie

One way of telling the history of the sociology of religion is in terms of a succession of paradigms or grand narratives. Here, as in the "hard" sciences, the paradigms appear to be few, and to succeed one another only very slowly, if at all. Secularization is one such paradigm or grand narrative, and is closely related to a second, that of "iron cage and anomie." As this mix of metaphors suggests, this narrative owes much to Weber and Durkheim, as well as to Marx, Toennies, Simmel, and Gehlen. In more recent times it has been influentially restated in the sociology of religion by thinkers like Peter Berger and Thomas Luckmann, but it emerges in a number of variants in the work of most sociologists of religion. In its simplest version, the theory holds that modernization involves the rationalization and technologization of public life, leading to a demystification of the natural world and the dissolution of the stable ties of local, kinship, and primordial relationships. Abandoned to the impersonal structures of impersonal institutions, modern men and women find themselves trapped in an iron cage of rationalized bureaucracy, which can supply neither meaning nor significance. Homeless, alienated, and anomic minds can now find purpose and value only in the realm of personal and private life. Religion, once part of the public realm, correspondingly shrinks in scope, and can work its enchantments – if at all – only in a severely delimited sphere. It becomes, in other words, a "privatized" means by which a declining number of people cope with the dislocations and restrictions of public life. (There are, of course, many, and much more sophisticated versions of this narrative.)

Like the sociology of religion more generally, this narrative has been gender-blind. As with the secularization paradigm, it is therefore interesting to look at it with a new sensitivity to issues of gender. To do so immediately prompts the thought that the narrative, whilst formulated in terms of a universal humanity, in fact takes men as its focus. If, instead, one were to retell the narrative with women as its subjects, would it retain its plausibility and explanatory power? The question is debatable, to say the least. Since women (at least in the West, and in modern times) have generally been excluded from the public realm, it may be that they have suffered the restrictions of the iron cage or an accompanying sense of normlessness and loss of meaning. The private and domestic realms which have long been women's sphere of operation remain so, and remain beyond the reach of the impersonal regulations of rationality and financial interest.

If the narrative of iron cage and anomie therefore has little application to most women's lives, it is necessary to ask whether its conclusion may also be inapplicable to women. In its stronger versions the conclusion is that religion *disappears* as disenchantment and demystification take place; in its weaker versions that religion becomes a matter of purely *private* significance, having to do in particular with the resourcing of the individual self. The stronger conclusion is clearly undermined if women remain outside the iron cage, whilst the weaker conclusion also becomes questionable. For if women live and work within the sphere of domestic and relational ties, then presumably their religion relates closely to this lifeworld. Indeed, as we would expect, religions of difference in modern times have served to resource and sanctify the domestic realm, whilst spiritualities of life have performed similar functions in relation to more loosely organized forms of intimacy.

Where many women are concerned then, one might expect that religion would continue to have as great a significance in modern as in premodern times. Equally, one would have to question the "iron cage and anomie" conclusion that their religion becomes "privatized" in the sense that it becomes a matter of concern only to the private individual or the self. Instead, one might say that religion becomes more thoroughly "feminized" and relational. The abandonment of gender-blindness in relation to old paradigms in the sociology of religion may, in other words, begin to prompt new ones.

Prompting New Paradigms: Feminization and Relational Religion

Though the sociology of religion has generally been blind to this fact, the distinction between private and public life which is so central in the narrative of iron cage and anomie is drawn from a masculine point of view. The sphere it uncritically designates as "public" is the world of (modern) men, and the distinction between private and public life makes much more sense from a male than from a female point of view. As many feminists have pointed out, the reality of women's lives tends to center not around a private realm, or a private "unencumbered" self, but around a "situated" and already relational self implicated in a network of connections (Gilligan 1982, Benhabib 1992). What is more, women exercise considerable power, even though this power becomes invisible from a masculine point of view for which "real" power is confined to the "public" realm of state and market (Elshtain 1990). From this masculine point of view, women are powerless and outside the realm of the political; from a feminist point of view, however, the classification of women's lives as private and apolitical can be seen as persuasive rather than neutrally descriptive.

Without disputing the reality of functional differentiation in modern times, it may therefore be helpful to reconceptualize the so-called privatization of religion. One way of doing so may be to adopt the language of feminization rather than of privatization. As Ann Douglas's classic study of *The Feminization of American Religion* (1978) shows, however, it is easy for this new language to carry over assumptions attaching to the old paradigm of privatization. Thus Douglas tends to assimilate the term feminization if not to privatization, at least to domesticization; for her the disestablishment of the churches in America led to the shrinkage of their sphere of activity to the domestic and private sphere, to women becoming the main agents in this sphere, and to Christianity being shaped by their distinct social needs and functions. In particular, Douglas argues, this led to the trivialization and "sentimentalization" of religion, as it became a matter of the emotions and lost all power to engage critically or intelligently with modern socioeconomic developments.

It may, however, be possible to develop the thesis of the feminization of religion, not in terms of privatization, but in terms of relationality. In this rendering, the feminization of religion can be seen to involve the shift of modern religion's center of gravity not just to the sphere of the emotions but to that of *relationships*, particularly noninstrumental relationships based on love, trust, and care. Of course there is already a great deal in many of the other world religions that lends itself to this relational turn. In Christianity, for example, an emphasis on the importance of love, peaceableness, and self-sacrifice has always been ill-suited to the cultivation of power and machismo and to the sustenance of purely functional relationships. Whilst, as Martin (1997) has shown so well, Christianity's alliance with social and political power has nonetheless turned it at many points in history into a martial faith, the loss of such opportunity within the context of modern secular polities has opened new possibilities of recovering and reactivating its pacific, feminine, and relational codes. Whilst these relational religious codes may be related to the family – as they continue to be in more conservative forms of Christianity – they can also sustain other forms of association. As noted above in relation to spiritualities of life, for example, religion can sanctify new patterns of post-familial relationship, including experimental sexual relationships and sacred friendships (Palmer 1994). Whether socially conservative or radical, religion in modern times thus appears to be playing an increasingly important role in offering conceptual and institutional space for relationships and activities of care, nurture, intimacy, and eroticism. In so doing it is clearly addressing the interests not only of women but, as gender roles become more fluid, of many men as well.

Evidence for this shift of weight towards the relational in religion in modern times is beginning to come from a number of studies of contemporary religious life and thought. In the first place, there is growing evidence that women in particular (but increasingly men as well) tend to think, speak, and value religion primarily in terms of its ability to sustain and validate forms of noninstrumental relationship. Often they even define true religion in these terms. Studies showing that women concentrate on a God of love, comfort, and forgiveness include those by Cox (1967), Martin and Pluck (1977), Nelsen, Cheek, and Au (1985), Sered (1987), Simmons and Walter (1988). Ozorak's study has already been mentioned. Her research yielded ample evidence that women's responses to their religious community "depended heavily on the extent of its connectedness, that is, the extent to which they perceived it as supportive, cooperative, and emotionally open" (1996:25). The women she interviewed repeatedly mentioned service to others as an integral part of religious practice. As one Unitarian said, "Going to church is nice, but I really feel religious when I am working. I enjoy working with dying people. So, I really feel like my God's work on earth is to do that sort of stuff" (Ozorak 1996:26).

These findings are amply confirmed by Nancy Ammerman and her team's recent and extensive research on contemporary congregations in the USA (1996), which uncovered the surprising fact that the most common form of religiosity within these congregations was not evangelicalism (29 percent of respondents), nor (social) activist (19 percent), but what Ammerman (1997) labels "Golden Rule" (51 percent). Like Ozorak's Unitarian, Golden Rule Christians view their religion as primarily a matter of loving relationship and care, and rate this more highly than correct belief or social action. Echoing the findings of Warner (1988), Ammerman also discovered that one of the most important features of religion for all her respondents, whatever their form of Christianity, was its ability to sustain local community ("localism") and thus to provide a certain form of social capital. Further evidence comes from Wuthnow's study of the rapid growth of small-group religiosity (1996), which reveals how this rapidly growing form of religion is typically highly affective, relational and "feminized." In the UK, the life of Princess Diana, and the reaction to her death, seem to furnish yet more evidence of the importance of a "religion of the heart" which imbues loving relationality with the aura of sanctity, and which is capable of tying together elements of Christianity, New Age, and other forms of religiosity on a golden thread of love (Woodhead 1999).

Secondly, the importance of relational religion is evidenced by new conceptions of divine–human relationship. No longer do most Christians view God as "Potentate Divine" looking down from "His Celestial Throne" on a sinful creation. Instead, God becomes "mother," "friend," and "lover" (McFague 1987), with whom one can have a "conversation" and a generally intimate involvement (Wuthnow 1996). This shift characterizes not only religions of humanity and spiritualities of life, but many religions of difference as well. Thus, for example, Christian evangelicals and charismatics believe that a "personal relationship" with Jesus lies at the very heart of faith, and have tended to move away from models of a punitive or vengeful God (Hunter 1987). Equally, Ammerman found that her interviewees' most common description of God was as "loving, caring, comforting, and protecting" (1997:205), and a Lutheran student interviewed by Ozorak said of God, "It just happens that He is as important to me as I feel I am to Him. It's a two-way relationship" (1996:26).

The temptation to think of such religion as privatized will no doubt recur, so powerful is the standard story of iron cage and anomie. By reconceptualizing the history of religion with the context of differentiation, however, the feminist perspective allows us to view modern religion in wider, relational, terms. From this point of view relational religion can be seen as far from the private matter that has so often been assumed, and can help broaden our understanding of the public and the political. As Ammerman says of her Golden Rule Christians, "Religiosity is not, for them, utterly 'private' . . . while they may not be eager to talk about religious issues while they are at work, and they might find it hard to articulate any coherent theological sense of 'vocation,' they claim that the practices they put at the center of the Christian life inform their everyday economic and civic activities" (Ammerman 1997:206). From this perspective, "public" religion begins to take on new meanings, and a fresh research agenda begins to present itself.

Conclusion

This chapter has attempted to offer a survey of the impact of feminism on the literature of the sociology of religion. It has suggested that a third wave of feminism has coincided with an analogous methodological shift in the sociology of religion in a way which has proved fruitful for the study of religion and gender, and given rise to a number of excellent ethnographically orientated studies. Nevertheless, much territory still remains untouched by a gendered perspective – the secularization paradigm and the preponderance of women in the churches were singled out as examples. Finally, this chapter has explored the impact that a feminist perspective may have on the sociology of religion, not only at the level of empirical study, but at the level of grand theory. The example was given of the way in which the grand narrative of iron cage and anomie and of the privatization of religion may be critiqued and rethought from a gendered perspective. My suggestion was that the conceptuality of privatization may need to be replaced by that of feminization and the rise of relational religion – with important gains for our understanding both of religion and of new forms of community and social organization in modern times.

One broader methodological conclusion may also be drawn from this discussion. As earlier studies of the impact of feminism on the sociology of religion point out, the feminist perspective questions the assumptions of neutrality upon which the "canon of objectivity" in the social sciences is based (Jacobs 1991). Such claims to objectivity are linked to the principles of research which mandate that a clear separation must be maintained between researcher (subject) and researched (object). This chapter has revealed the fragility of this distinction in a number of ways: first, by showing how a supposedly "objective" scientific study of religion has been profoundly affected by different phases of feminism (or, to give a different interpretation of the same phenomenon, how both feminism and the sociology of religion have been affected by the same changing intellectual and cultural currents); second, by showing how a theological agenda in feminist studies of religion has often carried over into the sociology of religion; third, by showing that religion is not unaffected by its study: as we have seen, some forms of contemporary religion are highly reflexive and have been shaped by an awareness of academic work in the study of religion. The application of a feminist perspective within the sociology of religion may thus lend support to the "standpoint" methodology championed by many contemporary feminists, which holds that a transformative knowledge emerges out of the multiplicity of truths which different subjective standpoints represent and in which all knowledge – including the myth of objectivity – is seen to be constructed by the social realities of race, class, and gender.

References

Adler, M. 1986. *Drawing Down the Moon: Witches, Druids, Goddess-Worshippers, and Other Pagans in America Today*. Boston: Beacon Press.

Ahmed, L. 1992. *Women and Gender in Islam: Historical Roots of a Modern Debate*. New Haven, CT and London: Yale University Press.

Ammerman, N.T. 1987. *Bible Believers: Fundamentalists in the Modern World*. New Brunswick, NJ and London: Rutgers University Press.

Ammerman, N.T. 1996. *Congregation and Community*. New Brunswick, NJ: Rutgers University Press.

Ammerman, N.T. 1997. "Golden Rule Christianity. Lived Religion in the American Mainstream," in *Lived Religion in America: Toward a Theory of Practice*, Ed. D.G. Hall. Princeton, NJ: Princeton University Press, pp. 196–216.

Beckford, J.A. 1989. *Religion and Advanced Industrial Society*. London: Unwin Hyman.

Beit-Hallahmi, B. and Argyle, M. 1996. *The Social Psychology of Religion*. London: Routledge.

Bellah, R.N., Madsen, R., Sullivan, W.M., Swidler, A., and Tipton, S.M. 1985. *Habits of the Heart: Individualism and Commitment in American Life*. Berkeley, CA: University of California Press.

Benhabib, S. 1992. *Situating the Self: Gender, Community and Postmodernism in Contemporary Ethics*. Cambridge and Oxford: Polity Press.

Burdick, J. 1996. *Looking for God in Brazil: The Progressive Catholic Church in Brazil's Religious Arena*. Berkeley, CA: University of California Press.

Burfield, D. 1983. "Theosophy and Feminism," in *Women's Religious Experience*, Ed. P. Holden. London: Croom Helm, pp. 27–56.

Campiche, R. 1993. "A Classical Question: Are Women Really More Religious Than Men?" Paper given to the SSSR, Raleigh, NC.

Carroll, J.W., Hargrove, B., and Lummis, A. 1983. *Women of the Cloth*. San Francisco: Harper and Row.

Casanova, J. 1994. *Public Religions in the Modern World*. Chicago and London: University of Chicago Press.

Christ, C. and Plaskow, J., Eds. 1979. *Womanspirit Rising: A Feminist Reader in Religion*. San Francisco: Harper and Row.

Comaroff, J. and Comaroff, J., Eds. 1993. *Modernity and its Malcontents: Ritual and Power in Postcolonial Africa*. Chicago and London: University of Chicago Press.

Cornwall, M. 1989. "Faith Development in Men and Women Over the Life Span," in *Aging and the Family*, Eds. S. Bahr and E. Peterson. Lexington, MA: Lexington Books/D.C. Health.

Cox, Edwin. 1967. *Sixth Form Religion*. London: SCM.

Crowley, V. 1989. *Wicca: The Old Religion in the New Age*. Wellingborough, UK: The Aquarian Press.

Cucchiari, S. 1991. "Between Shame and Sanctification: Patriarchy and Its Transformation in Sicilian Pentecostalism," *American Ethnologist* 18:687–707.

Daly, M. 1973. *Beyond God the Father: Toward a Philosophy of Women's Liberation*. Boston: Beacon Press.

Daly, M. 1979. *Gyn/Ecology: The Metethics of Radical Feminism*. London: Women's Press.

Davidman, L. 1991. *Tradition in a Rootless World: Women Turn to Orthodox Judaism*. Berkeley, Los Angeles, Oxford: University of California Press.

DeBerg, B. 1990. *Ungodly Women: Gender and the First Wave of American Fundamentalism.* Minneapolis, MN: Fortress Press.

Douglas, A. 1978. *The Feminization of American Religion.* New York: Alfred A. Kopf.

Eller, C. 1993. *Living in the Lap of the Goddess: The Feminist Spirituality Movement in America.* New York: Crossroad.

Elshtain, J.B. 1990. *Power Trips and Other Journeys: Essays in Feminism As Civic Discourse.* Madison, WI: University of Wisconsin Press.

Francis, L. 1997. "The Psychology of Gender Differences in Religion: A Review of Empirical Research," *Religion* 27(1):68–96.

Gilligan, C. 1982. *In a Different Voice.* Cambridge, MA: Harvard University Press.

Goldenberg, N.R. 1979. *Changing of the Gods: Feminism and the End of Traditional Religions.* Boston: Beacon.

Greeley, A.M. 1990. *The Catholic Myth: The Behavior and Beliefs of American Catholics.* New York: Charles Scribner's Sons.

Griffin, W. 1995. "The Embodied Goddess: Feminist Witchcraft and Female Divinity," *Sociology of Religion* 56(1):35–48.

Griffith, R.M. 1997. *God's Daughters: Evangelical Women and the Power of Submission.* Berkeley and London: University of California Press.

Hargrove, B. 1985. "Gender, The Family, and the Sacred," in *Sacred in a Secular Age: Toward Revision in the Scientific Study of Religion,* Ed. P. Hammond. Berkeley and London: University of California Press, pp. 204–14.

Hawley, J.S., Ed. 1994. *Fundamentalism and Gender.* New York: Oxford University Press.

Haywood, C.L. 1983. "The Authority and Empowerment of Women Among Spiritualist Groups," *Journal for the Scientific Study of Religion* 22(2):157–66.

Hertel, B.R. 1995. "Work, Family and Faith. Recent Trends," in *Work, Family and Religion in Contemporary Society,* Eds. N.T. Ammerman and W.C. Roof. New York and London: Routledge, pp. 81–121.

Huber, E. 1979. "A Woman Must Not Speak," in *Women of Spirit,* Eds. R. Ruether and E. McLaughlin. New York: Simon and Schuster, pp. 153–81.

Hunter, J.D. 1987. *Evangelicalism: The Coming Generation.* Chicago and London: University of Chicago Press.

Jacobs, J. 1989. "The Effects of Ritual Healing on Female Victims of Abuse: A Study of Empowerment and Transformation," *Sociological Analysis* 50:265–79.

Jacobs, J. 1990. "Women Centered Healing Rites," in *In Gods We Trust: New Patterns of Religious Pluralism in America,* Eds. T. Robbins and D. Anthony. New Brunswick, NJ: Transaction, pp. 373–83.

Jacobs, J. 1991. "Gender and Power in New Religious Movements. A Feminist Discourse on the Scientific Study of Religion," *Religion* 21:345–56.

Kaufman, D.R. 1991. *Rachel's Daughters: Newly Orthodox Jewish Women.* New Brunswick, NJ: Rutgers University Press.

Lehman, E.C. Jr. 1980. "Placement of Men and Women in Ministry," *Review of Religious Research* 22:18–40.

Lehman, E.C. Jr. 1993. *Gender and Work: The Case of the Clergy.* Albany, NY: SUNY Press.

Lenski, G. 1961. *The Religious Factor.* Garden City, NY: Doubleday.

Luhrmann, T. 1994. *Persuasions of Witch's Craft: Ritual Magic in Contemporary England.* London: Picador.

McFague, S. 1987. *Models of God: Theology for a Nuclear Age.* Philadelphia, PA: Fortress Press.

McGuire, M. 1994. "Gendered Spirituality and Quasi-Religious Ritual," in *Religion and the Social Order, vol. 4: Between Sacred and Secular*, Eds. A. Greil and T. Robbins. Greenwich, CT: Jai Press, pp. 273–87.

Marler, P.L. 1995. "Lost in the Fifties: The Changing Family and the Nostalgic Church," in *Work, Family and Faith in Contemporary Society*, Eds. N. Ammerman and W.C. Roof. New York and London: Routledge, pp. 23–60.

Martin, B. 1998. "From Pre- to Postmodernity in Latin America: The Case of Pente-costalism," in *Religion, Modernity and Postmodernity*, Ed. P. Heelas. Oxford and Malden, MA: Blackwell, pp. 102–46.

Martin, B. and Pluck, R. 1977. *Young People's Beliefs*. A Report to the Board of Education of the Church of England.

Martin, D. 1990. *Tongues of Fire: The Explosion of Protestantism in Latin America*. Oxford and Cambridge, MA: Blackwell.

Martin, D. 1997. *Does Christianity Cause War?* Oxford: Clarendon Press.

Marty, M.E. and Appleby, R.S., Eds. 1995. *Fundamentalisms Comprehended*. Chicago: University of Chicago Press.

Neitz, M. 1990. "In Goddess we Trust," in *In Gods We Trust: New Patterns of Religious Pluralism in America*, 2nd edn., Eds. T. Robbins and D. Anthony. New Brunswick, NJ: Transaction, pp. 353–72.

Neitz, M. 1994. "Quasi Religions and Cultural Movements: Contemporary Witchcraft As a Churchless Religion," in *Religion and the Social Order, vol. 4: Between Sacred and Secular*, Eds. A. Greil and T. Robbins. Greenwich, CT: JAI Press, pp. 127–49.

Nelsen, H., Cheek, N., and Au, P. 1985. "Gender Differences in Images of God," *Journal for the Scientific Study of Religion* 24:396–402.

Nesbitt, P.D. 1997. *Feminization of the Clergy in America*. New York and Oxford: Oxford University Press.

Nicholson, L., Ed. 1997. *The Second Wave. A Reader in Feminist Theory*. New York and London: Routledge.

Nightingale, F. 1991. *Florence Nightingale: Cassandra and Other Selections From Suggestions for Thought*, Ed. Mary Poovey. London: Pickering and Chatto.

Ozorak, E.W. 1996. "The Power, but Not the Glory: How Women Empower Themselves Through Religion," *Journal for the Scientific Study of Religion* 35(1):17–29.

Palmer, S. 1994. *Moon Sisters, Krishna Mothers, Rajneesh Lovers: Women's Roles in New Religions*. Syracuse, NY: Syracuse University Press.

Rendall, J. 1985. *The Origins of Modern Feminism: Women in Britain, France and the United States 1780–1860*. Chicago: Lyceum Books.

Roof, W.C. and McKinney, W. 1987. *American Mainline Religion: Its Changing Shape and Future*. New Brunswick, NJ: Rutgers University Press.

Ruether, R.R., Ed. 1974. *Religion and Sexism: Images of Women in the Jewish and Christian Traditions*. New York: Simon and Schuster.

Sered, S.S. 1987. "Ritual, Morality and Gender: The Religious Lives of Oriental Jewish Women in America," *Israel Social Science Research* 5:87–96.

Simmons, G. and Walter, T. 1988. "Spot the Men: The Relation of Faith and Gender," *Third Way* April: 10–12.

Stanton, E.C. 1985. *The Woman's Bible*, abridged edn. Glasgow: Bell and Bain.

Starhawk 1989. *The Spiral Dance: A Rebirth of the Ancient Religion of the Great Goddess*. New York: HarperCollins.

Steggarda, M. 1994. "The Social Location of Gender Differences in Religion," paper given at the conference *La Religion, Un Frein à L'Égalité*. Lausanne, 1–3 December.

Swatos, W.H. Jr., Ed. 1994. *Gender and Religion.* New Brunswick, NJ and London: Transaction.

Thompson, E.H. 1991. "Beneath the Status Characteristic: Gender Variations in Religiousness," *Journal for the Scientific Study of Religion* 30(4):381–94.

Tipton, S. 1982. *Getting Saved from the Sixties.* Berkeley and London: University of California Press.

van der Veer, P. 1994. *Religious Nationalism: Hindus and Muslims in India.* Berkeley, Los Angeles, and London: University of California Press.

Wallace, R.A. 1975. "Bringing Women In: Marginality in the Churches," *Sociological Analysis* 36:291–303.

Wallace, R.A. 1991. "Feminism: Expanding the Horizon of the Sociology of Religion," in *Religion and the Social Order Vol I. New Developments in Theory and Research*, Ed. D.G. Bromiley, Greenwich, CT and London: JAI Press, pp. 253–66.

Wallace, R.A. 1992. *They Call Her Pastor: A New Role for Catholic Women.* Albany, NY: SUNY Press.

Walter, T. and Davie, G. 1998. "The Religiosity of Women in the Modern West," *British Journal of Sociology* 49(4):640–69.

Warner, R.S. 1988. *New Wine in Old Wineskins. Evangelicals and Liberals in a Small-Town Church.* Berkeley, Los Angeles, London: University of California Press.

Winter, M.T., Lummis, A., and Stokes, A. 1994. *Defecting in Place: Women Claiming Responsibility for Their Own Spiritual Lives.* New York: Crossroad.

Woodhead, L. 1999. "Diana and the Religion of the Heart," in *Diana: The Making of a Media Saint*, Eds. J. Richards, S. Wilson, and L. Woodhead. London: I.B. Tauris.

Woodhead, L. and Heelas, P. 1999. *Religion in Modern Times: An Interpretative Anthology.* Oxford: Blackwell.

Wuthnow, R. 1996. *Sharing the Journey: Support Groups and America's New Quest for Community.* New York and London: The Free Press.

Wuthnow, R. 1997. "The Cultural Turn. Studies, Logic, and the Quest for Identity in American Religion," in *Contemporary American Religion. An Ethnographic Reader*, Eds. P.E. Becker and N.L. Eisland. Walnut Creek, CA and London: AltaMira, pp. 245–65.

CHAPTER 5

Melancholia, Utopia, and the Psychoanalysis of Dreams

Donald Capps

Melancholy has a very long history. In tracing its permutations from the ancient Greeks through the mid-twentieth century, Stanley W. Jackson (1986) views this history as "variations in a remarkable consistency." In his exploration of religious melancholy and Protestant experience in America, Julius H. Rubin (1994) shows that melancholy has been a constant feature of the American religious landscape from the New England Puritans to contemporary Christian authors, the common element being the sense of God-forsakenness. While the use of the term "depression" has become endemic to the late twentieth century (see Healy 1997), the word "melancholy" has survived and may well be staging a comeback. Melancholy is recognized as a specific expression of mood disorder in the official diagnostic manual of the American Psychiatric Association (1994); it is described as a depressed mood that does not improve, even temporarily, when something good happens, and as likely to reflect excessive or inappropriate guilt. It is also distinguishable from the sadness experienced after the death of a loved one (p. 383). The psychoanalyst Julia Kristeva characterizes melancholia as a suffering "that does not succeed in signifying itself," and as a "weird affect that the analyst will be looking for with utmost empathy, beyond the motor and verbal retardation of the depressed" (1989:189). William Styron, the novelist, employs the term "melancholy" to describe his own suffering, his "despair beyond despair." He complains that it has been usurped by a noun – depression – "with a bland tonality and lacking any magisterial presence, used indifferently to describe an economic depression or a rut in the ground, a true wimp of a word for such a major illness" (1990:37).

The word "utopia" has a somewhat shorter history, having been coined by Thomas More in 1516 (u = no, topia = place), but the idea goes back to "the oldest cultural stratum of Mesopotamia" (Manuel and Manuel 1979:35). More proposed that his own country be named "Eutopia," thus playfully suggesting through the emended prefix "eu" (Greek for "good" or "happy") that it was ideal, prosperous, and perfect. Utopia continued to attract scholarly attention in the late twentieth century, aided perhaps by the approaching millennium (Kumar and Bann 1993). The Manuels conclude their massive history of utopian thought in the Western world with the observation that "Experimenters tell us that as we sleep the eyeballs persist in going through their rapid movements four or five times a night, bearing witness to dreamwork. Western civilization may not be able to survive long without utopian fantasies any more than individuals can exist without dreaming" (Manuel and Manuel 1979:814).

As the only psychologist of religion invited to contribute to this sociology of religion text, it seemed to me that the most useful contribution I could make would be to illustrate ways in which the interests of the two fields might converge, possibly to the enhancement of both. By focusing on melancholy and utopia, I hope to indicate how the psychological study of melancholy may inform – and be informed by – the sociological study of utopia. While this may be only one of a vast number of illustrations of possible convergence, the melancholy–utopia association may be more than illustrative, for it seems to address the question of what religion itself is about. Wittgenstein observed that a "problem has the form: 'I don't know my way about'" (1958:123). I suggest that if religion is our shared problem, we psychologists and sociologists may begin to find our way about together by attending to melancholy, utopia, and their points of convergence.

That these two phenomena have something in common is not my original idea. I discovered the connection in Robert Burton's *The Anatomy of Melancholy* (1979), the first edition of which was published in 1621, nearly a century before Thomas More's *Utopia*. Burton introduces himself in the guise of Democritus, Jr., heir of the Greek philosopher who had searched for the cause of melancholy by cutting up several beasts. In his opening remarks to the reader, Democritus, Jr. contends that the disease of melancholy is especially apparent in societies where there are "many discontents, common grievances, complaints, poverty, barbarism, begging," and so forth. Such a society "must needs be discontent, melancholy, hath a sick body, and had need to be reformed" (1979:23). Burton does not need to travel the globe to find a society where melancholy is rampant. His own country, England, is such a place, and its reformation would require skills surpassing those of Hercules himself. Democritus, Jr., of course, is no Hercules. Nonetheless, "to satisfy and please myself," he decides to "make an Utopia of my own, a new Atlantis, a poetical Commonwealth of mine own, in which I will freely domineer, build cities, make laws, statutes, as I list myself" (Burton 1979:25). He provides a description of his own utopia (the details of which need not be recounted here), and then declares, "All the world is melancholy" (p. 28). Evidently, England is not exceptional in this regard.

This universal melancholy being the case, his own "purpose and intent" is "to anatomize this humor of melancholy" and "shew the causes, symptoms, and several cures of it, that it may be better avoided." He concludes: "Being then it is a disease so grievous, so common, I know not wherein to do a more general service, and spend my time better, than to prescribe means how to prevent and

cure so universal a malady, an epidemical disease, that so often, so much, cru-
cifies the body and mind" (p. 29). With this concluding statement, Burton, in
effect, sheds the guise of Democritus, Jr., and adopts his own identity as a physician. The rest of his massive text will reflect this professional identity – that of
the clinician or protopsychologist – as utopia gets more or less left behind. After
all, unlike an ersatz Greek philosopher, a physician lives in the real world of
human suffering.

It may be noted, in passing, that James Boswell once asked Samuel Johnson
what he did to combat "constitutional melancholy"?(1979). Along with such
diversions as taking a course in chemistry or in rope-dancing, Johnson recom-
mended reading Burton's *The Anatomy of Melancholy* (Boswell 1979:690).
Because it was the only book "that ever took him out of bed two hours sooner
than he wished to rise" (Boswell:438), we may assume that, for Johnson, reading
about melancholy was one of the methods he used to counteract it.

Melancholy is a vast topic, and a discussion of its history, the cultural meanings attached to it, the efforts made throughout the centuries to treat it, and so
forth, would be impossible here. Why Burton would make a connection between
melancholia and utopia is, however, a valuable question to ask and, as I have
intimated, the answers to this question promise to shed light on melancholy
itself. The preliminary question why a psychologist of religion might be interested in melancholy is relatively easy to answer. As I have shown in my *Men,
Religion, and Melancholia* (1997), major texts in psychology of religion (i.e.,
James' *The Varieties*, Otto's *The Idea of the Holy*, Jung's *Answer to Job*, and Erikson's
Young Man Luther), not only link melancholy to religion, but also (in my view)
reveal that the author struggled personally with melancholy throughout much
or all of his adult life. In the case of Otto, it resulted in his attempted suicide. In
all four cases, it manifested itself in rather unconventional views of religion.
While Freud's own writings on religion were not the focus of the book, I used
his essays, "Mourning and Melancholia" and "The 'Uncanny' " as the interpretive lens through which to understand the psychological dynamics underlying
the melancholia–religion relationship. A brief summary of this argument is
necessary here, as it provides the basis for the related connection between
melancholy and utopia.

Melancholia and the Lost Object

In "Mourning and Melancholia," Freud ([1917] 1957a) explores the similarities
and differences between the normal grieving process and the pathology of
"melancholia." The major similarity is that both are reactions to the loss of
someone or something deeply loved. In the case of mourning, one adjusts to the
loss in the normal course of time, whereas melancholia is a pathological condition that may require medical treatment. How to account for these divergent
outcomes? In his view, what characterizes melancholia is a profoundly painful

dejection, diminished interest in the outside world, loss of the capacity to love, inhibition of all activity, and a lowering of one's self-regarding feelings to such a degree that one engages in self-reproach and self-revilings, often culminating in a delusional expectation of punishment. Many of the same traits are found in grief: the same feeling of pain, the loss of interest in the outside world, an incapacity to adopt any new object or objects of love, and a turning away from active effort that is not connected with thoughts of the dead person. In mourning, however, there is little of the self-reproach that is always present in melancholia, and no anticipation of impending punishment. In mourning, the loss is deeply painful yet is experienced not as punishment but as a normal part of life.

Why this loss of self-esteem, this self-abasement, in melancholia? Why this "delusional belittling" of self, and expectations of chastisement? Some of this self-criticism is no doubt justified. After all, the patient is as lacking in interest and incapable of love and achievements as he says he is.[1] Moreover, in his self-criticisms, he has a keener eye for truth than nonmelancholics, for others cling to views of themselves and human nature that are much too sanguine. For Freud, however, the issue is not whether such distressing self-abasement is justified in others' opinion but whether the melancholic is correctly describing his experience of himself and its underlying reasons. If he has lost his self-respect, is there good reason for this, as he seems to believe? For Freud, the more he protests having lost his self-respect for unassailable reasons, the more hollow these protests seem.

Given the melancholic's loss of self-esteem, melancholia seems the very antithesis of grief, for grief involves loss of an object in the external world while melancholia involves the loss of self. This difference, however, is only apparent, and further probing reveals why. Like the griever, the melancholic has experienced the painful loss of a loved object. While the griever mourns the loss of the loved object, however, the melancholic experiences its loss with great ambivalence, as he feels that his loss is the object's own fault, that he is the victim of abandonment. This sense of abandonment is not one he can openly acknowledge because it is even more painful than bereavement, where the loved one has been "taken away" against her will. So his reproachful feelings toward the lost object are turned against himself. The lost object is not relinquished and released, as in grief, but internalized, becoming an aspect of the ego, so that the ego itself becomes the focus of reproach and delusions of future punishment. Thus, reproaches against the external object are redirected against the self. As a result, "in the clinical picture of melancholia, dissatisfaction with the ego on moral grounds is far the most outstanding feature: The patient's self-evaluation concerns itself much less frequently with bodily infirmity, ugliness or weakness, or with social inferiority" (Freud 1957a:247–8).

When the melancholic's self-reproachings are viewed as reproach of the lost object turned against the self, another puzzling feature of melancholia becomes more comprehensible. This is that the melancholic exhibits little if any "feelings of shame in front of other people" (Freud 1957a:247). We would expect that those who genuinely feel themselves to be worthless would shrink from the gaze of others. This is not, however, the case with melancholics: "On the contrary, they make the greatest nuisance of themselves, and always seem as though they feel slighted and had been treated with great injustice. All this is possible only because the reactions expressed in their behavior still proceed from a mental constellation of revolt" (p. 248). This means, in effect, that he has vengeful feelings toward the lost object, and his revenge is the pathology itself, for by this means he torments the one who has forsaken him. Such tormenting is possible because – unlike the lost object in mourning – the "person who has occasioned the patient's emotional disorder, and on whom his illness is centered, is usually to be found in his immediate environment"(p. 251). Thus, his relationship to the lost object takes two forms: internalization of the object, with resulting self-reproach; and punishment of the object via the pathology itself.

Is melancholia curable? Freud notes that it is more complicated than mourning because the lost object evokes deeply ambivalent feelings. In melancholia, "countless separate struggles are carried on over the object, in which hate and love contend with each other" (p. 256). Also, whereas in mourning the object is finally relinquished, its release in melancholia is greatly complicated because the melancholic is unconscious of the causes of his pathology. As grieving enables the ego eventually to relinquish the object, however, so in melancholia each single conflict of ambivalence, by disparaging and denigrating the object, loosens the fixation to it. Thus, the process in the unconscious may come to an end, either because the fury has spent itself or the object is abandoned. Which of these two possibilities will bring melancholia to a merciful end is impossible to determine. It concludes, however, when the sufferer experiences "the satisfaction of knowing itself as the better of the two, as superior to the object" (p. 257).

Freud emphasizes that the object is the internalized other, which only partially resembles the real-life other. The struggle is an internalized one in which the ego wrestles ambivalently – loving and hating – with the internalized other. Its internalization helps explain why the melancholic may experience symptoms of both mania and depletion. Mania usually accompanies the sense of triumph over the internalized other, while depletion reveals that the ego is weak, unable to hold its own against the superior power of the internalized other. When the ego feels strong, it has the ability to "slay" the object, bringing the melancholia itself to an end. Therapeutically, then, the goal is to strengthen the ego so that it may neutralize the internalized object, thus achieving through insight what may otherwise be acted out in manic reprisals against the internalized object.

Freud's essay concludes with a discussion of suicide and mania. Suicide occurs when the ego is too weak to defend itself against the desire to destroy the internalized hated object, and mania occurs when the ego "masters" the "complex" to which it has succumbed in melancholia. Freud admits that he finds mania difficult to account for, but suggests that it occurs as a consequence of the "long-sustained condition of great mental expenditure" involved in melancholia, during which time great psychic energy has been stored up, and – in the manic period – is finally discharged. He compares it to the experience of "some poor wretch" winning a large sum of money, who is "suddenly relieved from chronic worry about his daily bread," and "finds himself in a position to throw off at a single blow some oppressive compulsion, some false position he has long had to keep up" (1957a:254). Thus, the popular conception of someone in a manic state delighting in his movements and actions "because he is so 'cheerful'" is incorrect: "This false connection must of course be put right. The fact is that the economic condition in the subject's mind referred to above has been fulfilled" – that is, one is suddenly in a position to throw off at a single blow some false position – "and this is the reason why he is in such high spirits on the one hand and so uninhibited in action on the other" (p. 254).

The reader who is alert for connections between melancholia and utopia will certainly be drawn to Freud's comparison of the melancholic's sudden burst of mania to "some poor wretch" winning a large sum of money, and thus experiencing himself as suddenly relieved from a heavy burden long endured. This reflects the tenor – the mood – of utopia. Our more immediate concern, however, is the relationship of melancholia to religion, and here the question of the identity of the "lost object" is especially germane. While Freud does not identify the "lost object" in his discussion of melancholia – this appears to depend on the individual patient – he notes that this person is to be "found among those in his near neighborhood," and is considered by the patient to have "abandoned" him. It makes sense, therefore, to presume that the "lost object" was originally a parent, and that all subsequent abandonments are reminiscent of the original parental abandonment (e.g., Oedipus' abandonment by his father in a vain attempt to prohibit the oracle from coming true). In "A Seventeenth Century Demonological Neurosis" Freud ([1923] 1961) explicitly identifies the melancholic Christoph Haitzmann's "lost object" as his father.

Melancholia, Religion, and the Forsaking Mother

Freud's essay "The 'Uncanny'" ([1919] 1957b), published two years after "Mourning and Melancholia," leads one to suspect, however, that the deeper expressions of ambivalence felt toward a "lost object," as well as the more likely to inspire religious remedies, involve the mother. This essay addresses a phenomenon that was the focus of his earlier essay, "The Antithetical Meaning of Primal Words" (Freud [1910] 1957c), the fact that the German word *heimlich* (homelike) "is a word the meaning of which develops in the direction of ambivalence, until it finally coincides with its opposite, *unheimlich*" (1957b:226). He consults Grimm's dictionary, and finds the following notation that "From the idea of 'homelike,' 'belonging to the house,' the further idea is developed of something withdrawn from the eyes of strangers, something concealed, secret" (p. 255). Examples of its use are:

"I feel *heimlich*, well, free from fear"; *Heimlich*, in the sense of a place free from ghostly influences, familiar, friendly, intimate; *Heimlich* parts of the human body, pudenda, as in "the men that died not were smitten on their *heimlich* parts" (I Sam. 5:12); *Heimlich*, as used of knowledge, mystic, allegorical; *Heimlich*, as withdrawn from knowledge, unconscious; *Heimlich*, as that which is obscure, inaccessible to knowledge, as in "Do you not see? They do not trust me; they fear the *heimlich* face of the Duke of Friedland"; *Heimlich*, as the notion of something hidden and dangerous, as in "At times I feel like a man who walks in the night and believes in ghosts; every corner is *heimlich* and full of terrors for him." (1957b:225–6)

In several of the above examples, Freud notes that the word *unheimlich* would have been as appropriate as *heimlich*. He notes that whether we trace the meanings attached to the word *unheimlich* or focus on the properties of persons, things, sensations, experiences, and situations which arouse the feeling of the *unheimlich* in us, we come to the same conclusion, that "the uncanny is that class of the frightening which leads back to what is known of old and long 'familiar'" (p. 220). One point of the essay is to show how "the familiar can become uncanny and frightening." One way this occurs is where that which "ought to have remained hidden and secret"(p. 220) is revealed. In such cases, either word – *heimlich* or *unheimlich* – would be appropriate.

In the explicitly psychoanalytic section of the essay, Freud suggests that the experience of the "return of the repressed" accounts for the anxiety the uncanny evokes. The uncanny is "something which is familiar and old-established in the mind and which has become alienated from it only through the process of repression" (p. 241). An example of the return of the repressed "taken from psycho-analytical experience" is when

neurotic men declare that they feel there is something uncanny about the female genital organs. This *unheimlich* place, however, is the entrance to the former *Heim* [home] of all human beings, to the place where each one of us lived once upon a time and in the beginning. There is a joking saying that "Love is homesickness"; and whenever a man dreams of a place or country and says to himself, while he is still dreaming, "this place is familiar to me, I've been here before," we may interpret the place as being his mother's genitals or her body. In this case too, then, the *unheimlich* is what was once *heimisch*, familiar; the prefix "un" [un] is the token of repression. (1957b:245)

Thus, a man's mother is linked to the very ambivalence reflected in the shading of the *heimlich* into the *unheimlich*. Her body – especially aspects with which he was most intimately familiar – has been estranged, defamiliarized, no longer congenial. This defamiliarization, with all its anxieties, is implicated in every subsequent experience of the uncanny.

This invites the conclusion that the "lost object" of "Mourning and Melancholia" may be the mother who, having become *unheimlich*, now arouses anxiety in her son. This sense of uncanniness is greater for the male than for the female child because his physical difference from his mother is precisely where the *heimlich/unheimlich* ambivalence is so emotionally powerful. While he makes no explicit connection between the uncanny and melancholia, Freud's analysis of the uncanny suggests their relationship. Unlike mourning, melancholia is a state of anxiety where one is truly ambivalent, lamenting the loss of the familiar object, yet fearing her return. Thus, if the familiar object is given up and relinquished in mourning, in melancholia there is no final relinquishing of the object: its return in a new guise for the purpose of hurting or terrorizing its victim is an enduring threat. If Freud's analysis of melancholia alerts us to the loss of the loved object and the emotions this loss occasions – including feelings both of love and hate for the one who abandoned him – "The 'Uncanny'" directs us to the emotions aroused by the threat of its return in a new, unloving guise. The two essays together enable us to identify the anxieties underlying the melancholic condition, and to recognize that they are two sides of the same coin, for the object would not return to haunt him unless she had discovered his hateful feelings toward her, unless his awful secret had itself been revealed – when it ought to have remained hidden – to the very one from whom he most wanted to conceal it.

Although Freud does not identify the lost object as the boy's mother, the very intensity of the melancholic reaction suggests that she, the boy's first love object, is the object that has been lost. This would explain, for example, why one important feature of melancholia is the formation of a conscience and the fear of punishment. While her own objective may have been only that of helping him achieve separation from her in order that he would differentiate from her world and embrace the world of men (and manliness), the boy believes that he has done something to warrant the loss of his mother and that if he makes certain reparations and promises he might win her back. Because, for reasons of gender differentiation, the son's separation from his mother is more decisive than the daughter's, he is also more likely to form a false conscience, one more delusional as to his own personal culpability for the initial separation and the failure to restore the relationship. (For further discussion of the negative influence of separation from mother on boys, see Pollack 1998.)

Thus, his initial desire is to win her back. He believes that if he makes himself acceptable in her eyes she will return, and all will be well. He develops a conscience, becomes conscientious, and begins to exercise self-control over his actions and thoughts. To the mother, everything is working well, for through her withdrawal of her unconditional love (i.e., separation augmented by punishment), he is becoming a good and independent boy. But this is only the surface story. Under the surface, in the unconscious, an emotional storm is brewing. The calm, placid, well-behaved boy is inwardly furious with himself and with his shattered image of his mother. He continues to cherish this image but also wants to desecrate it. Love and hate wrestle together in a seemingly endless series of skirmishes. The "religious" side of him continues to cherish the loved object, now beatified. The "pathological" or iconoclastic side of him wants to have done with the object, to destroy it, so that he might get on with his life.

One way that conventional religion may conceivably help him to get on with his life is by teaching him that God is a Father, and that if he continues to be "a good boy," this Father God will not only *not* punish him but will reward him for his goodness. But this teaching has very little to do with, or to say to, his real distress, which is that he has lost the mother. He has experienced the withdrawal of her love, and he feels bereft, depleted, and angry. Thus, if it is true that "father religions have mother churches" (Erikson 1958:263), it is also true that father religions are a convenient cover for something much deeper, as these religions deceive sons into believing that if they appease the Father God, all will be well with them, when in fact nothing will be well with them until they come to terms with their melancholy, which has another basis entirely, that is, their underlying sense of having been forsaken by their mothers. This, I suggest, is the religious root of utopian longings.

The Psychological Impetus Behind Utopia

Freud's "The 'Uncanny'" essay also affords an association between the "lost object" of his "Mourning and Melancholia" essay and the experience of homesickness, which I will view as the psychological impetus behind the longing for utopia. The affliction of melancholia – which Burton likens to crucifixion – originates in a deep-seated anxiety about home, including the perception that it is actually a more dangerous place than the external world. This sense of home's inherent dangers has its roots in early childhood, and is specifically associated with the boy's anxieties over his relationship to his mother. (Jackson 1986:373–80 discusses nostalgia for home as a form of melancholia, but does not consider the perceived dangers attached to home, or related anxieties evoked by the mother.)

An especially relevant discussion of such anxieties is Norman Bryson's analysis of the male still life artist, which expands on Freud's essay on the uncanny to include male attitudes toward the place called "home." Citing Joshua Reynolds' view that "high focus and minute transcription are *the* dominant characteristic of the genre" of still life, Bryson notes:

> It is as if the world of the table and domestic space must be patrolled by an eye whose vigilance misses nothing. And in trying to understand this emphasis on gripping every last detail of that visual field through high-tension focus, the factors of gender asymmetry and male exclusion cannot be considered accidental. The male artist is peering into a zone that does not concern him directly. In a sense its values are alien to the masculine agenda. And spatially, it cannot be known from the inside. The result is often the production of the uncanny: although everything looks familiar, the scene conveys a certain estrangement and alienation. (Bryson 1990:170)

For Bryson, this estrangement and alienation is due to the fact that the home is the mother's milieu:

> The persistence of [the boy's] desire to remain within the maternal orbit represents a menace to the very center of his being, a possibility of engulfment and immersion that threatens his entire development and viability as a subject. . . . The seductiveness of the mother's body, together with her milieu and its mystique, become dangers he must escape; and he can do so by no other means than by claiming as his another kind of space, [one] that is definitely and assuredly *outside*. . . . Still life bears all the marks of this double-edged exclusion and nostalgia, this irresolvable ambivalence which gives to feminine space a power of attraction intense enough to motor the entire development of still life as genre, yet at the same time apprehends feminine space as alien, as a space which also menaces the masculine subject to the core of his identity as male. (Bryson 1990:172–3)

We may conclude from this that utopias – at least those conceived by males – have a direct connection to the affliction of melancholia. They arise out of the sense of having lost something of vital importance, that the loss feels like abandonment, and that the one who has done the abandoning is the mother. Because her domain is the home, he has been exiled to the world outside, condemned (this is his punishment) to make his way in this alien world, and challenged to see if he can find himself at home there.

The Place of Desire in Utopia

Among twentieth century utopian theorists, Ernst Bloch is especially cognizant of this psychological dynamic. In order to show this and its importance for melancholia, however, I need to locate his views within the larger context of utopian theory. The typical way in which sociologists of religion address the subject of utopia is to think of it in terms of religious movements and social experiments. Bryan Wilson (1973), for example, proposes a sevenfold typology based on the diverse ways in which people respond to the world when salvation from evil is no longer adequately found within the standard resources of their tradition. These comprise the conversionist, manipulationist, thaumaturgist, revolutionist, introversionist, reformist, and utopian types. According to Wilson, if reformists believe that God calls us to amend the world, utopians believe that God calls us to reconstruct the world. This presumes some divinely given principles of reconstruction and is much more radical than the reformist alternative but, unlike the revolutionist option, insists much more on the role human beings must take in the process.

Wilson, of course, is concerned here with religious movements, so it makes sense in this context to talk about the utopianist's impulse to "reconstruct the world." Our discussion thus far, however, suggests that leaders of such movements may be exploiting a deep longing among melancholic males which no amount of world reconstruction will assuage. For the melancholic, there may be very little distinction to be made between reformists who seek to amend, and utopianists who seek to reconstruct, the world. For the melancholic, utopian longings arise because he has experienced forsakenness, exile from mother and home, and carries a deep sense of grievance with him as he goes about in the world. To the extent that he is able to displace these longings onto "the world," his ambivalence is as likely to cause him to want to exploit or even destroy the world as to reconstruct it. This may help to explain why utopian social programs are as likely to fail from internal conflicts among the members as from outside opposition, and why men despoil and wage war on mother earth.

To gain a sense of what utopia (as opposed to radical social reform) is really about we need to review the work of theorists of utopia. Krishan Kumar notes (1991) that there are many varieties of utopias, including (1) the golden age, arcadia, or paradise; (2) the mythical land of Cockaigne; (3) the millennium; and (4) the ideal city. He emphasizes the class differences involved in the first two. The golden age and its various derivatives are considered the original state of humanity, and are the visions of the literate elite (poets and priests) with their devotion to simplicity and spirituality. The mythical Garden of Eden is such a vision. In contrast, the medieval land of Cockaigne is the "poor man's heaven," and is a kind of extravagance, exuberance, and excess: "Everything is free and available for the asking. Cooked larks fly straight into one's mouth; the rivers run with wine; the more one sleeps, the more one earns; sexual promiscuity is the norm; there is a fountain of youth that keeps everyone young and active." It is "a popular fantasy of pure hedonism: A cockney paradise" (Kumar 1991:6).

The third form, the millennium, connects with the golden age, linking the primitive Paradise and the Promised Land: "Both the beliefs and the movements associated with them oscillate constantly between the two poles, lending to millenarianism equally the characteristics of extreme conservatism and extreme radicalism" (1991:6–7). It is also, however, in "its forward-looking character that the millennium most clearly distinguishes itself from the Golden Age and Paradise. . . . The millennium faces the future more than it harks back to the past. . . . Of all ideal society concepts, it is the millennium which most forcibly introduces the elements of time, process and history" (p. 7). In Western thought, Christian millenarianism continues Jewish messianism, whereas the fourth type, the ideal city, is the contribution of the ancient near east (e.g., Egypt) and Hellenism. This is the philosophers' contribution to ideas of the ideal society. If poets and priests pictured the golden age, peasants yearned for the land of extravagance and excess, and devotees anticipate the millennium, philosophers "invented the ideal city as the earthly embodiment of the cosmic order which they deduced from first principles. The ideal city was the microcosmic reflection of the divinely regulated macrocosmic order" (p. 12).

To be sure, these four types have not remained entirely distinct, but have drawn upon one another, and the "religious connotations of many of these terms also point to their interconnection with overarching religious cosmologies" (p. 17). While utopia is more than an amalgam of these conceptions, each makes an "elemental" contribution to it. Cockaigne contributes the element of *desire*, paradise adds *harmony*, the millennium introduces *hope*, and the ideal city provides *design*. These four elements go into the making of utopia, but "utopia does not simply recombine these elements. It has its own inventiveness. Once established, it provides a map of quite different possibilities for speculating on the human condition" (p. 19). In Kumar's view, utopia distinguishes itself from other forms of the ideal society, and from other forms of social and political theory, by being "in the first place a piece of fiction." When we encounter utopia, "the first thing we encounter in most cases is a story" (p. 20). Its basic narrative pattern is one where a visitor from another place or time encounters a superior civilization. This device creates room for comic misunderstanding, thwarted intrigue, and romance. It also involves satire, "the holding up of an unflattering mirror to one's own society" (p. 26). This satirical strand led to the formation of a separate subgenre, the dystopia or antiutopia, where the narrator depicts a hellish society whose similarity to the author's own is all too apparent.

In contrast to abstract schemes of conventional social and political theory, through which we "are *told* that the good society will follow from the application of the relevant general principles," in utopia "we are *shown* the good society in operation, supposedly as a result of certain general principles of social organization" (p. 31). Because Christianity is so closely identified with millenarianism, this is a major reason why utopia has developed in the West and nowhere else. On the other hand, the millennium is not itself a utopia because "Its ideal order is predetermined. It is brought in by divine intervention. Human agency remains questionably relevant" (p. 36). In contrast to millenarianism, utopia – even for devout Christian thinkers – is:

> an order belonging unambiguously to this world, to be achieved with its materials and by the free agency of its human inhabitants. To Christian thinkers utopia might not be the summit and end of man's destiny; that must be for another world. But so far as this world was concerned it represented the best order that could be achieved by unaided human purpose and design. (Kumar and Bann 1991:36)

Thus, Christian formulations of utopia tend to integrate the millennium and the ideal city, and to elevate the elements of hope and design. No doubt this is the model of utopia that informs Wilson's description of utopianists in his typology of religious movements. This, however, is only one form of utopia, and is quite dissimilar to the utopia envisioned by peasant classes (as reflected, for example, in the medieval vision of the Land of Cockaigne).

Kumar argues that the element of *desire* – which he identifies with Cockaigne – is utopia's primary contribution to visions of an ideal society or ideal condition of humanity:

> Utopia opposes as well as proposes. Its pictures of a fulfilled and happy humanity are premised on the rejection of some social impulses and the elevation of others. It is through this willful suppression, by not showing certain things from our own

world, that it negates their persistence into the future. Things need not continue as they are. Out of this defiance, set in a context that proposes an alternative, comes the desire for change. (Kumar and Bann 1991:107)

Because desire is fundamental to utopianism, the peasant classes provide the fundamental stimulus for utopian visions. This is the social class among whom utopian visions tend to originate.

Ruth Levitas discusses the two elements of desire and hope in utopian thinking, and, like Kumar, concludes that desire is the more fundamental. She bases this conclusion on the fact that the idea of utopia as a "possible world" is too limiting, for an imagined world may carry out any of the functions of compensation, criticism, or change without being possible:

> To function as criticism or compensation, utopia does not even need to be believed to be possible. Thus while the questions of whether alternative worlds are theoretically or practically possible, and whether alternative worlds are theoretically or practically possible, and whether they are believed to be so by those who produce, peruse or pursue them, are important questions to ask, again, they cannot be definitional ones. (Levitas 1990:190)

The problem of restricting utopia to the "possible world" is that it conflates the categories of desire and hope, and "limits utopia to the question 'what may I hope?', and refuses the question 'what may I dream?' It implies also that the function of utopia is necessarily that of change" (p. 190).

For Levitas, examination of the Land of Cockaigne shows that the question of possibility is quite beside the point:

> There are rivers of oil, milk, honey and wine, as well as healing springs and springs of wine. The garlic-dressed geese that fly roasted on the spit and the cinnamon-flavored larks flying into the mouth do indeed, in [David] Riesman's terms, "violate what we know of nature." So too does the much later song, "The Big Rock Candy Mountain," with its little streams of alcohol, its lakes of stew and whiskey, where "The jails are made of tin, And you can bust right out again As soon as they put you in." Not only are these fantasies both theoretically and practically impossible – in other words, they are not possible worlds – but we have every reason to suppose that audiences knew this to be the case. Medieval peasants did not believe that larks could fly when cooked. American hobos did not believe in alcoholic lakes or totally ineffective jails. Yet both these examples are expressions of desire – desire for the effortless gratification of need and the absence of restrictive sanctions; they are not expressions of hope. (Levitas 1990:190)

Also, "if utopia is hoped for, then it must indeed be set in the future." Instead, utopia is fundamentally "the expression of desire." It may also include criticism of existing conditions, but this, too, is not absolutely necessary. Thus, Levitas notes that early utopias – including Sir Thomas More's – were more commonly located elsewhere in space than in some future time. The problem was not that they were temporally distant, but hard to get to. As Oscar Wilde quipped, "A map of the world that does not include Utopia is not worth glancing at" (quoted in Kumar 1991:95).

A third theorist who has relevance for our concern to link melancholia and utopia is E.M. Cioran (1987). In "Mechanisms of Utopia," he notes his amazement that some individuals have ventured to conceive a different society: "What can be the cause of so much naiveté, or of so much inanity?" To find out, he decided to spend several months steeping himself in utopian literature. From this, he arrived at several conclusions. One is that utopian systems are "dear to the disinherited" and that "poverty is in fact the utopianists' great auxiliary, it is the matter he works in, the substance on which he feeds his thoughts, the providence of his obsessions. Without poverty he would be empty; but poverty occupies him, allures or embarrasses him, depending on whether he is poor or rich" (pp. 81–2). Thus, if you question why another individual would engage in endless meditation, even obsessional thinking about another earth, this is because "you have not tasted utter indigence. Do so and you will see that the more destitute you are, the more time and energy you will spend in reforming everything, in thinking – in other words, in vain" (p. 82). By "reforming everything," Cioran means:

> not only institutions, human creations; those of course you will condemn straight off and without appeal; but objects, as they are, you will want to impose laws and your whims upon them, to function at their expense as legislator or as tyrant; you will even want to intervene in the life of the elements in order to modify their physiognomy, their structure. Air annoys you: let it be transformed! And stone as well. And the same for the vegetable world, the same for man. Down past the foundations of being, down to the strata of chaos, descend, install yourself there! When you haven't a penny in your pocket, you strive, you dream, how extravagantly you labor to possess All, and as long as the frenzy lasts, you do possess that All, you equal God, though no one realizes it, not even God, not even you. The delirium of the poor is the generator of events, the source of history: a throng of hysterics who want another world, here and now. It is they who inspire utopias, it is for them that utopias are written. But *utopia*, let us remember, means *nowhere*. (Cioran 1987:82)

Note Cioran's suggestion that true utopianists are obsessives and hysterics. Without challenging this diagnosis, my concern here is to make the case that they are fundamentally melancholics, at loose in a world where they are alien, dispirited, and feeling forsaken. What especially interests me, however, is Cioran's view that true utopianists envision far more fundamental changes than social institutions. Their grievances are with the very order of things. This being so, it is reasonable to assume that even their experience of being impoverished has a deeper basis than an unjust economic system, that their poverty pertains to the loss of the one object they needed the most when they were small and vulnerable.

Thus, for all their clarifications of what utopianism does and does not mean, an issue that receives inadequate attention by the theorists cited thus far concerns the psychological origins of desire. Ernst Bloch's views on utopia enable us to identify what these deeper psychological roots of utopian desire may be. In a conversation with Theodor W. Adorno on "the contradictions of utopian longing," Bloch (1988) suggested that "the decisive incentive toward utopia" is captured in Berthold Brecht's short sentence, "Something's missing." This something is perhaps best portrayed in a "picture," such as the picture "found in the old peasant saying, there is no dance before the meal. People must first fill their stomachs, then they can dance" (Bloch 1988:15). Thus, he uses a peasant saying about eating to illustrate the experience of "something's missing," and the desire, therefore, to address this sense of lack. The image of food, however, is part of a larger theme in Bloch's utopian theory, that of the desire to be at home in the world.

Bloch emphasized natural law and utopia as two essential features of human society, the essence of natural law being dignity or "the fundamental right not to be treated as scum," while the essence of utopia is the pursuit of happiness. Unlike natural law, however, utopia:

> includes a quest for an ontological state (as well as a social state which underpins it). The experience sought is . . . a "homeland of identity" or the "highest good" and can be prefigured in art through the experience of the "fulfilled moment." The goal, or One Thing Needful, is plainly the transcendence of alienation, construed here as a subjective experience which is anticipated in and communicated through art. (Levitas 1990:91)

This quest "for the transcendence of alienation, the overcoming of antagonism between humanity and the world," is essentially for the "feeling at home in the world" (Levitas 1990:95). The image of home – or homeland – is a recurrent one in Bloch's writings, reflected in the concluding words of *The Principle of Hope*: "But the root of history is the working, creating human being who reshapes and overhauls the given facts. Once he has grasped himself and established what is his, without expropriation and alienation, in real democracy, there arises in the world something which shines into the childhood of all and in which no one has yet been: homeland" (quoted in Levitas 1990:95).

For Bloch, in contrast to socialists of his day, the anticipation of the future has little to do with the process of production and much to do with "a process of contemplation," one which centers on the home that one experienced in childhood and the "home" where one has not yet been. Art is the primary locus of such a process of contemplation as it expresses the "fulfilled moments" in which the no-longer home of childhood and the not-yet home of the future meet. Such "fulfilled moments" are also, however, contemplated in religion. For Bloch, the biblical tradition, with its mystical notion of the kingdom of God as the locus of the overcoming of death, is the positive aspect of religion that stands in dialectical opposition to Marx's observation that religion is the heart of the heartless world and the spirit of spiritless conditions. The deep threat to all utopian visions is the reality of death. For Bloch, it is the religious impulse in works like Brahms' *Requiem* that:

intends a house, indeed a crystal, but from future freedom, a star, but as a new earth . . . all music of annihilation points towards a robust core which, because it has not yet blossomed, cannot pass away either. . . . In the darkness of this music gleam the treasures which will not be corrupted by moth and rust, the lasting trea- sures in which will and goal, hope and its content, virtue and happiness could be united as in a world without frustration, as in the highest good; – *the requiem circles the landscape of the highest good.* (Levitas 1990:91, her emphasis)

Bloch's association of the overcoming of death with a home that is both once lost and also not yet recalls Freud's "The Uncanny," where that which was once familiar has become defamiliarized; testifying, therefore, to our current estrangement from the world of the one in whose body we came to life. Levitas is critical of Bloch because, "although the passion and poetry of Bloch's writing is seductive, the criteria by which the utopian essence is extracted, or abstract and concrete utopia distinguished, remain obscure" (pp. 91–2).

The Dream as Locus of Utopia

While the preceding citations from Bloch's work justify Levitas's critique, I suggest that some of this obscurity is because the utopian essence is "the uncanny," that is, that which was once familiar but has been defamiliarized. On the other hand, I believe that Bloch makes a fundamental error in his construal of the contradictions of utopian longing when he, like so many others, futurizes utopia. He refers to utopia as "anticipatory consciousness," the subtitle of Part 2 of *The Principle of Hope*. It has two aspects, the "not-yet conscious" and the "not-yet-become," the former being its subjective, the latter its objective pole. Bloch's idea of the not-yet-conscious was developed through a critique of Freud, for, in his view, "Freud regarded the unconscious as a kind of rubbish bin of repressed material that was no longer conscious," and "this overly negative approach on Freud's part disregarded the additional and countervailing char- acteristic of the unconscious, that of being a creative source of material on the verge of coming to consciousness" (Levitas 1990:86). Bloch suggested that, in contrast to Freud's night dreams, the "daydream" is an important vehicle of utopian ideation. The first section of *The Principle of Hope* is concerned with day- dreams which are part of everyday life for people of all ages, although the pre- occupations of children, adolescents, and adults differ. They include dreams of revenge, of sexual conquest, of financial success and its consequences. Levitas notes: "Bloch agrees that these are essentially 'escape attempts,' involving the wish to break out of the world or change one's place within it, rather than to change the world itself. Nevertheless, they form part of the spectrum of utopian wishes" (p. 85).

Against Bloch, it may be noted that Freud was not at all oblivious to the cre- ative side of the unconscious. His writings on art are certainly indicative. More- over, his essay, "Creative Writers and Day-Dreaming" ([1908] 1959) anticipates

Bloch's own views on the wishes expressed through daydreams, though he believes that the daydream, like the night dream, is linked to repressed wishes. Thus, in daydreaming:

> The activity of phantasy in the mind is linked up with some current impression, occasioned by some event in the present, which had the power to rouse an intense desire. From there it wanders back to the memory of an early experience, generally belonging to infancy, in which this wish was fulfilled. Then it creates for itself a situation which is to emerge in the future, representing the fulfillment of the wish – this is the day-dream or phantasy, which now carries in it traces both of the occasion which engendered it and of some past memory. (Freud 1959:48)

Rather than getting involved in a discussion of the relative merits of daydreams over night dreams for the utopian impulse, I prefer to bring together the two strands of our preceding discussion – melancholia and utopia – by proposing that, for the melancholic, the locus of his utopian desire (locus here equals nowhere) is the dream itself.

In his essay "The Dream Specimen of Psychoanalysis" ([1954] 1987), Erikson discusses Freud's Irma Dream, noting that "The dreamer's [Freud's] activities (and those of his colleagues) are all professional and directed toward a woman. But they are a researcher's approaches: the dreamer takes aside, throws light on the matter, looks, localizes, thinks, finds. May it not be that it was the Mystery of the Dream which itself was the anxious prize of his persistence?" (pp. 269–70). Erikson suggests that, for Freud, "the Dream as a mystery had become to our dreamer one of those forbidding maternal figures which smile only on the most favored among young heroes." Freud alludes to two other women in his dream besides Irma – one was his wife – but confesses in a footnote (Freud 1953) that he has a feeling "that the interpretation of this part of the dream was not carried far enough to make it possible to follow the whole of its concealed meaning." If, however, he "had pursued my comparison between the three women, it would have taken me far afield. – There is at least one spot in every dream at which it is unplumbable – a navel, as it were, that is its point of contact with the unknown" (Freud 1953:111). Erikson suggests that:

> This statement, in such intimate proximity to allusions concerning the resistance of Victorian ladies (including the dreamer's wife, now pregnant) to being undressed and examined, suggests an element of transference to the Dream Problem as such: the Dream, then, is just another haughty woman, wrapped in too many mystifying covers and "putting on airs" like a Victorian lady. . . . In the last analysis, then, the dream itself may be a mother image; she is the one, as the Bible would say, to be "known". (Erikson 1987:270)

He adds: "It is clear that the first dream analyst stands in a unique relationship to the Dream as a 'Promised Land'" (p. 271).

What may we conclude from Erikson's suggestion that Dream itself is a mother image, and thus both the one to be "known" and the "Promised Land"?

Simply this: that the dream is the locus of utopia, the "no-place" where desires which are no longer possible – if they ever were – may be fulfilled. Freud, after all, said that the impetus behind dreams is the fulfillment of wishes. In one of his best known dreams, "The Three Fates," he meets three women, one of which – the inn-hostess – "was the mother who gives life, and furthermore (as in my own case) gives the living creature its first nourishment" ([1900] 1953:238. See also Freud ([1913] 1958), where he identifies "the three forms taken on by the figure of the mother as life proceeds: the mother herself, the beloved who is chosen after her pattern, and finally the Mother Earth who receives him again"). In another dream, his thirst was assuaged by his wife, who gave him a drink out of an Etruscan cinerary urn which he had brought back from Italy but since given away. In a footnote to this dream, he cites Isaiah 29:8: "It shall even be as when an hungry man dreameth, and, behold, he eateth; but he awaketh, and his soul is empty: or as when a thirsty man dreameth, and, behold, he drinketh; but he awaketh, and, behold, he is faint, and his soul hath appetite" (1953:124).

The Dream is the Land of Cockaigne, the melancholic's utopia. All other utopias are false and unreal, as they promise, at best, a haven in a heartless world. This does not mean, of course, that all of the melancholic's dreams are happy ones, but it *is* to say that if there is a place where he can be at home, it is here. Freud, to his infinite credit, had the temerity – which reveals his own melancholia – to demand not only access, but free run of the house. He assumed that the Dream was his to possess.

The next step in our inquiry, then, would be to explore the relationship between the melancholic disposition and the analytic temperament. As Philip Rieff (1966) points out, Freud, unlike his inheritors, was never tempted to ask the religious question ("How are we to be consoled for the misery of living?") for "His genius was analytic, not prophetic" (Rieff 1966:29–30). It was through his analytic powers that he sought to "triumph" over the lost object, to force her to make herself – once again – known to him. His book, *The Interpretation of Dreams*, is therefore his map to utopia. Had it been available to Samuel Johnson, one suspects that it would have shared honors with Burton's *The Anatomy of Melancholy* as compelling nighttime reading, for, in the final analysis, his book was the only possible response to Burton's search for melancholy's remedy.

Note

1   This chapter focuses exclusively on the male experience of melancholia. While melancholia has historically been viewed as an affliction to which men are most susceptible (even as women have been viewed as hysteria-prone), this may have much to do with cultural meanings assigned to melancholy at various periods in history. Julia Kristeva (1989) has written about women and melancholia, however, focusing on the daughter's relationship to her mother, but also taking into account the social conditions under which women bear and raise their daughters. By the same token,

there are many utopias written by women, and Jan Relf (1993) has explored this genre in light of the "coming home to mother" theme. I wish also to emphasize that the point of this essay is not to engage in mother-blaming. On the other hand, rather than moralizing about the tendency of the developmental literature to blame mothers for the eventual outcome of their children's lives, I take seriously here the psychological "fact" of mother-blaming among male melancholics. Whatever the justification may (or may not) be, male melancholics believe that they have a grievance against their mothers. It is this *belief* that I try to explore here.

References

American Psychiatric Association. 1994. *Diagnostic and Statistical Manual of Mental Disorders*, 4th edn. Washington, DC: American Psychiatric Association.

Bloch, E. 1988. "Something's Missing: A Discussion Between Ernst Bloch and Theodore W. Adorno on the Contradictions of Utopian Longing," in *The Utopian Function of Art and Literature*, Transl. J. Zipes and F. Mecklenburg. Cambridge, MA: The MIT Press, pp. 1–17.

Boswell, J. 1979. *Life of Johnson*, Ed. R.W. Chapman. Oxford and New York: Oxford University Press.

Bryson, N. 1990. *Looking at the Overlooked: Four Essays on Still Life Painting*. Cambridge, MA: Harvard University Press.

Burton, R. 1979. *The Anatomy of Melancholy*, Ed. J.K. Peters. New York: Frederick Ungar.

Capps, D. 1997. *Men, Religion, and Melancholia: James, Otto, Jung, Erikson*. New Haven, CT: Yale University Press.

Cioran, E.M. 1987. *History and Utopia*, Transl. R. Howard. Chicago: University of Chicago Press.

Erikson, E.H. 1987. "The Dream Specimen of Psychoanalysis," in *A Way of Looking at Things: Selected Papers From 1930 to 1980*, Ed. S. Schlein. New York: W.W. Norton, pp. 237–79.

Erikson, E.H. 1958. *Young Man Luther: A Study in Psychoanalysis and History*. New York: W.W. Norton.

Freud, S. 1953. *The Interpretation of Dreams. The Standard Edition of the Complete Psychological Works of Sigmund Freud*, vols. 4 and 5, Ed. and transl. J. Strachey. London: The Hogarth Press.

Freud, S. 1957a. "Mourning and Melancholia," in *The Standard Edition of the Complete Psychological Works of Sigmund Freud*, vol. 14. Ed. and transl. J. Strachey. London: The Hogarth Press, pp. 243–58.

Freud, S. 1957b. "The 'Uncanny'," in *The Standard Edition of the Complete Psychological Works of Sigmund Freud*, vol. 17. Ed. and transl. J. Strachey. London: The Hogarth Press, pp. 219–56.

Freud, S. 1957c. "The Antithetical Meaning of Primal Words," in *The Standard Edition of the Complete Psychological Works of Sigmund Freud*, vol. 11. Ed. and transl. J. Strachey. London: The Hogarth Press, pp. 155–61.

Freud, S. 1958. "The Theme of the Three Caskets," in *The Standard Edition of the Complete Psychological Works of Sigmund Freud*, vol. 12, Ed. and transl. J. Strachey. London: The Hogarth Press, pp. 291–301.

Freud, S. 1959. "Creative Writers and Day-Dreaming," in *The Standard Edition of the*

Complete Psychological Works of Sigmund Freud, vol. 9. Ed. and transl. J. Strachey. London: The Hogarth Press, pp. 143–53.

Freud, S. 1961. "A Seventeenth-Century Demonological Neurosis," in *The Standard Edition of the Complete Psychological Works of Sigmund Freud*, vol. 19. Ed. and transl. J. Strachey. London: The Hogarth Press, pp. 73–105.

Healy, D. 1997. *The Antidepressant Era*. Cambridge, MA: Harvard University Press.

Jackson, S.W. 1986. *Melancholia and Depression: From Hippocratic Times to Modern Times*. New Haven, CT: Yale University Press.

Kristeva, J. 1989. *Black Sun: Depression and Melancholia*, Transl. L.S. Roudiez. New York: Columbia University Press.

Kumar, K. 1991. *Utopianism*. Minneapolis: University of Minnesota Press.

Kumar, K. and Bann, S., Eds. 1993. *Utopias and the Millennium*. London: Reaktion Books.

Levitas, R. 1990. *The Concept of Utopia*. Syracuse, NY: Syracuse University Press.

Manuel, F.E. and Manuel, F.P. 1979. *Utopian Thought in the Western World*. Cambridge, MA: Harvard University Press.

Pollack, W. 1998. *Real Boys: Rescuing Our Sons From the Myths of Boyhood*. New York: Random House.

Relf, J. 1993. "Utopia the Good Breast: Coming Home to Mother," in *Utopias and the Millennium*, Eds, K. Kumar and S. Bann. London: Reaktion Books, pp. 107–28.

Rieff, P. 1966. *The Triumph of the Therapeutic: Uses of Faith After Freud*. New York: Harper & Row.

Rubin, J.H. 1994. *Religious Melancholy and Protestant Experience in America*. New York: Oxford University Press.

Styron, W. 1990. *Darkness Visible: A Memoir of Madness*. New York: Random House.

Wilson, B. 1973. *Magic and the Millennium: A Sociological Study of Religious Movements of Protest Among Tribal and Third-World Peoples*. New York: Harper & Row.

Wittgenstein, L. 1958. *Philosophical Investigations*, 3rd edn., Transl. G.E.M. Anscombe. New York: Macmillan.

CHAPTER 6

Georg Simmel: American Sociology Chooses the Stone the Builders Refused

Victoria Lee Erickson

Ever since the times of Jesus and the Buddha, parables have been used to emphasize a point, to force an encounter with truth and meaning.
Wade Clark Roof *(1993:298)*

The mission of a dialogical narrative is to display connections . . . and enjoy connections . . .
   Perhaps it is time for sociology to recover the robustly ecumenical outlook it evidenced when the discipline was established a century ago and to model, for the world community, a way of resolving the cultural crisis of our time.
Donald N. Levine *(1995:328–9)*

Social Crises and the Formation of Sociology

Our public life is in crisis. Sociologists have come to expect crises in public life, for that is the arena in which people struggle for power to control the future of culture and society. As a discipline sociology was in one sense created by the crisis of nineteenth century European industrialization as scholars responded to the human alienation and anomie precipitated by modernity. It is argued that our discipline is radically changing again as it responds to the social crises that some attribute to postmodern alienation. Regardless of the century in which one lives, the history of the discipline suggests that the way that one responds to the daily crop of public crises is a characteristic of one's sociological attitude as a scholar and researcher.
   Albion W. Small (1854–1926) had an attitude to recommend him for two posts that inaugurated American sociology. Professor Small held the first chair of

sociology at the University of Chicago (1892) and the first editorship of the *American Journal of Sociology* (*AJS*) in 1895. Sociology's *spiritus rector* (Coser 1976b:146, see also Coser 1976a, 1965) he wanted a public interdisciplinary conversation in which his discipline helped answer the question, "By virtue of what facts does it come to pass that [people] live together at all?" (Small 1902). Small found people "just now intoxicated with the splendid half-truth that society is what [people] choose to make it" (Small 1895:3). Finding "a little learning a dangerous thing," he sought to move beyond fragmentary knowledge to a social theory of human association complete with principles, precepts, rules, and predictions capable of making worthy judgments. Society's capacity for meeting its obligations to its members required professional judgment and intervention. *Investigation* became Small's substitute for the *riot of imagination* characteristic of the untrained mind, so that the desires of people could be interpreted and the general welfare of the people advanced (Small 1924:7). If we could understand "sociability," he reasoned, we might be able to address crises and establish such things as parks in cities, settlement houses for immigrants, transportation for workers, upward mobility for the poor, opportunities for women, newspapers that helped build a community, and school milk subsidies for children.

Addressing crises meant ending social pain and suffering in the human family. Small believed that "There is little likelihood that [sociologists] who personally observe actual social conditions, according to the methods we propose, instead of speculating on them in their study, will want to fold their hands and let social evil work out its own salvation" (quoted in Payne et al. 1981:374). Recognizing early on that the dazzling power of quantitative methods might overshadow the discipline's documentation of the narrative structure of society, Small wanted students to have an inductive understanding of the "provisional and mediate character of present institutions" (Small 1896:565). Blending qualitative and quantitative methods would give society a science capable of evolving methodological precision and a theoretical felicity that deciphered each new moment as one dissolved into the next.

Contrary and in resistance to the prevailing sentiment in the sciences, Small taught researchers to trust the insight and wisdom of people. "The plain truth about the so-called social sciences is this: Human beings have been in the world an unknown number of centuries" (Small 1924:11). They therefore knew something about their world. Working against a stormy reception by the other established disciplines, Small sought colleagues and students whose agitated minds were committed to a "radical social science" and to accepting one's status as the "stone the builders refused"(Small 1924:15). These exceptional sociologists were to use their marginality to artfully construct a capstone social science (Small 1902).

The Path Through Social Chaos

Small provided much in the way of attitude and methodological orientation for the nascent discipline of American sociology. But one thing he knew it still lacked: an adequate theoretical basis. As evidenced in the many articles published in *AJS* and his frequent references to his friend, Albion Small felt that American sociology needed the philosophical and theoretical insights of Georg Simmel (1858–1918). A founding partner of the German Sociological Association, Georg Simmel was, in the words of Max Weber, "simply brilliant." Weber was convinced that it was anti-Semitism that prevented his colleague, a Jew whose family had converted to Christianity, from holding a full university appointment. Simmel's inheritance never the less kept him stable and allowed him to pursue an intellectual life on the margins of German universities. His intellectual abilities, warmth, and compassion enabled him to become a powerful public intellectual. Hundreds of people attended his lectures. Students remember showing their gratitude by showering his lecture desk with rose petals, saying that his words gave them life (Laurence 1975).

Unlike Marx, Weber, and Durkheim, Simmel observed the ordering of chaos as the ongoing work of people who responded to one crisis after another by reforming their continuous conversation with the meaning-making practices left behind by the immortal dead. People rewrote history and sociality as they constructed the future out of the present. Like Marx, Weber, and Durkheim, Simmel found religion to be elemental to human relationality. The "world that the soul frames for itself" (Simmel 1950:4) is organized through the religious language of faith, a language Simmel spoke with great felicity.

> Without the phenomenon we call faithfulness, society could simply not exist, as it does, for any length of time. The elements which keep it alive – the self interest of its members, suggestion, coercion, idealism, mechanical habit, sense of duty, love inertia – could not save it from breaking apart if they were not supplemented by this factor . . . Faithfulness might be called the inertia of the soul. (Simmel 1950:379–80)

Simmel's success in describing how people construct society was partly responsible for his failure in the academy. His lectures attracted the wrong crowd – women, immigrants, Russians and Poles, and other nonelites. They were the strangers to society and its promises. Whereas Weber's, Marx's, and Durkheim's sociology moved to establish centers of analytical power through invariant methodological formulations and through universal theories of social action, Simmel's work flourished in the intuitive nature of society's margins. He argued that methodological diversity was needed because people do not live "random" lives that fit into algebraic equations. Rather, people's lives were both frozen and moveable, universal and local:

> The perpetual transformations of matter and energy bring everything in relation to everything else and make one cosmos out of all singularities . . . With respect to nature only humans are given the capacity to relate and to separate in the peculiar fashion that one is always the precondition for the other . . . Animals do not create the miracle of a path: the miracle to freeze movement into a permanent form which originates from movement and into which movement is channeled. (quoted by Kaern 1994:407–8)

The power-brokers of the discipline never really understood how to incorporate Simmel's path. Kaern argues that Simmel's puzzling theoretical and ahistorical approach was in service to his task of telling "the story beneath historical materialism" (Kaern et al. 1990:4; see also Aronowitz 1994, Etzkorn 1968; Frisby 1984, Wolff 1959). The translator, Horst J. Helle remarks that Simmel documented and defined religion as "an attitude or a perspective" capable of bridging the rift between people and their ideas (Simmel 1997:xii).

> In regard to these conditions of social life, faithfulness . . . bridges and reconciles that deep and essential dualism which splits off the life-form of individual internality [*Innerlichkeit*] from the life-form of sociation that is nevertheless borne by it. Faithfulness is the constitution of the soul (which is constantly moved and lives in a continuous flux), by means of which it fully incorporates into itself the stability of the super-individual form relation and by means of which it admits to life, as the meaning and value of life, a content which, though created by the soul itself, is, in its form, nevertheless bound to contradict the rhythm or un-rhythm of life as actually lived. (Simmel 1950:386–7)

This empathetic and sympathetic use of the people's paradoxical and nonscientific soul language was not well received by the Marxists or the Weberians. Surprisingly, it was his ability to reach beneath the data to uncover what is not systematically available to researchers that allowed Simmel to become an anchoring cornerstone in the foundation of modern sociology and at the same time, its enemy (Kaern et al. 1990:45).

"Simmel reminds us of things we tend to forget but would gain from remembering" (Wolff 1958:593). As strange as it sounds, he asked us to remember that:

> The preliminary forms are brought forth out of the teleological necessities [of life] . . . Nevertheless, all traces of the operation of these forms do not disappear when their job is done . . . all become products that have a career transcending the experience that brought them forth. (Wolff 1959:47)

Simmel also documented that people shaped sociation by utilizing an analytical and practical tool he called *form and content*. They did so even though ". . . life in all possible manifestations agitates against being directed into any fixed form whatever" (Simmel 1971:377).

Form and Content

The social world, according to Simmel, is made up of unities, forms that were brought into existence in order to make possible a connection between contents. Simmelian forms are strategies for organizing life (Molseed 1987, Quigly 1994). Forms are either visible, solid, and objective social institutions, or playful forms of the ruse, hunt, or games, that exist for their own sake (Simmel 1971). Social institutions are practices that structure human behavior in predictable patterns. Play forms are created for those moments when we need to imagine a world – a world that needs no materialization, just our imaginations. They allow people to associate in moments of gaiety that energize the hard work of constructing social institutions or of responding to the fixed forms of social life. Society would be impossible without both. How long forms stay in existence depends on the power of human experience that brought them forth. This power of association creates "fixed forms" like religion, art, law, education, and economic structures. In that forms are human constructions they are made up out of the content of human interactions.

Content itself is an ideal existence, made real through the mental process of "grasping hold" of it. However, since each person/group that grasps content does so through its particularity, the grasping changes the content into something else other than what it was in its ideational state. For example, the social institution we call marriage is a form of sociality that is found across the world. "No couple has by itself invented the form of marriage." What society wants from the form it regulates and historically transmits (Simmel 1950:130). In marriage, the individual is "confronted by the collectivity" that seeks "to tear down the borders of the ego and to absorb the I and THOU into one another" (Simmel 1950:128). That is why marriage is "super personal," he argued.

The contents of the marriage form are varied. For example, we have holy matrimony, civil marriage, and common-law marriage. Today as gay and lesbian couples seek the social support generated by this form, people have created "holy unions" and "common-law unions" and a movement to establish "legal civil and holy marriage" choices for homosexuals. What makes all of these unions "marriage" is that the relationship "transcends sexual intercourse" to be "whatever it is" (Simmel 1950:132). The solid institution of marriage, protected by law and custom, is also supported by play, by flirting and courting, and by ceremony and periodic anniversary celebrations. Simmel observed that when the power of the institution ceased, its "fixedness" would soften, allowing it to be reshaped.

To engage people in an understanding of their role in shaping the content of life and the unities they sought, Simmel became a great story teller. His lectures unfolded thick descriptions of bridges, doors, windows, ruins, clothing design, secret societies, strangers, faces, prostitutes, spendthrifts, enemies, religion, the arts, music, even handles on teapots. Mesmerized, people filled up his lecture hall by the hundreds. The resources of sociology, psychology, history, economics, law, religion, and philosophy were drawn into complicated webs of analysis that addressed the difficult questions of conflict, violence, subordination, race slavery, the role of women in culture, and the very possibility of society. Through vivid imagery, people were attracted to his ability to see, and in spite of what he saw, his serenity, and grace (Wolff 1959:236). If it were not for this attraction, he may not have been able to ask them to examine pain and suffering.

The Stranger as Social Form

Among Simmel's most well received concepts was the sociology of the stranger. Simmel understood the stranger to be a specific form of interaction. In contrast to the wanderer "who comes today and goes tomorrow," the stranger "comes today and stays tomorrow" (Simmel 1971:144). Constructed out of the social interaction between outsiders and insiders, "the stranger is an element of the group itself, not unlike the poor and "inner enemies' – an element whose membership in the group involves both being outside it and confronting it" (Simmel 1971:144). The stranger brings the outside in.

Simmel's primary examples were European Jews who were not organically bound to land through kinship and local dependence. This lack of land made the Jew appear mobile. The rest of the group, the landed majority, the oppressor, is relieved of worry about a member who appears to be able to establish life in another place. The lack of investment in the stranger's well-being insures the real and symbolic effect of creating detached people who, at their own expense, provide the social group with what it needs. In the case of the Jews, it meant being an economic middle-agent. It is precisely this role given to Jews by dominant society that makes society fear the Jew. The stranger confronts the group with a mirror that precipitates secret but startling revelations and confessions that are "hidden from everybody with whom one is close" (Simmel 1971:145).

The stranger's ability to listen and to theorize possibilities, from society's margins, allowed for a freedom not found in the group membership itself. But it is this freedom that threatens the group. Simmel found that the stranger's ability to name "dangerous possibilities," through an abstract and more global place, was established by society's ability to simultaneously construct the stranger as "close to us and far from us" (Simmel 1971:146–7). The dialogue the stranger convenes raises questions of freedom, power, duty, and kinship; therefore it also raises questions of equality and responsibility.

Sociology of the Soul and Relationships in Conflict

Another topic Simmel dealt with extensively was the concept of the soul. The soul is like a well that religion dips into for our stories, with which it teaches us how to structure sociability out of crises and conflict. Simmel's evidence was found in what people said and in what he saw them doing. A glance at the *Oxford English Dictionary* informs us that the soul people talk about through the English language is the "principle of life." The soul houses our emotions, feelings, thoughts, and conscience. It is the home of our intellectual powers. The soul has attributes as in "soul-power, soul-work, soul-blood." It has agency as in "soul-carrier, soul-healer, soul-mate, soul-saver, or soul-thief." People speak of the soul as the "self" of a person, that which is "deep and sure." However, when the soul is fragile and without courage, feeling, or inspiration, we say that the person "lacks soul," is "soul-sick," or "soul-dead." Our language allows us to evaluate a soul-sick person as one with a spiritual problem that science alone cannot heal.

Against the early sentiment of his peers, Simmel argued that the world science called "real" was only "one world" of many. The world framed by the soul was resistant to scientific methodological limitations and could only be "seen" in the "miracle" of the bridging work of people who created unities out of differences and fragmentation (Kaern 1994). The world the soul creates is a community with the capacity to construct a shared vision of wholeness out of chaos. Religion, the materialized language of the soul, is the meeting ground where differences are blended in the search for something higher: truth, justice, perfection, God.

Society lives only through its members, Simmel observed. The ability of its members to craft souls is critical to society's very being. However, the members rarely give themselves up freely and would "prefer liberty." In this sense, Simmel saw the member as "existing both inside and outside of society," as living in the tension of independence and subordination. As society is continually evolving, antagonisms between member and society exist in every area of life. They are continuously pulled into the religious sphere where differences are transcended in the search for unity: ". . . so religious behavior brings peace to the opposing and incompatible forces at work within the soul, resolving the contradictions they create" (Simmel 1997:36). Cooperation between society and the individual is an act of faith.

> Practical faith is the fundamental quality of the soul that in essence is sociological, that is, it becomes concretized as a relationship with some being external to the self . . . The purely social significance of this religious faith beyond that of the individual faith has not yet been investigated at all, but I feel sure that without it, society as we know it would not exist. Our capacity to have faith in a person or a group of people beyond all demonstrable evidence to the contrary is one of the most stable bonds holding society together. (Simmel 1997:169–70)

The Soul's Story

Through storytelling, the community of souls narrates a world. The soul's story frames reality by placing boundary markers around the human search for fulfillment. This story is archived in liturgies and festivals that anchor memory. Fully in the stream of German idealistic tradition, Simmel found the human search for wholeness and unity was expressed through the human search for a relationship with God, or with a God-consciousness. Being and the source of Being are now "ensouled" as one: ". . . Thou is our only peer or counterpart in the universe [and] . . . Thou also has an incomparable autonomy and sovereignty (Simmel 1980:105–7).

The space framed by the human search for Being is a geography marked by history, tradition, memory, and the present encounter with the material world.

Simmel called that space bounded by the activity of the soul, "society." Society is the product of human movement toward its Being, toward being who one really is, toward salvation. Human beings relate to each other in the same way they relate to Being itself. The self is created when the unique I encounters YOU. My encounter with YOU is shaped by your Being-consciousness, by your relation with Being-THOU (Simmel 1980:105). The human being, bound to a movement toward an ultimate goal, toward ultimate belonging called "salvation," surrenders to that goal all interactions and relationships (Simmel 1997:23). In that relationships are produced by bridging, all relationships are religious.

"Faith is, as it were, the sensory organ by which being is conveyed to us" (Simmel 1997:46). It is the task of the soul-community to sense the need for and to continually repair the tears and breaks that happen as human social relationships change, so that the production of the human being becomes an ongoing salvific event. The soul's diligence in connecting fragments depends upon its attitude toward its work. If beingness is well attended, a third thing, a new thing, develops between the searching soul and its God-consciousness. Simmel called this new thing "sociability"; sociability is the relationality that theology calls "hope." If there is no sociability, there is no hope. Sociability is possible when people simultaneously remain in the realm of immanent discourse and transcend, or rise above, the limits of the material world and its logic.

Faith is the Relationship Between Knower and Known

Simmel argued that human relationality is only possible through faith, through the power of believing in the possibility of knowing and being known (Simmel 1980). Knowing coordinates a communicative system that enables us to "express our essence with a paradox: we are bound in every direction, and we are bound in no direction" (Simmel 1971:355). He argued that we once understood that our lack of relationality, our lack of knowing each other, was a "soul-lack" directly linked to poor historical and philosophical training.

Claiming that life is the spirit's "court of last resort," Simmel wrote:

> These images of the past are conditions for the continuation of life itself . . . But this is not a consciousness of the past as vast, formless chaos of the totality of the material life that is contained in memory or tradition. On the contrary, the practical purposes served by the consciousness of the past depend upon an analysis and synthesis . . . emphasis and de-emphasis, interpretation and supplementation of this material. (Simmel 1980:97)

Our observations, our seeing and hearing, are interpreted through our ideas and emotions to produce a bridge that spans the gulf between ME and YOU. To really know someone, we must know empathetically (1980:105). Empathy makes the other, the YOU, irreducible. Face-to-face, the I and the YOU see themselves in each other. The process of empathy draws one to the other until the other is ensouled in the knower. We know when we embrace. To know, I approach YOU "with the same integrity that I approach my own ego." The "suspicion" I have of YOU disappears as I "intuitively" pull YOU toward me in an act that links our life moments together (Simmel 1980:109–10). Knowing creates a hope for a shared future. Understanding is hopeless, however, in those moments when ensoulment is rejected for reasons of fear, resistance, or a lack of desire. Simmel argued that the YOU produced by ensoulment is the "goal and practice" of sociology and historical studies. It is also the goal and practice of faith and its theologies. If this goal is not met, if there is no embrace, then there is no understanding, no history, and no sociology.

Simmel understood that the border regions where we embrace are places of surrender, thus places of natural resistance and fear. The self must surrender the self in order to authentically engage the other so that a new thing is produced from the encounter: a relationship. The tension between the self's unwillingness to give up its independence and its need for surrender places a value on the knowing. This value is the well from which the individual draws strength. The strength of individuals determines the strength of society.

Cooperation between differences removes "one sidedness" and presents individuals face-to-face with one another, with the "many-sided" reality of life (Simmel 1959:61). The individual personalities that must conform rightly protest the tragic kind of conformity that creates uniformity and harmonization. Conformity that produces equality between the differences seeks to dramatize our similarities and differences so that standing "next to each other" brings excitement, passion, wonder, and a shared vision. Mirroring God, who stands face-to-face confronting humans as an outsider to human society (Simmel 1959:65), an outsider who wants in – who has journeyed to the periphery seeking union with us – our Being transcends the human need for outsiders. We are invited into kinship, into a place where life is "blended" (Simmel 1959:19, 22).

Society is Faithfulness

Through the isolation and chaos of his life caused by anti-Semitism and his own resisting of the harmonization of the disciplinary voice, Simmel observed that faithfulness between institutions and citizens is much like faithfulness between spouses. Through faithfulness we come to love each other. Love built on faithfulness is "love without reservation" (Simmel 1950:328). It is this love that society needs in order to connect us "one to the other," be it in corporations, churches, schools, hospitals, or neighborhoods. Love-based connectedness preserves the self, the couple, the unit, the society. Love-based connection creates societal familihood where no one is the stranger. Love creates the embraced, included object.

When society is in chaos, as it always is, faithfulness rises above the fragmentation and builds footings on whatever ground it touches, making possible the bridging work of humans. Ernst Troeltsch, Simmel's colleague, argued that a country dependent on a citizenry that does not feel responsible for the well-being of the other, that does not feel responsible for creating form and bridging the fragments, totters on the brink of disaster (Starr 1996). Prewar Germany felt the coming chaos. Despite his friends' warnings and his own suffering, Simmel had faith in the fatherland's ability to produce a compelling secular version of morality that would support what he called "the coming formlessness."

Simmel as Practical Sociologist

The coming formlessness was directly linked to the demagicalization (Weber) of the world and its post-Enlightenment spirituality (Simmel). Like many others, Simmel did not find liberal Christianity up to the task of responding to the then present spiritual demands of people. Christianity, he believed, because it had not found a way toward reconciliation and peace, "had constructed the historical ground work for its own historical successor" (Starr 1996:151). The crisis of modernity was its failure to develop the individual personality, who remained "subjectively poor" in the context of overly developed objective culture. The continual crisis, the tragedy, was that there was no way out of this predicament. For Simmel what was missing was the very thing that gave life. There was no room after modernity for the soul. Lacking a soul and communication, underdeveloped and hyperindividualized, modernity resulted in a homicidal, anorexic, and schizophrenic culture (Weinstein and Weinstein 1993:217). Despairingly stuck in the eternal present, the soul commits murder.

Taking an agnostic and Nietzschean turn, Simmel suggested a secularized, objectless, religion that corresponded to the people's dissatisfaction with the churches and their growing attraction to the coming "formlessness." A people who could not create form could not see a need for it. Yet, his reasoning was not without its contradictions. History indicated that people tended to substitute one object for another. Simmel found that:

> Life wishes here to obtain something which it cannot reach. It desires to transcend all forms and to appear in its naked immediacy. Yet, the processes of thinking, wishing, and forming can only substitute one form for another. They can never replace the form as such by life which as such transcends form. (Simmel 1971:393)

Finding his era aggressively attempting to destroy form, Simmel found it destroying "the bridge between the past and the future of cultural forms." "Gazing into the abyss of unformed life," Simmel wondered if "formlessness is itself the appropriate form for contemporary life" (Simmel 1971:393).

Reasoning that "religion can only be robbed of its clothing but not its life," Simmel's "way out" was the "intransitive verb" *I believe*; not taking the object exempted the believer from church traditions but satisfied the spiritual need that persisted even after the "Enlightenment" (Simmel 1971:392). The objectless content of belief was the future. "The soul plays the melody of the contents of the form" (Simmel 1997:124). Following his prior argumentation, content is itself the product of human relationships. The absence of content is an absence of relationships. If religion is the attitude of human association, this new formless, objectless, belief system belonged to a people with no relationships, a fully fragmented and alienated humanity.

In the past, the community of belief needed a language; however, Simmel found people wanting a direct experience and therefore not needing "a language with a given vocabulary and fixed syntax. One might say (and it only appears to be a paradox) that the soul desires to preserve the quality of faith even though it no longer accepts any specific predetermined articles of faith" (Laurence 1976:239).

The reality of people who are resisting the language that previously created their world is both natural and terrifying. In that people are continually tearing down and rebuilding, a reconstruction of the language of faith is hardly remarkable. What people thought was new was their desire for a domesticated transcendence, life without God. The social theorists of the day had great empathy for this desire. However, as a historian of religion, Simmel knew at least this: the boundlessness of a protracted formlessness is ultimately a betrayal of the individual who cannot exist without boundaries (Simmel 1971:353). Psychosocial reality requires humans to continuously know and to be known. The knower is known in the ever evolving and materialized worlds of church, synagogue, mosque, and temple. The communities of church, synagogue, mosque, and temple form the soul. We would all be the same if people did not think that their religious formation process had something different to offer the world. Simmel's context was the German Christian and Jewish landscape that had formed social life in predicable ways.

Simmel argued from his context that the re-forming of the social world was a natural and ongoing process that took place at the margins of society, in the borderlands of the present and the future. In that the present and the future coexist, they are knowable. If we understand Simmel's research as he claimed it to be, a "fitting" response to people, we can hear him asking interesting questions about the present and future moment. Who are these people who resist cultivation and obligation, who favor play and coquetry? Why does this new world appear to be satisfied with whatever commonsense it can stir up? What world was coming if not the Kingdom of God? What happens to people who cannot balance the paradoxes of life? What is this place where belief is suspended, not necessary, inconvenient? Simmel had a hunch that it was not a particularly bad place, not hell as some of his contemporaries imagined. He had no name for "the coming formlessness."

Weinstein and Weinstein (1993) argue that the "coming formlessness" that Simmel was describing is what some theorists now call "postmodern life."

However, if we assume Simmel's method, we must assume that new realities materialize partially out of a debt owed to the past. In 14 complex, Simmel-like, sentences Giorgio Agamben (1993) swiftly names this coming community with an old name: "limbo."

A Sociology of the Theology of Limbo

Agamben, however, does not say anything about limbo that is not already known to students of the ancient Christian church. When theologians attempted to solve a theological riddle concerning the fate of an unbaptized, that is an unformed, soul that was nevertheless not guilty of sin, the result was the doctrine of limbo. A formless soul cannot enter heaven. The intense familial suffering created by high child mortality rates produced a public anguish that was at once sociological and theological. The people's terrifying question was, what happened to children who died before they were baptized – before they were saved? It became the practice of pastors to announce a child's soul peacefully existing in the neutral space between the judged and the unjudged. Because there is no hope of leaving limbo, people made it a pleasant place in their imaginations. Parents had visions of happy children. Clerics and theologians created a destination that had never existed before, a fantasy land where suffering and judgment could be avoided – like a land without parents. Being such a welcoming place, righteous pagans were sent there too. Limbo was a satisfactory alternative to salvation, its own kind of heaven.

Seen in another way, limbo was the place where people are permanently incarcerated, hemmed into oblivion or negation. Limbo exists permanently in the borderlands – some say next to hell, others say next to heaven. The language spoken in limbo is the language of the unbaptized, the uninaugurated, the unestablished, the unformed. Lacking baptism, inclusion, and identity, people assigned there will not enter heaven – they will never see the face of God. Their present will never become the future. Seeing God's face is, ultimately, seeing one's own face, thus they will never see their own faces. Excluded from the beautiful vision they exist forever in a land of natural happiness where there is no pain of sense or absence, just playful gaiety.

Limbo was an idea created by Western people who believed that life is what we make it. Out of their sorrow and suffering they made limbo a place of innocent immunity from sorrow and suffering. Limbo is a formless world where there is no redemption because there is no sin.

The innocents in limbo know God only as nature knows God. The human capacity for knowing God is not theirs. Not knowing, they happily exist in an intellectual sadness that seeks neither grace nor mercy. The continued lingering of limbo as a sociological and theological form affirms Simmel's observation that once created, form becomes frozen and everlasting. People created a social form that will not go away, a form where hope is unnecessary and maybe even dangerous.

Limbo has praxeologically always been open to discussion; the church never settled on a doctrinal stand. Catholic and Protestant theologians now say it was unfortunate that they once taught that babies needed to be baptized to enter heaven, and much more unfortunate that parents were ever told that their children would spend an eternity in limbo. Although people *hear* theologies that now speak about the wide mercy of God who takes loved ones straight away to heaven, they have not seen a ritual dissolve the prison walls and liberate the captive souls. Limbo has never been transcended.

It is even more dangerous, then, that as a public we no longer talk about the souls that were confined to a disappearing landscape for which we lost our map. We let the sign fall off its post, the grass grow up around the ruins, and the hot air of the centuries dry the souls out like seeds. Then the storm came. Another generation of refugees from chaos saw the cactus flowers in the desert, heard the singing of children and ventured inward. Leaving a path for others to follow, these adults, these righteous pagans, developed the inviting "culture of cute" where everything is a reason to giggle and where no change materializes in the world of the suffering because there are no entrances and exits from the court-yard where playtime and word games never end.

A sociology of limbo is a sociology of objectless secularism. Ironically, the church provided the space for this kind of secularism when it created limbo. In this permanently in between place there is no connection, no bridge to heaven. There would be, then, no bridge to the other. Limboland is a place not built on self-surrender and sacrifice, knowing and being known. It is an exhausting world of self-absorption.

From Simmel's documentation of modernism to the present day, a growing number of people name their existence as formless, boundless, and "postmodern." Their lives are like bridges with no footings, "like letters with no addressee" (Agamben 1993:6). People stuck in "postmodern" alienation need to conceptualize these spaces because their experience is in between and disconnected. People do not think alone. They depend on their wisdom sources for interpretation and direction. Cut off from history, tradition, and the dead – who took responsibility for their behavior and stood judged – these new people stumbled into an old form and gave it life by supplying new content. Limbo was the perfect form to house a playfully erotic culture opposed to seriousness, obligation, and accountability. These seemingly new people are only half right if they believe that they have created a new reality. Sociologically, what they have done is repeat a well-established practice. To construct a future, they sought a conversation with the dead; wanting an objectless secular future, they found the only place where the dead live without Being. Lacking subjectivity, a people who could not find themselves in the world created a world. This in essence is what Simmel perceived to be the fate of his era. Although he didn't name it as such, he provided for us a sociology of limbo, which might well be the sociology of postmodernity.[1]

Albion W. Small knew the American and European landscape. In an apparent attempt to bypass the European entrapment in disenchanted, formless, "postmodern" malaise, he translated and pulled into an American pragmatic sensibility a highly selective set of Simmel's writings – writings that had practical and therapeutic social goals. Horst J. Helle begins his new Simmel translation (1997) with a story about healing. The ability to heal requires an attitude of service to others. The healing function of sociology created by Simmel, for the people, was the ability to analyze the present moment. Although he attempted to find a way to make formlessness a working category of human sociality, in the end, Simmel held out hope for religious practices. People needed something to attach themselves to from one moment to the next. People need their stories.

Note

1   Ironically, Simmel's own life was not free from the entrapments of postmodernity. The tragic end of his family in Hitler's evil web obscures his own moral acting out of the alienation experienced by strangers (see e.g., Laurence 1975).

References

Agamben, G. 1993. *The Coming Community*, Transl. Michael Hardt. Minneapolis: University of Minnesota Press.

Aronowitz, S. 1994. "The Simmel Revival," *The Sociological Quarterly* 35(3):397–414.

Bierstedt, R. Ed. 1959. *The Making of Society: An Outline of Sociology*. The Modern Library. New York: Random House.

Coser, L.A. 1965. *Georg Simmel*. Englewood Cliffs, NJ: Prentice Hall.

Coser, L.A. 1976a. "Georg Simmel's Style of Work: A Contribution of the Sociology of Sociologists," *American Journal of Sociology* 63(6):635–41.

Coser, L.A. 1976b. "Sociological Theory From the Chicago Dominance to 1965," *Annual Review of Sociology* 2:145–60.

Etzkorn, K.P. "Introduction," in *Georg Simmel: The Conflict in Modern Culture and Other Essays*, Transl. K.P. Etzkorn. New York: Teachers College Press, pp. 1–10.

Frisby, D. 1984. *Georg Simmel*. Chicester/London: Ellis Horwood/Tavistock.

Kaern, M. 1994. "Georg Simmel's 'The Bridge and the Door.'" *Qualitative Sociology* 17(4):397–412.

Kaern, M., Phillips, B.S., and Cohen, R.S. 1990. *Georg Simmel and Contemporary Sociology*. Boston: Boston University Press.

Laurence, A.E. 1975. "Georg Simmel: Triumph and Tragedy," *International Journal of Contemporary Sociology* 12(1–2):28–48.

Laurence, P.A. 1976. *Georg Simmel: Sociologist and European*. New York: Barnes & Noble Books.

Levine, D.N. 1995. *Visions of the Sociological Tradition*. Chicago: University of Chicago Press.

Molseed, M.J. 1987. "The Problem of Temporality in the Work of Georg Simmel," *The Sociological Quarterly* 28(3):357–66.

Payne, G., Dingwall, P., Payne, J., and Carter, M. 1981. *Sociology and Social Research*. Boston: Routledge & Kegan Paul.

Quigley, T.R. 1994. "The Ethical and Narrative Self," *Philosophy Today* 38(Spring):43–55.

Roof, W.C. 1993. "Religion and Narrative (Presidential Address)," *Review of Religious Research* 34(4):297–310.

Simmel, G. 1950. *The Sociology of Georg Simmel*, Transl. K.H. Wolff. Glencoe: Free Press.

Simmel, G. 1959. *Sociology of Religion*, Transl. C. Rosenthal. New York: The Wisdom Library.

Simmel, G. 1971. *On Individuality and Social Forms*. Chicago: University of Chicago Press.

Simmel, G. 1980. *Essays on Interpretation in Social Sciences*, Transl. G. Oakes. Totowa, NJ: Rowman and Littlefield.

Simmel, G. 1997. *Essays on Religion*, Transl. H. Jurgen Helle with L. Nieder, Foreword by P. Hammond. New Haven, CT: Yale University Press.

Small, A.W. 1895. "The Era of Sociology," *The American Journal of Sociology* 1(1):1–15.

Small, A.W. 1896. "Scholarship and Social Agitation," *American Journal of Sociology* 1(5):564–82.

Small, A.W. 1902. "The Significance of Sociology for Ethics," in *The Decennial Publications*. Chicago: The University of Chicago, p. 150.

Small, A.W. 1924. *Origins of Sociology*. Chicago: Chicago University Press.

Starr, B.E. 1996. "The Tragedy of the Kingdom: Simmel and Troeltsch on Prophetic Religion," *The Journal of Religious Ethics* 24(Spring):141–67.

Weinstein, D. and Weinstein, M.A. 1993. *Postmodern(ized) Simmel*. New York: Routledge.

Wolff, K.H. 1958. "The Challenge of Durkheim and Simmel," *American Journal of Sociology* 58(6):590–6.

Wolff, K.H. 1959. *Georg Simmel 1858–1918*. Columbus, OH: Ohio State University Press.

CHAPTER 7

Transformations of Society and the Sacred in Durkheim's Religious Sociology

Donald A. Nielsen

The idea that modern society has undergone a pervasive process of rationalization and disenchantment is associated with the name of Max Weber. I want to suggest that Emile Durkheim has something valuable to say on this subject, although his view differs considerably from that of Weber and those following his leads. Durkheim's conception of this problem involves his ideas about the structural transformations of the sacred, the definition of religion, the role of ritual in social life, and the place of the individual in religion and society. It also implicates much of the rest of his sociology, from his earliest work on the division of labor, suicide, and professional groups, to his later theory of religion. Metaphysical and theological implications also emerge within the interstices of Durkheim's mature sociological project and there is reason to think that his work may represent a potential milestone in the foundation of a new theology of social immanence.

The Social and the Sacred

What is religion? Unlike some pioneering sociologists, Durkheim directly faces this issue. Religion is a system of beliefs and practices that bind a community together around those things which it holds sacred (Durkheim 1995:44). In defining religion's content in terms of the sacred, Durkheim seems to substitute one difficulty for another. What is the sacred? At a denotative level, Durkheim's answer is clear, if puzzling. Literally anything is capable of being sacralized: physical objects, persons, times, places, and so forth (Durkheim 1995:35). But how can something ordinary be made sacred? These things are transformed by a diffuse and generalized force or power capable of making them sacred. This force is expressed, for example, in the Melanesian term *mana*, an idea which plays a considerable role in the Durkheimians' work (Nielsen 1999: 168–74). However, for Durkheim, these powers or forces actually emerge from society, but can find fixed expression only if they become attached to objects (Durkheim 1995:327). Things, persons, times, places, actions, and so forth thus become vehicles of the sacred when they are touched by these diffuse and disengaged societal forces.

Durkheim's identification of the sacred with social power or force is intriguing. It points to an uncoupling of the sacred from religion (if the latter term is understood in its full Durkheimian definition). Durkheim distinguishes the fixed lodgings of the sacred in social institutions with the unbound social forces always also operating in society and perennially capable of gestating experiences of the sacred. While sociology focuses on institutions, these latter forces also require examination (Durkheim 1982:52–3). They figure prominently in Durkheim's *Suicide*, but are particularly relevant to the present discussion. On this topic, and despite their other differences, Durkheim and Foucault might be fruitfully compared (although I cannot now pursue this discussion at any length). Foucault's analysis of power avoids lodging it exclusively in law and the state and sees it as "a productive network which runs through the whole social body"(1984:61). Durkheim identifies social power with the sacred, which is its primary expression, a fact which may help explain why he gives so little attention to the manifestations of power in other spheres. However, like Foucault, Durkheim also sees this power diffused throughout society as a productive, unbound force. The points of appearance and fixation of this power include established religious institutions, but are not limited to them. Social powers are often found in oppositional forms, where groups attach their collective forces to new sacred objects disapproved by institutionally bound forces. The aura of power emanating in varying degrees from all social groups can readily become attached to and sacralize objects, persons, and practices in unexpected ways.

Religious practices, or rites, are especially central to Durkheim's conception of religion and the social genesis and reproduction of the sacred. In Jane Ellen Harrison's (1912:29,42–5) contemporaneous and very Durkheimian formulation, *dromenon* (things done) take a certain precedence over *legomenon* (things said). Durkheim's view of the relationship between rites and society focuses on the idea that periods of social concentration of populations alternate in a cycle with periods of social dispersion. The former are marked by emotionally intense rituals surrounding society's sacred things, while the latter are characterized by a reduced emotional intensity and a concern with profane activities. This cycle varies from society to society. Where the period of dispersion is long or the dispersion extensive, the ensuing concentrations are marked by heightened intensity, amounting in some cases to an orgy of collective sentiment. By contrast, where the interval between the two phases of social life is shorter, or the dispersion less extensive, the contrast between them is less extreme. The more societies develop, the less is their tolerance for interruptions that are too pronounced. Here, Durkheim combines the view of societal transformation, including changes in social morphology, developed in his earlier writings (Durkheim 1984), with his social theory of religion.

This later Durkheimian perspective is remarkable for its theoretical sweep and simplicity. It represents an elegant solution to many of the theoretical problems raised throughout his work. Durkheim insists on the centrality of religion, especially emotionally charged religious rites, and locates them in a more fully integrated theory of both societal transformation and social cycles. The significance of religion is expanded. It is now relevant to both "primitive" and "modern" societies, and to all those social types located between these two defining poles (Durkheim 1982:113–15). The more "evolutionary" theory of the early period is folded into a more comprehensive one which combines social "development" and "oscillation." This allows Durkheim to retain the empirical content of his earlier work on the division of labor (and related topics), yet recast it in a new form. He can now also root the cult of the individual in sociologically firmer ground. It is the logical outcome not only of Enlightenment ideals, but also of modern society's simultaneous intolerance for pronounced interruptions, and its need to sacralize its new social realities, which are marked by increasing individuation and moral autonomy.

Durkheim's book, *The Division of Labor in Society* (hereafter *Division*), argues that the transformations of whole societies from mechanical to organic solidarity diminished the role of the collective consciousness and, therefore, of religion (Durkheim 1984). Similar arguments appear in *Suicide*, where religious groups no longer exercise an adequate discipline over the individual, and egoism is the predominant type of modern psychopathology (Durkheim 1951:356,374–6). Durkheim's early writings seemed to argue for an overall "secularization" of modern society, indeed, at the very moment when he was taking an increased interest in religion and was already also insisting that modernity itself had instituted a new religious cult of the individual(Durkheim 1984:122, 1994:70).

Changes in Social Solidarity

Durkheim's early work lacked the benefit of his later theory of religion. *Division* provided an unsatisfactory place for the social concentrations which are so central to his maturing theory, conceiving of them in terms of an increasing social density which is the mechanical cause of the change in types of social solidarity. As social density increases, there occurs a movement away from a collective consciousness, segmentary social structures based on kinship groupings, and mechanical solidarity, and toward a more developed division of labor, with increases in individuation, an abstraction of collective ideas, and the potential (but not the certainty) of organic solidarity. The division of labor and organic solidarity are raised on the foundations of the continued existence, yet transformation of, segmentary social structure. Modern developments are impossible without the persistence, yet modification, of more "elementary" social ties. As we will see, the mature theory of religious rites and symbolism sketched above incorporates this idea. The rites of particular social segments persist and may be transfigured to serve larger units by being invested with more abstract, universal significance within a changed social dynamic.

At first glance, the earlier idea that modern society involves an increased social density seems difficult to reconcile with Durkheim's later view that emotional assemblies centered on the sacred are periods of greater social concentration, by comparison with the profane routine characteristic of less concentrated periods of social dispersion. If social differentiation were expanded at the expense of collective consciousness, would this not result in an eclipse of the sacred, an increased prominence of the profane, and, by implication, a general decrease in social density? This creative ambiguity can be resolved through a closer examination of Durkheim's mature theory.

One key is found in the role played by structural transformations of the sacred and modifications of the sacred–profane boundary. Durkheim's notion that the shortened cycle of concentration and dispersion in modern society is related to its intolerance of extensive social disruptions was already implied in Marcel Mauss's study of seasonal variations in Eskimo society. This seminal essay of 1904–5 sketched many of the elements of the larger Durkheimian thesis by focusing on a case involving a "long" cycle of dispersion and concentration and, therefore, an extreme alternation of highly emotional assemblies with a mundane and emotionally tepid dispersion (Mauss 1979, Nielsen 1999:157–9). In *The Elementary Forms of Religious Life* (hereafter *Forms*), Durkheim (1995) extends these findings as one instance of a wider set of possibilities. He compares them not only with other "primitive" cases, but also with modern society. In keeping with his thesis in *Division*, which broadly outlines a modern moral imperative of service within a specialized site in the division of labor, the routines of socially differentiated modernity are now seen to require a more seamless reproduction of social activities. This effort becomes focused especially on occupational groupings as the central sites of social activity and, therefore, ritual reproduction. Prolonged and excessively disruptive collective enthusiasms are incompatible with such social reproduction. Indeed, the demands of ritualized reproduction may even override creative cultural production.

Durkheim's distinction between the sacred and the profane is central to this image of sociocultural change and oscillation. The distinctive feature of the "primitive" sacred – sharp separation from the profane enforced by powerful interdictions – is transformed in modern society. The barrier between sacred and profane is breached. Extensive sacralizations and profanations occur. The latter are often emphasized (i.e., decline of the sacred), but we must also note the former. Such sacralizations make it difficult to unambiguously identify "the sacred" as a distinct category. Representatives of established religious institutions claim a hold over the sacred, through their many historically legitimated definitions of its sphere of activity. Yet, modernity opens up new avenues for expression of the sacred, in all its conceptual and moral ambiguity (Durkheim 1995:412, Pickering 1984). Both the gods and the demons become legion because, as Durkheim saw, society and the sacred are inextricably entangled. Wherever intense social gatherings occur, there are murmurings of the sacred, evidence of gods in *potentia*, waiting to show themselves. This helps us locate the emergence of "invisible" and marginal religious phenomena (Luckmann 1967, Tiryakian 1974) as well as the attempts by religious and other disciplinary institutions to confine heterodoxies and praxes by erecting boundaries between themselves and the other (Erikson 1966). Durkheim's argument implicates both the individual and the collective sides of the problem.

Modernity: The Ludic and the Religious

The paroxysms found in the more intense, but less frequent, societal rites of the past are displaced in the religious practices of modernity. There occurs a simultaneous increase in the number of rites across the calendar, that is, a shift in the contours of social time, yet a diminution in the emotional intensity of each of them. These two developments are interrelated. Although it is unclear which is cause and which consequence, it is likely that the increased number of ritual occasions would ultimately promote decreased emotionality by placing excessive demands on the individual's emotional economy. The proliferation of rites and dispersion of the sacred thus encourage a more disciplined and even distribution of emotional energies over a wider spectrum of activities.

In modern societies, with their complex fabric of social differentiations, not only among religions, but other groups and social activities, there thus appears a proliferation of rites. Since many rites are attached to the practices of specific groups and do not take on a societal-wide role, this proliferation does not necessarily impede societal integration. Even those rites that are societalized are modified to fit the profile described by Durkheim (i.e., combined with others in a larger number, with a reduced emotionality for each). The sum of societal rites themselves become routinized and more fully integrated into the workaday fabric of social order, reaching a variety of accommodations with other institutional spheres such as the state, the workplace, the market, the ethnic group, and the family.

The notion of a civil religion, brought to light by Bellah and others, fits well into Durkheim's expanded theory (Bellah 1970, Nielsen 1996). The rites of civil religion help bind society's temporal order. They fill in temporal gaps in the increasingly rapid flow of sociocultural change by combining a retrospective commemoration of the past with a reaffirmation of collective identity and future pursuit of collective ideals. They are well suited to modernity's simultaneous intolerance of excess, yet need for totalizing symbols and ritual reproduction.

Modern social structures also distribute collective labor across the social spectrum, generally reducing the time needed by any particular individual or group to reproduce its, and the society's, economic requirements. This contrasts with the longer, more extensive profane dispersions in primitive and archaic societies, ones necessitated by prolonged involvement of populations in economic reproduction. The seasonal festivals common to such communities reflect this dynamic (Durkheim 1995:353). With this shift, the older balance between intensely concentrated rites and extensive profane dispersion is disrupted and fissures emerge in society's temporal framework. Inherited ritual forms do not necessarily expand to fill this gap. Other activities compete for this time. In particular, a leisure sphere emerges within society's temporal dynamic. However, the proliferation of activities found under this heading cannot be viewed as entirely "profane." They are often sacralized, and take on religious characteristics, that is, they are set aside, covered by interdictions, develop ritual forms, and bind groups.

Durkheim sensed the primitive continuity between sacred rites and the "ludic" sphere, the point where mimetic representations in drama, art, team contest, and the erotic could become disengaged from religion (Durkheim 1995:385–7). Durkheim was unwilling to pay much attention to these play spheres, and his insistence that religion was, after all, a matter of the "serious" life, reflects his discomfort with them. However, it is clear that the "ludic" spheres have become permanently lodged in modern society. They have taken up much of the space previously occupied by religious rites, indeed, have often merged with them as well as with political and other "secular" rituals, sometimes with startling and explosive results. A large zone of competition, overlap, and merger has developed between the sacred and the profane. It is often difficult to disentangle them or identify which is at stake when we examine any given social activity.

Durkheim is strongly committed to the idea that society creates subjects. His view of the relationship between individual and society is highly asymmetrical (Nielsen 1999:223–6). The goods of civilization are entirely the work of society. Society constrains and disciplines individuals, yet they are also dependent on it. They owe a debt and are under obligation to society. This holds for all individuals. The great figures revered by a historical era, such as Abelard and Voltaire, are simply incarnations of society's own highest ideals, which society admires through the medium of these individuals (Durkheim 1977:70). The "great criminals" such as Socrates or Jesus express emerging collective sentiments and social opinions which will reach fruition only in the future (Durkheim 1982:102). All individuals instantiate social forces. The modern moral cult of the individual is no different. It is a creation of society. Durkheim hopes that it will give rise to new sorts of actual individuals, oriented not toward egoism and personal utility, nor even the autonomous use of their reason against authority, but dedicated instead to the advancement of society's moral aims (Durkheim 1994:70–1). This hope in the cult of the individual reflects his sense that individuals can be made to reinvest their moral energies in the improvement of society, which has literally "empowered" the subject, even while subjecting it to discipline, just as all religions have represented collective powers channeled through individuals. To fully realize this new cult, ritual processes must be developed corresponding to the new belief. In their absence, the belief cannot be sustained. In modern society, they necessarily take shape within the texture of everyday life in a wide variety of little rites.

Erving Goffman has developed Durkheim's notion of the proliferation and dispersion of the sacred in modern societies in his analysis of microrituals. They are not only the result of a new belief in the sacred character of the individual, as Goffman and Durkheim imply (Goffman 1967:47, 95, Durkheim 1994: 70–3). They are the small moral knots which bind the pieces of the social fabric into a continuous skein. They are rooted in the microreproductive requirements of this particular type of complex social structure. At the same time, microrituals are often also paralleled by highly individuated forms of belief (Bellah et al. 1986). From Durkheim's standpoint, it is to be expected that the modern individual becomes a *bricoleur*, to adapt the term of Lévi-Strauss (1966), who fabricates individuated forms of belief which combine fragments of past traditions with idiosyncratic experiences of the sacred.

Durkheim seemed skeptical of a future in which each person would not only individuate collective religious ideas (a structural feature of all religions), but where such practices would become the central focus of religious life (Durkheim 1995:43). Were not such "individual religions" merely another symptom of a pervasive modern egoism and anomie? Durkheim's own definition of religion requires reference to collective contents. Therefore, such cults would probably only find full legitimacy in Durkheim's eyes if they were individuated variants of collective themes, like the individual totems examined in the *Forms* (Durkheim 1995:181–2). However, Durkheim provides no "formula" for judging such developments, nor is it clear that he appreciated the problems raised by this aspect of his theory. A perspective which links religion and the sacred, yet allows them to be uncoupled under modern historical circumstances and, at the same time, focuses its hopes on a collective cult of the individual, certainly positions itself ambiguously toward the evaluation of the diverse historical outcomes likely to emerge from such combined circumstances. The cult of the sacralized individual introduces a very unpredictable element into Durkheim's theory of modernity. While Durkheim hoped this cult would place individuals in the service of collective ideals, it is antecedently unlikely that the varied creative outcomes of this newly valorized individual spirituality would all point in the same direction. It would be difficult for Durkheim, or anyone else, including those in positions of social and political "authority," to make definitive judgments about the potential collective value or social dangers of any particular individualizations of the sacred or label them in a facile manner as mere egoistic or anomic deformations.

The most general outcome of modern sociocultural change is a widespread diffusion of the sacred across society, in effect, establishing a modern "social pantheism." Many of the major historical findings of Weber and his followers concerning the effects of Protestant "innerworldliness" on work, the family, the division of labor, and modern culture generally can be understood in more systematic terms by placing them within Durkheim's perspective. These widespread sacralizations of the profane are the historical outcome of modernity's central structural tendency to diffuse the sacred in the interest of limiting the destructive impact of excessively violent cycles of religious and secular activity, while at the same time mobilizing collective religious energies for socially differentiated mundane pursuits. In this way, elements of the profane are selectively removed from the sphere of indifference or opposition to ultimate religious concerns and are made "transcendently" relevant.

However, since Durkheim sees religious forces and their capacity to sacralize "the world" as always already social, these sacralizations are theoretically displaced from the taken-for-granted symbolizations of transcendence current in any historical group into the realm of social immanence from which they initially emerged. Society turns back upon itself – not without risk – to selectively ratify its own mundane pursuits through varied sacralizations, even while the social actor believes – not wholly in vain – that "higher" forces are at work.

Durkheim thought that "collective effervescences," with all their intense emotionality, were the crucibles for cultural creativity or "renaissances" of ideas and ideals (Durkheim 1995:220, 1974:91–2). It might be imagined that any future moral transfiguration of modernity would also require such collective enthusiasms. Moreover, the relative absence of emotional intensity in modernity's ritualized routines might constitute a sort of Durkheimian "iron cage" barring such a collective rebirth. Indeed, decreased emotional engagement and declining capacity for moral indignation are often diagnosed as prime symptoms of a deformation in our current sensibility. However we may evaluate these phenomena – if, indeed, they are as pervasive as sometimes imagined – they are quite in keeping with Durkheim's description of modernity's routines.

The extensive social differentiation of modern societies allows for – perhaps necessitates – the proliferation of new rites. Most operate within limited social milieus, but some are selectively incorporated within wider societal structures and universalized as part of an ever-expanded "civil religion." There they operate as either shared ritual practices or goads to societal change in the name of shared cultural ideals involving either new images of the sacred or revivals of older ideals. While this may involve their emotional dilution, in line with Durkheim's main thesis, it also allows modern society to engage in a pluralistic, if competitive, process of moral self-correction on a more routine basis. Of course, conflicts regularly arise over the elevation of particular rites rooted in the values of particular "social segments" (e.g., ethnic, gender groups, etc.), or their individual representatives, to societal wide status. Whatever the outcome of these disputes, society gains sustenance from these emerging ideas, rooted in particular groups, yet the destructive tendencies of both societalized "primitive" excesses as well as segmentary group fragmentation are subjected to disciplinary control and "management."

Conclusion

Are the many new forms of ritual and belief gestated through the structural transformations of the sacred truly "religious"? Can we escape from the ambiguities and implications of Durkheim's basic definition of religion in terms of the sacred? Where people erect fences around things they hold sacred, separating them from the mundane, there are also found the lineaments of religion. Of course, Durkheim's definition of religion involves more than the sacred–profane distinction. For a religion to exist, there must be a "unified system of beliefs and practices" and they must have a social reference, create a moral bond among their followers. If we insist on measuring religion by the full range of terms in Durkheim's definition, many modern sacralizations are not strictly religious, but mere fragments of religious sentiment, rite, and belief; at best, protoreligions which might grow into new collective cults. However, we should not too hastily banish these manifestations of the religious impulse from Durkheim's defini- tional province. It is true that all things sacred do not necessarily constitute a religion. But the sacred is a broader category than religion, a fact clear even from Durkheim's own writings. Indeed, without this distinction, Durkheim's theory would become static. The ambiguous qualities of the unbound sacred as a social force provide a dynamic element which "religion" alone often lacks.

Religion has another feature relevant to our theme. As Durkheim noted in an 1899 letter to Gaston Richard, religion provides a sensory system for society, one parallel to that found in the individual. Just as the individual senses things in terms of colors, shapes, and other forms, religion represents things for society under the form of the sacred (Nielsen 1999:87). Durkheim implies that nothing could have collective relevance were it not first given a sacred "coloration" by religion. Society, like the individual, requires a sensory apparatus. Religion pro- vides one and thus occupies a crucial position in society. This "revelation" of religion's true significance had dawned slowly on Durkheim, emerging in the mid-1890s and coming to fruition only in his later writings. It is not clear that Durkheim understood its full implications. However, from his standpoint, it became necessary to emphasize the content of the representations (i.e., the sacred) in his mature definition of religion, and move beyond the excessively formal focus on obligation found in his definition of 1899 (Durkheim 1994:93, 1995:44, note 68). Since the sacred was embodied in physical objects which pro- vided for its visible symbolic expression, this necessitated increasing reference to the problem of nature.

If religion was society's sensorium, then it was also necessary to develop a social theory of the categories, as society's forms of cognitive universality about nature. The merger of these two perspectives provided a unified sociological solu- tion to Durkheim's two main problems: the nature of religion and the categories. As I have shown elsewhere, these theoretical moves also suggested a complex set of parallelisms within and between the individual and society, and a standpoint congruent with Spinoza's philosophy (Nielsen 1999:197–8, 224–6). To adapt Spinoza's language, religious rites are society seen under the mode of extension, while the religiously gestated categories are society seen under the mode of thought.

Durkheim's emphasis on religious rites, practices, collective actions and assemblies adds credence to this view. It is only through them that collective experience can be colored with the sacred. Religious beliefs are also important, as the cognitive residue of rites in the collective and individual memory.

However, they are also susceptible to greater variation and the contents of religious belief often succumb to the advance of knowledge. Religious rites can never be entirely eliminated, because the social body and mind must be periodically reanimated. In such emotionally charged religious gatherings, the social sensorium gains new experiences which can be crystallized into ideas and ideals. Collective representations achieve universality through the categories, but are first alerted to their relevant sensory contents through religion's transfiguration of the physical world. In turn, the individual's sensory apparatus provides access to the physical world, but its perceptions are molded by the forms of universality instantiated in the individual from the collective categories.

Durkheim argues that the individual cannot gestate categories, only society can. The individual partakes of these collective goods, but in a partial way, never appropriating them in their fullness. Durkheim is not entirely unambiguous on this score, for example, when he admits that perceptions are spatially organized around the embodied individual's location and orientation (Durkheim 1995:441). But this is not a true category of space. The inherent asymmetry of Durkheim's conception of the relationship between the individual and society demands that he retain religion and the categories as social products and forces. The individual can have little or no role in gestating them, and can only individuate them.

Another implication of this schema is found in the tension it creates between the collective and individual sensory structures, that is, between another aspect of the sacred and the profane. The collective sensorium of religion colors the external world with the sacred. But this sensory role does not encompass all the perceptions that are available to the individual. The latter's sensory system reveals a good deal more. Everything else remaining in the individual's perceptual field is profane. It exists and is also important for the person's (and the group's) mundane existence. Durkheim implies that profane perception is largely an individual affair. The group's collective perceptions are filtered through the sacred, and the individual sees sacredly through collective eyes. But the collective profane, all those aspects of shared everyday existence which are also an unavoidable part of the group's life, must derive from individuals, since the collectivity's sensorium is wholly a function of the sacred colors added to reality by religion. How can important profane group activities be collectivized without religion? This poses the most difficult problems for Durkheim, indeed, ones not entirely resolved, as Durkheim himself saw, by the notion of organic solidarity through functional differentiation of labor. As we have seen, his final theory of religion and society addresses these problems in a new way.

If the development of society is, in fact, a process of increasing individuation, resulting ultimately in a cult of the individual, this cult also necessarily results from religion's role as a social sensorium, which has now incorporated a new object in its sacred field of perception and imposed it on the individual as an obligatory reference point. The individual is required to perceive other individuals under the aspect of the sacred, and act accordingly, that is, in accordance with the rites appropriate to this new religious cult.

When the individual is sacralized within its modern cult, something else occurs. The individual cannot be sacralized without changing the terms of Durkheim's entire equation. The collective sensorium of religion paints the individual in sacred colors and makes it part of the totality of its sacrally delimited world. But when this happens individuals are no longer the same. The individual must then see both the other and the self as simultaneously sacred. One cannot be sacred without the other. They are bound together by a spirit of mutually sacralized reciprocity (Mauss 1990). By penetrating into the social body, disengaging its constituent cells and sacralizing them, religion modifies the image of society as an external force which constrains the individual, but also adds a new locus of force in its place. Individuals become increasingly self-constraining, because everywhere there are only other replicas of sacred individuality, but they also are free to create or destroy as godlike beings in their own right. This tension is inherent in the cult of the individual.

In sacralizing the individual, the religiously rooted social sensorium also takes on a new dimension. The collective cult of the individual empowers individuals to see religiously through their own individual, formerly profane eyes, while previously only the group, collectively, could sacralize experience. The individual's indirect collective perception of the world through the sacred is supplemented by the direct vision of the sacred through the sacralized self. The aura of the sacred can now be transferred to whatever the individual may see as sacred, because the society has transferred its collective power of sacralizing the world to the individual, who is now a legitimate sacralizing agent. Only some of the main sociological consequences of this idea are discussed in the foregoing analysis of the diffusion of the sacred in modern society. This wide-ranging set of developments is linked to the sacralization of the individual and, in turn, is deeply rooted in the changes in modern society's religious cycle.

The discussion moves us closer to the metaphysical and theological issues raised by Durkheim's theory. As I have noted elsewhere, Durkheim's religious sociology provides the basis for a distinctive theology of social immanence (Nielsen 1999), which cannot be discussed here. However, if we are to identify the outlines of a Durkheimian theology, we need to recall his key assumptions and aims. At the heart of this effort is a thoroughly sociologistic theory of religion. As he once wrote, between God and society lay the choice, one to which he was indifferent, since he saw nothing in God but society transfigured (Durkheim 1974:52). Although it has become unfashionable to view Durkheim as a "reductionist," it is difficult to avoid Durkheim's repeated declaration that all the elementary ideas and practices of religion are symbolic transformations of our experiences of society. In this respect, Swanson captures Durkheim's original spirit better than many other recent writers (Swanson 1966). Durkheim's theory of the categories provides a further, and very provocative, set of linkages among religion, society, and nature, thus extending his notion of religion's immanence in society to the immanence of nature itself in society (Nielsen 1999:232–4).

Durkheim's religious sociology ultimately locates religion at a limit point, on a boundary or surface between things. The sacred itself is the product of collective social activities, even while the material world serves as an infinitely expansible set of objective vehicles for the incarnation of these sacred forces. The sacred is therefore linked to material existence on its other boundary. It is fenced on both sides by material existence. It requires material objects for its symbolization, yet itself expresses the experiences of physically assembled gatherings. Durkheim's (1974:30–2) recognition that representations can become detached from their social origins, recombine in new ways, and take on new meanings, seemingly apart from any direct social influences, is quite irrelevant to this main point (Nielsen 1999:112–13). Religion is located at the boundaries between the material world and society, but is exclusively in neither one nor the other. On the one hand, there is active social substance, on the other, the physical world or nature. The former approaches and interjects its combined energies or forces into the latter, and even sometimes into its own bodily units, sacralizing them. It later withdraws these energies for new uses, but withdraws them merely to reinterject them again elsewhere, where another fold or surface is found. Gods and demons, both the propitious and unpropitious sacred, emerge eternally along these superficies between society and nature.

A theology of social immanence must also reconstruct inherited theological categories from the sort of sociological standpoint described above. It must see them as purely social facts. Durkheim wanted to offer a sociological alternative to the central Jewish and Christian ideas of Western European civilization as well as its core metaphysical perspectives. This seems clear from his critical dialogue with contemporary theological schools and religious thinkers as well as with more traditional philosophical perspectives associated with Plato, Aristotle, Descartes, Pascal, Kant and others (Allen et al. 1998, Nielsen 1987, 1999, Strenski 1997). But this means that the transcendent and otherworldly conceptions of God and salvation, as well as their ancillary ethical ideas, so dear to the West, must be reconceived as immanent in society. The transcendent, all-powerful God, the creation and fall of humankind, the incarnation and dual nature of Christ, the right path of moral conduct, the notions of sin, expiation, sacrifice, salvation itself – all the inherited categories – need to be recast in terms of the notion of social immanence. Durkheim never reached this goal. However, the Durkheimian focus on the sociology of the categories of the human spirit represented a step in this direction. The challenge of creating such a radically social theology, with all its potential risk and rewards, remains on the agenda.

References

Allen, N.J. et al., Eds. 1998. *On Durkheim's Elementary Forms of Religious Life*. Boston: Routledge.

Bellah, R.N. 1970. *Beyond Belief*. New York: Harper & Row.

Bellah, R.N. et al. 1986. *Habits of the Heart: Individualism and Commitment in American Life*. New York: Harper & Row.

Durkheim, E. 1951. *Suicide*, Transl. J. Spaulding and G. Simpson. New York: Free Press.

Durkheim, E. 1974. *Sociology and Philosophy*, Transl. D.F. Pocock and J.G. Peristiany, introduction. New York: Free Press.

Durkheim, E. 1977. *The Evolution of Educational Thought*, Transl. P. Collins, New York: Routledge.

Durkheim, E. 1982. *The Rules of Sociological Method and Selected Texts on Sociology and Its Method*, Transl. W.D. Halls, Introduction, S. Lukes. New York: Free Press.

Durkheim, E. 1984. *The Divison of Labor in Society*, Transl. W.D. Halls. New York: Free Press.

Durkheim, E. 1994. *Durkheim on Religion*, Ed., transl. W.H.C. Pickering. London: Routledge.

Durkheim, E. 1995. *The Elementary Forms of Religious Life*. Translator, introduction Karen Fields. New York: Free Press.

Erikson, K. 1966. *Wayward Puritans*. New York: John Wiley.

Foucault, M. 1984. *The Foucault Reader*, Ed. Paul Rabinow. New York: Pantheon Books.

Goffman, E. 1967. *Interaction Ritual*. Garden City, NY: Doubleday Anchor.

Harrison, J.E. 1912. *Themis: The Social Origins of Greek Religion*. Cambridge: Cambridge University Press.

Levi-Strauss, C. 1966. *The Savage Mind*. Chicago: University of Chicago Press.

Luckmann, T. 1967. *The Invisible Religion: The Problem of Religion in Modern Society*. New York: Macmillan.

Mauss, M. 1979. *Seasonal Variations of the Eskimo: A Study in Social Morphology*, Transl. J.J. Fox. Boston: Routledge.

Mauss, M. 1990. *The Gift*, Transl. W.D. Halls. New York: W.W. Norton.

Nielsen, D.A. 1987. "Auguste Sabatier and the Durkheimians on the Scientific Study of Religion," *Sociological Analysis* 47(4):283–301.

Nielsen, D.A. 1996. "Pericles and the Plague: Civil Religion, Anomie and Injustice in Thucydides," *Sociology of Religion* 57(4):397–407.

Nielsen, D.A. 1999. *Three Faces of God: Society, Religion and the Categories of Totality in the Philosophy of Emile Durkheim*. Albany, NY: State University of New York Press.

Pickering, W.H.F. 1984. *Durkheim's Sociology of Religion*. London: Routledge.

Strenski, I. 1997. *Durkheim and the Jews of France*. Chicago: University of Chicago.

Swanson, G. 1966. *The Birth of the Gods*. Ann Arbor: University of Michigan Press.

Tiryakian, E.A. Ed. 1974. *On the Margins of the Visible*. New York: John Wiley.

CHAPTER 8

Classics in the Sociology of Religion: An Ambiguous Legacy

Roger O'Toole

Introduction

Few issues in the discipline of sociology can provoke the emotional response which greets periodic public pronouncements on the role of the classics in contemporary theory and research. Eruptions of pent-up frustration can, apparently, be ignited as easily by occasional outbursts of nostalgia for a sociological Golden Age as by intermittent, impatient expressions of the increasing irrelevance of the founding fathers. The persisting presence of the classics, whether these are perceived as perspicacious or pernicious, is an indisputable feature of the sociological enterprise, which is not without irony in a profession which has often been viewed as debunking, muckraking, radical, and antiauthoritarian. In an intellectual climate of deconstruction, an image of sociologists as, in any sense, preservers and guardians of tradition has a certain poignancy which encourages further investigation of the nature of the disciplinary classical canon.

In the range of opinion it encompasses, the depth of disagreement it displays, and the odd alliances it invokes, the perennial though progressive debate over the significance of the classics offers insight into the practice of sociology at the most fundamental or metatheoretical level. From the perspective of the historian of ideas, the sociologist of science, or the sociologist of knowledge, there can be no better starting-point for characterizing the dimensions of the sociological imagination either at the disciplinary or subdisciplinary level. From the perspective of the sociology of sociology, the classics are social facts whose intellectual importance is matched by their symbolic, mythological, and functional relevance.

Classics and the Humanities

As Robert Merton (1968) has observed, the lingering presence of the classics is an affront to many sociologists, because it seems to belie the scientific aspirations of their discipline. Identified as the inextricable core of the humanities, the notion of a classical canon is taken to imply a static or circular conception of knowledge completely at odds with the progressive and cumulative growth envisioned by science. Evoking images of timeless truths, eternal wisdom, and perennial problems, classics are thus conceived as irredeemably rooted in older modes of thought and in a nostalgia for the absolute which undermines scientific method by its craven dependence on reputation, tradition, and authority. Before considering this assessment in the context of a broader social-scientific literature, it is worth noting its hazy perception of humanities classics and its shaky transposition of this notion into the sociological realm.

It is, of course, impossible to trace here either the variety of meanings historically associated with the term "classic" or the evolving literary and philosophical critique of the very idea of a classical canon. Instead, the views of a number of influential writers, scholars, and critics are briefly cited as indicators of contemporary opinion within the humanities. Emphasizing the maturity, amplitude, and catholicity of classics, T.S. Eliot denounces a provincialism in which "the world is the property solely of the living, a property in which the dead hold no shares" (1945:30). Discerning creativity in the balance between tradition and "the originality of the living generation," (pp. 14–15) he sees the achievement of the classics in their capacity "to suggest still undeveloped resources" while denying "that everything that can be done has been done." This open-ended perception of classics is endorsed by Italo Calvino (1986) who recommends both "re-visiting" them and alternating their perusal "with the proper dose of current affairs" in order to derive their maximum benefit. It gains further support from Alberto Manguel (1998) who stresses that horizons are widened by provision of "another way of looking, another manner of listening, another sense through which to perceive the bewildering world."

Frank Kermode contrasts an earlier imperial, authoritative, or authoritarian notion of the classic, insistent upon the identity of text and authorial intention, with a modern pluralist conception in which "the text is under the absolute control of no thinking subject"(1975:138–41). In the latter case, survival of the classic depends upon its surplus of meaning. It "must always signify more than is needed by any one interpreter or any one generation of interpreters." Such a conception clearly involves timeless truth only in the sense that it contains different truths for different times. It is apparent that, even within the humanities, changing conceptions and evaluations of the classic have entailed significant consequences for disciplinary practice in a number of fields.

Classics and Sociology

In the investigation of the role of the classics in sociology, certain literary, philosophical, and historical echoes of the previous discussion will inevitably be detected. While sociological classics do not, of course, exhibit the same range of form and content as those celebrated in the humanities, their kinship to the latter is a matter for serious meditation (Lepenies 1988).

It is unnecessary here to attempt any definitive depiction of the classical canon in sociology or to reiterate the role of such scholars as Talcott Parsons (1968) in its construction. Practicing sociologists are familiar enough with its main dimensions and its evolutionary character, even if they are not fully aware of the extent to which formerly prominent texts and writers have slipped into obscurity, or if they fail to appreciate how recently some major figures have been elevated to the pantheon. The presence of major classic thinkers, most notably Durkheim, Weber, and Marx, in the conversation of contemporary sociology is undeniable. What is equally indisputable, however, is the continuing centrality and prominence of their ideas in disciplinary and subdisciplinary debate, a fact underlined by the explicit and persistent use of such terms as "Durkheimian," "Weberian," and "Simmelian" in the depiction of specific theoretical orientations (Alexander 1988, Collins 1986). Evidence of the vitality of the classics is also readily apparent in the realm of widely used textbooks which stress continuity with the classics, emphasize the impact of classic thinkers on the main intellectual traditions of the discipline, and proclaim the virtues of confronting classical writers as if they were our contemporaries (Wallace and Wolf 1999, Orum 1989). In this context, classics emerge, not merely as distant fountainheads of current paradigms, but as scholarly resources with immediate and topical relevance (Sherman 1974, Collins 1994, Nisbet 1966, Poggi 1972).

While, for many sociologists, a sense that their discipline is still wrestling with the insights of its illustrious founders is a source of scholarly satisfaction, others regard this state of affairs with a more jaundiced eye. Four broad lines of criticism of the prominent role of the classics in contemporary sociological discussion may be discerned. The first of these, echoing Merton, essentially offers variations on Alfred North Whitehead's theme that "a science which hesitates to forget its founders is lost" (Merton 1968:1, Whitehead 1917:115). Rooted in a notion of science as a cumulative venture in which what is newer ought to be better, this approach applauds the divorce of history from systematics and bemoans a failure to construct propositional edifices in which identifiable individual insights are rendered anonymous and subsumed within a collective and convergent theoretical enterprise (Turner 1986:974).

Paralleling this critique, though by no means logically linked to it, is the simple perception that, in various ways, the classics have outlived their usefulness as instruments for comprehending the social world. In this conception, the classics have been wholly or partly overtaken and outdated by historical events

(Wallerstein 1991, Giddens 1976, 1987:26–9, Beckford 1992). Conceived in response to the shattering nineteenth-century processes of industrialization, modernization, and democratization, they are consequently inadequate to the tasks of description, analysis and prediction in a postindustrial, postmodern, and globalized world. Indeed, viewing contemporary social life through classical lenses can result only in grotesque reflections of already distorted images.

Distorted images are at the heart of a third attack on the role of the classics, which derives from philosophy and the history of ideas. In this assessment, "the classics" as collectively apprehended by sociologists, bear only the most tenuous relationship to the actual literary creations of the founding fathers. Determined to recover authors' intentions through analysis of both text and context, the proponents of this view assail the misguided notion of treating classical writers as contemporaries. Thus, they regard even the most erudite disciplinary discussions of the classics, whether in terms of adumbrations, unit ideas, convergences, or continuities as steeped in anachronism, illusion and mythology (Skinner 1969, Hawthorn 1976:1–7, Jones 1977, 1978, 1983, 1986).

The final critique of the role of the classics also strikes a mythological note by deprecating their intellectual relevance and stressing their disciplinary social functions. Here it is suggested that the classics are less important for their content than for their very presence as symbols of authority, tradition, continuity, and integrity in an increasingly polycentric and fragmented discipline. Utilizing the analogy of an ancestor myth, Becker expresses this sentiment exactly when he cites "the otherwise mysterious concentration on Marx–Durkheim–Weber, the Holy Trinity whose fathomless interconnections if they were charted would provide the final word on the integration of the field" (1979:24).

Defenders of the role of the classics have responded and continue to respond to these accusations in a variety of ways which also decisively dispel any impression that commitment to the classics is confined to conservatives, traditionalists, reactionaries, and retreatists. In reply to the proposition that persistence of the classics undermines sociology's cumulative character, two responses have occurred. One endorses the cumulative nature of disciplinary development while stressing that generic theory is a future goal rather than a present accomplishment. Thus, pondering Whitehead's maxim sympathetically, Gouldner (1958:vi) observes that it is impossible to forget something unless it is really known in the first place. Convinced that the ideas of the founders are not yet "known" in the sense of being fully interpreted, appreciated, exploited, and exhausted by subsequent scholarship, he insists that current concern with the classics is, in no sense, a symptom of intellectual inertia.

An alternative response firmly rejects the idea of sociology as a cumulative enterprise in the manner of the natural sciences (Freese 1972, Green 1977, Gans 1992, Gellner 1985:9, Wagner and Berger 1984). Emphasizing the high incidence of intellectual amnesia, the apparently static or cyclical nature of social ideas, and the prevalence of discourse as the predominant mode of communication within the discipline, many writers are inclined to underline sociology's kinship with the humanities. In so doing, of course, they endorse the legitimacy and pertinence of an abiding interest in the classics.

Belief that the classics are outdated may, of course, be met with counterarguments maintaining that, while specific elements are now clearly inadequate, disproved, or irrelevant, classic formulations essentially remain theoretically capacious enough to be profitably applied a century or more after their introduction. It may even be suggested that supposedly outdated myths perpetuated by the classics are products of subsequent misinterpretation rather than integral ingredients of classic texts in their pristine form. Many defenders of the classics' current relevance, however, frame their arguments in a way that transcends their specific theoretical utility or even the truth of their assertions. In the extreme case, indeed, some are even prepared (half-seriously) to celebrate the "uselessness" of the classics (Poggi 1996). This, however, is the exception that proves the rule. The resilience and longevity of the classics is mainly explained in terms of qualities which underscore the extent to which authority derives from utility in this context. In extolling the virtues of classical authors, admirers cite their imaginative vision, depth, and clarity of thought, complexity of mind, counterintuition, originality, creativity, and sense of style. Their works are portrayed as interesting, interpretive, and provocative touchstones of scientific elegance and excellence which generate insightful, powerful, and fundamental ideas in a comparative-historical atmosphere of equivocality and open-endedness (Hacker 1954, Levin 1973, Davis 1971, 1986, Rhea 1981, Szacki 1982). Naturally, the pricelessness of such an inheritance is forcefully and frequently contrasted with the tedious banalities, cliches, and truisms which are perceived as proliferating in contemporary sociological writing.

The case for the classics in these terms is perhaps expressed most eloquently in Mills's (1960) eulogy on the "classic tradition." Noting that his generation of sociologists is "still living off the ideas" of the sociological masters, he discerns the sources of the latter's greatness in the profound revelations and continuing relevance of the various broad and often contradictory "models" which they construct. For Mills, the classic tradition is defined not by any specific method or theory but rather by the questions which have guided its exponents. These are "generally of wide scope: they concern total societies, their transformations, and the varieties of individual men and women that inhabit them" (1960:2–4). The answers given offer broad conceptions of society, history, biography and the linkages among them. "Soaked in history," classic sociologists thus interweave analysis of individuals' private troubles with exploration of the great public issues confronting societies.

Defending the current role of the classics against those determined to rescue classic texts and their authors from misinterpretation, vulgarization, and debasement at the hands of working sociologists is a delicate assignment. While no genuine admirer of classic writings would presumably wish to discourage concerted attempts to historically reconstruct their authors' intentions by means of the most painstaking contextual analysis, nonetheless the intellectual anathemas imposed by this enterprise are regarded by many with dismay and foreboding. In a supreme irony, efforts to impose historical and philosophical rigor on the study of the classics threaten, not only to silence the lively debate which still envelops the works of the founding fathers, but to thwart the aspirations of both the history of sociological thought and the development of sociological theory in their customary disciplinary forms. To some commentators, a historicist or contextualist approach to the classics represents the divorce of history from systematics with a vengeance. It is an undertaking in which "we risk burying ourselves in pedantic, myopic antiquarianism" (Johnson 1978:174, Jones 1977, 1978, Peel 1978, Turner 1991).

Whatever its risks, there is no doubt that exact reconstruction of the intentions of classic authors is not the highest priority among those who uphold the importance of the classics to the contemporary sociological enterprise. While the founding fathers are respected and revered, their writings have long ceased to be regarded as their own exclusive intellectual property. In a manner which understandably incenses historicists and contextualists, the classic texts of sociology now possess a disciplinary meaning and scholarly significance which transcends the circumstances of their original inspiration and composition. Irredeemably "presentist" in their tendency to treat their great books in contemporary terms, sociologists have, in practice, long espoused a pluralist rather than an imperial conception of the text (Kermode 1975:140–1, Ricoeur 1971, LaCapra 1982). Whether in the building of a canon, the formulation of unit ideas, the explication of convergence or, for that matter, the generation of mythology, creative interpretations (or misinterpretations) of the classics have been conspicuous in the struggle to define the nature of sociology as an intellectual endeavor and a professional calling. While, in principle, a project to retrieve contextually what Marx, Durkheim, or Weber really meant to say would constitute a notable contribution to the history of sociology, well-rooted and resolute disciplinary resistance to the segregation of systematics from history would almost certainly deny such a reading the definitive or privileged status which its proponents would demand.

As social facts in disciplinary or subdisciplinary contexts, "the classics" are products of a vast, lengthy, and complex process of exegesis, classification, commentary, interpretation, and reinterpretation. They are palimpsests whose prevailing meanings are determined by dialogue, debate, and discussion among diverse readers armed (or burdened) with a century of scholarship, confronted by their immediate sociocultural and historical exigencies, and inspired by their own biographical predilections. No doubt, to some degree, this state of affairs represents "a bag of tricks we play upon the dead." But, as even its advocates admit, the intentionalist examination of texts cannot provide the "sole and sufficient approach" in the sociological encounter with the classics (Jones 1978:176–80, 1983:137). Just as the humanities resist restriction of the study of Shakespeare, Plato, and Nietzsche in this manner, a prevailing sociological presentism inevitably demands the treatment of classic texts as "open books" in the broadest sense of the term (Bloom 1994). This does not mean that they supply scriptural repositories of timeless wisdom or eternal truth but rather they lack occlusion, inspire imitation, invite elaboration, and provoke discussion. Where intentionalists attempt to restore the integrity of classical texts by narrowing their range of possible signifiers, presentists rejoice that resistance to such a strategy preserves that surplus of sociological signification which is the most indelible mark of a genuine disciplinary or subdisciplinary classic. From this point of view, classics are not terminal destinations but rather points of embarkation for departure on future intellectual journeys.

Far from undermining their legitimacy, revelation of the extrinsic disciplinary and professional functions performed by the classics actually enhances a conception of their scholarly centrality among many sociologists. Thus, for example, the suggestion that the classical "Holy Trinity" may function as a disciplinary or subdisciplinary ancestor cult is in no way seen to detract from the intrinsic intellectual significance of their ideas (Becker 1979:24, Jones 1980, Stinchcombe 1982). On the contrary, the very fact that founding fathers can be employed in such a symbolic manner is construed as convincing evidence of the continuing presence and vitality of classic ideas in the hearts and minds of sociological practitioners. The classics, it appears, can be collective representation of the sociological community without being entirely arbitrary symbols of scholarly accomplishment and creativity.

Sociologists have long recognized that, apart from their manifest intrinsic scholarly function as fountainheads of ideas, insights, models, and theories of exceptional imaginative brilliance, classic texts fulfill a range of extrinsic or latent functions relevant to both individual practitioners and disciplinary and subdisciplinary collectivities. Some of these are broadly pedagogical in nature while others concern the facilitation of professional communication and the reinforcement of commitment to a common scholarly enterprise. Noting that such functions derive from "the imperfect retrieval of past sociological theory that has not yet been fully absorbed in subsequent thought," Merton (1968:35–8) endorses contemporary sociologists' acquaintance, reacquaintance and "close familiarity" with their classical predecessors. In true presentist vein, he thus applauds the "interactive effect" of developing new ideas by turning to older writings within the context of contemporary knowledge. This "dialogue with the dead" provides models which constitute nothing less than the finest achievements of the sociological project, thus enabling current practitioners to devise worthy "standards of taste and judgment" while inspiring them to sharpen their critical, empathic, and creative faculties. For Merton, therefore, the classics contribute enormously to the socialization and professional motivation of sociologists in ways which include the "pleasure of coming upon an aesthetically pleasing and more cogent version of one's own ideas," the "satisfaction of independent confirmation of those ideas by a powerful mind," and the "educative function of developing high standards of taste for sociological work."

Stressing the need for a sociological canon and echoing some of Merton's views, Poggi asserts the pedagogical benefits of direct exposure to classical expositions of "huge, intellectually and morally exciting themes" (1996:43–4). As the products of "utterly superior minds," these writings of "unsurpassed scholarly texture and intellectual substance" reveal new dimensions of significance on each rereading. Sustained encounter with the classics induces "a certain sense of reverent yet critical awareness of the past" which lays a foundation for subsequent historicist or presentist exploration. Through the scrutiny of classic writings, students acquire hermeneutical skill, an appreciation of the complexity, profundity, and open-endedness of texts, and a sensitivity to the genesis of these texts in specific intellectual, social, and historical circumstances.

In a similar manner, Stinchcombe (1982) suggests that classics serve a pedagogical function as "touchstones" or models of possible ways in which "beautiful" scientific work can be executed. By articulating the complexity of social life, they induce a parallel complexity of mind in their readers, thereby ensuring long-term immunity from ever-present and highly infectious sociological simplifications, clichés, and banalities. While they are sources both of fundamental ideas and of specific puzzles and hypotheses for empirical research, the classics also perform a more mundane though still significant shorthand function as "small coinage." In the context of citations, references, and footnotes, they serve in almost totemic manner as "intellectual badges" which immediately identify particular traditions or styles of sociological work. Not surprisingly, therefore, the founding fathers and their works can be viewed in Durkheimian terms of shared myths and rituals which function to express and reinforce disciplinary and subdisciplinary "solidarity and common concerns."

Distinguishing the "intellectual-scientific" from the "functional" aspect of the classics, Alexander (1987) perceives the "functional necessity for classics" as deriving from a need for integration of theoretical discussion. Fulfilling an essentially boundary-maintaining function by providing minimum baselines for understanding and common points of reference for communication, classics reduce complexity by serving as symbols representing "a range of diverse general commitments" in the manner also denoted by Stinchcombe. Through such condensation of the innumerable formulations of an intellectual universe into a restricted number of representative works, theoretical conversation is simplified and facilitated. The assumption of a common knowledge of the classics permits the selective employment of familiar classical themes and arguments, a strategy which allows the circumvention of many otherwise essential preliminaries to general theoretical argument. By framing their assertions in terms of the classics, sociologists can be reasonably confident that their disciplinary peers will comprehend the main direction of their arguments and prove capable of intelligible response.

Where functions can be discerned, of course, so also can dysfunctions. Thus, in the opinion of a number of commentators, the most potentially dysfunctional aspect of the classics derives from their very recognition as the finest achievements of the sociological enterprise. If the rewards of classical erudition are sublime, the penalties for its misuse are grave. Misuse in this setting appears to be essentially indistinguishable from lack of use, a sentiment expressed most succinctly in Merton's observation that "the study of classical writings can be either deplorably useless or wonderfully useful" (1968:30, 1977:viii). An occupational hazard of prolonged exposure to the classics is, therefore, to fall under their spell and drift slowly away from utility and toward idolatry. Pious preoccupation with classics as ends in themselves rather than as means to an end is seen as leading inevitably to scholasticism and pedantry as well as to intellectual anemia, impotence, and sterility. From this perspective, antiquarianism constitutes the archenemy of sociological originality and creativity and its most authentic expression would appear to be that "thoughtless mimicry through which mediocrity expresses its tribute to greatness" (Merton 1968:37, Turner 1986:974). It is, incidentally, within the context of this broadly utilitarian conception of the classics that hostility to historicist and intentionalist proclamations may best be understood (Coser 1977, 1981, Johnson 1978).

As the preceding extended account indicates, sociologists have long pondered and debated the privileged place of classics in sociological conversation and they continue to do so in increasing numbers (Holton 1996, Calhoun 1996). No assessment of the enduring role of classical texts would be complete, however, without brief elaboration of what appears to be their prime virtue as a sociological resource. Such an undertaking, in its turn, cannot be concluded without contemplation of the distinctive disciplinary attribute which generates, sustains and perpetuates a reliance on the classics.

Frequent reference to their "open-endedness" and "complexity" underlies the often-repeated assertion that classic texts are not conclusive, hermetic, promulgations but foundations for continuing scholarly conversations. In this regard, it may be suggested that their propensity to intrigue, inspire, agitate, and provoke derives from their essential ambiguity. In explicating this concept in a sociological setting, Levine (1985b) contrasts a belief in the utter unambiguity of science with the intrinsic ambiguities both of human realities and the language used by social scientists in attempting to represent them. Discerning an obsession, in some scientific quarters, with the elimination of ambiguity and the replacement of the multivocal by the univocal, he offers "two cheers for ambiguity in science" and recommends tolerance of ambiguity as a way of dealing responsibly with issues of great complexity. The sociological classics have long been regarded as an ambiguous legacy (Hook 1955) in a number of ways, a fact which is a source both of frustration and exhilaration. Inconsistencies and contradictions within the texts and oeuvres of individual founding fathers, combined with fundamental disagreements among the major figures of the canon, ensure that the classical heritage is multivocal in the extreme (Levine 1985a, 1995, Calhoun 1996). If, in literary terms, any text is open to a plurality of meanings, this is surely true *a fortiori* of the classical canon of the sociological tradition. For defenders of the classics this is cause for celebration rather than dismay. From their point of view, the continuing capacity of the classics to incite novel forms of sociological creativity is due, in large measure, to that very ambiguity which periodically inspires adventurous interpretations of old formulations. In these circumstances, few sociologists now entertain hopes of disciplinary unity or even theoretical convergence based on the classical canon.

A more realistic and differentiated account of the sociological heritage, which stresses its dialectical or dialogical character, has thus emerged. Within this narrative, specific intellectual traditions are perceived as having "taken their shape partly in reaction to one another through progressively developed but contrasting solutions to common problems" (Levine 1985a:19, Shils 1970, Merton 1977:viii). The sociological "community" is thus, at best, a broad common enterprise which agrees to disagree and is rooted in radically different forms of classical contributions. In a sense, therefore, the writings of the founding fathers are simultaneously sources both of unity and disunity.

No contemporary scholar has done more than Alexander (1987) to justify and explain the centrality of the classics in contemporary sociology. Pondering the persistence of writings whose empathy, insight, interpretive adroitness, representational skill, and creative idiosyncrasy invite comparison with the great works of art, literature, and philosophy, he is drawn inexorably into a profound metatheoretical and postpositivist analysis of the nature of sociological activity. Confident that, in the aftermath of the Kuhnian revolution, old beliefs about the cumulative nature of sociology or the distinction between history and systematics are highly questionable, Alexander explores the practice of sociology in order to uncover its assumptions and procedures (Kuhn 1970, Jones 1983). Developing a now familiar disciplinary vision of fragmentation, polycentrism, and protracted internal conflict, Alexander underscores the degree of sociological disagreement even over basic background assumptions by observing that the "conditions that Kuhn defines for paradigm crisis in the natural sciences are routine in the social" (Alexander 1987:20). Sociology apparently exists in a permanent intellectual state of normal crisis in which arguments are not restricted to the empirical level but "cut across the full range of non-empirical commitments which sustain competing points of view" (1987:20). Fundamentally divided over facts, processes, and even definitions, sociology is inevitably differentiated by traditions, schools, or perspectives which not only express disagreement but promote and sustain it. Equally inevitably, in such circumstances sociological discussion is profoundly different in kind from intellectual interchange in the natural sciences.

Borrowing from the lexicons of Foucault and Habermas, Alexander suggests that social science is characterized by discourse as its major mode of communication (Alexander 1987:22, Foucault 1970, Habermas 1984:22–42). By this term he refers to forms of argument "which are more consistently generalized and speculative than are normal scientific discussions." Discourse is categorized as "ratiocinative" in that its focus is on the process of reasoning rather than the results of immediate experience and its significance arises "when there is no plain and evident truth." Seeking to persuade through argument rather than prediction, it places at a premium "such qualities as logical coherence, expansiveness of scope, interpretive insight, value relevance, rhetorical force, beauty and texture of argument" (1987:22). In Alexander's view, it is because of the prominence of discourse (in a number of forms) that social scientific theory is so multivalent and natural science models are so inappropriate to its development.

Having forcefully asserted the centrality of discourse within social science, Alexander investigates its relevance for the classics. In his judgment the link between discourse and the classics is far from coincidental and might be considered an elective affinity of the most powerful kind. Warning that the "existence of generalized nonempirical debate does not logically imply any privileged position for earlier works," he is convinced none the less that "the very conditions that make discourse so prominent also make the classics central" (1987:27). In practice, the prominence of discourse as a disciplinary mode of argument is connected inextricably with the conspicuousness of the classics in contemporary sociology. The classics indeed clearly embody the qualities which Alexander attributes to discourse, a fact which partly explains the almost unconscious "taken-for-granted" way in which sociologists weave interpretations of the classics into their specific arguments.

Noting that whether or not a discipline gives prominence to classics depends on its degree of consensus concerning nonempirical matters, Alexander acknowledges that the conditions for their emergence broadly correspond with the division between the natural and social sciences. The proportion of classic to contemporary writings is greater in the latter because "endemic disagreement makes the background assumptions of social science more explicit," (1987:27), a condition which, of course, generates discourse as its characteristic form of dialogue. The means by which this discursive form of argument takes a specifically classic turn have been indicated previously. It is unnecessary to deliberate on the functional or extrinsic significance of the classics other than to reiterate their key role in the generation and facilitation of discourse through the provision of common points of reference, the simplification of argument, and the legitimation of new ideas. However, further contemplation of their intellectual-scientific or intrinsic affinity with, and contribution to, disciplinary discourse is in order.

Alexander maintains that the more general a scientific statement, the more it supplies "compelling self-reflection on the meaning of social life" by encouraging aesthetic ability and social sensibility. He also proposed that "the more generalized a scientific discussion, the less cumulative it can be" (1987:30) because the truth criteria of generalized commitments cannot be anchored in an unequivocal way. Sustained less by "qualities in the object world" than by "the relative tastes and preferences of a particular cultural community," generalized discourse relies on "qualities of personal sensibility – aesthetic, interpretive, philosophical, observational – which are not progressive." In a statement crucial to the comprehension of the paramount place of the classics in disciplinary discourse, Alexander next muses that "variations in social science reflect not linear accumulation . . . but the essentially random distribution of human ability" (1987:28). The production of great social science is a gift like the capacity for the creation of great art and because it is dependent on a personal idiosyncratic ability "to experience, to understand and to know" (p. 29) life, it cannot be acquired merely by imitation of empirical problem solutions. It can, however, be vicariously experienced and conceivably nurtured through immersion in those great works where qualities of mind such as insight, empathy, and creativity have combined with critical, interpretive, and representational proficiency to produce many ideas which could not be fully appreciated in their own time and which, in a number of respects, have not yet been surpassed.

Alexander's examination of the intellectual and functional connections between discourse and the classical canon draws the inescapable conclusion that "the classics – not generalized discourse per se" are central to the practice of social science. It is because of such intrinsic and extrinsic considerations that certain earlier works are granted privileged status and are so venerated that their authors are often treated as a contemporary presence. As with the most outstanding works of the humanities, it has been the work of generations to recapture, repossess, and expand the arguments and implications of classical sociological texts. Far from constituting a sterile antiquarianism, such discourse represents, from Alexander's perspective, a laudable and "legitimate form of rational scientific dispute" (1987:31) in which sociologists express their "systematic ambitions" (p. 33). Given the centrality of the classics, new interpretations of old texts are not merely aids to theorizing but major forms of theoretical argument in themselves. There is thus an inextricable relationship between contemporary theoretical concerns and explorations of the meaning of historical texts. Indeed any erosion of such historical and textual concerns represents a threat "to the very practice of sociology itself" (p. 32).

While concurring that a sociological tendency to merge the history and systematics of social theory derives from the effort "to straddle scientific and humanistic orientations," Alexander firmly rejects the Mertonian view that such merging and straddling are pathological (Merton 1968:29, Jones 1983). He believes, on the contrary, that they have been "endemic to the practice of social science" (p. 31) since its earliest beginnings and that, because historical interpretation is so crucial to theory, "a merging of history and systematics must be made" (p. 48). The notion that sociology will eventually overcome its inclination to fuse history and systematics as it increasingly resembles a natural science is rooted not in empirical fact but in "unjustified speculative preconceptions." Affirming that "there are endemic irrepressible reasons for the divergence between natural and social science" (p. 31) and remarking that "in crucial respects the practices of natural and social science are not particularly alike" (p. 18), Alexander offers no encouragement to those who yearn for a pristine, systematic, and cumulative sociology freed of the burdens of its classical past and rooted firmly in the logic of the natural sciences. In fact, if sociology is, in Merton's phrase, "posed between the physical and life sciences and the humanities" (Merton 1968:29), it would seem to be situated much closer to the humanities than to either version of science by virtue of its embrace of both discourse and the classics. Alexander's analysis offers powerful theoretical support to those sociologists who believe that they can learn at least as much from their forerunners as they can from their contemporaries. Robustly rejecting the need to forget the disciplinary founding fathers, he insists that their presence, persistence, and prominence is vital to the continuing progress of sociology.

The Role of Classics in the Sociology of Religion

The role of the classics in the formation and evolution of specific sociological subdisciplines is a topic which merits greater attention than it has received. Few could doubt, however, that in any comparative survey of subfields, the sociology of religion would exhibit a long-standing and tenacious infatuation with the classics (O'Toole 1984, 1993). Indeed, there is little doubt that a sense of classical pedigree and a sentiment of keeping faith with the founding fathers are important ingredients in the subdisciplinary collective consciousness. Though any conception of an unbroken scholarly lineage reaching back to Comte and Saint Simon is, of course, mythological, the feeling of a special claim on the classics is grounded in the belief that sociologists of religion are guardians of a central classical insight long neglected by mainstream sociology. In their commitment to the analysis of religion as an indispensable component of the study of society, many subdisciplinary practitioners perceive themselves as participating in the preservation and protection of a vital part of the classical heritage.

The influence of the classics on the contemporary sociology of religion is not rhetoric but reality, a fact which even the most cursory examination of textbooks, journals, and professional publications can confirm. The founding fathers, especially Durkheim and Weber, loom large in all areas of this enterprise, either as the focus of investigation and interpretation or the inspiration for theoretical, methodological, and empirical explorations. Naturally, this circumstance is not cause for universal celebration. Some sociologists of religion view it with emotions ranging from vague unease to unremitting hostility, and their displeasure and frustration erupt in periodic calls for the subdiscipline to emerge from its tutelage, forget the founding fathers, and finally transcend the classics (Glock and Hammond 1973:409–18, Hammond 1985:1–6). Thus, while in some respects the classical legacy represents a source of subdisciplinary unity, it is also undoubtedly a source of serious tension and division.

For their defenders, classic texts remain repositories of intellectual riches worthy of continual revisitation and reinterpretation. Retaining a privileged status and authority deriving from their intrinsic and extrinsic utility, they are apprehended as apparently inexhaustible sources of ideas, perspectives, hypotheses, insights, and information which also provide perennial models of theoretical and methodological sophistication, subtlety, and ingenuity for successive generations of scholars. Some of those who resent, resist, and contest the persistence of the classics do so on the grounds that many of their theoretical formulations, factual descriptions, and empirical propositions have been erroneous since their inception. Others, however, concede the past validity of much of their content while denying its contemporary cogency. Most subdisciplinary appeals for movement beyond the classics tend to be in the latter category, essentially regarding the writings of the founding fathers as outdated and their ideas as now exhausted and irrelevant. Such a judgment can, of course, originate in a strongly held cumulative conception of scientific development or it may merely derive from a broad intuition that society has outpaced and evolved beyond the reach of nineteenth-century sociology. Both approaches possess considerable current theoretical significance. The former demands the construction of deductive theories, while the latter requires the repudiation and replacement of century-old concepts, categories, and theories perceived as appropriate to the analysis of industrial society but inadequate to the depiction, examination, and interpretation of contemporary realities (Stark 1997, Stark and Bainbridge 1985, Beckford 1992).

It is worthy of note that, within the sociology of religion, critiques of the persisting presence of the classics are empiricist rather than historicist in nature. Perhaps surprisingly in a subdiscipline attuned to the importance of texts, hermeneutics, and written authority, the contextualist and intentionalist assault on the nature of the classical canon has made little headway. This fact indicates a pronounced subdisciplinary commitment to the utility of the classics and an accompanying mistrust of activities which suggest either hero worship or antiquarianism. It also underscores the irredeemably presentist character of the subdisciplinary commitment to the classics.

Though the privileged role of the founding fathers undoubtedly incorporates an element of hero worship, this is coupled in the sociology of religion with such conspicuously utilitarian and presentist attitudes to classic texts that the scholarly Olympians are brought firmly down to earth. In theological terms, the classics are decidedly immanent rather than transcendent. Permeating both explicit theorizing and routine subdisciplinary conversation, they evoke a curious combination of reverence and routine which can be compared to the contemporary way in which religion appears less as an institutional source of authority than as a cultural resource to be drawn upon as required (Beckford 1992:170–1). In such circumstances, the practice of conversing with classic writers as if they are contemporaries is widely observed.

Among sociologists of religion, there are those who regard themselves as explicitly working in the tradition of a particular classic thinker and who are proud to define themselves as, for example, Durkheimians, Weberians, or Marxists. These, however, represent only a minority. The typical subdisciplinary practitioner demonstrates a diffuse, tolerant, and selective respect for the classics while resisting unreserved embrace of any particular perspective. This does not indicate any widespread espousal of explicit theories of classic intellectual convergence as much as it suggests the individually idiosyncratic quality of subdisciplinary commitment to the ambiguous legacy of the founding fathers and the evolving composition of the classical canon itself.

While rooted firmly in the sheer magnitude and quality of its achievements, the capacity of the classical heritage to nurture and provoke new scholarly developments in the sociology of religion derives, in large measure, from its fundamental ambiguity. This, in turn, is the result of disagreements and conflicts among the various classic authors, inconsistencies and contradictions among and within the texts of each individual author and, ultimately, the range of influential readings of those texts available to scholars at any given time. Thus, individually and collectively, the classics prominent in the sociology of religion contain a surplus of meaning and exhibit an open-endedness in the same way as the great books of the Western humanities tradition. Resoundingly multivocal, they display a propensity to sustain the most penetrating forms of exegesis and the widest varieties of interpretation, all of which may, in principle, be conscripted for use in subdisciplinary discussion, dialogue, and debate (O'Toole 1984, Alexander 1987:50–2, Levine 1985b, 1995).

Any doubts about the degree of ambiguity and open-endedness evident in classic texts may be laid to rest by perusal of the vast interpretive and critical literature generated by those twin pillars of the subdisciplinary canon, *The Protestant Ethic and the Spirit of Capitalism* (Weber 1958) and *The Elementary Forms of the Religious Life* (Durkheim 1961). Nearly a century after their initial appearance, these works continue to incite fervent arguments over fundamental theoretical and methodological issues as well as providing battlegrounds for rival explications and interpretations of their meaning. Indeed, there can be no more conspicuous case of radically opposed textual interpretations than the rival materialist and idealist versions of Durkheim's central thesis (O'Toole 1984:194–202). In the former reading, which forms a foundation for the perspectives of symbolic reductionism and metaphoric parallelism, Durkheim seems to agree with Marx that social being determines consciousness. In the latter construal, which inspires the theoretical approach of symbolic realism, a completely contradictory conclusion is drawn and Durkheim is understood to reverse Marx's formula entirely (Bellah 1967, 1970, Swanson 1964, Winter 1973, Bottomore 1981:913, Evans-Pritchard 1965:77). If, as Mills suggests, "a distinguishing mark of the classic is that it is subject to a variety of interpretations" (1960:2), Durkheim's seminal analysis of religion manifestly deserves its place of honor in the classical canon, a point reinforced by periodic scholarly revisits which elucidate its ambiguities from various angles (Parsons 1973, 1981, Jones 1977, Tiryakian 1981).

The extent to which the classics are regarded by sociologists as a resource, rather than a social-scientific form of holy writ, may be inferred from changes within the canon during the past half-century. Informal collective memory, even over one or two generations, is often a poor guide in this setting as relatively new elements rapidly acquire a hoary and hallowed character during the subdisciplinary invention of tradition (Halbwachs 1980, 1992, Hobsbawm and Ranger 1983). Thus, although Weber and Durkheim have constituted a continuous presence since the professional launching of the subdiscipline, having ascended by virtue of Parsonian canonization, it is sobering to note that few anglophone sociological writings on religion more than 50 years old are indebted to these figures (Beckford 1990:46, 1992:42–9). Again, though few practitioners would now contemplate Marx's exclusion from the canon, the freshness of his admission is noteworthy. A presence in the subdiscipline only since the decline of functionalism and the rise of "conflict sociology" in the discipline as a whole, he still remains a somewhat marginal figure in the pantheon (O'Toole 1984:188–94,

Marx and Engels 1958, Beckford 1991). Few practitioners describe themselves explicitly as Marxists but a number of Marx's ideas are certainly employed by less theoretically committed scholars in a variety of settings.

Three or four decades ago, in the heyday of obsession with church–sect typologies, it was impossible for a practicing sociologist of religion to ignore the writings of Troeltsch (1931) and Niebuhr (1957) which undoubtedly consti-tuted a central part of the subdisciplinary classical canon (Steeman 1984, Eister 1973, Beckford 1992:35–8, 54–5). The situation is very different today. Niebuhr is unread and largely unknown to younger scholars. Troeltsch is better known but little read, though significantly what is now read is what was mostly neglected at the time of his greatest influence. Thus, underlining a conception of classics as resources utilized in the solution of contemporary issues, a preoc-cupation with his analysis of church and sect has been succeeded by a more timely interest in his exploration of mysticism (Garrett 1975, Paul ⋅1993:677–8).

Despite his classic status in the discipline as a whole, and notwithstanding the fact that he wrote extensively on religious matters, Simmel has been accorded little attention within the sociology of religion until very recently. Current concern with the autonomization, individualization, and privatization of reli-gion has, however, prompted a notable interest in his difficult but illuminating religious writings published at the dawn of the twentieth century (Simmel 1997, Cipriani 1998). If sustained, such interest might significantly enhance his sub-disciplinary status in the next century, possibly at the expense of Marx.

The case of Simmel highlights an interesting phenomenon: the tendency of sociologists of religion, when faced with new theoretical, methodological, or empirical problems, to seek solutions in the familiar classics, and if this fails, to turn to classics from the broader disciplinary canon. Thus, just as Simmel has attracted attention among scholars concerned with the more individual and private aspects of religion, so a recent surge of interest in "rational-choice" theory in a religious context has led to a flurry of interest in Tocqueville and a novel subdisciplinary fascination with Adam Smith as a truly classic thinker (Tocqueville 1946, Smith 1937, Young 1997, Finke and Stark 1992, Stark and Bainbridge 1996, Iannaccone 1991).

The extent to which the classical canon is a product of contemporary needs through which scholars, in a sense, create their own predecessors, supports the suspicion that a subdisciplinary sense of a direct bond to the founding fathers is a cultural fiction emanating from a mythological narrative (Camic 1992, Manguel 1998). Thus, any doubts that "continuity between the classics of soci-ology and the modern sociology of religion is really as strong as has been claimed" are intensified by contemplation of the long "interval that separated the classical works of sociology from their widespread application in the study of religion." It is also undoubtedly true that, at least until recently, the subdisci-pline has "mainly pursued a limited range of topics" largely determined by modes of assimilation of the classics into "synthetic, all-purpose theories of industrial society" (Beckford 1992:43, 45, 48). Acknowledgement of all this, however, by no means negates the notion of the central importance of the classics in the contemporary activities of the subdiscipline. The fact remains that, whether or not they are bemused by myth or confused about their kinship to the founding fathers, many practitioners of the sociology of religion view the classic texts as the charter documents of their enterprise, hold them in the highest esteem, incorporate their ideas into current scholarship, and continue to find inspiration in their myriad meanings. Though this situation might be cause for dismay in intentionalist and other circles, it seems entirely consistent with a prevailing presentist perspective on the classics, as well as with functionalist accounts of their role in the generation and facilitation of scholarly discussion.

Whether diffuse or specific, formal or informal, the continuing sway of the classics over the sociology of religion appears undeniable. Thus, rightly or wrongly, a significant number of scholars believe that their work has been inspired by conversation with the classics while others assert their conscious effort to emulate, however imperfectly, the qualities they discern in classical writings. Though specific canonical influences may always be detected in explicit scholarly contexts, the commanding presence of the classics as a whole is most evident in the degree to which the broad theoretical and methodological ideas which animate the subdiscipline, together with the prime topics of scholarly interest, are infused with insights, examples, and arguments extracted from the writings of the founding fathers.

The ideas of Durkheim and Weber, in particular, are interwoven throughout every major discussion of every significant issue in a way which makes it virtually impossible for dialogue to be conducted without constant reference to their writings. Durkheim's influence, for example, is most prominent in discussions of myth, ritual, and civil religion while Weber's presence is felt in debates over a wide range of diverse topics such as sectarianism, prophecy, mysticism, and religious leadership (Durkheim 1961, Weber 1963, O'Toole 1984). In addition, no comparative discussion of issues such as religious authority, organization, institutionalization, stratification, and professionalization is likely to proceed far without recourse to Weber's analytical and documentary treasury (Kurtz 1995, Hamilton 1998a). Even debates over currently resonant topics such as New Religious Movements, Pentecostalism, or the New Age movement intermittently and inevitably incorporate insights from either Durkheim or Weber or both (Westley 1978, Barker 1993, Roelofs 1994, Heelas 1996). Their broadest influence on the subdiscipline, however, may be discerned within both the perennial definitional discussion and the dogged debate over secularization which has underlain and intersected conversation on every topic in recent decades. A brief exploration of these areas offers insight into the role of the classics in the sociology of religion by underscoring their ambiguity, equivocality, and open-endedness as intellectual resources.

The failure of sociologists of religion to agree upon a basic definition of their subject matter is for many subdisciplinary practitioners, especially those of positivistic orientation, a matter of shame and regret. For others of a more humanistic bent, however, this is an inevitable and acceptable aspect of scholarly conversation which in no way precludes fruitful dialogue and intellectual progress. Whatever their individual preferences, individual practitioners are aware that the work of their subdiscipline proceeds on the basis of a variety of functional and substantive definitions. In this, as in other lesser areas of dispute, they are compelled to agree to disagree, forging a professional unity out of their diversity (O'Toole 1984:10–51, Levine 1995, Merton 1977:viii).

In this situation, the role of the classics has been, and remains, significant. Weber's famous (or infamous) refusal to define religion at the outset of his researches (Weber 1963:1) is still invoked by advocates of definitional flexibility, and assailed by proponents of analytical exactitude. Whereas Weber's strategy is thus "open-ended" in the extreme, Durkheim's definitional formulation appears, on the surface at least, to be characteristically clear and precise. In fact, however, its attempt at universality, its functional character and, in particular, its depiction of the sacred, render it extremely inclusive in its application (Durkheim 1961:62, 257). For better or worse, subdisciplinary definitional dialogue has a tendency to begin with Durkheim and Weber, depicting them as functionalist allies in the struggle against substantive definitions in the Tylorian tradition (Tylor 1871:383, Horton 1960, 1968). In this way, for example, Luckmann (1967) draws primarily on Weber for his concept of "invisible religion" (perhaps the most open-ended definition available) and Bellah (1967, 1970) utilizes Durkheim in developing his themes of civil religion and symbolic realism. Such an emphasis has encouraged a general subdisciplinary distancing from "common-sense" or ordinary-language religious referents and this has contributed to the typically elusive, ambiguous, and inconclusive character of arguments about the most appropriate way of defining religion.

Acknowledgement of the deep disagreement which surrounds even this most fundamental concept in the subdiscipline is a reminder of Alexander's (1987) depiction of the sociological conversation as discourse, and his detection of its resistance to simple agreement on empirical referents, to say nothing of explanatory covering laws. If Alexander is correct, continuance of endemic disagreement concerning the nature of religion is likely to require the continued presence of the classics as permanent reference points in what is frequently an oscillating and cyclical debate.

The debate over secularization is, of course, inextricably linked to the problem of defining religion, in that the empirical absence or presence of this process is logically dependent upon the specific definition of religion in use. Thus, for example, secularization may be clearly discerned when a narrow substantivist definition of religion is applied only to disappear when a broad functional definition is substituted. One scholar has, in fact, applied the stage conjuror's formula "now you see it, now you don't!" to this aspect of the study of secularization (Hamilton 1998b). Participants in various phases of the ongoing subdisciplinary debate of the last three decades have frequently expressed their frustration over its inconclusive and interminable character. Arguments proceed at cross-purposes as rival definitions become entwined and indisputable facts are accorded entirely contradictory interpretations. The result is that few minds are changed, little clarification of the issue is achieved and, once again, disciplinary practitioners must be content to agree to disagree. In these circumstances, even the best-conceived and most carefully crafted efforts to clarify the parameters of debate and coordinate dialogue seem destined to end in disarray and confusion. Recalling again Alexander's notion of discourse as involving "modes of argument which are more consistently generalized and speculative than are normal scientific discussions" (1987:22) the secularization debate seems to offer a prime case in which "empirical underdetermination and theoretical overdetermination go hand in hand." After close scrutiny of the secularization debate, many observers would be inclined to agree that "from the most specific factual statements up to the most abstract generalizations, social science is essentially contestable," every conclusion being "open to argument by supra-empirical considerations" (Alexander 1987:25, Hammond 1985, Bruce 1992, Martin 1991, 1995, Wilson 1975, 1992, 1998, Hadden 1987).

These, of course, are ideal conditions, in Alexander's terms, for recourse to the classics as guideposts through the maze. Not surprisingly, therefore, the secularization debate is framed according to perceived classical agenda and is thus replete with classical referents marshaled by both defenders and opponents of the secularization thesis. In these circumstances, the extent to which this thesis is a part of the classical inheritance merits investigation. There is no doubt that many proponents of the thesis perceive it as inherited in this way and, in their support, offer an entirely plausible reading of Marx, Durkheim, and Weber (Wilson 1985, Wallis and Bruce 1989, 1992). A number of opponents of the thesis concur with this reading of the classics but cite selected empirical evidence to demonstrate the falsity of the secularization argument in both its classic and contemporary formulations (Hammond 1985:1–6). For some opponents of this sort, indeed, firm rejection of the secularization thesis seems to supply a convenient and strategic means of expressing a more fundamental and strongly felt hostility to the persistence of the classics. Other critics of the thesis, however, base their opposition specifically on the classics. Proposing a radically different reading of Durkheim and Weber in particular (with due recognition of Comte and Saint Simon), they reject the implication that the errors and misconceptions of what they regard as a misguided perspective can ultimately be blamed on the classic legacy (Thompson 1990a, 1990b, 1993).

It is possible that at least some of those proponents or opponents who see the secularization thesis as a central part of the classic legacy have been swayed by subdisciplinary mythology. As a minority secularist influence in the subdiscipline (though by no means an unambiguous one), Marx has been relevant for little more than a quarter-century, having been decisively excluded from the Parsonian canon (Parsons 1944, 1968). Granted the Parsonian imprimatur, Durkheim and Weber have loomed large in the subdiscipline since its earliest days but by no means primarily as secularization theorists. It is certainly noteworthy that Parsons, whose exegeses of Durkheim and Weber have made an indelible mark on the subdiscipline, was far from being an advocate of the secularization thesis. This is clearly evident, for example, in his writings on contemporary Christianity (Parsons 1960, 1963, Beckford 1992:60–3). Thus, in the 1950s and 1960s, sociologists of religion were inclined to follow Parsons' reading of the classics and contemplate, in Durkheimian terms, the eternal functional character of religion. Only later were they attracted to what many of its opponents regard as the "secularization myth" (Luckmann 1983, Lyon 1985).

To indicate these historical aspects of the subdisciplinary canon is to emphasize the fact that the role of the classics in the secularization thesis is often exaggerated and oversimplified because of a failure to appreciate the ambiguous and multivalent character of classic texts. In its most recent phase, the debate over secularization, together with significant related arguments concerning the emergence of a "new paradigm" in the sociology of religion, confirms the importance of this insight (Warner 1993, 1997a, 1997b, Hadden 1995, Lechner 1997). Thus, one of the effects of attempting to view the secularization thesis in terms of a Kuhnian paradigm has been to reveal its diversity and to challenge that belief in its firm grounding in the classics which has been held by so many for so long. Whether it is accurate to speak of a "new paradigm" and an "old paradigm" or whether, indeed, it is legitimate to use the term at all in a social-scientific context, its currency raises the thorny issue of the possibility of genuine cumulative knowledge within the subdiscipline (Eckberg and Hill 1979, Green 1977, Jones 1983:122–6, Gans 1992, Alexander 1987:20). It is hardly surprising, therefore, that among the most vigorous opponents of the secularization thesis are rational-choice theorists whose major goal in the forging of a new paradigm is to ground future disciplinary dialogue in scientific deductive theory (Stark 1997, Stark and Bainbridge 1996, Iannacone 1997). To the extent that the battle for deductive theory is a challenge both to discourse and the classics, it is appropriate to consider briefly the tenacity of their presence in the ongoing secularization debate as an indication of their current role. In this regard, there seems little doubt that within the subdisciplinary arena where attempts at deductive theorizing have recently made the greatest strides, a discursive form of argument with a strong classical component continues to prevail (Lechner 1997, Spickard 1998, Beyer 1998). The continuing stridency and proselytizing character of some rational-choice scholarship offers, perhaps, an indirect indication of this.

In recent years, the framework of the secularization debate has shifted significantly, and few would doubt that progress has occurred both in theoretical clarification and empirical documentation. Most notably, the balance of subdisciplinary opinion appears to have altered in such a way that proponents of the secularization thesis are decidedly on the defensive (Hadden 1987, 1995, Martin 1991, 1995, Wilson 1992, 1998, Thompson 1990b). However, in its essentially ratiocinative, noncumulative and inconclusive form, discussion of this issue has apparently retained the character of discourse as outlined by Alexander. It exhibits a generalized, speculative, persuasive and nonempirical quality in which clear, indisputable referents are rare and the propensity to operationalize propo-

sitions in a variety of different ways discourages definitive conclusions while perpetuating empirical and theoretical dissensus.

So far, all attempts to establish the plain and evident truth of this matter have
been unsuccessful. Having failed to achieve consensus around secularization
theory, its proponents must now ward off a growing opposition. Bloody but
unbowed, they continue to refine their perspective while condemning their opponents' arguments as logically incoherent, interpretively uninsightful, empirically dubious and theoretically confused. The proclamation of a new paradigm,
moreover, seems most unlikely to dampen debate. Attempts to characterize this
new subdisciplinary orientation and its relevance to the secularization issue
have already provoked an unrepentant, articulate, and highly critical response
(Tschannen 1991, Lechner 1991, 1997, Wilson 1992, 1998, Demerath 1995,
1998, Bruce 1996:25–68).

The prevalence of discourse implies a persistence of the classics, and in this
current debate there is no sign of their departure. Most conspicuously, the best-
known blueprint for the new paradigm explicitly indicates its grounding in specific classic texts. Thus, whereas the old paradigm was apparently rooted in a
reading of Weber's *Protestant Ethic* and Durkheim's *Division of Labor*, the perceived paradigm shift has resulted in inspiration now being drawn from Weber's
essay on the "Protestant Sects" and Durkheim's *Elementary Forms* (Warner
1993:1052). Finally, in a recent exchange focused on the significance of secularization processes, the close links between the secularization and definitional
debates and between discourse and the classics are succinctly and clearly articulated. Chiding proponents of the secularization thesis who discern "the apparent disappearance of large sections of (subdisciplinary) subject-matter,"
Kenneth Thompson condemns them for clinging to a "supernaturalist" and substantive definition of religion. Prescribing a classical antidote in the form of
Durkheim's theory of the sacred, he reminds his opponents that "for those who
follow the Durkheimian approach, their subject-matter does not decline but is
constantly reproduced, even if transformed" (Thompson 1990a:533–4, Wallis
and Bruce 1989, Luckmann 1991:169–70). Thus, by stressing the degree to
which the perception of secularization is dependent on definitional predilection,
he also emphasizes the continuing role of the classics as a fundamental resource
in the subdisciplinary conceptualization of religion.

Conclusion

Exploration of the role of the classics in current disciplinary and subdisciplinary
contexts is remarkably revealing in the light it sheds on the present nature of the
sociological enterprise. The fact that the classics are, and seem likely to remain,
a persisting presence on the sociological scene, is a matter of some significance
which has inevitably evoked rival interpretations and explanations. For those
espousing a cumulative conception of sociology and dedicated to a divorce

between history and systematic theory, continuing resort to the classics is essentially an indication of their discipline's failure to live up to its scientific expectations. For others, influenced by more recent conceptions of the characteristic role of ambiguity, dialogue, and discourse in sociological conversation, the continuing centrality of the classics is as desirable as it is inevitable. In the former case the classics represent the burden of the past, while in the latter they constitute resources for the present and the future.

The present discussion has been sympathetic to the latter conception and has accordingly attempted to apply some of its insights in the context of the sociology of religion. As befits a subject which, in some senses at least, is "at the heart of classical sociological theory"(Wilson 1982:9), the classics clearly remain a commanding subdisciplinary presence. Though their influence is far more multivalent than is often recognized, it is arguable that they represent the main means by which sociologists of religion come to know "what is central as opposed to peripheral, what is superficial as opposed to what is latent, what is material as opposed to a matter of appearance alone" (Fenn 1982:124). To acknowledge the current subdisciplinary centrality of the classics and the likelihood of its continuance in the future is not, of course, to regard the writings of the founding fathers as eternal and infallible sociological guides. It may be that emerging developments will render religion "sociologically problematic in ways that are virtually inconceivable in terms of the sociological classics" (Beckford 1992:172). It may also be necessary, as already indicated in the present discussion, for sociologists "to detach themselves from their own mythology in the future in order more clearly to assess the realities of the world around them" (Fenn 1982:125). None the less, it would be unwise to underestimate the capacity of the classics to generate novel interpretations and provoke fresh insights in the twenty-first century. For good or ill, the admonition that the "Twilight of the Classics" is at hand still carries less conviction than the proposition that "the future of sociology lies as much in its past as in the present" (Lukes 1966:203).

References

Alexander, J.C. 1987. "The Centrality of the Classics," in *Social Theory Today*, Eds. A. Giddens and J. Turner. Stanford, CA: Stanford University Press, pp. 11–57.

Alexander, J.C., Ed. 1988. *Durkheimian Sociology: Cultural Studies*. Cambridge and New York: Cambridge University Press.

Barker, E. 1993. "Charismatization: the Social Production of an Ethos Propitious to the Mobilization of Sentiments," in *Secularization, Rationalism and Sectarianism*, Eds. E. Barker, J.A. Beckford, and K. Dobbelaere. Oxford: Clarendon Press, pp. 181–201.

Becker, H.S. 1979. "What's happening to sociology?" *Society* 16(5):19–24.

Beckford, J.A. 1990. "The Sociology of Religion 1945–1989," *Social Compass* 37(1):45–64.

Beckford, J.A. 1991. "Quasi-Marxisms and the Sociology of Religion," in *Religion and the Social Order: New Developments in Theory and Research*, vol. 1, Ed. D.G. Bromley. Greenwich CT: JAI Press, pp. 17–35.

Beckford, J.A. 1992. *Religion and Advanced Industrial Society*. London and New York: Routledge.

Bellah, R.N. 1967. "Civil Religion in America," *Daedalus* 96:1–21.

Bellah, R.N. 1970. "Christianity and Symbolic Realism," *Journal for the Scientific Study of Religion* 9:89–96.

Beyer, P. 1998. "Sociological Theory of Religion between Description and Prediction: A Weberian Question Revisited," in *Secularization and Social Integration*, Eds. R. Laermans, B. Wilson, and J. Billiet. Leuven/Louvain: Leuven University Press, pp. 83–105.

Bloom, H. 1994. *The Western Canon*. New York, San Diego, London: Harcourt Brace.

Bottomore, T. 1981. "A Marxist Consideration of Durkheim," *Social Forces* 59:902–17.

Bruce, S., Ed. 1992. *Religion and Modernization: Sociologists and Historians Debate the Secularization Thesis*. Oxford: Clarendon Press.

Bruce, S. 1996. *Religion in the Modern World*. Oxford and New York: Oxford University Press.

Calhoun, C. 1996. "Whose Classics? Which Readings? Interpretation and Cultural Difference in the Canonization of Sociological Theory," in *Social Theory and Sociology*, Ed. S.P. Turner. Oxford and Cambridge, MA: Blackwell, pp. 70–96.

Calvino, I. 1986. "Why Read the Classics?" in *The Uses of Literature: Essays*, Transl. P. Creagh. San Diego, New York, London: Harcourt Brace Jovanovich, pp. 125–34.

Camic, C. 1992. "Reputation and Predecessor Selection: Parsons and the Institutionalists," *American Sociological Review* 57:421–44.

Cipriani, R. 1998. "Sociology and Religion: Durkheim and Simmel," in *Secularization and Social Integration*, Eds. R. Laermans, B. Wilson, and J. Billiet. Leuven/Louvain: Leuven University Press, pp. 37–43.

Collins, R. 1986. *Weberian Sociological Theory*. Cambridge and New York: Cambridge University Press.

Collins, R. 1994. *Four Sociological Traditions*. New York and Oxford: Oxford University Press.

Coser, L.A. 1977. *Masters of Sociological Thought: Ideas in Historical and Social Context*. San Diego, CA: Harcourt Brace Jovanovich.

Coser, L.A. 1981. "The Uses of Classical Sociological Theory," in *The Future of the Sociological Classics*, Ed. B. Rhea. London: George Allen & Unwin, pp. 170–82.

Davis, M.S. 1971. "That's Interesting! Towards a Phenomenology of Sociology and a Sociology of Phenomenology," *Philosophy of the Social Sciences* 1:309–44.

Davis, M.S. 1986. "'That's Classic!' The Phenomenology and Rhetoric of Successful Social Theories," *Philosophy of the Social Sciences* 16:285–301.

Demerath, N.J. 1995. "Rational Paradigms, A-Rational Religion and the Debate Over Secularization," *Journal for the Scientific Study of Religion* 34(1):105–12.

Demerath, N.J. 1998. "Secularization Disproved or Displaced?" in *Secularization and Social Integration*, Eds. R. Laermans, B. Wilson, and J. Billiet. Leuven/Louvain: Leuven University Press, pp. 37–43.

Durkheim, E. 1961. *The Elementary Forms of the Religious Life*, Transl. N.W. Swain. New York: Collier.

Eckberg, D.L. and Hill, L. 1979. "The Paradigm Concept and Sociology: A Critical Review," *American Sociological Review* 44:925–37.

Eister, A.W. 1973. "H. Richard Niebuhr and the Paradox of Religious Organization," in *Beyond the Classics?*, Eds. C.Y. Glock and P.E. Hammond. New York: Harper and Row, pp. 355–402.

Eliot, T.S. 1945. *What is a Classic?* London: Faber and Faber.

Evans-Pritchard, E.E. 1965. *Theories of Primitive Religion*. Oxford: Clarendon Press.

Fenn, R.K. 1982. "The Sociology of Religion: A Critical Survey," in *Sociology: The State of the Art*," Eds. T. Bottomore, S. Nowak, and M. Sokolowska. London and Beverly Hills: Sage, pp. 101–27.

Finke, R. and Stark, R. 1992. *The Churching of America: 1776–1990*. New Brunswick, NJ: Rutgers University Press.

Foucault, M. 1970. *The Order of Things: The Archaeology of the Human Sciences*. London: Tavistock.

Freese, L. 1972. "Cumulative Sociological Knowledge," *American Sociological Review* 37:472–82.

Gans, H.J. 1992. "Sociological Amnesia: The Noncumulation of Normal Social Science," *Sociological Forum* 7(4):701–10.

Garrett, W.R. 1975. "Maligned Mysticism: The Maledicted Career of Troeltsch's Third Type," *Sociological Analysis* 36:205–23.

Gellner, E. 1985. *Relativism and the Social Sciences*. Cambridge: Cambridge University Press.

Giddens, A. 1976. "Classical Sociological Theory and the Origins of Modern Sociology," *American Journal of Sociology* 81(4):703–29.

Giddens, A. 1987. "Nine Theses on the Future of Sociology," in *Social Theory and Modern Sociology*. Stanford, CA: Stanford University Press, pp. 22–51.

Glock, C.Y. and Hammond, P.E., Eds. 1973. *Beyond the Classics? Essays in the Scientific Study of Religion*. New York: Harper & Row.

Gouldner, A. 1958. "Introduction," in E. Durkheim, *Socialism and Saint-Simon*. Yellow Springs, OH: Antioch Press.

Green, B.S.R. 1977. "On the Evaluation of Sociological Theory," *Philosophy of the Social Sciences* 7:33–50.

Habermas, J. 1984. *Reason and the Rationalization of Society*, Transl. T. McCarthy. Boston: Beacon Press.

Hacker, A. 1954. "Capital and Carbuncles: The 'Great Books' Reappraised," *American Political Science Review* 48(3):775–86.

Hadden, J.K. 1987. "Toward Desacralizing Secularization Theory," *Social Forces* 65(3):587–611.

Hadden, J.K. 1995. "Religion and the Quest for Meaning and Order: Old Paradigms, New Realities," *Sociological Focus* 28(1):83–100.

Halbwachs, M. 1980. *The Collective Memory*, Transl. F.J. and V.Y. Ditter. New York: Harper & Row.

Halbwachs, M. 1992. *On Collective Memory*, ed. and transl. L.A. Coser. Chicago: University of Chicago Press.

Hamilton, M.B. 1998a. *Sociology and the World's Religions*. London: Macmillan.

Hamilton, M.B. 1998b. "Secularization: Now You See It, Now You Don't," *Sociology Review* 7(4):27–31.

Hammond, P.E., Ed. 1985. *The Sacred in a Secular Age: Toward Revision in the Scientific Study of Religion*. Berkeley, Los Angeles, London: University of California Press.

Hawthorn, G. 1976. *Enlightenment and Despair*. Cambridge: Cambridge University Press.

Heelas, P. 1996. *The New Age Movement: The Celebration of the Self and the Sacralization of Modernity*. Oxford and Cambridge, MA: Blackwell.

Hobsbawm, E. and Ranger, T., Eds. 1983. *The Invention of Tradition*. Cambridge: Cambridge University Press.

Holton, R.J. 1996. "Classical Social Theory," in *The Blackwell Companion to Social Theory*, Ed. B.S. Turner. Oxford and Malden, MA: Blackwell, pp. 25–52.

Hook, S. 1955. *Marx and the Marxists: The Ambiguous Legacy*. New York: Van Nostrand.

Horton, R. 1960. "A Definition of Religion and its Uses," *Journal of the Royal Anthropological Institute* 90:201–26.

Horton, R. 1968. "Neo-Tylorianism: Sound Sense or Sinister Prejudice?" *Man: The Journal of the Royal Anthropological Institute* 3:625–34.

Iannaccone, L.R. 1991. "The Consequences of Religious Market Structure," *Rationality and Society* 3:156–77.

Iannaccone, L.R. 1997. "Rational Choice: Framework for the Scientific Study of Religion," in *Rational Choice Theory and Religion*, Ed. L.A. Young. New York and London: Routledge, pp. 25–44.

Johnson, H.M. 1978. "Comment on Jones's 'On Understanding a Sociological Classic'," *American Journal of Sociology* 84(1):171–5.

Jones, R.A. 1977. "On Understanding a Sociological Classic," *American Journal of Sociology* 83(2):279–319.

Jones, R.A. 1978. "Subjectivity, Objectivity, and Historicity: A Reply to Johnson," *American Journal of Sociology* 84(1):175–81.

Jones, R.A. 1980. "Myth and Symbol Among the Nacirema Tsigoloicos: A Fragment," *American Sociologist* 15:207–12.

Jones, R.A. 1983. "On Merton's 'History' and 'Systematics' of Sociological Theory," in *Functions and Uses of Disciplinary Histories*, vol. 7, Eds. L. Graham, W. Lepenies, and P. Weingart. Dordrecht, Boston, London: Reidel, pp. 121–42.

Jones, R.A. 1986. *Emile Durkheim: An Introduction to Four Major Works*. Beverly Hills, CA: Sage.

Kermode, F. 1975. *The Classic*. New York: Viking.

Kuhn, T. 1970. *The Structure of Scientific Revolutions*. Chicago: University of Chicago Press.

Kurtz, L. 1995. *Gods in the Global Village: The World's Religions in Sociological Perspective*. Thousand Oaks, CA, London, New Delhi: Pine Forge Press.

LaCapra, D. 1982. "Rethinking Intellectual History and Reading Texts,"in *Modern European Intellectual History: Reappraisals and New Perspectives*, Eds. D. LaCapra and S.L. Kaplan. Ithaca, NY and London: Cornell University Press, pp. 47–85.

Lechner, F.J. 1991. "The Case Against Secularization: A Rebuttal," *Social Forces* 69:1103–19.

Lechner, F.J. 1997. "The 'New Paradigm' in the Sociology of Religion: Comment on Warner," *American Journal of Sociology* 103(1):182–92.

Lepenies, W. 1988. *Between Literature and Science: The Rise of Sociology*. Cambridge: Cambridge University Press.

Levin, M. 1973. "What Makes a Classic in Political Theory?" *Political Science Quarterly* 88(3):462–76.

Levine, D.N. 1985a. "On the Heritage of Sociology," in *The Challenge of Social Control*, Eds. G.D. Suttles and M.N. Zald. Norwood NJ: Ablex, pp. 13–19.

Levine, D.N. 1985b. *The Flight from Ambiguity*. Chicago and London: University of Chicago Press.

Levine, D.N. 1995. *Visions of the Sociological Tradition*. Chicago and London: University of Chicago Press.

Luckmann, T. 1967. *The Invisible Religion: The Problem of Religion in Modern Society.* New York: Macmillan.

Luckmann, T. 1983. "Secularization – a Contemporary Myth," in T. Luckmann, *Life-World and Social Realities.* London: Heinemann, pp. 124–32.

Luckmann, T. 1991. "The New and the Old in Religion," in *Social Theory for a Changing Society,* Eds. P. Bourdieu and J.S. Coleman. Boulder, San Francisco, Oxford: Westview Press, pp. 167–88.

Lukes, S. 1966. "On the History of Sociological Theory," *British Journal of Sociology* 17:198–203.

Lyon, D. 1985. *The Steeple's Shadow: On the Myths and Realities of Secularization.* London: SPCK.

Manguel, A. 1998. "Review of J.L. Borges, Collected Fictions," *Toronto Globe and Mail,* October 17:D9.

Martin, D. 1991. "The Secularization Issue: Prospect and Retrospect," *British Journal of Sociology* 42(3):465–74.

Martin, D. 1995. "Sociology, Religion and Secularization: An Orientation," *Religion* 25:295–303.

Marx, K. and Engels, F. 1958. *Marx and Engels on Religion.* Moscow: Foreign Languages Publishing House.

Merton, R.K. 1968. "On the History and Systematics of Sociological Theory," in *Social Theory and Social Structure.* New York: Free Press, pp. 1–38.

Merton, R.K. 1977. "Foreword," in L.A. Coser, *Masters of Sociological Thought: Ideas in Historical and Social Context.* San Diego, CA: Harcourt Brace Jovanovich, pp. vii–ix.

Mills, C.W. 1960. "Introduction: the Classic Tradition," Ed. C.W. Mills. *Images of Man.* New York: George Braziller, pp. 1–11.

Niebuhr, H.R. 1957. *The Social Sources of Denominationalism.* Cleveland, OH: World Publishing.

Nisbet, R. 1966. *The Sociological Tradition.* New York: Basic Books.

Orum, A.M. 1989. *Introduction to Political Sociology.* Englewood Cliffs, NJ: Prentice-Hall.

O'Toole, R. 1984. *Religion: Classic Sociological Approaches.* Toronto: McGraw-Hill Ryerson.

O'Toole, R. 1993. "Classical Statements on Religion and Society," in *The Sociology of Religion: A Canadian Focus,* Ed. W.E. Hewitt. Toronto: Butterworths, pp. 19–27.

Parsons, T. 1944. "The Theoretical Development of the Sociology of Religion," *Journal of the History of Ideas* 5:176–90.

Parsons, T. 1960. "Some Comments on the Pattern of Religious Organization in the United States," in *Structure and Process in Modern Society,* Ed. T. Parsons. New York: Free Press, pp. 295–321.

Parsons, T. 1963. "Christianity and Modern Industrial Society," in *Sociological Theory, Values and Sociocultural Change,* Ed. E. Tiryakian. New York: Harper and Row, pp. 33–70.

Parsons, T. 1968. *The Structure of Social Action.* Glencoe, IL: Free Press.

Parsons, T. 1973. "*Durkheim on Religion Revisited: Another Look at The Elementary Forms of the Religious Life,*" in *Beyond the Classics?* Eds. C.Y. Glock and P.E. Hammond. New York: Harper & Row, pp. 156–80.

Parsons, T. 1981. "Revisiting the Classics Throughout a Long Career," in *The Future of the Sociological Classics,* Ed. B. Rhea. London: George Allen and Unwin, pp. 183–94.

Paul, G.E. 1993. "Why Troeltsch? Why Today? Theology for the 21st Century," *Christian Century* 110:676–81.

Peel, J.D.Y. 1978. "Two Cheers for Empiricism; or, What is the Relevance of the History of Sociology to its Current Practice?" *Sociology* 12:347–59.

Poggi, G. 1972. *Images of Society*. Stanford, CA: Stanford University Press.

Poggi, G. 1996. "Lego Quia Inutile: An Alternative Justification for the Classics," in *Social Theory and Sociology*, Ed. S.P. Turner. Oxford and Cambridge, MA: Blackwell, pp. 39–47.

Rhea, B., Ed. 1981. *The Future of the Sociological Classics*. London: George Allen & Unwin.

Ricoeur, P. 1971. "The Model of the Text," *Social Research* 38:529–62.

Roelofs, G. 1994. "Charismatic Christian Thought: Experience, Metonymy and Routinization," in *Charismatic Christianity as a Global Culture*, Ed. K. Poewe. Columbia, SC: University of South Carolina Press, pp. 217–33.

Sherman, L.W. 1974. "Uses of the Masters," *American Sociologist* 9:176–81.

Shils, E. 1970. "Tradition, Ecology and Institution in the History of Sociology," *Daedalus* 99(4):760–825.

Simmel, G. 1997. *Essays on Religion*, Transl. H.J. Helle. New Haven and London: Yale University Press.

Skinner, Q. 1969. "Meaning and Understanding in the History of Ideas," *History and Theory* 8(1):3–53.

Smith, A. 1937. *An Inquiry into the Nature and Causes of the Wealth of Nations*. New York: Modern Library.

Spickard, J.V. 1998. "Rethinking Religious Social Action: What is 'Rational' about Rational-Choice Theory?" *Sociology of Religion* 59(2):99–115.

Stark, R. 1997. "Bringing Theory Back In," in *Rational Choice Theory and Religion*, Ed. L.A. Young. New York and London: Routledge, pp. 3–23.

Stark, R. and Bainbridge, W.S. 1985. *The Future of Religion*. Berkeley, Los Angeles, London: University of California Press.

Stark, R. and Bainbridge, W.S. 1996. *A Theory of Religion*. New Brunswick, NJ: Rutgers University Press.

Steeman, T.M. 1984. "Troeltsch and Modern American Religion," *Archives de Sciences Sociales des Religions* 58(1):85–116.

Stinchcombe, A.L. 1982. "Should Sociologists Forget Their Mothers and Fathers?" *American Sociologist* 17:2–11.

Swanson, G.E. 1964. *The Birth of the Gods*. Ann Arbor: University of Michigan Press.

Szacki, J. 1982. "The History of Sociology and Substantive Sociological Theories," in *Sociology: The State of the Art*, Eds. T. Bottomore, S. Novak, and M. Sokolowska. London and Beverly Hills: Sage, pp. 359–74.

Thompson, K. 1990a. "Religion: The British Contribution," *British Journal of Sociology* 41(4):531–5.

Thompson, K. 1990b. "Secularization and Sacralization," in *Rethinking Progress*, Eds. J.C. Alexander and P. Szompka. London: Unwin Hyman, pp. 161–81.

Thompson, K. 1993. "Durkheim, Ideology and the Sacred," *Social Compass* 40(3):451–61.

Tiryakian, E.A. 1981. "Durkheim's 'Elementary Forms' as 'Revelation'," in *The Future of the Sociological Classics*, Ed. B. Rhea. London: George Allen and Unwin, pp. 114–35.

Tocqueville, A.C. de. 1946. *Democracy in America* (2 vols.), Transl. H. Reeve and F. Bowen. New York: Alfred Knopf.

Troeltsch, E. 1931. *The Social Teaching of the Christian Churches* (2 vols.), Transl. O. Wyon. New York: Macmillan.

Tschannen, O. 1991. "The Secularization Paradigm: A Systematization," *Journal for the Scientific Study of Religion* 30:395–415.

Turner, J. 1986. "Review: the Theory of Structuration," *American Journal of Sociology* 91:969–77.

Turner, S.P. 1991. "Salvaging Sociology's Past," *A.S.A. Footnotes* 19(5&6):6.

Tylor, E. 1871. *Primitive Culture* (vol. 1). London: John Murray.

Wagner, D.G. and Berger, J. 1984. "Do Sociological Theories Grow?" *American Journal of Sociology* 90(4):697–728.

Wallace, R.A. and Wolf, A. 1999. *Contemporary Sociological Theory: Expanding the Classical Tradition*. Upper Saddle River, NJ: Prentice-Hall.

Wallerstein, I. 1991. *Unthinking Social Science: The Limits of Nineteenth-Century Paradigms*. Oxford: Polity Press.

Wallis, R. and Bruce, S. 1989. "Religion: The British Contribution," *British Journal of Sociology* 40(3):493–520.

Wallis, R. and Bruce, S. 1992. "Secularization: The Orthodox Model," in *Religion and Modernization*, Ed. S. Bruce. Oxford: Clarendon Press, pp. 8–30.

Warner, R.S. 1993. "Work in Progress Toward a New Paradigm for the Sociological Study of Religion in the United States," *American Journal of Sociology* 98(5):1044–93.

Warner, R.S. 1997a. "A Paradigm is Not a Theory. Reply to Lechner," *American Journal of Sociology* 103(1):192–8.

Warner, R.S. 1997b. "Convergence Toward the New Paradigm," in *Rational Choice Theory and Religion*, Ed. L.A. Young. New York and London: Routledge, pp. 87–101.

Weber, M. 1958. *The Protestant Ethic and the Spirit of Capitalism*, Transl. T. Parsons. New York: Scribner.

Weber, M. 1963. *The Sociology of Religion*, Transl. E. Fischoff. Boston: Beacon Press.

Westley, F. 1978. "'The Cult of Man': Durkheim's Predictions and New Religious Movements," *Sociological Analysis* 39:135–45.

Whitehead, A.N. 1917. *The Organization of Thought: Educational and Scientific*. London: Williams and Norgate.

Wilson, B.R. 1975. "The Debate Over 'Secularization'," *Encounter* 45(10):77–83.

Wilson, B.R. 1982. *Religion in Sociological Perspective*. Oxford: Oxford University Press.

Wilson, B.R. 1985. "Secularization: The Inherited Model," in *The Sacred in a Secular Age*, Ed. P.E. Hammond. Berkeley, Los Angeles, and London: University of California Press, pp. 9–20.

Wilson, B.R. 1992. "Reflections on a Many Sided Controversy," in *Religion and Modernization*, Ed. S. Bruce. Oxford: Clarendon Press, pp. 195–210.

Wilson, B.R. 1998. "The Secularization Thesis: Criticisms and Rebuttals," in *Secularization and Social Integration*, Eds. R. Laermans, B. Wilson, and J. Billiet. Leuven/Louvain: Leuven University Press, pp. 45–65.

Winter, J.A. 1973. "The Metaphoric Parallelist Approach to the Sociology of Theistic Beliefs," *Sociological Analysis* 34:212–29.

Young, L.A., Ed. 1997. *Rational Choice Theory and Religion: Summary and Assessment*. New York and London: Routledge.

CHAPTER 9

Individualism, the Validation of Faith, and the Social Nature of Religion in Modernity

Danièle Hervieu-Léger
Translation by Michael Davis

For a quarter of a century all descriptions of the religious situation in Western European and North American societies have presented the same established theme. On the one hand, it is observed that the cultural and political power of the mainline churches is diminished, as is their capacity to organize the symbolic life of society. In certain countries of northern Europe, it is a matter of the virtual collapse of mainline religion, a process that began two centuries ago. In other countries the phenomenon is quite recent and subtle. But the tendency is a general one and makes tenable – at least with respect to the development of religious institutions – the classic thesis of an ineluctable "secularization" of modern society. On the other hand, empirical investigations dealing with beliefs within these very societies attest with the same consistency that individual interest in the spiritual and the religious has not undergone any decline, despite a disenchantment introduced by the pervasive expansion of instrumental reason in all regions of life. Paradoxically, modern societies, confronted with the uncertainties to which the rapidity of technological, social, and cultural change gives rise, are societies where belief proliferates. This explosion of belief is the work of individuals who cobble together, in their own fashion, systems of signification which give a subjective meaning to their own experience, and who independently choose (for their own gratification) the communal affiliations which they themselves recognize.

"Religious modernity is individualism" – in various guises this proposition constitutes the central contemporary motif of sociological reflection upon religion. But what exactly does this signify? And what are the implications of this individualization of the forms of "communalization" (as Weber calls it) which provides believers with means of exchanging, sharing, and validating together their personal convictions? These are the two questions that guide the reflections of the present chapter (see also Hervieu-Léger 1999).

Religious Individualism and Modern Individualism

Let us first return to the paradigm that makes individualism the very core of religious modernity. This notion can give rise to confusion if it suggests that religious individualism is essentially a completely new reality along with modernity. In reality, one can speak of religious individualization ever since the differentiation between ritualized religion and interior religion. The first only requires of the faithful the observation of the minutiae of prescribed actions. The second implies, in a mystical or ethical fashion, the personal and continuous appropriation of religious truths by each believer. In all the great religious traditions, this differentiation was manifest well before the emergence of modernity.

From this point of view, the history of Christian mysticism can be read entirely as the construction of the history of the religious subject. But this history is supremely paradoxical, for the mystical quest for union with God occurs through the work of divesting oneself of self. This requires an emptying out of passions, interests, thoughts, emotions, and representations within which is inscribed the uniqueness of the individual. Nevertheless, this tearing away of individuals from the peculiar determinations of their life constitutes, for those who travel this path, a way of accessing the self. It likewise opens the highest possible awareness of the self: that which proceeds from the ineffable experience of union with God. On the one hand, this mystical way, described in the accounts of all the great Christian mystics, constitutes an extreme path of individualization of religious experience, reserved, in fact, for a small number of virtuosi. On the other hand, it is through the "rational and systematic fashioning" of the life of the individual that an ethical way constitutes the individual as a believing subject (Weber 1996: 431). Within the Christian context, Calvinism has pushed this ethical logic of religious individualization the furthest, in developing the idea that everyone must confirm their personal destiny and salvation in every aspect of everyday life in the world, and particularly in their professional life. In the absence of any mediation between the self and God, believers are thus confronted, in a radically individual manner, with the question of their own salvation.

What link holds this religious individualism, whether of a mystical or ethical kind, to modernity? It is not helpful to insist at length upon the classical Weberian thesis which has emphasized an elective affinity weaving together ethical individualism, the "this-worldliness" of Calvinist Puritanism, and the spirit of modern economic capitalism in a nascent state. But it would be improper to deduce that the trajectory of Christian religious individualism, which is found in its most radical form in Calvin, anticipates, in a perfectly continuous, linear fashion, the emergence of modern individualism. To establish an unbroken continuity between religious individualism of a mystical or ethical kind and the modern conception of the individual, is as absurd as the opposite point of view that consists in making religious individualism a recent achievement of modernity. For religious individualism is separated from modern individualism – whose origin is found in the recognition of the autonomy of the subject – from at least two points of view: one of these constitutes the individual in the very process of self-renunciation in order to achieve a state of surrender before God; the other wholly devalues the mundane barriers to this union with the divine. These two points not only characterize the other-worldliness of mysticism or ethics, as Catholic tradition has developed them. They are present again in the worldly conception of ethics which prevailed in the Reformation. For this reason, the German theologian and sociologist Ernst Troeltsch firmly criticized the view that worldly religious individualism, born of the Reformation, had directly prepared the emergence of the modern conception of the individual and opened the way for the advent of democracy. Troeltsch does insist upon the fact that the Lutheran valorization of work in the world permitted the development of a functional religious ethic in relation to the development of capitalism. But at the same time he underlines that this ethic is in contradiction with a modern ethic which recognizes and magnifies the autonomy of worldly realities.

Therefore, Luther was situated within a neoplatonic perspective which devalued the world. Troeltsch equally rejected the idea that in developing his doctrine of predestination, Calvin laid the foundations for the modern process of individualization. Thus, for Calvin, the elect are not valued in themselves: rescued by pure grace, they only find their meaning in the service of the Kingdom. If believers are intensely engaged in worldly tasks, they are engaged in this way exclusively for the glory of God, for God wills the world itself. But this activity as such is insignificant. It does not allow individuals an assurance of their salvation, nor can they derive any benefit from the personal accomplishment which it offers to them. Calvinistic individualism denies the autonomy of the individual and dwells, therefore, in contradiction with rational individualism – the true offspring of the Enlightenment:

> Calvin does not affirm the freedom of man. This notion is excluded from his systematic theology and his social system. The kingdom of God does not offer an unconditional acceptance of the human; without doubt it establishes itself through persuasion, but also through repression of all rebellion, through coercion. . . . The honor of God is maintained when humans are reined in under the Law in an attitude of free or constrained submission. (Troeltsch 1912:635, n. 330)

This Calvinistic insistence upon obedience is fundamentally opposed to the modern conception of individual autonomy.

It also separates Calvinism from the Puritan sects, in so far as the latter require of their members a free and voluntary adherence to the community. In fact, if there truly ever were a "Protestant modernity" it would be at the heart of those current neo-Calvinist pietists and Puritans principally singled out by Troeltsch. This modernity proceeds for the most part from political conflicts which have led communities to claim freedom of conscience, to promote a community founded upon the free will of each member, and to affirm their independence by generalizing the practice of electing pastors. In reaction to the guardianship of the churches and their formalistic rituals, these communities have radicalized the

Lutheran problematic of the ethical interiorization of the relationship to God. However, in seeking to be separated from a world that is considered evil, they have paradoxically accorded to this world recognition of its autonomy. From this point of view, the sectarian spirituality of the radical Reformation maintains positive elective associations with modern individualism. However, Protestant spirituality – both Lutheran and Calvinist – essentially remains within a problematic of a negative affirmation of the individual which is characteristic of pre-modern religious individualism (Troeltsch 1912). Religious individualism no more makes for modernity than modernity invents religious individualism. What characterizes the contemporary religious scene is not religious individualism as such; it is rather the absorption of religious individualism within modern individualism.

The Modern Mutation of Religious Individualism: The Case of "New Age" Religion

This modern mutation of religious individualism is particularly visible within the ensemble of heterogeneous groups and spiritual networks which are designated as "New Age." What constitutes the unity of this ensemble is a religious belief entirely centered upon individuals and their personal accomplishment, and characterized by the primacy accorded to personal experience which guides everyone according to their own way. It is not a matter of discovering and committing oneself to a truth outside the self: it is a matter of experimentation – everyone finding their own truth for themselves. In spiritual matters, no authority defines and imposes an external norm upon the individual. The objective pursued is the perfection of the self, perfection which is not concerned with the moral accomplishments of the individual, but with access to a higher state of being. This self-perfection is made available through physical and spiritual practices borrowing from a wide range of techniques adapted from the great traditions of mysticism and spirituality. However, recourse to these techniques implies complete optimism concerning the human capacity to arrive at a full realization of the self by taking the way that one has chosen responsibly (Champion 1993).

The salvation sought through this work of self-perfection is exclusively concerned with life here below. It is a question of attaining, in as complete a manner as possible, the goals which modern society offers as something attainable by all: health, well-being, vitality, and beauty. This conception of a strictly "this-worldly" salvation is set within a monistic understanding of the world: it rejects all dualisms (human–divine, natural–supernatural, etc.). It also questions the fragmentation of knowledge and practices that frustrates the modern ambition of individual and collective progress. Such a perspective of spiritual reunification of the life of the individual and the collective ensures the reign of an "ethic of love," which manifests the convergence of the ways of truth explored by individuals. Likewise this implies a new alliance with modern science. The goal of power over nature, which modern science pursues, links with the goal of realizing one's physical and psychological capacities which guides individuals in their spiritual quests. From this arises the importance which many of these believers accord to "paranormal phenomena" (out-of-the-body experiences, journeys through previous lives, communication with spirits or extraterrestrials). The fact that humankind might be able to access these by personally developing its uniquely spiritual capacities does not contradict scientific ambition. On the contrary, it completes it, as it constitutes a way for the individual to enter into the project of knowledge and power over the world which modern science develops along other lines.

The groups and networks of the nebulous New Age movement constitute a fine instrument for analyzing contemporary religious reality because they bring to the fore, with all their implications, the tendencies generally present in renewal movements which shape historic religions: a search for personal authenticity, the importance given to experience, the rejection of faith systems which offer ready keys to reality, a this-worldly conception of salvation conceived of as a form of individual self-perfection, and so forth. These different tendencies illustrate well the phenomenon of the absorption of religious individualism within modern individualism under the aegis of the valorization of the world on the one hand and of the affirmation of the autonomy of the believing subject on the other. "Religious modernity" is, fundamentally, a product of this process. It incorporates the spiritual quest into a psychological modernity characterized by individual concern for the perfection of self. These tendencies – consistently emphasized by empirical inquiries into the subjectivization of traditional religions, the rejection of received "truth" from others, along with the valorization of the authenticity of the spiritual journey which everyone is supposed to conduct according to their dispositions and interests – are the principal indicators of this movement.

The Individualization of Faith and Religious Communalization

The question which arises then, is one of knowing which forms of social religion are able to exist despite the imposing presence of a religious individualism so fully integrated into modern individualism. If one produces by oneself, in an autonomous fashion, a small-scale "ordering of meaning" which allows one to orient one's own life and respond to "ultimate questions" concerning one's own existence; if one's spiritual experience is condensed into an intimate and purely private relationship with what one may or may not choose to call "God"; if this eminently personal experience does not require action in the world; then membership within a believing community is of secondary importance, if not completely useless.

This predisposition to "belief without belonging" (Davie 1994) is confirmed even in the case where individuals give a religious sense to their spiritual quest; or in other words, when they establish a self-referential relationship between their personal belief and a traditional, institutionalized faith. "I feel spiritually Christian, but I don't belong to any church"; "I feel close to Buddhism"; "I am attracted to Islamic mysticism": to cultivate such personal preferences, commonly expressed with ease by free-floating believers, it is not necessary to join a particular religious group. It is enough to read a particular journal, to shop at a particular bookstore, to watch a particular program on television, or even – and more and more frequently – to log on to a particular Internet site. At the extreme, one is able to imagine that the logic of a "patchwork belief" renders the formation of believing communities, joined together by a shared faith, impossible. In this extreme hypothesis, the communal realization of any sort of lineage of believers that is based upon a continuity with a tradition which produces the very substance of a religious bond, tends to disappear. The expansion of a modern spirituality of the individual might well signal, given this point of view, the end of religion. For the atomization of individual spiritual quests not only dissolves the religious bond consisting of the assent to a shared truth by a past, present, and future community: it also prohibits, in the name of a purely subjective conception of the truth to be attained, the reconstitution of this bond in any form. (This is, for example, defended by Steve Bruce, 1996, within a perspective which elaborates and radicalizes the vision of secularization defended by Bryan Wilson.)

Here again, the example of the "New Age" movement illustrates this phenomenon of "decomposition without recomposition" well. The social bond between the aficionados of this nebulous spirituality is, in effect, comprised of episodic recourse to resource centers: bookstores, educational facilities, convention centers, and so forth. To the degree that these individuals meet there regularly and create more or less stable bonds between themselves, these resources can constitute spiritual cooperatives, at the core of which are exchanges of information, addresses, the titles of books, and so forth. These bonds bear witness to spiritual affinities more or less recognized by the participants, but do not bind them "religiously" together. What prevents one from being able to speak of "religion" is a common reference to a shared reality, constitutive of a tradition-making authority (Hervieu-Léger 1993). The validation of faith remains, at the core of these cooperatives of spiritual resources, a truly individual discipline: to each his or her truth. The purely subjective regime of truth which the individualistic atomization of belief leads to can preserve a form of individual religiosity (note that, for individuals, there is still a recognition of their subjective affinity to various particular traditional faiths). However, it potentially does away with all forms of religious communalization.

This schema obviously constitutes a limiting constraint. It is concretely realized only when a regime of self-validation of faith is imposed, in which the believing subjects recognize within themselves only the capacity to define the truth of belief. This tendency exists in certain spiritual currents, but is far from being the only one that one can observe. The dissemination of belief likewise gives rise to a completely contrary movement of the proliferation of communities. This tendency can be summarized as follows: the more people "cobble together" a small-scale system of belief adapted to their own needs, the more they aspire to share this experience with others who share in the same type of spiritual aspiration. This seeming contradiction accords with the intrinsic limits of the self-validation of faith. For individuals to stabilize the meanings they produce to give significance to their daily experience, they must find outside of themselves a confirmation of the validity of these meanings. Deprived of the strong confirmation that secure global codes of meaning guaranteed by institutions (religious or philosophical systems, political ideologies, etc.), it is above all in mutual exchange that individuals can hope to find a way to establish a personal universe of meaning with which they might equip themselves. In the absence of such a support – if no one ever affirms, "What makes sense to you also makes sense to me" – the odds are high that individually produced meanings (supposing that they succeed in emerging as such) will not make sense in the long term.

The logic of self-validation of belief, which marks the definitive escape from the spiritual quest out of the world of confirmed certitudes of religion, also encounters this limit. It encourages to an astonishing extent the consumption of cultural products (books, movies, journals, etc.) which support the exclusively individual search for the confirmation of faith. Evidence of this is the success of works of this spiritual genre, such as books of interviews with those the media designates as athletes in the quest for meaning, or even the boom of esoteric literature which, for the last twenty years has occupied whole shelves in all the big bookstores. Indeed, the sharing of this reading material constitutes one of the motivating factors in binding together networks of individual searchers after meaning: fluid, flexible, unstable, and even virtual networks which constitute the degree zero, as one might say – of a spiritual communalization. This communalization is likely, if it allows for the subjective and objective incorporation of those interested into a faith lineage recognized by them as such, to evolve towards a form of religious communalization.

In the latter case, self-validation gives way to a regime of mutual validation of faith, founded upon personal testimony, the sharing of individual experiences, and eventually upon the search for ways of their collective deepening. This regime of mutual validation is not only a principle of the constitution of the "New Age" networks. It also invades the world of institutionalized religions. The contemporary landscape of churches is characterized by the development of groups and networks which make use of, on the margin or at the center of parishes and movements, supple and unstable forms of social affinity, founded upon the spiritual, social, and cultural proximity of the individuals who are involved. When individuals are engaged in a militantly religious group, they adhere to communal belief and place themselves at the service of the objectives of the group. In these groups of spiritual interests, things are very different: the individual finds in the fellowship of the other participants a disposition of "mutual comprehension" at the disposal of each member (see Wuthnow 1988).

Here it becomes apparent what separates those forms of religious sociability corresponding to a regime of mutual validation of faith and those which establish themselves, within and without the major religious traditions, starting from a regime of communal validation of faith. In this latter case, believers make use of the certitudes which they share in organizing daily life and/or action in the world. The "militant" model of the movement, of the fellowship or apostolic order, as well as the "monastic" model of a religious life lived totally outside the world, imply, among those who assemble according to one of these models, an adherence to a common regime of faith wagered upon, so to speak, the intensity of their individual and collective engagement. Communal cohesion attests, for each, to the truth of the common faith.

Institutional religions, in principle, make good an institutional regime based on the validation of faith, making use of secure precedents according to the authoritative organizations proper to each tradition, in continuity with the faith lineage. The institutional authorities define the rules and the norms which are, for individuals, the stable benchmarks of conformity to the faith. This regime is valid for the assembly of believers. But this does not preclude the fact that, at their core, regimes based on the validation of faith differentiate themselves in response to the desire for religious intensity proper to the particular group. Hence, communities unite more narrowly and specifically in "spiritual families" sharing a common interpretation of their relationship to the world and a way of life which this common interpretation implies. Religious congregations and orders, movements, devotional groups, "new" communities, inscribe their own regimes of validation within the general regime of institutional validation, though not without frequent conflicts which have left their traces in the history of the foundation of religious orders.

But this communitarian validation of faith can equally develop in an autonomous fashion, by opposing to the "least common denominator of faith," which institutions tend to establish among their faithful, an intensive regime of shared truth among personally converted individuals. This involves a personal step toward adherence on the part of regrouped individuals within the community, and it is the intensity of the engagement undertaken by each which validates, for the others, the shared significances at the core of the group. The rise of religious individualism has reinforced the pluralistic affirmation of communal regimes of faith, which contractually bind the individuals involved in the same fashion in their religious life, over against institutional definitions of formal faith shared by a congregation of believers.

This tendency manifests itself in an exemplary fashion in the history of Christianity, with the development of communities and movements of the Radical Reformation. But the tension between the institutional regime and the communal regimes of the validation of truth (of the true faith) is present in all religious institutions. Pushed to the extreme, it tends to isolate from the mass of believers the nuclei of pure individuals, capable of witnessing with integrity, on behalf of the others, to the truth which they share, and capable, therefore, of doing without the legitimization of the institution. The period of "communal salva-

I

Regime of Validation: Institutional
Referent for Validation: Institutionally Qualified Authority
Criterion for Validation: Conformity

II

Regime of Validation: Communal
Referent for Validation: The Group as Such
Criterion for Validation: Coherence

III

Regime of Validation: Mutual
Referent for Validation: The Other
Criterion for Validation: Authenticity

IV

Regime of Validation: Self-validation
Referent for Validation: The Individual Him or Herself
Criterion for Validation: Subjective Certainty

Figure 9.1   Typical forms of the validation of faith

tion," identified by the French historian A. Dupront (1996: 137–230) as the first
stage of the historic trajectory of Christianity, was typically that of the institutional validation of faith. The second stage is that of affirmation, sealed by
the Reformation, of an individual conception of salvation. This was a conflict
between a dominant regime of institutional validation of faith and of multiple
regimes of communal validation of faith. The third stage is one of religious
modernity, in other words that of the absorption of religious individualism into
modern individualism. The latter is consistent with a worldly and subjectivized
conception of individual salvation. This stage is also one of the overlapping of
these two models in tension by an intervening regime of mutual validation of
faith, which makes the exchange of personal experiences the support of subjective access of each to his or her truth.

Figure 9.1 summarizes the traits of these four typical regimes of the validation of faith, according to the referent for validation (who declares the true
faith?) and the criterion for validation made use of in each case (what is it that
makes the truth of faith?).

The regime of the institutional validation of faith turns over to religious
authority (the authorities with the power to proclaim the truth of faith) responsibility for confirming the beliefs and practices of the faithful. The criterion maintained is one of conformity in beliefs and practices to the norm fixed by the
institution. In Catholicism, the institutional magisterium, for which the bishop
is the guardian, assumes this function. In Protestantism, the theologian takes

on this role in the ideological regulation of the faith. But in every case, an institutional authority holds the legitimate power to fix the rules of adherence and affiliation which delineate the boundaries of the religious groups.

In the regime of communal validation of faith, it is the group as such which constitutes the validation. In this case, the coherence of the behavior of each of the members with regard to norms, objectives, and more broadly relations, to the world, as defined by the group, constitutes the principal criterion of the truth of a shared faith. Egalitarianism is supposed to govern the relations within the group. This does not mean that some leader is not able to emerge as its center, but that leaders are always supposed to express themselves in the name of the whole group: they are the voice of the group.

In the regime of mutual validation, the illumination of faith's truth is accomplished within intersubjective interaction. The only criterion recognized in this exchange is the authenticity of the individual quest which expresses itself there by all who are participating. No exterior precedent – neither institution nor community – can prescribe for the individual an assemblage of truths of faith. There is no "true faith" but that which is personally appropriated.

In the regime of self-validation, all instances of validation other than the individual vanish. It is in individuals themselves, in the subjective certitude of possessing the truth, that the confirmation of the truth of faith is found.

Church, Sect, and Mysticism

In making the regime of the validation of faith the principle of the differentiation of forms of religious society, one inevitably recognizes the classical typology of the forms of Christian communalization focused upon by Weber and Troeltsch. The principle of differentiation, they hold, is the particular relation that each person maintains with the world. This relation finds its legitimation in the preaching of the gospel itself. Let us recall briefly what the classical typology is. The church is a natural community within which one is born, and an "institution of salvation"; it is in charge of universal redemption. It assures the transmission of grace for all humankind and must, in order to realize its mission, embrace all societies and all cultures. A sacred institution, whose purity does not depend upon that of its members, it imposes upon its ordinary faithful a minimum of religious requirements and reserves religious intensity for a small number of virtuosi. At the same time, it requires a body of specialists specifically formed in order to manage and distribute the benefits of salvation. This universal objective, along with this regime of a "double ethic," predisposes the church to maintain relations with contemporary culture and political establishments based upon compromise, in order to extend its hold over society.

In contrast to the inclusive activity which characterizes the church, the sect is a voluntary grouping of believers into which one enters after personal conversion. It is characterized by the intense engagement which it demands of its members. No ministerial specialization, no mediation in relationship to the scriptures is imaginable in an egalitarian community founded upon a contractual bond which ties together regenerated and converted believers. Religious fidelity demands of them the work of perpetual personal purification and sanctification. The sanctity of the group depends upon the purity of each and upon mutual correction exercised from within. The church struggles to incorporate the largest number of faithful, while the sect opens itself exclusively to "religiously qualified" individuals whose collective witness (be it simply by example, aggressively militant, or even revolutionary) must disconcert "worldly" culture and polity in order to efface it before the divine order. Beyond all compromise with the profane world, from the margin of society, the sect asserts the radicality of the requirements of the gospel.

Troeltsch has clarified the tension between the two conceptions of the realization of the Christian ideal, which lead to different relations with the world – negotiation or secession – and which are crystallized in opposite forms of religious communalization. This tension, present in the origins of Christianity, unfolds even as it transforms itself subject to the social, economic, political, cultural, and intellectual conditions over the duration of its history. But to these two clearly different types of groups, Troeltsch would add a third type, one less clearly identifiable because it develops as a movement at the very heart of the church and, when it stabilizes, often evolves towards a sect. This is the type called mysticism (*Spiritualismus*).

This form of Christian regrouping finds its theological justification in the fact that Jesus himself created neither church nor sect: he assembled individuals who were unified by their choice to serve the Master. The time of the Reformation – the time *par excellence* of religious individualism – gave a forceful impulse to this type of regrouping into a network, reuniting individuals (essentially the intelligentsia) who shared the idea that the Kingdom is within everyone. Each can, therefore, in a direct, personal and unmediated manner, experience this presence. Founded upon the idea of the presence of a divine principle in each person (Christian or not), this immediate, concrete, and antidogmatic conception of Christian experience rejects rigid doctrinal formulations, stereotyped ritual routines, and, more generally, any form of communal organization, church as well as sect. It privileges individual exchange and spiritual companionship in intimate circles of mutual edification. From the Troeltschian perspective, the mystical type crystallizes the principle of individual religiousness characteristic of modernity.

One sees that it is perfectly possible to make a correspondence between each of these types of religious groupings – church, sect, and mystical network – and a dominant regime of the validation of faith. The church employs a regime of institutional validation of faith; the sect knows only the communal validation of faith with immediate reference to scripture; the mystical network, finally, orients itself towards the mutual validation of faith. Why, then, do we not simply go with the classical categories?

To answer this question, it is first necessary to recall that the notions of sect and church have been forged as ideal types of Christian groupings combining two types of distinctive traits. On the one hand there are characteristics touching upon the organization of the groups (size, conditions for membership, hierarchy, the degrees of permeability to the social, political, and cultural environment, etc.). On the other hand are the elements which engage the content itself of faith (conceptions of the role of the Church in the economy of salvation, theology of the sacraments, relations with the world, etc.). When one uses the word "sect" to designate an intensive religious group with a small number of adepts, whose beliefs and mode of life separate them from the rest of society, one forgets that the definitions established by Weber and Troeltsch find their origin in irreducible divergences in theology, concerning the conception of Christian salvation itself. A "bracketing of context" of the classical typology, worked out in order to conceptualize Christian diversity during the Reformation, tends to produce, in a totally perverse manner, a static classification of religious groups, without much relationship to the original works of the two German sociologists.

The classical typology of Christian groups conflates two principles of classification. The first differentiates the modes of affirmation of Christianity in history. The second identifies the modes of social existence of religion. The typology of regimes of validation of faith exclusively concerns the second principle. Its primary interest is to function as a tool for the ordering of reality outside the Christian camp. Independent of validated religious or spiritual content, it can be applied to the case of Judaism or Islam, serve to discriminate between the different currents of Buddhism in the West, or differentiate the logical differences of "new religions" and "cults." The typology of the regimes of validation, by exclusively concentrating upon the internal logic of the legitimating function of faith, and on the different forms of possibilities for the administration of the truth employed by religious groups, can serve to identify the characteristic moments in the trajectory of a religious group, as well as to identify stable, distinct forms of religious communalization. It allows one to mark the permeability, characteristic of religious modernity, between the networks governed by the mutual validation of faith and a purely individual regime of self-validation. It can serve to highlight the transitions (in every sense of the word) which a group can make from one regime of validation to another, depending on its internal dynamic, of the dispositions of its members, or of the demands of its environment, and so forth. It authorizes a flexible method of analysis of the possible combinations between these different regimes at the very core of groups which show "church" or "sect" type in terms of their formal characteristics (number, relation to the environment, internal organization of authority, etc.). The approach of communalization forms through the methods of validation of belief, therefore, gives the means to mark the dynamics at work in the mobile and fluid landscape of religious modernity.

The Double Movement of the "Deinstitutionalization" of Religion

The collapse of regular observances, the development of an à la carte religion, the affirmation of the personal autonomy of believers, the diversification of trajectories of religious identification, religious "nomadism": all of these phenomena are indicators of a general tendency towards the erosion of institutional regimes of the validation of religious faith. In modern Western societies all the Christian churches and most religious institutions are confronted, in diverse ways, with the collapse of their own ability to regulate faith. They are no longer, or less and less, the guardians of the central values of society (see Hammond 1992). This crisis involves the relation of the individual believers to those institutions whose exclusive authority to declare the truth of faith and to fix an ultimate definition of communal identity is now contested. If, in the future, the authenticity of the personal spiritual journey becomes more important than the conformity of belief demanded of the religious faithful by the institution, the legitimation of religious authority will be attacked at its very foundation.

One might rightly judge that this presentation of contemporary "deinstitutionalization" of religion is excessively crude. Indeed, religious institutions survive, they still gather the faithful together and often make themselves heard in society. I am not suggesting that the movement leads to a disintegration, pure and simple, of institutional religion; rather, I want to emphasize a tendency that shapes religious institutions and profoundly transforms them while also provoking a global reorganization of the religious landscape. Religious institutions must come to terms, at their core, with the encroachment of a regime of mutual validation of faith which dissipates the traditional orderings of institutional validation gently, by progressively imposing a "weak model" of true faith. They must at the same time face, both internally and externally, the proliferation of "small-scale" regimes of communal validation that opposes the previous group's resistance to the "strong models" of shared truth. From the viewpoint of those who adhere to them, this is the only way of facing the irresistible wave of individualization and subjectivization of faith (the war of cultures).

In order to describe this situation more precisely, one can say that the religious landscape of contemporary modernity is traversed by two movements which proceed in opposite directions. The first movement, in direct relation to the culture of the individual which dominates in all areas, tends to relativize the norms of belief and church practices fixed by religious institutions. It places emphasis above all upon the value of the search for and the personal appropriation of meaning. It dilutes and sometimes contests explicitly the notion of "obligation" attached to these beliefs and practices. If there is a community, it is not its vocation to attest to an *a priori* homogeneity of faith. Rather, its vocation is one of manifesting a "convergence" that is mutually recognized in the personal journeys of its members. The accepted acknowledgment of differences is as important, from this perspective, as the affirmation of faith references shared by believers within the group. The communal bond should permanently form and reform itself from the "spiritual credit" which the individuals engaged in the search for a communal expression give themselves. The identification of the limits within which this common expression remains possible is therefore based upon the principle of a continually recast definition of communal identity. One notes that this conception of the community, more or less clearly formulated, is often associated with the idea of a "converging ethic" of the major religious traditions, a convergence which looks to the utopian horizon of a possible unification of individual "quests for meaning."

The other movement is in a radically contrary direction and opposes this "process-oriented" conception of the community. Solidarity is collectively proven by small-scale universes of certitude which efficiently assure the ordering of the experience of individuals. The community concretizes, then, the homogeneity of truths shared by the group; and the acceptance of this code of communal faith, which embraces beliefs and practices, in turn fixes the boundaries of the group.

The "process-oriented" conception of a community always in the making corresponds to a regime of the mutual validation of faith. The "substantive" conception of the community accords with a communal regime of the validation of faith. Not only are they directly opposed to each other, but they both challenge the institutional conception which makes the "community" a transcendental given, preexisting before the concrete groups in which membership to the lineage of belief is realized in varying ways. In the regime of institutional validation, it is the assembly of believers past, present, and future, who constitute the authentic "community." The small-scale communities are historical condensations of the lineage of faith. They do not exhaust the reality of the "great community" (the chosen people, the umma, or the church) that is their reference. Institutional religious authority is that which has the recognized right to speak legitimately in the name of the "larger community."

Guaranteeing the community and its unity, this authority checks centrifugal or separatist forces which can spring up at the core of diverse groups testifying to their affiliation to the lineage of belief. When this institutional regulation is weakened, or when it does not exist, the dynamics of individualism and communitarianization develop their contradictory effects. Moreover, they tend to set each other into motion by accentuating the polarization of the regimes of mutual validation and communal validation of faith within a religious landscape undergoing "deinstitutionalization." This tension between the two movements manifests itself outside of the major institutions where one observes both the expansion of a world of individually cobbled-together beliefs and the proliferation of small-scale communities – "sects" or "cults" – which claim for their membership a monopoly over truth. But this tension also crosses the major institutions, which are dismissed, at least partially, from their legitimacy in fixing a uniform regime of faith for the assembly of their adherents.

The major churches busy themselves then with overseeing the widening gap between two contradictory imperatives. The first imperative is to feed a theological consensus and an ethical minimum, capable of absorbing and encircling, without breaking them, the increasingly diverse trajectories of believers' identities. The second imperative is to maintain, at the same time, a sufficiently strong model of shared truth so as to avoid being overwhelmed by the aggressive offensive of small-scale communal orderings of meaning, and to be prepared to offer the security of a "code of truth" as a key available to those faithful dismayed by the absence or the loss of the collective benchmarks of faith.

References

Bruce, S. 1996. *Religion in the Modern World: From Cathedrals to Cults.* Oxford and New York: Oxford University Press.

Champion, F. 1993. "Religieux flottant, éclectisme et syncrétismes," in *Le Fait Religieux,* ed. J. Delumeau. Paris: Fayard, pp. 741–72.

Davie, G. 1994. *Religion in Britain Since 1945.* Oxford: Blackwell.

Dupront, A. 1996. *Qu'est-ce-que les Lumières?* Paris: Folio.

Hammond, P.E. 1992. *The Third Disestablishment in America.* Columbia, SC: University of South Carolina Press.

Hervieu-Léger, D. 1993. *La Religion Pour Mémoire.* Paris: Cerf. (English translation, 2000 *Religion and Memory.* Oxford and New Brunswick, NJ: Polity Press and Rutgers University Press.)

Hervieu-Léger, D. 1999. *Le pèlerin et le convert: La religion en mouvement.* Paris: Editions Flammarion.

Troeltsch, E. 1912. *Soziallehren des christlichen Kirchen und Gruppen.* Tübingen: Mohr.

Weber, M. 1996. *Sociologies des religions.* Paris: Gallimard.

Wuthnow, R. 1998. "The Decline of Denominationalism and the Growth of 'Special Purpose Groups'," in R. Wuthnow, *The Restructuring of American Religion.* R. Wuthnow. Princeton, NJ: Princeton University Press, pp. 100–31.

CHAPTER 10
The Origins of Religion

Richard K. Fenn

A Hypothesis Concerning the Sources of the Religious Imagination

What is it that keeps generating religious interest and even enthusiasm from one generation to the next, even in fairly large and complex, relatively open and democratic societies? In all the vast changes in the way modern societies are organized, in what they stand for, in the peoples they include, and in the way they go about understanding and seeking to control their social and natural environments, religion continues to find new forms, new ways of appealing even to a disenchanted and skeptical populace, and new ways of guiding individuals in their encounters with finitude and death. Just as Durkheim made it clear that he was examining not the origins *per se* but only the proximate causes of religion, I wish to point out that our inquiry here is only into some of the conditions and the contingencies that enable people to discover new sources of inspiration and authority in old traditions or to generate new practices and beliefs out of the remnants of old disciplines.

In this chapter I inquire into the origins of religious beliefs and practices by putting forward a hypothesis about the sources of the religious imagination. I will argue that religious imagery reflects an experience of primitive and irrevocable loss. Further, I will suggest that the experience of that loss overwhelms the mind's capacity to reconcile contradictions between desire and reality. Thus religious illusions form a sort of unhappy compromise between the necessary and the possible. This is not a novel hypothesis. Indeed it is in keeping with general notions about the function of religious myth and ritual: that they restore order and harmony to natural and social relationships that have been broken and plunged into chaos. Thus they make up for lost time and give individuals and societies a new lease, as it were, on time itself. No wonder, then, that myth and

THE ORIGINS OF RELIGION 177

ritual embody themes of death and regeneration, loss and recovery. However, my thesis assumes that beneath the surfaces of ritual and myth there are other motives at work. As Catherine Bell puts it:

> Methodologically, psychoanalytic ethnographers might begin with the ritual, but they must work backward, even past the etiologic myth, to uncover what is thought to be the 'real' story of desire and repression, fear, and projection that is at the root. Unconscious motives are the profoundest and most explanative; the unconscious myth is the true one. (Bell 1997:15)

Catherine Bell gives us a masterful summary of the early ethnographic literature that argued for an original relationship between myths of death and resurrection and certain rituals: for example those of the king renewing the social and natural orders at critical points in the seasons or during crises of succession. These studies purported to show that the associated myth also was the original source of comparable themes of death and resurrection in art, drama, and literature (Bell 1997:5–7). In many of the myths the king is thought to have descended into hell and returned triumphant over chaos and death. In others the myth merely describes an attempt to recover associations with the departed whose souls had gone to an underworld, but who were still of vital importance to the living (p. 4).

In both sets of myths, however, the focus is on the recovery of lost souls. Even in the myths that portray a slain king descending to the underworld, the journey is the same: an effort heroically to make up for lost time and thus renew the hold of the living on life itself.[1] The perennial nature of these myths is due, I would argue, to the fact that individuals in every generation do tend to seek to rescue and recover the presence of the dead, affection or hatred for whom lingers long after their departure. What is essential is the attachment of the living to the souls of the departed.

Thus the search for the origins of religion takes us into the realm of what is true of every generation, rather than to some hypothetical departure in antiquity. From a psychoanalytic viewpoint, as Freud argued, every generation renews a "primitive" experience of helplessness before the forces of nature and of fate itself. Furthermore, societies that become large and complex in order to defend individuals from the sudden onslaught of disease and death, of enemies and intrusions, themselves can make an individual feel helpless and small. Even within the shelter of the family, the child may feel overwhelmed by the powerful presence of parents who are crucial to the survival of the child but also both potent and threatening. They are threatening in part because they are rivals in the child's eyes: competitors for the scarce resources of affection and particularly for the possession of the parent on whom the child has set his or her primary affections. Thus Oedipal conflicts, rivalry with siblings, and rebellion against the imposition of limitations, can drive the child into longings for a return to the safety and permanence of the womb.

What then do these infantile longings have to do with the descent of a mythical king into the underworld? Among these longings is the desire of the infant to own and control all the sources of life, including those represented by the parents. Alongside these desires is the infant's sense of entitlement: the fantasy that the infant is entitled to the pleasures normally reserved for royalty. It is this assumption of a right to royalties, so to speak, that allows infants to imagine that they can indeed usurp the father's authority or possess the mother; after all, Oedipus was a young king. The king therefore must die for two reasons. First, such a punishment indeed fits the imaginary crime of being a royal pretender. Secondly, the illusion of such entitlements itself must die as the child grows older, discovers his or her mortality, and seeks to live life more or less on its own terms.

The Descent into Hell

For illustration of such original fantasies and beliefs, let us turn to poetic and mythological notions of a descent into hell. They are among the earliest and also among the more sophisticated and imaginative sources for our inquiry into the sources of religious imagery, idiom, and illusion. Later in this discussion we will turn to Homer, Augustine, Dante, the author of *The Cloud of Unknowing*, and finally to Freud and Heidegger in an effort to document the persistence of the desire to go to hell and back, as it were, to rescue and recover lost loves, to satisfy old grievances, and to rebel against the passage of time. Here we begin with perhaps the earliest known descent into hell, that of Gilgamesh, and I will draw on that epic here to suggest what may well be the basic structure of all later descents. (In this account I will be relying heavily on what is probably the best secondary source, Alan Bernstein's 1993 discussion of *The Formation of Hell*.) What is essential to the myth is the attachment of the living to the souls of the departed.

The myth begins with a sudden and tragic loss. Gilgamesh, perhaps a Babylonian King (of Uruk) nearly three thousand years before the beginning of the Christian era, loses his dear friend Enkidu. I mention this here as something more than incidental to the descent into hell. Such a loss, I will suggest, is the very beginning of that descent, since it plunges the individual into the experience of time and mortality. Later in this chapter we will see that it was the loss of Augustine's most intimate friend that plunged the fourth century theologian into a contemplation of the passage of time. Certainly it was just such a loss that prodded Freud into contemplating his conscious and unconscious ways of avoiding the fact of death and the experience that it is too late to fulfill one's deepest desires. Augustine took his consolation from contemplating his friendships under the aspect of eternity; his soul took refuge in the timeless presence of God and there found its rest. Freud demythologized his own psyche. Gilgamesh, like Augustine and Freud, associated the death of his friend with their own mortality: "How can I be still? My friend, who I loved, has turned to clay! Must I, too, like him, lay me down, not to rise again for ever and ever?" (Bernstein 1993:4).[2]

At the very beginning of the descent into hell, then, we find two steps, very closely related to one another: the experience of irrevocable loss, and the realization that one is mortal. "Uruk's king [i.e., Gilgamesh] then understood that he too would die and he determined to seek a remedy" (Bernstein 1993:4). Thus the descent begins with an implicit awareness that part of the self has perished with the friend.

It is this awareness, perhaps, that prompts the question of whether I, "like him," must die, "not to rise again for ever and ever?" The possibility of recovering the part of the self that seems to have accompanied the friend into death is a real one; the slow withdrawal of emotion and identity from the departed is part of the perennial and universal task of those who mourn. This self-recovery, however, may be accompanied by another wish that is not to be fulfilled: the wish never to die. Augustine, as I will note later in this discussion, took comfort in his belief that friendships held in and through the mind of God would not come to an end, and thus the basis was laid for a rejection of the experience of mortality. Freud found that it was his unfinished, and often unconscious business, not God, that refused to allow the dead to die.

Thus I will be tracking two descents into hell: one complete, in its acceptance of the irreversibility of time and the finality of death; the other magical or romantic, in its advance knowledge that the experience of time and death is temporary and reversible. One descent is undertaken in faith, that is, with the knowledge that there is no rescue from death, and if there is more life to come it is wholly beyond one's knowledge and control and may well not come at all. The other descent is undertaken under the auspices of religion and is characterized by the magical thought that one can overcome death through some mental or emotional activity or symbolic gesture. As I will point out later in this discussion, even the early Christian views of hell were colored by these two images: the one that leads into the darkness where there is no vision of rescue and only blind hope in the mercies of God; the other that leads into the underworld with some hope of a rescue and return or, at the very least, a predictable calculus of pains and rewards in the afterlife. Like Gilgamesh, one seeks "a remedy." For Gilgamesh, the penultimate remedy was magical: a root that he fetched from the depth of the ocean, only to lose it again in a moment of inadvertence. For Augustine, the remedy was to see all friendships under the aspect of eternity. For Freud, the remedy was to accept the passage of time and to seize time itself. In the end, for both Gilgamesh and Freud, magic has failed. Gilgamesh ultimately returns home, accepting his mortality; there he dies. Freud leaves his home for exile in Britain, where he dies.

The descent into hell, then, begins with an experience of losing someone who was both an intimate friend and whose death was not expected or imagined. One seeks to recover oneself through a period of testing in which one is tempted by the impossible. Having tried magic only to find it wanting, in the end one returns from the descent to face and accept the particularity of one's own being; one can only be who one is, where one is. That being, finally, is temporary at best and wholly subject to the passage of time. One finally then accepts one's inevitable death.

It would be hard to find a more acute awareness of hopeless desire than is contained in the following passage describing the descent of Odysseus into "The Kingdom of the Dead." Here he waits for his mother to come to him, and when she does her first words sound a knell of anguish across the distance that separates them still:

> She knew me at once and wailed out in grief
> and her words came winging toward me, flying home:
> "Oh my son – what brings you down to the world
> of death and darkness? You are still alive!
> It's hard for the living to catch a glimpse of this . . .
> Great rivers flow between us, terrible waters,
> The Ocean first of all – no one could ever ford
> That stream on foot, only aboard some sturdy craft. . . ."
> (Homer 1996:254, II.177–85)

Those winged words flew like arrows; it is not only the mother's heart that is pierced with grief. Odysseus's own sorrow is intensified by the irrevocable lapse of time between them: a time span depicted in terms of space. It is a river, that is, nature, that separates the living from the dead and makes life hell for both.

I mention Odysseus because the invention of hell as a place of intense and hopeless longing did not lose its classical roots in the process of becoming Christian. There is no tendency in Dante, for instance, to treat earlier work as "mythic, archaic, and false," as did Virgil with Homer (Pike 1997). Whereas in Dante's *Inferno*, however, it is the dead who inquire of the living for news of family and friends on the surface of the earth, for Homer it is the living who inquire of the dead. Odysseus asks his mother for word of the fate of his wife, his father, and son, and he assumes that his mother is aware of his wife's "turn of mind, her thoughts" (Homer 1996:255, II. 201–2). The association between wife and mother is intimate indeed.

The bond between Odysseus and his mother is one of grief, and it is a passion that can be lethal. First it is Odysseus's mother who acknowledges that it was her sorrow over his long absence that had killed her:

> No, it was my longing for you, my shining Odysseus –
> you and your quickness, you and your gentle ways –
> that tore away my life that had been sweet.
> (Homer 1996:256, II.230–2)

It is also Odysseus who is suffering in anguish and heartbreak:

> And I, my mind in turmoil, how I longed
> to embrace my mother's spirit, dead as she was!
> Three times I rushed toward her, desperate to hold her,
> Three times she fluttered through my fingers, sifting away
> like a shadow, dissolving like a dream, and each time the grief cut

to the heart, sharper, yes, and I,
I cried out to her, words winging into the darkness:
"Mother – why not wait for me? How I long to hold you! "
                         (Homer 1996:256, II.233–40)

This is mortal grief, capable of causing the heart to break. Homer portrays the oneness of mother and son in ways that are not only poignant but that make him almost our contemporary. The close succession of the narrative of heart-break, first the mother's and then the son's, points not only to the closest of emotional identifications between the two but to the reciprocity of crime and punishment. If the son's departure had caused his mother's heart to fail, it is only fitting that the son's heart, too, should fail him precisely at the moment that he realizes his irrevocable separation from her. Hell is indeed the experience of longings that are intense enough to fill one's entire being and are yet known at the moment of passion to be hopeless.

For the living, however, there is still time to experience life as a form of deathly suspense. Waiting is the lot of the living. Indeed, Odysseus begs his mother to wait, and his mother assures him that his wife is:

                         . . . still waiting
There in your halls, poor woman, suffering so,
Her life an endless hardship like your own . . .
Wasting away the nights, weeping away the days.
                  (Homer 1996:255, II.207–10)

His wife's life of endless waiting, then, is as his mother says, like his own. The chain of suffering continues. His wife must be punished for the mother's crime of keeping him forever waiting; his wife, too, must be kept waiting. Sons whose affections are tied to their mothers are not ready to go home to their wives, and thus their marriages are in a sort of emotional limbo until the final separation between the son and mother occurs. No wonder that Odysseus recognizes among the dead the mother of Oedipus, "beautiful Epicaste," who went down to Death who guards the massive gates.

Lashing a noose to a steep rafter, there she hanged aloft,
strangling in all her anguish, leaving her son to bear
the world of horror a mother's Furies bring to life.
                  (p. 258, II.307, 314–17)

An inordinate affection of a son for a mother or of a mother for a son can become a hopeless and fatal desire that brings condemnation to both the living and the dead.

There is, in psychoanalytic terms, a conflict between what the individual feels is necessary and yet knows to be impossible. Nowhere is this conflict more apparent than in the loss of someone who was deeply loved and was never fully imagined to be mortal. Let us now return to Augustine of Hippo, who like Gilgamesh mourned the death of a friend and found himself grieving for the loss of a secular eternity. Instead of speaking of unconscious fantasies, however, he faulted himself for having believed in "one huge fable, one long lie" (Augustine 1963:78, Book IV, 8). The lie, of course, was that his friendship could go on forever. As Augustine put it, "For the reason why that great sorrow of mine had pierced into me so easily and so deeply was simply this; I had poured out my soul like water on to sand by loving a man who was bound to die just as if he were an immortal" (p. 78, Book IV, 9).

Along with the fantasy that a relationship can go on forever, however, was another delusion: Augustine's belief that he and his friend were merged in a single consciousness:

> For I felt that my soul and my friend's had been one soul in two bodies, and that was why I had a horror of living, because I did not want to live as a half being, and perhaps that was why I feared to die, because I did not want him, whom I had loved so much, to die wholly and completely. (p. 76, Book IV, 6)

Not only does Augustine recognize a belief in a timeless relationship as a "lie" or a "fable." He has traced the origin of that experience of timelessness to an imaginary merging of two psyches: "one soul in two bodies." Although he did not argue the psychoanalytic point that such an imaginary fusion is a desperate attempt to recover the feeling of timelessness associated with the womb, Augustine did insist that this attempt to find a perfect accord of two souls in a "timeless" relationship was an abortive effort to recapture and recapitulate eternity itself. It took some time for Augustine to trace his loathing of death to the fear that his dying would complete, and make irrevocable, the death of his deceased friend.

What is lost when one imagines that one is fused with another? Augustine answers that question quite simply: one's own soul. In her perceptive discussion of Augustine's grief, Genevieve Lloyd goes on to argue that "The loss of a friend loved as another self makes the soul a burden to itself. But this loss only makes visible a wretched state of separation from himself which was already there, fuelled by the attachment to something external" (Lloyd 1993:17).

It is just such an attachment that Augustine had in mind when he talked about pouring out his soul like water onto sand. The soul is thus dissipated; Augustine speaks of the "distension" of the soul as one confuses one's own psyche with that of another. Thus ". . . for Augustine . . . time itself is to be understood in terms of the distension of the soul" (Lloyd 1993:36). To project the self forward into the future, into an indefinite present, or backward into the past thus ensures that one will experience time itself as serious, fateful, yet perhaps under one's control.

The danger of such a "distension" of the soul, of course, is that the soul will be encased in – and thus confused with – its trappings. If the inner self becomes fused with another person, the memory of that person displaces the individual's own experience of the self and becomes its surrogate. To be a lost soul is precisely to be forced to search for oneself, whether by retracing one's journey or by seeking to recover the immediacies of childhood. Mourning becomes a perpetual attempt to recover one's own inner self. Thus there is indeed a large element of self-loss in such relationships as a result of the imaginary fusion of the self with another. Augustine goes on to report that he looked everywhere for his dead friend, in all the familiar places where he used to be found, but he looked in vain.

To recover the soul, however, it is necessary to realize that one cannot preserve attachments over time or complete unfinished loves, once death intervenes. Thus there is an original tendency to self-mortification underlying the desire for the fusion of one's soul with another's. Although, for the libido, as Freud might have put it, it is never too late to complete the partial gestures of love, time being a stranger to the id, after death of the beloved, however, it is in fact always too late to complete and fulfill old loves, no matter what lies one tells oneself, and no matter what delusions one entertains. Those who refuse to accept the fact that death has broken an intimate relationship thus hold on to the residues of the dead within themselves: harboring in their psyches the presence of the past. As Freud noted in his reflections on dreams in which dead friends and colleagues reappeared, it was he, himself, who felt that he was too "late." He, too, was not only tardy but a mere ghost of his former self.

The notion that one is in a timeless relationship feeds on an illusion of spiritual unity that originated in the womb and may have survived into the first weeks of infancy. In the womb, of course, two hearts did indeed beat as one: hence the fantasy of a merger of selves like that between the mother and child prior to birth. The wish to restore that unmediated unity, moreover, lies at the root of the desire for self-mortification and for access to eternity, because only an obliteration of one's separateness, uniqueness, and autonomy could restore such a primitive union. For Augustine, therefore, the problem is that he is looking for the eternal where it cannot be found; he is seeking to find in a friendship with a mortal the everlasting joys that can only be found in a relationship that is literally selfless. The memory of the lost attachment can then be subsumed within a belief that one was once in an unmediated relationship to the divine: the problem thus becomes one's separation from God. Perpetual mourning is then transformed into a longing for eternity. To sublimate grief into religious strivings for eternity, however, only encourages a this-worldly experience of hell. As Genevieve Lloyd puts it, in her discussion of Augustine: "Reflection on the idea of eternity serves to focus and intensify the experience of incompleteness and fragmentation that goes with being in time" (Lloyd 1993:39). Earlier, I mentioned an alternative, less exhaustive and more authoritarian, calculated, punitive view of hell as a place where one gets what one perhaps unfortunately deserves. Thus Dante's descent into hell reveals the punishments of those whose desires became transgressions of the ordinances of the church. The descent into hell has lost some of its existential character of a journey to recover lost elements of the self, however, and has been mixed with the ideology of religious intellectuals and professionals. These status groups, as Weber called them, have a vested interest in providing reasons for torment and suffering that reinforce their own authority. Even there, however, one can find the more primitive and existential elements of grief and mourning, and of the attempt to recover the soul from its earlier attachments.

For Dante, hell is the "realm of grief," whose "emperor" is Lucifer, Satan himself (Dante 1996:297, Canto XXXIV.31). There is no forgetting in hell, despite the knowledge that it is too late to fulfill one's obligations: too late either to undo the damage that one has done, to take revenge for old injuries, or to fulfill old longings and recover lost loves. Forgetting, as Dante reminds us, is allowed only those who, being in Purgatory, are well away from the abyss of hell: "There where, repented guilt removed, souls gather/To cleanse themselves" (Dante 1996:117, Canto XIV.117–18). Hell simultaneously exposes the naked soul to the ravages of time and of unfulfilled passion.

Dante's hell is a reminder that passions may be undying, but that the objects of such passions are usually mortal. Mourners are therefore left with their unsatisfied affections, divided loyalties, and unfulfilled sense of duty. Hell is a place of negatives, as we shall soon see. It is too late to satisfy these passions or discharge these old obligations, but the debts and passions remain unforgotten as well as unfulfilled. To be in hell is thus to be "too late."

Although Dante himself as pilgrim has the hope of a final restoration, those he meets in Hell have no such prospects. Take, for example, the first circle in hell; it is the Limbo that contains the souls of all those who died before the time of Christ and who were not among those rescued by Christ in his descent into hell. Some indeed were taken captive then: notables of past revelation like Abel and Abraham, Moses, and David. The remainder became an abandoned remnant with no hope of salvation; as Virgil, who belongs in this Limbo, explains it to Dante:

> We are lost, afflicted only this one way:
> That having no hope, we live in longing.
> (Dante 1996:29, Canto IV.31–2)

That is precisely the point of hell. There the damned know that it is too late for them; there will be no other life, no other possibilities, no restoration to an "encompassing state" of eternal communion with the source of life. On the other hand, they do not cease to long for such a redemption. For those in Purgatory, as Dante later argues, there is yet hope; they have time, and in Purgatory time itself is registered on the face of various clocks: the calendar there being the same as the one that orders the life of the living. In hell, however, there is no time at all. Dante speaks more than once of the "timeless air" that the souls breathe who constitute "the population of loss" (pp. 19, 27, Cantos IV.21, III.3).

There is a form of suffering, then, peculiar to hell. It is not as if the past is forgotten; on the contrary, the past can be a source of memories of bliss as well as a prod to shame and remorse. One adulterous lover therefore explains to Dante that "No sadness/ Is greater than in misery to rehearse/Memories of joy, as your teacher well can witness" (Dante 1999:43, Canto V.107–9). This rehearsal would not be sad, of course, if there were any hope of restoration or reunion, but in Hell there is no such possibility. It is "too late," although longings do not cease and perhaps even intensify.

There is nothing that more concentrates the mind than the knowledge that one's most heartfelt desire will remain forever unassuaged and undiminished. As Erich Auerbach put it in his discussion of Dante's *Inferno*,

> And still more: from the fact that earthly life has ceased so that it cannot change or grow, whereas the passions and inclinations which animated it still persist without ever being released into action, there results as it were a tremendous concentration. (Auerbach 1953:192)

Those in hell therefore have no time; the past eclipses the present. One might think that the souls in hell have only the present, but – as Auerbach notes – they do not have any sense of real time as it is on earth: ". . . they are passionately interested in the present state of things on earth, which is hidden from them" (Auerbach 1953:193). Remember that Odysseus's mother had no such difficulty in knowing what was happening on earth. Under the auspices of the church and of the clergy, a new torment has been added to the experience of being late: the hell of being totally shut off from the land of the living. It may be a particularly monastic punishment devised by those who know what it means to be unable to see and imagine what is happening on earth.

Dante offers us one more image of hell as a "realm of grief": an image that combines these complex themes into a single explanation for hell itself. The rivers of hell, that drain into a blood-red stream seething with passion, are simply the end result of a "rain of tears." Somewhere within a mountain on the island of Crete, Dante reminds us, stands an Old Man, made from gold, silver, bronze, iron, and clay from head to right foot: an allegorical depiction of various themes culled by Dante from classical and scriptural sources and suggesting the passage of time from one kingdom or civilization to the next (Dante 1996:237, note to Canto XIV.86–98). From cracks in this inanimate Old Man flow the tears that become the torrents of hell: grief turning sour and bloody-minded before being spent in forgetfullness.

Clearly social systems and civilizations are no proof against the passage and ravages of time. Dante therefore goes on to have Virgil describe Crete as a "waste land," "like some worn thing by time decayed" (Dante 1996:115, Canto XIV.78,82). For Dante, hell is a place of "naked souls, all of whom mourned/ Most miserably." Mourning, furthermore, is a state in which life itself seems suspended. In confronting the city of Satan, for instance, Dante reported that he "neither died nor kept alive . . ." but that he was "denuded of death and life" (p. 295, Canto XXXIV.28,30).

The source of mourning, however, and of the rage that accompanies it, is love for one's place of birth. As if to make the point more baldly, Dante describes the island of Crete as the place where Rhea hid her son, Jove, in a mountain away from the wrath of Saturn. Just as Mars threatens Florence for abandoning him, Saturn seeks to take his fury out on Rhea by seeking to kill their son, whom she hides in Mt. Ida (p. 327, note to Canto XIV.78-85). There, too, is the statue of the Old Man, from whose cracks flow the tears of mourning for a lost birth place. For that loss no civilization can provide redemption, just as no kingdom can transcend the passage of time. It is as if there were a fatal contradiction, the perennial warfare between father and son: the son seeking to recover the maternal space from which he came, while the father stands guard to ensure that no one returns through the maternal gates from which, as Dante reminds us, all once have passed on their way into life and into their own encounter with time.

The descent into hell, then, is at the very least an anticipation of one's own death. It entails a conscious apprehension of the time when it is too late to fulfill old desires or satisfy ancient animosities. At that time there is indeed no future; one's character and identity are forever fixed, and there is no possibility of further development. The passage of time is itself suspended, and there is no present, just as one in hell is weightless and without substance. It is a dangerous descent, since those who are tempted to predict their future or flee from that certain prospect have their character fixed forever in the form of one who is constantly looking backwards and seeking to make up for lost time. This descent requires more, therefore, than a *memento mori*; it requires a guide into the depths of one's own suppressed or forgotten passions, that burn unassuaged by the passage of time. Along with the experience of unmitigated desire, however, comes the simultaneous experience that such longing is forever hopeless. One lives on the cusp of despair.

I have further suggested that this descent not only into the limits of one's existence but into the realms of the libido requires a secular guide, one who like Virgil is no longer distracted or confused by the fantasy of rescue, because hell has been harrowed once and for all. For the pilgrim, however, there is always the hope of being returned to the temporal without the burden of the past and of one's character. That is why the Christian pilgrim, even one like Dante, cannot really undertake this spiritual descent. For the poet, moreover, the end is never out of sight, and it is one of ecstatic reunion with one whose love transcends the passage of time.

Thus Dante's descent into hell is only figurative: a foreshadowing of a later ascent at the end of which he is transported by joy and reunited in ecstasy with the objects of his adoration. At first he is touched by the suffering of others, but under Virgil's direction he learns to curb his pity. Therefore other souls suffering in hell are not recognized as shades of himself, nor is he ever subject to the infernal regime of time in which it is too late to satisfy soul-destroying passions. On the contrary, for Dante as for Virgil, the temporal regimen of the world above still exercises its constraints, and they are both under pressure to pursue their journey without staying overlong in the very place to which these unhappy souls are consigned forever. That is why I cannot agree with Freccero's assessment that

> The descent into hell, whether metaphorical as in the *Confessions* [of Augustine], or dramatically real as in Dante's poem, is the first step on the journey to the truth.

It has the effect of shattering the inverted values of this life (which is death, according to Christian rhetoric) and transforming death into authentic life. (Freccero 1986:4)

Unavoidably, then, there is a certain "as if" quality to the Dantean descent into hell, just as Augustine reminisces in the sort of tranquility that comes from seeing things under the aspect of eternity. Neither Augustine nor Dante have renounced the transcendence of the soul that lives in God and thus experiences all loss as merely provisional: contained, as it were, within the reach of everlasting arms. Their search for that transcendence has indeed taken a roundabout route through the depths of vicarious despair, but they are still a long way from the depths of the unconscious and from the acceptance of an existential point of no return.

I am arguing that one can find the perennial origins of religion in the existential refusal to submit to unbearable loss; religion begins with a conscious rebellion against the passage of time. Thus the poet, philosopher, and convert all short-circuit their descent into hell by viewing it from the vantage-point of eternity or at least from a point of transcendence over the passage of time. They may regard it as a pilgrimage whose end is never in doubt. They may allow old passions to endure in a compartment of the psyche, or they may turn the descent itself into a dramatic or liturgical performance. Thus the journey of the pilgrim becomes a substitute for the actual descent, a mere "dramatization," to use Freccero's apt term. The journey becomes a substitute, as it were, for arriving at the destination. So long as one is on such a spiritual trek, one is allowed to postpone the act of will that consigns certain longings and parts of the self to the past; one can keep potentiality alive without a radical confrontation with one's limits and limitations. Thus the journey keeps one in a condition of being delayed or arrested in one's development: a chronic supplicant or arriviste.

Neither convert nor poet therefore truly leave the past behind. Just as Augustine in his *Confessions* spoke of a "maimed and half-divided will, struggling, with one part sinking as another rose," Dante spoke of an arduous journey up the mountain, with his left foot lower than his right: the left foot standing for a spirit that lacks animation from the heart and guidance from the intellect (Freccero 1986:43–4). Hampered in his journey, then, by a fear that hinders the directives of the will, Dante the pilgrim proceeds like one who is only partly converted and who drags with him the burden of the past.

However, he also walks with the certainty and hope of the poet whose guide, also a poet, is sure to find the way out of hell and lead him to the threshold of the beatific vision. That is why pilgrims are always in danger of running late, not only because the past impedes their progress, but because each footstep is a reminder of their distance from the everlasting. Until they have renounced their desire for a taste of the infinite, they will not have really undertaken the descent into temporality. Both the poet and the convert hold on to a hope for the recovery of timeless love. The decision to consign such a longing, along with the moribund parts of the self, to the past is yet to be made. Their descent into hell is only metaphoric. For those who have truly undertaken the descent into hell, it is already too late to satisfy those longings.

The road to hell is not always paved with good intentions. No wonder that the experience of the poet, as a pilgrim through hell, differs from the experience of those in hell itself. Poets, being on a pilgrimage, are privileged to witness and even to have pity for those suffering from these passions without fully recognizing themselves in those unhappy shades. A demythologized descent into hell will expose the self to its own passions: emotions so intense that they may previously have been numbed or attributed to others, and the day for their fulfillment, if ever there was one, has long passed. Furthermore, murderous affections and rivalries of childhood may leave a legacy of guilt for imaginary crimes and of nostalgia for a grandiose selfhood that was never realized. In the process of experiencing the passions that have no hope of fulfillment, or that have led to real or imagined disaster and loss, one may experience the self as being a shade – shadowy – because one had been mortified, whether by humiliation, rejection, or the loss of love. The self may also seem to be moribund because one is still attached to those toward whom one has had murderous feelings and fantasies.

The shades in hell are often crucial parts of the self, and their recovery may therefore be essential. Like veterans of combat, the survivors of disasters, or children who have been abused, these shades may represent the deadening of fundamental elements of the self. Perhaps the deadened self may simply have been mortified by verbal aggression. It is nonetheless crucial to recognize and express those parts of the self that have been numbed or deadened, whether because they were too painful or merely too shameful to acknowledge.

In the lives of most persons, however, there are often little psychic deaths along the way that cannot later be undone: mortifications of the self that are beyond redemption. It is important to be able to accept these irreversible losses of the self as preparation for the final act of renouncing outdated attachment and emotion; otherwise the attempt to recover the lost self may lead to a perennial pilgrimage through hell rather than to a descent and, later, to a genuine termination of the past. Without such a termination, one goes through life seeking to reestablish primitive and primordial ties of imaginary mutuality: a communion of the spirit that defies the facts and logic of difference, separation, and loss. If one is ever to ascend from such a descent into hell, therefore, one eventually will necessarily allow earlier and outdated, but not yet outgrown, aspects of the self to wither and die.

The origins of religion in every generation are thus to be found in the inability of the psyche to accomplish two feats. One is to place certain desires and aspirations firmly in the past: to finish old quarrels, abandon old ambitions, part with old loves. The other is to allow these desires to die a slow death: not to split them off from the psyche but to deprive them of the nourishment that comes from a sense of possibility. One feat requires the soul to give the devil of time its due: to acknowledge the passage and irreversibility of time itself. The other requires the soul to let a cherished part of itself atrophy and perish in a slow but determined renunciation of desire. Otherwise the soul is anchored in the past. Old loves still demand satisfaction, as do old grievances. The past, however, remains to be created. The soul lives as though it were not too late, even though it knows that there is no hope whatsoever for these longings to be fulfilled. On the horns of this dilemma, so to speak, the soul is impaled, unable to move forward and yet unwilling to part with the past.

Among the perennial and proximate causes of religious interest and enthusiasm are the mind's strategies for playing games with the passage of time. Religion helps the psyche to live with the legacy of traumatic experience by attenuating suffering rather than enduring and resolving acute and unavoidable anguish. In a delaying reaction to psychic pain, the self seeks to 'buy time' by thinning out traumatic experience, but in so doing the psyche goes into debt once again to the temporal reservoirs of the unconscious. Only a descent into the actual experience, however long delayed, in the full recognition that it is too late to do anything but suffer for the time being, sets the stage for the creation of the past as that which has been truly superseded.

It is, after all, the earlier stages of the self that seek to keep opportunities and possibilities wide open, whereas the later and more adult stages inevitably face the limits and end of time. However, in Christianity the individual is asked to convert, in the sense of leaving behind old loves and attachments, unassuaged grief and hopeless longings, in order to undertake a new life under the auspices of the Christian spirit. Nonetheless, the "old Adam," we understand from the Pauline epistles, remains, and so does the conflict between the earlier and later self. Sometimes it is the elder self that condemns the younger; sometimes it is the younger that seeks to convince the elder that the latter is a fraud and has not yet graduated or arrived. Other sources of temporal anxiety emerge from parts of the self that are split off and are beginning to die in solitary confinement, as it were. These parts of the self also send out desperate messages about time running out and seek to convince the dominant self that it is moribund. Conversion is no antidote to the legacy of infancy or to the trauma of loss.

A Secular Descent: Psychoanalysis

In contrast to Christianity, psychoanalysis places the full responsibility on individuals for saving their own souls from psychic death. The individual's will must be strong enough to confront and reject the passions and forces that wound the "inward self." Hell is the experience of passions so intense that in self-defense individuals numb, mortify, and deaden part of themselves; for such people, who have undergone a partial psychic death, it is indeed too late to feel, let alone to satisfy, those old longings. The Freudian demand that the obscurity and complexity of mixed and negative feelings be articulated in analysis, so that they can become parts once again of a more integrated and therefore more vital self, is itself closely related to the romantic tradition's embrace of all that is human.

That is one danger of the descent into hell; one can seem permanently alienated from oneself; the death agony of the soul becomes a way of life.

A masochistic journey into night, so to speak, is a perennial danger; it poses the threat of self-destruction. The tendency of the individual to dissolve the self in the milieu of infancy is what Freud came to understand as a primary form of masochism. Formerly Freud had thought that the masochist was a person who took aggression that was initially directed outward and turned it inward. Later, however, Freud came to the conclusion that sadism was initially directed toward the self and only later came to be directed outward in a move toward self-protection. Thus Freud preferred to speak of a "primary masochism" that is ". . . still strange to us" and went on to ask:

> But how can the sadistic instinct, whose aim it is to injure the object, be derived from Eros, the preserver of life? Is it not plausible to suppose that this sadism is in fact a death instinct which, under the influence of the narcissistic libido, has been forced away from the ego and has consequently only emerged in relation to the object? It now enters the service of the sexual function. (Freud 1961:48)

Thus the path to the development of the self requires that the self-destructive impulse be turned outward, and that one become aggressive toward objects. The oral sadism of infants is crucial to their freedom from primary masochism. Augustine's oral sadism in the courts of law, which was so horrifying to him later, was simply part of his development: the price others had to pay for his freedom from primary masochism. It was a short-lived freedom, as he turned his aggression inward into techniques of self-examination that were lacerating and destructive. (Witness his ending his life weeping as he examined himself according to the penitential psalms.)

Freud earlier was at some pains to separate instincts that were self-destructive (the ego-instincts) from the sexual instincts, which seemed free from the need to repeat and to reproduce the past (1961:38–9). In Freud's constant splitting and resplitting of the self into ego and sexual instincts, or into life and death instincts, or into love and hate instincts, we find him wrestling with a need to purify the self or the organism of some form of internal opposition that he is loathe to confront directly. Nonetheless, in the end he was forced to suggest that the most primitive of all tendencies was one toward self-destruction: the dissolution of the self into the elements of inanimate nature.

That is why the descent into hell may be so dangerous. It is not only because one may get into an internal struggle between one's earlier and emerging self, or because one can waste one's life in such infernal preoccupations; there is in the nether regions of the psyche itself a wish to self-destruct. Until and unless one emerges from this descent, one can live, like the shades, in a wholly insubstantial and tormented half-life. Such a permanent descent is indeed self-destructive, and it is therefore important at least to be warned in advance against undertaking such a descent without the presence of a guide. In *The New Introductory Lectures*, Freud suggests that self-destructiveness itself is entirely primitive:

Let us go back to the special problem presented to us by masochism. If for a moment we leave its erotic components on one side, it affords us a guarantee of the existence of a trend that has self-destruction as its aim. If it is true of the destructive instinct as well [as of the libido] that the ego – but what we have in mind here is rather the id, the whole person – originally includes all the instinctual impulses, we are led to the view that masochism is older than sadism, and that sadism is the destructive instinct turned outwards, thus acquiring the characteristic of aggressiveness. . . . It really seems as though it is necessary for us to destroy some other thing or person in order not to destroy ourselves, in order to guard against the impulsion to self-destruction. A sad disclosure indeed for the moralist! (Freud 1965:105)

In the midst of this passage Freud goes on to mention that this tendency toward self-destruction is visible when it appears as sexual masochism or as aggressiveness toward others. Once the impulse to self-destruct has been combined with the more pleasurable pursuits of sexuality, masochism takes the familiar form of finding pleasure in what to an observer would seem unpleasant or painful. This characteristic, which for some commentators defines masochism, is for Freud merely one of its side-effects: a later development of the original impulse to dissolve the self. Later Freud goes on to trace this impulse to a universal desire to return to inanimate nature, that is, to a death instinct.

Freud's notion of a primitive masochism is more radical than Ferenczi's observation that some individuals seem to dissolve in the presence of others, but both are directed toward understanding a fundamental tendency toward self-obliteration. Ferenczi notes that a certain "narcissism . . . is indispensable as the basis for personality," and without it "the individual tends to explode, to dissolve itself in the universe, perhaps to die" (Ferenczi 1995:129). He argues that the "environment" of the individual should provide a "counterpressure," perhaps in the form of a "positive interest" in the individual that will keep the individual's love and attention from being dissipated into the world. This would seem to suggest that narcissism may emerge as a defense against primitive masochism and that self-love is a far more fragile plant than self-hatred. In this regard, Freud makes a telling, even a radical comment:

Theoretically we are in fact in doubt whether we should suppose that all the aggressiveness that has returned from the external world is bound by the super-ego and accordingly turned against the ego, or that a part of it is carrying on its mute and uncanny activity as a free destructive instinct in the ego and the id. *A distribution of the latter kind is the more probable; but we know nothing more about it.* (Freud 1965:109)

Freud's argument is radical because, pursued to its conclusion, there is an inner tendency toward masochism which is exceedingly self-destructive and yet hard to locate: "mute and uncanny."[3]

But there is no difference in principle between an instinct turning from an object to the ego and its turning from the ego to an object – which is the new point now under discussion. Masochism, the turning round of the instinct upon the subject's own ego, would in that case be a return to an earlier phase of the instinct's history, a regression. The account that was formerly given of masochism requires emendation as being too sweeping in one respect: there *might* be such a thing as primary masochism – a possibility which I had contested at the time. (Freud 1961:48–9)

Notes

1   Unfortunately the historical evidence for an underlying rite is lacking, which leaves us looking elsewhere for rituals in which the noblest, most potent and representative individual must make a journey to the place of departed souls.
2   Bernstein is quoting from Pritchard 1969; the Assyrian Version, tab.X, ii, lines 13–16, and iii, lines 29–32.
3   It may not be possible to observe the primary masochistic tendency but only to see it embodied in what the psychoanalyst, Jill Montgomery, calls imaginary "archaic torturers" (Montgomery 1989:29–36). Given a mind that is host to these images, it is difficult for such a person to be at peace or in solitude; they need internal sources of benign support and protection. Thus when the psychoanalyst goes on vacation, these "archaic torturers" pose a renewed threat to the psyche of the patient. Indeed, Montgomery notes that a masochistic individual may seek time and again to return to infantile states of mind: e.g. a timeless association with the mother, and yet also struggle, as though in a womb, for space and freedom of movement.

References

Auerbach, E. 1953. *Mimesis. The Representation of Reality in Western Literature*, Transl. W.R. Trask. Princeton, NJ: Princeton University Press.
Augustine 1963. *The Confessions of St. Augustine*, Transl. R. Warner. New York and Scarborough, Ontario: New American Library.
Bell, C. 1997. *Ritual Perspectives and Dimensions*, New York, Oxford: Oxford University Press.
Bernstein, A.E. 1993. *The Formation of Hell. Death and Retribution in the Ancient and Early Christian Worlds*. Ithaca, NY and London: Cornell University Press.
Dante 1996. *The Inferno*, Transl. R. Pinsky. New York: The Noonday Press.
Ferenczi, S. 1995. *The Clinical Diary of Sandor Ferenczi*, Ed. J. Dupont, Transl. M. Balint, and V. Zarday Jackson. Cambridge, MA: Harvard University Press.
Freccero 1986. *Dante. The Poetics of Conversion*.
Freud, S. 1961. *Beyond the Pleasure Principle*. Ed. and transl. J. Strachey. New York: W.W. Norton.
Freud, S. 1965. *New Introductory Lectures on Psychoanalysis*, Ed. and transl. J. Strachey. New York: W.W. Norton.
Goethe, J.W. von 1994. *Faust*, in *Goethe. The Collected Works*, Ed. and Transl. S. Atkins. Princeton, NJ: Princeton University Press.
Homer 1996. "The Kingdom of the Dead," Book II of *The Odyssey*, Transl. R. Fagles, introduction and notes by B. Knox. New York: Penguin.
Lloyd, G. 1993. *Being in Time. Selves and Narrators in Philosophy and Literature*. London and New York: Routledge.

Montgomery, J.D. 1989. "The Return of Masochistic Behavior in the Absence of the Analyst," in *Masochism: The Treatment of Self-Inflicted Suffering*, Eds. J.D. Montgomery and A.C. Greif. Madison, WI: International Universities Press.

Pike, D.L. 1997. *Passage Through Hell: Modernist Descents, Medieval Underworlds*. Ithaca NY: Cornell University Press.

Pritchard, J.B. 1969. *Ancient Near Eastern Texts Relating to the Old Testament*, 3rd edn., Princeton, NJ: Princeton University Press.

PART II

Contemporary Trends in the Relation of Religion to Society

Editorial Commentary: Whose Problem is it? The Question of Prediction versus Projection 197

11 Secularization Extended: From Religious "Myth" to Cultural Commonplace 211

12 Social Movements as Free-floating Religious Phenomena 229

13 The Social Process of Secularization 249

14 Patterns of Religion in Western Europe: An Exceptional Case 264

15 The Future of Religious Participation and Belief in Britain and Beyond 279

16 Religion as Diffusion of Values. "Diffused Religion" in the Context of a Dominant Religious Institution: The Italian Case 292

17 Spirituality and Spiritual Practice 306

18 The Renaissance of Community Economic Development among African-American Churches in the 1990s 321

19 Hell as a Residual Category: Possibilities Excluded from the Social System 336

Editorial Commentary: Whose Problem is it? The Question of Prediction versus Projection

Richard K. Fenn

In Part 2 we explore in more detail and in particular contexts the general tendencies that were introduced in more theoretical terms in the first section. Of these terms none is more controversial or misused than the concept of secularization. It has been misused by those who see religion either as the enemy of secularization or its victim. In fact, as a number of sociologists have long argued, Christianity itself has been a major carrier of secularization and a force behind it for many centuries. Not only has Christianity, in alliance with the state, repressed and destroyed the native pieties of particular groups and regions. Christianity has also secularized the world from within through its theology, which advocates a highly transcendent God whose ways are not the ways of human beings. Under the auspices of such a theology very little can be held to be sacred, and what is sacred is always open to the challenges of faith, inspiration, and fresh revelation. No force is more secularizing than a religion of the spirit that refuses to make the customary sacrifices to the old shrines, whether they be of the temple and its priesthood or of the Christian church itself. Certainly there has been a process of secularization from within and below, as suppressed peoples and communities newly endowed with the authority of Christian faith have failed to render tribute to Caesar or to venerate the church itself. The Reformation is the prime example of a movement that broke the monopoly of the church on the sacred, and the Pentecostal movements of Latin American and Africa are, as we have seen in Part 1, contemporary cases in point.

Christianity has also been a force for secularization in its long and relentless attack on magical thinking and practice. The theological notion that in Christ all the principalities of this world and the elemental forces of the universe have been overthrown is a case in point. Under the auspices of such a theology Christianity has often attacked all those whose sources of inspiration and authority by-passed the authorized channels, ignored the clergy, transcended the hierarchy, and engaged in conversation with unseen spirits on their own terms. In constructing a rational system of theological thought and in enforcing a thorough, detailed discipline of thought, emotion, pedagogy, and sexual practice, the church has at times been able to uproot and destroy competing claims to sacred authority. Rationality and social control are no less secularizing when they are conducted under the auspices of the clergy than of, say, a modern bureaucracy. There has also therefore been a secularization from outside and from above under the auspices of the church itself.

What becomes secularized therefore depends on who is doing the secularizing. That is precisely the point of Demerath's chapter, with which we begin Part 2. Drawing on his comparative study of religion and politics in 14 nations, Demerath liberates the concept of secularization from its long captivity in the arguments of religionists and their sociological friends or despisers. Noting that conventional and institutionalized religion has no monopoly on the sacred, Demerath finds the sacred itself to be an attribute of any culture that has taken on the mantle of authority and is thus accepted on faith: a development that can as well apply to the nation-state or a political ideology, to an institution or to a way of life, as to what traditionally or conventionally has been considered to be religious. Thus the sacred is produced in the marketplace of cultural change, on the battlefield, in the halls of the state, and in the home or on the streets. As with most of the relationships studied by sociologists, the relationship between the sacred and the secular is variable and depends on a wide range of conditions and circumstances.

To reduce the contingencies of the sacred to manageable conceptual proportions is no mean feat, but Demerath may well have offered the readers of this volume a way to do it. The process of secularization may appear to rise up from the indigenous or local levels of a society or it may come from outside influences. In either case the process threatens what had previously been taken for granted and held to be sacred in a society: its beliefs, perhaps, or its limits on the acceptable range of political or sexual freedom. Similarly, Demerath goes on to argue, the secular may be imposed from the top down by authoritative edicts from a dictator or high court. Conversely, the secular may be imposed on a society from outside by the force of arms. Imperialism, he notes, has long been a major source of secularization.

In this way Demerath argues simultaneously that societies inevitably tend to hold sacred their most important beliefs and institutions and that processes of social change from within and from outside any society are not only inevitable but inevitably secularizing in their effects on the sacred. As societies become more democratic, therefore, and more susceptible to influences from the grass roots and from the social periphery, the center will increasingly be subject to secularizing influences. As the state grows in its ability to permeate all aspects of social life and to intrude on spheres previously regarded as inviolate or private, moreover, the less it will be possible to hold sacred any aspect of life. The so-called sacred confidences exchanged between priest and penitent, doctor and patient, lawyer and client, are cases in point. In addition, as societies become more open to outside influences, the more will these imported notions of authority or the good life bring into question what any society has hitherto regarded as sacred. Some of those changes, moreover, may not be imported voluntarily but are brought in by force. That is, of course, a very old tendency exhibited by the church whose evangelizing monks and priests were often accompanied by military retinues and thus brought peace not only by the sacraments but also by the sword.

These are what are sometimes called macrosociological considerations; they pertain to society as a whole rather than to more specialized or local practices and institutions. However, it is also necessary to see secularization as a process that goes on quite often in the practices of everyday life without the dramatization offered by major events or cultural displays. In this regard it is especially helpful that we have Bruce's review of the process by which religion has lost its mono-poly on major functions, from teaching and social control to administration and warfare. These functions were taken up, he argues, by institutions that developed their own values, rules, procedures, and means of ensuring compliance. There was little scope in these newly autonomous areas for religious services or private devotions. Indeed, religion became not only more differentiated from the secular world, but the sacred became increasingly distinct from the profane.

As societies became more complex, they also became more organized and able therefore to overpower the traditional communities, like the ethnic group and the family, in which individuals had been raised and had lived the better part of their lives. Even sanctuaries of privacy and trust, affection and devotion, have been invaded by the larger society's techniques for monitoring behavior and ensuring compliance. Little is therefore left that can be called sacred.

It is precisely such a threat to traditional communities that Gill discusses in his chapter on long-term trends in religious participation. Especially among immigrant communities and sectarian groups, Gill argues, religion will continue to serve important functions for the defense of social identity. For individuals who are identified with the dominant institutions of their countries, further-more, certain traditional civil or religious institutions and rituals will perform the function of preserving their social identity. The future may thus represent two contrary trends: one of overall decline in formal religious participation, the other of an increasingly sharp public defense of the religious markers of com-munal identity.

Bruce is particularly helpful in pointing out that religion, so far from being a helpless victim in this process, has been a major agent of secularization. To begin with, Christianity, like Judaism, has had a tendency to demystify the world and remove from it the sources of enchantment. The world becomes knowable, understandable, even to some extent subject to prediction and control. The indi-vidual believer's ideas and beliefs, practices and relationships, are also subjected to the same sort of rational scrutiny and control, and they display the same sort of consistency as does a universe deprived of irrationality and mystery. Further, the deinstitutionalization of organized religion has proceeded largely under Protestant auspices. Individuals demanded the right to speak in their own voices rather than listen solely to the clergy. Individuals began to make their own spiritual choices rather than to follow received doctrine and authorized versions of belief and practice. Individuals demanded direct access to the sources of grace and got them without benefit of the clergy. In these ways religion not only became more diverse, competitive, less authoritative, and less plausible. Religion also became a function of individual decision and personal preference.

One result of this process of secularization is an expansion in what is considered possible. As individuals gain access on their own terms to the sources of grace, interpret the Bible according to their own insights, choose their sources of livelihood, and raise their children in their own fashions, they become increasingly able and likely to think of – and for – themselves. Bruce makes it clear that in modern democracies a tendency toward economic betterment and technological innovation were the unintended by-products of the changes brought about through the Reformation. The Christian religion defeats itself, so to speak, by its own successes.

As the individual becomes freed from traditional statuses, enabled to play a variety of roles, and authorized to hold property and make political decisions, it is the individual in the long run who becomes the arbiter of what is sacred and what is not. That is an outcome that is implicit in the Protestant notion of the priesthood of all believers, but it is a notion with radical and sometimes disruptive implications. No doubt those implications were very much on the mind of Emile Durkheim, who, as we have seen in the first section, sought to describe modern societies as being integrated around the notion of the individual as sacred. That theoretical move would give radical individualism essentially the conservative function of providing a focus of loyalty and the basis for a consensus on values in a society otherwise too complex and fragmented to be integrated.

A heightened sense of the possible, of course, expands the range of uncertainty that individuals must accept and overcome if they are to make their way through a bewildering array of occupational and ethical choices over the course of a lifetime. The sacred is no longer confined to specific times and occasions or kept under clerical lock and key. The world of the profane becomes increasingly open to the promptings of the sacred. In the 1960s, therefore, consciousness raising became a practice that engaged students and teachers, workers, and those too disenchanted with American society to join the workforce. It was a practice that challenged individuals to become aware of the many ways in which the larger society was constraining them, limiting their chances for fulfillment, or using their gifts for purposes that they themselves would not have intended.

Sociologists reminded those who were elevating individual consciousness that liberation required the change of social structures and not just personal enlightenment. Furthermore, even the practice of consciousness raising itself was the object of sociological scrutiny. Predictably, sociologists found that individuals who thought they were free were in fact acting out the unwritten prescriptions that they learned in their families: prescriptions that varied, of course, according to one's social class and ethnicity. The more individuals thought they were free, the more sociologists reminded them that their freedom itself was a social product and was constrained by social facts that often lay beyond the horizon of everyday consciousness.

In Part 2 you will find sociologists making similar points about the diffusion of the sacred. As an experience that apparently allows individuals to come to terms with the transcendent in their own way, spirituality nonetheless is a practice that follows rules, depends on shared understandings, relies on a tradition, and replicates the past even while opening the door to possibilities for personal growth and relatedness in the future. In his fine chapter on contemporary practices devoted to enhancing individual spirituality, Wuthnow makes precisely these points.

This viewpoint, you will remember from Part 1, owes perhaps more to Durkheim than it does to Weber. To understand the individual as a being derived from the larger society, dependent on it for instruction and guidance, for purpose and even for the definition of personal experience and identity, is typically, but not exclusively Durkheimian. Those who derive their sociological imagination from Weber will tend to emphasize the freedom of the spirit even though acknowledging that spiritual freedom is inevitably, and sometimes very quickly, channeled into social containers where it may remain confined for years. There it may spoil, so to speak, corrupted by its social context into uses that were initially never foreseen or intended. The cross, as David Martin put it, becomes a sword, even though the sign of the cross retains over the long term its freedom to challenge the structures of social power.

In the accounts that constitute Part 2, you will find these different tendencies: to emphasize, on the one hand, the fate of the free spirit as it inevitably comes to terms with its social context, and, on the other hand, to emphasize that individual freedom and spirituality are themselves the products of social institutions that are prior to individual experience. On this latter view, priority of the social over the individual is not only causal but also has moral implications for the individual's experience of the sacred. That experience is properly constrained by social standards; otherwise it ignores and perhaps destroys its own basis in the social order.

In their chapter on the concept of hell, for instance, Fenn and Delaporte trace two different strands over many centuries. One strand places the individual largely at the mercy of a God who has an uncanny resemblance to a Roman emperor: a god on whose mercy the individual is entirely dependent in the next life as in this. On the other hand, there has also been a tendency to see individuals in the next life as working out their salvation through a variety of punishments in places that are clearly extensions of this world: mountains and islands, for instance, on which souls are imprisoned for an unspecified length of time until they have sufficiently regretted the past. It is a hell that for many years was indistinguishable from purgatory. The second view of hell, then, is like the sociological view that allows individuals considerable latitude in working out their fate while recognizing the inevitable interference or even eventual domination of social facts and forces.

Beckford's chapter brings to light the paradoxes of the current religious situation in a variety of countries. On the one hand are the developments that reflect the process of differentiation. Certain traditionally religious institutions are losing some of their distinctiveness, authority, control, and members in complex societies. Professional organizations, community agencies, and support groups have learned to do for themselves what has been done in the past under the auspices of churches, synagogues, mosques, and temples. Education, health, welfare, the management of conflict, the disciplining of the emotions: these functions are now being performed by other institutions and by occupational groups that are licensed by secular authorities and monitored by the state. Differentiation also permits a variety of other religious communities to compete with the churches for influence, membership, public support, and recognition by the state. At the same time, the churches have long been losing their monopoly on what is legitimately considered religious as a wide range of groups and communities define themselves and their goals in religious terms. In something approaching market conditions, religious groups now have to compete with one another for their identity, support, and membership.

Where differentiation is less advanced, of course, religion still operates as a way of binding together ethnic, political, and economic issues under the authority of the transcendent or the supernatural. Beckford notes the conservative religious and political movements in the United States, where race is so potent a factor in defining religious differences, and he calls attention to the radical Islamic movements in Iran and parts of the former Soviet Union. Even in relatively homogeneous societies, however, the process of differentiation has led to a wide range of allegiances and viewpoints that cause conflict among members over organizational policy and activist strategies.

As a result, religious communities and organizations have not only become more numerous and diverse; they also have become more like social movements. That is, even the more conventional churches enter the public sphere as advocates and contestants for particular goals and policies. In this role they resemble social movements in the way they mobilize their constituencies for particular purposes. Although participation is optional and membership fluid, the fact of intense mobilization puts a premium on intense moral commitments to values that are heralded as timeless or even eternal. Beckford speaks at this point of the intensely "spiritual" aspects of participation in efforts to affect public opinion and mobilize support.

In an interesting development of his argument, Beckford notes that it becomes increasingly difficult to distinguish the religious from what he calls the "spiritual" in "industrial societies." Both refer, he argues, "to levels of meaning and significance which go beyond the surface of everyday realities . . . [and] convey a sense of the ultimate significance of things, often creating the impression that human life is part of a comprehensive, timeless scheme." This is very much like what Durkheim called the sacred itself: *"la vie sérieuse."* Although Beckford does not subscribe to the notion of the quasi-sacred, he does suggest that as the sacred is becoming more pervasive and ambiguous, diffuse and problematical, so also is the definition of religion itself.

Religion is the place where the past and the future come together in significant moments, critical incidents, hallowed places, and sacred occasions. Time becomes serious under the auspices of the sacred. The many moments of personal life, and the momentous events in the life of a community, come together in religious forms that create a collective memory. That memory enshrines decisive moments in the past, ennobles loss by transforming it into sacrifice, and turns defeat into holy surrender. These tragedies then become the seeds of new life: the moments at which the shape of the future is to be seen sprouting from the soil of human agony.

To put it another way, the sacred gives place to time. Those places, as Davie points out, have been cathedrals and shrines, churches at the ends of long pilgrimages that traverse the landscape of Europe and turn it into the map of religious memory. That map of the past becomes the pathway into the future: the path along which impulse turns into obligation and desire into duty. With each new generation comes not only a new installment of the past but a fresh deposit, so to speak, on the altar of the future. Generations surrender their lives in the sure and certain hope that their sacrifices will not have been in vain. One lives, in a quiet way, in an eschatological world that is difficult to distinguish from common sense.

What happens when that collective memory begins to fade? Davie makes it very clear that the past itself in Europe is increasingly beyond the reach of personal memory. No longer a living memory, the collective past remains only in the custody of institutions like the church. The church becomes what Davie aptly calls a public utility. It does for individuals what they are no longer able to do for themselves. Memory is thus preserved, but in the form of a museum rather than as a living memory that dignifies and stimulates the lives of individuals and communities.

In this way Davie makes a contribution to the literature on secularization. The secular world is indeed about time: the *saeculum* being another word for the age that is indeed present but passing away. One gets a sense of the temporality of religion in Europe as Davie speaks of the ways in which the past is not localized but rather held in custody, and thus kept at some distance from the daily and immediate experience of individuals who experience their own collective past vicariously at best and, at the worst, in a form of amnesia.

Of course there are contradictions to be found in Europe, and Davie is very quick to point out that not all of Europe fits this picture of religion that is increasingly voluntary, vicarious, optional, and thus also evanescent and temporary. She also points to the numerous immigrant communities in Europe: Muslims and Jews, Turks and Arabs, Slavs and Lithuanians, where the past is anything but distant and fading. On the contrary, in these communities collective memory is vital, vivid, obligatory, enduring, and it commands assent to the point of personal and collective sacrifice. These communities exist on the fringes of each European country, where they live in more or less tension with a center that is rapidly becoming empty of sacred memory. These communities also live on the fringes of Europe as a whole. In Ulster or Kosovo, for instance, people have long memories, plenty of ammunition, and a drive to self-determination that is capable of mobilizing ethnic and political reprisals on a grand scale.

If the sacred has escaped the confines of traditional religious institutions, what passes for authentic religious experience will depend on a wide range of personal and social factors. In his chapter on spirituality, Robert Wuthnow takes up precisely this more diffuse encounter with the sacred and observes that the popularity of the notion of spirituality, as something apart from traditional or conventional religion, is itself a fairly recent development: "Spirituality is somehow more authentic, more personally compelling, an expression of their search for the sacred, while religion connotes a social arrangement that seems arbitrary, limiting, or at best convenient."

As the process of secularization advances, spirituality breaks the institutional frame formerly placed around the experience and definition of the sacred. As Wuthnow says, spiritual practice is no longer the monopoly of religious institutions but is being promoted and regulated in a variety of secular contexts from television and publishing to the schools.

Wuthnow also points out that students of secularization have been more concerned with the position and influence of religion in public life than with the ways in which people actually practice and experience the sacred. His chapter helps to redirect our understanding of secularization toward the more diverse and diffuse aspects of the sacred in complex societies and to the depths with which people are now encountering the sacred in ways that may be very difficult for religion to bind together into a single, overarching system of belief and practice. Indeed, Wuthnow suggests that it may be precisely because of the "erosion" of traditional beliefs and practices that people seek new practices for a "common experience of the sacred." Secularization, then, underlies the proliferation of spiritual practices in search of the sacred itself.

What matters, however, is not the relevance or irrelevance of institutional religion, but what Wuthnow aptly calls the practice of "spirituality in everyday life." By thus freeing the study of spirituality from the domain either of the idiosyncratic or the entirely conventional, Wuthnow places it on the same footing as any other practice, like talk and conversation, that informs and constructs everyday life. Thus practices are ways in which people define who they are in relation to others, engage in some form of interaction with people who are present or absent, and in so doing they often follow or change the rules that govern relationships and communication.

To think of spirituality as a practice thus brings people and what they do back into the center of the picture and marginalizes the institutional contexts which cater to, or seek to control, those practices. Remember that Erickson finds in Simmel precisely this same emphasis on spiritual practice as a way of placing individuals in new relationships to others. Because the spiritual emanates from what Simmel called the soul, spirituality as a practice exemplifies the role of the stranger who brings in influences from outside that may threaten or subvert a particular social order. Because, however, spiritual practice is also partly social-ized, it acts like an insider in fostering relationships, although perhaps in new and creative ways.

To put it another way, the practice of spirituality changes the horizons of everyday life. The practice of spirituality may introduce the possibility of new relationships, alter ways of expressing the self and of experiencing others. It may release impulses and energies into consciousness that have long been ignored or suppressed, and in so doing may undermine or reinforce the familiar world of everyday life. As Capps put it in his chapter in Part 1, the sacred makes the fa-miliar seem strange by allowing the repressed aspects of the self to return in new disguises. In so doing, spirituality opens the door to longings and fantasies that may make individuals less rather than more comfortable in the world to which they have been accustomed. Wuthnow, too, points out that the practice of spirituality allows individuals degrees of spiritual freedom that place them well beyond the limits of spiritual experience that have been approved by the local church or synagogue or by denominational headquarters. Those who pursue the sacred must therefore do so in ways that open themselves up to uncertainty and ambiguity. The goal of spiritual practice is always ambiguous, the way to achieve it uncertain, and the stakes extremely high. It is precisely the sort of practice that is suitable to a world in which the sacred has escaped from its institutional confines.

Even more to the point, the practice of spirituality prepares the individual for a virtual world of interaction and communication with others who are strangers, whom one will never meet, and yet whose lives may impinge closely on one's own. In a cybernetic world there is little immediate connection between one's actual social status or physical location on the one hand, and the limits of available interaction on the other. The horizon of possibility expands, as do the benefits and risks of interaction and uncertainties about the rules.

If individuals are practicing spirituality for themselves, it means that they are now by-passing the institutions that used to mediate between themselves and the divine. Just as individuals are now leaving their brokers to invest on-line for themselves, with little in the way of commissions to be paid, the costs of transaction with the divine are being assumed by the persons engaged in spiritual practices themselves; they are not being paid by any spiritual mediator whose sacrifice alone makes it possible to communicate with the divine. The implications for a Christian faith that has long stressed the importance of a mediator who permits humans to have transactions with the divine could not be greater.

As Beckford has also pointed out, to understand the seriousness of social conflict it is necessary to grasp that for many their participation in a particular cause or movement is filled with sacred significance. The sacred may be a source of awe at the forces unleashed, for example, by nuclear power, or a source of joy at participating in powers that unite humans with nature and thus heal the body, the environment, and the world. As the sacred has become more dispersed, however, and its boundaries more diffuse, it has become more difficult for any institution to gather, organize, and define its members around a particular set of beliefs and values. Religious belief and practice in complex societies becomes more sporadic and occasional, more interactive and fluid, more negotiable and easily contested.

If religion becomes more contingent on a variety of circumstances and agreements, that is because social life itself is coming to depend more on the sort of provisional agreements and understandings that make communication among strangers possible in cyberspace. Social life itself comes to resemble a chat room on the Internet far more than an assembly of true believers ready to subscribe to a creed or to engage in an authoritative collective act. Individuals increasingly engage in the frequent exchange of ideas and symbols, negotiate their mutual commitments and meanings, and revise the conditions for participating in discussion and action. Whether communication occurs in face-to-face gatherings, in more loosely organized social movements, or over the Web, it will become increasingly difficult for any meaning or commitment to be enshrined in any religious creed or to be controlled by any religious institution. Indeed the nature of religious authority is itself contestable and negotiable as the sacred takes on an independent life of its own in these wide-ranging and fluid social contexts. It is this process of increasing uncertainty and fluidity in the location and shape of the sacred that is called the deinstitutionalization of religion.

In view of the arguments so far advanced, it will not be surprising to find that more of our contributors in Part 2 are seeking to define religion in novel ways that avoid sharp boundaries between religion and other aspects of social life. Not only does Cipriani, for instance, wish to blur the conventional sociological distinction between what religion is and what it does, between the substance and function of religion; he also wishes to avoid any sharp demarcation between what is empirically verifiable and nonverifiable. His disrespect for analytical boundaries is forced on him, he suggests, by the development of what he calls diffused religion. Religion is, Cipriani argues, the transmission of values, and that constitutes both its substance and its function. In ordinary language, one might say that religion is the process of assigning worth, that is, of worthship or worship, not only through ritual but through the dissemination of a system of values that affects decisions over a varying range of social life.

Diffused religion, in Cipriani's view, is the form that religion takes in a society that has long been subject to the influence of a particular religious tradition. In the Italian case, Cipriani notes, Catholicism has been able to have an enduring impact, not only on the formal religious beliefs and behavior of Italians but on a wide range of values and attitudes that carry over into political and economic life regardless of any specific religious consciousness on the part of the citizens themselves. Some social classes are more likely than others to carry this diffused form of religion, and some are more likely than others to do so in a way that is consistent with the Catholic tradition, but there can be no doubt that the religious past is very much alive in the present.

Even under the guise of apparently secular choices in politics, for instance, the Italian citizen is living from a tradition that has deeply shaped popular values and therefore constrains and directs secular choices. Granted that there is more freedom of choice outside the context of institutionalized religion than within it, still even in the secular fields of work and politics there is a connection and continuity with the religious tradition that has informed Italian culture and society for nearly two millennia. As Cipriani points out, the diffusion of religion expresses but also limits the process of secularization. Diffused religiosity breaks the monopoly of the church on the sacred but keeps open the door of secular societies to a wide range of sacred aspiration and meaning.

One could say something very similar about the role of African-American churches in developing urban communities in the United States. As in the Italian case, there is a strong tradition of religious training and commitment to the community that provides social capital for a wide range of investments in the larger society. The difference between political, religious, and economic issues is anything but clear-cut in the African-American community. Certainly the churches of that community have long combined aspects of the sacred and the profane in their organization and ministries. The minister may well be an entrepreneur, politician, community organizer, and capitalist, even at the same time that he or she is also a pastor, preacher, and prophet. Prayer is mixed with politics, intercession with investment.

In her contribution to this section, Katherine Day acknowledges the leadership of the African-American church in community organization and development. This blurring of the boundaries between the sacred and the profane is one aspect of the process of dedifferentiation, and in the case of the African-American church it is closely associated with a contrary process of preserving the boundaries of the African-American community itself. The church may be making common cause with other congregations for the sake of the well-being of the metropolitan community as a whole, but it is also devoted to preserving the integrity and increasing the prosperity of the African-American community itself.

As with Cipriani's discussion of the Italian case, so in Day's analysis of the role of the African-American church in the United States, it is clear that the blurring of the boundaries between the sacred and the profane (Cipriani's "diffused religiosity") opens up a wide range of possibilities for social action. Housing programs that turn urban waste areas into livable neighborhoods are understood prophetically to be part of the vision of Ezekiel of a valley of dry bones being given new life. Along with the blending of the sacred with the profane comes new access to the centers of power and of social credit. This access is still mediated to some extent by the pastor of the African-American church, but it is also increasingly available to the lay leadership of the community. Dedifferentiation and disintermediation are thus two of the processes by which the world of the profane becomes opened up to the possibilities previously contained in the sacred.

In Day's account of changes in the African-American churches there is also a brief discussion of the churches' loss of a monopoly on the sacred. That is, lay organizations as secular as the Industrial Areas Foundation in assumptions and background are seeking to give to the leaders of the local community the powers and authority previously monopolized by the clergy of the African-American churches. No doubt the intrusion of these new techniques of community organization is causing some conflict within and between the churches. Some are following the new drumbeat of community organization, while others are relying on the pastor's role as spiritual, economic, and political leader of the community to bring new development. However, the deinstitutionalization of religion in the African-American context does not seem to have proceeded as far as it has among the churches of the liberal, "mainline" denominations. The church remains the primary institution through which the community pursues its interests and defines its identity.

In both the Italian and African-American communities there is a strong defense of the natural community: of the family and the ethnic group. As Cipriani notes, the Italians surveyed in various studies place by far the highest value on the family. This is not surprising, of course. Previous analysts of Italian society have noted the absence of a civic culture and an emphasis on loyalty to the family at the expense of more general or universal attachments to the society or the state. What Edward Banfield (1974) once called "amoral familism" may well still be a source of indifference or cynicism with regard to the larger society.

It is therefore worth asking how the primary emphasis on building up the resources of the African-American community affects that community's relationship to the larger society. Day is quite clear that some African-American churches do join coalitions for the improvement of the larger metropolitan community and enjoy considerable benefits from alliances with other groups. Nonetheless, she argues, the primary emphasis is on the development of the African-American community rather than on the cooperative organization of various communities in pursuit of more jobs, better housing, improved schools, and access to capital. In the context of a history of oppression and of continuing racism in American society, that choice is understandable. To put it another way, the survival of racial and ethnic stereotypes, of ethnic hegemony, and of the churches' role in perpetuating social distance among ethnic groups appears to have placed limits on the process of secularization, at least in the American case.

Whether or not secularization is irreversible, as Bruce argues, is a question that will take on additional meaning as you read each of the contributors to Part 2 of the volume. In making this argument Bruce cites Europe as a prototype of irreversible secularization: Europe which is, as Grace Davie argues out, something of an exception among the world's societies. Indeed, Bruce cannot imagine a return to a religious consensus that is binding on all members of a nation, let alone one that is reinforced by the power of the state. Diversity, fragmentation, complexity, the autonomy of separate regions of social life, the churches' loss of institutional authority, the dissemination of religious goods to the individual, the demand for immediate and equal access to centers of political and cultural authority, the relative equality of individuals vis à vis matters of choice and opinion, and above all the individual's insistence on the right to make these choices without apology, influence, or coercion, are points of no return at least for the part of the world – Europe – that is the focus of his chapter. There the gods of fascism, of ethnic and national hegemony, apparently have died, along with the capacity of the nation-state to call for human sacrifice.

I dwell on the issue of ethnic or familial loyalties in order to focus on what is not emphasized by our contributors: the continued vitality of ethnic or familial loyalties even in complex societies. Certainly the religious right continues to further the interests of white communities in limiting the public resources that are allocated to minorities and especially to African-Americans: the attack on welfare, on affirmative action, and on the rights of immigrants being the more obvious examples. The point is simply that the erosion of boundaries between the sacred and the profane, the deinstitutionalization of religion, and the increasing access of individuals and groups to central sources of economic and political capital may easily be reversed by a reactionary political movement.

If there should be rising levels of unemployment, higher interest rates, increased rates of alcoholism and other addiction, of divorce, suicide, and crime, it would not take long for social movements to demand tighter controls over immigration, over the flow of capital to minority communities, and over access to the schools and the courts. New attempts would be made among both minority and majority communities to strengthen ethnic boundaries and monopolize ethnic loyalties. The boundary between the sacred and the profane would likewise be strengthened, as dominant groups seek to exclude individuals, ideas, artistic expressions, and various forms of entertainment as forms of profanation of values and institutions. The attempt to outlaw flag-burning or to exclude homosexual art from federal funding are cases in point.

It is therefore well to remember Bruce's point about the limits to the process of secularization. These are reached when ethnic groups, especially those who rely on religion to defend their embattled identities, tend to regard other groups as beyond the pale of any salvation. There is under such conditions a return to the most primitive forms of secularization, when one group claims to transcend the passage of time by relegating another group to the world that is passing away. Under these conditions, as Bruce goes on to point out, the penalties for changing one's religious affiliation are high. All one's social and emotional eggs, not to mention one's ideological investments, are in one basket. Where religion and ethnicity are still largely coterminous, religious differences remain a matter of ideological, social, and sometimes physical, life or death.

Institutionalized Christianity, I would argue, has been suffering from what anthropologists used to call cultural fatigue. It has been dying the death of too many contradictions and paradoxes. The more that Christians have adhered to a God that transcended this world, the more they have succeeded in secularizing society and nature. To confine the sacred to certain institutions and to mediate the sacred through a professional elite is indeed what is necessary if God is to be lifted above the mundane, but the effect of such institutionalizing is to take sacred mystery and possibility from the world. In their attempts to invest everyday life, work and politics, the family and education, the economy and the state with religious significance, however, the churches continued to rely too heavily on official communications and professional expertise.

Certainly Protestantism has sought to emphasize the individual's responsibility for belief and practice, but in doing so that has made every belief more or less relative: one among many. The optional nature of belief and practice is thus a side-effect, unwanted, perhaps, but inevitable, of the rigorous Protestant emphasis on personal responsibility. In that emphasis the church has succeeded in destroying an ethos in which belief and practice were second nature: part of a taken-for-granted world of possibility and obligation. In its attempt to inculcate an ethic of responsibility on the part of the laity, institutionalized religion has helped to create a bureaucratized society in which responsibility is diffused in large, complex organizations. In such a bureaucratic society no one is personally responsible; as President Clinton put it, one only makes "honest bureaucratic mistakes."

As many of the contributors to this volume have already indicated, however, we are entering – have entered – a relatively unstable world in which the Spirit, so to speak, moves wherever it will without the benefit of clergy and without being contained within religious institutions. That horrendous or revolutionary possibilities both for life and death can crystallize in particular places has always been an object of sociological fascination; Durkheim's preoccupation with "collective effervescence" is a case in point. The crowds in Munich, waving their red flags and shouting "Heil Hitler," are not easily forgotten, so much so that the presence of crowds outside Kensington Palace on the death of Princess Diana triggered once again fears of latent fascism. If there are fascist movements in the future it will in part be because of the churches' failure to mediate and contain the sacred, and they will also arise partly because it is too frightening to live in a world in which the ultimate possibilities both for life and death are ubiquitous and immediate.

Reference

Banfield, E. 1974. *The Unheavenly City Revisited*. Boston: Little, Brown.

CHAPTER 11

Secularization Extended: From Religious "Myth" to Cultural Commonplace

Nicholas J. Demerath III

Today anyone who raises the issue of "secularization" or religious decline in the company of religious scholars runs the risk of being labeled antichurch, antediluvian, or a bore. At least in some circles, a concept that was once an unquestioned staple of scholarly work has been shunted to the unmucked stables of scholarship past. In the eyes of its critics, secularization is a hypothesis that has been proved false and a term that should be expunged from proper usage. The very fact that religion persists and often thrives is ample rebuttal to the "secularization thesis" and a signal to abandon both its explicit assumptions and its implicit agenda.

In disagreeing with this position, I am not alone. The debate over it has become deeper and more raucous than is common in the academy, perhaps because the issues concern not just scholarship but religion with all of its potentially personal overtones. In fact, one of my objectives here is to recapture the argument for social science and rid secularization of connotations that mistakenly threaten both religion and the religious.

This chapter tries not only to salvage secularization but extend it. The first section will argue that criticisms of the concept are based on a greatly – and perhaps purposely – exaggerated statement of its argument that is understandably vulnerable to attack. The second section will review a different version of secularization which is far more plausible, in part because of an oscillating linkage to its seeming opposite, "sacralization." Finally, the last two sections will move the discussion and debate beyond the narrow province of conventional religion into the broader sphere of culture. They will argue that secularization is a primary factor in cultural dynamics and cultural change of all sorts; this includes, but is by no means restricted, to religion.

The Myth of the Myth of Secularization

In its earliest formulations at the hands of such Enlightenment sages and heirs as Voltaire ([1756] 1963), Marx ([1844] 1983), Comte ([1852] 1891), and Spencer ([1874] 1915), there is little question that secularization involved the prophetic end of religion itself. Although such prophecy has been rare among more measured twentieth century analyses, recent critics have preferred to concentrate their fire on the earlier and more extreme versions of the argument and then generalize the results to secularization of any sort and form.

At the hands of critics such as Rodney Stark (Stark and Iannaccone 1994, 1999, Finke and Stark 1992), Laurence Iannaccone (1994), and Stephen Warner (1993), secularization has come to mean the transition between a world where religion is all to a world where religion is nothing at all – that is, between societies where religion is dominant at every level from politics to personal piety, to societies in which religion has disappeared.

Put in this extreme form, it is not hard to reject the "secularization thesis," as it has come to be known. Both of its extreme poles buckle beneath the weight of evidence. Critics point out properly that the very notion of a totally religious society is a mythical construct unsustained by either historical or anthropological evidence. Whether reaching back to ancient societies or reaching out to isolated tribes, one may find religion as a potent force but never omnipotent. Competing interests, rival claims, status jostling within and without the priesthood – all of these have taken their toll on religious domination. Nor is secularity itself unknown in such settings; people on the margins often become alienated from or indifferent to religion.

At the other extreme, where is the society with no traces of religion? Certainly not in the USA or anywhere else in the West. Nor for that matter in the several countries around the globe who have mounted official campaigns against religion – the People's Republic of China or the former USSR. True, religion is sometimes a minority phenomenon in these and other countries, but in no instance can it be described as fully dormant, much less dead.

So much for secularization. Or is it? There is a sense in which the critics have inflated the argument to make it more vulnerable to pricking. Using an all-versus-nothing criterion is a very stringent test indeed, and it ignores the important dynamics and variations that may occur in between these extremes. Even if secularization is seen as a straight-line, linear process from high to low – and I shall argue momentarily that it should not be – one can surely imagine a society whose religion is powerful but not all-powerful, from which there is a religious decline that does not reach demise. To deny conceptual standing to any process of change along a continuum because it does not involve a shift from the extreme maximum to the extreme minimum is to deny scientific examination of everything from temperature gradients to growth patterns. The critical dynamics in virtually all matters of change occur within the midrange of the distributions rather than at the ideal–typical poles.

But having reached this point without a definition of secularization, such a definition is overdue. Consider the following:

> Secularization is the process by which the sacred gives way to the secular, whether in matters of personal faith, institutional practice, or political power. It involves a transition in which things once revered become ordinary, the sanctified becomes mundane, and things other-worldly lose their prefix. Whereas "secularity" refers to a condition of sacredlessness, and "secularism" is the ideology devoted to such a state, secularization is a historical dynamic that may occur gradually or suddenly and may be replaceable, if not reversible. (Demerath in press)

This is a more "middle range" conception of secularization that allows for differences of both degree and kind. In fact, these are both matters for empirical investigation. In principle, one can imagine a massive displacement of religion altogether, but in practice the shifts are likely to be more shaded and more subtle. Moreover, there are different forms of secularization at different levels of society that may or may not accompany each other. For example, in any given society or community, there may be a secularization or diminution of religion's political role but not necessarily a decline in its personal salience for individual adherents.

This is a far cry from the triumphal predictions of Voltaire, Comte, and Marx, or from the Cassandra-like jeremiads of threatened religionists. Virtually all of the major sociological work on behalf of secularization over the past 75 years has occurred in this more closely grounded and finely raked terrain. This includes a wide span of works from Bryan Wilson (1966) to Daniel Bell (1976), David Martin (1978), Richard Fenn (1979, 1993), Karel Dobbelaere (1981, 1993), Robert Bellah et al. (1985), W.C. Roof and William McKinney (1987), Robert Wuthnow (1988, 1999), and Mark Chaves (1993). It even includes the seminal statement of Peter Berger (1967), though Berger has recently felt obliged to clarify, if not recant, his earlier position by indicating that religion is most assuredly not disappearing and is actually flourishing in some settings (Berger 1997).

All of these authors have described some aspect of religious decline in the complex societies of the West, but none has made so bold as to claim or predict religion's disappearance. All would concur that the traditions of every faith have changed over the years and generally in a way that involves less strict adherence to older standards, but none would suggest that doctrine and ritual have evanesced entirely or that the faithful have totally given way to the faithless. All have argued for some sort of long-term linear loss in religion's overall political power and personal salience, but none would deny shorter-term instances of religious surges manifest by spurts of personal religiosity and/or spirituality, church growth, and the proliferation of sects and cults – or "new religious movements" as the latter are now called euphemistically.

With such a caveat, most of the professed critics of the "greater" secularization thesis have, when pressed, admitted to a "lesser" form of the concept with its various middle-range shifts. Recently Rodney Stark (1999) acknowledged ". . . a decline in the social power of once-dominant religious institutions . . . nor are primary aspects of public life any longer suffused with religious symbols, rhetoric, or ritual" (p. 252) and "Of course, religious changes [with] more religious participation and even greater belief in the supernatural at some times and places than in others . . ." (p. 269). Stark contends – unpersuasively, in my view – that the real issues of secularization involve personal piety rather than public religion. But on another point, he is sustained. Secularization proponents may fault Stark's second point above for not specifying a linear trend to his admitted fluctuations in participation and belief. Yet there is no reason why it should. There is nothing inherently linear over the long run about secularization. I am among those persuaded that secularization does constitute an inevitable long term, for reasons I shall elaborate shortly. But it is always important to examine the possibility that periods or episodes of secularization may be followed by plateaus of relatively little change or, indeed, phases of the reverse process of "sacralization."

Sacralization as a Nonhostile, Countervailing Process

Turning the earlier definition of secularization on its head, sacralization "is the process by which the *secular becomes sacred or other new forms of the sacred emerge*, whether in matters of personal faith, institutional practice or political power." As this suggests, sacralization may take a number of forms. These may range from the tendency of religious "sects" to revive or revitalize older religious beliefs and practices, to the tendency of "cults" to develop new religious forms, whether through the innovation of a prophetic and virtuosic leader within the society or by importing a religion from outside the society that is effectively new within it.

The USA has long been a fertile field for religious movements of both types. Virtually every Protestant denomination began as either a sectarian effort to recapture a lost religious truth or a theological and organizational innovation. Groups like the Christian Scientists, Mormons, Adventists, the Jehovah's Witnesses, and Waco's Branch Davidians continue to bear strong traces of their original efflorescence. Imported movements such as the Unification Church (South Korea), the Hare Krishna (India), and the Soka Gakkai (Japan) have also had deeply sacralizing effects for their members in the USA.

Sacralization is also apparent at certain points in the history of US "civil religion," that is, any nation's sense of its shared overall heritage and commitments. It is not unusual for a country's civil religious sensibility to wane and wax over time. It would be too simple to argue that its shared Judeo-Christian legacy tends to secularize during relatively uneventful periods of collective complacency, only to sacralize during times of national crisis. A sense of common religious dedication does tend to surge during and immediately after major external crises, for example, a world war. However, contrary to the old axioms, there are atheists in both foxholes and deathbeds and some types of internal societal crises may reduce religion's credibility, as happened during the 1960s.

Historians of American religion (e.g., McLoughlin 1978) have long tended to chart the country's changes with reference to the several "great awakenings" of the early eighteenth, nineteenth and possibly mid-twentieth centuries. But it is important to bear in mind that every great awakening requires a preceding nap, and that every episode of sacralization generally follows a preceding period of secularization. The important point is that neither secularization nor sacralization alone is adequate to describe the USA or any other nation in holistic and linear terms. While both short-term and long-term trends in one direction or another are common, the two tendencies often oscillate and even play off one another. And while they are often adversaries responding dialectically to each other's pulls in the opposite direction, they can also be allies. Secularization often serves as a form of adaptation to historical change, and it can prepare the way for a sacralization that is more attuned to contemporary circumstances once the detritus of tradition is cleared away.

The point here is not to advocate some law-like proposition by which secularization and sacralization are always linked to insure some constant level of sacredness in an individual or social unit. Nor is it to posit a rigid model of religious crop rotation by which secularization clears the ground for a new sacred planting. New forms of the sacred may precede and influence the secularization of older forms. The major argument is that tendencies in each direction generally check each other to ward off all-or-nothing extremes of either sort. Still, exceptions do occur, and there is at least a loose sense in which sacralization without secularization is the equivalent of "premodernity"; secularization without sacralization is not a bad definition of "postmodernity," while the two in tandem are central to much of what "modernity" itself entails. Of course, premodernity, modernity, and postmodernity are far more defensible as iterative cyclical moments rather than static phases of a single linear trend.

Meanwhile, how does one measure secularization? There are a variety of barometers ranging from the standard counts of church membership, church attendance, and religious media consumption to legislative and judicial decisions, and the uneven compliance with both. However, all of these indices are suspect in one way or another. As a steady stream of research has long indicated, one can be a church member without being a faithful and/or believing adherent – and vice versa. Church membership totals generally exceed church attendance rates by 50 percent, and recent work by Haddaway, Marler, and Chaves (1993) has shown that claimed church attendance routinely exaggerates actual church attendance by 50 percent or more.

Moreover, religious media sales and ratings may reflect active minorities swimming against the current more than the phlegmatic majorities drifting down a secularizing stream. On the other hand, judicial decisions may be subject to the opposite error. When the US Supreme Court ruled against prayer in the public schools in 1963, this was by no means a reflection of dominant public sentiment. As with most decisions in the area of religion since World War II, the plaintiffs were aberrantly nonreligious types resisting an encroaching religious establishment, rather than heirs of the pilgrims of old seeking religious freedom. And once the school prayer case was decided by the court, it remained on problematic trial within the nation's communities. Many ignored the decision, and school prayers continued as a matter of informal local policy with few objections. It is likely that even today some 25 percent of the USA's public classrooms begin with some form of spoken or silent prayer – the Court notwithstanding.

Clearly secularization and its strangely related concept of sacralization require careful analysis rather than demagogic debate. As all students of religion know full well in their mind of minds, both phenomena are here to stay. Eradicating either term will do nothing to obviate the often subtle yet critical realities at issue.

Shifting from Religion to Culture at Large

To some readers, the earlier definitions of secularization and sacralization may suffer from a glaring omission: there is no mention of religion *per se*. This is not an oversight. In stressing the broader phenomenon of the "sacred," I want to push beyond religion to consider "culture" more generally.

Of course, secularization is no stranger to cultural analysis. Virtually every major cultural theorist and cultural historian has taken religious secularization into account as either an effect or a cause of historical change. For Karl Marx (1983), religion's decline and demise awaited that crucial point when class consciousness replaces false consciousness and social actors become aware that their roles are determined by economic relations rather than other-worldly fantasies. On the other hand, for Max Weber ([1905] 1993), secularization was more of an independent than a dependent variable. The emergence of "the Protestant Ethic" was a cause of subsequent social and economic change involving "the Spirit of Capitalism."

France has been a special source of secularization accounts. The 18th century decline of the French monarchy and the ensuing French Revolution involved a fundamental "de-sacralization" of the link between church and crown that has been widely analyzed by historians (cf. Merrick 1990, Darnton 1995, Gordon 1998). This in turn is linked to France's role as a seedbed for Enlightenment thought, which provided such critical intellectual second-guessing of religion from Voltaire forward. One strand of this tradition took the form of French positivism. As represented by the mid-nineteenth century visionary, Auguste Comte, positivism – like Marxism – both sought and prophesied the replacement of religion by social science.

An important mollifying heir to this tradition was the turn of the twentieth century sociologist, Emile Durkheim. He, Weber, and even Marx provided conceptually sympathetic accounts of religion without being personally religious. But the three also shared a mantle as prophets of secularization, though none ever used the term. Beyond this, there were certainly differences among them. Durkheim and Marx were both self-conscious social scientific theorists, while Weber remained ambivalent on the cusp of historiography. And whereas Weber viewed a "disenchanted" Western future pessimistically as an end to meaning, both Marx and Durkheim were more optimistic – the first as a political-economic revolutionist and the second as a cultural evolutionist.

Durkheim ([1912] 1995) acknowledged that early twentieth century France was experiencing "a period of transition and moral mediocrity." But he went on to envision new surges of enthusiasm for new forms of "the sacred." In fact, one of his less remarked upon convergences with Weber involved a broadened sense of sacred meaning that went beyond religion itself. Weber's famous dark reference to the "iron cage" of capitalism suggested – perhaps erroneously – that capitalism was unable to replace Protestantism with a sacred value system of its own. Durkheim noted

> [the civic] origin of ceremonies that, by their object, by their results, and by the techniques used, are not different in kind from ceremonies that are specifically religious. What basic difference is there between Christians' celebrating the principal dates of Christ's life . . . . and a citizen's meeting commemorating the advent of a new charter or some other great event of national life? (Durkheim [1912] 1995:249)

This, of course, is a seminal passage that was later reborn in Robert Bellah's (1967) famous account of "civil religion" with specific reference to the US national polity. However, it is worth remarking that Bellah gave the concept a far more narrowly religious thrust than had Durkheim – or for that matter, Durkheim's own predecessor in these matters, the eighteenth century social philosopher, Jean-Jacques Rousseau (1960).

Subsuming religion within a larger category of the sacred has a more extensive pedigree. The great comparativist, Mircea Eliade (1959), was consistently at pains to talk of "hierophanies" that afforded contact with the "sacred," rather than concentrate on religion itself. For him conventional religion by no means exhausted sacred possibilities. If religion was explicitly sacred, other forms qualified implicitly. In fact, Edward Bailey (1998) has made explicit the notion of "implicit religion" that is itself implicit in the work of Eliade and others. As Rousseau, Durkheim, and Weber would also have agreed, sacred meanings may emanate from the political, the familial, and the quotidian. The quality of sacredness is not inherent in a thing or idea; rather, sacredness is imputed from within a social context.

Meanwhile, if religion is only one form of the sacred, the sacred in turn is one important dimension of something broader still; namely, culture. The relation between religion and culture can be so close as to be confusing. Consider the two definitions below from the anthropologist, Clifford Geertz, and see if it is immediately obvious which refers to religion and which to culture:

___ is 1) a system of symbols which acts to 2) establish powerful, pervasive, and long-lasting moods and motivations in men by 3) formulating conceptions of a general order of existence and 4) clothing these conceptions with such an aura of factuality that 5) the moods and motivations seem uniquely realistic. (Geertz 1973:190)

___ is . . . . the framework of beliefs, expressive symbols and values in terms of which individuals define their world, express their feelings, and make their judgments. [It] is the fabric of meaning in terms of which human beings interpret their experience and guide their action. (Geertz 1973:144–5)

Both definitions have that element of abstraction that qualifies them as social scientific; both share an emphasis on the kind of "control system" that Geertz found essential. The first refers to religion and the second to culture, but in the often arbitrary world of conceptual definitions one could do far worse than reverse them.

And yet Geertz's emphasis on cognitive control neglects another element that both phenomena have in common. It is true that both religion and culture are symbol systems that perform powerful directive functions. But one of the reasons for their power is precisely a shared quality of sacredness. The point scarcely needs elaboration for religion. But arguing that culture carries a sacred dimension may be more controversial.

Take the very word "culture." In strict etymological terms, it traces back to the notion of "horticulture" and the spreading of manure – something many critics of culture's conceptual softness will have no difficulty crediting. But if one adds a historically indefensible but conceptually strategic hyphen to produce the term "cult-ure," this produces a more instructive story. "Cult" in its older, non-pejorative, Durkheimian sense refers to that behavioral core of religious beliefs and practices that constitute the center of any religion – and perhaps any cultural system as well.

Can a culture operate effectively without having a cultic or sacred component? In responding no, I am using the term "sacred" in its broader connotation rather than as a synonym for the conventionally religious. Taken in this way, any cultural system of symbols, beliefs, and values is a sacred system in that its components must be accorded a reverential status that allows for the leap of faith required in converting what are often relative and arbitrary judgments into absolute normative standards. Culture's credibility depends less upon the objective and empirical standing of its tenets than upon a subjective and nonempirical belief in its guidance. This requires a special status that involves the quality of sacredness in at least a latent, if not always manifest, sense. So much for a bridge to our concluding section.

Secularization as a Cultural Dynamic

If secularization is alive and well within religion, and if religion is only part of the wider sphere of the sacred which is in turn a crucial component of culture, then it follows that secularization should be an active dynamic within culture itself. The insight is surely not an original revelation. However, it is little acknowledged in the various discussions of cultural change that have occurred in the social science literature. While older theories of history and the more recent but now largely recessed literature on "modernization" refer to secularization, both refer almost exclusively to the secularization of religion *per se* (e.g., Germani 1981). Secularization of culture as distinct from religion is commonly neglected.

Virtually any form of cultural change both reveals and depends upon the opposite but often symbiotic processes of secularization and sacralization. Take any episode of change, and it is not hard to find the waning of older "sacred" beliefs and values, along with the frequent waxing of new ones. This applies to every type of symbol, belief, or value – whether political, economic, scientific, or indeed religious. As indicated above, all cultural components require a sacred quality, and generally this quality must erode before the components may decline and possibly give way to new commitments.

Cultural secularization may involve various syndromes which have rarely been disentangled. As noted previously, even within the narrow sphere of religion, secularization is generally discussed in all-or-nothing terms. When gradations are admitted, they are gradations of degree, not of kind. But in what follows, I want to delineate four basic kinds of secularization that are framed by the intersection of two fundamental distinctions.

The two distinctions involve *internal* versus *external* sources and *directed* versus *nondirected* scenarios. The former distinction refers to the difference between secularization that emerges from within the social context of the cultural system at issue versus secularization that is imported or imposed from outside. The latter distinction refers to secularization that stems downward from authorities in control versus secularization that seeps upwards from within the cultural system itself. Putting the two distinctions together produces four combinations or types of secularization: "emergent," "coercive," "imperialist," and "diffused." In describing each, I shall draw on a wide array of examples, including some drawn from a recently completed 14-nation comparative study of religion and politics around the globe (Demerath 2000). This applies the types to whole societies, but they could also be relevant to the secularization of subcultures, communities, institutions, or even social movements within a society.

Emergent secularization

This form of internally evolved and nondirected secularization is the classic model for religion. Here secularization is seen as a kind of drift to the left –

the unintentional product of increasing education, industrialization, modernization, and differentiation in the social context. This is the secularization described in a stanza of Matthew Arnold's "Dover Beach," (cited in Gordon 1988:150):

> The sea of faith
> Was once, too, at the full, and round earth's shore
> Lay like the folds of a bright girdle furl'd
> But now I hear
> Its melancholy, long, withdrawing roar,
> Retreating to the breath
> Of the night-wind down the vast edges drear
> And naked shingles of the world.

Arnold wrote in England in the mid-19th century when a number of Western intellectuals generally had begun to sense that perhaps the Enlightenment had gone too far and produced saddening changes on the part of the many, not just the few. The historian, James Turner (1985), dates the legitimation of unbelief among American intellectuals at the end of the Civil War. But the Enlightenment altered more than religion; it affected a whole conception of human self-consciousness that included what Arthur Lovejoy (1936) called "the great chain of being" and what Owen Chadwick (1975) termed "The Secularization of the European Mind." Moreover, the Enlightenment was not just an assault upon faith, but a substitution of one faith for another. The notion of progress through thought became a sacred cult in its own right, albeit one that has been subject to secularization since. Meanwhile, there is little question that the rise of Newtonian and Darwinian science as well as the advent of major universities set apart from religious seminaries represented a major cultural change (cf. Koyre 1957, Foucault 1966).

There was no single event, let alone decree, that produced the shift. Certainly this was not the result of any authoritative edict. Rather, it depended on cultural forces that were themselves dependent upon forms of nonreligious secularization. Weber was right to point to the rise of the Protestant Ethic as a historical watershed, but most historians now agree that he overestimated the effects of religion and theology themselves. Insofar as Protestantism broke the spell of Catholic dominance over a tightly undifferentiated world, it released a series of developments in the newly differentiated and autonomous spheres of society. Gradually, politics, the economy, and the world of science and education began to march to their own cultural drummers, but not before drumming out some of the older sacred tenets that had conserved the past and inhibited change. In each case, new sacred commitments depended upon the secularization of older cultural faiths.

In politics, democracy took various structural forms, but its cultural core arose only after "desacralization" was well under way for the French monarchy and other absolutist regimes in the West. It is true that part of the legitimating code of the *ancien régime* involved its ties with the church. But it also involved a conception of top-down civil authority that went far beyond religion.

The rise of capitalism – and most especially its Weberian "spirit" – depended upon the secularization of a prior economic stage with its attendant economic rituals. Here structural changes influenced the cultural shift, and one might paraphrase Karl Marx to stress the importance of changing modes of economic production in desacralizing old social practices. Later, Max Weber saw Puritanism as a new source of commitment to capitalism, one in which earning success in this world at least offered hints about one's predestined salvation in the world beyond. Weber saw religion fall away from surging capitalism by the end of the nineteenth century, and this led him to prophesy a world of disenchantment within a materialist "iron cage." The theme has continued to resonate within twentieth century "critical theory" that began in Germany between the two world wars. Themes of materialistic disenchantment resonate deeply within Herbert Marcuse's lament for "one-dimensional man" (1964); Daniel Bell's concern for the "end of ideology" (1964) and the loss of meaning within the "cultural contradictions of capitalism" (1976), and Jurgen Habermas's sense of the "colonization of the (private) life world by the (public) system (1989).

But all is not lost, and somehow enchantment has persisted (cf. Schneider 1993). The historian Daniel Gordon offers a telling rebuttal to Weberian despair:

> But when Weber spoke of an "iron cage," he meant an absence of meaning, an economy that had no moral ground at all . . . . Yet, had Weber known more about the Enlightenment and its sacralisation of capitalism, he would not have created such a radical antithesis between the Reformation and modernity. (Gordon 1998:151)

Here then is the cultural cycle of secularization and sacralization enacted within the economic sphere itself. The spirit or culture of capitalism had achieved autonomous standing but it had become sacralized in its own terms and for its own sake. While Weber and others might quarrel with the quality of meaning involved, there is little question of its quantity.

The rise of science and education, of democracy and capitalism are among the great cultural transformations in Western history. Each depends upon a succession of secularization and sacralization, even though none is conventionally religious. All of this illustrates an internal, nondirected, "emergent" form of secularization that is more glacial than explosive. It is a cultural dynamic that nevertheless moves mountains.

Coercive secularization

Here is another form of internal secularization but one that is purposely directed by some type of effective authority. There are many types of direction, and the term "coercion" is meant to suggest a top-down exercise of power – legitimate or not. There are also many loci and levels of coercion, but for simplicity's sake, I shall focus here mainly on the societal.

Surprisingly, there are those who would place the USA in this category. Although no political leader would dare exert public influence on behalf of secularization, this is at least one interpretation of the first part of the First Amendment to the Constitution: "Congress shall make no laws respecting an establishment of religion. . . ." Of course, the clause goes on to support the "free exercise of religion." But the establishment ban and the judicial decisions in its wake concerning prayer in the public schools, Christmas celebrations on public property, and so forth have often been construed as governmental coercion on behalf of "secular humanism."

This is not the place to debate the greater wisdom of the establishment clause, especially since I have elsewhere defended an expansive treatment of it as the often neglected but unique mark of genius within the First Amendment (Demerath 2000). However, the opposing arguments are by no means ludicrous, even though the preponderant views of the Amendment hold that prohibiting an establishment and fostering free exercise was an important combination in fostering the USA's unique religious competition and vitality.

Meanwhile, there are other instances of coercive secularization in the USA. On the one hand, consider the federal government's role in restricting Native Americans, both territorially and culturally, with secularizing consequences. On the other hand, the federal government has also played a secularizing role in reining in racism and racial segregation. There is little question that racism has long been a part of American culture, especially following the Civil War when emancipation of the slaves required new doctrines of racial inferiority to justify continued discrimination. But how does one change racism? Put more familiarly, how can one secularize the values, norms, and rituals that provide cultural reinforcements? The great liberal faith in education had been little rewarded by the 1960s. But when the government stepped in to produce and implement civil rights legislation integrating schools, public accommodations, and voting practices, the required changes in behavior ultimately brought about corresponding changes in both social psychology and culture. This is a clearer instance of coerced secularization paving the way to change, though some might argue that the coercion was more external than internal because it came from Washington and the Federal government rather than the South.

Insofar as laws and political regimes can influence change, and insofar as virtually every social change requires some secularizing of an older culture to make way for or accommodate the new, virtually every country offers examples of coercive secularization. Turkey, Japan, and China offer three especially instructive cases that combine religious and other cultural changes.

Turkey was once the center of Orthodox Christianity and later became the center of the once great Islamic Ottoman Empire. Turkey straddles the border between Asia and Europe, and the vicissitudes of its culture reflect its geography. This was especially clear shortly after World War I when the young military officer, Kemal Attaturk, seized control of the state and essentially pivoted the

nation 180 degrees to face the West. Influenced by his sympathetic understanding of the European Enlightenment, French positivism, and Emile
Durkheim, Attaturk declared that Turkey would henceforth be a secular state
rather than officially Muslim. Over the next several years in the mid-1920s, he
was able to pass a series of statutes that amounted to no less than a cultural
transformation. These included bans on certain forms of Islamic practice – such
as the Sufis' mystical "whirling dervishes" – and on such items of traditional
Islamic dress as the men's "fez" and the women's veils. Here too the secularization reached beyond religion to other aspects of the traditional culture. It
included a Westernization of the written numerical system and mandated
alterations in the language itself.

More than 70 years later, Attaturk continues to be revered, and his changes
endure. Although there is now a resurgence of Islamic identity in lifestyle and
politics, this is a minority movement and one held in tight check by an ever-vig-
ilant military. Clearly Attaturk was one of the twentieth century's most effective
statesmen, and his example of directed secularization was not lost on others of
his generation, including Lenin and Stalin in Russia, Nasser of Egypt, Ben-
Gurion of Israel, Sukarno of Indonesia, and Mao Zedong of China.

Of course, Mao's regime in China offers a particularly infamous example of
coercive secularization, especially its hypercoercive "cultural revolution" during
the 1960s and 1970s. One might quarrel with the term "secularization" here
because many Chinese suggest that theirs was never a religious culture to begin
with – superstitious and philosophical, yes, but religious, no. But whatever one
calls Confucianism, Taoism, and Buddhism, the larger point involves a secularization of sacralized culture embedded in traditional forms. This was most
assuredly Mao's objective – again as a way of preparing the nation for a new
sacred system, namely, communism.

Japan also offers ambiguities with regard to religion, but at least two instances
of coercive secularization stand out. First, during the 1860s, a small group of elite
figures behind the throne were eager to spark a new sense of Japanese nationalism
and industrialization. They fomented the "Meiji restoration" with the Emperor as
the divine head of a new system of "state Shinto," which was deliberately grafted
on to the traditional and localistic "folk Shinto." Buddhism was vigorously suppressed (i.e., secularized) throughout the country to create a cultural space for the
new national faith so zealously promoted as a way of binding the country together
and prodding it forward, both economically and militarily. Some 80 years later,
following the ill-fated venture known in Japan as "the great Pacific war," the
country experienced another form of directed secularization, this time aimed at
state Shinto itself. But because here the direction came from the USA, I shall use it
as a segue into a third form of secularization.

Imperialist secularization

This is another form of directed secularization, but one that emanates externally,
that is, from forces outside the society at issue. It strains no credulity to begin

with the USA as an imperialist exemplar, though its role in Japan following World War II is not often seen in imperialist terms. The USA was understandably eager to uproot state Shinto, downgrade the Emperor's status, and insure that religion would never again serve to mobilize the nation. A new Japanese constitution was the vehicle for these purposes. But just as the earlier secularization under the Meiji restoration was unable to totally eliminate all Buddhist influence, the more recent secularization of state Shinto has not been completely successful. It is one thing to change a political structure with the stroke of a constitutional pen, but quite another to transform a culture so quickly.

Meanwhile, there are ample instances of imperialist secularization in other places and other times. India has been a reluctant host to outside powers for almost 500 years. The Muslim Mogul emperors began their succession in the early sixteenth century, only to be followed by the British "raj." Both empires exerted secularizing influence over Hinduism, though Hinduism has certainly survived. Both also had secularizing impacts on other aspects of the subcontinent's culture. For weal and for woe, the British altered the area's entire political, economic, and educational infrastructure with wrenching cultural changes. The imposition of modernity on India's traditional culture has had a lasting impact through older sacred patterns left behind and newer ones uneasily accommodated.

There have been few more imperialistic forces in world history than the converting armies of Christianity. These mobilizations on behalf of new sacred systems have been perhaps more effective in secularizing older ones, sometimes leaving a confused void as a result. In addition to their obvious effects on indigenous religions, they have had important consequences for nonreligious cultural elements. For example, Lamin Sanneh (1991) notes that missionary activities in Africa were not all negative from the standpoint of African political development. Because they offered educational programs with a new common language, they tended to break down (secularize) older tribal cultures and divisions, thus clearing the way for new nationalistic bonds.

Nationalism is itself both a secularizing and sacralizing phenomenon, though it is frequently misunderstood. Beginning in the mid-nineteenth century, the spoils of warfare often produced new nation-states. These were assembled at the end of wars out of the remains through acts of statecraft that frequently had no regard for cultural communities and affinities. The new nations were often cultural hodgepodges in which those exercising power were often strangers to those affected by it. Imperialist secularization was an important means of holding onto power insofar as it diluted competing sources of loyalty – whether ethnic, tribal, regional, or religious. The Soviet Union and its Eastern European satellites were, of course, prime examples. However, as we have seen over the past decade, there are limits to the processes of secularization and resacralization. Older cultural identities and enmities have asserted themselves throughout the region with tragic consequences in Bosnia and the former Yugoslavia, including Kosovo. Because the new forces of separatism are quite different from the motives behind older nation-states, they might better be termed "cultural-ism" than "nationalism."

Diffused secularization

Our fourth and final scenario of secularization involves external forces that spread more by diffusion than direction. These are often the unintended consequences of culture contacts. They result from transmitted cultural innovations that become hegemonic in new locales, and in the process serve to displace old practices, rituals, and beliefs, whether formally or informally sacred.

Imagine the reactions of the New Guinea fishing villagers who, some time in 1943, awoke to see for the first time a substantial fleet of the US Navy anchored offshore and establishing beach installations with jeeps, guns, and communications equipment, which the villagers were seeing for the first time as the wondrous bounty of a divine providence. It was incidents like these that led to the famous "cargo cults" of Oceania. These cults worshipped new gods of Western materialism and waited – largely in vain – for their own cargo to materialize. Of course, any new religion comes at the expense of the old. In this instance, sacralization preceded secularization.

Today's "globalization" offers parallels to the cargo cults, except that here the materialism does materialize. Accounts are legion of television sets aglow in dark slum dwellings in Calcutta, cosmetic sales on the upper Amazon in Brazil, Internet communication between stay-at-home families in China and their migrating children, and surgical miracles being performed in African villages. I have written elsewhere (Demerath 2000) that globalization has some of the qualities of a Western middle class conceit – as if the world were now totally enthralled by American high tech innovations, mass media programming, consumer products, and medical advances, not to mention its environmental depredations and political manipulations in pursuit of its economic interests.

Globalization is neither as new nor as totalizing as popular treatments would have it. Cultural exchanges have followed trade currents for millennia, and the spread of Western culture into the far corners of the world has only begun to be reciprocated in the last century. But wherever one culture diffuses into another, the former is likely to have a diminishing, secularizing effect. Of course, the effect is greatly accentuated when the invading culture enjoys a favorable power differential.

I have used the term "diffused secularization" for this syndrome in a double sense. Obviously it refers to the diffusion of culture around the world. But it also suggests a corresponding tendency for every culture to suffer some diffusion and dilution as a result. We have certainly witnessed aggressive assertions of traditional faiths and identities as sacralizing responses to this general secularizing trend. "Fundamentalist" Islamic and Hindu movements as well as more direct political opponents of Western culture have become major players on the world stage.

Conclusion

At a time when many are ticketing the concept of secularization for extinction, this chapter has sought to reverse the direction, and not only salvage the concept but extend it. After rescuing secularization from its critics' purposely bloated and mythological overstatement, it offered a more nuanced and less extreme statement. In arguing that religion is subject to oscillating moments of both secularization and sacralization, it avoided the overdrawn implication of the death of religion.

In addition to providing a defense of secularization, the chapter also took to the offensive. It argued that secularization applies not only to religion writ small but to the sacred writ large and to culture writ larger still. Not unlike religion, culture generally must have a sacred component if it is to compel allegiance. These sacred elements are no less subject to the same tendencies of secularization and sacralization. But in order to move beyond a single, over-reaching concept, the chapter ended by suggesting four different scenarios of secularization – the emergent, coercive, imperialist, and diffused.

In sum, secularization has a permanent and increasingly relevant place in the conceptual repertoire of the social sciences, and this is a far cry from the oblivion some have wished for it. As one of the basic dynamics of culture, it is a crucial source of insight in understanding past, present, and future, and the critical paths between them.

References

Bailey, E. 1998. *Implicit Religion: An Introduction*. London: Middlesex University Press.

Bell, D. 1964. *The End of Ideology*. Cambridge, MA: Harvard University Press.

Bell, D. 1976. *The Cultural Contradictions of Capitalism*. New York: Basic Books.

Bellah, R.N. 1967. "Civil Religion in America," *Daedalus* 96:1–21.

Bellah, R., Madsen, R., Sullivan, W.M., Swidler, A., and Tipton, S.M. 1985. *Habits of the Heart*. Berkeley: University of California Press.

Berger, P.L. 1967. *The Sacred Canopy*. Garden City, NY: Doubleday.

Berger, P.L. 1997. "Epistemological Modesty: An Interview with Peter Berger," *Christian Century* 114:972–8.

Chadwick, O. 1975. *The Secularization of the European Mind in the Nineteenth Century*. Cambridge: Cambridge University Press.

Chaves, M. 1993. "Denominations as Dual Structures: An Organizational Analysis," *Sociology of Religion* 54:147–69.

Comte, A. 1891. *The Catechism of Positive Religion*, third edn. London: Routledge.

Darnton, R. 1995. *The Forbidden Best-Sellers of Pre-Revolutionary France*. New York: W.W. Norton.

Demerath, N.J. III 2000. *Crossing the Gods: Religion, Violence, Politics and the State Across the World*. New York: Rutgers University Press.

Demerath, N.J. III in press. "Secularization," in *The Encyclopedia of Sociology*, 2nd edn. New York: MacMillan Publishers.

Dobbelaere, K. 1981. "Secularization: A Multi-Dimensional Concept," *Current Sociology* 20:1–216.

Dobbelaere, K. 1993. "Church Involvement and Secularization: Making Sense of the European Case," in *Secularization, Rationalism, and Sectarianism*, Eds. E. Barker, J.A. Beckford, and K. Dobbelaere. Oxford: Clarendon Press, pp. 19–36.

Durkheim, E. 1995. *The Elementary Forms of the Religious Life*, Transl. K. Fields. New York: Free Press.

Eliade, M. 1959. *The Sacred and the Profane*. London: Harcourt, Brace, Jovanovich.

Fenn, R. 1979. *Toward a Theory of Secularization*. Provo, UT: Society for the Scientific Study of Religion Monograph.

Fenn, R. 1993. "Crowds, Time, and the Essence of Society," in *Secularization, Rationalism and Sectarianism: Essays in Honor of Bryan Wilson*, Eds. E. Barker, J.A. Beckford, and K. Dobbelaere. Oxford: Clarendon Press, pp. 287–304.

Finke, R. and Stark, R. 1992. *The Churching of America, 1776–1990: Winners and Losers in Our Religious Economy*. New Brunswick, NJ: Rutgers University Press.

Foucault, M. 1966. *The Order of Things*. New York: Vintage Books.

Geertz, C. 1973. *The Interpretation of Culture*. New York: Basic Books.

Germani, G. 1981. *The Sociology of Modernization*. New Brunswick, NJ: Transaction Books.

Gordon, D. 1998. "The Great Enlightenment Massacre," in *The Darton Debate*, Ed. H.T. Mason, Oxford: Voltaire Foundation, pp. 129–56.

Habermas, J. 1989. *On Society and Politics*, Ed. S. Seidman. Boston: Beacon Press.

Hadaway, C.K., Marler, P.L., and Chaves, M. 1993. "What the Polls Don't Show: A Closer Look at Church Attendance," *American Sociological Review* 58:741–52.

Iannaccone, L.R. 1994. "Why Strict Churches Are Strong," *American Journal of Sociology* 99:1180–1211.

Koyre, A. 1957. *From the Closed World to the Infinite Universe*. Baltimore, MD: Johns Hopkins University Press.

Lovejoy, A.O. 1936. *The Great Chain of Being*. Cambridge, MA: Harvard University Press.

McLoughlin, W.G. 1978. *Revivals, Awakenings, and Religious Change*. Chicago: University of Chicago Press.

Marcuse, H. 1964. *One-Dimensional Man*. London: Routledge and Kegan Paul.

Martin, D. 1978. *A General Theory of Secularization*. New York: Harper and Row.

Marx, K. 1983. "A Contribution to the Critique of Hegel's Philosophy of the Right," in *The Portable Karl Marx*, Ed. E. Kamenka. New York: Penguin Books, pp. 115–24.

Merrick, J.W. 1990. *The De-Sacralization of the French Monarchy in the 18th Century*. Baton Rouge: Louisiana State University Press.

Roof, W.C. and McKinney, W. 1987. *American Mainline Religion*. New Brunswick, NJ: Rutgers University Press.

Rousseau, J.J. 1960. "Of Civil Religion," in *Social Contract*, Ed. E. Barker. London: Oxford University Press.

Sanneh, L. 1991. "The Yogi and the Commissar: Christian Missions and the New World

Order in Africa," in *World Order and Religion*, Ed. W.C. Roof. Albany, NY: SUNY Press, pp. 173–92.

Schneider, M. 1993. *Culture and Enchantment*. Chicago: University of Chicago Press.

Spencer, H. 1915. *Essays Scientific, Political, Speculative*, 3 vols. New York: Appleton.

Stark, R. 1999. "Secularization R.I.P.," *Sociology of Religion* 60(3):249–74.

Stark, R. and Iannaccone, L.R. 1994. "A Supply-Side Interpretation of the 'Secularization' of Europe," *Journal for the Scientific Study of Religion* 33:230–52.

Turner, J. 1985. *Without God, Without Creed*. Baltimore, MD: Johns Hopkins University Press.

Voltaire, F.-M.A. 1963. *Essai sur les Moeurs et l'Esprit des Nations*, 2 vols. Paris: Garnier.

Warner, S. 1993. "Work in Progress Toward a New Paradigm for the Sociological Study of Religion in the U.S." in *American Journal of Sociology* 98:1044–93.

Weber, M. 1993. *The Protestant Ethic and the Spirit of Capitalism*, Transl. T. Parsons. Introduction R. Collins. New York: Roxbury Press.

Wilson, B. 1966. *Religion in Secular Society*. London: Penguin.

Wuthnow, R. 1988. *The Restructuring of American Religion*. Princeton, NJ: Princeton University Press.

Wuthnow, R. 1999. *After Heaven: Spirituality in America Since the 1950s*. Berkeley: University of California Press.

CHAPTER 12

Social Movements as Free-floating Religious Phenomena

James A. Beckford

The "Religious Turn"

One of the ironies of the sociology of religion is that it became institutionalized
as a flourishing academic specialty in the 1960s at the very moment when the
dominant currents in Western sociology lost interest in religion. I described the
result as the insulation and isolation of the sociology of religion (Beckford
1985). But the "parting of the ways" between the sociology of religion and
mainstream sociology has been showing signs of coming to an end since the late
1980s. There are strong indicators of a rapprochement from both sides. Several
factors can help to account for this change.

In the first place, some developments in religions have been sufficiently surprising and challenging to catch the attention of social scientists who were previously uninterested in it as a topic of professional study (for surveys of relevant
developments, see Haynes 1998, Marty and Appleby 1991). For example, the
mobilization of very large numbers of North, Central, and South Americans in
pursuit of conservative political ends in the name of conservative Protestantism
could hardly be ignored. The perception that "fundamentalist" forms of various
world religions were beginning to shape the lives and outlooks of increasingly
large proportions of the population in many countries also called for scrutiny.
Furthermore, the growing salience of religious identity among the younger generations of communities of Hindu, Muslim, and Sikh migrants and settlers in
many European countries began to force a rethink of the priority which had previously been given to ethnicity and "race." Finally, the collapse of the Soviet
Union and of its client states in Central and Eastern Europe highlighted not only
the latent capacity of Orthodox churches to meet the needs of their followers but
also the strenuous attempts that some of these churches were making to prevent
other religious movements from benefiting fully from increases in religious

freedom. In their different ways all of these developments have forced religion back on to the agenda of mainstream sociology because it is clearly an important dimension of the central processes of identity formation, social inclusion, and boundary maintenance. At the same time, sociologists of religion have come to see that many of the phenomena that had previously been intrinsically interesting to them were also connected to large-scale social processes involving much more than religion alone (Smith 1996).

Secondly, religion has become more interesting to social scientists because in some cases it calls in question or complexifies other social phenomena. Debates about the contribution of religion and spirituality towards physical and mental health are a good example. The huge growth of public interest in, or curiosity about, therapies, remedies, and healing practices that draw on spiritual or religious resources is not only helping to raise fresh questions about the sociology of health and healing but is also giving rise to questions about the necessity for some measure of control and monitoring of the entire field of "alternative healing." Since the training, certification, licensing, and monitoring of practitioners of spiritual and religious healing are under discussion in many countries, specialists in the sociology of professions, health and healing, and legal regulation are necessarily having to take more account of the specificity of religion.

The growing concern with "clergy malfeasance" also owes much to the professionalization and commodification of the counseling and psychotherapeutic services routinely provided by ministers of religion in some places. Again, religion has become interesting to a wider variety of social scientists because it is now inseparable from activities that had previously had relatively few religious connections. A similar argument can be made about the increased attention shown these days by constitutional lawyers, political scientists, and human rights specialists in the situation of religious minorities who consider themselves to be oppressed in various parts of the world. Numerous official reports have inquired into the activities of such sectarian and/or new religious movements as Jehovah's Witnesses, Scientology, and the International Society for Krishna Consciousness on the grounds that they might be, for example, damaging to the well-being of their followers, economically fraudulent, or prejudicial to the security of the state. Whereas the sociological study of these movements might have been considered frivolous or strictly of interest only to sociologists of religion in the past, there can be no doubt that the associated political and legal issues are now of much wider concern. This is another instance of religion forcing itself back on to the agenda of mainstream social science.

Thirdly, the significance of religion for social scientists and scholars of the humanities has grown in recent decades as a consequence of "the cultural turn." This refers to the widespread recognition that our understanding of human societies and cultures has not been best served by positivistic methods of research or by theoretical perspectives that prioritized material, economic, and organizational factors. Partly in reaction against these features of social science, scholars in many disciplines came to emphasize the need to take better account of the specificity and the significance of cultural symbols, meanings, and values in social life. As a result, aspects of language, identity, rituals, and symbols all acquired a higher profile in the research of some scholars who had previously shown little interest in these phenomena. Examples include Manuel Castells' *The Power of Identity* (1997) and Jacques Derrida and Gianni Vattimo's *Religion* (1998). Some have even gone so far as to claim that a new opening to the transcendental (Flanagan 1996) and the sublime (Milbank 1990) has occurred in the conditions of postmodernity. I am deeply skeptical about these claims (Beckford 1992), but for present purposes the more important point is that the cultural turn in the social sciences has at least raised the level of many scholars' interest in the meaning of religion. The main aim of this chapter is to show that the rapprochement between social scientists and the study of religion can be taken further by examining the relationship between social movements and religion.

The Paradox of Institutional Decline and Political Salience

Religion has become more interesting to social scientists in the past decade or so, but not all are agreed about the meaning of the changes observed in religions. Some regard the "big picture" as one of continuing secularization in the sense that religion's capacity to shape, for example, the policies of governments, social policies, economic ethics, personal morality, and so on has been steadily declining since the early modern era. In this view, religion no longer provides the coherence or the control of local communities, national societies, or international systems of states.

Skepticism about the reality of secularization is exceptionally strong in the United States, where a growing number of sociologists began to claim in the early 1990s that religion, in the sense of supernatural compensators for rewards that are not easily available in the human world, was an inexhaustible but highly variable phenomenon (see Warner 1993, Stark and Bainbridge 1987). From this point of view, the alleged decline of religion was either an ideological ruse or a product of European history. The situation in the United States is described, by contrast, as a never-ending process of the death of old forms of religion and the birth of new ones in a competitive marketplace.

Other scholars are prepared to accept that religious organizations are continuing to lose their capacity to shape social life, but are unwilling to acknowledge that this amounts to secularization. They wish to argue, instead, that religion is being "restructured" in such a way that it is actually becoming more powerful in the sphere of private life and in that of small-scale intentional communities of believers (Champion and Hervieu-Léger 1990). The argument is that religion's capacity to arouse strong feelings and personal commitments is an increasingly important antidote or counterweight to the dominance of late-modern societies by the impersonal forces of economic markets and of state bureaucracies. Still other scholars hold to the view that the late-modern era is far from secular because a variety of implicit, customary, diffused, or folk forms of religiosity continue to flourish amidst or alongside the remains of formerly commanding religious organizations (Bailey 1998, Cipriani 1989, Hornsby-Smith, Lee, and Reilly 1985).

Each of these skeptical views of secularization is focused mainly on changes taking place in religious phenomena. An alternative position, as I shall argue in this chapter, holds that changes have also taken place in public "uses" of religion, regardless of whether the "big picture" is secularization or merely the restructuring of religion. In particular, it seems to me that some aspects of religion have become significantly more controversial at the end of the twentieth century and that this is partly due to the relatively new ways in which religion is now being "used."

There has been a marked tendency in many countries where Christianity has long been dominant for religion to lose some of the features of a social institution (Beckford 1989). This means that, instead of operating as a "sacred canopy," permanently providing identity, meaning, inspiration, and consolation to very large numbers of people, religion increasingly serves as a resource to which individuals and groups may have recourse from time to time. The death of Diana, Princess of Wales, was one such time both in the UK and in other countries. The number of people for whom religion still functions as an overarching and massive institution, meeting many of their perceived needs on a continuous basis, is in decline. At the same time, the institution of religion, at least in the form of religious organizations, exerts less and less influence over other social institutions such as the law, politics, economics, health care, science, and the family. In this sense, the significance of religion as a social institution is diminishing in many societies.

Yet, it also seems clear that, as the influence of religious organizations has waned, religious symbols, meanings, and values have been deregulated and made more exploitable. "Religion has come adrift from its former points of anchorage" (Beckford 1989:170) and is increasingly available for use in a bewildering variety of ways. This is why I described religion as a "free-floating phenomenon." In this context, deregulation means more than the relaxation of legal or constitutional restraints on religious activity. It also means that religious organizations are able to exercise less control over the uses made of their own religious symbols. For example, the Advertising Standards Authority in the UK now receives proportionally more complaints about advertisements containing religious symbols than about any other category of advertisements. The British are not becoming more sensitive about religion, however. What is happening is that advertising companies are exploiting religious symbols more frequently than in the past when religious organizations were more powerful and when belief in customary Christian doctrines was more widespread (see Gill, Hadaway, and Marler 1998). Communication via the Internet also seems likely to accelerate the pace at which the use of religion is leaving its institutional anchorages (Dawson and Hennebry 1999).

Of course, religion is not necessarily withering away, for there is undeniable evidence of vitality in many religious organizations, vigor in the spiritual lives and religious experiences of some people, and strength in the attachment to collective religious identities in some places. There is no need to deny this evidence or to reduce it to the status of an epiphenomenon. Religious vitality is neither unreal nor ephemeral. But it must be kept in perspective. That is, the persistence of religious vitality must be set alongside the equally compelling evidence of decline in the power, influence, and significance of religion as an institutional force. As such, religion has lost much of its capacity to shape the social action and cultural values of people other than those who choose to align themselves with religious norms.

In short, the religious situation in many advanced industrial societies is sociologically complex. One feature is the diminishing capacity of religion to serve as an overarching institution. Another is the absolute and proportional decline in the number of people who actively participate in the activities of religious organizations – at least in Christianity and Judaism. A third feature is the buoyancy and liveliness of selected religious movements and organizations ranging from conservative fellowships to New Age spiritualities. A fourth feature of the current situation in many advanced industrial societies is the growing size, self-confidence, and effectiveness of Buddhist, Hindu, Muslim, and Sikh faith communities. The situation is further complicated by the fact that each of these four features also conceals wide variations. This means that rates of decline and growth vary from time to time, place to place, and group to group. It is as if we were looking at a kaleidoscopic image which is constantly changing in shape, color, and intensity. There is no single dominant trend. And nothing is to be gained from trying to show that the kaleidoscopic pattern lends itself to a single "trump card" explanation.

The complexity and unevenness of changes in religion call into question the value of would-be explanations which rely on a single factor or which try to freeze the flux in a single image. There will certainly be no attempt in this chapter to reduce the complexity to a single formula along such lines as "the return of the repressed" (Giddens 1991) or "faith without dogma" (Ferrarotti 1993). Instead, I shall merely tease out the significance of my earlier claim that one of the features of religious change in advanced industrial societies is the process whereby religious symbols and meanings, having floated free from their origins in religious traditions and organizations, can be appropriated for use by nonreligious agencies. This is why it makes good sociological sense to think of religion less as a social institution and more as a cultural resource susceptible to many different uses.

It also makes good sense to deny that religion necessarily possesses fixed and timeless characteristics. It is better to think of religion, from a sociological point of view, as a highly variable set of social and cultural practices credited by many people with conveying the ultimate significance of anything and everything. In other words, religion amounts to the bewilderingly varied symbols, values, feelings, experiences, actions, and forms of association which are usually regarded by religious believers as ultimately real or significant because they derive their meaning from belief in the existence of supernatural, superhuman or superempirical forces.

It is important for me to be clear about this point because my argument in this chapter is different from some apparently similar arguments about religious change. I do not claim that an entity called "religion," which used to be found in institutionalized religious groups, has migrated to new locations or has undergone "restructuring." Nor is my argument that the form in which religion is expressed has changed from collective to personal, or from explicit to implicit. I am not even in agreement with the view that ambiguity about whether something is religious or not is evidence of "quasi-religion" (Rudy and Greil 1989, Greil and Robbins 1994), for I do not hold the assumption that religion is a fixed territory separated by a "no-man's-land" of quasi-religion from an equally fixed territory of the secular. And I am certainly not claiming that unregulated competition between religious groups raises a society's level of religious vitality. In fact, my general thesis is more radical: the definition of what counts as religion is at stake in the course of people's attempts to make use of it in various ways. The waning capacity of mainstream religious organizations to control the definition and use of religious symbols and practices has created opportunities for more extensive experimentation with their use *and* for corresponding attempts to denigrate or block such usage. There is a struggle to influence the outcome, and this helps to place religion in a position similar to that of social movements in most advanced industrial societies.

I shall argue that one way of understanding the uses to which religion can be put nowadays is to examine the mutual relations between religion and social movements. But my argument differs significantly from that of Zald and McCarthy (1998) who advocated that religion be analyzed from the perspective of Resource Mobilization Theory. While this is certainly a productive way of understanding social movements, it neglects some of the most important features of religion and therefore needs to be supplemented by the more "cultural" approach that I shall take in what follows. My position is much closer to that of Armand Mauss (1993:131) who advocated "more extensive 'cross-fertilization'" between studies of social movements and studies of new religious movements. In fact, my main reason for urging a closer connection between studies of religious and social movements has to do with the view that advanced industrial societies have become "social movement societies" (Meyer and Tarrow 1998). This means, among other things, that changes in social inequalities, political divisions, education, and the mass media of communication have facilitated a mode of conducting politics that allows generous space to institutionalized social movement protests, pressure groups, single issue campaigns, and lobbies. Religion has been affected by the same changes and has in some respects become just one, albeit distinctive, resource for a variety of social movements.

Religion and Social Movements

The term "social movement" refers to collective attempts to identify, challenge, and change situations that movement supporters consider unjust or unacceptable. They pursue their grievances and campaigns mainly outside the channels of institutionalized politics.

Although there are overlaps between religion and social movements, religion clearly has aspects to which there are no obvious counterparts in social movements. For example, notions of prayer, worship, intercession, salvation, and immortality are remote from the core claims and activities of nonreligious social movements. Religion cannot be reduced to a social movement. Indeed, in everyday life the boundary between religion and social movements is relatively unproblematic. On the other hand, there is a gray area between them where ideas, sentiments, and activities closely associated with conventional definitions of religion are used in ways that are characteristic of social movements and *vice versa*. For example, the promotion of values considered to be ultimately significant is common to religion and many social movements. So are the diagnosis of serious problems in social life and the framing of putative solutions. Collective identity and communal solidarity are highly valued in religions and social movements alike; and a sense of obligation to participate in them in the face of problems requiring an urgent response is usually well developed in both. In other words, as I shall argue below, there may be more in common between religion and social movements from a sociological point of view than scholars have commonly acknowledged. (For exceptions, see Hannigan 1991, 1993, Mauss 1993, Smith 1996, Zald and McCarthy 1998, Yarnold 1991a, Hart 1996.) In particular, three social and cultural changes have made it important to examine the things in common between religion and social movements.

First, social and cultural changes in the twentieth century have tended to drive religious organizations towards positions similar to those occupied by social movements. My starting point for this assertion is that in early industrial societies religious identity and practice involved participation in local groups of worshipers which, in turn, provided some sense of incorporation into the wider community and civil society. This close association between participation in religion and participation in a local community was progressively eroded by increasing rates of geographical and social mobility, urbanization, suburbanization, and the strengthening of forces favoring outlooks that transcended local differences and refracted social class and regional differences. The result, in most advanced industrial societies, is that formal membership of, and participation in, local religious groups has ceased to be the norm for most people – just as rates of participation in local branches of many voluntary associations have also declined. Those who *do* participate in local religious groups are now much more likely to do so by choice than out of a sense of tradition or obligation. In this sense religious activities are increasingly a matter of choice. Not surprisingly, rates of switching between religious groups or of switching between participation and nonparticipation also increased during the twentieth century. Consequently, religious groups now share many of the sociological features of other intentional communities and mobilizations such as social movements. That is, they are subject to "enrollment economies" in competitive "markets" where a premium is placed on the skills of framing their distinctive message, packaging it attractively, communicating it persuasively, and retaining the loyalty of their "clients."

The fact that active participants in organized religious activities are nowadays in the minority in most advanced industrial societies is a second reason why religious organizations and social movements have more in common with each other than used to be the case. Both of them are in tension with aspects of their surrounding societies. This used to be the case for radical sectarian or minority groups which departed from the norms of mainstream Christianity, but it has become characteristic of even the most popular religious organizations. In other words, tension between religious organizations and some of the norms and values prevailing in society is virtually endemic and is no longer confined to religious radicals. As a result, religious organizations find themselves in a position shared by social movements. Both kinds of collectivity define themselves as defenders and promoters of change, seeking to air their respective grievances and to combat what they regard as the evil, dangerous, or unjust aspects of the world around them. Admittedly, religious organizations usually emphasize the timelessness of the truths underlying their activities, but it is also common for social movements advocating, for example, human rights, civil rights, environmental protection, or peace to stress the "eternal" nature of their values. Again, the sharp distinction between religious organizations and social movements is increasingly questionable from a sociological point of view.

A third reason why the conceptual gap between religion and social movements has begun to close is that long-standing assumptions about the benign and beneficial nature of religion have come under pressure in many advanced industrial societies. Leaving aside countries with a sharp separation between religion and the state, the constitutions and legal systems of many other countries confer privileges and responsibilities on particular religious organizations and, in some cases, on the entire category of religious activities. Exemption from some forms of taxation, recognition that their activities are considered "charitable" or "for the public good," official membership of statutory bodies, and accreditation of their religious professionals have all been conferred on religious organizations by state agencies in some places. Courts of law have often interpreted these privileges as applying only to the historically and locally dominant religious organizations of the Christian faith, that is, state churches or national churches. But these "cozy" arrangements between privileged religious organizations and state agencies came under close scrutiny in the latter half of the twentieth century, thereby calling in question the principle of treating "religion" as a privileged category.

Several factors have contributed to this change: declining rates of membership and participation in the major churches; growing public interest in, and understanding of, other religions; substantial increases in the number of people belonging to faith communities excluded from legal privileges; significant growth in support for the view that no religion should receive any official privileges. As a result, divisions are appearing in public opinion between the majority, who continue to regard the historically dominant religious organizations as the only "normal" forms of religion, and the minority, who believe either that no religions should receive official privileges or that a much wider set of religious organizations should receive them on the principle of "equal respect" for all religions in multifaith societies. The stakes are high in relation to matters such as religious education in schools, access to public broadcasting facilities (Beckford 1999), control over the dress code of school students (Khosrokhavar 1997), exemption from military conscription, and access to state-funded chaplaincy services in prisons and hospitals (Beckford and Gilliat 1998).

It is therefore becoming more contentious, even in the USA and France, where religion is constitutionally separate from the state, to take for granted the difference between acceptable and nonacceptable forms of religion and to defend the official or unofficial privileges traditionally enjoyed by selected churches. Against this background, religion is perceived as more controversial. This applies most clearly to the case of new religious movements (NRMs), some of which are widely regarded as extremely problematic. The growing number of official inquiries into NRMs in European countries and Japan is merely one piece of evidence of how seriously the "problem" is perceived in some quarters (Introvigne 1997). According to Cuddihy (1978), religion was regarded almost by definition as benign and worthy of strong protection by the US Federal Constitution, but Robbins (1983) and Wuthnow (1988) have argued, for different reasons, that this long-standing American assumption has been eroded since the 1950s. The acrimony surrounding the short-lived Religious Freedom Restoration Act of 1996 has also emphasized the extent to which the legal status of religion has become a matter of controversy (Richardson in press). Current struggles to establish the operational boundaries of religious freedom in the former state socialist countries of Central and Eastern Europe are further evidence of the increasingly controversial character attributed to NRMs and Orthodox Churches alike (Barker 1999). The enactment of the International Religious Freedom Act in the USA and the appointment in 1999 of the first ambassador-at-large of the office of International Religious Freedom at the US State Department are further indicators of the growing controversy about religious freedom issues.

One of the common features in all these different situations is the heightened sensitivity of politicians and agencies of the state to the expectation that they should protect "consumers" against actual or potential exploitation. Since participation in religious activities has become a matter of individual choice, and since religious organizations compete for participants in an increasingly deregulated market in many countries, unease about the risks of malpractice by religious groups has also grown. This unease resonates with the readiness of politicians in advanced industrial democracies, where the strength of communal and collective bonds has been sapped by fragmentation and diversification, to legitimate their authority in terms of "consumer protection." The result is that, in the absence of a clear consensus about the value of competing religious groups and ideals, agreement can only be sought on the neutral criterion of "least offence." That is, legal recognition, protection, or tolerance will be extended only to those religious groups that comply with standards ensuring their public accountability and, hence, their conformity with dominant social and cultural norms. In other words, the marketization of religion has made the latter more controversial and, consequently, more analogous to social movements in so far as both phenomena are seen as potentially disruptive of social order, and therefore in need of regulation.

If there are good sociological reasons why religion is increasingly used in ways that resemble the uses to which social movements are put in advanced industrial societies, what does the investigation reveal? I shall divide my answer into two parts: the first part will document the direct input of religion into social movements, while the second part will tease out the religious or spiritual issues that emerge in social movements.

Religious Contributions Toward Social Movements

There is nothing new about religion providing social and ideological support for many major social movements (Yarnold 1991a). In the language of Resource Mobilization Theory, religious organizations have supplied the social infrastructure for movements as diverse as antislavery, temperance, pacifism, and civil rights. It was through the social networks in which members of religious groups frequently came into contact with each other that support for these movements also circulated. These networks provided the foundations of material, social, and moral support with which the movements could be constructed, as demonstrated in McCarthy's (1987) comparison between the "social infrastructures" of the prolife and prochoice mobilizations in the USA. To take the example of the Campaign for Nuclear Disarmament (CND) in the UK, 23 percent of activists in the mid-1980s were members of religious organizations (Byrne 1988). This figure is roughly twice as high as the proportion of the British population who are members of religious organizations. Moreover, about 10 per cent of these particular activists were Quakers, who nevertheless represented only 0.05 per cent of the general population. The Religious Society of Friends constitutes one of the most important social networks from which support has come for a wide variety of peace movements and other humanitarian campaigns. (See Epstein 1990:109–10 for details of the Quaker underpinnings of many peace initiatives in the USA.) Similarly, the support of Roman Catholics for the Sanctuary movement in the USA is well-documented (Golden and McConnell 1986, Wiltfang and McAdam 1991, Yarnold 1991b).

Even more attention has been given to the central role played by historically black churches in channeling support towards the American civil rights movement (Morris 1984, 1996, McAdam 1982). In more recent times Christian churches in many countries of Central and Eastern Europe (Weigel 1992) as well as South Africa (Villa-Vicencio 1990) and Central and South America (Adriance 1991, Smith 1991) fostered the social networks through which support for movements of democratic political reform or revolution was mobilized. Less well-documented are the religiously supported countermovements that opposed these changes, but Aho's (1990, 1996) writings on right-wing Christian patriot groupings in the USA give a good insight into the confluence of conservative politics and religion at the extremes. Religious contributions to social movements can be negative as well as positive.

None of this is surprising, although the proponents of the strongest versions of secularization theory may find it difficult to take proper account of these important contributions of religion to social change. What is less acknowledged, even among sociologists of religion, is that religion can still operate on some occasions as the *central* focus of social change – not just as a tributary of political change. Examples include the Nation of Islam's program for a separate, religiously governed social world for people of African descent in North America, Western Europe, and elsewhere (Gardell 1996, Lincoln 1973); the mobilization of millions of supporters for the conservative Christian Coalition in the USA; the Islamic Revolution, which transformed the nature of Iran from 1979 onwards; and movements for the Islamicization of various Central Asian republics following the collapse of the Soviet Union (Mickulsky 1993). The fact that these movements for the creation or regeneration of a whole way of life are animated by the desire partly to defend entire cultures and partly to underline the religious identity of ethnic or "racial" groupings does not weaken my claim that religion can still serve as the main motive and legitimization for comprehensive social change. Indeed, the national and cross-national social networks that link religious activists together constitute in some cases virtually the only effective infrastructure for would-be transformative movements.

The Religious in Social Movements

The direct contribution of religion toward social movements is only one side of the coin. The other, less understood side concerns the processes whereby religious, or at least spiritual, issues emerge in social movements. This is a relatively neglected area of study. Neither sociologists of religion nor analysts of social movements have paid much attention to it (exceptions include Eder 1982, 1985, Melucci 1985, 1989, 1995, 1996), but I would like to argue here, expanding my earlier thoughts (Beckford 1989:143–65) and drawing upon Hannigan's (1990, 1991, 1993) insights, that the central preoccupation of some social movements in supposedly secular societies has a spiritual or religious quality or, to borrow the formulation of Demerath and Schmitt, "seemingly nonreligious" movements for change in civil rights, gender relations, the environment, and welfare "are religious at their edges, if not their core" (1998:390).

The terms "religious" and "spiritual" are often used more or less interchangeably, and this in itself is indicative of changes in the way that religion is used in advanced industrial societies. They both refer to levels of meaning and significance which go beyond the surface appearance of everyday realities. They both point to the possibility that ostensibly routine taken-for-granted, matter-of-fact phenomena may conceal deeper or higher levels of reality. Spiritual insights convey a sense of the ultimate significance of things, often creating the impression that human life is part of a comprehensive, timeless scheme. The "spiritual," defined in this way, shades off into the "religious." The latter term embraces the former but adds the implication that supernatural, superhuman or superempirical powers are responsible for the ultimate significance of everything. This accounts both for the requirement that they should be worshiped or venerated and for the belief that the truth about their intentions is contained in revelations, relics, scriptures, artifacts, hierophanies, and so forth. The most important sociological implication of the differences between the two terms is that the "religious" provides a better basis for the development of communities of believers subject to control by authoritative knowledge and religious specialists. Nevertheless, communities of believers invariably provide opportunities for the cultivation of spiritual interests in the context of preaching, prayer, worship, and pastoral activities. How do religious and spiritual issues emerge in social movements?

Importing religion

In the first place, social movement members may simply seize the opportunity to articulate their particular, religiously based views of social movements' aims and methods. Thus, many activists in antiabortion movements have been able to draw on formal statements made by the Roman Catholic Church and conservative Protestant churches in support of their protest. They may even form their own caucuses within wider movements or join coalitions with other groupings. The radical Christian section of the nonviolent direct action wing of the American peace movement in the 1980s (Epstein 1990:107) is a good example of religious affinities within social movements, although it is never easy categorically to separate the religious from the nonreligious input to social movements. Another example concerns Solidarity, the Polish nationalist movement for an independent trade union and for democratic political reforms (Touraine 1983). Solidarity undoubtedly benefited from the distinctive contribution that Catholicism made to its early popularity in 1980, but many other ideological influences shaped the movement as well. Emerging at the end of more than 20 years of deliberate attempts to revive the notion that Poland was a fundamentally Catholic country, symbolized in the famous image of the Black Madonna of Czestochowa, many of Solidarity's ordinary supporters drew heavily on religious symbolism and practices. Its "semiology connected the movement to Poland's Catholic mythology and the touchstones of the Great Novena: the Black Madonna, the suffering Christ, the Christian nation. Elaborate ceremonies and symbolic displays were as essential to Solidarity as the sit-down strike" (Osa 1996:82). Yet, opinions are divided on the question of whether placing Solidarity in a religious frame of meaning provided an adequate basis for the movement's long-term political strategy.

A further complication arises from the possibility that members of social movements who make connections between their religious or spiritual convictions and the movements' objectives may not agree with each other. It is well established that ideological divisions within many religious organizations sometimes outweigh the agreements between them. Current tensions within the worldwide Anglican communion, for example, are related in part to disagreements about the propriety of ordaining women to the priesthood and consecrating them as bishops (Nesbitt 1997). Anglicans who participate in various women's movements, feminist movements, and antifeminist movements witness to the existence of these deep-seated tensions and conflicts. In this way, the ideological problems within the Anglican communion may be replayed and elaborated in the broader struggles being conducted by these various movements.

In other words, there is no guarantee that religiously motivated activists in movements that appear to be based on a shared ideology actually think alike. Williams and Blackburn (1996), for example, highlight the discrepancies between the formal ideology of Operation Rescue, a high-profile antiabortion movement organization in the USA, and the "operative ideology" of its activists. The activists' practical understanding of their own protest activities departs from the organization's official views in several important respects concerning relations between church and state, the primacy of political over evangelical strategies, and the defensibility of civil disobedience. The conclusion is that "Holding a movement together, even among people as generally homogeneous as white, born-again, Conservative Protestants is a difficult business" (Williams and Blackburn 1996:183). The findings of research into support for the cause of animal rights among the American public also revealed a puzzle. Higher levels of church attendance accompany disagreement with animal rights ideology, whereas subscription to four religious beliefs (biblical literalism, a "gracious" image of God, a relationship between God and nature, and a negative relationship between religion and science) was correlated with support for animal rights ideology (Peek, Konty, and Frazier 1997). The conclusion is that religion is subtle and complex and therefore unlikely to bear a simple relationship to social movements.

Generating the sacred

Secondly, some social movements give rise to spiritual and religious associations not only because activists draw on ideas previously shaped by religious organizations but also because these activists detect a sense of the sacred or the ultimate in the ideology, sentiments, or collective actions of the movements. The term "sacred" signifies phenomena which, from a religious or spiritual point of view, are infused with such power and significance that they command strong reverence or fear. For example, they may associate the sacred with feelings of awe or dread in the face of problems perceived to be overwhelming. A good case in point concerns the perception of many activists in movements against nuclear weapons that "never . . . have people collectively, in the midst of life and health, been subject to the threat of sudden extinction we now face" (Soper 1983:174). The response of many activists in American peace movements was religious or spiritual (Knudson-Ptacek 1990).

Alternatively, a sense of the sacred may be linked to feelings of optimism, or at least hope, that good will ultimately triumph over evil. This is a common theme among therapeutic movements, especially those that incorporate the 12-step program associated with Alcoholics Anonymous (Rudy and Greil 1989). The character of participants' spiritual experiences varies with each movement's ideology or its claims about the causes of problems and the preconditions for their solution (Antze 1976, Rice 1994). Nevertheless, therapeutic movements are often the setting in which participants not only come to believe that they can transcend their problems but also come to experience their therapy as a form of transcendence revealing sacred power (Jacobs 1990). Furthermore, there is mounting evidence about the gendered character of the spirituality encountered in healing groups (McGuire 1994). And animal rights activists who talked to Groves (1997:102) about religion, "preferred doctrines in which God lives 'within' rather than above people." Their concern was with "concepts such as love and discipline, being connected to the universe, not wanting to hurt anything, living in harmony, respecting earth, respecting each other." Similarly, in the ecology movement "alternative spiritualists assert that *all* aspects of life are sacred, both the sky-like 'heavens' and the 'matter' of earth and that activities involving protection of the earth should be conceptualized as part of one's spirituality" (Bloch 1998:57, emphasis original).

Transcendental experiences may also be attributed to the "collective effervescence" (Durkheim 1915, Mellor and Shilling 1997) accompanying selfless immersion in a movement's enthusiastic activities and celebration of its unity of purpose. Yet, a recurrent theme in studies of new social movements is the weakness of their formal organizations (Melucci 1989, 1996). This is why some observers use terms such as "collection action" (Diani and Eyerman 1992) in preference to "social movement." The latter is felt to imply too much rigidity, formality, and substance. Instead, emphasis is placed on the networks of social relations, ideological commitments, and symbols of identity which form the framework for collective action.

If this is a feature of present-day social movements it is also reflected in the reluctance to create formal groupings of "alternative or countercultural spiritualists" in the ecology movement. According to Bloch, spiritually motivated activists in ecology are "geared more toward changing social meanings than rig-orously associating as a collective . . . One need not belong to a highly-organized group to consider oneself to be part of and contributing to the larger social movement" (1998:59). This is true, but it ignores the spiritual excitement stim-ulated by the occasional embodied celebrations of collective identity and purpose that occur among even the least formally organized activists. Indeed, some "eco warriors" have developed elaborate collective rituals, often drawing on pagan or Wiccan sources, in celebration of their common purpose. A well-documented example concerns a loosely structured group of protesters in the UK against the construction of major roads in areas of natural beauty or in human neighbor-hoods. Ironically taking the name "the Donga tribe" from a Matabele word which was applied in the nineteenth century to medieval paths criss-crossing British hillsides, these radical protesters live rough near construction sites and deploy a range of nonviolent direct action tactics to obstruct road building pro-jects. Moreover, "There is a strand of spirituality and ritual in Dongas experi-ence, which taps into the usual diverse New Age sources such as Celtic myth, stone circles, world music and drumming, equinox and solstice celebrations . . . They have developed rituals and festivals celebrating the seasons" (McKay 1996:139). It is also common for ecological movement activists to pepper their language with religious terms such as "the sacred," "sacrilege," "profanation," and "redemption."

Conclusion

Two of the social and cultural changes that have occurred in advanced indus-trial societies in the latter half of the twentieth century have affected relations between religion and social movements. The first concerns the declining power of religious organizations to shape social life and to control the public usage of religious symbols except for the relatively small proportion of people, in societies other than the USA, who choose to associate themselves with religious organi-zations. Since organized religion has become a minority activity which is in tension with some of the values prevailing in major social institutions, religious organizations have come to occupy a societal position similar in some respects to that of social movements. That is, they are heard by outsiders as voices of dissent or protest; and they are often regarded as controversial. The second change concerns shifts in the criteria for categorizing things as "religious." Just as uses of terms such as "art," "sport," and "culture" have changed, so the meanings attributed to "religion," "religious," and "spiritual" have also under-gone modification. The direction of change has been towards using these terms in ways that come close to the usage of terms referring to the activities of social movements. This conceptual shift is a strong justification for further sociologi-cal research into the intertwining of religion and social movements.

One of the possible objections to my claim that religions and social movements have more and more in common in most advanced industrial societies may be that it only applies, at best, to "quasi-religion" (Greil and Robbins 1994). Perhaps my examples are not about "authentic" or "genuine" religion at all. My critics may charge me with ignoring "real" religion or of confusing it with phenomena that bear only a superficial resemblance to it. Such accusations would be serious – but far from fatal for my argument. My response would be that, from a sociological point of view, there is no reason to believe that religion is a phenomenon with fixed, timeless properties. On the contrary, I consider religion to be constellations of immensely variable beliefs and practices by means of which human beings attribute the highest significance to all manner of objects, events, ideas, values, sentiments, and ways of living. The boundaries of the religious are constantly being negotiated, contested, and renegotiated.

My argument is that the boundary between religion and social movements became progressively more confused in advanced industrial societies towards the end of the twentieth century. This blurring of the boundary is partly due to the declining capacity of religious organizations to control the use made of religious symbols, and partly due to the growing belief that many of the era's most pressing political, social and economic problems would be better redefined as spiritual or religious.

References

Adriance, M. 1991. "Agents of Change: The Roles of Priests, Sisters, and Lay Workers in the Grassroots Catholic Church in Brazil," *Journal for the Scientific Study of Religion* 30(3):292–305.

Aho, J. 1990. *The Politics of Righteousness. Idaho Christian Patriotism.* Seattle: University of Washington Press.

Aho, J. 1996. "Popular Christianity and Political Extremism in the United States," in *Disruptive Religion*, Ed. C. Smith. New York: Routledge, pp. 189–204.

Antze, P. 1976. "The Role of Ideologies in Peer Psychotherapy Organizations: Some Theoretical Considerations and Three Case Studies," *Journal of Applied Behavioral Science* 12(3):323–46.

Bailey, E. 1998. *Implicit Religion: An Introduction.* London: Middlesex University Press.

Barker, E. 1999. "But Who's Going to Win? National and Minority Religious Movements in Post-Communist Society," *Facta Universitatis: Series Philosophy and Psychology* 2(6):49–74.

Beckford, J.A. 1985. "The Insulation and Isolation of the Sociology of Religion," *Sociological Analysis* 46:347–54.

Beckford, J.A. 1989. *Religion and Advanced Industrial Society.* London: Unwin-Hyman.

Beckford, J.A. 1992. "Religion, Modernity and Postmodernity," in *Religion: Contemporary Issues*, Ed. B.R. Wilson. London: Bellew, pp. 11–23.

Beckford, J.A. 1999. "The Politics of Defining Religion in Secular Society: From a Taken-for-Granted Institution to a Contested Resource," in *The Definition of Religion: Concepts, Contexts and Conflicts*," Ed. J.G. Platvoet and A.L. Molendijk. Leiden: E.J. Brill, pp. 23–40.

Beckford, J.A. and Gilliat, S. 1998. *Religion in Prison. Equal Rites in a Multi-Faith Society.* Cambridge: Cambridge University Press.

Bloch, J.P. 1998. "Alternative Spirituality and Environmentalism," *Review of Religious Research* 40(1):55–73.

Byrne, P. 1988. *The Campaign for Nuclear Disarmament.* London: Croom Helm.

Castells, M. 1997. *The Power of Identity.* Oxford: Blackwell.

Champion, F. and Hervieu-Léger, D., Eds. 1990. *De l'émotion en religion.* Paris: Centurion.

Cipriani, R. 1989. " 'Diffused Religion' and New Values in Italy," in *The Changing Face of Religion,* Eds. J.A. Beckford and T. Luckmann. London: Sage, pp. 24–48.

Cuddihy, J. 1978. *No Offense: Civil Religion and Protestant Taste.* New York: Seabury.

Dawson, L.L. and Hennebry, J. 1999. "New Religions and the Internet: Recruiting in a New Public Space," *Journal of Contemporary Religion* 14(1):17–39.

Demerath, N.J. III and Schmitt, T. 1998. "Transcending Sacred and Secular: Mutual Benefits in Analyzing Religious and Nonreligious Organization," in *Sacred Companies: Organizational Aspects of Religion and Religious Aspects of Organizations,* Eds. N.J. Demerath III *et al.*, New York: Oxford University Press, pp. 381–400.

Derrida, J. and Vattimo, G., Eds. 1998. *Religion.* Cambridge: Polity Press.

Diani, M. and Eyerman, R., Eds. 1992. *Studying Collective Action.* London: Sage.

Durkheim, E. 1915. *The Elementary Forms of the Religious Life,* Transl. J.W. Swain. London: George, Allen & Unwin.

Eder, K. 1982. "A New Social Movement?" *Telos* 52:5–20.

Eder, K. 1985. "The 'New Social Movements'," *Social Research* 52:869–90.

Epstein, B. 1990. "The Politics of Moral Witness: Religion and Nonviolent Direct Action," in *Peace Action in the Eighties,* Eds. S. Marullo and J. Lofland. New Brunswick, NJ: Rutgers University Press, pp. 106–24.

Ferrarotti, F. 1993. *Faith Without Dogma: The Place of Religion in Post Modern Societies.* New Brunswick, NJ: Transaction.

Flanagan, K. 1996. *The Enchantment of Sociology: A Study of Theology and Culture.* London: Macmillan.

Gardell, M. 1996. *Countdown to Armageddon: Louis Farrakhan and the Nation of Islam.* London: Hurst.

Giddens, A. 1991. *Modernity and Self-Identity.* Cambridge: Polity Press.

Gill, R., Hadaway, K., and Marler, P.L. 1998. "Is Religious Belief Declining in Britain?" *Journal for the Scientific Study of Religion* 37(3):507–16.

Golden, R. and McConnell, M. 1986. *Sanctuary: The New Underground Railroad.* New York: Orbis.

Greil, A.L. and Robbins, T., Eds. 1994. *Between Sacred and Secular: Research and Theory on Quasi-Religion.* Greenwich, CT: JAI Press.

Groves, J.M. 1997. *Hearts and Minds: The Controversy over Laboratory Animals.* Philadelphia: Temple University Press.

Hannigan, J.A. 1990. "Apples and Oranges or Varieties of the Same Fruit? The New Religious Movements and the New Social Movements Compared," *Review of Religious Research* 31:246–58.

Hannigan, J.A. 1991. "Social Movement Theory and the Sociology of Religion," *Sociological Analysis* 52:311–31.

Hannigan, J.A. 1993. "New Social Movement Theory and the Sociology of Religion," in *A Future for Religion?*, Ed. W.H. Swatos Jr. Newbury Park, CA: Sage, pp. 1–18.

Hart, S. 1996. "The Cultural Dimension of Social Movements: A Theoretical Reassessment and Literature Review," *Sociology of Religion* 57(1):87–100.

Haynes, J. 1998. *Religion in Global Politics*. London: Longman.

Hornsby-Smith, M.P., Lee, R.M., and Reilly, P.A. 1985. "Common Religion and Customary Religion: A Critique and a Proposal," *Review of Religious Research* 26:244–52.

Introvigne, M. 1997. "Religious Liberty in Western Europe," *ISKCON Communications Journal* 5(2):37–48.

Jacobs, J. 1990. "Women-Centered Healing Rites," in *In Gods We Trust: New Patterns of Religious Pluralism in America*, Eds. T. Robbins and D. Anthony. New Brunswick, NJ: Transaction, pp. 373–83.

Khosrokhavar, F. 1997. *L'Islam des jeunes*. Paris: Flammarion.

Knudson-Ptacek, C. 1990. "Self-Conceptions of Peace Activists," in *Peace Action in the Eighties: Social Science Perspectives*, Eds. S. Murullo and J. Lofland. New Brunswick, NJ: Rutgers University Press, pp. 233–45.

Lincoln, C.E. 1973. *The Black Muslims in America*. Boston: Beacon Press.

McAdam, D. 1982. *Political Process and the Development of Black Insurgency, 1930–1970*. Chicago: University of Chicago Press.

McCarthy, J.D. 1987. "Pro-Life and Pro-Choice Mobilization: Infrastructure Deficits and New Technologies," in *Social Movements in an Organizational Society*, Eds. M.N. Zald and J.D. McCarthy. New Brunswick, NJ: Transaction, pp. 49–66.

McGuire, M.B. 1994. "Gendered Spirituality and Quasi-Religious Ritual," in *Between Sacred and Secular: Research and Theory on Quasi-Religion*, Eds. A.L. Greil and T. Robbins. Greenwich, CT: JAI Press, pp. 273–87.

McKay, G. 1996. *Senseless Acts of Beauty: Cultures of Resistance since the Sixties*. London: Verso.

Marty, M. and Appleby, S., Eds. 1991. *Fundamentalisms Observed*. Chicago: University of Chicago Press.

Mauss, A.L. 1993. "Research in Social Movements and in New Religious Movements: The Prospects for Convergence," in *The Handbook on Cults and Sects in America*, Eds. D.G. Bromley and J.K. Hadden. Greenwich, CT: JAI Press, pp. 127–51.

Mellor, P. and Shilling, C. 1997. *Re-Forming the Body: Religion, Community and Modernity*. London: Sage.

Melucci, A. 1985. "The Symbolic Challenge of Contemporary Movements," *Social Research* 52(4):789–816.

Melucci, A. 1989. *Nomads of the Present: Social Movements and Individual Needs in Contemporary Society*. Philadelphia: Temple University Press.

Melucci, A. 1995. "The New Social Movements Revisited: Reflections on a Sociological Misunderstanding," in *Social Movements and Social Classes*, Ed. L. Maheu. London: Sage, pp. 107–19.

Melucci, A. 1996. *Challenging Codes: Collective Action in the Information Age*. Cambridge: Cambridge University Press.

Meyer, D. and Tarrow, S., Eds. 1998. *The Social Movement Society*. Lanham, MD: Rowman & Littlefield.

Mickulsky, D. 1993. "Muslim Fundamentalism in Soviet Central Asia. A Social Perspective," in *Religious Transformations and Socio-Political Change. Eastern Europe and Latin America*, Ed. L. Martin. Berlin: Mouton de Gruyter, pp. 141–8.

Milbank, J. 1990. *Theology and Social Theory: Beyond Secular Reason*. Oxford: Blackwell.

Morris, A.D. 1984. *The Origins of the Civil Rights Movement*. New York: Free Press.

Morris, A.D. 1996. "The Black Church in the Civil Rights Movement: The SCLC as the

Decentralized, Radical Arm of the Black Church," in *Disruptive Religion*, Ed. C. Smith. New York: Routledge, pp. 29–46.

Nesbitt, P.D. 1997. *The Feminization of the Clergy in America*. New York: Oxford University Press.

Osa, M. 1996. "Pastoral Mobilization and Contention: The Religious Foundations of the Solidarity Movement in Poland," in *Disruptive Religion: The Force of Faith in Social Movement Activism*, Ed. C. Smith. New York: Routledge, pp. 67–85.

Peek, C., Konty, M., and Frazier, T. 1997. "Religion and Ideological Support for Social Movements: The Case of Animal Rights," *Journal for the Scientific Study of Religion* 36(3):429–39.

Rice, J.S. 1994. "The Therapeutic God: Transcendence and Identity in Two Twelve-Step Quasi-Religions," in *Between Sacred and Secular: Research and Theory on Quasi-Religion*, Eds. A.L. Greil and T. Robbins. Greenwich, CT: JAI Press, pp. 151–64.

Richardson, J.T. (in press) "The Religious Freedom Restoration Act: A Short-Lived Experiment in Religious Freedom," in *Religion, Pluralism and the Law*, Eds. C. Parrigan and D. Sinacore-Guinn. Atlanta, GA: Scholars Press.

Robbins, T. 1983. "The Beach is Washing Away: Controversial Religion and the Sociology of Religion," *Sociological Analysis* 44(3):207–14.

Rudy, D. and Greil, A. 1989. "Is Alcoholics Anonymous a Religious Organization?" *Sociological Analysis* 50(1):41–51.

Smith, C. 1991. *The Emergence of Liberation Theology: Radical Religion and Social-Movement Activism*. Chicago: University of Chicago Press.

Smith, C., Ed. 1996. *Disruptive Religion: The Force of Faith in Social Movement Activism*. New York: Routledge.

Soper, K. 1983. "Contemplating a Nuclear Future: Nuclear War, Politics and the Individual," in *Over Our Dead Bodies: Women Against the Bomb*, Ed. D. Thompson. London: Virago, pp. 169–79.

Stark, R. and Bainbridge, W.S. 1987. *A Theory of Religion*. New York: Peter Lang.

Touraine, A. 1983. *Solidarity: Poland 1980–81*. Cambridge: University of Cambridge Press.

Villa-Vicencio, C. 1990. *Civil Disobedience and Beyond: Law, Resistance, and Religion in South Africa*. Grand Rapids, MI: Eerdmans.

Warner, R.S. 1993. "Work in Progress: Toward a New Paradigm for the Sociological Study of Religion in the United States," *American Journal of Sociology* 98(March): 1044–93.

Weigel, G. 1992. *The Final Revolution*. New York: Oxford University Press.

Williams, R.H. and Blackburn, J. 1996. "Many Are Called but Few Obey? Ideological Commitment and Activism in Operation Rescue," in *Disruptive Religion: The Force of Faith in Social Movement Activism*, Ed. C. Smith. New York: Routledge, pp. 167–85.

Wiltfang, G.L. and McAdam, D. 1991. "The Costs and Risks of Social Activism: A Study of Sanctuary Movement Activism," *Social Forces* 69(4):987–1010.

Wuthnow, R. 1988. *The Restructuring of American Religion*. Princeton, NJ: University of Princeton Press.

Yarnold, B.M., Ed. 1991a. *The Role of Religious Organizations in Social Movements*. New York: Praeger.

Yarnold, B.M. 1991b. "The Role of Religious Organizations in the US Sanctuary Movement," in *The Role of Religious Organizations in Social Movements*, Ed. B. Yarnold. New York: Praeger, pp. 17–46.

Zald, M.N. and McCarthy, J.D. 1998. "Religious Groups as Crucibles of Social Movements," in *Sacred Companies: Organizational Aspects of Religion and Religious Aspects of Organizations*, Eds. N.J. Demerath III, P.D. Hall, T. Schmitt, and R.H. Williams. New York: Oxford University Press, pp. 24–49.

CHAPTER 13
The Social Process of Secularization

Steve Bruce

Introduction

The peoples of preindustrial Europe were thoroughly religious. The extent to which they were orthodox Christians varied considerably but most understood the world through basically Christian lenses. Most knew by heart the Lord's Prayer and the Hail Mary, and could make the sign of the cross. They knew the Ten Commandments, the four cardinal virtues, the seven deadly sins, and the seven works of mercy. They paid their tithes, brought their babies for baptism, and married in church. They believed sufficiently in hell, the power of the church, and the unique status of Holy Writ for the swearing of oaths on the Bible to be an effective means of social control. They avoided blaspheming. They spent considerable sums of money supporting priests whose function was to say mass for their benefactors. Most seem to have accepted that it was necessary to make reparation to God for serious and willful sins either in this life or in the next. When the clergy complained of irreligion it was not because their people were secular but because they persisted in pre-Christian superstitions and used the church's rituals in an instrumental magical manner (Bruce 1997).

As societies industrialized, their people divided. Some became thoroughly educated literate "true believers" while others fell away completely. The once-pervasive religious worldview was replaced by an increasingly secular public culture. By the middle of the nineteenth century, the separation of religion from everyday life had become sufficiently advanced for us to be able to count those who were active supporters of organized religion and those who were not. The introduction of social surveys and opinion polls in the twentieth century allowed us to get some statistical sense of religious belief. Whether we measure church membership, church attendance, the popularity of religious ceremonies to mark rites of passage, or the more nebulous matter of religious belief, we find that, though each index starts at a different level, and the rate of decline differs for each society, nonetheless, across the industrial world there is a steady and to-date unremitting decline in all religious indices.

Put in the familiar organizational types, the religion of premodern societies was of the "church" type, encompassing an entire people and making elevated claims for its own authority while tolerating considerable laxity in individual performance. Particularly in Protestant cultures, the church of the early modern world faced increasing competition from a range of "sects": voluntary associations of pious committed believers. Gradually the need to live with increased diversity forced both the dominant church and the contending sects to converge on the "denomination"; a form of religion that was tolerant of alternatives and made no claim to unique possession of the truth. In particular social and geographical pockets, the sectarian spirit survives but most religious innovations of the second half of the twentieth century have been of the "cult" form, in which individual consumers determine their levels of interest and commitment and synthesize their own ideological packages from a global cafeteria of spiritual traditions and therapies.

This is not just a story of change. It is also a tale of decline. The road from religion embodied in the great European cathedrals to religion as personal preference and individual choice is a road from more to less religion. From the Middles Ages to the end of the twentieth century, religion in Europe (and its offshoot settler societies) declined in power, prestige, and popularity.

To illustrate the changes for Britain, in 1851 about 60 percent of the available adult population of England and Wales attended church (Crockett 1998:131). At the end of the twentieth century the figure was about 10 percent (Brierley 1991). Between 1900 and 1984, despite the population growing by 35 percent and becoming considerably more affluent, the clergy of the Church of England halved, from just over 20,000 to 10,000. In 1900 there were about 3,600 Presbyterian ministers in Scotland, in 1990 no more than 1,450. The number who, in response to social surveys, claim to be religious or to believe in God, is considerably greater than those who are active in the life of a religious organization, but these indices too show decline. A thorough review of all available survey data shows "an increase in general skepticism about the existence of God [and] the related erosion of dominant, traditional Christian beliefs" (Gill, Hadaway, and Marler 1998:507). Even in the United States, long held to be an exception to secularization, the last quarter of the twentieth century saw declining church membership and attendance (Bruce 1996:129–68, Hadaway, Marler, and Chaves 1993).

Explaining Secularization

Before presenting a synthetic summary of a number of sociologists associated with the secularization thesis, I will preempt unnecessary and unwarranted criticisms. First, the thesis explains the *past* of a particular part of the world.

There is no implication that societies of the "second" or "third" worlds must follow the patterns of development found in the old world: secularization is not inevitable. Of course, the West's power and prestige give its characteristics a degree of preeminence as a model for others to emulate (or react against) but the changes described here will be repeated elsewhere only if new circumstances match the old. Second, the secularization thesis is not part of any "Enlightenment" project. On the contrary, it supposes that the major changes are inadvertent and unintended consequences. Third, and this is related, there is no assumption that modern people are too mature or too clever to believe the old superstitions.

Structural Differentiation

Modernization entails the fragmentation of social life as specialized roles and institutions are created to handle specific features or functions previously embodied in or carried out by one role or institution. The family was once a productive as well as a reproductive unit; by the nineteenth century most economic activity was conducted in distinct settings that had their own values. The public sphere became instrumental, pragmatic, and rational; the private sphere expressive, indulgent, and emotional. Increased specialization had the direct effect of "secularizing" many social functions (public administration, diplomacy, education, health, welfare, and social control) which in the Middle Ages were either the exclusive preserve of the Christian church or were dominated by the clergy.

Social Differentiation

Structural differentiation was accompanied by social differentiation. The economic growth implicit in modernization led to an ever-greater range of occupations and life-situations. The emergence of social classes was usually accompanied by increasing class conflict; it was certainly accompanied by class avoidance. In feudal societies, masters and servants lived cheek-by-jowl; such physical proximity was possible because everyone knew their place. The plausibility of a single moral universe in which all people had a place depended on the social structure being fixed. With the proliferation of new social roles and increasing social mobility, traditional organic communities began to fragment. As classes and social fragments became more distinctive so they generated metaphysical and salvational systems along lines more suited to their interests. Thus feudal agricultural societies had a hierarchical religion in which the great pyramid of pope, bishops, priests, and laity reflected the social pyramid of king, nobles, gentry, and peasants. Independent small farmers or the rising business class preferred a more democratic religion; hence their attraction to such early Protestant sects as the Presbyterians, Baptists, and Quakers.

However, modernization was not simply a matter of the religious culture responding to social, economic, and political changes. Religious innovation itself was a cause of differentiation and influenced its shape. The Reformation removed the institution of the church as a source of authority between God and human beings, made all people equal in the eyes of God, reduced the importance of priestly ritual, and thus inadvertently made schism easier. Instead of one Christian church purified and strengthened, because it coincided with increasing social differentiation, the Reformation produced a large number of competing churches and sects. In Protestant countries, social differentiation took the form not of a radical divide between clerical and secular elements but of a series of schisms from the dominant traditions. Rising social classes were able to express their new aspirations and ambitions by reworking the familiar religion into shapes that accorded with their self-image.

Societalization

As Wilson (1982:154) uses the term, "societalization" describes the process of close-knit, integrated communities losing power and presence to large-scale industrial and commercial enterprises, to modern states coordinated through massive, impersonal bureaucracies, and to cities. As the society rather than the community increasingly became the locus of the individual's life, organized religion lost many points of contact with the people. The church of the Middle Ages baptized, christened, and confirmed children, married young adults, and buried the dead. Its calendar of services mapped on to the temporal order of the seasons. It celebrated and legitimated local life. In turn it drew considerable plausibility from being frequently reaffirmed through the participation of the local community in its activities. When the total, all embracing community of like-situated people working and playing together gave way to the dormitory town or suburb, there was little held in common left to celebrate. The contemporary societal system relies less on the inculcation of a shared moral order and more on the use of efficient technical means of eliciting and monitoring appropriate behavior. The oath sworn on the Bible has been replaced by the skin galvanometer lie detector.

Differentiation and societalization reduced the plausibility of any single overarching moral and religious system and thus permitted competing conceptions that, while they may have had much to say to privatized, individual experience, could have little connection to the performance of social roles or the operation of social systems. Religion retained subjective plausibility for some people, but lost its objective taken-for-grantedness. It was no longer a matter of necessity.

The fragmentation of the religious tradition that resulted from the Reformation hastened the development of the religiously neutral state and public sphere.

The successful economy required a high degree of integration: effective communication, a shared legal code to enforce contracts, a climate of trust, and so on. And this required an integrated national culture (Gellner 1983, 1994). Where there was religious consensus, a national "high culture" could be provided through the dominant religious tradition. The clergy could continue to be the schoolteachers, historians, propagandists, public administrators, and military strategists. Where there was little consensus, the growth of the state tended to be secular. In Ireland and the Scandinavian countries, a national education system was created through the Catholic and Lutheran churches respectively. In Britain and the United States it was largely created by the state directly. However, even where a dominant church retained formal ownership of areas of activity, those still came to be informed primarily by secular values.

Rationalization

The Judeo-Christian tradition involved a considerable rationalization of religion. According to the religions of Egypt and Mesopotamia, the human world was embedded in a cosmic order which embraced the entire universe, without any sharp distinction between the human and the nonhuman, the empirical and the supraempirical. The ancient Romans and Greeks had a horde of gods or spirits, who behaved in an arbitrary fashion and at cross purposes, and thus made the relationship of supernatural to natural worlds unpredictable. First Judaism and then Christianity were rationalizing forces. By having only one God, they simplified the supernatural and allowed the worship of God to become systematized. Pleasing God became less a matter of anticipating the whims of an erratic despot and more a matter of correct ethical behavior. As the Christian church evolved, the cosmos was remythologized with angels and semidivine saints. The Virgin Mary was elevated as a mediator and coredeemer with Jesus. The belief that God could be manipulated through ritual, confession, and penance undermined the tendency to regulate behavior with a standardized and rational ethical code. However, this trend was reversed as the Protestant Reformation demythologized the world, eliminated the ritual manipulation of God, and restored the process of ethical rationalization.

Formalizing God's requirements made it possible for morality and ethics to become detached from the supernatural. The codes could be followed for their own sake and could even attract alternative secular justifications. In that sense, the rationalizing tendency of Christianity turned against its progenitor.

A similar point can be made from the way in which people thought about various aspects of the social and material world. Science was not easy for cultures that believed the world pervaded by unpredictable supernatural spirits and divinities. Systematic exploration of regularities in the behavior of matter required the assumption of regularities. The less God was implicated in the day-to-day operations of the universe, the freer people were to elaborate theories of its operations that paid only lip service to the creator. Many early scientists wanted to demonstrate the wonders of God's creation and thus to prove the existence of God, but the development of rationalistic scrutiny in time subverted what it had been intended to protect. By freeing the way for empirical inquiry, and for pragmatic and instrumental treatment of this world, the Judeo-Christian tradition created its own problems.

The Reformation played a particular role in demystifying the world. Just as the medieval church retarded and temporarily reversed the ethical rationalization inherent in Judaism and early Christianity, so the development of science was retarded by the church's imposition of orthodoxy on all fields of thought. The Reformation, by breaking the power of the church (albeit in many places replacing it with the power of a national church), made way for a variety of thought and for the questioning of tradition which is so vital to natural science. There is also a positive connection, argued for by Robert Merton (1970). He shows that a strong desire to demonstrate the glory of God by displaying the majesty of his creation, the rational and systematic attitude of the Protestant ethic, and the Puritan's wish to control the corrupt world, all combined to produce in seventeenth century England a great interest in natural science.

Science played a relatively small part in displacing religion. Often the two are seen as competing systems of explanation and it is supposed that the latter was pushed out by the former showing that many Christian beliefs are wrong. The earth is round and not flat. The earth moves round the sun and not vice versa. The earth and human life are vastly older than the ages taken from Biblical accounts. While scientists recognize that there is still much we do not know, most agree that an evolutionary model along the lines of Darwinism offers a better explanation of the origins of species than does the account of divine creation given in the Old Testament book of Genesis. However, to insist that one set of beliefs lost popularity because another proved it wrong is to miss the difference between truth and plausibility. There are all sorts of ways in which we can insulate our beliefs from apparently contradicting evidence. We can avoid hearing the troublesome evidence or we can dismiss it by blackening the character of those who bring the bad news. But to maintain a shared belief system one needs shared defenses against the cognitive threats. Where such resources are available, new ideas, no matter that they might be better supported by the evidence, can readily be ignored or rejected. It is far less easy to avoid being influenced by widespread and powerful but subtle assumptions about the nature of the world.

One such set of assumptions came with our increased reliance on effective secular means of securing this-worldly ends. Technically efficient machinery and procedures reduced uncertainty and thereby reduced reliance upon faith. The domain over which religion offered the most compelling explanations and the most predictable outcomes shrunk. Innovating farmers found that crop rotations did more to clean the soil of weeds and parasites than did prayer. This did not prevent pious farmers using prayer as a supplement, and some may even have elaborated the theory that break crops only clean the ground if accompanied by religious rituals but experience would soon have refuted that claim. The growth of technical rationality gradually displaced supernatural influence and moral considerations from ever-wider areas of public life, replacing them by considerations of objective performance and practical expedience.

As Martin says, with the growth of science and technology: "the general sense of human power is increased, the play of contingency is restricted, and the over-whelming sense of divine limits which afflicted previous generations is much diminished" (1969:116). Religion is most often and extensively used for the dark recessive areas of human life over which control has not been established by technology: unhappiness, extreme stress, and the like. When we have tried every cure for cancer, we pray. The "gaps" in our rational control and intellectual understanding of our world may loom very large. But they do so in an individualized manner. They are personal, not social problems.

To summarize, the clash of ideas between science and religion is less significant than the more subtle impact of naturalistic ways of thinking about the world. Science and technology have not made us atheists, but underlying "rationality" – the material world as an amoral series of invariant relationships of cause and effect, the componentiality of objects (Berger, Berger, and Kellner 1974), the reproducibility of actions, the expectation of constant change in our exploitation of the material world, the insistence on innovation – makes us less likely than our forebears to entertain the notion of the divine.

Egalitarianism and Cultural Diversity

In replacing feudal "stations" with modern classes, industrialization brought a basic egalitarianism. Religious innovation made an important contribution here. Although the Protestant reformers were far from being democrats, one major unintended consequence of their religious revolution was a profound change in the relative importance of the community and the individual. By denying the special status of the priesthood and by removing the possibility that religious merit could be transferred from one person to another (by, for example, saying masses for the souls of the dead), Luther and Calvin asserted that we are all severally (rather than jointly) equal in the eyes of God. For the reformers, that equality lay in our sinfulness and in our obligations but the idea could not indefinitely be confined. Equality in the eyes of God laid the foundations for equality in the eyes of others and before the law. Equal obligations eventually became equal rights.

Gellner (1983) has plausibly argued that egalitarianism was a requirement for industrialization; a society sharply divided between high and low cultures could not develop a modern economy. The spread of a shared national culture required the replacement of a fixed hierarchy of stations and estates by more flexible class divisions. Economic development brought change and the expectation of further change. And it brought occupational mobility. People no longer did the job they always did because their family always did that job. As it became more common for people to better themselves, it also became more common for them to think better of themselves. However badly paid, industrial workers did not see themselves as serfs.

Medieval serfs occupied just one role in a single hierarchy and that role shaped their entire lives. A tin miner in Cornwall in 1800 might have been sore oppressed at work but on Sunday he could change his clothes and his persona to become a Methodist lay preacher of prestige and standing. Once occupation became freed from an entire all-embracing hierarchy and became task-specific, it was possible for people to occupy different positions in different hierarchies. In turn, it became possible to distinguish between the role and the person who played it. Roles could still be ranked and accorded very different degrees of respect, power, or status but the people behind the roles could be seen as in some sense equal.

The fragmentation of the organic community allowed the radical individualism inherent in the Protestant Reformation to emerge in three closely-related ideas: that everyone was much of a muchness, that the individual was (at least in theory) autonomous, and that in future societies would have to deal with individuals and not communities. The practical consequences of these ideas were slow to be worked out and many changes came only with considerable struggle and bloodletting. The old elites were not keen to give up their powers, but gradually the principles of egalitarianism and individual autonomy gave birth to the universal right to own property, to be free from the arbitrary exercise of power, and to select one's political leaders. Many rising groups on achieving liberty were less than keen to allow those behind them to benefit, but the modernization of the economy allowed the gradual expansion of the notion of rights and of the scope of those rights.

Modernization brought with it increased cultural diversity in three different ways. First, populations moved and brought their language, religion, and social mores with them into a new setting. Second, the growth of the increasingly expansive nation-state meant that new groups were brought into the state. But, even without such changes in the population that had to be encompassed by the state, modernization created cultural pluralism through the creation of classes and class fragments with increasingly diverse interests. Especially in Protestant societies, where such class formation was accompanied by the generation of competing sects, the result was a paradox. At the same time as the nation-state was attempting to create a unified national culture out of thousands of small communities, it was having to come to terms with increasing religious diversity.

It should be stressed that diversity need not force secularization. An authoritarian hierarchical society can ignore or suppress religious minorities (and even majorities). Dissenters need not be tolerated; they can be massacred or exiled. But a society that was becoming increasingly culturally diverse and egalitarian and democratic had to place social harmony before religious orthodoxy. Religious establishments were abandoned altogether (as in the case of the constitution of the United States), or neutered (the British case). As already noted, this reduced the social power and scope of organized religion. While freedom from embarrassing entanglements with secular power may have allowed churches to become more clearly "spiritual," the removal of the churches from the center of public life reduced their contact with, and relevance for, the general population.

The separation of church and state was one consequence of diversity. Another, equally important, was the break of the chain of church, community, everyday life, and plausibility. In sixteenth century England, every significant event in the life cycle of the individual and the community was celebrated in church and given a religious gloss. The church's techniques were used to bless the sick, sweeten the soil, and increase animal productivity. Every significant act of testimony, every contract, and every promise was reinforced by oaths sworn on the Bible and before God. But beyond the special events that saw the majority of the people in the parish troop into the church, great credibility was given to the religious worldview simply through everyday social interaction. People commented on the weather with "God be praised" and on parting wished each other "God speed" or "Goodbye" (which we forget is an abbreviation for "God be with you"). With that constant affirmation, the Christian worldview had immense plausibility because it was not one of a range of alternatives but simply an accurate account of how things were.

The elaboration of alternatives provides a profound challenge. Of course, believers need not fall on their swords just because they discover that others disagree with them. Where clashes of ideologies occur in the context of social conflict (of which more below), or when alternatives are associated with people who can be plausibly described as a lower order and thus need not be seriously entertained, the cognitive challenge can be dismissed. But such explanations of diversity could only work for so long as they were widely shared. They were thus undermined by the condition they were designed to treat: diversity. And that condition was most virulent when it was internally produced. When the oracle speaks with a single clear voice, it is easy to believe it is the voice of God. When it speaks with 20 different voices, it is tempting to look behind the screen. As Berger (1980) puts it, in explaining the title of *The Heretical Imperative*, the position of the modern believer is quite unlike that of the Christian of the Middle Ages in that, while we may still believe, we cannot avoid the knowledge that many people (including many people like us) believe other things.

Diversity and differentiation fundamentally changed the relation of the church to the state and to the community and forced it to become increasingly denominational. Most sects, unable to maintain the sacrificial commitment of their members over many generations, also became increasingly tolerant and ecumenical. The result was a liberal form of religion that had little binding address. Having abandoned the claims that it had any particular access to the will of God and that any great evil would befall those who did not accept its teachings, the denominational form of religion found it ever more difficult to sustain the psychological pressure on members that would ensure subsequent generations were raised in the faith. As the dominant tradition lost the power to stigmatize and punish deviation, there was considerable growth in religious experimentation and innovation. However, most (and the most popular) of the new religions had little impact on their members and even less on the wider society. For all its fondness for claiming to be "alternative" and "counter-cultural," because it accepts the primacy of the autonomous individual, most New Age spirituality offers little or no prophetic challenge to the modern world.

There are three major results of modernization. The number of those who are religious is much smaller than at any time before. The sectarians who continue to hold to the sort of beliefs that were orthodox for the last three centuries survive only where they can create relatively autonomous subcultures; their isolation constrains their effect on the wider world. The rest of the Christians and the New Age innovators hold their beliefs in a liberal and relativistic manner. As Clark Roof put it: "the religious stance today is more internal than external, more individual than institutional, more experiential than cerebral, more private than public" (Roof 1996:153).

Retarding Tendencies

The secularization thesis can be summarized as arguing that social and structural differentiation, societalization, rationalization, and increasing social and cultural diversity, undermine religion. However, its proponents would want to add an important qualification: "except where religion finds or retains work to do other than relating individuals to the supernatural." The many and varied instances of that work can be summarized under the headings of cultural transition and cultural defense.

Cultural transition

Where social identity is threatened in the course of major social transitions, religion may provide resources for negotiating such transitions or asserting a new claim to a sense of worth. Ethnoreligious groups provided a mechanism for easing the transition between homeland and the new identity in the new world. The church offered a supportive group that spoke one's language, shared one's assumptions and values, but which also had experience of, and contacts within, the new social and cultural milieu. Hence the common phenomenon of immigrant groups not only being more religiously observant than their hosts but also more observant than they were in their old setting.

There is another manifestation of the tendency for religion to retain significance, even temporarily to grow in significance, and that is in the course of modernization itself. Modernization disrupted communities, traditional employment patterns, and status hierarchies. By extending the range of communication, it made the social peripheries and hinterlands more aware of the manners and mores, lifestyles and values, of the center and metropolis, and vice versa. Those at the center of the society, the carriers of modernization, were motivated to missionize the rest, seeking to assimilate them, by educating them and socializing them in "respectable" beliefs and practices. They were moved to improve and elevate the masses in the rural areas and those who moved to the fringes of the cities and there posed the threat of an undisciplined or radical rabble on the doorstep. Sectors of the social periphery in turn were motivated to embrace the models of respectable performance offered to them, especially when they were already in the process of upward mobility and self-improvement.

Industrialization and urbanization therefore tended to give rise to movements of revival and reform, drawing the lapsed and heterodox into the orbit of orthodoxy. The new converts and their overenthusiastic religion often offended the dominant religious organizations. They solved the awkwardness of their position by seceding (or being expelled) and forming new sects. Methodism in late eighteenth and nineteenth century Britain is a prominent example, as is Laestadianism in nineteenth century Norway.

Cultural defense

The second great role for religion is as guarantor of group identity. Where culture, identity, and sense of worth are challenged by a source promoting either an alien religion or rampant secularism, and that source is negatively valued, secularization will be inhibited. Religion can provide resources for the defense of a national, local, ethnic, or status group culture. Poland and the Irish Republic are prime examples, but Northern Ireland can also be included, as, in more attenuated form, can other "dual" societies (such as the Netherlands), or the peripheries of secularizing societies, resistant to the alien encroachment of the center.

It is worth going back over the basic elements of the secularization thesis and noting how ethnic conflict inhibits their development. In the classic model of functional differentiation, the first sphere to become freed of cultural encumbrances is the economy. Yet even in the preeminent site for rational choice, ethnic identification may be a major constraint on the maximizing behavior that is the fundamental principle of economic rationality. In Northern Ireland attempts to use the law to impose universalism on the world of work have largely failed to prevent the exercise of religioethnic preferences in hiring policies (especially in small firms that do not depend on the state for contracts and thus cannot be easily controlled). People also exhibit their ethnic identity in personal consumption, which is beyond state regulation. The Northern Ireland small business sector is irrational in that small towns often support one Protestant and one Catholic enterprise where the market can profitably sustain only one. Especially at times of heightened tension, Protestants and Catholics boycott each others' businesses and travel considerable distances to engage in commerce with their own sort.

Consider next what Wilson (1982) called "societalization." A beleaguered minority may try to prevent the erosion of the community. Deviants who attempt to order their lives in the societal rather than the community mode may be regarded as disloyal and treacherous and punished accordingly. For example, in the ethnic conflicts in Bosnia and Northern Ireland, those who marry across the divide have been frequent targets for vigilantes keen to clarify and maintain their boundaries.

Finally, ethnic conflict mutes the cognitive consequences of pluralism because the prevalence of invidious stereotypes allows a much more thorough compartmentalizing and stigmatizing of alternative cultures. The gradual shift to relativism as a way of accommodating those with whom we differ depends on us taking those people seriously. Where religious differences are strongly embedded in ethnic identities, the cognitive threat of the ideas of the others is relatively weak. Thus Scottish Protestants in the nineteenth century deployed caricatures of the social vices of the immigrant Irish Catholics as a way of avoiding having to consider them as Christian.

The Rational Choice Alternative

There is a radically different reading of the consequences of diversity. Rodney Stark and his colleagues have argued that the greater religious vitality of the United States (compared with most European countries) is explained by it having a free market in religious goods and considerable competition between the providers of such goods. Diversity allows everyone to find a form of religion that suits their interests, keeps down costs, and thus makes the creation of new religions easier, and provides the clergy with incentives to recruit and sustain a following (Young 1997).

Although there is some evidence to support small parts of the rational choice or "supply-side" model, only those studies produced by the small group of the model's proponents claim to find strong support for the general approach. Almost all attempts to replicate the work, either by comparing religious vitality and diversity for different areas within one society or by cross-cultural comparison have failed to find any positive effects of diversity on religion. Across Europe, church attendance and membership is far higher in those countries where almost everyone belongs to the same religion (Poland and Ireland, for example) than in places such as Britain where there is considerable pluralism. If we take a clutch of states that are in many respects similar (the Baltic countries of Lithuania, Latvia, and Estonia, for example), we find that overwhelmingly Catholic Lithuania has far higher rates of church attendance and adherence than the more mixed Latvia and Estonia. Iannaccone, one of the leading rational choice theorists, has admitted that while (to his mind) church attendance rates in Protestant societies are positively related to diversity, those in Catholic countries are not. This rather undermines the status of what is purported to be a universal theory of human behavior (Iannaccone 1991:169).

Elsewhere I have offered a detailed critique of the supply-side approach (Bruce 1999). Here I will confine myself to making three points. First, whatever support the supply-side model might find in comparing diversity and religious vitality in different places in the same time frame (the urban and rural areas of the USA in 1906, for example) is overwhelmed by the conclusions drawn from looking at changes in one place over time. Whether we take Canada, Australia, Norway, Scotland, or Holland we find that religion was far more popular and powerful in 1850, 1900, or 1950 than it is at the beginning of the twenty-first century. As societies have become more diverse (and more urban and industrialized) so they have become secular.

Second, rational choice models work best for fields where general demand is high but "brand loyalty" is low. We are not socialized into a culture of norms that bans us from buying one kind of refrigerator. Hence we feel free to "maximize." But for most of the world, religion is not a personal preference; it is a social identity in which one is socialized, that is closely tied to other shared identities and that can only be changed at considerable personal cost. Hence this paradox. Only in largely secular societies, where there was little religious behavior left to explain, would people have the attitude to religion supposed by the rational choice model.

My third criticism continues the observation that the rational choice approach is profoundly unsociological into a more general observation about individual needs and will be dealt with below in a prediction.

The Irreversibility of Secularization

As the future is unknowable, it is always possible to argue that the decline of indices of religious interest in the twentieth century was merely temporary and that there will be a resurgence of religious interest. Sometimes this claim rests on a theory that makes people enduringly religious. For example, Stark and Bainbridge (1985, 1987) have argued that the human condition is such that people will always need religion. Humans desire rewards but, as these are in short supply, they will be in the market for "compensators," which explain why the desired rewards have not been forthcoming, promise that they will arrive in the future, and explain how they might be achieved. Because they can invoke the supernatural, religious compensators are more persuasive and powerful than secular ones. Hence so long as the demand for rewards outstrips their supply, people will be essentially and enduringly religious. It follows that long-term and widespread secularization is impossible. If one religious tradition declines then another should appear to fill the gap.

The problem with this is that it neglects the role of social interaction in the creation and maintenance of culture. It supposes that individual needs translate into outcomes in an unmediated fashion. It misses entirely the point that individual needs are a result of biological and psychological drives being shaped and articulated in a particular culture. Even if we suppose that there are basic questions that most people will ask themselves (such as "what is the meaning of life?"), we cannot assume that large numbers will frame the question in the same terms, let alone embrace the same answer. On the contrary, the modern assumption of the authority of the autonomous individual prevents such consensus emerging or being sustained. While it is common to berate the high place we give the individual, to ascribe to it every manner of social vice, and to yearn for a return to a more communal way of life, there is no sign that the people of the Western world are willing to give up their autonomy. In the mainstream Christian churches and in the cultic milieu of the New Age, believers insist on their right to determine their beliefs and the extent of their commitment.

The brevity of this chapter requires me to state this bluntly: shared belief systems require coercion. The survival of religion requires that individuals be subordinated to the community. In some settings (religioethnic conflicts, for example) individual autonomy is constrained by shared ascribed identities. But in the stable affluent democracies of the Western world the individual asserts the rights of the sovereign autonomous consumer. We believe we have the right to choose our electrical goods; we claim the same right in delineating the supernatural. Unless we can imagine some social forces that will lead us to give up that freedom, we cannot imagine the creation of detailed ideological consensus. It is not enough to point out that some social calamity may disrupt our complacency. Without a preexisting common culture, large numbers will not interpret a disaster in the same way and hence will not respond collectively. There was no religious revival in Europe during either of the twentieth century's world wars. When the common culture of a society consists of operating principles that allow the individual to choose, no amount of vague spiritual yearning will generate a shared belief system.

To conclude, the secularization thesis argues that the decline of religion in the modern West is not an accident but is an unintended consequence of a variety of complex social changes that for brevity we call modernization. It is not inevitable. But unless we can imagine a reversal of the increasing cultural autonomy of the individual, secularization must be seen as irreversible.

References

Berger, P.L. 1980. *The Heretical Imperative: Contemporary Possibilities of Religious Affirmation*. London: Collins.

Berger, P.L., Berger, B., and Kellner, H. 1974. *The Homeless Mind*. Harmondsworth: Penguin.

Brierley, P. 1991. *Prospects for the Nineties: Trends and Tables from the English Church Census.* London: MARC Europe.

Bruce, S. 1996. *Religion in the Modern World: From Cathedrals to Cults.* Oxford: Oxford University Press.

Bruce, S. 1997. "The Pervasive Worldview: Religion in Pre-Modern Britain," *British Journal of Sociology* 48:667–90.

Bruce, S. 1999. *Choice and Religion: a Critique of Rational Choice Theory.* Oxford: Oxford University Press.

Crockett, A. 1998. "A Secularising Geography? Patterns and Processes of Religious Change in England and Wales, 1676–1851," Unpublished Ph.D. thesis, University of Leicester, UK.

Gellner, E. 1983. *Nations and Nationalism.* Oxford: Blackwell.

Gellner, E. 1994. "From Kinship to Ethnicity," in *Encounters with Nationalism,* Ed. E. Gellner. Oxford: Blackwell, pp. 34–46.

Gill, R., Hadaway, C.K., and Marler, P.L. 1998. "Is Religious Belief Declining in Britain?," *Journal for the Scientific Study of Religion* 37:507–16.

Hadaway, C.K., Marler, P.L., and Chaves, M. 1993. "What the Polls Don't Show: A Closer Look at Church Attendance," *American Sociological Review* 58:741–52.

Iannaccone, L.R. 1991. "The Consequences of Religious Market Structure," *Rationality and Society* 3:156–77.

Martin, D. 1969. *The Religious and the Secular: Studies in Secularization.* London: Routledge, Kegan and Paul.

Merton, R.K. 1970. *Science, Technology and Society in the 17th Century.* New York: Fetting.

Roof, W.C. 1996. "God is in the Details: Reflections on Religion's Public Presence in the United States in the Mid-1990s," *Sociology of Religion* 57:149–62.

Stark, R. and Bainbridge, W.S. 1985. *The Future of Religion.* Berkeley: University of California Press.

Stark, R. and Bainbridge, W.S. 1987. *A Theory of Religion.* New York: Peter Lang.

Wilson, B.R. 1982. *Religion in Sociological Perspective.* Oxford: Oxford University Press.

Young, L.A. 1997. *Rational Choice Theory and Religion: Summary and Assessment.* London: Routledge.

CHAPTER 14

Patterns of Religion in Western Europe: An Exceptional Case

Grace Davie

Introduction

The following chapter has three sections. The first outlines the patterns of religion in Western Europe, suggesting that these are unusual in the modern world. The second begins to inquire *why* this might be the case, looking at the European case from the inside; it draws heavily on a recent publication (Davie 2000). The third section continues the discussion of exceptionalism but using a very different starting point. It looks at Europe from the outside, asking, in effect, what European religion is not. What are the much talked about forms of religion that exist in the modern world (or at least in major parts of it), which do not gain a purchase in Europe? Is it possible to explain this absence in sociological terms?

With this in mind, it is necessary to make a further introductory point. This chapter will deal with Western Europe – in the sense of Western Christianity – rather than a wider (or narrower) definition, of the continent. The marker in question derives from the split between Roman Catholicism and Orthodoxy that divided the continent a millennium ago, a far more fundamental division in my view than the relatively recent opposition between communist and noncommunist Europe in the postwar period. Indeed the terms "Eastern" and "Central" Europe have significance in this respect, for Eastern Europe (Romania, Bulgaria, and most of European Russia) belong to the Orthodox tradition, whereas the Central European countries (Poland, the Czech Republic, Slovakia, Hungary, and what was East Germany) developed within Western Catholicism. The position of the Baltic states is equally revealing. Roman Catholic Lithuania and Poland are closely linked historically; in contrast, Latvia and Estonia belong essentially to Western (Lutheran) Europe. None of them face East.

The continuing vicissitudes in the Balkans exemplify the same point. The postwar entity known as Yugoslavia combined within one country not only contrasting Christian traditions but a sizable Muslim presence as well. For a relatively short space of time (two generations, perhaps) the country held together under the personal authority of Marshall Tito. As that authority – and the creed that underpinned it – collapsed, it is hardly surprising that Yugoslavia's pseudo-unity began to fall apart. Ethnic nationalisms, bolstered by religious differences, interacted with a multiplicity of factors (linguistic, historical, and economic) to create an explosive situation. At the same time, the presence of sizable ethnic minorities within the borders of each state rendered the dissolution of the country as problematic as its retention. Long-term stability remains elusive. In more ways than one, Europe reaches its limits in the Balkans; the essentially European patterns that will emerge in the following section start to disintegrate at the margins of the continent.

Patterns of Religious Life in Europe

What, then, do the countries of Western Europe have in common from a religious point of view? There are several ways of looking at this question. There is, first, a historical perspective. O'Connell (1991), amongst others, identifies three formative factors or themes that come together in the creation and re-creation of the unity that we call Europe: these are Judeo-Christian monotheism, Greek rationalism, and Roman organization. These factors shift and evolve over time, but their combinations can be seen forming and reforming a way of life that we have come to recognize as European. The religious strand within such combinations is self-evident. Other very different sources reinforce this conclusion. One of these, the European Values Systems Study Group (EVSSG),[1] provides a principal source of data for this chapter. In contrast with O'Connell's primarily historical approach, the European Values Study exemplifies, for better or worse, sophisticated social science methodology (see introductory sections of Abrams, Gerard, and Timms 1985). Using careful sampling techniques, the EVSSG aims at an accurate mapping of social and moral values across Europe. It has generated very considerable data and will continue to do so. It is essential to pay close, but at the same time critical, attention to its findings.

Two underlying themes run through the EVSSG study. The first concerns the substance of contemporary European values, and asks in particular to what extent they are homogeneous. The second takes a more dynamic approach, asking to what extent such values are changing. Both themes involve, inevitably, a religious element. The first, for example, leads very quickly to questions about the origin of shared value systems: "If values in Western Europe are to any extent shared, if people from different countries share similar social perceptions on their world, how had any such joint cultural experience been created?" (Harding, Phillips, and Fogarty 1986:29). As the European Values Study indicates, the answer lies in deep-rooted cultural experiences which derive from pervasive social influences that have been part of our culture for generations, if not centuries. A shared religious heritage is one such influence.

So much is unproblematic and confirms O'Connell's historical conclusions. But as soon as the idea of value change is introduced, the situation becomes more contentious. A series of unavoidable questions immediately present themselves. How far is the primacy given to the role of religion in the creation of values still appropriate? Has this role not been undermined by the process known as secularization? Can we really maintain at the turn of the millennium that religion remains the central element of the European value system? The influence of religion is becoming, surely, increasingly peripheral within contemporary European society. *Or is it?* There can be no doubt that these somewhat provocative suggestions pertain to Western Europe (they and some possible answers are developed at length in Davie 2000), but an additional point follows: is this situation unique to this part of the world – and if so, why – or can it be found elsewhere? Herein lies the central argument of this chapter.

The first task, however, is to indicate the principal findings of the 1981 and 1990 EVSSG surveys for a variety of religious indicators. There are, broadly speaking, five religious indicators within the data: denominational allegiance, reported church attendance, attitudes towards the church, indicators of religious belief, and some measurement of subjective religious disposition. These variables have considerable potential: they can be correlated with one another and with a wide range of sociodemographic data. In this respect the survey shows commendable awareness of the complexity of religious phenomena and the need to bear in mind more than one dimension within an individual's (or indeed a nation's) religious life. What emerges in practice, however, with respect to these multiple indicators is a clustering of two types of variable: on the one hand, those concerned with feelings, experience, and the more numinous religious beliefs; on the other, those which measure religious orthodoxy, ritual participation, and institutional attachment. It is, moreover, the latter (the more orthodox indicators of religious attachment) which display, most obviously, an undeniable degree of secularization throughout Western Europe. In contrast, the former (the less institutional indicators) demonstrate considerable persistence in some aspects of religious life. The essentials of this contrasting information are presented in tables 14.1 and 14.2, reproduced from the EVSSG data. These tables can be used in two ways: either to indicate the overall picture of the continent or to exemplify some of the marked national differences that can be found within the continent as a whole. In this chapter the emphasis will lie on the former.

We should start, perhaps, by echoing one conclusion of the European Values Study itself: that is, to treat with caution statements about the secularization process – particularly unqualified ones – both within Europe and elsewhere. For the data are complex, contradictory even, and clear-cut conclusions become correspondingly difficult (Harding et al. 1986:31–4). Bearing this in mind – together with the clustering of the variables that we have already mentioned – it seems to me more accurate to suggest that Western Europeans remain, by and large, unchurched populations rather than simply secular. For a marked falling-off in religious attendance (especially in the Protestant North) has not resulted, yet, in a parallel abdication of religious belief. In short, many Europeans have ceased to

Table 14.1   Frequency of church attendance in Western Europe 1990 %

	At least once a week	Once a month	Christmas, Easter etc.	Once a year	Never
European average	29	10	8	5	40
Catholic Countries					
Belgium	23	8	13	4	52
France	10	7	17	7	59
Ireland	81	7	6	1	5
Italy	40	13	23	4	19
Portugal	33	8	8	4	47
Spain	33	10	15	4	38
Mixed Countries					
Great Britain	13	10	12	8	56
West Germany	19	15	16	9	41
Netherlands	21	10	16	5	47
Northern Ireland	49	18	6	7	18
Lutheran Countries					
Denmark	11 }				
Finland	– }				
Iceland	9 }	attendance once a month or more			
Norway	10 }				
Sweden	10 }				

Source: Adapted from Ashford and Timms (1992: 46); additional figures for the Lutheran countries from EVSSG data.

belong to their religious institutions in any meaningful sense, but they have not abandoned, so far, many of their deep-seated religious aspirations. One of the crucial questions raised by the EVSSG material concerns the future of European religion. Are we on the brink of something very different indeed: a markedly more secular twenty-first century? It is, however, very difficult to tell how the relationship between believing and belonging will develop. Nominal belief could well become the norm for the foreseeable future; on the other hand, the two variables may gradually move closer together as nominal belief turns itself into no belief at all.

Two short parentheses are important in this connection. The first may seem obvious, but the situation of believing without belonging (if such we may call it) should not be taken for granted (as it is by many Europeans). This relatively widespread, though fluctuating, characteristic within European religion in the late twentieth century should not merely be assumed; it must be examined,

Table 14.2   Extent of religious belief in Western Europe 1990 %

Belief in:	God	A soul	Life after death	Heaven	The Devil	Hell	Sin	Resurrection of the dead
European average	70	61	43	41	25	23	57	33
Catholic Countries								
Belgium	63	52	37	30	17	15	41	27
France	57	50	38	30	19	16	40	27
Ireland	96	84	77	85	52	50	84	70
Italy	83	67	54	45	35	35	66	44
Portugal	80	58	31	49	24	21	63	31
Spain	81	60	42	50	28	27	57	33
Mixed Countries								
Great Britain	71	64	44	53	30	25	68	32
West Germany	63	62	38	31	15	13	55	31
Netherlands	61	63	39	34	17	14	43	27
Northern Ireland	95	86	70	86	72	68	89	71
Lutheran Countries								
Denmark	64	47	34	19	10	8	24	23
Finland	76	73	60	55	31	27	66	49
Iceland	85	88	81	57	19	12	70	51
Norway	65	54	45	44	24	19	44	32
Sweden	45	58	38	31	12	8	31	21

Source: Adapted from Ashford and Timms (1992: 40); additional figures for the Lutheran countries from EVSSG data.

probed, and questioned. The second point both illustrates this need for questioning *and* introduces the issue of exceptionalism. To what extent is the pattern described so far unique to Western Europe? Or, to put the same point in a different way, where else can it be found in the modern world?

The first contrast can be found very close to home. In Eastern and Central Europe prior to 1989, the two variables were (in some places at least) reversed. Here the nonbeliever quite consciously used Mass attendance as one way of expressing disapproval of an unpopular regime. The Polish case is the most obvious illustration of this tendency (Michel 1996). One of the most interesting questions that the former communist parts of Europe poses for the sociologist of religion concerns, moreover, the extent to which the patterns of religious life found therein will follow those of Western Europe once (or now that) conditions have returned to "normal". It is probably too soon to answer this question with any conviction. In the first decade of independence (i.e., since 1989) the region has been characterized not only by diversity but by considerable volatility in almost all the religious indicators.

Elsewhere in the world (and for the time being sticking to predominantly Christian countries), the cases that conform most readily to the type already described are those to be found in the English-speaking Dominions – Canada, Australia, and New Zealand. (Interestingly, Canada looked more like the United States in the first half of the twentieth century than in the second, when it moved in a more "European" direction.) Each of the Dominions presents a rather different case and each will move away from the European "norm" as non-European populations begin to predominate (especially in Australasia). All, however, are markedly different from the United States where vibrant forms of religious life compete in a flourishing religious market – a phenomenon more or less unknown in Western Europe and the Dominions. Exactly how many Americans do attend their churches on a regular basis has been considerably disputed (Bruce 1996), but the situation in that (and other) parts of the New World seems set to develop along lines very different from either the European or the Dominion case.

If we return now to the Western European data and begin to probe more deeply, there is evidence of consistency in the shapes or profiles of religiosity obtained across a wide variety of European countries. Significant here are the correlations obtained between religious indices and a range of socioeconomic variables, all of which confirm the existence of socioreligious patterning across national boundaries. Throughout Western Europe, it is clear that religious factors correlate – to varying degrees – with indices of occupation, gender, and age (social class as such is more problematic). The correlation with age is particularly striking, prompting one of the most searching questions of the European Values Study: is Western Europe experiencing a permanent generational shift with respect to religious behavior, rather than a manifestation of the normal life cycle? The EVSSG findings indicate that this might be so. If this really is the case, the future shape of European religion may be very different indeed. The questions posed by this chapter may, or may not, resonate in the middle of the twenty-first century.

There are additional changes occurring in Western Europe, one of which needs careful underlining. The EVSSG sample sizes for each country are too small to give any meaningful data about religious minorities. It would, however, be grossly misleading to present even an overview of European religion at the end of the twentieth century without any reference to these increasingly important sections of the European population.

The first of these, the Jews, has been present in Europe for centuries; a presence, moreover, that has been inextricably bound up with the tragedies of recent European history. Nor can it be said, regrettably, that anti-Semitism is a thing of the past. It continues to rear an ugly head from time to time right across Europe, itself an accurate indicator of wider insecurities. Estimations of numbers are always difficult, but there are, currently, around one million Jews in Western Europe, the largest communities being the French (500,000–600,000) and the

British (300,000) (Wasserstein 1996, Webber 1994). French Judaism has been transformed in the postwar period by the immigration of considerable numbers of Sephardim from North Africa; it forms a notable exception within the overall pattern of declining numbers (Wasserstein 1996:viii).

Former colonial connections also account for other non-Christian immigrations into Europe. The Islamic communities are, probably, the most significant in this respect though Britain also houses considerable numbers of Sikhs and Hindus. Islam is, however, the largest other-faith population in Europe, conservative estimates suggesting a figure of six million.[2] Muslims make up approximately 3 percent of most Western European populations (Lewis and Schnapper 1994, Nielsen 1995, Vertovec and Peach 1997). More specifically, the links between France and North Africa account for the very sizable French Muslim community (three to four million). Britain's equivalent comes from the Indian subcontinent (1.2 million). Germany, on the other hand, has absorbed large numbers of migrant workers from the fringes of South-Eastern Europe, and from Turkey and the former Yugoslavia in particular. The fate of these migrants in the face of growing numbers of ethnic Germans looking for work within the new Germany remains an open question.

One further source of diversity remains: the presence of new religious movements in all European societies, a somewhat controversial area in many respects. There can be no doubt, on the one hand, that new religious movements attract considerable media attention (often negative in tone); the numbers involved are, however, tiny. Be that as it may, such movements fulfill an important function for the sociologist of religion. Inadvertently, they have become barometers of the changes taking place in contemporary society (Beckford 1985, 1986). New religious movements "represent an 'extreme situation' which, precisely because it is extreme, throws into sharp relief many of the assumptions hidden behind legal, cultural, and social structures" (Beckford 1985:11), notably those that relate to the concepts of pluralism and tolerance. New religious movements extend the range of choice for modern Europeans.

Europe from the Inside: a Memory Mutates

The distinctiveness of the European case is – and probably always will be – disputed. Wilson (1998) and Bruce (1996) argue that the patterns of religion found in Western Europe are substantially those that pertain in considerable parts of the Western world, whereas Berger (1992), Martin (1991), and Casanova (1994) are increasingly drawn to emphasize the atypical nature of religion in Europe – notably the relatively low levels of religious activity and institutional commitment. My own inclinations lead me to support the latter view – that is, that European patterns of religiousness are indeed unusual in the modern world and should be seen as one strand in what it means to be a European, rather than in terms of any necessary relationship between religion and modernity or religion and the process of modernization. What then has been the nature of this strand in the latter part of the twentieth century and what will it be like in subsequent decades? It is this essentially *European* (and indeed Durkheimian) question that this section considers in more detail; it draws heavily on the argument presented in Davie (2000).

This in turn builds on to the theoretical approach developed by a leading French sociologist of religion, Hervieu-Léger, whose point of departure (Hervieu-Léger 1993) lies in trying to identify and to refine the conceptual tools necessary for the understanding of religion in the modern world. An answer gradually emerges in the definition of religion as a specific mode of believing. The crucial points to grasp in this analysis are (a) the *chain* that makes the individual believer a member of a community – a community which gathers past, present, and future members – and (b) the tradition (or collective memory) which becomes the basis of that community's existence. Hervieu-Léger goes further than this: she argues that modern societies (and especially modern European societies) are not less religious because they are increasingly rational but because they are less and less capable of maintaining the memory which lies at the heart of their religious existence. They are, to use her own term, amnesic societies. Through what mechanisms, then, can modern European societies overcome their amnesia and stay in touch with the forms of religion that are necessary to sustain their identity? That seems to me the challenge set by Hervieu-Léger's analysis.

The paragraphs that follow are a response to that challenge, albeit a selective one. They must start, inevitably, with the churches themselves. Europe's churches have undergone a metamorphosis in course of the last century.[3] No longer do they supply a sacred canopy embracing every citizen within the nation in question, but nor have they have disappeared altogether. They have become *de facto*, if not always *de jure*, influential voluntary organizations, capable of operating in a whole variety of ways – traditional as well as innovative. Placing the churches in the sphere of the voluntary sector or civil society is, in fact, the crucial point. In this sector of society – both in Western Europe and in the former communist countries[4] – the churches are key players; they are central to the structures of a modern democracy and attract more members than almost all their equivalents, with the partial exception of sporting activities, if these are taken as a whole. Churches, moreover, imply churchgoers (the social actors who carry and articulate the memory). Who these people are in modern Europe and how they are placed in the nexus of social relations – an essentially Weberian question – is central to the understanding of both formal and informal patterns of religion in the late modern period. The data from the first section of this chapter provide a partial answer. These people are relatively well-educated, often professionals, older on average than the population as a whole and disproportionately female.

A crucial concept begins to emerge from these analyses: that of vicarious religion (Reed 1978). Might it not be the case that Europeans are not so much less religious than populations in other parts of the world, but differently so? For particular historical reasons (notably the presence of a state church), significant numbers of Europeans are content to let both churches and churchgoers enact a memory on their behalf (the essential meaning of vicarious), more than half aware that they might need to draw on the capital at crucial times in their individual or collective lives. The almost universal taking up of religious ceremonies at the time of a death is the most obvious expression of this tendency.

The churches, however, do not work in isolation: they are surrounded by a whole web of institutional mechanisms which, again for historical reasons, have become important carriers of religious memory in the European context. Education is but the most obvious of these; in terms, first, of the role of the churches as the owners/managers of significant numbers of schools in many European countries. An important focus of this debate concerns which religious communities may or may not have access to this privileged position. It is significant that the newly arrived (European Muslims, for example) compete for this privilege, they do not despise it. A second aspect of education introduces the teaching of moral, social, and religious education within the school system, an increasingly sensitive issue which needs to be set against the prolonged and often confused exchanges about the transmission of values more generally. The place of religion in the lives of young people forms a background to this discussion, an area in which the aspects of the religious memory quite clearly become not only vicarious but precarious.

The role of religion in the media at a time when technology has permitted exponential growth in the number of broadcasting outlets is similarly important. The relationships between religion and the public media are, moreover, complex, for what is portrayed either in print or on the screen both reflects the realities of modern religion and creates new and persuasive images (or memories). Hence the need to discover who has access to broadcasting outlets and which categories of people are most likely to be influenced by them. For many Europeans a crucial question dominates the scene: will American style televangelism make inroads into the European market? If it does, will this change the nature of European religion as a whole? If it doesn't, what are the likely forms of religious broadcasting in the foreseeable future in the European context? Indirectly, moreover, such a debate will contribute to a better understanding of televangelism *per se*: if it cannot penetrate the European market, but does relatively well elsewhere, why is this so? Might this not be further evidence of European exceptionalism (see below)?

A final area of discovery concerns the growing popularity of sacred places in contemporary Europe – whether these be traditional shrines (for example Santiago or Lourdes) or more recent places of pilgrimage (notably Iona or Taizé). The argument leads naturally to the relationship between tourism and pilgrimage and the importance of the aesthetic (architecture, art, and music) as a carrier of the sacred. It is not an exaggeration to consider Europe's cathedrals as a form of European museum – they are embodiments as well as carriers of memory. Their relationship with secular museums is a significant if underresearched area of investigation, and opens up fruitful lines of inquiry: just how are the artifacts of memory assembled? Liturgical changes provide another route into the discussion; so, too, the contemporary significance of Europe's religious festivals, a growing rather than declining phenomenon. If, for example, a million young people come together to hear the Pope celebrate Mass (as they did in Paris in August 1997), they will hear the words "Do this in remembrance of me": articulating memory lies at the heart of Christian liturgy.

A conceptual framework is important to all these discussions. It emerges from a closer look at the concept of memory itself. The following elements can be discerned within the concept, some of which have already been introduced. The others demonstrate just how far this type of analysis can be extended in order to encompass the growing diversity as well as the unity of European religion:

- *vicarious memory* (through which a minority maintains the tradition on behalf of the majority – an essentially European idea);
- *precarious memory* (especially among young people);
- *mediated memory* (and the confusion between the medium and the message);
- *cultural or aesthetic memories* (with an emphasis on art, architecture, and music);
- *alternative memories* (for example, disputes within as well as between the historic churches, the gradual establishment of faiths other than Christian in modern Europe, the emergence of alternative foci for the sacred which replace or exist alongside more traditional forms of religion);
- *conflicting memory/memories* (European versus national memory and the role of religion in each, the Balkan and Irish cases);
- *extinguished memory* (is this likely and what might be the consequences for other aspects of European life if certain religious memories were to disappear altogether?);
- and, finally, *mutating memory* (the on-going reconstructions of European religion(s) as the twentieth century gives way to the twenty-first).

All-important in the whole analysis is the specificity not only of Europe's religion, but of the culture in which this has been embedded for the best part of a millennium. Europe's religious memory is part of what it means to be a European.

Europe from the Outside

A second way into the area of exceptionalism looks at European patterns of religion from the outside rather than from within. Again it is necessary to work selectively, but it seems increasingly clear that certain forms of religious life that flourish in the modern world (itself made up of a multiplicity of different examples), either do not feature in the European context at all or feature only minimally. The most obvious of these is the much talked about phenomenon known as fundamentalism. A glance at the contents of the multiple volumes emanating from the "Fundamentalism Project" (Marty and Appleby 1995) is sufficient to illustrate the point. Only three case studies from Europe are cited, none of which fully meets the criteria of the ideal-type central to the working of the project. These are traditional Catholicism (the movement associated with Archbishop Lefebvre), the Italian youth movement known as *Communione e Liberazione*, and Ulster Protestantism. The first of these is, clearly, reactionary rather than fundamentalist, the second is described by Italian commentators as at best a "*fondamentalismo ben temperato*" (Pace and Guolo 1998), and the third is effectively an ethnic nationalism.

There is, similarly, no parallel in Europe to the widespread and rapidly growing Pentecostal movements, so evident in Latin America, North America, sub-Saharan Africa, and parts of the Far East. Such movements do not fit well within the fundamentalist frame; they represent, none the less, a form of religion that attracts enormous numbers of adherents in different parts of the world, but not in Europe. It is true that the Pentecostal or charismatic movement resonates in Europe like everywhere else; it does not, however, have widespread popular appeal – the distinctive feature in other parts of the world. (Partial exceptions to this statement can be found in Transylvania, the West Ukraine, Southern Italy, and in the gypsy populations of both Western and Eastern Europe.)

Why is this so? Within the sociology of religion two lines of thinking are emerging which can be applied to the question of European exceptionalism seen from the outside. The first of these is Jose Casanova's work on *Public Religions in the Modern World* (1994). Casanova initiates his analysis by offering a clearer articulation of what exactly is meant by secularization:

> A central thesis and main theoretical premise of this work has been that what usually passes for a single theory of secularization is actually made up of three very different, uneven and unintegrated propositions: secularization as differentiation of the secular spheres from religious institutions and norms, secularization as decline of religious beliefs and practices, and secularization as marginalization of religion to a privatized sphere. If the premise is correct, it should follow from the analytical distinction that the fruitless secularization debate can end only when sociologists of religion begin to examine and test the validity of each of the three propositions independently of each other. (1994:211)

With this in mind, Casanova examines five case studies; two of these are European, two are from the United States, and one is from Latin America.

Two points emerge from these cases, both of which relate to the unusual nature of Europe's religious life. The first is that *secularization as differentiation* constitutes the essential core of the secularization thesis. "The differentiation and emancipation of the secular spheres from religious institutions and norms remains a modern structural trend" (Casanova 1994:212). It is not the case, however, that modernity necessarily implies either a reduction in the level of religious belief or practice or that religion is necessarily relegated to the private sphere. Indeed the evidence outside Europe indicates the reverse: religious enthusiasm is a normal feature of modern living and needs to be considered as such both by the sociologist of religion and by the sociologist *per se*. The latter, in particular, is all too ready to dismiss the presence of religion in the modern world as really something else (nationalism for example), or as a hangover (necessarily limited) of a former civilization. The second point follows from this: it is precisely those churches that have resisted the structural differentiation of church and state – notably the state churches of Europe – which have had the greatest difficulty in coming to terms with the pressures of modern lifestyles. Hence the decline, relatively speaking, of religious vitality in much of modern Europe where state churches remain a dominant mode of organization.

The second line of thinking evokes the approach to religion primarily associated with Rodney Stark, William Bainbridge, and Larry Iannaccone – an approach known as rational choice theory (RCT; for a summary see Young 1997). RCT offers a supply-side approach to religion, suggesting that a demand for religious activity will increase if the supply is both sufficiently diverse and sufficiently attractive to entice the religious consumer. Following Stark and Bainbridge (1985, 1987), there will always be a need for religion, given the predicaments of the human condition. Such needs, however, will only be translated into demands if the suppliers of religion have sufficient freedom to create and to market an appropriate range of commodities.

RCT has generated a wide range of empirical studies, not to mention considerable controversy. A number of the case studies have focused on the European situation (Stark and Iannaccone 1994), suggesting that it is the restrictions of the European market (notably the monopoly or quasi-monopoly of the state churches) that account for the limited supply of religious commodities in this part of the world. Demand is correspondingly depressed. The situation, however, could be reversed if market conditions allowed this. Opponents of RCT (notably Bruce 1995, 1999) will have none of this. The explanation for low levels of religious activity in Europe lie elsewhere, not least in the traditional accounts of secularization, which – noting Casanova's refinements to the term – have more relevance to the European case than they do elsewhere.

Conclusion

As a brief conclusion to this chapter, I would like to place both Casanova's analysis of secularization and at least some elements of RCT into a wider context. A formula emerges which acknowledges (a) the significance of market forces in some aspects of religious life, and (b) the undeniable importance of the state church in Europe's past, but at the same time indicates the limitations of both approaches to the *present* situation. In my view, the lack of religious activity in modern Europe must have explanations other than an overly restricted market. For those who want it there is an endless choice of religion in most parts of the continent (the most obvious exception is Greece where membership of the Orthodox Church remains almost coterminous with Greek citizenship); such choices, moreover, are proliferating all the time. It is equally clear that the state churches of Europe have become *de facto* if not *de jure* a set of voluntary organizations, functioning far more effectively as contributors to civil society than as the partners of state. Structural separation has happened in many parts of Europe, both inside and outside the historic churches – even within those that are formally linked to the state. The old antagonisms no longer resonate (Martin 1991).

The present situation is better explained by a particular European mentality – the real legacy of the state church. Or to put the same point in a different way (echoing the principal conclusion of the previous section), significant numbers of Europeans operate vicariously in their religious lives – a concept central to the understanding of Europe's religious awareness. Europeans do not, on the whole, view their churches as centers of activity that will collapse without their support; they are much more inclined to regard them as a necessary public provision, anticipating their services to both individuals and communities at the turning points of life. Churches should be maintained for the good of society as a whole, whether or not they attract significant numbers of worshippers on a regular basis. In the past such a presence was ensured by the state church, a sacred canopy that encompassed all citizens; increasingly, however, the same effect is achieved in the voluntary sector. Churches are maintained by the few for the many – remembering that this is an equation with two parts. Too much attention to the few distorts the picture. A proper understanding of religion in Europe requires that the subtle, shifting but crucial relationship between the active few and the passive many is scrutinized in detail.

One way of doing this picks up metaphors from economic life. Europeans approach their churches not so much as firms but as public utilities. Herein lies the essence of the state church mentality: churches exist (rather like the water or electricity supply) to be made use of when necessary. Such a mentality, moreover, is ill-suited almost by definition to the market, be this financial or cultural. In this connection, televangelism offers an excellent final example, once again linking this section with the last. Televangelism is an aspect of the cultural market strongly resisted both by Europeans and by European state churches. These are attitudes that can be interpreted in two ways: as a failure to respond to the exigencies of the market (a negative view), or as naturally resistant to extreme and, some would say, distasteful forms of religion in the modern world (a much more positive spin).

Either way, the questions posed by the notion of European exceptionalism open up an exciting sociological agenda. The answers not only challenge the traditional methodologies (notably the narrowly quantitative), they require in addition new ways of sociological thinking.

Notes

1   The European Values Study is a major cross-national survey of human values, first carried out in Europe in 1981 and then extended to other countries worldwide. It was designed by the European Values Systems Study group (EVSSG). Analyses of the

1981 material can be found in Harding, Phillips, and Fogarty (1986) and in Stoetzel (1983). A restudy took place in 1990. Published material from this can be found in Timms (1992), Ashford and Timms (1992), Barker, Halman, and Vloet (1993) and Ester, Halman, and de Moor (1994). The longitudinal aspects of the study enhance the data considerably.

2   Estimates of the size of Europe's Muslim population are, inevitably, related to questions about immigration. Statistics related to illegal immigration are particularly problematic. See Nielsen (1995:170–1) for a discussion of the statistical question and related difficulties.

3   Exactly when and why these changes were initiated is subject to debate amongst historians; starting dates vary considerably from place to place.

4   The considerable, if disputatious efforts to reinstate churches and other religious organizations in those parts of Europe where their existence was threatened in the communist period illustrates the same point. These institutions are not considered irrelevant to modern living, however problematic the logistics of reinstatement might be.

References

Abrams, M., Gerard, D., and Timms, N., Eds. 1985. *Values and Social Change in Britain: Studies in the Contemporary Values of Modern Society*. London: Macmillan.

Ashford, S. and Timms, N. 1992. *What Europe Thinks: a Study of West European Values*. Aldershot: Dartmouth.

Barker, D., Halman, L., and Vloet, A. 1992. *The European Values Study 1981–1990: Summary Report*. Aberdeen: Gordon Cook Foundation on behalf of the European Values Group.

Beckford, J.A. 1985. *Cult Controversies*. London and New York: Tavistock Publications.

Beckford, J.A. 1986. *New Religious Movements and Rapid Social Change*. London: Sage/UNESCO.

Berger, P.L. 1992. *A Far Glory: The Quest for Faith in an Age of Credulity*. New York: Doubleday.

Bruce, S. 1995. "The Truth About Religion in Britain," *Journal for the Scientific Study of Religion* 34(4):417–30.

Bruce, S. 1996. *From Cathedrals to Cults: Religion in the Modern World*. Oxford: Oxford University Press.

Bruce, S. 1999. *Choice and Religion: A Critique of Rational Choice Theory*. Oxford: Oxford University Press.

Casanova, J. 1994. *Public Religions in the Modern World*. Chicago and London: University of Chicago Press.

Davie, G. 2000. *Religion in Modern Europe: A Memory Mutates*. Oxford: Oxford University Press.

Ester, P., Halman, L., and de Moor, R. 1994. *The Individualizing Society: Value Changes in Europe and North America*. Tilburg: Tilburg University Press.

Harding, S., Phillips, D., and Fogarty, M. 1986. *Contrasting Values in Western Europe*. Basingstoke: Macmillan.

Hervieu-Léger, D., 1993. *La religion pour mémoire*. Paris: Cerf.

Lewis, B. and Schnapper, D., Eds. 1994. *Muslims and Europe*. London: Pinter.

Martin, D. 1991. "The Secularization Issue: Prospect and Retrospect," *British Journal of Sociology* 42(4):466–74.

Marty, M.E. and Appleby, R.S., Eds. 1995. *Fundamentalisms Comprehended.* Chicago: University of Chicago Press.

Michel, P. 1996. "Les églises dans le monde post-communiste," *Cahiers D'Europe* 1(1):466–74.

Nielsen, J. 1995. *Muslims and Western Europe.* Edinburgh: Edinburgh University Press.

O'Connell, J. 1991. *The Making of Modern Europe: Strengths, Constraints and Resolutions.* University of Bradford: Peace Research Project.

Pace, E. and Guolo, R. 1998. *Il Fondamentalismo.* Rome and Bari: Editori Laterza.

Reed, B. 1978. *The Dynamics of Religion.* London: Darton, Longman and Todd.

Stark, R. and Bainbridge, W. 1985. *The Future of Religion: Secularization, Revival and Cult Formation.* Berkeley: University of California Press.

Stark, R. and Bainbridge, W. 1987. *A Theory of Religion.* New York: Peter Lang.

Stark, R. and Iannaccone, L. 1994. "A Supply-Side Reinterpretation of the 'Secularization' of Europe," *Journal for the Scientific Study of Religion* 33(3):230–52.

Stoetzel, J. 1983. *Les Valeurs du temps présent.* Paris: Presses Universitaires de France.

Timms, N. 1992. *Family and Citizenship: Values in Contemporary Britain.* Aldershot: Dartmouth.

Vertovec, S. and Peach, C., Eds. 1997. *Islam in Europe: The Politics of Religion and Community.* Basingstoke and Warwick: Macmillan and CRER.

Wasserstein, B. 1996. *Vanishing Diaspora: The Jews in Europe Since 1945.* London: Hamish Hamilton.

Webber, J., Ed. 1994. *Jewish Identities in the New Europe.* London and Washington: Littman Library of Jewish Civilization.

Wilson, B. 1998. "The Secularization Thesis: Criticisms and Rebuttals," in *Secularization and Social Integration: Papers in Honor of Karel Dobbelaere*, Ed. R. Laermans, B. Wilson, and J. Billiet, Leuven: Leuven University Press, pp. 45–65.

Young, L. 1997. *Rational Choice Theory and Religion: Summary and Assessment.* London: Routledge.

CHAPTER 15

The Future of Religious Participation and Belief in Britain and Beyond

Robin Gill

Futurology is a risky business. By definition the unpredictable cannot be foreseen, and most of us are aware at both personal and national levels just how often the unpredictable happens. At best we can extrapolate from past and present trends how things might turn out if everything continues as it broadly has so far. Yet detecting social regularities, which might in theory be projected into the future, has always been one of the functions of sociology. Indeed, the pioneer sociologists were often rather bolder than their present-day successors in making such projections. Whilst the failure of many of the latter should make sociologists today duly humble, it should not, I believe, warn us off futurology altogether.

It is in this spirit that I offer this chapter on the future of religious participation and belief in Britain and elsewhere in the Western world (it is quite beyond my competence to speculate about the future of Christianity or other religions in the non-Western world). This is intentionally a speculative essay, albeit one grounded in data on longitudinal trends which can now be mapped out over a considerable period of time. Precisely because data on changes of levels of religious participation and belief in Britain, as well as their wider cultural interconnections, is now so extensive, speculation based upon established regularities becomes a serious possibility. In turn these regularities can be compared with data from other Western countries, suggesting that they are not entirely idiosyncratic. Nevertheless, none of this gainsays the possibility of major changes in the future caused by unpredictable factors. They lie outside the scope of this chapter.

The first part of this chapter will examine longitudinal statistical evidence of religious decline in Britain, in terms of a decline both in participation in religious institutions and in specifically Christian beliefs. The patterns of decline that emerge from this will then be compared with evidence from elsewhere in the Western world and projected tentatively into the future. The second part of the chapter will examine countertrends in British data: the apparent increase of churchgoing in the first half of the nineteenth century; high levels of religious participation in new immigrant groups such as Roman Catholics between the mid-nineteenth century and the mid-twentieth century, Jews in the early twentieth century, and Muslims in the late twentieth century; persisting patterns of beliefs within religious groups; and persisting non-traditional beliefs within the population at large.

In the third part of this chapter my central thesis will emerge, suggesting that there is an intimate connection between formal religious participation and social identity. Here I will speculate about the future of religion within three groups: immigrant and migrant minorities for whom religious belonging can be an important focus of identity, albeit one which tends to fade over time; exclusivist sectarian groups, with a strong sense of religious identity but also a tendency to be increasingly fissiparous; and individuals within a settled population at large who, faced with the ambiguities of modern life, are likely still to participate in key civic and religious rituals, seek to pass values to the young through religious participation, but may regard religious boundaries as increasingly fluid. A common feature of these three groups is that the more social identity is threatened by external changes, the more likely individuals are to participate in formal religious groups. At more settled times this participation is likely to decline, yet, so far at least, it does not totally disappear. Social mobility, identity, and formal religious participation are thus seen as strongly connected with each other.

Long-term Religious Decline

Evidence of long-term decline in formal religious participation in Britain is overwhelming. Wherever overall participation rates can be compared longitudinally over the last hundred years they typically show this decline across Christian denominations, and even allowing for some recent growth in Eastern religious traditions. The twentieth century has seen a sharp and continuous decline, albeit with some denominational variations, in active support for both Christian churches and Jewish synagogues in Britain, without any clear indication that this decline has yet halted. There are technical problems in collecting comparable data to map this decline in a linear fashion. However, when like is carefully compared with like, within most denominations and from one area to the next, the extent of this decline becomes obvious. Such zig-zag mapping makes accurate analysis of religious participation possible for most of the nineteenth and all of the twentieth century – a task difficult or impossible to achieve so comprehensively elsewhere in the world.

A series of examples help to demonstrate this. In each of these, census data are used combining morning and evening church attendance (excluding Sunday school attendance) across denominations on a particular Sunday, measured as a percentage of the population at large (Gill 1993). In some instances it is possible that there may be variations in the proportions of individuals attending both services (most church censuses count heads and not individuals). However, the overall levels of decline are too sharp to account for the decline solely in these terms. In addition, individual questionnaire data in the second half of the twentieth century confirm that fewer and fewer individuals go to church (and not simply that the same proportion of the population goes to church but less frequently) (Gill 1999).

Churchgoing rates in Inner Greater London provide a clear indication of decline. They amounted to 29.1% in 1851, to 28.7% in 1887, and then declined sharply to 22.4% in 1903 and to just 10.7% in 1989. Anglican attendances declined earliest in London, from 15.6% in 1851, to 14.1% in 1887, to 9.6% in 1903, and then to just 1.8% in 1989. Free Church attendances combined increased from 11.3% in 1851, to 12.5% in 1887, but then declined to 10.7% in 1903, and to 4.6% in 1989. Roman Catholic attendances were just 2.3% in 1851, had grown to 4.7% in 1979, but then declined to 4.2% in 1989.

In Liverpool, with a much larger Roman Catholic population, churchgoing rates have long been considerably higher than those in London. Nevertheless, there has been a similar pattern of churchgoing decline there – first amongst Anglicans, then amongst the Free Churches, and finally amongst Roman Catholics. Overall churchgoing rates there were 39.9% in 1851, 32.9% in 1881, 31.9% in 1891, 29.4% in 1902, and 26.6% in 1912. By 1989 overall attendance in Merseyside as a whole had declined to just 14%. Anglican attendance declined sharply from 15.3% in 1851, to 9.8% in 1881, and then to 7.7% in 1912. Free Church attendance increased to 12.7% in 1881, then declined to 11.9% in 1891, and to 8.7% in 1912. With a large Irish workforce, Roman Catholic attendances in Liverpool already amounted to 13.9% in 1851; in Merseyside as a whole they were still 11.5% in 1979, but then declined sharply to 8.9% in 1989.

York provides an instructive example of a smaller urban area with a more dominant Anglican Church. It is possible to map churchgoing patterns there accurately from 1837 until the present with remarkably few long gaps. At the start of this period Anglican attendances amounted to 16.8% of the population. They had increased to a high 26.0% in 1851, but then declined to 20.7% in 1865, to 17.0% in 1884, to 11.1% in 1912, to 8.6% in 1931, to 4.8% in 1953, and to 3.4% in 1989. Free Church attendances in York amounted to 19% in 1837, but had declined to 13% in 1901, to 5% in 1935, and to 3% in 1989. In 1837 these Free Church attendances were almost entirely Methodists, whereas in 1989 only half were. In proportion to the population of York, Methodist attendances, now just a twelfth of what they were a century-and-a-half earlier, have experienced the sharpest decline of any denomination. In contrast, Roman Catholic attendances in York amounted to 3.4% in 1837, increased to 6.6% in 1851, but then declined to 4.9% in 1901, to 3.9% in 1948, and remained at 4.1% in 1989. Taken together, attendances at morning and evening church services across denominations in York, having risen from 39.2% in 1837, declined from a high point of 50.6% in 1851 to just 10.9% in 1989. So, if London and

Liverpool experienced almost a threefold decline in overall attendances between 1851 and 1989, in York the decline was nearer fivefold.

Census data also show that rural areas of Britain have been just as affected by a decline in attendances as urban areas, albeit perhaps more recently. Two remote rural areas, both of which have experienced considerable depopulation, illustrate this. In north Northumberland 31 percent of the local population attended local churches (mainly Anglican and Presbyterian) on Mothering Sunday morning in 1851 and 7.9 percent in the afternoon or evening. In contrast, at Pentecost 1988 just 9 percent of the population was in church in the same area (all services were now held in the morning). In the Welsh-speaking area of Glan-Llyn near Bala, Meirionnydd, it is possible to pinpoint the start of rural churchgoing decline more accurately. In 1851 there were two Anglican churches and ten chapels serving a population of little more than one-and-a-half thousand. More than a third of this population attended the evening services at the chapels alone. Each church and chapel had at least one service, and some up to three, on the Sunday of the 1851 census. Well over half of the young people in the area were at the morning Sunday schools, and afternoon Sunday school and adult attendances amounted to 44 percent of the total population. A survey in 1950 showed that church attendance still remained high: in every age and gender group more than half and, for the most part, two-thirds attended church or chapel at least once on a Sunday. However by 1990 attendances in Glan-Llyn had dropped very sharply: four out of five people in the population were still registered as church or chapel members, yet only 18 percent of them now attended at any point on a typical Sunday.

Another way of illustrating this long-term decline in religious participation is to compare statistics from a single denomination over a period of time. Church of England twentieth century statistics serve this purpose well. Clergy estimated average Sunday attendances that we recorded from 1968 until 1995. During this time attendance declined continuously: 3.5% of the population in 1968, 3.0% in 1973, 2.7% in 1978, 2.5% in 1985, 2.4% in 1989, and 2.2% in 1995. The proportion of infant baptisms to live births declined from 67% in 1950 to 55% in 1960, to 47% in 1970, to 37% in 1980, 28% in 1990, and to 22% in 1996. Statistics for confirmations, electoral rolls, Sunday communicants, and Easter and Christmas communicants, all show similar patterns of persistent decline.

It is now possible to make a number of crucial comparisons from sample data from attitude surveys over the last 50 years (Gill 1999, Gill, Hadaway, and Marler 1998). In response to the question "Would you describe yourself as being of any religion or denomination?" 23 percent of the sample in 1950 responded negatively. By 1996 this no-religion group had grown to 43 percent. In the earlier survey there was very little difference between age groups, yet by the 1990s there was a very striking difference. Whereas those aged 65 and over had changed little, two-thirds of the 18–24 age group now gave a no-religion response.

With this declared secularity there is now clear evidence of a general decline in Christian beliefs within the British population, as well as a marked increase in skepticism. Measuring these changes using data from more that one hundred national surveys conducted since the 1940s, it is now possible to map them with some accuracy. For example, a generalized belief in God shows some evidence of change, declining as a belief held by fourth-fifths of the population to two-thirds. However, stated disbelief increased sharply from just a tenth of the population to over one-quarter. The more specifically Christian belief in a personal God also shows clear signs of change, declining as a belief held in the 1940s by 43 percent of the population to just 31 percent in the 1990s. Belief in Jesus as the Son of God declined from just over two-thirds of the population to under one-half, whereas belief that Jesus was "just a man" or "just a story" increased from under one-fifth to some two-fifths of the population. A generalized belief in life after death is still held by something less than half of the population, but disbelief has doubled over 50 years, now almost matching belief.

Even though they cannot be mapped as fully, similar changes can be detected in other parts of the Western world. For example, in Australia those recording a no-religion option in the national population census have increased from 6.7% in 1971 to 16.6% in 1996, and those claiming in opinion polls to go to church at least once a month have declined from 47% in 1950 to 24% in 1993 (Hughes 1997, Hughes et al. 1995). Similarly, in Canada opinion polls suggested a decline in those claiming to have gone to church or synagogue in the last seven days from 65% in the 1940s to 30% in the 1990s, with this decline just as evident amongst Catholics (especially in Quebec) as amongst Protestants, and a decline in the same period of children going to Sunday school or church from 60% to 26% (Bibby 1987, 1997).

Even in the United States, despite much evidence of comparative resilience of religious participation, there is now also evidence of decline. Gallup polls over the last 50 years have suggested comparatively high levels of regular church-going at approximately two-fifths of the population, yet in the 1950s this rose to almost half of the population. And the blunt Gallup question "What is your religious denomination?" shows an increase in no-religion responses in five decades from 2% to 11%. Until the mid-1960s the *Yearbook of American and Canadian Churches* charted overall membership of religious bodies in the United States, both Christian and non-Christian, measured against the total population. This suggested a remarkable rise from 16% in 1850 to 36% in 1900, to 47% in 1930, to 57% in 1950, rising finally to 64.3% in 1965. Using the same basis of measurement, this level was still 64.5% in 1970, but had declined to 59.5% in 1980 and to 59.3% in 1990.

Many European countries have also seen a decline in churchgoing, especially since the 1960s, and with it a measurable decline in specifically Christian beliefs. For example, the two sets of surveys conducted by the European Value Systems Study Group, first in the early 1980s and then in the early 1990s, showed a decline in mean weekly churchgoing rates in 10 European countries from 49% to 29%, with a particularly sharp decline in the 18–24 age-group from 43% to just 18% (Kerkhofs 1988, Abrams, Gerard, and Timms 1985, Timms 1992). These surveys also detected a decline in the same countries in belief in God from

85% to 79% and in heaven from 53% to 49%. In addition, they provided evidence of clear generational differences. For example, in Britain in 1990 only 31% of those in the 18–24 age group reported that they had been "brought up religiously at home," compared with 58% of the 35–44 age group and 82% of those over 64 years old.

Again, using a rather longer time-frame, *Der Spiegel* commissioned an attitude survey in West Germany in 1967, which it repeated in 1992 (Shand 1998). During that 25-year period declared weekly churchgoing declined sharply from 25% to 10% and, amongst a series of beliefs, a belief in God declined from 68% to 56% and in Jesus as the Son of God from 42% to 29%.

Evidence, then, of growing secularity in the Western world appears to be overwhelming. The future seems clear. Participation in religious institutions (predominantly Christian) will continue to decline. Within two generations we can expect, on current trends in Britain, that only 31 percent of the elderly there will report that they had been "brought up religiously at home," 22 percent of the middle-aged, and just 12 percent of the young. As a result, explicitly Christian beliefs of any variety will be held by only a small section of the population and most people, old as well as young, will see themselves as having no religion and will be increasingly prepared to express skepticism about any form of religious (especially theistic) belief. Thus within two generations secularity and religious skepticism will have triumphed both in Britain and in most other countries within the Western world. The population of the United States, apart from the more secular California, may be comparatively resilient, but on this basis it too will eventually follow the ineluctable process of secularization evident elsewhere in the West.

Countertrends

Yet there are other, more awkward, pieces of evidence suggesting that growing Western secularization is not the whole of the story. There are already indications in the data just set out that churchgoing decline has not been an entirely linear process, either between or across denominations, either in Britain or elsewhere in the Western world. In addition, to focus so exclusively upon declining Christian participation and beliefs may be to miss other religious forms brought with new immigrants or reemerging within the indigenous population. As a result, predictions based only upon linear secularization may well be far too simplistic. Despite the fact that such predictions have often been made by sociologists going all the way back to Comte, they may owe more to ideology than to empirical observation.

Evidence pointing to a rise in churchgoing in York between 1837 and 1851 has already been noted. Throughout Britain in the first half of the nineteenth century there was very extensive building of new churches and chapels, as well as a general increase in the number of services that they offered on a Sunday.

Anglican parishes that had been neglected for years received a resident incumbent, sometimes for the first time since medieval times, with a new parsonage and a renovated or newly built church. Rural churches, which had often had an irregular provision of Sunday services, now had a regular pattern of two or three services. Urban churches, which frequently had a single service in the afternoon in the eighteenth century, now had morning and afternoon services and Sunday schools as well as evening services for adults. Free Churches competed vigorously in both rural and urban areas, providing an abundance of new churches and chapels and frequently several alongside each other even in larger villages.

The 1851 census reveals clearly just how successful all of this was. In some areas of Britain more than half of the total population was in church or chapel at a single point on the census day and there was sufficient space in all of these churches and chapels for most of the population. Ironically, the conductors of the census were worried that not everyone *was* attending church on that Sunday and that a reason for this might be that there were still insufficient church buildings to serve the population. In reality, 1851 may well have been a high point both in British churchgoing and in church provision compared with the immediate centuries before, rivaling the remarkable period of church building by immigrant Normans in the eleventh century. The mid-nineteenth century appears to have been the most recent peak of religious participation in Britain, just as the mid-twentieth century was apparently that for the United States.

Again, although regular attendances within most denominations in Britain and in much of the rest of Europe have been declining since the 1960s, their pattern is much more varied before that date. It has already been seen that in urban areas Anglicans have experienced the longest-term decline, whereas Roman Catholics had a century of steady growth or consolidation in many areas, as they did in the United States, before experiencing recent decline. It has also been the inclusive denominations, such as Episcopalians, in the United States that have experienced long-term decline, whereas more exclusive denominations, such as Southern Baptists, or "sects," such as the Mormons, have experienced considerable growth (Finke and Stark 1992). The relative resilience, until recently, of overall levels of churchgoing in the United States has often been contrasted with European decline. Yet in both contexts predictions about linear secularization appear far too simplistic. There seems to be more than one process operating between and across denominations even within Europe, let alone within the United States.

Migration appears to be a highly important variable accounting for such variations. In Britain in the first half of the nineteenth century, rural migration to cities and large towns was associated less with estrangement from churches (as so many sociologists have supposed) than with new religious attachments. The dramatic rise of Barrow-in-Furness in northern England illustrates this well. In 1821 the Anglican parish of Dalton-in-Furness had a total population of some two-and-a-half thousand. Of these 29 percent attended the Anglican church and, beyond this, there was just a single Wesleyan Methodist chapel with two dozen members. By 1851 the population had doubled and now 34 percent attended the five Anglican churches and chapels and a further 4 percent the two Methodist chapels. However, by 1881 the ship-building town of Barrow-in-Furness had been created within this once rural parish with a population of over 47,000. A third of the population still attended church, yet Anglicans accounted for only 9 percent of this population and Roman Catholics a further 3 percent. Within a generation this had become a predominantly Free Church town, with six Wesleyan chapels, three Primitive Methodist chapels, two each belonging to the Methodist New Connexion, the United Methodists Free Church, and the Congregationalists; a large Baptist chapel, an active Salvation Army mission, and smaller chapels belonging to the Bible Christians, Plymouth Brethren, Christadelphians, Welsh Calvinists, Catholic Apostolic, and Spiritualists. Rapid migration thus brought with it a fascinating mixture of traditional and novel denominations and a radical change in the dominant religious culture.

A more recent example of a similar process is that of South Korea. There the three decades up to 1990, but not beyond, were characterized both by extremely rapid urbanization and industrialization and by a phenomenal growth of a rich variety of Protestant churches (as well as Buddhist temples). In contrast, Japan, which urbanized much earlier (like Britain), has experienced no comparable twentieth century growth in formal religious participation.

Immigration has also been strongly associated with religious growth and change in Britain. The steady growth from the mid-nineteenth century of Roman Catholics after emancipation, until the mid-twentieth century, closely matched patterns of Irish immigration. Interestingly, it was accompanied by an Irish rather than a Continental European pattern of church building. Characteristically a single building was used on a Sunday morning for multiple masses with churchgoers expected to travel in from some distance. In contrast, Anglicans and many Continental European Catholics expected to have a local church even within small communities. This pattern persists to the present with Catholic churches typically placed in small towns rather than villages. In York today, overall Anglican and Roman Catholic attendance levels are fairly similar, yet there are still 24 Anglican churches there to the Catholic six. Roman Catholics now represent approximately a third of total churchgoers in England as a whole, and yet they own only a tenth of the churches.

The first half of the twentieth century saw a series of waves of Jewish immigration following persecution in Russia and continental Europe. In cities such as London and Liverpool this resulted in the building of many Orthodox, Liberal, and Reform synagogues. Towards the end of the twentieth century other waves of immigration have seen a considerable growth in the Muslim population of Britain (accounting now for 3 to 4% of the general population). With this has also come a rapid building of rival mosques – there are now more than 50 in Bradford alone and prestigious central mosques in cities such as London and Edinburgh. Although fewer in number, Sikh and Hindu temples have also been built in urban areas. Taken together they have radically changed the visible religious map in Britain and offer a serious challenge to a theory of linear secularization.

This varied pattern is also reflected in the data from attitude surveys already mentioned. Alongside a pattern of declining Christian beliefs and growing skepticism is another pattern of persisting, and sometimes increasing, nontraditional or noninstitutional religious beliefs. Belief in reincarnation and in horoscopes has been held consistently by a quarter of the population over the last three decades. About half of the population also apparently believes in those foretelling the future (presumably in a more dramatic sense than the present chapter!). Over the last 50 years the proportion of people believing in ghosts has also doubled: a third of the population now has this belief, even though only half claims actually to have seen a ghost. Although many people express skepticism about these beliefs, they hardly support a theory of linear secularization.

Attitude data also suggest that there are remarkable continuities (as well as some changes) in the beliefs and values of churchgoers across several decades and across different cultures. Perhaps it is not surprising that British churchgoers in the 1960s and 1990s have similarly high levels of belief in a personal God or in life after death – and, indeed, that similar levels can be detected amongst churchgoers in continental Europe, Australia, and North America. It is, though, interesting that British and Northern Irish, or Canadian and American, churchgoers have very similar levels of belief even though these levels differ widely amongst nonchurchgoers in their countries. So in Britain and Canada, where churchgoing levels are comparatively low, differences between the beliefs of churchgoers and nonchurchgoers are more pronounced than those in Northern Ireland and the United States, where churchgoing levels are higher. Yet in all of these contexts the levels of Christian belief among churchgoers themselves are remarkably similar. More significantly, there is now abundant evidence that participation in voluntary service work in the community is characteristically high among churchgoers. In terms of a wide set of stated attitudes and behavior, churchgoers throughout the Western world have a strong sense both of moral order and altruism (Gill 1999).

The Future

A more complex picture of the past and present is beginning to emerge. There are indications of growing secularity and skepticism, but alongside these there appear to be other countertrends. What responsible speculations might be made about possible future patterns of religious participation and belief in Britain and elsewhere in the Western world?

Perhaps the common factor prompting renewed religious participation, both amongst at least some migrants to urban areas and amongst some overseas immigrants, is a concern for identity. It is well known that English expatriates, missing their culture, can become regular churchgoers, more involved in the English-speaking Anglican Cathedral in Hong Kong, say, than they might have been back at home. Throughout Britain's former colonies it is, perhaps, not surprising that there are a disproportionate number of St. George's churches built by the English and St. Andrew's churches built by the Scots. Indeed, as a retired section of the British population gravitates to the coast of Southern Spain, so English-speaking congregations are still being established there to serve their need for cultural identity. If the future in the West is characterized at all by radical internal migration (perhaps this time from urban to rural areas) or by immigration from overseas, then renewed religious participation may well be a result. A part of the continuing vitality of American churches may be a result of this. Successive waves of new religious minorities, as well as distinctive immigrant groups within long-established denominations (such as the fast growing Hispanic Catholics in Southern California), continue to bring their own religious enthusiasm to the United States. This is not, of course, to claim that migration and/or immigration are always and everywhere associated with religious enthusiasm, but simply to note that they can indeed be.

However, in Britain immigrant groups have not usually been able to retain their distinctively religious identity intact indefinitely. Just as the effects of rural–urban migration eventually wear off, so do those of immigration from overseas. Many of the synagogues built in London and Liverpool by newly arrived Jewish immigrants have now been closed. Intermarriage between Jews and Gentiles has contributed to a sharp decline in the practice of religious rituals in the household, and religious skepticism is expressed by many British and Continental European Jews today. Cultures of observant Jews, such as the pocket of observant Sephardic Jews in Gibraltar, are becoming increasingly rare outside the United States and, of course, Israel. British Catholics have also experienced a considerable increase in intermarriage with non-Catholics in the second half of the twentieth century and increasing difficulties in retaining the religious loyalties of their young. Set within a dominant culture in which a majority of neither young nor old are religious participants, it becomes increasingly difficult to retain a separate religious identity. Inevitably the young ask, "Why do I have to go to mass?" or "Why do I have to eat kosher food or go to synagogue?" when a majority of their other friends have no corresponding religious practices.

Will young Muslims in Britain (or, indeed, in continental Europe, Australia, or the United States) be any different? At present they represent a distinctive set of religious enclaves, concentrated particularly in a number of urban areas. Muslim leaders and parents naturally press for the establishment of Muslim schools in Britain, mock Christians for not taking their own faith seriously, and demand a more significant role for Muslim institutions in British life. If they are as successful in retaining this distinctive cultural identity as British Catholics have been, then this may remain an important part of the religious map both within Britain and within Continental Europe for several generations to come. Yet if the young rebel, as British Jews soon did and as Catholics eventually did, then this culture may not be as secure as it seems to be at present. Whatever its longevity, its eventual demise appears likely. More than that, even if it survives relatively intact for several generations, it is likely to remain a religious enclave. The broader populations may well visit the more spectacular central mosques out of interest or curiosity, but they are unlikely themselves to become practicing Muslims in any significant numbers. Unlike the conquering Norman immigrants in the eleventh century, who themselves may have remained as enclaves within England for several decades, more recent Irish Catholic, Jewish, or Muslim immigrant enclaves have been in no position to eventually "persuade" the population at large to join them.

Even the attitude data suggesting a strong minority persistence of nontraditional religious beliefs in the British population does not modify this judgment. As yet there is little clear evidence that these beliefs are grounded in any particular institution or communal practice. So-called New Age beliefs are characteristically eclectic and may well lack wider social significance. Nevertheless, problems of personal identity will remain for individuals, especially when confronted with the vicissitudes of life. New Age beliefs, however lacking in social function, may well be symptomatic of problems of personal identity – as well a general dissatisfaction with Christianity and secularism alike. What institutional religious options are likely to remain to meet these problems in the future?

One obvious option is exclusive religious groups with a strong sense of separate identity, whether in the form of small-scale sects or new religious movements, or in the denominational form of congregations that become more exclusive and sectarian. At present the latter appear to be growing everywhere in the Western world at the expense of inclusive denominations, sometimes ensuring that overall religious participation remains comparatively high (as in the United States or Northern Ireland) but more often not (as in Britain, Europe, Canada and Australia). As a growing section within most Western societies becomes explicitly secular and skeptical, so those religious groups who are confident about their own separate identity and beliefs are apparently more likely to survive than those who are not. The current situation in the West is sometimes depicted as the culture of postmodernity, or at other times as simply the fragmented nature of postindustrial societies. In either case it is argued that the future will increasingly consist of incommensurable groups (some religious and some secular) in which individuals will seek reassurance and certainty in a situation of confusing pluralism. In terms of this scenario, there will no longer be *any* dominant metanarratives in Western societies – neither those of the long-distant Christian past nor those of the more recent secular Enlightenment.

Now this is a distinct possibility for a map of the future in the West. Nonetheless, it still has some flaws. The most obvious is that it is remarkably difficult in a changing world for groups, whether religious or not, to retain a consistent reassurance and certainty that remains credible to all of their followers. Rigorous exclusive sects such as the Jehovah's Witnesses have long known that such consistency is only possible if members are excluded as soon as they deviate from official teaching. In a skeptical world they lose or exclude many members and, despite mighty efforts in evangelism, find overall growth in the West extremely slow. Other groups, such as Pentecostalists, tend to become fissiparous. They typically recruit strong-minded individuals looking for reassurance and certainty, who then fall away or form new groups when they disagree with their leaders or fellow members. The higher the demand for commitment, the more likely the possibility of disillusionment.

Attitude data again confirm that absolute levels of consistency and distinctiveness are not apparent even amongst regular churchgoers. As already mentioned, churchgoers are more concerned with moral order and altruism than the population at large. Yet neither value is absent in the general population nor consistently present among churchgoers. Furthermore, on specific moral or belief issues there are usually variations of opinion amongst churchgoers themselves. So, whereas it is true that most Catholic churchgoers tend to oppose abortion or euthanasia, there are some who do not. And, throughout the Western world, it has long been established that lay Catholic opinion on contraception differs markedly from that of the Pope. Even Mormon birthrates in the United States are at variance with conservative Mormon teaching on birth control.

What of those individuals who continue to take an active part in more inclusive religious denominations? In terms of present data this is the group which still appears to be declining throughout the Western world. In Britain and Europe more widely this group is closest in ethos to a general population which has learned from the bitter experience of past centuries to be deeply suspicious of religious zealots. This is a group that is particularly active in the community at large and, without which, much community service would be lost. Yet, for the moment at least, it faces an uncertain future. In the first half of the twentieth century most children in the West were socialized through Sunday schools and their equivalents. Thus familiarized with church culture, they retained many of its beliefs and values as adults and returned to its worship at key moments of the calendar or life cycle. Faced with some crisis in identity (migrating, having children, retiring, or being bereaved) they could even return to regular attendance. Now changes in the second half of the twentieth century – especially in Britain, most other European countries, Australia, and Canada – have made all of this more difficult for the twenty-first century. Children became more reluctant to go to Sunday school or church while their parents stayed at home, or they came with their parents but never established a pattern of independent churchgoing once they left home and were amongst nonchurchgoing friends. As a result, few adults in the future, even when faced with a crisis of identity, will be able to "return" to church. They will never have acquired the language, symbols, or ritual of church culture and are likely to find it strange rather than reassuring. Searching for meaning beyond the ambiguities of life, they will find difficulty in decoding the meanings offered within institutional worship.

In this situation boundaries between inclusive denominations are likely to become increasingly fluid for new churchgoers. A pattern already becoming established among British university students today may become more widespread in all age groups. Some denominations committed to older but disappearing loyalties will face further attrition, if not extinction. In contrast, those inclusive denominations seeking to attract new members may find that much of their worship is family-oriented nonsacramental worship. Whereas many inclusive denominations in the late twentieth century became accustomed to a diet of eucharistic worship, those in the twenty-first century may discover that this is actually a recipe only for socialized Christians. To attract the religiously unsocialized at a point when they are searching for meaning in their lives, they may need to provide less formal worship and, indeed, provide it less often than once a week. In many rural areas there is already developing a pattern of fortnightly or monthly worship.

If this is the future then it will involve some social cost. Attitude data suggest strongly that those who attend monthly have less distinctively Christian beliefs and values than those who attend weekly. And those who attend weekly, having become accustomed to a regular Eucharist, are likely to be impatient with a nonsacramental diet. Perhaps they will have to resort instead to conferences or retreats to supplement this diet.

All of these options assume that thoroughgoing secularity is not the only option remaining in the future within Western societies. Secularity is likely to be a strong and growing feature in many Western countries. Nonetheless, other more varied patterns, resulting from migration, immigration, and a natural tendency to search for meaning, especially at moments evoking a crisis of personal identity, may also remain features of the Western religious map in the future. Time, of course, will show.

References

Abrams, M., Gerard, D., and Timms, N., Eds. 1985. *Values and Social Change in Britain: Studies in the Contemporary Values of Modern Society*. London: Macmillan.

Bibby, R.W. 1987. *Fragmented Gods: The Poverty and Potential of Religion in Canada*. Toronto: Irwin Publishing.

Bibby, R.W. 1997. "Going, Going, Gone: The Impact of Geographical Mobility on Religious Involvement," *Review of Religious Research* 38(4):289–307.

Finke, R. and Stark, R. 1992. *The Churching of America: Winners and Losers in Our Religious Economy*. New Brunswick, NJ: Rutgers University Press.

Gill, R. 1993. *The Myth of the Empty Church*. London: SPCK.

Gill, R. 1999. *Churchgoing and Christian Ethics*. Cambridge: Cambridge University Press.

Gill, R., Hadaway, C.K., and Marler, P.L. 1998. " 'Is Religious Belief Declining in Britain?" *Journal for the Scientific Study of Religion* 37(3):507–16.

Hughes, P.J. 1997. *Religion in Australia: Fact and Figures*. Kew, Victoria, Australia: Christian Research Association.

Hughes, P.J., Thompson, C., Pryor, R., and Bouma, G.D. 1995. *Believe It or Not: Australian Spirituality and the Churches in the 90s*. Kew, Victoria, Australia: Christian Research Association.

Kerkhofs, J. 1988. "Between 'Christendom' and 'Christianity'," *Journal of Empirical Theology* 1(2):88–101.

Shand, J.D. 1998. "The Decline of Traditional Christian Beliefs in Germany," *Sociology of Religion* 59(2):179–84.

Timms, N. 1992. *Family and Citizenship: Values in Contemporary Britain*. Dartmouth: Aldershot.

CHAPTER 16

Religion as Diffusion of Values. "Diffused Religion" in the Context of a Dominant Religious Institution: The Italian Case

Roberto Cipriani

Introduction

There has been much discussion concerning possible definitions of religion. Generally a distinction is made between a substantive and a functional approach. The substantive approach may be exemplified by Durkheim (1995) when he speaks of "beliefs and practices" as the ground of the "moral community" called a "church." Luckmann (1967) is said to demonstrate the functional approach when he refers to "symbolic universes" as "socially objectified systems of meaning" by way of "social processes" considered as "fundamentally religious," "which lead to the formation of the Ego" and the "transcendence of biological nature."

However, when we make a thorough exploration of Durkheim's and Luckmann's writings, we observe that Durkheim is also alive to function (religion helps solidarity), and that Luckmann is not concerned only with function (religion is a conception of the world made up of specific contents). Thus in reality those quoted as exemplary champions of one or the other perspective emerge as more open to less rigid, more polyvalent formulations. In short, content and function are inseparable, and should be considered as a unique whole which permits the realization of much more complex and interconnected analytical and interpretative procedures.

For example, we might start from the idea that the metaempirical referent in attributing meaning to human existence is a particular characteristic of religion. At the same time, however, it is sensible to leave an opening for responses that do not envisage an explicit referral to the dimension of the empirical non-verifiability and the inaccessibility of direct experience. Thus, a metaempirical referent would possess a merely indicative character, or, in Blumer's (1954) term that of "sensitizing."

In this way there is no conflict between the transcendent level and that of the real. It is rather as though we were to look at the same object from two different view-points; the canalizing of a non-human presence within reality. One vision does not exclude the other. They are not in opposition and indeed at times they may converge on the same conclusion – the understanding-explanation of life in a religious key. (Cipriani 1997a:15)

From Diffused Religion to Religion of Values

Certainly, the presence of values is a constant both in the historic religions, more deeply rooted at the cultural level, and in the new religious movements still in a phase of growth and recomposition. These values represent idealistic motives, key concepts, basic ideas, parameters of reference, and ideological inclinations which watch over the personal and interpersonal actions of individuals and make them reasonable, socially relevant, and sociologically classifiable.

Every religious experience involves dedication to a cause or an ideal, with socioindividual involvement, which is more or less marked according to the individuals' intentions, utility (also in "rational choice" terms), life history, opportunities offered, encounters, and the challenges faced. To say one belongs to a particular religion means essentially to share its general principles, basic choices, and ritual procedures. The latter allow membership to become visible, permit encounters with coreligionists, legitimate executive roles (real, not merely symbolic, power), reinforce belonging, and deepen value-based motivations.

In other words, every performance of a ritual has multiple functions, but above all focuses the total values promoted and diffused by a particular religion through its members: the more these participate, the more they become convinced their choice was correct.

The latter effect is so portentous that it remains in a weakened condition even without further continuing participation. Thus, the experience of religious practice (and belief) forms of its own accord an ideal, value-laden habitus which tends to persist far beyond visible religiosity. Indeed, those who no longer practice religion and may be ever less believers retain a kind of imprinting which cannot easily be erased, and which presents them as disaffected members with continuing meaningful links to the former reference group.

Undoubtedly much is owed to primary (essentially family) socialization rather than to secondary (school and friendship within peer groups) socialization. The Berger and Luckmann (1966) teaching in this regard remains authoritative: in fact, the social construction of reality is the basis from which the value system branches out, a circuitry that directs social action and rests on an objectified and historicized worldview, which is thus endowed with a religious character that is hard to lose. The ultimate meaning of life itself is clearly written therein and orientates attitudes and behaviors.

However, it may now be more convenient to aim at disarticulating religious phenomenology from within, following a reading with more stratified dynamics and multiple facets. This is an alternative to distinguishing to the utmost between traditional religiosity, linked to church structures and quite visible in its forms, on the one hand, and a more individualized, privatized, and thus less visible religiosity, on the other. In practice it is not clear that there is only church religion and invisible religion *à la* Luckmann (1967). Rather, we may propose another hypothetical solution which envisages intermediate categories to the two extremes, defined in terms of visibility and invisibility.

An initial post-Luckmann interpretation was articulated in 1983 and applied to the Italian situation during the International Conference of Sociology of Religion (held at Bedford College, London):

> besides the interests and pressures coming from ecclesiastical sources, are there any other premises or factors which can explain religious bearing on Italian politics? In particular, it is important to verify first of all how the institution fares under the pressure of an extended "religious field" containing varied and attractive options, including anti-institutional purposes. Secondly, we must ask ourselves whether in practice religious influence in political choices concerns only Catholicism (or Christianity) or any religious expression in general. Thirdly, we must see whether the country's history or its national culture mark the existence of fixed elements, bearing common values leading (directly or indirectly, in specific or vague ways) to a widespread model of religious socialization (based prevalently on patterns of Catholic reference). (Cipriani 1984:32)

The starting point was thus represented by the influence of Catholic religion on politics in Italy. This was a fortuitous indicator that showed itself to be very illuminating, because it became increasingly possible to show that such influence involved, and involves, circles much wider than politics. Indeed, after nearly 20 years it can be asserted that the weight of religion in matters regarding decisions of a party and government nature has been reduced, but remains quite solid as regards society in general. Meanwhile the anti-institutional spirit has lessened, given that the Catholic Church is the institution least contested by Italian citizens, who moreover assign it a noteworthy portion of their taxes (0.8% of taxable income).

While the preponderant influence of official Catholicism has waned, other religious confessions have not replaced it. Only Judaism has managed on a few special occasions to have its celebrations and customs recognized. The ability of Muslims, Jehovah's Witnesses, and others to gain a hearing at a political level is negligible.

On the other hand, the connection between Catholic religious values and values diffused in the social environment has been amply demonstrated. In many instances the two are superimposed, if not wholly identical. In fact, having started from the concept of "diffused religion" referring mainly to links with the political dimension, we then arrived at a conception of religion in Italy as a web of value elements directly derived from the baggage of Catholic socialization.

Before going further, however, I should clarify what we originally intended to investigate in our research.

The leading concept, in this research, is that of "diffused religion." The term "diffused" is to be understood in at least a double sense. First of all, it is diffused in that it comprises vast sections of the Italian population and goes beyond the simple limits of church religion; sometimes in fact it is in open contrast with church religion on religious motivation (cf. the internal dissension within Catholicism on occasion of the referendum on divorce and abortion). Besides, it has become widespread, since it has been shown to be a historical and cultural result of the almost bi-millennial presence of the Catholic institution in Italy and of its socializing and legitimizing action. The premises for the present "diffused religion" have been laid down in the course of centuries. In reality, it is both diffused *in* and diffused *by*. As a final outcome, it is also diffused *for*; given that – apart from the intents of so-called church religion – we can remark the spread of other creeds (the easy proselytism of other Christian churches, of the "Jehovah's Witnesses," of "sects" of oriental origin etc . . .), as well as the trend towards ethical and/or political choices (an eventual conflict – far from disproving this hypothesis – confirms, from the outset, the existence of a religious basis, be it weak or latent). In brief terms, it is licit to think of religion as being "diffused" through the acceptance of other individual or group religious experience, and also because it represents a parameter which can be referred to with regard to moral and/or political choices. (Cipriani 1984:32)

First of all, it is still valid to claim that diffused religion concerns broad strata of the Italian population. More than one study has established this conviction over time, and it has been enriched gradually, without distortion, by new variations on the theme. In itself church religion should also be basic to the origin of diffused religion itself. However, for reasons of exposition and to avoid misunderstandings, it is preferable to regard it as a category by itself, to be deconstructed, if required, on the basis of attitudinal and behavioral differences of the subjects interviewed (usually grouped together according to stratification derived from cluster analysis). Moreover, as regards diffused religion's diversification as compared to institutional Catholic religion, this should be stressed from a sociological point of view so as to determine the differences between orthodox and heterodox modes in relation to the official Catholic model.

However, the most relevant aspect is still the strong historico-geographical – and thus cultural – rootedness of the religion most practiced in Italy. It is precisely the strength of tradition, the practice of habit, the family and community involvement, which make membership of the prevalent religion compelling and almost insurmountable. Where socialization does not arrive within the family home, pastoral and evangelizing activity carried out in a systematic way in the area by priests and their lay parish workers moves in. In fact, Catholicism is diffused in every part of the country by means of a church structure well-equipped over time and particularly able to draw on its effective know-how.

These characteristics of diffused religion make it a nonautocratic experience, open to other options, careless of the theologicodoctrinal boundaries between manifold confessional memberships. The subjects of diffused religion are little inclined to join battle in the name of their ideal referents, and they do not contest others over viewpoints that cannot always be shared. The best proof of this is provided by the easy proselytism effected by other religious groups and movements that have arrived in Italy, particularly the Christian ones, though not only these. Another piece of evidence can be found in ethical and, especially in the past, political inclinations.

> What "diffused religion" consists of can be understood even by means of its peculiarities. In a broad sense, its presence is clearly visible in forms which are not as evident as church religion, but which are not totally invalidated. This visibility may appear somehow intermittent. (Cipriani 1984:32)

Thus diffused religion also runs the risk of being classified as an "invisible religion" *sui generis*, though in reality it manifests that peculiarity of partly relating to church religion by way of participation in liturgical practices and religious rites, and partly to a "semimembership" or even nonmembership (in its most peripheral forms, almost bordering on total absence of socioreligious indicators).

> It is easy to presume that the widespread model of "diffused religion" is different from that of its source of origin, that is, this widespread religious dimension ends up by differing from the system it derives from (the institution). In this way, however, it reaches degrees of freedom which the concentrated and centralized pattern of church religion would not favor. (Cipriani 1984:32)

We might even speak of diffused religion as a perverse effect of the dominant religious system, which thus generates what is different from itself, even though in continuity with it. The greater freedom in putting ourselves outside the church permits spaces for action otherwise prohibited. In short, there is no clear opposition, nor yet a clear link of diffused religion to church religion.

> The fragmentation of the areas of diffusion and distribution cannot, however, cover all existing spheres; all aspects are not equally widespread and reach vague, undefined limits which empirically are difficult to define. This diffusiveness broadens foreseeably into complex and multiple options (especially political options: from extreme right to extreme left). Meanwhile, original religious contents diminish and lose their intensity, they disperse, they mingle, they are integrated in new syntheses. Consequently, this expansion also causes a certain lack of positive reactions with respect to the center of propulsion, either because of increased separateness or because of a weakening of the basic ideological nucleus. It is thus a "passive" religion which may become active again in specific circumstances. Rather than the dynamics of accelerated religious transformation, this provokes a certain stagnation. Even within the prevailing passivity, the underlying echo remains persistent and pervasive, it penetrates large groups of persons. At this stage "diffused religion" appears rather under false pretenses: as a feeling, a sensation which "contaminates" both the religious and political fields. Thus re-emerges the link with processes of socialization. It remains, however, to be seen if the future generations will maintain such a religious form which becomes more and more socially diluted to the extent of losing all influence on politics. (Cipriani 1984:32–3)

Despite its pervasion, diffused religion is not present in every case and every context. Indeed, it cannot easily be catalogued using homogeneous indicators. Usually, cluster analysis outlines three levels of diffused religion: the first seems closest to church religion, the second departs partially from it, and the third is situated on the margins of the continuum between church religion and diffused religion. If we look particularly at political placement, the whole ideological party spectrum has its followers distributed among the three large areas of diffused religion. The members of these classes of diffused religion prefer solutions running from the right to the extreme left, thus excluding the extreme right, as is shown by a study carried out in Rome in 1994–5 (Cipriani 1997b). At the level of values, the area of strictly religious ones seems to be narrowing, but there is an increase in the area of lay principles – lay but vaguely inspired by, or capable of drawing inspiration from, orthodox religious models. It thus seems that diffused religion is destined to remain inert, at the mercy of other confessions, though its greatest attraction lies in relation to ongoing socialization.

The problem of change within diffused religion was posed some years ago. In fact:

> even for someone who has always kept his sociological interest in current events alive, it is not easy to disentangle the guiding threads of the social, political, and religious dynamics which have characterized Italy in the last two decades. The fact is that one finds oneself in the present situation almost naturally, as though it had been expected, without even letting questions, doubts, or scientific curiosity about what has been happening to more than 50 million citizens, from the mid-1960s to the threshold of the 1990s, break the surface. (Cipriani 1989:24)

The fact is that while the contents of diffused religion change almost imperceptibly, the sociological approach also mutates, hones its instruments of empirical research, digs deeper into reality and searches for verifications and falsifications of its guiding hypotheses.

Until the end of the 1980s, there were no scientific results available providing adequate reliability as products of serious, thorough representative studies at that statistical level in relation to the whole of Italy. It was thus in the wake of the questions raised by theorizing about diffused religion that a fruitful season of field research began – from the Sicilian study on "the religion of values" (Cipriani 1992) to the major national research on "religiosity in Italy" (Cesareo et al. 1995) and the most recent one, on an international level and with a comparison between Europe and the United States on "religious and moral pluralism," is still awaiting publication.

Especially during the last decade, it has been argued that relations between the Catholic Church and the Italian state, though they have not wholly disappeared as a strategic point for examining the interinstitutional political–religious link based on citizens' interest in problems of a legislative kind, are no longer a key test of the ability of the dominant religion to influence Italian political affairs. For the past, consider the diatribes of the 1970s and 1980s on divorce and abortion, which are not comparable to the current one on financing Catholic schools. Once the major questions on the diplomatic level had been regulated solemnly on February 18, 1984 and by law on 20 May, 1985, which renewed the Concordat of 1929 between the Italian state and the Vatican hierarchy, the so-called "Catholic question" seems to have lost its bite and its interest. The movement defined as Catholic contestation has also long ago shipped its oars and seems now reduced to a sporadic attempt at dissent as regards the Establishment – unless the Holy Year of 2000 provides new possibilities for a recovery of a critical kind, taking its lead from the jubilee program. To some extent it is diffused religion itself that also represents a kind of functional substitute for divergence from the ecclesiastical structure. This differentiation appears through other ways of believing and practicing, even though the real base remains Catholic, thanks to primary socialization in the initial phases of life.

It should thus be stressed that:

> "diffused religion" refers to the characteristic conduct of believers who have received at least a Catholic education and who relate to it in a general sense. In fact, it refers to citizens who appear to be less than completely obedient to the directives of the Catholic hierarchy but who, on the other hand, refuse to reject completely certain basic principles which form part of the set of values promoted by Catholicism. (Cipriani 1989:28)

The essential core of diffused religion is to be found precisely in those sets of values that are the basis for the sharing of outlook and practices that bring together Catholics and non-Catholics, believers and nonbelievers, on the same terrain of social action. In fact, through this cultural mediation of shared values, there runs a large part of decisions for enactment by social subjects. The ecclesiastical Establishment stays in the background, intervening in a mediated way, thanks to its prior socializing activity. There is no longer, if there ever was, a close adherence to orthodoxy and orthopractice as taught by the Catholic Church, although the essential parameter remains Catholicism as the ideology determining perspective. It is precisely this which permits collaboration between the Italian state and the Catholic Church without major disturbance and indeed with a formal, legitimated agreement which has now lasted over 70 years.

As Calvaruso and Abbruzzese emphasize,

> diffused religiosity then becomes the dominant religious dimension for all those who, immersed in the secular reality of contemporary society, though not managing to accept these dimensions of the sacred cosmos which are more remote and provocative compared with the rational vision of the world, do not thereby abandon their need for meaningfulness. In the immanent dimension of individual everyday existence, diffused religiosity, rather than bearing witness to the presence of a process of laicization in a religiously oriented society, seems to enhance the permanence of the sacred in the secularized society. (1985:79)

Thus diffused religion appears as an antidote to the process of secularization of which it is, at the same time, an expression which is meaningful as a distancing from church religion. In fact

> diffused religiosity is located in an intermediate area between a secular society in crisis and a resumption of the ecclesiastical administration of the sacred. It remains too "lay" to accept the more specific elements of church doctrine and too much in need of meaning to survive in an epoch which is "without God and without prophets." (Calvaruso and Abbruzzese 1985:80)

In particular,

> the variables in "diffused religion" are, by contrast, more changeable according to the syntheses which it produces from time to time. They are achieved on levels determined by the dialectic between the basic values of primary and secondary legitimation and the "different" ones which appear on the horizon in the long confrontation with other ideological perspectives. The "new" value is internalized but almost never taken up in a wholly pure form or according to a formula that could totally replace the previous perspective. The new way of seeing reality, the different *Weltanschauung*, is, however, the result of the collision-encounter between what already exists and what is still in the process of becoming. (Cipriani 1989:29)

Diffused religion is thus quite dynamic as regards its development, despite the constancy of the chief frame of reference. However, "diffused religion lacks the kind of clear-cut characteristics which would be visible in, for example, church attendance, but it works through long-range conditioning, which is due, above all, to mass religious socialization, and to which there is a corresponding kind of 'mass loyalty' of a new type" (Cipriani 1989:46). We can discover these links between the social and the religious, between implementation in the everyday and the context of origin by way of certain value indicators.

A particular example of this is provided by

> a piece of empirical research conducted in Sicily by means of questioning a group of people selected by statistical sampling. The results were compiled from the completed questionnaires of 719 subjects, and the objective was to illuminate the concept of "diffused religion" as observed in the presence of common social values which tend to unify behavior and attitude deriving from both the religious and lay perspectives. Cluster analysis was used to identify six different groupings: religious (church) acritical; religious (church) critical; religious (diverging from the church) critical; religious (diffused) as a condition; religious (critical and distancing self from the church); and not religious. The starting point for the research is the hypothesis that Catholicism (as the dominant religion) pervades many sectors of social life and maintains its influence over common values, despite the effect of increased distance between people and institutionalized religion. This appears to refute the theory of secularization. (Cipriani 1993:91)

Table 16.1 Numbers in each grouping

Groupings	
Religious (church) acritical	101 (14.0%)
Religious (church) critical	261 (36.3%)
Religious (diverging from the church) critical	79 (11.0%)
Religious (diffused) as a condition	190 (26.4%)
Religious (distancing self from church) critical	47 (6.5%)
Nonreligious	41 (5.8%)
Total	719 (100%)

Source: Cipriani 1992.

Table 16.1 shows the general data from the study.

On the basis of these results, we have argued that the religion of values embraces the central categories of table 16.1. In particular the area that can be ascribed to the religion of values runs from the category defined as "religious (church) critical" to that described as "religious (distancing self from church) critical," and thus includes both a part of church religion (the less indulgent part) and the whole gamut of diffused religion, along with all forms of critical religion. Thus the framework of noninstitutional religion appears much broader, being based on shared values which are represented essentially by choices acted upon (to a maximum of four responses) by those interviewed in terms of guiding principles of their life, commencing with education received up to the age of 18.

As can easily be deduced from table 16.2, reflecting different value elements, it is reasonable to maintain that we are faced not only with a religion based on values largely shared, since they have been diffused chiefly through primary and, later, secondary socialization, but that these very values can be seen in themselves as a kind of religion. This religion has lay, profane, secular threads.

In essence, we have gone from a dominant church religion to a *majoritarian* diffused religion, and then to a religion *compounded of values*. As we shall attempt to show later, the conclusion is that religion can be defined as a mode of transmission and diffusion of values; indeed, that it performs especially this functional task and does so efficiently.

Thus we resolve the polemic between substantive and functional definitions. In the substantive sense the constituent elements of a religion are the values it teaches and propagates, whilst in the functional sense the task of religion, especially when it appears prevalently in a particular historicogeographical framework, is that of providing key linkage points for community life, social action, and the "rational choices" to be made in the light of established guidelines, and to be brought to life in everyday life and basic existential choices.

Table 16.2 Values of respondents

Particularistic values	
Attachment to the family	450 (62.6%)
Love of one's children	232 (32.3%)
Good use of money	69 (9.6%)
Managing by oneself	66 (9.2%)
Earning a lot	32 (4.5%)
Universal values	
Honesty, probity	532 (74.0%)
Faith in God	386 (53.7%)
Respect for others	213 (29.6%)
Having a clear conscience	131 (18.2%)
Attachment to work	120 (16.7%)
Friendship, solidarity	105 (14.6%)
Being content with little	99 (13.8%)
Generosity, charity	96 (13.4%)

Source: Cipriani 1992.

Content and Function of Religion

Our reading of the Italian situation is largely applicable to those social realities where a specific religious confession is conspicuously present and active in the area, with a hegemonic position.

> In fact, religion, which never really stopped playing its part in society, has reappeared beneath the surface of secularization. Even if we admit that there has been a significant occlusion, this has only involved secondary, external and formal aspects, especially at the level of ritual. The decline in participation at official, preordained services has not thus meant the end of every resort to the sacred. The trajectory of religiosity is not set towards definitive extinction. Simultaneously, secular impulses seem also to have exhausted their impetus. Their efficacy now affects only the less fundamental aspects of belief, which tends to remain in essence more or less stable. Between religiosity and secularization there seems to reign almost a tacit compromise. They are reinforced and weaken virtually in unison. Aspects steeped in religion continue (or return) to manifest themselves in secular reality, whilst in the reality of the church and of religious culture we see a progressive surrender to demands that are less orthodox from the viewpoint of the official model. (Cipriani 1994:277)

The case of Rome, described as the Holy City *par excellence*, even though it is heavily secularized, is emblematic. The world capital of Catholicism, the meetingplace of universal import for millions of pilgrims in the jubilee year, 2000, manifests rather low levels of religious practice. That which is described as regular, once a week, stands at 23.3% (Cipriani 1997b), whilst 22.1% never go to mass. Yet the number who pray is significant – 71.5% of those interviewed. Some turn to prayer only a few times a year (14.9%) and some much more often, like the 32% who do so one or more times every day. This means that there is at once slight attachment to practice and a broad interest in prayer, so religion lies not wholly in ritualism. Rather, the most frequent link with divinity runs through prayer, a direct conversation, at the interpersonal level. In this regard we might argue that whereas practice of the festal mass is linked more to church religion, that of recourse to prayer may have a more spontaneous character, free and removed from social control, but nonetheless an index that reveals a belief, a tie, a sensitivity at the religious level. In practice, if Rome is not by any means a city of many practitioners, neither is it one with many atheists, agnostics, or religiously indifferent people (however, it should be noted that 21.3 percent of those interviewed – the highest number in all the country – show no sign of religiosity at all). The capital of Italy manifests in a heightened manner some of the characteristics revealed in the 1994–5 study on "religiosity in Italy" through a national sample (Cesareo et al. 1995). For example, in a year a mere 7.6 percent had taken part in pilgrimages and 13.6 percent had made or satisfied a vow. Essentially, the Romans' religion is two-sided: on the one hand it appears imbued with a dramatic crisis, on the other it seems quite lively (though at a due distance from the habits of the official church). The religious future of the city seems destined to proceed along these two parts, divergent yet parallel.

The same may be said in general for Italy, though with certain essential differences.

> A double religion is the result: a majority and a minority religion, explicable also in terms of the historic presence of the Catholic church in Italy in the past century and especially since the Second World War. The Italian minority religion is for those who identify with the church quite closely and also involve themselves significantly in religious practices. The majority religion, on the contrary, lacks these characteristics. (Cipriani 1994:281)

This majority religion is rooted in the individual conscience, guided by the law of God, according to 40.4 percent of those interviewed in a systematic sample of 4,500 (Cesareo et al. 1995:180): in individual conscience alone in 36% of those sampled, and exclusively in the law of God for 22.1%. On the level of values lived with satisfaction, we find first the family that can be depended upon (73% of the sample), followed by working honestly and with commitment (68%) and having friends (38%). A smaller response was obtained as regards devotion to others (25%) and commitment to changing society (22%).

The overall picture is a varied one, but it confirms the image of religiosity diffused but fractal, tattered, with heterogeneous outlines. According to the results of the cluster analysis, 32% of the sample could be classified as belonging to church religion, 59.1% to diffused or modal religion, and 8.9% to no religion.

Table 16.3   Attitudinal and behavioral groupings

Groupings	Percentages
1 Church-oriented religion (heterodirected)	9.4
2 Reflexive church religion (self-directed)	22.6
Church religion total (1 + 2)	*32.0*
3 Modal primary (diffused) religion	16.5
4 Modal intermediary (diffused) religion	21.6
5 Modal perimetric (diffused) religion	21.0
Diffused or modal religion total (3 + 4 + 5)	*59.1*
Continuing religion total (1 + 2 + 3 + 4 + 5)	*91.1*
6 No religion	8.9
Overall total (1 + 2 + 3 + 4 + 5 + 6)	*100.0*

Source: Cesareo et al. 1995: 146.

The proportions of Italian religiosity demonstrate the typology shown in table 16.3.

As can be seen from the percentage of the six attitudinal and behavioral classes, religion in the broad sense (church or diffused/modal) is largely preponderant and clearly almost all of Catholic type. Church religion is in a minority percentage-wise, and diffused religion (called modal, as statistically it is in practice the mode, the characteristic with the greatest frequency) is the majority. But between minority and majority there is no break. Indeed it is often hard to establish the distinction between one and the other, especially between reflexive church religion (more autonomous and individualized, less inclined to accept the directives of official ecclesiastical teaching), and primary diffused or modal religion (more diversified as regards church membership). In fact, church and diffused or modal religion are in close relation with one another, the second arising from the first, whereby one can speak of a genuine religious continuum which involves 91.1 percent of those interviewed, without breaks or interruptions in the religious argument and its content, especially in the field of values.

Even more convincing, if that is possible, is what emerges from the more recent (March–April 1999) international comparative study on Europe and the United States on "religious and moral pluralism," involving in Italy the universities of Turin, Padua, Trieste, Bologna, and Rome. The Italian sampling was carried out by Doxa and involved 2,149 interviews (1,032 males and 1,117 females from 18 and upwards), carried out in 742 cases in provincial capital cities and in 1,407 cases in noncapital centers: 97.5% said they were Catholic; 31.2% said they were very close to the church and 45.5% close to it; 51.1% remembered that at 12 years old they went to church at least once a week, but 21.7% spoke of more than once a week, and 6.7% of daily participation in religious functions.

Significant confirmation of satisfaction with religion comes from the judgment of whether it was more or less important: 22.2 percent said a little more, and 12.8 percent much more.

As for the relation between education and religion, a very close link is taken for granted, especially if we bear in mind that 35.9 percent seemed to be much influenced by the education they received.

It should also be noted that 81.2 percent of those surveyed explicitly owned to belonging to a church, confession, group, or religious community.

Finally, 86.4 percent said they used prayer, though with differences both quantitative (once or more) and temporal (daily or during the year).

The following characteristics seem definitely established:

1   The essential content of religion is values, much more than rituals and beliefs.
2   The function of religion appears to be that of diffusing values.

Thus religion can be understood as basically an agent for diffusing values.

Conclusion

The concept of diffused religion has often been employed over the last 15 years to test its heuristic efficacy. Starting from an initial applicability to the Italian case, it is possible to move on to presenting it in other contexts in which the centrality and size of a specific religious confession are characteristic.

However, the most significant result is the demonstration of the centrality of values as the base of every religious expression. Beyond the socializing, consoling participation in ceremonies and belief or faith in something which in sociological terms escapes any empirical analysis, it is perhaps values which serve as the master key of the religious system.

The Italian philosopher Giambattista Vico (1983:600) was thus correct when about three centuries ago he wrote that "religions are the only means by which men can understand virtuous behavior and practice it."

References

Berger, P.L. and Luckmann, T. 1966. *The Social Construction of Reality*. Garden City, NY: Doubleday.

Blumer, H. 1954. "What is Wrong with Social Theory?" *American Sociological Review* 19(1):3–10.

Calvaruso, C. and Abbruzzese, S. 1985. *Indagine sui valori in Italia. Dai postmaterialismi alla ricerca di senso* [*An Inquiry into Values in Italy: From Postmaterialism to the Quest for Meaning*]. Turin: SEI.

Cesareo, V., Cipriani, R., Garelli, F., Lanzetti, C., and Rovati, G. 1995. *La religiosità in Italia* [*Religiosity in Italy*]. Milan: Mondadori.

Cipriani, R. 1984. "Religion and Politics. The Italian Case: Diffused Religion," *Archives de Sciences Sociales des Religions* 58(1):29–51.

Cipriani, R. 1989. " 'Diffused religion' and New Values in Italy," in *The Changing Face of Religion*, Eds. J.A. Beckford and T. Luckmann. London: Sage, pp. 24–48.

Cipriani, R. 1992. *La religione dei valori. Indagine nella Sicilia centrale* [*Religion of Values. A Survey in Central Sicily*]. Caltanissetta-Roma: Sciascia.

Cipriani, R. 1993. "De la religion diffuse à la religion des valeurs," *Social Compass* 40(1):91–100.

Cipriani, R. 1994. "Religiosity, Religious Secularism and Secular Religions," *International Social Science Journal* 140(June):277–84.

Cipriani, R. 1997a. *Manuale di sociologia della religione* [*Handbook of Sociology of Religion*]. Rome: Borla.

Cipriani, R. 1997b. *La religiosità a Roma* [*Religiosity in Rome*]. Rome: Bulzoni.

Durkheim, E. 1995. *The Elementary Forms of Religious Life*. New York: Free Press.

Luckmann, T. 1967. *The Invisible Religion. The Transformation of Symbols in Industrial Society*. New York: Macmillan.

Vico, G. 1983. *Autobiografia. Poesie. Scienza Nuova* [*Autobiography. Poems. New Science*]. Milan: Garzanti.

CHAPTER 17
Spirituality and Spiritual Practice

Robert Wuthnow

One of the more important developments in sociology of religion has been its recent interest in spirituality and spiritual practice. Earlier studies examined such aspects of personal religiosity as belief in God, views of the Bible, and church attendance, and some research focused on religious experience and religious consciousness. But it has been only in the past 15 years that spirituality has come to be regarded as a topic that is not entirely understandable in terms of these familiar concepts.

This scholarly interest in spirituality has emerged because of the growing popularity of the term in the wider culture. Although they may have only vague ideas about the meaning of spirituality, many people distinguish it from religion. "Religion is structure, an institution. It limits you. Spirituality is something you are." This statement by a man in his sixties is typical of the distinction many Americans draw between religion and spirituality.

The distinction between spirituality and religion frequently casts the former in a more favorable light than the latter. A woman in her forties says she is more comfortable with spirituality than with religion because "spirituality is about an experience" whereas "religion is more about a belief system and a doctrine describing that experience." Another woman expresses the same preference "because religion feels restrictive and spirituality feels inclusive." A middle-aged man elaborates: "Religion represents the institutionalized essence of spirituality, and the nature of the process is that as it becomes institutionalized it becomes encrusted with traditions and inflexibility, and eventually becomes polluted with egotism and power."

These examples are notable because they point to a wider development in contemporary culture. Many people say their interest in spirituality is increasing, but they may or may not pursue this interest through organized religion. Spirituality is somehow more authentic, more personally compelling, an expression of their search for the sacred, while religion connotes a social arrangement that seems arbitrary, limiting, or at best convenient.

This sharp distinction between spirituality and religion has roots in religious teachings that encourage adherents to seek the truth on their own or to trust ultimately in God rather than in clergy or religious organizations. Yet it also raises questions about the character of contemporary religion and about the meaning of spirituality.

Spirituality in Social Context

For present purposes, spirituality can be defined as a state of being related to a divine, supernatural, or transcendent order of reality or, alternatively, as a sense or awareness of a suprareality that goes beyond life as ordinarily experienced. Interest in spirituality is commonly expressed in beliefs about God and other divine beings, such as angels, and in experiences of such beings. But spirituality is not limited to such beliefs. For instance, some people refer to the spiritual as that which lies beyond the filtered experiences available to us because of our cultural categories; others use the term spiritual to designate that which encompasses all of physical, emotional, and mental experience.

One way of thinking about the spiritual transformation of the past century is in terms of rising individualism (Luckmann 1967, Bellah et al. 1985). Seeing the lack of seriousness with which many Americans take religious institutions, some observers argue that we are becoming increasingly private about our faith. The emphasis on *spirituality* (as opposed to "religion"), they would say, attests to this shift. People are retreating inward, focusing on themselves, and searching in a vacuum, rather than relying on their friends and neighbors, bearing their social responsibilities, and finding sustenance from congregations and clergy.

But this theory does not correspond well with the facts. Many people who practice spirituality in their own ways still go to church or synagogue. They may not be social activists who attend every meeting of the city council, but they vote, stay abreast of important community issues, do volunteer work, and contribute to the social good through their jobs. Their spirituality is an important part of their private life, but they participate in groups, talk about the sacred with friends, and try to help them with their spiritual journeys. They contribute in relatively small ways to their community and are willing to move on and make new friends when the need arises. But this does not mean they are devoid of community attachments.

Another way of interpreting changes in American spirituality is to argue that the country is experiencing a prolonged culture war in which the defenders of tradition are squaring off against the proponents of change (Hunter 1991). In this interpretation, interest in spirituality is sometimes associated with progressive worldviews that are morally relativistic, whereas commitment to traditional religion is taken as a mark of a more orthodox worldview. The culture war argument makes sense of debates that have surfaced in recent decades over such issues as abortion, pornography, homosexuality, school prayer, family values,

and decency in art and literature. These debates are not unrelated to realign-
ments in religious institutions, such as the declining authority of separate
denominational traditions and the rise of special interest groups. Yet the culture
war thesis is better at making sense of the rhetoric of interest groups than of the
hearts and minds of average Americans (Brint 1992, Himmelstein 1990, Wolfe
1998).

We might also think about changes in spirituality by drawing from the literature on secularization. This literature emphasizes the decline of religion's influence over other realms of social life, such as politics or the economy (Wilson
1982, Martin 1978). These declines have been widely discussed in recent years,
especially by writers who decry the maginalization of religion in public life. Yet
their concern is almost entirely with government and with the ramifications of
church–state issues in the courts. They have paid little attention to the quality
of spirituality in the personal lives of ordinary Americans. If secularization
theory is relevant to the study of spirituality, it certainly needs to focus more on
the ways in which cultural changes influence the quality of personal religiosity
and not simply the ways in which religion is positioned in public life.

The problem with all these interpretations is that they fail to consider seriously enough *how* we are spiritual. Inadvertently, they often perpetuate an antiquated way of looking at religion, namely, describing spirituality in terms of
conformity with established religious institutions. Those who say that nothing
has changed rely on evidence reported by religious institutions rather than
looking at qualitative differences in the ways that people are spiritual. Arguments about individualism stress the value of institutions, but fail to consider
how institutions are changing or to see that nonparticipation in established
institutions can mean something other than rampant individualism. Discussions of culture wars and fringe movements ostensibly focus on the quality of
spirituality, but take their cues from the public pronouncements of leaders and
groups. Much of the literature on baby boomers, while hinting that something
fundamentally new is happening, has been concerned with whether or not baby
boomers are returning to the religious communities in which they were reared.
And secularization theory has been preoccupied with influence and decline,
rather than qualitative changes in spirituality itself.

A generation ago, Thomas Luckmann diagnosed the underlying problem. He
observed that individual spirituality was seldom understood in the social sciences as being anything but a set of attitudes and opinions that were "naively,"
in his words, "for or against a given church or denomination" (1967:25). As a
result of this failure to better understand the peculiar position of the self in
modern society, Luckmann believed, sociology of religion had cut itself off from
the most important theoretical and practical questions of our time.

Given the attention that religion has received in scholarly studies in the intervening decades, this problem should have been overcome. Yet most discussions
of personal religion, including Luckmann's own, have made little headway –
precisely because they still take religious institutions as their starting point.
Thus, many discussions of contemporary religion focus on its private character

and emphasize the fact that people do not go to church. Others, especially among those who advocate a new paradigm for the sociology of religion, argue that Luckmann and others fail to understand American religion because organizational involvement is still quite widespread in American society (Warner 1993). What neither side has adequately dealt with, however, are the changing ways in which individuals are involved religiously and what the social dimensions of these involvements may be. For all these reasons, then, it seem valuable to focus less on institutions and institutional membership and more on the spiritual practices that constitute spirituality in everyday life.

Spiritual Practice

Spiritual practice refers to those activities in which individuals engage in order to become more aware of their spirituality or to enrich and grow in their spiritual lives. Whereas spirituality indicates a transcendent state of being or an ineffable aspect of reality, spiritual practice is a more active or intentional form of behavior. For example, people often regard prayer or reading religious books as a spiritual practice, while others emphasize meditation, chanting, or participation in group rituals.

The main theoretical orientations toward religion in the social sciences have always paid some attention to spiritual practices, although it is often difficult to glean much from these works that is directly relevant to the present situation. Weber, for example, deals with prayer and Bible reading in only a few scattered passages in his extensive treatment of religion in *Economy and Society* ([1992] 1978) and Troeltsch's *Social Teaching of the Christian Churches* ([1931] 1960) is valuable mostly in suggesting the inherent tensions between institutional religion and those forms of private devotion that lead to a "purely spiritual religion." Among this generation of writers, William James is perhaps most worthy of continuing attention because of his insistence on the centrality of prayer to any understanding of religion. He writes:

> Religion is nothing if it be not the vital act by which the entire mind seeks to save itself by clinging to the principle from which it draws life. This act is prayer, by which term I understand no vain exercise of words, no mere repetition of certain sacred formulae, but the very movement itself of the soul, putting itself in a personal relation of contact with the mysterious power of which it feels the presence. . . . Wherever this interior prayer is lacking, there is no religion; wherever, on the other hand, this prayer rises and stirs the soul, even in the absence of forms or of doctrines, we have living religion. (James [1902] 1958:352)

James also correctly sees that spiritual practices must be understood in relation to different conceptions of the self; yet his emphasis on the contrast between healthy and sick conceptions of the soul needs to be superseded. What these and other perspectives in the social sciences suggest is mainly the idea that spiritual practices should not be examined in isolation, but should be considered to have *meaning* – both to the practitioner and to the wider society – and thus must be understood in relation to the cultural circumstances in which they arise.

From its inception, systematic empirical research on American religion recognized the importance of spiritual practices, although the term itself was generally not used. These studies were often limited, focusing more on organized religion than on spiritual practices, or treating the latter as a kind of mystical or deviant expression of spirituality. Nevertheless, measures of devotionalism were included, for instance, in Gordon Allport's (1950) surveys of college students in the 1930s and 1940s and in the Detroit, Episcopal, and Catholic surveys conducted by Gerhard Lenski (1961), Charles Glock et al. (1967), and Joseph Fichter (1951). Glock's influential article on the "five dimensions" of religiosity paid particular attention to "religious practice" and his subsequent work among California church members provided evidence on the extent of prayer and other spiritual practices (Glock and Stark 1965). In Glock's conception, devotionalism was a norm of institutional religion; church members could conform or deviate from this norm. There was little effort to move toward a more complete understanding of spiritual practices.

During the 1970s and 1980s, most large-scale surveys of American religious life dealt with spiritual practice to a limited degree by including an occasional question about frequency of prayer; occasionally, evidence about Bible reading, meditation, and personal religious experiences was also obtained. Besides surveys, some evidence on spiritual practices has also been gathered in community studies, through in-depth interviews and participant observation in congregations and religious movements, and by historians. The qualitative evidence has been relatively sparse, but adds a great deal in interpreting exactly what people do devotionally, why they do it, and what it means to them. Some of this research is rich, but deals with spiritual practices more in fringe groups than in mainstream settings; much of it treats spiritual practice as a peripheral issue in relation to questions focusing on congregational leadership and organization, the growth and decline of denominations, or theological education. Some of this literature suggests that spirituality is changing, but does not examine how spiritual practices may be implicated in these changes.

It is safe to say that the major scholarly interpretations of how American religion is changing – and of the challenges facing it – have paid relatively little attention to the spiritual life. One thinks, for example, of the literature on the decline of mainline Protestant denominations, controversies over abortion and homosexuality, gender, culture wars, changes in American Catholicism, theological education, religion in higher education, congregations and clergy leadership, new immigrants, black churches, and baby boomers. Many of these studies argue that major changes have been taking place in the institutional life of American religion. Yet the assumption seems to be that these crucibles of spirituality can change without influencing significantly how ordinary people pray or meditate or understand their relationships to God in everyday life.

As a result of this neglect, questions have been asked both in the media and in scholarly studies, as well as in churches and synagogues, that cannot be answered very well: are people really interested in cultivating their spirituality, or is the present interest in spirituality superficial (if not flaky)? Is this current interest in spirituality different than in previous decades; for instance, are people more obsessed with themselves now and less influenced by theological wisdom? Is the very tendency to speak of "spirituality" symptomatic of some shift in how we believe the sacred can be approached in daily life?

In grappling with these questions, scholars and religious leaders have, of course, been talking about personal spirituality. But the conversation often fails to be joined because so many different things are meant by this term: everything from mysticism to introspection to broader world views. Indeed, some of the debate seems to focus on institutional questions to the point that there is little awareness of what people "out there" are really saying, while other discussions focus so much on subjective beliefs that it is hard to tell if anything concrete is known about the actual practice of spirituality.

Despite the growing emphasis on spirituality in the wider public, there are thus at least three reasons why greater attention to spiritual practices is needed in scholarly research. First, we still know relatively little about what people do and how they understand what they do. Most studies of spiritual practices have been limited to a few questions about frequency of prayer, table grace, and the like. Some studies have focused on isolated spiritual activities, such as prayer, and have compared people who pray with those who do not, rather than examining the full cluster of spiritual practices in which people engage. Other studies treat prayer only as one among several indicators of "religiosity." For these reasons, one finds reports in the national media that are truly difficult to interpret – for instance, *Life* (1994) magazine's report a few years ago that 28 percent of the American public prays for an hour or more daily.

Few studies have tried to examine the ways in which spiritual practices develop and change over the course of a person's lifetime or to situate these in relation to changing patterns of institutional affiliation. Nor has much attention been paid to the ways in which people interpret these activities in terms of their understandings of spirituality or in relation to official church teachings about spiritual practices. And much less attention has been given to the possibility that changes in American culture may affect the quality and meaning of these practices, rather than simply influencing the likelihood of people doing them at all.

A second reason for research to focus on spiritual practice is the debate already mentioned concerning the nature of spirituality. Researchers studying baby boomers, small groups, feminism, and new religious movements have observed the growing number of people who disclaim interest in religion but who are vitally concerned with spirituality. Some conclude that spirituality is so private – and perhaps narcissistic – that it does not amount to much. Others argue that the current interest in spirituality indicates an awakening to the sacred that may have far-reaching consequences. The problem in settling this debate – or even shedding light on it – is that spirituality is too vague a term to

have concrete meaning. The discussion needs to move beyond vague generalizations about a new mood or a new voluntarism or me-ism. It needs to benefit
from examining what people actually do to pursue their spirituality. Spiritual
practices are clear observable activities that people can talk about. What people
do devotionally gives us a window into their spirituality.

And third, the relationship between spiritual practice and organized religion
appears to be increasingly problematic. In addition to the fact that many people
now distinguish "religion" and "spirituality," there has probably been a shift
toward a greater variety of spiritual practices as well. Until as recently as the
1950s, most Americans' spiritual practices were performed under the direct or
indirect auspices of a congregation or denomination. Many Catholics, for
instance, followed "paraliturgical" practices, and many Protestants said
morning and evening prayers or conducted family devotions using guides provided by their churches (Taves 1986:48). That clearly is no longer the case. The
information explosion of the past 30 years has influenced spiritual practices as
well. People can now shop among a wide variety of meditation guides, attend
groups of all kinds, and take their cues about devotionalism from any number
of sources.

This does not mean, as some have tried to argue, that churchgoing itself is
becoming less important. It does mean that the *meaning* of religious participation may be changing. There may be a looser connection between it, for instance,
and one's spiritual practices. Indeed, this possibility suggests that we may need
to reorient our thinking about how best to understand spirituality and religion.
Rather than assuming that congregations are the main places where spirituality happens, it may be valuable to entertain the possibility that everyday life is
the main place where spirituality happens – through spiritual practices, among
other things – and that congregations are merely one (albeit important) place
where individuals seek to enrich or to express their spirituality.

The concept of practice has a distinct meaning in the social sciences owing
to the work of Alasdair MacIntyre (1984), Jeffrey Stout (1988), and others. Mac-
Intyre writes:

> By a "practice" I am going to mean any coherent and complex form of socially
> established cooperative human activity through which goods internal to that form
> of activity are realized in the course of trying to achieve those standards of excel-
> lence which are appropriate to, and partially definitive of, that form of activity, with
> the result that human powers to achieve excellence, and human conceptions of
> the ends and goods involved, are systematically extended. (1984:187)

Practices are thus clusters of activities in which individuals engage deliberately,
alone or in the company of others, and they follow social norms that define and
govern the pursuit of certain ends that are deemed intrinsically worthwhile.
Spiritual practice is a cluster of intentional activities concerned with relating to
the sacred. It may result in extraordinary experiences, but it generally takes place
in ordinary life.

In contrast to institutions (that focus our attention on organizations, leadership, power, status, and conformity), practices feature the loosely structured behavior of individuals. Practices are not performed without rules and they are not devoid of rewards. One thinks of chess or medicine as practices. But most practices are embedded in ordinary life and their rules are difficult to codify. A focus on practices helps orient our thinking to the fact that spirituality exists in the complex and fragmented arena of contemporary society. It frees us from thinking of religion only in terms of participation in congregations or other communities and focuses attention on the fact that individuals exercise "agency" in their choice of activities through which they seek a relationship to the sacred.

The current emphasis on practice reflects a broader shift in our understandings of how we come to know what we know and of how we apply our knowledge to the ways we live. This shift is actually a return to the wisdom of earlier civilizations and of ancient religious traditions. Throughout most of history, people absorbed knowledge through the stories they heard, retold, and invented. These stories provided them with practical knowledge about how to live. Gradually, between the sixteenth and nineteenth centuries, however, science, metaphysics, and philosophy attempted to develop abstract conceptions of knowledge and to create complex intellectual systems by which people were expected to live. These developments were enormously helpful in broadening intellectual horizons and in imposing rational processes on social behavior. But these developments were *not* effective in providing formulae for everyday life. Increasingly, we are coming back to the realization that our knowledge is rooted more in stories and in partial understandings of what we do than in abstract theoretical formulae.

Because many different activities may qualify as spiritual practice, it is useful to draw some distinctions among them. *Devotional practices* are activities performed for the purpose of focusing one's attention on the divine and they usually include efforts to communicate petitions or expressions of worship or gratitude to the divine. Devotional practices have generally been regarded as an essential aspect of religious life in all religious traditions. Drawing inspiration from the Bible or comparable sacred texts and from the lives of saints and other religious leaders, clergy have encouraged the faithful not only to attend public worship services but also to allocate some time in their personal lives to prayer, meditation, study, inspirational reading, or other activities, such as ritualized breathing or chanting. Among Christians, most church constitutions and catechisms refer to the value of private prayer and other acts of worship or religious observance in daily life. In recent years, there appears to be a resurgence of interest in devotional practices. Classic works, such as those of Teresa of Avila, John of the Cross, and Francis de Sales, are being reexamined. Congregations sponsor small groups aimed at teaching members how to pray and meditate, seminaries are offering popular continuing education courses on these topics for laity, and countless devotional guides and meditation books have appeared in the popular market.

Practices aimed at *enriching a person's spiritual life* point to a somewhat wider variety of possible activities, such as attending catechism classes, participating in small Bible study or fellowship groups, attending weekend retreats, reading books about religious history or going to a seminary. These practices are seldom aimed at communicating directly with the sacred in the same way that devotional activities are, but they contribute to the understandings and inter- pretations that surround devotional activities. They are typically regarded as important activities to be sponsored by religious organizations, providing struc- ture that encourages spiritual "growth" or "formation." The fact that they are regarded as means toward the attainment of a closer relationship with the divine is one reason people mention for distinguishing religion from spirituality.

Practices aimed at *expressing spirituality* may also be distinguished from devo- tional activities: rather than focusing on direct communication with the divine they result from an awareness of this relationship. Some people say they sing, for example, not to gain contact with the divine, but to give praise for their expe- riences of divine guidance and comfort. Art appears to be one of the enduring ways in which people express their spirituality. For some people, visual arts such as painting and sculpture provide a way to articulate half-formed feelings about the existence of the sacred; for others, poetry or music may serve a similar purpose.

Practices that *derive from a person's relationship to the sacred*, such as service or hospitality, are also worth distinguishing. These practices may be similar to those that express spirituality because they arise from a feeling or awareness of divine love. But they may also be guided more by intellectual reflection on religious teachings; for example, people may be motivated to serve others by reading sacred texts advising them to do so. Most religious teachings in fact draw a con- nection between the more direct sense of relationship to the divine that may be experienced during times of devotion and the desire to be of service to others or to be faithful in one's work. Other such practices include stewardship or the responsible use of time and money, attempts to utilize personal talents for divine glory, such as in sports or through scholarly endeavors, and efforts to lead exem- plary moral lives (Bass 1997).

The common aspects of spiritual practices are that they are intentional, they are oriented toward the attainment of internal or intrinsic goods, they are embedded in social institutions, they imply moral obligations (or a commitment to follow certain norms), they require interpretation or self-reflection, they have histories, and they are interlaced with other practices. Each of these character- istics requires some explanation.

Intentionality

Some discussions treat spirituality as a set of convictions or an implicit world- view that is largely taken for granted. Contrary to this view, the idea of practice treats spirituality as something people decide to do. Practicing architecture or becoming good at soccer requires deciding both to learn it and to do it on any given day. Spiritual practice points to deliberate ways of seeking contact with the divine, rather than only taking for granted the divine's existence. This is not to deny that practices become habitual. Unlike a set of techniques, they become sufficiently part of people's lives that they do not have to think about each step. Still, *human* practice is deliberate as long as one can choose to do otherwise. And deliberate actions are not only voluntary, but actions about which we deliberate. They are actions, Aristotle argued, "where the result is obscure and the right course not clearly defined" (1976:119). They require us to determine how best to proceed.

Intrinsic rewards

The primary rewards that come from participating in a practice are, by definition, internal to the practice itself. The joy of worship, for example, is an *internal good* that can be obtained only by worshiping. In contrast, external goods are the prestige, status, and money that may result as by-products of a practice, but have no specific connection with that practice. Worshipers may elevate their status in the community, for example, but could achieve the same results by playing golf at an exclusive country club. The internal goods that derive from spiritual practice are still aptly described in the words of William James: "the feelings, acts, and experiences of [individuals] in their solitude, so far as they apprehend themselves to stand in relation to whatever they may consider the divine" (1958:42).

Practices are embedded

Resources – time, energy, money, facilities, guides, instructional material – are required to engage in any practice (Little League baseball is an example). Institutions develop as ways to organize these resources. Practices thus depend on institutions and these institutions help to encourage practices. Despite people's insistence that spirituality is different from religion, spiritual practice depends on a vast network of churches and synagogues, clergy, seminaries, church-related colleges, religious studies departments, publishing houses, bookstores, periodicals, recording artists, speakers' bureaus, and retreat centers. A person wishing to read the writings of a desert monk, for instance, is aided by the fact that some publishing company has printed the monk's works. Nevertheless, tension is inherent because institutions and practices are fundamentally concerned with different things. As one writer observes, religion is "a hodgepodge of funds, properties, projects, and offices, all urgently requiring economic support." Maintaining these activities may be contrary to some of the principles of religion itself. As this writer further observes, "the building fund can be preserved by crude applications of money, but the fowls of the air and the lilies of the field can be preserved only by . . . the *practice* of a proper love and respect for them as the creatures of God" (Berry 1990:96).

Practice implies moral responsibility

By learning the rules of a practice and by choosing to observe (or violate) these rules, practitioners are inevitably engaged in moral choices (moral in the Durkheimian sense of feeling constrained by social norms that carry authority). They learn that actions have consequences and they feel constrained by the logic of their practices, rather than feeling entirely free to do whatever they please. Spiritual practice always involves mastering a certain degree of technical knowledge – say, knowing where favorite passages of a sacred text are located, memorizing a prayer, or knowing what bookstores to shop at for books about prayer. But practices involve a shaping of the person as well: becoming habituated to the practice to the point that one can exercise wisdom when new situations face one with difficult judgments, learning how to get along with other practitioners, being willing to pay the costs that may be associated with one's principles, and knowing how to relate the practice to one's other obligations and areas of life. To practice is to accept the standards of evaluation that are part of a practice, such as the rules of a chess match or the expectations that govern whether one player is considered better than another. These standards need not be accepted blindly. Practitioners are often in the business of challenging norms as well as conforming to them. They may do this either by rebelling against some and accepting others or by staging collective movements aimed at altering the rules or creating a new game. But practitioners do recognize that there is a *binding* quality about these standards. They recognize, for instance, that other people (past and present) say that doing X is necessary for achieving Y. Practitioners may also recognize that if they make up their own rules they will pay certain costs for doing so.

Practice involves interpretation

Two people can operate spinning wheels: for one, this is a spiritual practice; for the other, it is not. The difference is interpretation (one thinks of Gandhi's spinning as a means of spiritual liberation). Practice requires us to know what we are doing. Interpretation occurs in many ways, ranging from grand theories to homespun advice. One of its key ingredients is what might be called "an understanding": a core narrative that provides coherence to a practice over time. Understandings are generally less concerned with abstract or theoretical knowledge than with practical wisdom for ordinary life. They are organized around stories, personal experience, and role models. Often they are fragmentary and difficult to articulate. But understandings are vital to the way we gain competence in a practice. We become habituated to a practice by engaging in it over an extended period of time. Understandings are ways to make sense of the chronology of our practices. We do this by telling stories about where we began, how we changed, and where we are going. Stories fix meaning to events by organizing them chronologically.

Practice implies history

This is because practices develop over time. They are emergent, unfolding, evolutionary. We do not engage in practices devoid of memory. Instead, we do things with partial knowledge of things that have worked or not worked in the past and with a sense of linking ourselves to or dissociating ourselves from the past. MacIntyre observes: "To enter into a practice is to enter into a relationship not only with its contemporary practitioners, but also with those who have preceded us in the practice, particularly those whose achievements extended the reach of the practice to its present point" (1984:194). Personal history (autobiography) lies at the core of spiritual practices. We make sense of what we are doing by telling stories that place ourselves in an unfolding series of actions and events. The stories we tell about our practices inevitably engage us in a conversation with the past. We talk about our current activities by comparing them with previous ones. We make significant comparisons between our own journeys and those of our parents. Having witnessed our parents' lives first hand, we readily make judgments about how similar – or different – our lives are from theirs. In this process, we also use public tales about the past as landmarks. These include theories – or public narratives – that try to depict social change. Even more significantly, they include public events: the noted happenings that provide us with a way of telling others how and when we have changed.

Practices are interlaced

We generally learn a practice in a specific setting (baseball on the ball field). Families and congregations remain the cradle of spiritual practices. Once learned, however, practices become intertwined with other practices. There is also the possibility that practices may be engaged in vicariously, that is, through reading or viewing, rather than firsthand participation. We would want to maintain the distinction between actually playing football and viewing it on television, of course. But it is also important to include vicarious participation in our understanding of practices because much of how we learn practices is, indeed, vicarious. Few of us, for example, have been desert mystics, yet we may have cultivated our own spirituality by reading their writings. Certainly spiritual practice includes the time one spends reflecting on the observations and experiences of others.

Research on spiritual practice suggests that it varies considerably in the self-consciousness and intensity with which people engage in its component activities. Many people pray occasionally, asking for divine help in emergencies or offering habitual statements of thanksgiving; relatively few expend time and energy on spiritual practices to the point that they master these practices in the way an expert chess player may master the game of chess.

The Social Construction of Spirituality

A sociological perspective on spiritual practice emphasizes the ways in which people's experience and understanding of spirituality may be influenced by social conditions. This perspective neither denies nor assumes that people's claims about spirituality are true or that the spiritual realm actually exists. Indeed, sociologists take differing views of these issues. For purposes of sociological investigation there is nevertheless strong agreement that claims about spirituality can usefully be examined in relation to social conditions but cannot be fully explained by or reduced to these conditions.

Spiritual practices are influenced by social conditions, just as other religious beliefs and activities are. Age, gender, level of education, region, and religious background are all likely to shape people's propensities to engage in spiritual practices as well as the content of these practices. For example, anecdotal evidence suggests that women are more likely to express interest in spiritual practices than men, and some evidence suggests that growing up in affluent circumstances gives people greater opportunities for exposure to esoteric or eclectic practices than growing up in less advantaged circumstances. Yet the relationships between spiritual practices and these kinds of demographic factors are inadequate for understanding the complex ways in which people use cultural materials to construct and interpret the meaning of their practices.

Many of these materials are of course learned as children, even though they may be reinterpreted as people mature. Accounts of spiritual journeys are rich with what is sometimes termed the "material culture" of religion: family Bibles, crucifixes, altars, wall hangings, pictures of Jesus, Mary, or an ancestor, stained glass windows, story books, and the like. These objects appear to be retained in adults' memories more vividly than creeds or abstract theological teachings. Adult spiritual practices often take shape around ways of retrieving the experiences associated with these objects. People often remember prayers they recited at bedtime as children and continue to say these prayers on special occasions. Some remember pictures of angels or saints who continue to guide their spiritual activities.

Holidays appear to be particularly rich influences on spiritual practices. Along with more regularly practiced rituals, such as Friday night Shabbat or Sunday dinners, they create sacred times that people remember with fondness and try to recreate in their own practices. It is for this reason that many people express concerns about the commercialization of holidays or speak favorably about efforts to promote voluntary observances of family rituals.

As people mature, their spiritual practices frequently undergo some distancing from the religious routines and institutions in which they have been raised. For many people, this distancing consists of switching to another denomination or faith tradition, while for others it includes a temporary break from or psychological rethinking of their tradition. Turning points, such as conversion experiences, crises of faith, divorces, illnesses, near-death experiences, and bereavement, often provide the occasions for such distancing.

Many people have well-rehearsed spiritual autobiographies that come from repeated efforts to make sense of their spiritual practices. Rather than describing their faith as a one-time commitment, they use the imagery of journeys to suggest how their spiritual practices have changed. This imagery gives legitimacy to the idea that practices should be pieced together in ways that people find personally rewarding and that they should change as new life situations emerge.

With many practices available in the wider religious marketplace, people often emphasize the immediate gratifications they receive from particular practices, or acknowledge that their practices are arbitrary. If exposure to diverse religious teachings erodes the plausibility of particular beliefs, practices appear to be somewhat more resistant to such erosion because they can be defended less as absolute truths and more as interchangeable activities through which people seek a common experience of the sacred. This may be one reason for the contemporary interest in spiritual practices.

Social Criticism and Spirituality

In addition to examining and attempting to understand spiritual practices, social science can contribute to critical reflection on the quality of these practices. When a society is driven by advertising and the quest for consumer markets, spiritual practices are likely to be influenced by these impulses as well. Critics of contemporary spiritual practices argue that they are often superficial because people expect instant gratification or switch from one activity to another rather than spending the time and energy necessary for mastering any particular tradition. Critics also assert that spiritual practices can easily become self-interested if they are not pursued in the context of communities and traditions that restrain them or discourage excesses that have created problems in the past.

Whatever the validity of these criticisms, spirituality appears to be attracting widespread attention not only among people who are interested in religion but among therapists, members of other helping professions such as medicine and nursing, artists, writers, and the media. Studies of spiritual practice are needed both to sort out its varieties and to understand how it is shaped by the culture.

References

Allport, G.W. 1950. *The Individual and His Religion: A Psychological Interpretation*. New York: Macmillan.

Aristotle. 1976. *Nicomachean Ethics*, Transl. J.A.K. Thomson. Baltimore, MD: Penguin Books.

Bass, D.C., Ed. 1997. *Practicing Our Faith: A Way of Life for a Searching People.* San Francisco: Jossey-Bass.

Bellah, R.N., Madsen, R., Sullivan, W.M., Swidler, A., and Tipton, S.M. 1985. *Habits of the Heart: Individualism and Commitment in American Life.* Berkeley and Los Angeles: University of California Press.

Berry, W. 1990. *What Are People For?* San Francisco: North Point Press.

Brint, S.B. 1992. "What If They Gave a War . . . ?" *Contemporary Sociology* 21:438–40.

Fichter, J.H. 1951. *Dynamics of a City Church.* Chicago: University of Chicago Press.

Glock, C.Y. and Stark, R. 1965. *Religion and Society in Tension.* Chicago: Rand McNally.

Glock, C.Y., Babbie, E.R., and Ringer, B. 1967. *To Comfort and To Challenge.* Berkeley and Los Angeles: University of California Press.

Himmelstein, J.L. 1990. *To the Right: The Transformation of American Conservatism.* Berkeley and Los Angeles: University of California Press.

Hunter, J.D. 1991. *Culture Wars: The Struggle to Define America.* New York: Basic Books.

James, W. 1958. *The Varieties of Religious Experience: A Study in Human Nature.* New York: New American Library.

Lenski, G. 1961. *The Religious Factor.* Garden City, NY: Doubleday.

Life. 1994. "Why We Pray." March:54–62.

Luckmann, T. 1967. *The Invisible Religion: the Problem of Religion in Modern Society.* New York: Macmillan.

MacIntyre, A. 1984. *After Virtue: A Study in Moral Theory*, 2nd edn. Notre Dame, IN: University of Notre Dame Press.

Martin, D. 1978. *A General Theory of Secularization.* New York: Harper & Row.

Stout, J. 1988. *Ethics After Babel: The Languages of Morals and Their Discontents.* Boston: Beacon.

Taves, A. 1986. *The Household of Faith: Roman Catholic Devotions in Mid-nineteenth-Century America.* Notre Dame, IN: University of Notre Dame Press.

Troeltsch, E. 1960. *The Social Teaching of the Christian Churches.* New York: Harper & Row.

Warner, R.S. 1993. "Work in Progress toward a New Paradigm for the Sociological Study of Religion in the United States," *American Journal of Sociology* 98:1044–93.

Weber, M. 1978. *Economy and Society*, vol. I, Eds. G. Roth and C. Wittich. Berkeley and Los Angeles: University of California Press.

Wilson, B. 1982. *Religion in Sociological Perspective.* Oxford: Oxford University Press.

Wolfe, A. 1998. *One Nation After All.* Boston: Viking.

CHAPTER 18

The Renaissance of Community Economic Development among African-American Churches in the 1990s

Katherine Day

Church-based Community Organizing and Community Economic Development

Currently there are two social movements seeking to address the quality of life in local communities throughout the United States. During the 1980s, community organizing experienced a renaissance, particularly as it came to be based in religious congregations. The increased popularity of church-based community organizing (CBCO) in the USA was aided by the reorientation of the Industrial Areas Foundation (IAF) towards congregations as a primary vehicle for organizing. Other community organizing networks, not nearly as large, but also based on the work of Saul Alinsky, followed suit. The recent growth of CBCO as indicated by the growth of community organizing networks has been stunning. For example, the IAF developed 12 new organizations around the country in as many years, between 1973 and 1985. In the next five years they doubled that number. Currently, there are over 40 local chapters in the USA, UK, and South Africa, all training members of their affiliated churches in leadership skills and organizing them to bring about change in their communities. By "organizing people and organizing money" – IAF's fundamental approach to developing power – local chapters have cultivated enough clout to have an impressive record of changes in policies and services to show for it: housing constructed, schools reorganized, jobs created, banks reoriented to community investment and community policing instituted.

There has been a concurrent growth trend of community economic development (CED). This umbrella incorporates all efforts to attract capital to a community or neighborhood and keep it there. It includes housing development, capital formation (credit unions and banks), job creation, and commercial development. Like community organizing, this resurgence of such locally based activity in the 1990s, after two decades of relative dormancy, recalls the "glory days" of the 1960s. Community organizing flourished during that decade of activism. Fueled (and funded) by the Great Society, and more specifically, the War on Poverty of the Johnson Administration, community economic development also found a fertile context in which to grow.

In their 1999 census of community development projects, the National Congress for Community Economic Development (NCCED) found that there are currently 3,600 organizations involved in bettering the economic health of poor and working-class communities. Their research shows that 600 of these organizations were newly formed during the 1990s and already had produced housing, jobs, and businesses in their short histories.

As with community organizing, it is the increasing involvement and leadership of communities of faith in this renaissance that is particularly noteworthy. The census showed that 14 percent of the CED organizations identified themselves as faith-based. This increase at the local level has been supported by a proliferation of resources at the national level which provide much-needed technical assistance. For example,

- The NCCED has a special program for the religious sector (Faith-based Community Economic Development Program), complete with staff and newsletter.
- A quasi-public training organization, the Neighborhood Reinvestment Training Institute, now regularly includes a two-day course on faith-based CED in its well-resourced and well-attended training conferences held twice a year.
- In addition, denominations often provide funding and training resources that provide further support of CED efforts initiated by local congregations or small coalitions of congregations.

Of course, community organizing and economic development often have parallel outcomes, low-income housing being the most visible. Both efforts seek to impact the lived quality of life in communities. However, relationships between community organizations and CED groups are often fraught with tension, even among faith-based activists. The inherent tensions revolve around two issues which are fundamental to the identities of CBCO's and CED organizations: their ultimate goals and the strategic approaches they employ.

While CED efforts focus on the economic well-being of a community, community organizing sees development projects only as the means to the larger goal – the empowerment of the people for self-determination. For many the CBCO, facilitated by the IAF and similar groups, represents the only viable hope for social change. One observer representing that perspective is political journalist William Greider: "American political history suggests that this kind of politics, difficult as it is, is the only kind that leads to genuine change" (Greider 1992:235).

Out of the goal of political empowerment and participation for CBCOs flows a strategic approach in which the differences with CED come into high relief. For

CBCO efforts, leadership is sought at the grassroots level and training is made available to cultivate confident and articulate "lay" activists. Further, organizational power is broadly shared rather than being concentrated in a few staff or clergy. As community organizations name issues and seek change, there can be confrontational tactics with those representing the status quo.

While there is, at times, overlap between the two orientations to community change represented by a few "hybrid" projects, the debate continues. In my own research with congregations employing the two different approaches in Philadelphia (Day 1996, in press), I identified four points of tension between the two models representing their differing goals and strategies:

1   *Clerical vs. shared leadership.* Central to CBCO is a commitment to expanding the leadership base to include representation of the constituency. Church-based CED projects tend to have centralized leadership, usually clergy acting as entrepreneur on behalf of a congregation and community. As a project matures, professional staff are hired to manage it.

2   *Parochial vs. coalitional organizing.* Economic development projects are more often sponsored by one church and focused on one clearly defined service area. In contrast, CBCO is generally broad-based – that is, bringing together a number of churches as a way of expanding the power base. Resulting projects (such as housing) may be scattered throughout a wider geographical area and impacted services (such as policing or educational reforms) benefit the whole city.

3   *Empowerment vs. access to power.* The most striking distinction between the two models is in their understanding of power. CBCOs seek to build a power base out of a broad foundation of people to leverage for change. Those organizing CED projects seek to access the power structure – rather than confronting it – to get much-needed resources.

4   *Change vs. status quo.* Those seeking resources for economic development projects do so through existing channels for the distribution of resources in both the public and private sectors. Community organizations also want "a piece of the pie," but if they encounter policies and programs of distribution they consider unjust, they will seek to change the recipe of the pie as well. CED projects are not willing to bite the hands that feed them.

African-American Church Social Movements

As congregations engage their communities, gravitating to either CBCO coalitions or the more entrepreneurial CED projects, there is a striking third social movement that is making a significant impact on the life of American cities. African-American churches are experiencing their own renaissance of community engagement. Yet they are less attracted to the CBCO strategy and are increasingly pursuing CED projects, often on a grand scale.

For many within the African-American community, it is the congregations, not the community organizing coalitions, that hold the key to more economically viable, self-determining communities. "If the black church doesn't do it, who will?" is often heard in conversations about community development.

This sentiment is more fully explored by Harold A. McDougall in his book, *Black Baltimore*. He credits much of the development in the neighborhoods of that city to the efforts of the African-American churches. He has a high level of respect for BUILD (Baltimoreans United In Leadership Development, an affiliate of IAF), yet shares a Weberian pessimism that large organizations eventually become bureaucratized, hierarchical, and indeed coopted by the very powers they initially seek to confront and change. Instead, he puts more faith in smaller units of development which are "more indigenous, more flexible, and more intimate" (McDougall 1993:110). Local congregations (not the "megachurches," he specifies) as well as smaller ministry groups, such as Habitat for Humanity, are better equipped to generate microenterprise development, rooted in what he calls the "vernacular culture" of the African-American community which values smaller social groupings.

My own research in Philadelphia churches (Day 1996, in press) suggests that the vernacular culture of many African-American churches seems more naturally suited to CED than to CBCO. The subcultures of these congregations maintain an understanding of leadership that is decidedly centralized in the pastor, rather than shared. There is a history of pastors, acting as representatives of their people, cultivating contacts within the power structures that might be accessed. These preachers then take on the role of entrepreneur, developing housing, credit unions or commercial strips within their immediate neighborhood. There is a suspicion that joining coalitions diffuses energy and dilutes the possibility of improving the quality of life within their corner of the city. While very few African-American pastors (and none in my study) would argue that the system of distribution of resources is entirely just, entrepreneurial pastors are not willing to challenge it.

Many African-American churches do join community-organizing coalitions in order to pursue the same goals of neighborhood betterment. The pastors of these congregations are more open to models of shared leadership. They have come to believe that as individual churches they cannot access enough power to bring significant change. Therefore, they are willing to defer their goals for local projects in order to participate in a larger power base. Emboldened by linking with like-minded communities of faith, they are more willing to participate in confrontational tactics involved in "holding accountable" public officials and bringing about political change.

However, black congregations are far less represented in CBCOs than in individual CED efforts, a source of frustration for the IAF and other organizing networks. There is a history, of course, of grassroots mobilization in the civil rights movement, which might be expected to have bred an affinity for CBCO. However, the contemporary multicultural coalitions do not pursue overtly race-based politics. Affiliating with these interracial coalitions represents the adoption of a new strategic approach among African-American members. While there is often an uneasiness expressed, and a sense of chosen compromise, those black clergy who do join CBCOs find that the understandings of leadership, power, and change resonate with their own understandings. Their political pragmatism often pays off in terms of housing development in the neighborhood, improvement in services, job creation, and the increased participation of their own people in the democratic process.

Still, as the century turns, it is clear that the resurgence of CED among black churches is the stronger stream – and better resourced – of the two approaches to community betterment. Within the resources developed to support CED in general, there is a more dramatic rise in the number of high caliber programs geared specifically toward supporting CED efforts within the African-American churches:

- Harvard Divinity School (in partnership with their Kennedy and Business Schools) holds an annual two-week program for clergy on CED. The 50 ministers who are selected ante up $3,300 in tuition.
- Under HUD secretary Henry Cisernos, an office was organized to link local faith-based CED efforts with federal programs – the Center for Community and Interfaith Partnerships. Staffed by African-Americans, it has continued to target black church development efforts.
- The training component for the Neighborhood Reinvestment Training Institute mentioned earlier has been contracted out to Interdenominational Theological College (ITC), a consortium of seminaries for the historic black churches, based in Atlanta. This puts flesh on President Robert Franklin's call to seminaries to "build the church's capacity to engage in comprehensive community development" (Franklin 1997:127).
- A plethora of publications by and for African-American clergy have come out in recent years which provide both theological rationale and how-to information on developing housing, credit unions, small businesses, and shopping centers.

This new wave of involvement with CED is not without strong historic precedent. African-American churches have always been involved in economic development, as "mutual aid," out of necessity. For example, Philadelphia has a rich history of church-based economic development in, by, and for the African-American community. W.E.B. DuBois documented a wide variety of economic activity in Philadelphia congregations during the late nineteenth century, ranging from employment services to cooperatives (DuBois [1899] 1970). Later, North Philadelphia served as the home base for Rev. Leon Sullivan (now retired) who, through his impressive development work in the community and through the establishment of the Opportunities Industrial Centers (OIC), left a strong legacy which continues to be a model for church-based CED. He has been described as "perhaps the most prominent example of the modern black minister involved in the complexities of economic development issues" (Lincoln and Mamiya 1990:264).

Sullivan's philosophy was that African-Americans needed more educational and employment opportunities in order to function as full participants in the economic system. During his tenure as the pastor of Zion Baptist Church on North Broad Street (1950–88) the OIC developed Progress Plaza, the first and largest shopping plaza developed by and for the African-American community. Beyond North Philadelphia, the OIC created training programs in 160 cities; by 1980 almost 700,000 people had received job training and employment placement. His influence extended beyond the United States. He is widely known as the author of the Sullivan Principles in the late 1970s (incorporated by the Reagan administration in its foreign policy) which were voluntary ethical guidelines for multinational corporations in South Africa. Rev. Sullivan did not attack apartheid directly or call for economic divestment until the end of the Reagan era. Until then he had hoped to preserve the corporate presence and employment opportunities for South African blacks, while urging their fair treatment.

Sullivan's operational philosophy of stressing self-help while maximizing opportunity, whether at an individual or collective level, has set a standard for many pastors interested in becoming involved in economic development. His approach relies on lone entrepreneurial pastors who access the system in order to get resources for development projects in their immediate neighborhoods. It has been, and continues to be, the dominant model for CED among African-American clergy.

African American Churches and Social Movement Theory

The historic roots of community development by black churches are easily identifiable. However, less clear are the factors contributing to the growth surge of CED activity among African-American churchfolk in the 1990s and into the next century. After all, the legacy of mutual aid and entrepreneurship leading to self-sufficiency have been part of the fabric for generations. But what is driving this renaissance?

In searching for an analytical tool with which to work on this question, the rubric of social movement theory appears to be helpful, although it is not a perfect fit. While clearly the widespread organization of resources and effort among African-American churches in the arena of CED is a social phenomenon, it does not meet the criteria of a *movement* as defined by sociologist Doug McAdam: "those organized efforts on the part of excluded groups to promote or resist change in the structure of society that involve recourse to non-institutional forms of political participation" (1982:25). Unlike community organizing, the current generation of CED activity does not seek to challenge or change the system of distribution of resources. Still, it is arguable that increasing the capital resources of the black community is, *de facto*, an effort aimed at "change in the structure of society," through accepted forms of participation in the political and economic system. Given that, it is defensible to utilize the tools of social movement theory in understanding the current increase in CED activity among black churches.

An important critic of earlier work on social movements, Doug McAdam expanded the field of factors which must be examined out of his own study of the political movements among African-Americans between 1930 and 1970. His approach, as well as more recent contributions of others writing in the field, provides a helpful lens for analyzing the dynamics at work leading some African American churches beyond traditional forms of ministry into participation in CED efforts.

McAdam's analysis begins with an examination of the external context, particularly the political realities. More specific than attention to the political culture stressed by others (e.g., Tarrow 1992), McAdam is looking for shifts in *political opportunities* – that is, those reversals of political fortunes, changes in policy makers, the sudden propulsion of a public issue, or social changes over time – any factors which alter the political landscape making it possible, although not inevitable, for new voices to emerge. But political changes only become opportunities when there is some preexisting organizational strength which becomes a vehicle for mobilization (*resources*). Congregations bring a number of critical elements to a social movement – members, leadership, communication networks, and capital (including buildings, funds, and the capacity to raise money). The institutional stability and resources they offer expedite movement-building when compared to the prospects of recruiting individuals.

McAdam goes on to argue that political opportunities and organizational strength are but preconditions to mobilization for social change. There also has to be a *transformation of consciousness*. Congregations come with their own collective identities, which have evolved out of their history and context, and find expression in their symbols, language, and ritual. The shared meanings that exist in congregations can, of course, serve to inhibit change. However, they can also promote change as they interpret grievances as injustice, and provide an ideological framework for understanding social suffering as morally intolerable. Interpreting unnecessary suffering as injustice is part of the moral discourse of religious communities. Elevating the grievance to moral outrage and a call to action can occur within the public expression of a congregation, through liturgy and sermon.

McAdam introduces a fourth component of social change movements which he considers the most critical. Even when grievance has been framed as injustice through the transformation of consciousness, even when there is a sense of intolerance and imperative (i.e., "This cannot continue! We must do something!") collective action is not inevitable. The potential actors must also be convinced that effectiveness is possible. Participation in a movement must be seen as a viable means for bringing change.

In summary, McAdam traces the potential for social change movement to the interaction of five variables, all necessary for mobilization to occur. As with any formula, timing is everything.

Shift in political opportunities → sense of grievance + moral imperative (if resources) + sense of viability = social action

Using this approach, the marked rise in economic development efforts on the part of African-American churches in the last decade becomes more understandable.

Shifts in political opportunities

After the infusion of federal resources into urban areas during the War on Poverty in the 1960s, with its myriad of programs for economic and social empowerment, there was a gradual retreat throughout the 1970s. Urban policy changes redirected monies to states, which could then parcel out "block grants" to cities, which in turn allocated support for economic development projects. The direct access to federal resources, which had been critical to the development of so many local CED projects, was lost. Additional layers of bureaucracy ate up resources and diffused the original goals of economic development.

The erosion of resources for local CED efforts accelerated dramatically during the Reagan administration. Federal programs for housing development and job creation were reduced to near extinction, as were resources for other social supports for the urban poor. This put additional burdens on local cities, particularly in the North, which were feeling the double stress of reduced federal (and tax) revenue and increased demand for social services.

This trajectory continued through the Bush administration. Although President Clinton did restore some of the federal government's attention to local economic development (such as through the development of "enterprise zones"), the legacy of the 1980s urban policy culminated in the near dismantlement of the welfare system in 1996. African-American churches particularly felt the brunt as increasing numbers of people in urban neighborhoods came to their doors with basic needs for food, clothing, shelter, health care and employment. For those with memory of programs such as Model Cities, which enabled housing development through local leadership, the state of urban policy in the late 1990s represents nothing short of a sea change. Political opportunities had shifted.

A heightened sense of grievance

As it was becoming clear that the federal government was no longer the major source of support for poor communities that it had once been, and a sense of abandonment was setting in, black churches began burning again, and in large numbers. During 1996 the media was filled with images of houses of worship in flames. Not all were black churches, and an organized national conspiracy was not found to be at work. Still, African-American churches were disproportionately targeted and racial hatred was often evident in the arson. Black churches, already feeling increasingly alone in responding to the economic needs of their people, now began to feel under siege. "If the black churches doesn't do it, who will?" was no longer a well-worn rhetorical question, but a realistic assessment of the economic and social conditions.

An emerging sense of imperative

Much of the historical and sociological study of African-American religion has revolved around the question of whether black churches are a vehicle of resistance or protest, or are agents of accommodation to the dominant culture (Marx 1967, Marable 1983, Wilmore 1983, Baer and Singer 1992). This is particularly evident in studies of clergy.

Given the current context, the heightened sense of moral imperative ("We've got to do something in light of these injustices!") is being articulated in forms that might not appear as expressions of resistance if using the lens of earlier models of analysis. Even the Million Man March, with its stress on family and community commitment, might have been judged as "accommodationist" by researchers a generation ago.

Yet the African-American church is an enormously complex set of traditions and institutions. The tensions that exist internally, in relation to the African-American community and to the dominant culture, are not easily understood in historical or sociological analyses. African-American churches are perhaps best understood in paradoxical terms, having seemingly contradictory realities which exist in "dialectical tension" (Lincoln and Mamiya 1990) or "ambiguity" (Marable 1983). That is to say, African-American religious expression can be at once accommodationist and resistant in relation to the dominant culture. Therefore, as voices such as Cornel West, Manning Marabel, ITC's Robert Franklin, Harvard Divinity's Preston Williams or Rep. Floyd Flake issue a call to action out of a heightened sense of grievance, it is to action which works through the existing economic system for the empowerment of the disenfranchised. The call is not to separatist or revolutionary goals which would challenge the fundamental principles of the economic system; rather the call is to understanding and utilizing economic structures with greater sophistication and commitment, and to greater advantage. Robert Franklin writes:

> public theologians should be stewards of community economic development. They should recognize the potential economic power of billions of dollars in aggregate income that African Americans receive and organize ways to harness it for community development. As we discovered in the Hampton survey, 57 percent of

(Black) clergy believe that churches should own for-profit businesses. Good stewards identify and seize opportunities to make financial resources work more effectively for the improvement of living conditions. (1997:123)

While that might sound accommodationist to earlier theorists, strains of resistance to the political and economic status quo are identifiable in what is communitarian strategy. The current articulations of moral imperative are not an encouragement for individualistic upward mobility. Rather they are rooted in racial politics: CED efforts should be of, by, and for the African-American community.

The 1990s also saw the mainstreaming of the cultural Afrocentrist movement. Kente cloth, African drumming, and exploration of traditional forms of tribal leadership could be found in the most conservative of churches, not signifying cultural separatism but ethnic identity. Reminiscent of the "black is beautiful" movement of the 1960s, the current expressions of Afrocentrism in churches reinforce cultural distinction.

This reinforces the paradoxical nature of African-American religion, particularly regarding economic betterment: economic development is needed in the community, utilizing existing structures, but not at the expense of a loss of cultural identity.

Resources in place

As the African-American community is confronted by the contemporary realities of diminishing government support as well as employment opportunities in areas of greatest need, it is only possible to contemplate social action in the context of a recognized set of resources.

A recent *Newsweek* article (Cose 1999) documented the increased upward mobility of African-Americans (as well as the persistent economic discrepancy with whites). Rates of college attendance, life expectancy, and income were rising while unemployment, infant mortality, and birth rates were on the decline. The same percentage (48%) of blacks and whites indicated in a survey that they felt that their family situation was better now than it had been five years before. When asked what had contributed to the improved conditions for African-Americans, more credited "black churches" (46%) than any other factor, governmental or social. The article highlights one church in Oakland, California (Allen Temple Baptist) as a critical factor in the survival of its neighborhood, having generated 20 million dollars worth of new construction projects.

This finding indicates that not only is there increased wealth among African-Americans – an important resource in itself – but that the church continues to have trust and legitimacy within the black community. Because of their historical commitment to economic development and its current momentum in this area, African-American churches stand poised to continue to serve as the center of CED activity for the community.

Churches, for the most part, represent a variety of resources: buildings, people, leadership training, legitimacy, connections, and media outlets. But other institutions and organizations, beyond the local churches, have also provided important resources, enabling increased participation in CED. The philanthropic community has focused considerable resources for black churches wanting to be involved in economic development, providing seed monies and technical assistance. Denominations, seminaries, and training programs (mentioned earlier in this article) have targeted black churches for leadership development in CED. Federal support, such as loosening up restrictions on the funding of faith-based programs, has added further fuel to the movement.

In summary, it is apparent that as black churches continue to engage economic development in their communities more frequently and effectively, they do not operate in a vacuum but in a context of acknowledged internal and external resources which are accessible.

A sense of viability

When a group of black clergy from Philadelphia were considering the possibility of establishing a local affiliate of the IAF, they began by visiting St. Paul's Baptist Church in East Brooklyn. The pastor, Rev. Johnnie Ray Youngblood, is well known for his dynamic pastoral ministry and for his community leadership. He had been instrumental in organizing an ecumenical coalition which took on the bombed-out neighborhood of Brownsville and transformed it into a redeveloped community of several thousand newly constructed town houses for low and moderate income first-time homebuyers. It is the modern equivalent of Ezekiel's field of dry bones which miraculously find flesh and new life. Even before the book documenting Youngblood's story was published (Freedman 1993) the Nehemiah homes of Brownsville had become somewhat of a pilgrimage destination for those church leaders hungry for demonstration of what was possible. There is nothing like bricks and mortar and an inspiring preacher telling the story to inspire a sense of viability.

The clergy returned to Philadelphia, exhilarated. They took the first steps toward establishing a community organizing coalition. The IAF group was launched and within a few years had 180 units of their own Nehemiah housing to show off. However, the original clergy did not feel comfortable with the IAF – particularly its notions about shared leadership. They withdrew from the ecumenical effort to pursue their own CED projects.

The predominant strategy for developing a sense of viability remains exposure to successful case studies, or models. A resulting taste of what is possible is the critical variable which can lead a community of faith from a heightened sense of grievance and imperative into action, rather than disillusionment, cynicism, rage, or despair. Currently many such successful CED projects exist, and they are widely utilized. Such case studies are peppered throughout the plethora of books and articles on black church involvement in economic development (whether foundation material or how-to manuals). The training programs, such as that at Harvard, rely heavily on case studies. There is an awareness of the importance of such exposure to developing a sense of viability for those just contemplating CED. It is also consistent with the face-to-face mentoring which has always been a part of the ongoing education of African-American clergy.

Conclusions

The past decade has seen a resurgence of grassroots organizing efforts across all racial lines. In the post-Reagan era, faith-based groups have become increasingly involved in the local democratizing strategies of community organizing as well as more entrepreneurial efforts for community economic development. Both streams continue to gain in momentum and share the goals of improving the quality of life in local communities through self-determination.

African-American churches have bought into this trend, but have gravitated to the CED stream. Because of historical precedent and contemporary shared understandings among black church members of leadership, power, social change, and racial politics, congregations are more comfortable acting as entrepreneurs on behalf of their neighborhood than they are joining broad-based coalitions.

The dramatic proliferation of CED activities on the part of local black churches has taken on the characteristics of a *social movement*, rather than a *social phenomenon*, consisting of a number of simultaneous yet organizationally unrelated actions. Coming out of the political shift in the 1980s, which had enormous implications for the African-American community, as well as the continuing development of the black middle class, the social conditions were ripe for such a response. The level of grievance was high, as social programs to the poor were cut. The reemergence of hate crimes directed against the black church contributed to a sense of moral imperative – the African-American community was under assault, and something had to be done. If not the black church – the historic heart and soul of the community – then who? Resources were available aiding the mobilization: a history and religious tradition in which economic development activities had always been valued as being foundational to the mission of the church. Organizations beyond the local churches also generated much-needed resources for the efforts. Foundations, denominations, academic institutions, publishers, government, and quasi-government agencies all stepped to the plate, providing encouragement, training, funds, and outlets for communication. Local congregations were no longer on their own in responding to the increased numbers of people coming to their door needing safe, affordable housing, job training and placement, as well as food, education, and health care. What had seemed like an overwhelming economic reality could now be framed as an opportunity for an effective response.

A strictly Weberian analysis might not have predicted this movement. Most of the more sophisticated CED activities are based in the larger congregations (Billingsley and Caldwell 1994), which tend to attract a majority of members from the rising and established middle classes. Within these churches, conservative theology coexists with progressive political views (Day in press). However, the beneficiaries of the economic development projects are largely poor people.

In a Weberian framework, socioeconomic class is predominant in identifying political beliefs and behaviors that best represent class interest. Weber further explained religious belief as also being related to class interest. There had been a long-standing tenet in the sociology of religion which linked conservative theology and political views. More recent research challenges this assumption. Because conservative religious beliefs cannot be a predictor of conservative political views, however, does not mean that they are unrelated. The poor, or underprivileged, classes seek "a sense of honor," "just compensation," and "a release from suffering" (Weber 1964). Salvation-oriented religion (such as fundamentalist or conservative Christianity) offers them such rewards, as could political activism; acquiescence is not inevitable. Religion does not necessarily only serve to legitimate the status quo, especially for the poor.

That being the case, how does class function in large, middle-class African-American churches as they become involved in CED? It could be predicted that those from higher socioeconomic strata would not be attracted to community organizing, which so often is an active critic of the political and economic systems. Those from the middle and upper classes have benefited from the system; it would be in their interest to access it, but not seek to change it. Why would those who have escaped poverty and benefited from the system work so intently in the interest of others? Here is the theoretical conundrum of explaining altruism.

Clearly, middle-class churches would find an affinity with the methodology of CED. As those who are more likely to function within bureaucratized institutions with articulated specialization, they would expect their pastor to function in a specialized role; they would be comfortable with clerical leadership in CED project development. In addition, a parochial orientation could also be in the interest of those members from higher socioeconomic status. Development projects around the church improve the neighborhood, making it a safer destination for commuters and contributing to the future viability of the church. But prior to forms, how do we understand the basic motivation of investing such capital (human and exchange) into the creation of shopping centers, housing projects, credit unions, job training programs and even banks that will primarily serve the interests of others?

It is critical to remember that black churches exist because of, in spite of, and always in the context of a racist society. Those who are socially and economically upwardly mobile do not have an unambiguous class identification. Despite the fact that they have benefited from the system, African-Americans in the middle and upper social strata remain all too aware of racism (Cose 1995). Racial consciousness increases with education and African-Americans do not easily abandon their communities of origin.

Therefore, many journey in from the suburbs every Sunday morning to worship in urban churches which draw members from a diversity of social strata, and which are deeply committed to improving the quality of life for the urban poor. Racial politics within the African-American context are marked by a "dual agenda" of political and economic gains. In other words, class interest here is defined more by racial, rather than social/economic parameters: to work in the interest of all African Americans is to work in one's class interest. In this context, class interest cannot be reduced to individualistic terms, or even economic interests alone.

As African-American churches take on more ambitious CED projects, and their pastors become more sophisticated in their entrepreneurial skills, social scientists and policy makers alike should follow closely how the movement is articulated. How will the momentum affect the models of CED among black churches and their communities? Will the emerging models reflect a more parochial focus; that is, even more narrowly targeting a geographical area? Perhaps experience will lead pastor-developers to see a need for a broader power base, making collaboration with other churches more attractive. Will pastors garner enough capital resources and technical assistance to build their sense of confidence and reinforce their primary leadership role? Or will the growing complexity of CED contribute to a pragmatic choice of sharing leadership? How will African-American churches encounter "institutionalized racism" as they engage the financial and governmental sectors? Will it have a "radicalizing impact" on their activities, leading them toward greater critique of the system of distribution and a willingness to challenge it?

Finally, where are the boundaries between cultural identity (racial and religious) and CED activity? At what points is tension created in following the call to be both faithful and effective? That is to say, at what points do congregations feel as if they are compromised by the CED process? How then is that tension exhibited and how is it resolved? Economic development could be infused with religious meaning – or church folk might react to the sense of being compromised and disengage from CED altogether.

Certainly there are many factors at work as the drama unfolds: opportunities and dynamics within the larger political and economic systems, resourcing by public and private enterprise, and the degree of visible effectiveness of efforts. As the millennium turns, the conditions are ripe for turning a lament into a call to action: "If the black church doesn't do it, who will?"

References

Baer, H. and Singer, M. 1992. *African American Religion in the Twentieth Century: Varieties of Protest and Accommodation*. Knoxville, TN: University of Tennessee Press.

Billingsley, A. and Caldwell, C.H. 1994. "The Social Relevance of the Contemporary Black Church," *National Journal of Sociology* 8:1–24.

Cose, E. 1995. *The Rage of a Privileged Class*. New York: Harper Perennials.

Cose, E. 1999. "The Good News about Black America," *Newsweek*, June 7:29–40.

Day, K. 1996. "Prelude to Struggle: African American Clergy and the Resurgence of Community Organizing," PhD dissertation, Temple University, PA.

Day, K. in press. *Prelude to Struggle: African American Clergy and the Resurgence in Community Organizing in Philadelphia*. Lanham, MD: University Press.

DuBois, W.E.B. 1970. *The Philadelphia Negro: A Social Study*. New York: Schocken Books.

Franklin, R.M. 1997. *Another Day's Journey: Black Churches Confronting the American Crisis*. Minneapolis: Fortress Press.

Freedman, S.G. 1993. *Upon This Rock: The Miracles of a Black Church*. New York: Harper Collins.

Greider, W. 1992. *Who Will Tell the People: The Betrayal of American Democracy*. New York: Simon and Schuster.

Lincoln, C.E. and Mamiya, L.H. 1990. *The Black Church in the African American Experience*. Durham, NC and London: Duke University Press.

McAdam, D. 1982. *Political Process and the Development of Black Insurgency 1930–1970*. Chicago: University of Chicago Press.

McDougall, H.A. 1993. *Black Baltimore: A New Theory of Community*. Philadelphia: Temple University Press.

Marable, M. 1983. *How Capitalism Underdeveloped Black America*. Boston: South End Press.

Marx, G.T. 1967. "Religion: Opiate or Inspiration of Civil Rights Militancy among Negroes?" *American Sociological Review* 32:67–8.

National Congress for Community Economic Development (NCCED) 1999. "Coming of Age: The Achievements of Community-Based Development Organizations." Washington, DC: NCCED.

Tarrow, S. 1992. "Mentalities, Political Cultures, and Collective Action Frames: Constructing Meanings through Action," in *Frontiers in Social Movement Theory*, Eds. A.D. Morris and C. McLurg Mueller. New Haven, CT: Yale University Press, pp. 174–202.

Weber, M. 1964. *The Sociology of Religion*. Boston: Beacon Press.

Wilmore, G. 1983. *Black Religion and Black Radicalism: An Interpretation of the Religious History of Afro-American People*, 2nd edn. Maryknoll, NY: Orbis Books.

CHAPTER 19

Hell as a Residual Category: Possibilities Excluded from the Social System

Richard K. Fenn and Marianne Delaporte

In this chapter we will suggest that the notion of hell is essentially a residual category for all the possibilities that a society is unable fully to include within its own moral and cultural order. As mentioned in the Preface, every social system is a conspiracy against reality in the sense that there are far more possibilities for both life and death than any society can imagine, let alone encompass within its own set of symbols and under its own set of controls. These are the familiar "contingencies" of social system theory, and it is religion that in the past has both helped a society to imagine them and to put some of them, at least for the time being, beyond the pale of possibility. Religion, however, has also constricted the social imagination and offered a set of controls that have often proved to be contestable or illusory. Hell, for instance, has been one perennial concept for possibilities for domination or submission, satisfaction or frustration, bestiality or spiritual error, that a particular society might wish to exclude. Because social boundaries are notoriously permeable and shifting, however, hell has long been seen as a clear and present danger or even a state into which a society, or even a mind, can descend especially in times of social crisis.

On the one hand, then, societies tend to reduce the possibilities for life and death, for love and hate, for hope and despair, to proportions that are manageable given the limits of their own resources, their own expertise, their tokens of authority, and their skills in medicine or warfare, in child-raising or pacifying the dead. Societies must make choices and then justify these choices as necessary. Any society must create a partial world of possibility and yet portray itself as offering a wider universe of possibilities for fulfillment, for relationships, and for life itself. Furthermore, the convenience and interests of groups in a position to set limits on the range of human aspiration have been concealed under the cloak of notions of inevitability, necessity, or right thinking and doing. To expose the role of status groups like the clergy in setting unnecessary limits on human aspiration and desire has long been one of the major functions of folklore about the private lives of the religious. It is also one of the functions of the sociology of religion and of the critique of ideology.

No wonder, then, that any society is more or less haunted by the possibilities that it has excluded from its order. Take, for example, the separation of one society from another. As soon as social boundaries are drawn, it no longer becomes possible, perhaps, to marry certain outsiders, or it becomes prohibited to live among them or to speak their language. That universe of possibility is excluded from the pantheon of the society in question, and yet it remains a source of perennial temptation or rivalry. The onions and garlic of Egypt, so to speak, always remain a source of rival satisfaction to what poor Israel can offer. Thus other societies also offer an alternative object of loyalty or allegiance; no wonder that many societies have had to institute loyalty oaths in order to maintain and reinforce the invisible boundary between themselves and their enemies. Apart from invasion, the simple flow of ideas and people across social boundaries makes it possible for one society to penetrate and pervade another. No wonder, then, that oaths of loyalty have often been required to separate those who have divided allegiances from those who are of a single minded devotion to their own society alone.

Societies, we are arguing, are perennially haunted by the possibilities that they have excluded but that remain available in rival social orders. Thus hell has been a place where those are consigned who have broken the moral order of the society in question and whose allegiances have been divided. To hell go all manner of sinners, spies, traitors, dissidents, and apostates who have succumbed to the appeal of another social system. We will discuss them, and in so doing we will argue that dreams and visions, doctrines and teachings, concerning a more universal form of salvation represent a society's attempt to overcome the contradiction between the possibilities enshrined in its own order and those that remain outside its normative boundaries. On the one hand these boundaries are mere inventions, but on the other hand they must be presented as necessary to life itself and as part of an ultimate moral order. In order to keep open the possibility of transcending the limits of its own system of social control, a society may portray hell as a penultimate destination for traitors and dissidents, who in the final judgment will be encompassed once again in a more inclusive social order of transcendent justice. Indeed, theological speculation has long imagined at least parts of hell to be reserved for those who are just doing time, as it were, and who can look forward at least to being released on eventual probation.

Second, however, note the possibilities that are excluded as societies distinguish themselves from their natural surroundings. It is the bush surrounding the civilized village where ghosts and sorcerers are to be found; these are the perennial bearers of excluded possibility. There in the natural world are also to be found wild animals and evil spirits, which can tear apart the flesh and reduce the human to the bestial. Nature thus becomes the repository of passions and spirits, people and relationships, that can disturb the fragile peace of the human community as it is defined in a particular social system. It is where the uncultivated and thus the wild are to be found: cannibals and witches with insatiable desires, for instance, or the forces of fire and flood that can decimate a society. Sorcerers and wild animals, demonic beasts and insatiable desires, have often been portrayed as staples of hell itself. It is in hell that a society can imagine those forces of nature that it has been unable to include but without which it apparently cannot fully thrive.

Of course, any society is likely to be haunted by the possibilities it has excluded by consigning them to the world of nature. The living long for the presence of the dead. Young men are badly in need of their animal spirits if they are to go to war. The leaders of the community need the services of sorcerers if they are to defend or recover their positions of authority in the community. Thus religion legitimates the distinction between the natural and the social by making social infractions and disorders appear to be unnatural. It is Satan who is the source of unnatural affections and desires: loves that know no legitimate boundaries but by going beyond acceptable limits have violated the laws of nature itself. We will discuss the role of nature in the imagery of hell toward the end of this chapter, where we take up the possibilities for life and death that not even institutions like the church are capable of transcending. It is in nature, after all, that we find the arrow of time: that irreversible forward thrust of life into death from which there is no recourse or return. Thus if a society is to be able to proclaim a final judgment that restores all possibilities to the fold of the social order, it will also have to proclaim a way of transcending the passage of time.

We have been suggesting why in images of hell one finds traitors and sinners, or bestial individuals and all too human demonic animals, psychics and seers, sorcerers and magicians, who seemed to have tapped on their own, outside the approved channels, the forces of nature itself. In hell, however, we also find souls cut off from their bodies: pure, lost, passionate, and hopeless selves who had sought to be – or to find – their own sources of inspiration and authority. In descents into hell individuals discover the possibilities for a selfhood that is not mediated by the social order. It is indeed a nightmare of any social system that claims to have a monopoly on grace or fortune, that individuals may find salvation on their own terms or even merely think and decide for themselves what it is worth living – and dying – for, through unauthorized descents into hell. It is with the soul, therefore, that we begin.

Thus hell has been a way of reminding adventurous souls of their eventual fate if they stray too far on their own spiritual journeys. The descent into hell has been one way of reminding the devout of the perils of salvation on any other terms than those offered by the church. That vision has served political purposes in reminding kings of their duties to the church, and it has reminded sensitive and gifted souls of the perils of making up one's faith on one's own terms.

Hell as the Set of Excluded Possibilities for Authentic Selfhood

It is well recognized, of course, that the church has long mounted an attack on the soul. In the name of saving the soul the church – both Protestant and

Catholic – has at times been engaged in a process that has been aptly called "soul murder." The telling of horrific stories to children about the tortures of the damned, the onslaught of evangelists on the souls of the spiritually oppressed, who subsequently suffer or even die from wasting away and anorexia: these are the well-documented excesses of evangelical Protestant spiritual discipline. Although these are conspicuously Protestant forms of spiritual sadism and masochism, they have their roots in the Catholic piety that inspired evangelicals in the nineteenth century, and before them the Puritans themselves. Indeed, it was in part to relieve children of this oppressive pedagogy that John Locke argued for forms of education that, while preparing souls for the next life, would spare them unnecessary terrors of the soul in this one. Individuals would still be on spiritual probation for a lifetime, and citizens would be required to demonstrate their good faith through daily repentance. Nonetheless, liberal democratic political theory sought to limit the more destructive elements of Christian pedagogy and to entice rather than crush the soul in order to control it.

In the more repressive forms of religious pedagogy, the doctrine and prospect of hell have been essential ordinances. As we will point out later in this discussion, however, there has been a wide range of terrors associated with hell. At one extreme, release from hell required the intervention of a God whose mercies and judgments resembled those of a Roman emperor. On the peripheries of the empire, however, hell was more likely to be a place in this world where the dead could work out their punishments with less fear and trembling and finally qualify for a happy spiritual existence. For contemporaries, however, it may be difficult fully to grasp the agonies to which the prospect of hell has introduced sensitive and believing souls. Consider, for instance, the following passage from Teresa of Avila's *Life*, in which she recounts a sudden spiritual descent into hell:

> one day when I was at prayer, I found myself, without knowing how, plunged, as I thought, into hell. I understood that the Lord wished me to see the place that the devils had ready for me there, and that I had earned by my sins. All this happened in the briefest second; but even if I should live for many years, I do not think I could possibly forget it. . . . I felt a fire inside my soul, the nature of which is beyond my powers of description, and my physical tortures were intolerable. I have endured the severest bodily pains in the course of my life, the worst, so the doctors say, that it is possible to suffer and live, among them the contraction of my nerves during paralysis, and many other agonies of various kinds, including some, as I have said, caused by the devil. But none of them was in any way comparable to the pains I felt at that time, especially when I realized that they would be endless and unceasing. But even this was nothing to my agony of soul, an oppression, a suffocation, and an affliction so agonizing, and accompanied by such a hopeless distress and misery that no words I could find would adequately describe it. To say that it was as if my soul were being continuously torn from my body is as nothing. (Teresa of Avila 1957:233)

No doubt the torments here are physical; she suffers excruciating pain. However, the torments are also deeply emotional and spiritual. She encounters herself as forever beyond the reach of the grace of God, with no hope for any reprieve, let alone redemption. It is too late for her to experience anything other than the prospect of endless agony. Furthermore, this descent into hell is no momentary lapse or aberration; it is "the Lord's will" and " a great favor" that she should have been allowed not only to see, but to experience acutely, the agony from which she believed she would be spared in the end.

The priestly religious imagination nonetheless may obscure the real depths to which spiritual torment can descend. The margins of psychological experience are often far more terrifying or passionate than might be suggested even by some of the more graphic, authorized versions of hell. Teresa of Avila reports reading many accounts of hell, but none of these had awakened the appropriate fear or contrition in her soul. In retrospect, she says, these books "are like a picture set up against the reality." They stood between her and the thing itself. Once she had actually experienced her soul being torn from her, and an excruciating "interior fire and despair" that "were the worst of all," she was no longer impressed either by these visions of hell or by the actual sufferings of life itself.

It is no accident, of course, that this sudden episode of spiritual torture occurred to Teresa while she was praying. It had long been one element of the spiritual discipline of the Church to encourage the individual to contemplate the terrors and pangs of the souls in hell. In *The Spiritual Exercises of St. Ignatius*, the fifth of these meditations requires the individual to employ all the senses in imagining hell itself. Not only is the individual to imagine the spatial contours and dimensions of hell, but to "ask for a deep awareness of the pain suffered by the damned." Thus the believer is encouraged to see "souls enveloped, as it were, in bodies of fire, or to hear their "screaming cries, and blasphemies," to "smell the smoke" and "Taste bitter things, as tears, sadness, and remorse of conscience," and finally to imagine touching the flames (Ignatius 1964:59).

In the church's earliest visions of hell one can find this experience of hopeless desire, of inevitable and irreversible mortality, despite a heavy overlay of theodicy and warning by the professional clergy. For instance, a river runs through Gregory of Tours's vision of a place of departed spirits (Turner 1993:94–5). On one side was a beautiful white house to which the faithful could go, but those who were unworthy fell from the bridge into the river where they could remain tormented by the sight of inaccessible refreshment. Such a view of unending and hopeless desire was meant as a cautionary tale for the living. Certainly in the eyes of a contemporary, Pope Gregory, the descent of the soul into hell prior to death was meant for the edification of the believer and as a warning to others who might be tempted to ignore the prospects of eternal torment. Thus Pope Gregory recounted the story of a soldier who died and, before returning to life, saw in hell the usual river spanned by a bridge on which souls were tested. On one side of the river there was a place of exquisite satisfaction, but on the other were the souls condemned to longing in vain. The river itself was infested with beings who would torment any soul who fell from the bridge in an attempt to cross over to the meadows and mansions on the other side. Stripped of the mythology and the setting, hell is simply a state of the soul in which one contemplates for ever the object of a hopeless desire that is made all the more intense by aggravated suffering (Turner 1993:93). The fact that for some souls it has been possible to cross the bridge makes the torment even worse. The meadow on the far side is a possibility for some: hence the capacity of that prospect to torment the soul.

As this vision attributed to Pope Gregory suggests, the church had a vested interest in intimidating the warlike soul. Indeed, the church sought to pacify the gangs of young men in armor and to subject knights to the civilizing moral code of the church, that is, chivalry. Take, for example, *The Vision of Tundal*. There a knight is given an appalling view of Lucifer himself, "the Prince of Shadows," a frightening monster who "inhaled and exhaled all the souls into different parts of hell." This is Lucifer incarnate in a charred and tormented beast (Gardiner 1989:178). The cautionary elements of this tale are evident in the question posed by the soul of the knight, "why this monster is called the Prince of Shadows when he can defend no one and he is not able to free himself" (p. 180). Not even Lucifer can free himself or anyone else from the chains – or pangs – of mortality. Although the soul of the knight gets no closer to hell itself than this final vision of the beast that bedevils every soul, he is allowed to witness the agony of souls seeking to atone for their sins (p. 157). The moral is apparent: "We cannot complete our journey in any other way unless we pay attention to this very torment" (p. 159).

It is not only warlike young men who came under the control of a priestly status group with a very strong interest, both ideal and material, in exercising social control. Women were also beneficiaries of the church's interest in controlling their impulses and especially their sexuality. Take, for example, Margery Kempe, the fourteenth century mystic, who leaves us in little doubt that she knew intense and occasionally hopeless desire. She reports that she had long struggled not only with sexual desire but with intense guilt for her "lechery." Indeed, she may have been temporarily driven out of her mind when a priest failed properly to hear her confession of guilt, and she was subjected to physical restraints for a time because she was inclined to harm herself. After a visit from her Lord, however, she enjoyed a respite of two years, in which she regained her composure and was released from the intensity of the desires that had been tormenting her. On one occasion, however, she experienced renewed sexual interest for a man who had propositioned her, although no new liaison came about. Nonetheless, she felt that she had forfeited the good graces that she had been enjoying, and she goes on to report the pangs of hell very succinctly: "I thought I might be in hell itself for the sorrow I felt in my heart. . . . I was in continual mourning and full of sorrow as if God had forsaken me for good" (Kempe 1998:36).

It can be too late not only to fulfill sexual desires but to have any hope of reestablishing a primordial connection to the source of life itself. That is a primitive form of mourning for which talking is not very helpful, since separation from the original matrix occurs long before one has any capacity to speak. That God should be thought to have forsaken her "for good" confirms that Margery

Kempe has fast forwarded, as it were, to some point in the future from which ret-rospective grief reaches back into the present. Her eschatology is "realized"; the end is already at hand. She has run out of time for repentance to do any good or for future grace to lift the weight of past sin. This is just the opposite of a retrospective involvement in a Holocaust that one has avoided; it is to imagine oneself already to have been consigned to the consuming fires of hell: a suitable punishment, as it were, for the perennially unsatisfied passions to which she had been prone. It is only after this experience of total and irrevocable abandonment to a nature that had already taken its course that Margery Kempe reports the experience of being restored to the presence of God. The necessary but the impossible had occurred. She claims to have heard God saying to her:

> I, the very same God, forgive you all your sins. And you shall never go to hell or even purgatory; but when you come to pass out of this world, in the twinkling of an eye, you will have my bliss in heaven, for I am the same God who brought these sins to your mind and made you confess them all. Therefore I grant you true contrition until the end of your life. (Kempe 1998:37)

In this account of her sufferings, Margery Kempe describes an intensity of remorse for a sin that remains unnamed, and therefore unconfessed, through-out the book. An earlier attempt to confess this sin to a priest ends disastrously, as we have mentioned, and the rest of the book reflects the anguish caused by that peremptory confessor. It is thus not too much to say that she first descended into hell through the spiritual malpractice of a priestly status group that had a vested interest in her suffering.

Under these conditions it would not be surprising to find in Margery Kempe's account of her ordeal signs of emotional and psychological regression. Her image of herself as suffering from the sin of lechery, her longing for restoration to an ideal mother, and her ecstasy in the presence of the Virgin Mother suggest the persistence of intense infantile longings. So does her devotion to a Lord who calls himself her lover and who refers to Margery as his daughter. Whether or not her unconfessed sin was incestuous and included memories as well as feelings is not essential for us to know or understand. The point is simply that her leap forward to a day of judgment in which she consigns herself to hell is also a projection of the past into the future. The present thus becomes filled not only with the memory of old passions but the sense that they are hopeless and, in her case, damning. It is literally too late for her to fulfill those passions or to undo them. Therefore she projects them into the future to a moment, real-ized in the present, where she can resolve them once and for all. That is after all what the eschaton is: the fullness of times. It is also more than many souls can bear, and it helps to explain why Margery Kempe wept prodigiously until her death.

If the descent into hell were only a descent, never to be finished into an ascent up and out of hell, it would be too much for all souls to endure. In the case of

Margery Kempe we get a glimpse of what the ascent looks like. Toward the end of her life she dictated these words to her scribe:

> Our Lord too, in his mercy, visited me so frequently and so generously with holy conversation and talk of love that quite often I did not know where the day had gone. I would sometimes imagine that, say, five or six hours had been but an hour. It was all so sweet and full of consolation that I might have been in heaven. It never seemed to be a long while; I did not feel that time dragged – it simply passed, without my noticing. If I could have lived a hundred years in this way (supposing that were possible), I would have preferred it to a single day in my former lifestyle. . . . I even believe that if I were in hell itself, I could weep and mourn for love of you just as much as I do here; hell would not bother me, it would turn into a kind of heaven. (Kempe 1998:92)

This suggestion of living in a timeless heaven on earth is associated, as we have seen, with fantasies of infantile reunion with the maternal breast or womb. Certainly Margery Kempe's own account here causes us to wonder whether her lifetime of mourning had been for the loss of a maternal presence, perhaps of the womb itself, from which separation had been a sort of hell. In such moments as the one described above, where Kempe no longer notices the passages of time, she has received the assurance that "Devils in hell may not, angels in heaven will not, and man on earth shall not" ever separate her from the presence of her loving God (p. 38).

We should therefore not be surprised to find Western monks comparing their surroundings favorably to Paradise, as though they had already found a place where their spirits could soar unimpeded to the presence of God. On the other hand, the same context provided a place where they were to be tested within by the devil. No longer were the temptations largely external, of "the world" and "the flesh." The devil had found a more intimate quarry; as Constable (1996:151) puts it: "What had previously been a war against the external forces of evil and the devil was now increasingly seen as an internal struggle against the evil proclivities of man."

We have seen that visions of hell were used to control the violence of young men and the sexual impulses of women; it should not be surprising to find that monks also were placed under this sort of spiritual intimidation. In their descent into hell monks endured not only the temptations of the devil but a final encounter with the forces of damnation. Some critics of monasticism charged monks with succumbing to the devil's temptations simply by withdrawing from the world; others accused the monks of trying to ward off ultimate damnation by undergoing a foretaste of hellish suffering: they "damn themselves in order to avoid perpetual damnation," in the words of Theobald of Etampes (Constable 1996:134–5). In another of Pope Gregory's early medieval visions of hell, a monk named Peter has had what would now be called a near-death experience. His discovery of hell is enough to make him wish to mortify himself in this life as a form of prophylaxis against the real thing. It is as if one could fight hellfire with the fires of self-mortification: again a primitive form of magical thinking that seeks to enable the individual to escape the finality of death but makes the individual vulnerable to external sources of suggestion and control. Thus Peter is reported to have ". . . devoted himself to such fasting and vigils that, although he said nothing, his very life and conversation still spoke of the torments he had seen and still feared" (Gardiner 1989:47). His life itself became a form of descent into hell.

Young men, monks, and women all represent types who might seek out their own sources of inspiration and authority. However, societies have a tendency to stigmatize those who represent such a threat to their symbolic orders. Young men, women, and strangers represent various forms of threat: new ideas, new ways of life, independence of judgment, and the importation of genes from other pools. To identify and isolate that threat, societies place a stigma on the person. It is a wound: a warning that the person so marked is slated for death. The vision of hell was just such a psychological wound, and it was sometimes accompanied by wounds to the body. Ignatius encouraged a monk who did his spiritual exercises to "scourge oneself with light cords, which cause exterior pain, [rather] than in another way that might cause internal injury" (St. Ignatius 1964:62).

In patriarchal societies it is women and the young who represent the danger of new ideas or foreign genes being brought into the social order. They can subvert the society from within, and so they are the most vulnerable to being stigmatized. Conversely, however, those who wish to assert their individuality against the social order will discover that they are mortal. It is the social order that endures, and so to stand out as a person, to identify what is unique and particular to the self, is to place oneself at the mercy of time.

If these notions about the stigma of time seem a little abstract, consider Paul Binski's detailed account of a certain kind of late medieval tomb (Binski 1996:139ff.). The upper deck, so to speak, of the tomb presents the individual in the full regalia of station and office: a bishop in his vestments, or a knight in armor. The lower deck of the tomb had a different sort of effigy: not the social individual but the natural one, in the form of a corpse well advanced in the stages of internal decay. The stigma of time was thus reserved for what was most uniquely and particularly personal, the individual's own body. Only in that aspect of the person that conformed to the social order and represented its highest values could one see the form of a victory over time:

> tombs of this type at their most elaborate possess the structural character of divi-
> sion and confrontation – between the social and the natural, between the timeless
> and the time-bound, between the perfect and the fallen, and so on: again the body
> is deployed as a sign, and the themes of the uncanny (such as repetition and
> doubling) are equally present. (Binski 1996:139)

There is much more than a patriarchal ideology on display in these noble or ghastly effigies. Note the primitive magic by which persons have long sought to preserve themselves by doubling. Indeed the soul itself, as an essence of the person that would survive death, is perhaps the most primitive form of such doubling. Inconceivable as it may have been to individuals that they would not persist after death, the soul represented that ongoing identity that not even time and nature could destroy. Indeed, the medieval church was adorned not only with tombs but with chapels devoted to prayers for the departed, that their souls might be purified of the remaining taints of time and thus have all their stigmata removed. On the day in which the soul is finally freed from all temporal burdens, it is ready for beatitude.

It was not only chantry chapels in the larger churches, however, that carried forward this concern for the soul. As Binski points out, colleges at Oxford and Cambridge were the functional equivalent of chapels in which prayers were said repeatedly for the souls of the dead (p. 115). Instead of prayers, however, the living offered their own life and work in memory of the founder of these colleges; their scholarship was not only a memorial to the founder, but carried out his original vision and purpose in founding the college. Thus the afterlife of the individual was guaranteed by the community of scholars whose ideas and works removed the stigma of time from the founder and, through virtuous association, from themselves as well. However, it was not, of course, individuals *per se* that were being allowed to transcend the passage of time of only their achievements. These represented the vicarious contributions of the mind, so to speak, of the founder. All versions of the self therefore had to be authorized by prior authority and benefaction.

Indeed, the Archbishop of Canterbury, whose transi tomb perfected the art of doubling the self, not only in vestments and the regalia of office but in the decaying body, founded All Souls' College at Oxford as precisely such a scholarly chantry. There, however, the element of humor or debunking that could be found in the original tomb may have been harder to discern. In the tomb itself, as Binski points out, the effigy of the corpse appears to be mocking the stately effigy lying above it in episcopal repose. There is indeed something macabre about the corpse's presence, and it exposes the self "to the naked truth of time": the college being the upper portion of the tomb (Binski 1996:137).

Therefore, the corpse is stigmatized, as it were, for revealing the individual, the unique person, who would otherwise be cloaked by the vestments of the archbishop. It is as if one can endure this exposure of the unique person that is disguised by the office if, and only if, one is willing to accept the punishment of death. Here is Binski once more, going right to the point: "With the rise of the individual came a renewed sense of the individual in history, of the individual in life; and with that realization came its correlate, the sense of loss, of failure in death" (p. 131). That loss begins, however, in the original projection of the self into an authorized version of the individual that can be expected to endure beyond death. So long as the soul is willing to be split into a part that is mortal and a part that transcends the passage of time, psychological duality offers a symbolic victory over death, and individuality itself will be stigmatized by time. If individuals find their existence guaranteed in the form of a soul that will not perish at death, then the ultimate terror comes from contemplating the death of the soul. That was the fate reserved for those who not only died but went to hell, where they faced perpetual death throes rather than the total extinction of the soul in the darkness of nonbeing.

Of course residues of this bifurcation of the self, this primitive doubling into a part that will perish and a part that will live on forever, can still be found in modern societies. Instead of effigies, however, individuals are more concerned about their images. Those with images that seem to be prominent and enduring are the ones who seem to have the strongest purchase on the eternal. Thus celebrities in sports or the cinema are sometimes referred to as immortals. Even the ordinary obituary tells us far less about the unique and particular, hence time-bound qualities of the deceased than about their achievements that presumably have stood the test of time or their memberships in organizations that will endure without them. Those who have dealt with abstractions, produced information or texts, or designed symbols or products that have endured, all have a greater chance of having an obituary in the major newspapers than those whose presence, however real, has been confined to a more intimate circle of associations. Those whose work has focused primarily on the body itself are particularly forgettable. Nature and the uniquely personal share the stigma of time.

It is no accident that individuals are left in hell to their own unhappy devices and desires. Their fault is that they have thought and acted for themselves, as heretics, or as sexually impulsive or otherwise greedy persons. Thus the punishment for individuality must fit the crime, and the sinners in hell are left to their own spiritual isolation even in the company of fellow sufferers. Even on the Celtic periphery, the souls in hell are on islands, where indeed they can be visited, as by St. Brendan on his mythical voyage, but their lot is generally solitary until they are restored to the company of the more faithful departed. The experience is one of total alienation from a community that might be open to one's own soul; in hell one is closed back into the small circle of one's own psyche.

To avoid hell, then, one must make the most of one's time on earth and act as an emissary to those whom death at any moment might condemn to eternal torment. Thus the living suffer the constant apprehension of being too late. In fact, Pope Gregory embellished his stories of souls that had traveled to hell with accounts of how they had sometimes succeeded, and sometimes failed, to warn the living in time (Turner 1993:93). Freud, too, was a visionary whose accounts of his dreams include revelations of the fate of those who had died. Like the accounts reported by Pope Gregory, Freud's own analysis of his dreams serves the purpose of warning the living to make the most of the time in which they live. They, too, are to take responsibility for their affectionate and murderous passions, and renounce desires that are destructive or that death has placed beyond the prospect of any fulfillment.

For the religious visionary the descent into hell provided an opportunity for the living to beat hell at its own game, as it were. To subject the body and the soul to deprivation and torment in this life would be prophylactic against hell in the next. It is as if one could fight fire, so to speak, with fire. Christian asceticism attempts to engage in self-mortification as a way of preempting the sufferings of the damned. Those who have been seared by fire or frozen in ice during their descents into hell return to this life scarred but immune to death.

For Augustine, those in hell would have no prospect of a second chance. It was for the living, whose life was at best purgatorial, to renounce Satan and his works once and for all (Turner 1993:82). That is why notions of a second birth and a new dispensation became so intensely important not only in Catholic piety but in evangelical devotion. Those in a this-worldly purgatory have the opportunity and the obligation to place certain desires not in a spiritual limbo but to consign them to a past from which there could be no return. The past, as a world from which there could be no reprieve, is a cultural invention.

To summarize: it is in visions of hell that individuals finally confront their own mortality, and there one is haunted by the memory of impossible desires. The longings even persist, but they are intensified and made bitter and remorseful by the stinging awareness that it is too late ever for them to be satisfied. That is why the dead continue to burn without being consumed, with no hope of reprieve or final satisfaction as icons of self-mortification.

If there is one threat to social institutions that supersedes all others, it is the possibility that individuals will confront their own mortality on terms and under auspices that owe little or nothing to the larger society. That encounter relieves people of the necessity of finding their protections against death from the disciplines offered by the larger society or its more intrusive institutions, such as the church: hell being a gateway to personal freedom.

If individuals confront their own mortality and deprive it of its power to terrorize the soul, they may become impervious to the promises of transcendence offered by the larger society. Those who face death on their own terms may not be enthralled by the pantheon of the larger society's heroes or be willing to model (read sacrifice) themselves on the altar of these authorized lives and deaths. Take, for example, Joyce's description of the enticements offered by the church to captivate the souls of young men seeking a model for heroic encounters with life and finally with death itself. In *The Portrait of an Artist as a Young Man* he describes several of these, notably a litany of reminders of how St. Ignatius heroically died in the struggle to win souls for Christ in his travels through Asia. Indeed Ignatius was said to have saved over 10,000 of them through his preaching in one month alone. This heroism is contrasted with the lives of those who have succumbed to the passions of their own souls and who are thus headed for a painful and endless sojourn in the depths of the hell. The young should anticipate the possibility of being far removed from the grace of God and thus haunted by the reminder of the possibility of salvation that they had forfeited through their sins. As Joyce recalls the clerical harangue on the subject of hell, the damned in hell will be reminded of the possibilities for pleasure or other forms of sin that were first suggested to them by their associates, whom they will see suffering like themselves in an eternal fire that gives off not light but only an excruciating flame. Indeed, "They turn upon those accomplices and upbraid them and curse them. But they are helpless and hopeless: it is too late now for repentance" (Joyce 1992:117). Even in the fires of hell, the memory of possible satisfaction comes back to haunt one, but so does the memory of possible lost opportunities for forgiveness. These memories haunt rather than entice or save their souls, however, since it is "too late" for repentance.

The Roman Catholic Church has long known, as Joyce puts it in the mouth of one of Stephen Dedalus's early instructors, that

> of all these spiritual pains by far the greatest is the pain of loss, so great, in fact, that in itself it is a torment greater than all the others . . . This, then, to be separated for ever from its [the soul's] greatest good, from God, and to feel the anguish of that separation, knowing full well that it is unchangeable, this is the greatest torment which the created soul is capable of bearing, *poena damni*, the pain of loss. (Joyce 1992:122–3)

Other institutions besides the church also lay claim to the soul of the person and thus may stifle it, sometimes beyond hope of recovery. Take, for example, the family. Joyce makes it clear that Stephen Dedalus's father often compared himself favorably to his son and counseled his son to model himself after those who were good at something: singing, perhaps, or rowing. In this more secular form of spiritual testing and probation the father found a form of salvation that would work in a society that was based on skills and knowledge rather than on inherited social status or nepotism. His son, however, seemed little inclined to be good at anything in particular. Had he been an American Protestant, perhaps Stephen would have been offered various forms of social probation and testing that would eventually have qualified him for membership in one of the Protestant voluntary associations and entitled him to the social credit that his father had long forfeited through alcohol and insolvency.

This is not to suggest that Joyce's Catholic Ireland relied solely on the church and the family for the process of spiritual and social testing in this life. Besides his father and the Jesuit priests, Stephen Dedalus had to contend with schoolmates who also demanded that he confess or merely admit to something: an infraction against the discipline of the school, perhaps, or a love for some young girl. It was the prospect of private devotion that seemed to outrage both the church and his peers, his father and the schools. It appears that the soul should not be allowed to worship at a secret altar of personal inspiration and authority.

What distinguishes the church from other agencies of social control is the transparency of its attack on the soul of the individual. The church remains very much concerned about the possibility that individuals will confront their mortality, and the prospect of hell, on their own terms. Recently the Roman Catholic Church has expressed concern for individuals whose ideas of hell seem exaggerated or antiquated. These are people who presumably believe in a place called Hell and, worse yet, believe that God sends people there. In a recent document, "Hell: Reflections on a well-debated topic," the Magisterium has sought to counteract the distortions caused by "the popular imagination or the exaggerations and amplifications of preachers."[1] Religious art over the centuries has also been a source of distorted notions of hell as a place of torment, and so was Dante's Divine Comedy. Among these unhappy notions of hell are the notions that God judges some people as worthy of hell and that hell is a place where the damned reside eternally. The document makes it very clear that it is people who judge themselves by seeking their happiness and destiny apart from the grace and presence of God. Thus they consign themselves not to a place but to a "state of being" which is hell, as it were, by definition: hell being the condition of Godlessness.

So far there is little in this document that Weber would not have easily understood as a typical theodicy by a religious status group seeking to blame indifferent followers for their own eternal problems. One does not have to be a Weberian sociologist, however, to see in this document the ideal and material interests of the clergy coming into play. They are still helping people find a rationale for their sufferings and their fate, and the rationale has the function of justifying the continued influence and ministrations of the clerical profession and of blaming individuals for not having taken the offerings of institutionalized grace when they were made available. One could wish for the church that it would be so easy to lay to rest these distortions of which they disapprove. Unfortunately, in citing the New Testament as an authority on the subject of hell, the anonymous authors of "Hell: Reflections on a well-debated topic," quote a number of passages in which hell does appear to be a place to which people are consigned by the judgment of God and of Christ himself. Typical is the passage from Matthew 25:41 in which Christ will say to those who have no acts of charity, "Go away, far from me, oh damned ones, in the eternal fire which was prepared for the devil and his angels." Thus it is not likely that "the popular imagination" or even over-enthusiastic preachers will lack support for their archaic notions. Neither do many Protestants who take the Bible literally wish to be instructed by those who typically turn biblical myths into metaphors. Hell is here to stay.

Whatever the theological contradictions and dilemmas with which the Roman Church still has to wrestle, this document does suggest that the unfinished project of modernity requires official as well as popular interest in the problem of hell. It is no longer sufficient or satisfying that life should be a continual this-worldly purgatory of spiritual testing and social probation. As the widespread popular interest in apocalypse and the Rapture attests, there is a strong demand for images of a resolution of the problem of time: an encounter with death that is final and, for some, a matter for rejoicing. For some, by necessity, this final encounter with the end of time will be the discovery that it is too late even for repentance, and that damnation goes on endlessly and for an eternity. For others, the descent into hell is a way to selfhood.

Thus we would suggest that the Roman Catholic Church's recent document on hell is a sign that the church would like to preempt the discussion of hell. Not only is hell too important a topic to be left to the laity. It is the concept by which individuals do indeed confront their own selfhood in its most mortal aspect. Left to their own devices, the laity may come up with a wide range of beliefs or practices that would enable them to face their mortality on their own terms. This religious apocalypticism enjoys a very large audience and readership willing to face death and discover their own selfhood without the benefit or control of the clergy.

Hell as the Repository of Possibilities Contained in Other Societies: The Problem of Identity and Allegiance

As we have seen in Grace Davie's account in chapter 14 of religious belief in a variety of countries, belief in hell seems a remarkably resilient conviction. From a Weberian viewpoint, of course, we should not be surprised. Religious beliefs in places of punishment served the initial purpose of making sense of suffering. The good die young, and the evil typically continue to prosper. To be saved from the agonies of suffering and death, and to assuage the desire for vengeance on those who suffer less and get away, so to speak, with murder, the doctrine of a place of eventual suffering and punishment for the unworthy dead served the purpose of what Weber often called theodicy. It explained what on the surface seemed a sort of divine indifference to those who had done their best to deserve a better fate. There is therefore in the human condition a desire not only for relief from suffering and death but a desire also for a set of reasons as to why things should work out as they do. Out of this initial drive toward a rationale, of course, came what Weber called the various ethics of people: some calling for more, others for less asceticism; some calling for more, others for less engagement with the mundane.

We would suggest that there is more to the survival value of the notion of hell, however, than a mere desire for a practical ethic. Hell is not only the place, mythologically speaking, in which the dead get their just deserts. To be sure, such a vision of hell has often been encouraged by what Weber called status groups: by religious professionals with a vested interest in convincing people that their own failings were responsible for their fate: failings which often had to do with the individual's lack of faith in what the religious professional had prophesied or taught. Sin becomes unbelief. However, let us take a closer look at what hell might be, apart from the distorting effects of the ideology of professional groups (from what Weber called the ideal and material interests of priests and prophets, for instance).

Hell was thus a place where those were consigned who betrayed the social order: sinners who violated its norms, aliens who diverted and consumed its resources, traitors who betrayed its trust. In images of hell we therefore see just how haunted a society could be by the possibilities of other allegiances. Certainly such a fate bothered Jews and Greeks who gave divine justice much thought. In their view it was intolerable that the good should share the same fate or be buried in the same place as the bad. Surely the devout or the pure should be allowed a victory over death. Therefore the wicked dead should be required to endure not merely the anguish of knowing that it is too late for them to enjoy any further satisfactions at the expense of the good but also suffering for such wickedness. Contrast Jonah, whose descent into the belly of the whale had placed him within the grasp of hell and thus had made him more humane, vulnerable, and aware of his mortality (Bernstein 1993:141). Similarly, for some psalmists death was still the Mesopotamian underworld of dryness, dust, and clay; there it is too late even to praise God. Thus all the dead lie beyond the remotest hope for divine presence, let alone rescue and redemption (Bernstein 1993:143). Under the influence of priestly editors, perhaps after the return from exile, however, ancient stories were rewritten to allow God to scourge even hell of his enemies and to visit retribution upon the souls consigned to that hopeless place (Bernstein 1993:144–5). God could also purify the community of sinners and send the wicked to a place where they would not only languish but suffer eternal punishment (Bernstein 1993:148). Hell is thus the social order's last revenge.

The use of the doctrine or myth of hell to serve authoritarian purposes is precisely what Weber would have expected; it served the material and ideal interests of various priestly or prophetic status groups. However, it is important not to forget Weber's other argument, that these status groups could make use of the widespread and perennial need to explain the disappointment and frustration of desires and good intentions in this life. Consider, for example, the Book of Job, for a treatment of the desires of the good to have a fate different from that of the wicked. Neither for the Greeks nor the Jews was what Bernstein calls a "neutral afterlife" entirely satisfactory; only a "reward and punishment after death" could serve the purpose of human, let alone divine, justice (Bernstein 1993:160–1). Note, of course, the extension of magical thinking: the dead are not merely shades but have a consciousness capable of entertaining regret or resentment over the presence or absence of divine retribution; for some time will pass very slowly indeed as part of their punishment (Bernstein 1993:150). Hell is thus the individual's last resort.

Note also the increasingly mythical attributions of divine intent and activity with regard to the dead; the work of God extends to the departed, as does the reach of divine justice. No wonder, then, that in Ezekiel the mythical and the magical combine to create a picture of a God who is busy bringing about the shame of the wicked departed, who are even consigned to a different section of Sheol from that inhabited by the faithful and the good (Bernstein 1993:162–3). Indeed, "The former oppressors suffer the scorn of the other shades" (p. 166). In later developments, Bernstein goes on to note, it is not enough that the good see the wicked suffer or even that the good be resurrected to a new life on earth. It is essential, by the time the Book of Daniel comes to be written, that both the good and the bad be resurrected to face their respective judgments and be sent to their entirely separate fates (pp. 174–5). Thus the ideology of the righteous increasingly developed the mythology of a final judgment that would vindicate their own sacrifices and punish those who had lived too well in this life.

In the Synoptic Gospels, furthermore, we can encounter a critique of this mythology of reward and punishment. In his discussion of the biblical concept of hell, for instance, David Powys argues that by the time of Jesus and his movement the Pharisees had largely rewritten the biblical expectation of a divine intervention to establish justice among the dead as well as the living. They believed, on the contrary, that they would naturally inherit paradise precisely because of their merits in this life. That there was a sort of quid pro quo, paradise for righteousness, thus obviated the need for divine intervention and placed those who could afford to observe law at a considerable advantage over the poor. As Powys goes on to explain, in Jesus' critiques of the Pharisees we have an attack on a "form of hope which motivated most of Jesus' contemporaries," one that was "individualistic, concerned with life after death, and preoccupied with compensation for good and evil deeds. In contrast to earlier Jewish formulation of hope, it was anthropocentric and spatial rather than theocentric and temporal . . . Its impact was quietist, at least in political terms" (Powys 1997:228).

We mention this conflict between the Pharisaical and the apocalyptic or theocentric views of life after death in part because it reflects the tension we described earlier between magical or romantic views of a descent into hell, and one that acknowledges one's total dependence on a fate that one cannot know in advance or control. Such a tension also keeps returning in some of the later medieval visions of the progress of the soul toward either heaven or hell that we have already discussed. Further, the magical notion of redemption rests, as we have suggested, on the notion of the sinner's helplessness before the power of God. It is a notion, as Peter Brown has argued, that is derived primarily from a form of amnesty or mercy modeled by a Roman emperor. Its origins, then, are imperial and authoritarian (Brown 1997:1247–61). Brown argues that the notion that the judgment of the sinner should be individualized, that is, based on the sinner's merits, and that it should be determined at the time of one's death rather than at an apocalyptic moment beyond the imagination and reach of the living or the dead, was far closer to lay or pagan sentiments. These flourished precisely where the power of state authority, especially of the imperial kind, was weakest, as it was in Ireland. Indeed, as Brown has argued, it is this sense of the individual as responsible in this life and the next for the working out and purification of the soul that laid the groundwork for the later doctrine of Purgatory.

Consider this twelfth century Irish imaginative treatment of a journey toward hell, the *Vision of Tundal*. In this vision a tormented soul is torn between fearing that he will receive the just deserts of his occasional sins, and hoping, on the other hand, that divine mercy will outweigh heavenly justice (Gardiner 1989:149–96). The soul is that of a knight who is undergoing what moderns would call a near-death experience. His journeys are harrowing, and his soul suffers many but not all of the torments of those who have been too greedy or lustful, too violent or prideful, and who have signally failed to live up to their religious vows or pretensions. The knight's soul had clearly been prepared for the nice calibration of merit and reward associated with Pharisaism, and yet he is also mortally afraid of receiving what now appears to be the reward for the sort of demerits he had accumulated from occasional sexual or violent excesses during his lifetime. Thus he complains to the guardian angel who is accompanying him on his trip toward hell that God "revives" and "mortifies" souls "as he wishes" but not "as he promised: to give back to each one according to his or her merit and work" (Gardiner 1989:155). As the tale progresses, it becomes increasingly apparent that the authoritarian version will prevail, and it is also increasingly apparent that the knight's only hope is not in the Pharisaical calculus but in the divine prerogative to relieve and save those whom God wishes. Magical control over one's postmortem fate competes unsuccessfully against the clerical insistence on the need for divine rescue.

In the light of Brown's comments about the survival of a more individualized sense of justice outside the scope of Roman influence, we should not be surprised, therefore to find in Ireland a tradition, derived largely from outside the church, of a belief in a life after death that has a strong sense of person and place along with a rich legacy from Irish folklore. Thus, as Carl Watkins has demonstrated, there were several Irish visions of the dead that located individuals in specific islands in the sea; there they took the punishment for their sins or enjoyed the happier consequences of their virtues until the final day of judgment (Watkins 1996). The vision is thus a compromise between Christian notions that the ultimate fate of souls depends on divine judgment and mercy, with the more laicized or folkloric view of the afterworld as a place where the dead live out the punishment or reward for their lives on earth according to a version of natural law.

So long as a society is haunted by the possibility of defection, betrayal, and disobedience or dissent, it must entertain notions of a final reconciliation. The normative boundaries of the society will be reasserted, and the damned reconciled to the social world they had forfeited by their preference for another allegiance. Death and damnation will in the end be conquered by the transforming and reconciling grace of the social order itself. In the meantime, however, a society that is troubled by corrupt clergy, vicious judges, warlords who rape and despoil their victims, and kings who allow their kingdoms thus to be wasted will be under the influence of hell itself.

Just such a view of a moribund kingdom is to be found in the ninth century among the visionary texts written to attack or defend the hapless son of Charlemagne, Louis the Pious, who was in the process of losing control of his empire not only to alien influences like Northmen and Saracens but to corrupt officials of the church and state: not to mention a household alleged to be riddled with incest and attempted parricide (Dutton 1996:81–112). There was at the time what Dutton aptly calls "a royal textual community that communicated in written dreams" (p. 108). Some monks created dreams of a trip to the underworld where the king's corrupt allies were being justly punished, while others created similar visions of a noble and just king, surrounded by those who have lent themselves to the domination of "evil impulses"; thus "the politics of dreaming shifted as power shifted; with its corrective mandate, it was not bound exclusively to the criticism of kings, but to the chastisement of all the world's wicked, especially those who would be king" (Dutton 1996: 109).

The point is that hell was even in the ninth century a highly contested affair. There was no doubt in the mind of many of these dreaming monks that as Dutton puts it, "hell seemed to have spilled over into the waking world of the Carolingians" (p. 96). Even demons from hell, once exorcised, gave prophetic judgment about the extent to which the kingdom had fallen under satanic influence. Certainly the floods and famines, the brutality and corruption of the regime all testified to "the Devil's oppression of the land" (Dutton 1996:98). Not only were its geographical boundaries breached by invaders; its moral boundaries had been violated by bribery and incest, fratricidal and parricidal impulses, and by the corruption of the church itself.

At the heart of the church's dilemma is an inescapable contradiction between notions of the love of God and notions of inevitable and final judgment. In the past the Roman Church has rejected various ways out of that dilemma. A notion that there would be a final reconciliation of sinners with Christ after a long, indeterminate period of suffering was condemned by the Council of Constantinople in 543: an opening but not final victory for the authoritarian version of hell.

Hell as the Mirror of Nature Itself: The Reservoir of "Unnatural" Possibilities

One way to soften the contradiction between endless damnation, then, and the love of God is to point out that damnation is self-imposed by the sinner and is irrevocable because, once one dies, it is indeed too late to change one's state of being. Hell thus becomes a this-worldly state, and its irreversibility is due not to the meanness of a punitive deity but to nature. It is one of the natural facts of life that end in death: "the decision that man makes consciously during his life is confirmed upon his death – for God or against God – and is definitive and irrevocable in nature", as it says in the Roman Catholic Church's recent document on hell mentioned earlier. It is nature's fault, not God's, that a state of hell is forever.

If that makes God seem to be an unwitting accomplice of a nature that he created, one can therefore only cite "the mystery of God" and the divine nature. Salvation would be for everyone, if God were to have his way, but not everyone will be saved, since some successfully resist the grace of God until it is too late, even for God, to save them. It will be too late even for God because God will be true to his nature to the end. That nature requires him to respect the freedom and dignity of individuals to choose their own fate. Although the church may continue to pray for "its sinning children," according to this document, God will only and forever treat humans as grown-ups.

It is therefore not surprising that there is renewed interest among sociologists, psychologists, historians, and theologians in the notion of hell. For sociologists and others to discuss hell without being caught up in the discourse of the church over doctrinal issues, or in the ideal and material interests of a religious profession determined to explain to people the reasons for their suffering in ways that reinforce the authority of the church, it will be necessary to approach the topic of hell without a mythological bias. Here we have employed the notion of hell to describe a state of being in which the individual knows that it is too late to realize certain possibilities that nonetheless remain the object of desire. The possibilities are real, in the sense that they can be imagined or known and, in different circumstances, could be realized, but in fact it is too late to realize them. Take, for example, the love of someone for a friend or family member who is terminally ill. One knows that in other circumstances (more advanced medicine, an earlier diagnosis, a lifetime of different habits etc.) one could go on enjoying the presence of this other person. One also knows, however, that it is too late; the end has begun, and the person soon will be dead. The sentence of death is irrevocable; the disease is irreversible. What will endure is the longing and the will to accomplish what nature, as the Roman Catholic document on hell puts it, makes impossible. Like Lazarus in the parable of hell described by Jesus (Luke 16:19–31), the longing is intensified by the awareness that "there is a great gulf fixed" between the person and the possibility of refreshment. That "great gulf" is a metaphor, drawn from nature, for the passage of time: irreversible, irrevocable, and in the end fatal. Nature has taken its course. A longer life would be unnatural, and it is only a new creation, a new heaven, as it were, and a new earth, that can bring the dead back to life. That is, of course, the eschatological hope that Western Christianity has long offered to overcome the loss of possibility represented by nature itself. On that day the dead will no longer haunt the living with unfulfilled possibility, since the living and the dead will be reunited in a community that transcends the boundaries of nature itself.

The prospect of certain death puts a crimp in the possibilities embodied in the notion of the sacred. Put theologically in terms of the Roman Catholic Church's document on hell, even God must accept that with death a person's choice to refuse the gift of God's presence becomes "irrevocable." It is because of nature, then, that any hell exists whatsoever. A demythologized notion of death, then, begins with the prospect of the coincidence of two opposites: the unlimited and unfathomable possibilities of the sacred, and the certainty that with death it is too late for one to enter into any of these possibilities.

It is simply mortality and the notion of the sacred that create the contradiction between too-lateness and the continuing sense of open and compelling possibility. It is a contradiction that exists in life and only becomes logically intractable when one adds to the sacred the notion of a loving God whose will it is that no one be without God's presence. The sacred is a reservoir of possibility, whether or not one reaches a time in life or at death when those possibilities lie forever beyond one's reach. For the sacred to be itself, of course, it must contain every possibility. One of those possibilities is eternal death and suffering. As the new teaching on hell puts, it, "Therefore, Hell always remains a 'real possibility.'" (Put theologically, this notion produces the contradiction of a God whose love *and power*, according to the Roman Catholic document on hell, are "infinite" and yet who chooses to allow people to remain estranged and tormented forever.)

Conclusion

Not only social conflict and the threat of war underlie contemporary interest in images of the end of time. We would argue that hell will be of continued popular interest so long as time is a category filled with personal and societal notions of unfulfilled possibility. *The Persistence of Purgatory* (Fenn 1995) traced the process by which individuals have been instructed to treat time in this life with the seriousness that has long been believed to weigh on souls in Purgatory itself. This life became purgatorial, under the aegis of Dominican preachers, saints like Catherine of Genoa, preachers like Richard Baxter, political theorists like John Locke, and their followers on the North American continent who took it upon themselves to civilize and perfect a new people.

Western culture became, as it were, a conspiracy against time: an agreement to come to terms with the past continually, over the lifetime of the individual, as a sign of the *bona fides* of the citizen. Thus it was never too late to fulfill old longings, to pay old debts, to satisfy old grievances; there was no statute of limitations on earlier sin, even for those who repented and converted in an allegiance to Jesus Christ. On the contrary, that allegiance ensured that they would carry the responsibility for daily and perpetual signs of repentance, expressed in the outward forms of good citizenship over their lifetime. The resulting social contract provided the masses with an exemption from being considered beyond the pale of redemption. No longer being listed among the damned in hell, they were consigned to a secular purgatory of continuing possibility.

In every attempt to control the past, certain central tendencies of a society are reproduced, and the past is thus renewed. The debt to the past is thus never paid in full, so long as the methods of payment are culturally prescribed. No wonder that the project of modernity has been so difficult to complete; so long as one uses the past to overcome the past, no new cultural invention will suffice.

For the individual, however, the past is always a quite specific past rather than a generic one. Even when the individual's past is caught up in the tragedy of a whole generation or people, as in the case of the Holocaust and of the great wars of the twentieth century, the past is still a living memory of quite particular suffering. For any person, moreover, the past may be present in daydreams, in longings for a return to a primitive matrix, in memories of childhood conflict, in feelings of guilt for imaginary psychological crimes, in the return of moments of ecstasy that rekindle first loves, or in chronic quarrels with our earlier selves. Given the choice between the hell of knowing that it is too late to satisfy desire and the illusion that purgatorial rumination may be redemptive, many, perhaps most, have chosen the open-ended past represented by purgatory.

Such agonizing and internal contradiction deserve the notice of sociologists, who as a whole assume that the past permeates and even dominates the present. The French sociologist, Pierre Bourdieu, perhaps more than any other contemporary theorist, assumes, quoting Emile Durkheim, that

... in each of us, in varying proportions, there is part of yesterday's man; it is yesterday's man who inevitably predominates in us, since the present amounts to little compared with the long past in the course of which we were formed and from which we result. (Bourdieu 1977:79, quoting from Durkheim 1938:70)

Durkheim goes on to argue that one is usually unconscious of the past, as if to imply that there is a certain false consciousness in what passes for modernity: an ignorance of the extent to which the past is still embedded in the present. In any event, the presence of "ancestral spheres" in the human psyche is a staple of sociological discourse. Sociologists understand that individuals may seek refuge in a transcendent sphere above the passage of time, even while they also are seeking self-discovery and spiritual confirmation in the moment. The sacred is the cultural expression of this contradiction, and it is found in an underlying ethos that seeks to reconcile time and transcendence, the present and the past, the knowledge of death and the affirmation of life. As Grace Davie has argued, however, in her chapter in this volume, modern Europe may increasingly present us with an exception to this generalization. To be sure, the collective memory of many European peoples and nations is enshrined in the church and especially in its cathedrals, but that memory is now held, as it were, in trust for a people who have learned to forget it or at least to hold it in high disregard except where they wish to make an occasional and highly personal appropriation of sacred time and space for themselves.

From Bourdieu's viewpoint, for instance, even an immersion in the present moment does not enable one to escape the grip of the past. As Bourdieu puts it:

Unlike the estimation of probabilities which science constructs methodically on the basis of controlled experiments from data established according to precise rules, practical evaluation of the likelihood of the success of a given action in a given situation brings into play a whole body of wisdom, sayings, commonplaces, ethical precepts ("that's not for the likes of us") and, at a deeper level, the unconscious principles of the *ethos* which, being the product of a learning process dominated by a determinate type of objective regularities, determines "reasonable" and "unreasonable" conduct for every agent subjected to those regularities. (Bourdieu 1977:77)

Of course, what one perceives as an opportunity rather than a threat is determined to a large extent by one's past; the present, as a set of possibilities, therefore exists in the mind's eye: the mind itself being prepared only to see a limited field defined and shaped by the past itself. Within that field, the mind's eye is thus prepared to find relevance or meaning only in various limited ways. The present may exist, but it is very hard to see it apart from the lenses and the field provided by the past.

One implication of the earlier work on purgatory (Fenn 1995) is that the dead are contemporaneous with the living in the sense of being part of the same moral community. As purgatory became this-worldly, the living thus came under the same spiritual discipline as the dead. In particular, the living became obligated to make the most of their allotted time in order to fulfill old obligations and to prepare themselves for future beatitude. (Few had the spiritual temerity of a friend of ours who refuses, as she puts it, "to improve one more damn shining hour".) Individuals in the West therefore have inhabited a relatively "traditional" or "primitive" world precisely because the past does remain contemporaneous with the present.[2] The project of modernity is therefore yet to be completed.

To be sure, modernity began, as Fenn (1995) argued, as a result of serious efforts at distinguishing the present from the past and at developing a psyche that is no longer haunted by spirits, ghosts, and biblical horror stories. That was precisely the intention of John Locke, who went on to develop the notion of a pedagogy that would create citizens capable of self-mastery, freed from the burden of the past, and anxious for the good approval of others, just as they had learned as children to seek the approval of their parents. This life became purgatorial. American society itself became the scene of continuous preparation for the life to come: a continuing purgatory, albeit first under evangelical, and later under secular auspices.

This time of continuing probation does indeed impose a severe psychic burden and may well inspire a demand for images of a temporal resolution of the quandaries of salvation. For this sense of this world as a scene of spiritual trial and probation we have to thank, among others, John Locke. Although Locke was concerned to create a new dispensation freed from the ghosts of the past, he nonetheless regarded the institutions of family, school, and the state primarily as settings for the purification of the soul to make it fit for life everlasting. The soul and character of the converted Christian were thus placed on continuing probation. The modern break with the past was therefore incomplete. On the one hand, individuals were being trained to distinguish their own will from the promptings of unseen spirits and from the dead hand of past obligations and affections. On the other hand, however, the present opened up into a future of continuous social and spiritual probation, which implied that the past was still to be overcome. That is precisely what Max Weber saw as the contribution of Protestant sects to an American ethos. Individuals could be admitted to these voluntary associations only after they had been subjected to a process of testing and probation. If they could satisfy the demands of Protestant asceticism, they could also be trusted with money. Thus the marriage between the Protestant ethic and the ethos of capitalism was consummated in these sectarian associations. However much these groups were the carriers of modernity, however, they were the vehicles by which the past also entered into the present and the future: a past of subjecting all claims to gifts of grace to a severe process of probation over one's lifetime. If America is indeed a secular evangelical purgatory, it is because the sects that Weber so rightly observed were placing the individual on continuous trial.

To be complete, the project of modernity needs to be able to draw a line between past and present which allows the individual to expand, not into a spiritual future which is a replay of the past, but into an indefinite, open-ended present. That is, the continued blurring of the distinction between the past and the present, which is called the "purgatorial complex" in Fenn (1995) stands in the way of entering into a truly modern world. To complete the project of modernity, therefore, requires a truly secular spiritual discipline: a willingness to live in the indefinite present, knowing that time is running out, without the comforts of enchantment, and in full knowledge of one's own limits. Such a discipline requires a willingness to let some parts of oneself perish, that the rest may live: a willingness to undertake a spiritual descent into hell.

The notion that the past is active within the present makes the present something of a facade for the past. For many a sociologist, such a thought is entirely welcome and even fashionable. As we have noted, no one has argued more persuasively than Pierre Bourdieu that one can only understand human communities if one fully appreciates the presence of the past. Similarly Connerton (1989) recently has demonstrated the role of memory in forging even those revolutionary societies that pride themselves on making a sharp break with the past. Sociologists and anthropologists have long argued that ritual imprints individual characters with the seal of the larger society and that such imprinting survives generations, even centuries. No longer is Freud's insight into the role of the past in determining the present alien to sociologists; it is too late to separate the so-called "diachronic" study of a society over the course of time from the "synchronic" analysis of processes in the present. It is also too late to regard earlier societies as existing in a benighted cultural world that is inaccessible to the modern psyche, since so much of the past is present and so much of the apparently modern masks the primitive. Thus if there is to be a modern, even a secular project of self-recovery, it will require us to reveal the spirit of past ages within the spirit of the living person: again, a descent into hell.

It is not enough, however, to discover the presence of the past. One must somehow be able to turn the past into a world that can be remembered rather than recovered or relived. Otherwise, there is no present, let alone a future. The argument here is that to complete the project of modernity requires the ability and the willingness to experience the past in all of its intensity, yet in the full knowledge that there is no prospect of restoration, of recompense, or recovery. Such a spiritual resignation is easier said than done, of course, and meets with resistance at almost every level of the psyche. That is why it is the heart of Freudian psychoanalytic technique not only to become conscious of past feelings, fantasies, injuries, and longings, but also actively to distinguish them from the present. The so-called "transference" that makes the past come alive in the conversations of the analytic hour is only half of the battle; the other half is waged by the patient who must decide whether to continue to entertain the past as though it were the present or to recognize it for what it is: namely, the past.

Notes

1   The quotation is from a mimeographed copy of a recent teaching document issued by the Roman Catholic Church, for which I thank Gustav Niebuhr of *The New York Times*.

2   "There remains 'only' the all-pervading denial of coevalness which ultimately is expressive of a cosmological myth of frightening magnitude and persistency. It takes imagination and courage to picture what would happen to the West (and to anthropology) if its temporal fortress were suddenly invaded by the Time of its Other" (Fabian 1983:35).

References

Bernstein, A.E. 1993. *The Formation of Hell. Death and Retribution in the Ancient and Early Christian Worlds*. Ithaca, NY and London: Cornell University Press.
Binski, P. 1996. *Medieval Death*. Ithaca, NY: Cornell University Press.
Bourdieu, P. 1977. *Outline of a Theory of Practice, Cambridge Studies in Social and Cultural Anthropology, No. 16*. Transl. R. Nice. Cambridge: Cambridge University Press.
Brown, P. 1997. "Vers La Naissance du Purgatoire. Amnistie et pénitence dans le Christianisme occidental de l'Antiquité tardive au Haut Moyen Age," *Annales, Histoire, Social Sciences*, November–December (6):1247–61.
Connerton, P. 1989. *How Societies Remember*. Cambridge: Cambridge University Press.
Constable, G. 1996. *The Reformation of the Twelfth Century*. Cambridge: Cambridge University Press.
Durkheim, E. 1938. *L'évolution pédagogique en France*. Paris: Alcan.
Dutton, P.E. 1996. *The Politics of Dreaming in the Carolingian Empire*. Lincoln and London: University of Nebraska Press.
Fabian, J. 1983. *Time and the Other: How Anthropology Makes its Object*. New York: Colombia University Press.
Fenn, R.K. 1995. *The Persistence of Purgatory*. Cambridge: Cambridge University Press.
Gardiner, E. Ed. 1989. *Visions of Heaven and Hell Before Dante*. New York: Italica Press.
Ignatius, St. 1964. *The Spiritual Exercises of St. Ignatius*. Transl. A. Mottola, Introduction R.W. Gleason. Garden City, NY: Doubleday, Image Books.
Joyce, J. 1992. *A Portrait of the Artist as a Young Man*. Toronto: Bantam Books.
Kempe, M. 1998. *The Book of Margery Kempe*. Transl. and Introduction J. Skinner. New York: Doubleday, Image Books.
Powys, D. 1997. *"Hell": A Hard Look at a Hard Question. The Fate of the Unrighteous in New Testament Thought*. Carlisle, UK: Paternoster Press.
Teresa of Avila, St. 1957. *The Life of Saint Teresa of Avila By Herself*. Transl. and Introduction J.M. Cohen. London: Penguin Books.
Turner, A.K. 1993. *The History of Hell*. New York: Harcourt Brace and Co.
Watkins, C. 1996. "Doctrine, Politics, and Purgation: The Vision of Tnuthgal and the Vision of Owein at St. Patrick's Purgatory," *Journal of Medieval History* 22(3):237–48.

PART III

The Sociology of Religion and Related Areas of Inquiry

Editorial Commentary: Looking for the Boundaries of the
Field: Social Anthropology, Theology, and Ethnography   363

20   Acting Ritually: Evidence from the Social Life of Chinese
Rites   371

21   Moralizing Sermons, Then and Now   388

22   Health, Morality, and Sacrifice: The Sociology of Disasters   404

23   Contemporary Social Theory as it Applies to the
Understanding of Religion in Cross-cultural Perspective   418

24   The Return of Theology: Sociology's Distant Relative   432

25   Epilogue: Toward a Secular View of the Individual   445

Part III

The Sociology of Religion and
Related Areas of Inquiry

Editorial Commentary: Looking for the Boundaries of the Field: Social Anthropology, Theology, and Ethnography

Richard K. Fenn

As the boundaries between anthropology and sociology begin to be more per-meable, or even to disappear, it will be more difficult for sociologists to document the world that has been lost. No longer are sociologists specializing in the study of societies that are more or less differentiated and complex, nor are anthropol-ogists closer to the lost Eden of relatively primitive harmonies between the self and society, between the human and the social, and between society and nature itself. The range of possibility in so-called primitive societies is seen to be as open and complex as those in more advanced societies. Given the globalization of social interaction, no society is far removed from the impact of foreign ideas, the opportunities offered by the Internet, and the introduction of alien ideas, ways of life, and organisms. Conversely, in societies that are relatively complex, certain archaic boundaries are becoming more ambiguous and problematical. For instance, the distinction between what is human and what is animal is con-tested, as is the distinction between society and nature itself. Animals are known to have social organization and to grieve, while humans are known to share most of their DNA, and much of their social and emotional life, with the animal kingdom. Relationships between the individual and the larger society are becom-ing both more complex and diffuse, so that the boundary separating the self from society is no longer easily defined or described. The depths of the psyche are pro-foundly socialized, and the larger society is found to exist largely in the imagi-nation as a set of individual projections. No wonder, then, that the supernatural, the world of angels and of the departed, appears to share increasingly the same social space as the living.

If there is a single activity in which such boundaries are both created and destroyed, it is the study of ritual. There sociology learns from history and ethnography, anthropology and semiotics, sociolinguistics and ethology. No one has discussed the literature in ritual studies more thoroughly or in greater depth than Catherine Bell, who was herself trained as a historian of religion. Her specialization in the history of the religions of China enables her to speak with an uncommon authority, and her comments on the limitations of conventional sociological approaches to the study of ritual therefore carry a particular weight. From her we have learned to see power at work not only in rituals but in the way that sociologists discuss them. To be sure, she has argued, it is important to understand rituals as a form of action; individuals know what they are doing and what rituals mean to them. On the other hand it is also important to understand what the rituals are doing to the participants without their knowledge or consent. To keep both these insights in tension at the same moment is difficult, but it is necessary if one is to keep in sight both poles of the world that ritual itself embraces: the human and the divine, the individual and the social, the personal and the public, the deviant and the regulated, the subversive and the compliant.

Clearly, it is the usual frameworks within which sociologists have discussed religion in general and ritual in particular, their background assumptions and typical interests, that may have made it difficult for sociologists to understand the ambiguity and complexity of rituals. Ritual, as Bell points out, may be able to create unity out of difference, a single lineage out of the divisions that separate classes and generations from one another. However, they do so in ways that are often highly creative and ambiguous. It would be easy for a sociologist intent on discovering order and compliance therefore to miss the anomalous and subversive, the innovative, "uncoercive and experiential" aspects of any rite.

Bell's work therefore helps us to reassess the assumptions that underlie conventional distinctions between religion and the secular, the sacred and the profane, the traditional and the modern, the institutional and the popular. Bell is particularly acute in criticizing the sociological tendency to define religion in opposition to the secular or to magic, to rationality, or to the law. These are the "inflated" and "static" conceptions of a sociology that is far too much informed and shaped by the separation between the secular state and the nation, between rationality and enthusiasm, between law and subversion. These polarities may exist, but in ritual they exist in a state of fluidity as well as tension, and the individual actors do not lose their capacity to invent or modify the social order even when they appear to be subject to it or doomed to replicate and reproduce it. The sacred is where it is created, and it emerges where individuals invoke the blessings of the cosmos on their own self-created communities and lineages.

Remember David Martin's work on the Pentecostal groups that create their own communities in ways that liberate them from the tutelage of the church or from their debts to landowners and their subjection to conventional notions of masculinity. In creating these new open spaces, however, these practitioners of the spirit claim descent from a more ancient lineage and invoke an authority that is subject to no church or state, priest or official. There is, as both David and Bernice Martin and Bell appear to agree, something very modern about the primitive and very primitive about the modern form of the sacred. These scholars have a native respect for those whose piety may seem outdated to those habituated to the assumptions of secular professions and to the order imposed by a system that claims a monopoly on the rational. Like Linda Woodhead, Bell stresses the emptiness of the distinctions between the sacred and the profane and seeks to liberate sociology from the taken-for-granted assumptions embedded in theories of secularization.

There is another way in which Bell's work contributes to the central concerns of this volume. If individuals are finding new ways to express their relation to the ultimate in a world where religion has lost its monopoly on the sacred, it will be necessary to revise our notions of the sacred itself. No longer is it opposed to the profane, since there is a new accessibility and openness to the sacred. No longer is it a "given" that provides an aura of permanence to some institutions and ways of life. Instead, it is itself clearly created and constructed, contrived and contingent on the consent of the devotees themselves. This new element of the provisional and profane in the midst of the sacred is, however, not entirely new. Bell has reminded us that in some of the most ancient practices of Chinese religion there are many degrees of individual freedom in the ways that obeisances such as the bow are made. Similarly, in the use of the trance individuals are placed in immediate touch with divine powers, some benign and others demonic, whose blessing they must seek or whose bane they must avoid. This directness of accessibility is as ancient as it is characteristic of societies in which individuals have become entrepreneurs of their own "spirituality."

Note the lack, in Bell's chapter, of what Erickson so perceptively called "intellectual sadness" in her chapter on Simmel. There is no European sense of a permanent limbo here in which the generations yearn for each other without being able to make fundamental contact with one another across the divides of time and mortality. There is no limbo here, in which individuals seek hopelessly for the immediate and intimate human contact without which they can never know another soul or be known in the depths of their own psyches. In this introduction to the study of ritual in the Chinese context, Bell pays tribute to a capacity that is very ancient although it is of peculiarly modern significance. That is the capacity to entertain the other, to engage in an open-ended conversation with those who are beyond us in some way: beyond us in social status or education, in time and in their acquaintance with death itself. Bell thus reminds us of the capacity for cultural invention, in which individuals find ways to address those who are beyond them and to come in contact with the inaccessible. In this way they create a community or a lineage that they can believe transcends the passage of time. The point is simply that the contingent and fluid, the negotiable and open-ended character of the sacred may not only link the modern world with the ancient but will allow humans to feel at home in a world that remains elusive and changing, ambiguous and risky, demanding and yet obscure in what is being demanded: a world that requires radical commitments with no guarantee of comfort or reward.

If Bell's chapter reminds us of the close ties between disciplines that engage in the study of ritual, so Davies's study reminds us of the need for cross-fertilization between psychology, sociology, and perhaps above all, anthropology. That is in part because anthropologists have long studied social systems that scarcely differentiate between the social and the natural, the human and the social, and between self and society. The need for anthropological insight is also due to the peculiar relationship between the sacred and violence: an affinity long studied by social anthropologists and perhaps less well understood by their sociological colleagues. Thus Davies concludes his argument by developing a model in which he demonstrates how various forms of ritual, especially sacrificial rites, are designed to restore or create a sense of personal well-being combined with a belief that the social order is inherently just.

Whatever may be the liaison between sociology and anthropology, however, both disciplines will need to focus on the sacred in a world where its forms are highly problematical. As Davies points out in his study of various public demonstrations of protest and grief, the symbols and practices of these occasions owe as much to politics and the media as they do to traditional forms of the sacred or to personal devotion. Indeed these events are sometimes contrived, require the interaction of celebrities and celebrants with the ordinary citizen, and they are ambiguous and sometimes subversive of existing authorities. Furthermore, many of these public events are international in scope and involve citizens of many countries reacting together and simultaneously to an event that has captured their very different imaginations. That is, they exhibit the forms of the sacred as we have come to expect them in the course of this book.

Modern societies now host sacred demonstrations of grief and protests over violence that are very traditional, just as the so-called traditional world no longer seems so very different from what we have taken to be the modern. Clearly the sacred emerges, if only temporarily, in these public and yet highly personal responses to deaths that are accidental or otherwise lacking in meaning and justice. Indeed, it would appear that calls for justice carry the freight of a deep sense of personal loss and injury in modern societies. Further, in many of these cases it is difficult to perceive the line separating personal malaise from social injustice, so closely intertwined is the self with the society. Even the line separating the personal and social from the purely natural is broken at these moments, as the body bears not only the weight but also the marks of social injustice and psychological loss.

If the modern world is not so different from the traditional as was once thought, that is in part due to the ritualization of everyday life and of the public sector. In his essay on moral communication in the German context, Luckmann reminds us that much of what passes for secular speech is really modeled after a traditional homily: a sermon on moral topics intended to change the attitudes and behavior of the listener. Such communication thrives in a secular society such as Germany, he argues, in part because the traditional sermon has now lost its institutional context, and the function of moral exhortation has passed to political leaders and to mundane authorities such as parents. Thus he examines a presidential address in which he finds a monologue that follows a traditional pattern of description, prophecy, and exhortation. However, he also analyzes a conversation between a mother and her daughter, in which also a traditional monologue is embedded in their dialogue. The monologue, given by the mother, follows the traditional pattern of the homily and thus describes her daughter's current behavior, warns of its consequences, and appeals for a change.

Note the familiar changes associated with the process of secularization: a transfer of religious functions to secular contexts, a decline in the public authority of institutionalized religion, the loss of an institutionalized framework for the sacred, the lack of an authority mediating the sacred to the profane, and thus the mixing of the sacred with the profane in everyday life. It is therefore not clear, as Luckmann himself points out, how much the pattern of moral communication is indeed following traditional patterns and how much it is a cultural invention whose form is fairly universal.

As Bell's argument about ritual reminds us, therefore, we need to look for the inventive and the subversive, the interactive and the ambiguous, even in behavior that conforms to traditional patterns. Thus Luckmann notes the conversational strategies in the presidential monologue, for example, the attempts to include the speaker in the same category as the listener, and the rhetorical devices designed to elicit guilt and to ward off defensive responses. In the very process of decomposing the President's speech into its rhetorical strategies, moreover, Luckmann reduces serious communication to the merely strategic and compares presidents with each other more or less unfavorably. There is a subversive element in the chapter itself, therefore: one that is more clearly evident in his analysis of the conversation between the mother and daughter. There the mother engages in a serious speech to her daughter on the subject of the latter's smoking, even as the daughter attempts to dilute, divert, and subvert the mother's authority. The somewhat improvised nature of moral communication in modern societies is further illustrated by Douglas Davies in his chapter on social and psychological responses to disasters. Like Luckmann, he finds that there is an implicitly religious structure to what appears otherwise to be wholly secular communication. Indeed he compares the formulae of public language and legal documentation regarding disasters with that of seventeenth century liturgy.

Note also how Luckmann is reluctant to draw any grand conclusions from his study of moral communication. Especially missing are inferences to the social order itself or abstract conceptual schemes in which Luckmann might be tempted to generalize to universal patterns of communication. Like Bell, he prefers to avoid any "inflated" and "static" concepts. Allowing that the latter may exist, he prefers to stay within the text of his conversations without even drawing modest inferences from the conversation or the speech to the actual relationships existing between mother and daughter, the President and the public.

In Beyer's chapter we have a further assessment of the ways that sociologists of religion need to rethink their relationship to other disciplines and to imagine religion itself in entirely new ways. Beyer notes that the difference between sociology and anthropology has hinged on distinctions that are now relatively meaningless in a global social system. Anthropologists are thus looking at cities, and sociologists are examining the smaller-scale and face-to-face worlds previously studied in exquisite detail by anthropologists. The distinction between the traditional and the modern is also becoming anachronistic in a world where societies and individuals that are very far apart nonetheless take each other carefully into account. Also on the list of anachronisms is the distinction between societies in which the sacred is relatively complex and institutionalized and those in which the sacred is more amorphous, endemic, and episodic. There is indeed something very primitive and traditional in the ways that religion is taking shape in the most complex and modern of circumstances.

Beyer notes other concepts that now should be given a decent burial. One is the notion of forms as a source of religious variation and of functions as a basis for comparing similarities in religious belief and practice across social boundaries. The forms used to be thought to vary while the functions were remarkably similar: a convenient handle for interpreting "primitive" religion in relation to "modern" societies. Now, Beyer notes, these varied forms may be mirror images of each other as individuals and groups in a wide range of societies see themselves through others' eyes. Furthermore, not only are the forms increasingly a result of symbolic interaction rather than a source of religious difference; they are becoming so fluid and amorphous as to defy easy recognition and comparison. Finally, Beyer notes, it will be necessary to rethink what it is we mean by religion itself: a point made earlier by others in this volume, notably Beckford.

If there is a sociological version of the "Fall," it is in the notion of differentiation: the process by which traditional and primitive societies became complex. Individuals became discrete entities demanding their own identity and autonomy; the self came into conflict with society. In the earlier stages of the process of differentiation, the social defined itself in opposition to nature. Later in the same process, notions of what constitutes the human came to be distinguished from what was merely and particularly social. Ideas of a universal human nature came to offer a far greater range of possibility than the social.

Now, if Beyer is right, we will find sociologists and anthropologists alike studying a world in which these distinctions no longer make a difference. As individuals expand their social networks they will adapt their own lives and self-conceptions to what they imagine to be the views of their counterparts in far-flung societies. This is not a new phenomenon, as anthropologists know who have found "natives" defining themselves in anthropological terms as a result of earlier studies. However that process is no longer singular to field work. Field work, so to speak, has become universalized by travel, the flow of ideas and people across boundaries, and by the Internet itself.

Similarly problematical is the boundary between the social sciences and the humanities. The Gulbenkian Commission (1996) has explored these boundaries in some detail, noting the variety of trends that have created a state in which the social sciences are ready to be opened to the natural sciences and to the humanities. The subjectivity of the researcher, the role of hermeneutics in the social and natural sciences as well as in the humanities, dynamic interaction between the observer and the observed even in the physical sciences, the role of contingency even in apparently stable social and natural processes, and the awareness of a wide range of possibilities in systems whose boundaries are at best diffuse: all these contribute to a moment in which the boundaries between the physical, the natural, and the social are increasingly ambiguous. It is not surprising, then, that the boundaries between the fields that study them should also be problematical and contested.

Not only the boundary between sociology and anthropology but that between sociology and theology is now open for discussion and revision. That is the argument made by Kieran Flanagan, who goes so far as to suggest that sociology could once again be seen as a form of theology. That is because, like theology, sociology seeks to interpret, give form and coherence to, and evaluate the testimonies of individuals and groups not only to their religious experience but to their faith. The sociological task is made more pressing, he argues, because the sacred has indeed escaped the confines of institutionalized religion. Theology therefore stands in need of sociological assistance if it is to grasp the range of the sacred in social life, in its particular contexts, and in the depth of the individual's encounter with it. The world is hardly as disenchanted as those have thought who have uncritically adopted an oversimplified notion of the process of secularization.

However, as Flanagan goes on to argue, sociologists themselves need the assistance of theology. Following Simmel, Flanagan notes that social life itself is deeply rooted in the search of the soul for an anchor, for response and recognition, and finally for a sense of purpose and destiny. Even secular societies are therefore the product of a spiritual quest. If sociologists are to grasp the spiritual dimensions and consequences of social life in general and of secularized societies in particular, they will need to learn from theology how to recognize, interpret, and evaluate testimonies to religious experience. In this task they will be well advised, Flanagan argues, to return to Simmel's work. It is worth reading his chapter, then, in relationship to the chapter by Victoria Erickson. Flanagan also takes note of David Martin's capacity to find in religion an expression and an embodiment of the deep contradictions of social life: not only those between races and genders, but between the capacity for surrender and self-assertion, between life and death.

If indeed sociologists are now called upon to understand individuals as those who can at least partially imagine themselves outside of any given or particular social context, they will need to revise their conventional understandings of what constitutes individuality. For some, notably those with a Durkheimian viewpoint, individuals are largely a social product and can best be understood as unwittingly replicating the social contexts in which they have been able to develop. On the other hand, those with a more Weberian outlook have seen society itself as the often unintended consequence of individuals striving to enhance their control over the symbols and statuses, goods and services that make life possible. Neither viewpoint, I argue in the epilogue, really equips contemporary sociologists with the ability to understand those who seek to define themselves over and against any and all forms of social life. In doing so they face high levels of ambiguity and uncertainty and seek increasingly to define even their mortality in their own terms.

Reference

Gulbenkian Commission 1996. *Open the Social Sciences*, Report of the Gulbenkian Commission on the Restructuring of the Social Sciences, Stanford, CA: Stanford University Press.

CHAPTER 20

Acting Ritually: Evidence from the Social Life of Chinese Rites

Catherine Bell

The religious rituals and ceremonial activities commonly found in social life can appear to be rather straightforward objects of scholarly interest. Yet the way we scrutinize these activities is, in fact, complicated by a variety of cultural perspectives, disciplinary assumptions, and historical agendas. Certainly the secular humanist decrying the credulous piety of the devout, or the born-again minister entreating the hard of heart to fall to their knees represent very different orientations to ritual within our culture. Likewise, the missionary, the tourist – and the scholar – have projected distinct frames of reference on rituals of cultures more distant in history, geography, or purported stages of civilization. Since the early theories of William Robertson-Smith ([1889] 1969) and Emile Durkheim ([1915] 1965) on the cultic origins of social community, scholars have used a succession of interpretative frameworks to address the social function of ritual activities, the cultural meanings of their symbolic gestures, and the most effective ways to analyze this particular mode of human behavior. In addition, on-going debates over basic interpretative approaches to ritual, and the agendas that they imply, have been important occasions for social analysis to reflect on itself.

This chapter will trace several major issues in the sociological conceptualization of ritual in a context that illuminates key tensions in current thinking. To do this, it will look to China, both the phenomenon of ritual in China and the history of sociological attempts to analyze Chinese ritual. In 1938 Bronislaw Malinowski argued that systematic social analysis of China was a landmark, pushing fieldwork and theory beyond their early and limited focus on so-called simpler societies to grapple with the full complexities of civilization as such. Paying tribute to Malinowski some 25 years later, the social anthropologist Maurice Freedman argued that the study of China not only *could* change the fields of sociology and anthropology, it absolutely *must* change them (Freedman 1979:380–97). Although both arguments recognized the challenges that Chinese culture presents to the deep-seated assumptions and agendas of traditional European-American social analysis, there are few areas where these challenges have been more interesting than the study of ritual.

For those who think about ritual, China certainly presents an embarrassment of riches. The "riches" not only include a particularly long and complex history of ceremonial practices, but one accompanied by the oldest continuous written tradition of systematic reflection – simultaneously philosophical, moral, religious, and political – on what rites are and should be. When compared to those sociological projects that attempted to focus on the most "elementary forms" of social and religious life, the study of China presents too much material – a thick history of ritual terminology and writings, as well as a vast panorama of folk customs, mediums and shamans, canons of etiquette, divinely revealed liturgies, and politically significant imperial ceremonies. There are esoteric rites for highly trained specialists, government bureaus for ritual affairs, and manuals of simplified ceremonies for popular consumption. There are tightly transmitted ritual formats and radically fresh cultic creations. And there is ample evidence that people share basic assumptions about these practices even while they engage in them in quite individual ways. The "embarrassment" of these riches surfaces in two painfully obvious facts. First, no general theory of ritual can begin to address adequately the sheer scope of relevant information; all attempts to analyze even the most prominent dimensions of this material must simplify, reduce, and exclude to a truly discomforting extent. Second, the pragmatic choices we make in this necessary reductionism may inadvertently promote our most conventional assumptions and limit what we learn from China.

History of Chinese Sociology

Chinese ritual practices have always intrigued foreign visitors who inevitably bring their own particular interpretative categories with them to Asia. Whether or not Marco Polo actually had as much firsthand knowledge about China as his *Travels* suggest, his account of thirteenth century "Cathay" voiced the European dilemma of reconciling Chinese "idolatry" with accounts of the "excellence of their manner and their knowledge of many subjects" (Polo 1958:160, Wood 1995). Several centuries later, Catholic missionary orders and the Vatican argued for decades about the complex place of ancestor rituals in Chinese social life and, more to the point, whether Chinese converts to Roman Catholicism must renounce these practices. Jesuits working in China at the time praised what they saw as the enlightened rationalism of China's ethic of filial piety, but castigated what they saw as the irrationalism of the rites of Buddhist "asceticism" and Taoist "magic" (Spence 1992:79). The Rites Controversy, as the seventeenth and eighteenth century debate over ancestor rites came to be known, remains a particularly illuminating example of multiple, self-interested views on what constitutes ritual and religion. The French Enlightenment philosopher Voltaire concluded that "the great misunderstanding over Chinese rites sprang from our judging their practices in the light of ours: we carry the prejudices that spring from our contentious nature to the ends of the world" (quoted in Spence 1992:82). Yet this pithy insight could do nothing to forestall subsequent judging and the inevitable misses in understanding.

Among the fresh flood of Protestant missionaries that entered China after the Opium War (1839–42), many were gradually drawn into the excitement of classical translation or amateur ethnography. With commentary that ranged from admiration to abhorrence, the latter group recorded even the most humble rituals observed among the people of China's towns and villages – despite repeated entreaties from their mission boards at home to spend more time documenting the number of souls they were supposed to be saving. More formally trained scholars followed them, giving rise to the first important sociological studies of Chinese religion. Their concerns differed from missionary impulses to condemn, praise, or simply inventory the variety of beliefs and practices found in China. In vast projects such as J.J.M. de Groot's six-volume study, *The Religious System of China* (1892–1910), in focused monographs like Edouard Chavannes's ([1910] 1970) *Le T'ai chan: Essai de monographie d'un culte chinois*, and in trenchant syntheses like Marcel Granet's *La religion des Chinois* ([1922] 1975), scholars began to look self-consciously beneath the surface of Chinese ritual activities in order to uncover implicit cultural categories organizing Chinese society and culture as a whole.[1]

By the middle of the twentieth century, Chinese sociologists such as Fei Hsiao-t'ung, Francis L.K. Hsu, and C.K. Yang were also contributing major studies of the central role of ritual practices in shaping Chinese family life, social organization and cultural attitudes (Fei 1939, Hsu [1948] 1971, Yang 1961). Since the 1960s, the amount of scholarship published in Western and Asian languages on Chinese ritual, both ancient and modern, is truly staggering, spanning the fields of history, sociology, anthropology, religious studies, and political science. (For the scholarship in Western languages, see Thompson 1985, Thompson and Seaman 1993, 1998.)

Looking back over the more sociological examples of this scholarship, it is apparent that a few basic concerns have dominated the questions pursued and the methods used. For the most part, interest in ritual in general and Chinese ritual in particular has been greatly shaped by the desire to understand how groups maintain their social unity and cultural coherence (Bell 1989). For the scholar, an interest in the essential unity of Chinese culture became closely tied to the project of understanding its cultural distinctiveness – its "Chineseness" so to speak (Vandermeersch 1976, Freedman 1979:352, Nathan 1993:932). The tendency to see ritual as some sort of functional mechanism for creating social unity reinforced the nearly tautological view that what makes Chinese culture so different is precisely its ritualism – that is, its reliance on ceremony as the most important medium of socialization. Studies have not only explored the ritual nature of Chinese family and village life, but also the ritual dominance of its political institutions (Chang 1983, Wheatley 1971) and cultural style of governing (Wechsler 1985, Smith 1989, Kuhn 1970). At times contrasts with the self-described rational, secular, progressive, and law-based cultures of the West have been very starkly drawn.

For example, in older studies, such as Granet's work on ancient matrimonial and funeral rites, a focus on ritual is linked to a grand narrative (seen in *La civilisation chinoise* [1929] 1951 and *La pensée chinoise* [1934] 1950), which lays out the manifold differences in Chinese and European forms of thought, and roots them in contrasting forms of social organization and stages of history. Even recent studies of Chinese religion continue to look, quite self-consciously, for the principles that form the coherent holism underlying the manifest diversity of Chinese culture. In this quest, social analysts have seen ritual life as basic to the deep order of Chinese society and frequently seen one set of rituals – ancestor rites – as a type of key to the culture (Freedman 1979:352–3, Watson 1985, 1988, Ebrey 1991:3–4).

Underlying this continuity of approach, however, analyses of how ritual functions – that is, how it actually manages to promote social unity and cultural coherence – have become increasingly complex. Distancing themselves from Durkheim's description of the enthusiastic experience of the social group in the guise of transcendent power, recent approaches describe cultic ritual as a more procedural medium of socialization in which the variety of surface concerns is subtly and flexibly recast in terms of the deeper structures buried in the rite. For Freedman and James Watson, for example, the deep structure of ritual is unique in its ability to express and impose social unity despite a diversity of imagery, symbols and styles (Freedman 1979:367, Watson 1985, 1988). In this context, a richly nuanced study of the cult of the goddess Tianhou in southern China can point to how standardized ritual activities allow them to mediate different sociopolitical groups and concerns to form a loose but accommodating sociocultural coherence (Watson 1985). This approach identifies ritual, more than any other set of social activities (such as the written language or the governing apparatus of the state) as the basic social mechanism for consolidating key social groups (such as family, village, and nation) and transmitting key cultural values (such as hierarchy and authority) in a society in which there has been no national church and little standardization of belief.

This role for ritual is evident even in those studies that start out considering the major divisions in Chinese culture, variously defined as high versus low culture, official versus peasant classes, elite versus popular, or local versus regional identities. Very few studies have taken the divisions in Chinese culture so seriously that they resist emphasizing China's basic social and cultural unity. In a notable example, Stephan Feuchtwang (1992) uses a particularly polarized model of the relationship between local cults and more national traditions. He argues that local cults are predominantly autonomous institutions with long and fixed traditions of their own that are fundamentally opposed to the more embracing institutions of the state, as well as Taoist and Confucian institutions, which constantly attempt to appropriate them. Feuchtwang's ethnography suggests that this deep opposition is expressed in the notions of demonic power routinely evoked by local cults. For such cults, the cosmos is always mobilized for a war against demonic forces. Not only is this local cosmos in stark contrast to the imperial cosmos of centralized harmony and order, but for the local village cult, Feuchtwang argues, the imperial cosmos itself is experienced as a demonic force. From this perspective, the rites and festivals of village cults present alternative and dissenting histories at odds with official history and culture. In contrast to the many ritual theories emphasizing cultural unity, this type of analysis is at pains to demonstrate that popular religious practices are not just regional reflections of the dominant ideology, but deeply heterodox visions of an alternative one. Nonetheless, ritual is still the essential means by which local culture defines itself in opposition to more central and inclusive models of religious and cultural life. In other words, it is the ritual activities of the village that provide the defining ethos of a unified local identity.

The same role for ritual is seen in a series of new studies of Chinese secret societies in both premodern and modern periods (Naquin 1985, Haar 1992, Ownby and Heidhues 1993). They show that such groups are not simply an assemblage of people acting on shared political beliefs that they express in ritual; rather, ritual is the very means by which the group assembles itself with a distinctive religiopolitical identity and agenda. Studies of Taoism employ a similar form of analysis, as when Kenneth Dean (1993) argues that the coherence of Taoism today lies in how it functions as a liturgical framework that links local customs and festivals to a translocal or regional network of groups. Hence, Taoist liturgy, which gives the Taoist tradition its defining identity, mediates high culture and low culture, local culture and national culture, and in this way helps create the warp and woof of Chinese society as a whole.

Whether the scholarly perspective favors a unified and holistic picture of Chinese culture or a more fractured view of social tension and contention, these studies invariably find ritual to be central to the dynamics by which people generate a socially consolidating view of the cosmos and its divine powers. In that sense, sociological theory of ritual finds what it is looking for – an essential place for ritual in the construction of social life. Yet the success of this search raises some pertinent questions: what would we learn from China if we were less sure what we were looking for? Does our interest in and approach to ritual impose an agenda on the data that subordinates Chinese experience to a predetermined set of categories and a predetermined model of social dynamics? Have we allowed China to change sociology in the ways Malinowski and Freedman envisioned?

To raise these questions is not to suggest that the sociological literature on China is wrong or misguided. These studies have not only uncovered a great deal of factual information, they have generated very useful depictions of cultural dynamics for scrutiny and testing. At the same time, however, this research may be unduly constrained in its goal of better understanding ritual by its own assumptions and methods. Certainly there is an assumption that ritual is an essentially well-defined phenomenon; specifically, the high-profile role it is given in the construction of social groups is apt to reinforce a rather monolithic view of ritual as a *very* distinctive way of acting, usually characterized by a distinctive internal structure (Turner 1969, Geertz 1973:112–13). By virtue of this structure, ritual is then credited with the ability to effect nothing less than a type of social alchemy. But exactly how ritual does all that it is credited with doing is more often inferred than actually demonstrated.

There are also critics of the theoretical tendencies in Western scholarship, such as Talal Asad, who suggest that universalized categories like ritual are implicated in the way scholars identify the ethnographic "other" as an object of analysis. These categories also may inherit the legacy of the history of social analysis in the West which emerged as part of an effort on the part of the secular state to control religion (Asad 1993). Further, it can be argued that secular scholarship actually defines much of its own enterprise of objective research by its polarized scrutiny of ritual as the quintessentially social subjective datum (Bell 1992:47–54, 1997:253–67).

Despite these problems, there is embryonic evidence in the preceding scholarship that China can teach us a number of useful things for broadening our thinking about the dynamics involved in what we mean by ritual. In brief, Chinese data demonstrates that much depends on who gets to define what is ritual. Chinese examples remind us that what we lump together as "ritual" is basically a wide spectrum of ways of acting that do what they do with a whole vocabulary of physical and linguistic gestures. Finally, we learn that this medium of activity is a very flexible one, amenable to promoting unity or division, but always invoked to root this unity or division in embracing cosmological orientations – religious, secular, with divine beings or without.

Vocabulary

In an attempt to clarify the influence, if any, of external categories and agendas on Chinese data, a handful of studies have focused on the various terms used in Chinese history to piece together basic understandings of ritual in Chinese culture (Wechsler 1985, Ebrey 1991, Schipper 1995, Bastid-Bruguiere 1995). It is quickly apparent that for the most commonly cited term, *li*, the translation "ritual" obscures its most interesting features. Closely associated with wine libations in ancient usage, *li* became the focus of Confucian teachings for centuries, but as such it often had little to do with worship of deities and routinely included features not usually central to our notion of ritual, such as personal morality, musical aesthetics, and even sartorial rules for the official classes. Schipper concludes that other terms – *fa* (rules, forms of sacrifice), *dian* (canon, rules), and *yi* (right conduct, ceremonies, rule, deportment) – are closer equivalents, at least in premodern China, based on how they were used and what they usually included (Schipper 1995:4–6).

When analyzed in their historical contexts, it is also apparent that the variety of terminology used for activities like ritual, ceremony, sacrifice, incense offerings, and etiquette is not the result of a simple proliferation of neutral vocabulary by a highly ritualized people – as tropical peoples are credited with many more words for mosquito or Arctic peoples with words for ice. Rather, these terms are associated with real tensions over proper and improper ceremonies, such as concerted efforts to draw or muddle boundaries between social classes, or the struggles between government-approved and nonapproved cults (Stein 1979, Weller 1987, Ebrey 1991). The shifting purview of all these terms also demonstrates constant historical fluidity rather than timeless consensus. China's long historical record provides many examples of how terminological distinctions are closely tied to one institution attempting to control definitions of what is authentic or orthodox ritual on the one hand as opposed to vulgar custom, impropriety, foreign parallels, or even sorcery on the other. Through such attempts at control, and the counter attempts to promote practices and terms that challenge control, people who deploy ritual are reifying understandings of the cosmos that empower them to construe reality in ways that often conflict with each other.

The lesson about who defines ritual does not mean that sociologists should simply accept Chinese distinctions at face value. Chinese terms are as tied to their historical context as our own conventional terminology for ritual. But sociological analysis must incorporate understandings of these terminological dynamics into any approach that attempts truly to engage the Chinese experience. No one's terms are neutral. (On the analogous difficulties of applying the terminology – and Western notion of "religion" – to China see Yang 1961:1–27 and Schipper 1993:2–3.) There is some evidence that only a secular state, distancing itself from much tradition and most religion (which are both strategically defined in the process), would find the enormous consolidations of the single term "ritual" useful. Insofar as the sociology of religion developed in the context of a secularizing state, it may be prone to make the same basic assumptions. The more monolithic the terminology and the more essentialist the view of ritual, the more this approach imposes a powerful set of assumptions about objectivity, religion, and other societies.

Realizing that traditional usage would not readily lump together the complex *jiao* rites (rites of renewal) of the Taoists, the domestic incense offerings to the ancestors, and the elaborate state-sponsored celebrations at the Confucian temple on the sage's birthday, it is easier to see that in fact there is no generic Taoist *jiao* ritual, no uniform style of domestic offering, and no standardized imperial enthronement ritual (Bell 1998:215). On the contrary, there are many specific performances that differ from each other even as they carry over recognizable features. A more effective approach would be one that could track the way traditional forms are freshly codified, appropriated, nuanced, and manipulated. To do this would be to focus on how the activities themselves define and distinguish what they are doing – that is, to approach ritual as human activity that must be grasped in terms of action itself – as much as we can (Bell 1992:69–74).

Take, for example, the activity of bowing, which was once ubiquitous in China. It is a fully physical gesture that people learn by seeing and doing, and in most cases knowledge of how to bow is part of people's socialization and, ultimately, their particular effectiveness in social communication. There is no one formula for bowing; while there are various formal styles and numerous informal styles, all have lots of room for personal touches whether one is making three quick bows in front of an altar, the infamous kowtow demanded of all who would be received by the Qing emperors, or the finely calibrated exchanges of courtesy bows involved in greeting friends and strangers. Analysis of the semantics of bowing – the major styles used, when and where, to what degree, with what cultural assumptions or self-conscious purposes, and how nuances are introduced and read by others – would provide a great deal of information about the Chinese sense of ritual in the social and religious spheres, the way individuals can manipulate standardized ways of acting, and the specific ways in which such nuanced courtesies can affect and effect social relations. Such a study would have trouble maintaining distinctions among ritual, etiquette, and morality on the one hand, and social formulas and individual creativity on the other – because bowing seems designed to be effective in ways that confound all such distinctions. Nonetheless, we might see in the full spectrum of bowing a perpetuation of a stratified vision of society and cosmos, even as individual bows work this system to their own advantage. (For an interesting analysis of refusal to bow see Hevia 1995.)

To get beyond our overly determined category of ritual (as well as the self-interested categories of various Chinese institutions) and explore how Chinese ceremonial activities are constructed and wielded, we need to focus on the physical vocabulary. Since this cannot include analysis of every bow, hand gesture, or chant, a relevant unit must be defined. The relevant units should be distinct sequences, visible in different contexts, that establish meaningful cosmological orientations (cf. Dean's notion of "key ritual paradigms" 1993:175). A ritual performance might involve just one sequence, several juxtaposed, or a more complicated dynamics by which some sequences reinterpret others. How these sequences are deployed is basic both to how ritual activities do what they do, and to how tradition is both established and modified. Naturally, any attempt to delineate a full repertoire of Chinese ritual sequences – that is, to construct some sort of comprehensive semiotic system – would probably result in an ethnographic abstraction as inflated and static as the notion of "Chinese ritual" itself. Still, such sequences clearly have semiotic relationships with each other; they derive much of their significance and effect by virtue of their contrasts to other sequences and even to nonritual ways of acting (Bell 1992:90).[2]

Examples of Ritual Sequences

There are a few ritual sequences, frequently distinguished from each other and just as often compounded in various arrangements, which can serve to demonstrate this analytic focus on the physical actions of ritual – namely, the trance, the incense burner, cosmic ordering of space and time, and the offering of bureaucratic petitions. While there are many more sequences that may be identified in the spectrum of ritual practices in China, these four appear to be particularly basic.

Trance

Trance, one of the earliest and most enduring postures in Chinese ritual activities, is regularly described as the very "substratum" of Taoism in particular and Chinese religion in general (Schipper 1993:6). It includes shamanic journeys to other worlds and mediumistic possession by a descending spirit; naturally, it is also closely linked to states of possession by intrusive forces that the medium must exorcise. The trance services of a medium or shaman include communicating with the gods, spirits, and ancestors, conveying offerings, and bringing back charms and messages. In the nineteenth and twentieth centuries, most temples (particularly visible today in Taiwan, Hong Kong, Malaysia, and Singapore) have employed a trained medium or two (*jitong*, literally "divining-stick child") who is consulted by individuals but also participates in festivals and major rituals, sometimes alongside ordained Taoists and Buddhists.

In general, trance appears to be most associated with local cults and the particular type of cosmos that such cults project. The medium or shaman in trance is essentially acting among visible and invisible beings who do not keep to neatly separate spheres of reality; instead, the dead, living, and divine interpenetrate in numerous ways. The medium wields power in this confluence of forces by virtue of his or her authority to command. Some command authority is built on personal relationships established with particular deities who can be summoned when needed, but command authority is also seen in the medium's ability to recruit an army of spirits that agree to serve him or her. Summoned with the blow of a horn, mediums regularly direct this spirit army to roust demons and impurities. In contrast to the use of an incense burner, mediums do not mediate cosmic realms; they join the fray of forces as a type of military commander ready to do battle in the interest of the client or community. When leading a temple procession, the medium engages local demons in battle, brandishing sword and halberd and incurring bloody wounds, in order to purify the temple area. Generally, in such a cosmology, power is accessible to anyone who appears to be chosen by the gods to train in the techniques of trance. It is a cosmos where power is elemental and fluid, good or demonic, to be seized and wielded by those who can display prowess.

The ritual posture of trance is one that the earliest Chinese political institutions attempted to coopt, with some scattered instances in later history as well. For the most part, however, the standard government position has been to outlaw or marginalize trance as much as possible because the cosmos and empowerment evoked by trance can subvert the type of authority claimed by the state or other religious experts. In essence, trance gives an individual immediate and direct access to cosmic power while defining the cosmos in ways that collapse distinctions critical to the definition of other experts. So, while trance may have been central to the earliest forms of political authority, when the state grew to embrace multiple regions and subcultures, and adopted more formal, invested, and bureaucratically defined forms of power, trance constituted a threat.

Lighting incense

Lighting incense in an incense burner is another physical sequence quite distinct from trance, but an equally ancient and ubiquitous element in Chinese ritual life. In fact, some scholars conclude that the incense burner is the basic requirement of any Chinese "cult," that is, the formal worship of a deity by a community. No temple, image, or clergy is needed for worship – only the incense burner is indispensable. A Taoist text makes this explicit: "You have only to set up the incense burner for the divine empyrean to be present" (Schipper 1993:85). Yet an incense burner communicates only with the gods, not the demonic or ambivalent spirits invoked in trance. Reflecting perhaps the physical significance of focusing on an external object, or the visual experience of watching rings of incense smoke waft upwards to disappear, the incense burner sets up a formalized mediating relationship between two realms, the human and the divine, which are in this process more clearly distinguished from each and made dependent on an organized form of intercommunication.

The burner thus links two polarized realities with a formal method of exchange: for their incense, prayers and devotion, supplicants are given the deity's patronage and blessings. But more, gathered around an incense burner, a group of people do not only become a unified community but a type of lineage established by the deity, sons and daughters of the deity, brothers and sisters, aunts and uncles to each other. The type of clan bond suggested here, rooted in ritual, can be constructed by incense offerings in the small burner on a domestic ancestral altar, in the huge bronze brazier that dominates the courtyard of a village temple, or in the urn around which secret societies swear oaths of brotherhood. When a community grows too large, or some of its people decide to emigrate, the ashes in the community's brazier are divided (*fenxiang*) with a portion placed in a new brazier that will forever see itself as the "child" of the first.

The lineage-style community formed by a cult of the burner tends to be a relatively egalitarian one. Use of a burner does not generate ranks among the living, rather it funnels all the living to this one point of contact with all the divine. Hence, recourse to use of the burner is a powerful invocation of a human–divine opposition and reciprocity that empowers those who can mediate it successfully – gathering a community made whole and harmonious by its patronage of a deity who becomes their divine parent.

Cosmic ordering

A third ritual pattern distinct from trance and the incense burner, cosmic ordering is a sequence that realigns the spatial and temporal order of the earthly realm to put it in full harmony with the natural divine order of the universe. Various studies identify a type of "correlative thought" or "principle of synchronicity" underlying this form of ritual action by which the cosmos is envisioned as an interrelated whole (Jung 1950:xxiv–v, Needham 1956:216). While cosmic ordering is seen most clearly in imperial rites and some forms of divination, it also turns up as a component of other ritual activities, such as Taoist *jiao* liturgies and village processions that take the local temple deity on a formal tour of his or her realm. Most commonly, this ritual pattern focuses on an altar of tiered steps, carefully oriented to the four directions and forming a sacred mountain and cosmic axis to connect the zenith and nadir. The passage of the imperial retinue through these directions is carefully choreographed with temporal considerations, both seasonal and quotidian. In the elaborated imperial cult of later dynasties, the emperor would conduct a series of rites throughout the year in a succession of suburban altars keyed to each season's central symbols and activities.

This form of ritual action invokes a cosmos centered and unified by virtue of an appeal to intrinsic forces of order and harmony. But it is a cosmos that can be dominated from the particular pivotal position marked out. It is interesting to note that in this ritual pattern human beings do not claim to be the center, simply to step into a center that exists. As such, the ritual movements establish a pivotal point in such a way that the agency of the emperor or ritual officiant almost disappears (Zito 1987:343).

Cosmic ordering depends on a number of popular correlative systems of classification that link human physiology, psychology, and even morality to corresponding phenomena in the natural and celestial world. These classification systems create complex analogies between the microcosm of the human body and the macrocosm of the country and even the universe. The imperial state used such systems to naturalize its own authority and institutional forms, elaborating at various times the connections between government offices and spatial directions, the seasons, and the constellations. This form of ritual action is closely linked to astronomical prognostications and the determination of the annual calendar, two activities strictly controlled by imperial authority. Popular forms of divination, from use of the Classic of Changes (*Yijing*) to marriage partner prognostications itemized in the annual almanac, are all based on the logic underlying this ritual pattern.

Cosmic ordering is far from being the only pattern employed in imperial ritual. Although it is one of the earliest, and closely associated with claims to centralized dominion and a type of divine right, many other ritual patterns came to overlay it in developing the institution and rituals of imperial authority. The emperor might pace out the order of time and space, adjusting the synchronic order by rounding the altar to heaven in the south at the winter solstice and squaring the altar in the north at the summer solstice; but he would also use an incense burner to invoke lineage relationships that cast him as the dutiful son and heir of the lineage of lineages. He would also invoke the contractual relations with the divine pantheon that is implied in the ritual use of written memorials.

Written memorials and petitions

Written memorials and petitions to the gods invoke a type of bureaucratized cosmos in which the wielder of the texts has a type of contractual right to be heard, to expect effective action, and to hold the spirits addressed accountable for the quality of their response. Written petitions can be drawn up by shamans, Taoist priests, and imperial officials among others, usually following explicit models but allowing room for personal concerns; these are usually burned but may also be buried or, in more ancient practice, cast into ravines or rivers or left on mountain tops. These petitions assume the existence of an organized hierarchy of spiritual beings, that is, a heavenly pantheon, but they also assume a human hierarchy in which literary skills or ordination into a priesthood confers the ability to address the very highest forms of divinity in this way. In effect, simply wielding a written petition posits a cosmos organized around a legitimate set of ranks and rungs of authority.

This cosmic bureaucracy is, as Weber would put it, more rationalized (predictable, formal, depending on office) than the cosmos of the entranced shaman or medium, but potentially more oppressive by virtue of its remove from human affairs. At the same time this style of ritual cosmos offers more ways to manipulate the system as such – if one has access to those people who are trained to do that. The use of written memorials also formalizes a particular style of ritual authority and mediation that goes well beyond the form invoked by the incense burner. The liturgists wielding a formal petition to the gods are themselves part of a vast bureaucracy that spans the human and divine realms, not a specialist orchestrating a powerful moment or point of contact between these two realms. Such officiants usually undergo more formal training and initiatory rites, with grades of career and spiritual advancement. The net effect of this ritual posture is to subordinate many other ritual patterns (and authorities) by identifying them with various tiers of the larger cosmic bureaucracy. This posture has proven to be a powerful stance for Taoist liturgists in defining an expertise that dominates local shamans and mediums on the one hand, and that respects the imperial cosmos while still transcending it, with access to the ultimate realms of the Tao, on the other.

The development of scholarly studies of the Taoist liturgical tradition in the last twenty years has made it possible to recognize more of these sequences and to appreciate the various ways in which they are deployed in actual practice (Schipper 1993, Lagerwey 1987, Saso 1972). In an elaborate Taoist rite like the *jiao* various sequences are layered and juxtaposed so as to define a special cosmological realm and mediational expertise. The *jiao* combines trance, an incense burner, cosmic ordering and written petitions in ways that enable the Taoist master to subordinate local ritualists and their local cosmos on the one hand, while embarking on imperial-style cosmic ordering on the other.[3] The physical sequences are orchestrated to reify a multitiered cosmos of spiritual ranks that, nonetheless, can be aligned by ordering and petitions so that the whole stratified edifice of the cosmos temporarily collapses into complete oneness, with the

highest realm of the Tao descending to fill the Taoist master, flood the community, and renew the whole earthly realm (Bell 1988). In this way, the Taoist
claims powers that transcend those of other ritual experts, while sufficiently
complementing them and supporting a place for them that is not a direct threat
to their world views and social positions.

Such examples suggest that a few physical sequences can generate diverse
evocations of cosmos, community, and mediating authority. They do so simply
by virtue of how the body physically moves about and handles various imple-
ments. We can say that with these movements people are *constructing* a universe,
although the participants actually see themselves as *responding* to a universe that
facilitates such actions on their part. The special logic of most ritual appears to
turn on this feature: it is the type of practical medium by which people can
visibly, formally, and explicitly *attest* to a whole cosmos of implicit *assumptions*
about the nature of reality. Ritual activities, from the elaborate *jiao* to the modest
bow, promote particular attitudes toward reality in a notably uncoercive and
experiential way.

Conclusion

If the sociological theories described earlier are correct – ritual is a central
medium for the construction of social groups and the emphasis in Chinese
society on this medium has a generally unifying effect – then analysis of the
vocabulary of physical sequences may help explain exactly how. It does not
appear that a particular structure underlying all ritual is the cause of its social
alchemy. Rather, physical sequences create temporal unities by evoking familiar sets of symbolic orientations or providing convincing experiences of less
familiar ones. Sequences can be performed in ways that claim to reproduce
time-honored traditions or claim to revolutionize them. As a medium ritual
tends to be conservative simply because it is always making use of an established
physical vocabulary, but it still orchestrates fresh permutations in which tradition resonates within and legitimates new connections and meanings. Unities
across regional or class differences appear to operate in the same way. The
literate Taoist masters who inscribe petitions to the upper bureaucracy of the
realms of Tao are evoking the upper class stance of the *literaté*, even as their
meditative trances link them to the concerns of the local community. Another
dimension of the unifying effect of ritual may lie squarely in the performative
force of physical enactment and multisensory spectacle. Certainly Chinese
writers themselves have long pointed out that the conventions of public performance give ritual a special effect on people's hearts and minds. For the classic
Book of Li (*Liji*), when a host and guests are seated in the correctly prescribed
directions, and the proper utensils are used in the correct order, then virtue
can occur, the body is "moralized" by this very physical ordering (see Yang
1961:225–6).

The implicit cosmological framework of ritual sequences appears, in the examples from Chinese history, much more constant than a focus on supernatural beings. This is particularly clear in the more Confucian liturgical traditions, where commentators regularly interpret the rite in terms of its moral effects, even denying any sort of spiritual presence. These examples challenge our tendency to equate ritual with religion and religious notions of divinity (Lawson and McCauley 1990). China may be suggesting that our conventional categories of the religious and the secular are more historically contingent than usually granted. In fact, if we question our use of this distinction, we may find that the physical sequences associated with ritual are more ubiquitous and open-ended, that is, less confined to "religion" and more a quality of a way of acting in the world.

The challenges to ritual theory posed by China's historical and cultural wealth, as well as its distance from traditional Euro-American categories, do not obscure the fact that people on both sides of the globe use ceremony in ways that are closely tied to what it means to be human, social, and expressive. This continuity of human experience should certainly encourage all efforts to understand phenomena so various and complex. Still, the sociology of religion, as it becomes increasingly global, must continue to learn from other cultures in ways that help sociologists to keep pushing their own premises. It is even possible that the fruits of this approach for the study of ritual could lead to the retirement of "ritual" in favor of another term, like *yi*, which may come to seem more inclusive or less encumbered by culturally specific assumptions. Then again, a closer focus on meaningful sequences of physical action might lead to fresh categories that do not single out "ritual" as such, since most or all action will be thought to contain performative or cosmological dimensions.

Notes

1 Chavannes (1865–1918) was a colleague of Durkheim at the Ecole Normale Supérieure, although less influenced by him than was Granet (1884–1940), who was Durkheim's student.
2 The model for this type of analysis is Claude Lévi-Strauss's structural comparisons of multiple versions of myths (or kinship relations) in order to distinguish general principles underlying all the permutations. Max Weber also delineated a type of limited semiotic system when he identified keys ("pure types") of religious leadership; his contrasting descriptions of the priest, prophet, magician, and mystic illuminated how these styles of religious mediation exist less as autonomous institutions than as critical foils or complements for each other (Weber 1963 [1922]). In terms of Chinese religion, an interesting prototype of this form of analysis has focused on the grades of spirit money, and the contrast with real paper currency, used in ritual offerings (Wolf 1978).
3 While classical Taoist texts contrast the abilities of the sage and the shaman, the development of liturgical Taoism in the third century CE is marked by explicit criticism of the singing, dancing, and blood sacrifices of local mediums who are said to

traffic promiscuously with the spirits and delude the people. Intent on distinguishing themselves, the Taoists argued that their liturgies did not involve possession by any external spirits, a claim for greater purity (Stein 1979).

References

Asad, T. 1993. *Genealogies of Religion*. Baltimore MD: Johns Hopkins University Press.

Bastid-Bruguiere, M. 1995. "Classification et terminologie usuelles dans la littérature lettrée chinoise du XVIIIème et XIXème siècle." Paper delivered at Conference on State and Ritual in East Asia, Paris.

Bell, C. 1988. "Ritualization of Texts and the Textualization of Ritual in the Codification of Taoist Liturgy," *History of Religions* 27(4):366–92.

Bell, C. 1989. "Religion and Chinese Culture: Toward an Assessment of 'Popular Religion'," *History of Religions* 29(1):35–57.

Bell, C. 1992. *Ritual Theory, Ritual Practice*. New York: Oxford University Press.

Bell, C. 1997. *Ritual: Perspectives and Dimensions*. New York: Oxford University Press.

Bell, C. 1998. "Performance," *Critical Terms for the Study of Religion*, Ed. M.C. Taylor. Chicago: University of Chicago Press, pp. 205–24.

Chang, K.C. 1983. *Art, Myth, and Ritual: The Path to Political Authority in Ancient China*. Cambridge, MA: Harvard University Press.

Chavannes, E. 1970. *Le T'ai chan: Essai de monographie d'un culte chinois*. Paris. Taipei reprint.

Dean, K. 1993. *Taoist Ritual and Popular Cults of South-East China*. Princeton, NJ: Princeton University Press.

Durkheim, E. 1965. *The Elementary Forms of the Religious Life*, Transl. J.W. Swain. New York: Free Press.

Ebrey, P.B. 1991. *Confucianism and Family Rituals in Imperial China*. Princeton, NJ: Princeton University Press.

Fei Hsiao-t'ung 1939. *Peasant Life in China: A Field Study of Country Life in the Yangtze Valley*. New York: Oxford University Press.

Feuchtwang, S. 1992. *The Imperial Metaphor: Popular Religion in China*. London: Routledge.

Freedman, M. 1979. *The Study of Chinese Society*. Stanford, CA: Stanford University Press.

Geertz, C. 1973. *The Interpretation of Cultures; Selected Essays*. New York: Basic Books.

Granet, M. 1950. *La pensée chinoise*. Paris: Michel.

Granet, M. 1951. *Chinese Civilization*, Transl. K.E. Innes and M.R. Brailsford. New York: Barnes and Noble.

Granet, M. 1975. *The Religion of the Chinese People*, Ed. and Transl. M. Freedman. New York: Harper and Row.

Groot, J.J.M. de. 1892–1910. *The Religious System of China*, 2 vols. Leiden: E. J. Brill.

Haar, B.J. 1992. *The White Lotus Teachings in Chinese Religious History*. Leiden: E. J. Brill.

Hevia, J.L. 1995. *Cherishing Men from Afar: Qing Guest Ritual and the MaCartney Embassy of 1793*. Chapel Hill, NC: Duke University Press.

Hsu, F. 1971. *Under the Ancestors' Shadow*, revised edn. Stanford, CA: Stanford University Press.

Jung, C.G. 1950. "Foreword," *The I Ching or Book of Changes*. Transl. R. Wilhelm and C.F. Baynes. Princeton: Princeton University Press, pp. xxi–xxxix.

Kuhn, T.S. 1970. *The Structure of Scientific Revolutions*, 2nd edn. Chicago: University of Chicago Press.

Lagerwey, J. 1987. *Taoist Ritual in Chinese Society and History*. New York: Macmillan.

Lawson, T.E. and McCauley, R.N. 1990. *Rethinking Religion: Connecting Cognition and Culture*. Cambridge: Cambridge University Press.

Lévi-Strauss, C. 1969. *The Raw and the Cooked: Introduction to a Science of Mythology*, vol. 1, Transl. J. and D. Weightmann. New York: Harper and Row.

Nathan, A.J. 1993. "Is Chinese Culture Distinctive? – A Review Article," *Journal of Asian Studies* 52(4):923–36.

Naquin, S. 1985. "The Transmission of White Lotus Sectarianism in Late Imperial China," in *Popular Culture in Late Imperial China*, Eds. D. Johnson, A.J. Nathan, and E.S. Rawski. Berkeley: University of California Press.

Needham, J. 1956. *Science and Civilization in China*, vol. 2. Cambridge: Cambridge University Press.

Ownby, D. and Heidhues, M.S., Eds. 1993. *"Secret Societies" Reconsidered: Perspectives on the Social History of Modern South China and Southeast Asia*. Armonk, NY: M.E. Sharpe.

Polo, M. 1958. *The Travels*, Transl. R.E. Latham. Harmondsworth, UK: Penguin Books.

Robertson-Smith, W. 1969. *Lectures on the Religion of the Semites: The Fundamental Institutions*. New York: KTAV Publishing House.

Saso, M.R. 1972. *Taoism and the Rite of Cosmic Renewal*. Pullman: Washington State University Press.

Schipper, K. 1993. *The Taoist Body*, Transl. K.C. Duval. Berkeley: University of California Press.

Schipper, K. 1995. "Vocabulary and Taxonomy of State Ritual," paper delivered at the Conference on State and Ritual in East Asia, Paris.

Smith, R.J. 1989. "Ritual in Ch'ing Culture," in *Orthodoxy in Late Imperial China*, Ed. Kwang-Ching Liu. Berkeley: University of California Press, pp. 281–310.

Spence, J.D. 1992. "Looking East: The Long View," *Chinese Roundabout: Essays in History and Culture*. New York: W.W. Norton, pp. 78–90. Originally published in *Heritage of China: Contemporary Perspectives on Chinese Civilization*, Ed. P. Ropp. Berkeley: University of California Press, 1990.

Stein, R.A. 1979. "Religious Taoism and Popular Religion from the Second to Seventh Centuries," in *Facets of Taoism: Essays in Chinese Religion*, Eds. H. Welch and A. Seidel. New Haven, CT: Yale University Press, pp. 53–81.

Thompson, L.G. 1985. *Chinese Religion in Western Languages: A Comprehensive and Classified Bibliography of Publications in English, French, and German through 1980*. Association for Asian Studies Monograph, no. 41. Tucson, AZ: University of Arizona.

Thompson, L.G. and Seaman, G. 1993. *Chinese Religions: Publications in Western Languages 1981 through 1990*. Ann Arbor Association for Asian Studies.

Thompson, L.G. and Seaman, G. 1998. *Chinese Religions: Publications in Western Languages, 1991–1995*. Ann Arbor, MI: Association for Asian Studies.

Turner, V. 1969. *The Ritual Process: Structure and Anti-Structure*. Chicago: Aldine.

Vandermeersch, L. 1976. "La conception chinoise des rites," *Cahiers linguistique d'orientalisme et de slavistique* 8(July):75–86.

Watson, J.L. 1985. "Standardizing the Gods: The Promotion of T'ien Hou ('Empress of Heaven') along the South China Coast, 960–1960," in *Popular Culture in Late Imperial China*, Eds. D. Johnson, A.J. Nathan, and E.S. Rawski. Berkeley: University of California Press, pp. 292–324.

Watson, J.L. 1988. "The Structure of Chinese Funerary Rites: Elementary Forms, Ritual Sequence, and the Primacy of Performance," in *Death Ritual in Late Imperial and Early Modern China*, Eds. J.L. Watson and E.S. Rawski. Berkeley: University of California Press, pp. 3–19.

Weber, M. 1963. *The Sociology of Religion*, Transl. E. Fischoff. Boston: Beacon Press.

Wechsler, H.J. 1985. *Offerings of Jade and Silk: Ritual and Symbol in the Legitimation of the T'ang Dynasty*. New Haven, CT: Yale University Press.

Weller, R.P. 1987. *Unities and Diversities in Chinese Religion*. Seattle: University of Washington Press.

Wheatley, P. 1971. *The Pivot of the Four Corners: A Preliminary Enquiry into the Origins and Character of the Ancient Chinese City*. Chicago: Aldine.

Wolf, A.P. 1978. "Gods, Ghosts, and Ancestors," in *Studies in Chinese Society*, Ed. A.P. Wolf. Stanford, CA: Stanford University Press, pp. 131–82.

Wood, F. 1995. *Did Marco Polo Go to China?* Boulder, CO: Westview Press.

Yang, C.K. [Ch'ing-k'un] 1961. *Religion in Chinese Society*. Berkeley: University of California Press.

Zito, A.R. 1987. "City Gods, Filiality and Hegemony in Late Imperial China," *Modern China* 13(3):333–71.

CHAPTER 21

Moralizing Sermons, Then and Now[1]

Thomas Luckmann

Moral Communication and Moralizing Sermons

Moral communication takes many forms. Societies differ from one another, and from epoch to epoch, quite noticeably in this regard. However, the basic purposes of instruction in the good life, of blame and praise, are intrinsic to human life in society. They find some communicative expression everywhere that human beings live together, generation by generation. To put it in somewhat more abstract terms: the construction and maintenance of a social order presupposes social interaction, more particularly, communicative interaction. All of it will have a moral aspect – but only some communicative processes will have a pre-dominantly moral function, will be what we may call "moralizing." The forms of moralizing may be direct, as in blaming and praising, or they may be oblique, ironical, and so forth; they may consist of simple communicative activities or of elaborated forms such as genres.[2]

The moral(izing) sermon, as a direct and elaborated genre of moralizing, although based on elementary forms of moral communication, such as threats and appeals – which are used almost everywhere and at all times – is anything but universal. Its characteristic form developed in early Christianity. The genre, emerging as a special type of sermon along with other varieties (such as exegetic or evangelizing, sermons), made use of elements with older roots, in particular prophesies of doom and appeals for a change of heart, which were not uncom-mon in ancient Israel. The ecclesiastic sermon developed from the patristic period, flowered through the Middle Ages to its peak in the late Baroque era and went into decline during and after the Enlightenment.

Sermons, especially moralizing sermons, were of inestimable importance in the Christianization of the societies that succeeded the Roman Empire. With varying effectiveness at different times, church sermons helped to shape the worldview of all social strata, from the nobility to the peasantry, and directly influenced the way they conducted their lives. Without a doubt, they were one of the most important means of communication. They were instrumental in creating a basically unified moral order across all variations of mentality and of discourse that were characteristic of different social strata and regions of the Western world.

Church sermons no longer have much to do with the moral condition of modern societies. The influence of the Christian churches on the thoughts and lives of the vast majority of people in Europe has waned in the urban centers since the nineteenth century and even earlier times, somewhat later in the countryside. Analogous changes occurred to a significantly lesser degree, and much later, in North America. This is true even of people who haven't lost all sense of identification with the church of their ancestors (cf. Kaufmann 1989, Luckmann 1991). In the communicative budget, as one may call the "economy" and "ecology" of communicative forms and processes, of most modern societies with a Christian past – again, with the partial exception of the USA – the church sermon plays an insignificant part. The circle of its addressees has been dwindling steadily for generations.[3] Protestant and Catholic theologians complain that the sermon is in a serious state of crisis, and that, in any case, moral(izing) sermons are no longer an appropriate way to spread the message of Christianity.[4] Inasmuch as recent homiletic discussion permits an inference concerning the actual practice of the moralizing sermon in church, it can be said that in Europe it is a moribund genre. As a form of *authoritative* moralizing, the morality sermon has lost much of its credibility even within the narrow circle of its immediate addressees (see Ebertz 1993).

Does this mean that the morality sermon has disappeared altogether, except for some small remnants within the Church? Or are there extraecclesiastic forms of moralizing which show so much structural and functional similarity to moralizing sermons that one could speak of a genre to which the term can be appropriately attached? Did the moral(izing) sermon, fading in the churches, find another habitat outside of them?[5]

A "Secular" Metamorphosis?

If anywhere, one would expect to find the moralizing sermon whenever and wherever citizens are admonished to do their duty in public speeches. Let us look at an example, a fairly recent Christmas address by a president of the Federal Republic of Germany, selected from the many public speeches broadcast through the mass media.[6] Does it resemble a moral(izing) sermon? It should be noted that such addresses are an expected annual event. A slot is reserved in the public calendar for this symbolic occasion. The communicative form is unilateral and indirect, and the social relationship between speaker and addressee is established from the outset as asymmetrical: between a concrete person with official charisma and an anonymous public who doesn't respond, ask, comment. Therein lies yet another resemblance to the moral(izing) sermon in church.

1	Today I wish you, my dear fellow Germans,
	and all those who live here in Germany
	with all my heart a Merry Christmas.
	I hope that the holidays bring you closer
5	to your fellow human beings
	and give you strength and confidence.
	It may be hard to
	reach with these wishes all of you
	in your hearts – I am thinking
10	of your worries if you are unemployed
	and don't know what the future brings or
	if you feel alone in a world that overwhelms
	with stimuli rather than
	offering true meaning. And some live in
15	depressing confrontations
	with the past in East Germany.
	The Christian Christmas Legend
	tells of the Holy Family that could find no
	shelter at the inn, nothing but a
20	stable with a manger. Before the Savior was
	born a shelter had to be found.
	The worry about a roof over one's head
	connects us, at Christmas, most particularly
	with large families and retired people, with
25	the unemployed and the homeless,
	students, with single
	mothers and fathers who worry about
	their apartments or their
	rooms, in fear of rent increases
30	or of being evicted or (moved to) substandard
	housing. The inn of which
	the Christmas Legend tells represents
	safety and security.
	Depressing living conditions threaten the
35	peace among human beings . . .

The address opens with a personalizing formula. (For the tendency toward personalization in various forms of moral communication cf. Bergmann et al. 1999.) It signifies that the speaker does not address the public as an anonymous mass. The speech format is far from that of a somber "Address to the Nation." Its wishes are directed at "dear fellow Germans" (l.1). They are not the only intended recipients, however. The somewhat cumbersomely named non-Germans, "those who live here in Germany" (l.2), are also immediately included. It soon becomes clear that such inclusiveness in the public address of a German president pursues a moral end.

An undefined subcategory among the compatriots and noncompatriots is singled out: "it may be hard to reach all of you in your hearts with these wishes" (ll.7–8). The specification follows: first the unemployed (l.10) "if you are unemployed," then all those who are alone, overwhelmed by stimuli and [without] "true meaning" (ll.12–14), then "some [who] live in depressing confrontations with the past" (ll.14–16). Finally, (ll.17–23) an analogy to the Christmas legend is established by referring to the "worry about a roof over one's head" (l.22). Now, all who might be listening are addressed once again.

There has been an almost imperceptible shift regarding the addressees of the speech (the *apostrophe* of rhetoric). While those afflicted with woes are initially addressed directly, they are now spoken *of*, and the new addressee is another. Further categories of social misery are named in something of a jumble ("large families" and "retired people" (l.24), the "unemployed and the homeless" (l.25); "students," "single mothers and fathers" (ll.26–7), those who live "in fear of rent increases or of being evicted" (ll.29–30) or in "substandard housing" (ll.30–1). The rhetorical opposition of safety and security (l.33) to depressing living conditions (ll.34) underlines the moral aspect of the list. Those listeners who do not themselves live in misery are to feel at least emotionally affected if not outright guilty.

The listing of various aspects of collective and private misery refers to present and acute evil. For Jeremiah, it was the betrayal of God by Israel; in traditional moral(izing) sermons, it was the sin committed by the Christian congregation or its individual members. In this secular address, however, evil is *not* depicted as having been caused by the victims. Only those addressees who do not suffer from the evils described, and who live in comfortable circumstances, are to feel at least partially responsible for the misery of the others. They are the ones to whom the moral message implied by the listing of miseries is addressed. Evidently, the listeners have been divided into two groups once again, the sufferers and those who should help them.

In structural analogy to the ecclesiastical genre, here, too, the present evil is at the roots of greater misery to come (there, the wrath of God, here, the threat to peace). The "prophecy of doom" in the secular address is not particularly dramatic compared to the portentous words of Jeremiah or the damnation forecast by the baroque preachers. It is articulated without strong emotion in the cautiously circumstantial form: (conditions that) "threaten the peace among human beings" (ll.34–5). Nonetheless, the resemblance to the prophecy of doom, one of the chief structural elements of ecclesiastical morality sermons, is evident. Averting the threat to inner or outer peace was no weaker a motivation for action for twentieth century people than avoiding punishment in hell was for a medieval Christian.

As in the traditional moral(izing) sermon, the present misery, once understood as sin, and the coming doom, formerly threatened as punishment, also appear as two complex, interdependent speech parts in our example of a "secular address". They appear in canonic form and sequence.

In the ecclesiastical moral(izing)sermon (and formerly, in Old Testament prophecies of doom) the bipartite description of disaster was the beginning, not the end of a speech. Nor is it the end in our case. In an address that is not mere description, but shows strong moralizing aspects (above all, the emphatic topos of nearness to one's fellow human beings, such as "I am thinking of your worries" (ll.9–10) and the emotional list of miseries: "feel alone" (l.12), "depressing confrontations" (l.15), "being evicted" and "substandard housing" (ll.30–1)), one need not be an experienced listener to expect a continuation in which moral implications of the list of miseries will be spelled out.

```
35                    . . . this is
          what we should all think of at Christmas.
          And as politicians we have every reason to
          let ourselves be emphatically admonished.
          Safety and security are to be
40        found in one's faith, in one's family, but
          also in day-to-day human
          contact. There we can not only
          find comfort and safety, but also and especially
          offer them through our willingness
45        to communicate. Sometimes it is already enough
          to have a little more time for one another.
          Or to give help spontaneously
          when someone is in difficulties: a greeting
          or simply showing an open and friendly
50        face to an unknown neighbor.
```

A moral appeal follows the description of present, and prophecy of conditional future, calamity. It commences in a general and subdued tone (ll.35–6: "this is what we should all think of") and continues with a list of increasing and action-specifying variations specifying desirable action (l.38: "let ourselves be emphatically admonished," ll.42–4: "not only find comfort and safety, but also and especially offer them"; ll.44–5: "willingness to communicate"; l.48: "a greeting"; l.49–50: "an open and friendly face to an unknown neighbor"). The addressees of the first appeal are once again "we all" (l.36) and remain so (l.42: "we can"), albeit following an interim self-category-directed appeal ("as politicians we have . . ." l.37) for which no clear motivation is apparent, unless it is an attempt to curry the listeners' favor by presenting himself as one to be equally reproved – (". . . every reason to let ourselves be emphatically admonished," ll.37–8) – a stratagem well known to classical rhetoric as a *confessio criminis*. (Lausberg 1990).

The description of individual and collective misery and the resulting (conditional) prophecy of internal and external discontent in the Christmas address is reminiscent of the descriptions of present evil that were paired with prophecies of future doom in traditional moralizing sermons in church. Similarly, the subsequent appeal appears as a secular counterpart to the prophetic warning cry and call for repentance in the ecclesiastic tradition. The sequence of present and future doom and of the appeal, the three basic elements of these genres of ecclesiastical speech, is also found in our example of a festive public speech by the representative of a modern state.

The Christmas address is not yet over.

51   The military salute, hand raised to
      one's cap, goes back, the legend says, to the
      knight in armor who
      opens his visor to show others
55   his face and to signal his readiness
      to come to communicate and to help.
      We do not live in the Middle Ages,
      but we also often wear
      an invisible armor. Even more
60   good can be wrought by a gesture in
      a traffic jam on the highway, in the store
      at the corner, or at work. It should
      simply say: we are strangers but
      not enemies, we all are
65   denizens of the same earth.

The direct appeal (ll.44–5 "willingness to communicate"; l.46 "more time for one another"; l.47 "to give help spontaneously"; ll.49–50 "open and friendly face") acquires additional meaning in the continuation of the speech, continuing where the "open, friendly face" left off, in order to develop an allegorical figure: the knight's open visor, signaling his peaceful intentions and his readiness to communicate and help (ll.54–6), in contrast to the "invisible armor" (l.59) surrounding contemporary men and women, a point made in the description of present-day evil. The appeal continues by calling for a sign which is to emulate the knight's gesture, and work "even more good" (ll.59–60).

65   . . . We
      humans react strongly to differences
      between the familiar and the strange, between
      the accustomed and the unknown.
      This need not be necessarily
70   linked to skin color, religion, or
      nationality. Familiar are those
      who, in the pattern of our lives
      have their accustomed place, thus
      the foreign colleague
75   at work, the owner of the
      pizzeria, the
      soldier of a friendly
      nation stationed nearby. However,
      the behavior of hooligans and radical
80   rowdies is alien to us even if
      they are fellow nationals. To its
      causes and consequences
      we must not remain indifferent.

The opposition "familiar/strange" and "accustomed/unknown" (ll.67–8) is elucidated in an unusual turn of phrase which, however, fits in the attempt at naturalization of foreigners: *alien* compatriots (hooligans and radical rowdies, ll.79–80) and *familiar* noncompatriots ("the foreign colleague" etc., ll.74–8). And then, once again, an appeal: "we must not remain indifferent" (l.83).

This forms a consistent pattern. In the course of the speech, each description or mention of contemporary social ills is followed by an appeal to remedy them.

```
83     . . . and then there
       are the foreigners in the hostel on the
85     outskirts of town. There is the
       danger of our excluding them or that
       we might feel threatened by them, perhaps
       as competitors for our jobs and our
       apartments, or their getting everything for
90     free from our social welfare.
       Two tasks presents themselves, a personal
       and a political one. Our own
       behavior towards foreigners is
       not a matter of politics but
95     of our humanity and not least
       of our own dignity. It is a dictate
       of our self-respect to
       meet the weak without violence and to help them
       whether they happen to be foreigners
100    or not.
```

The ills named are the exclusion of "foreigners in their hostels on the outskirts of town" (ll.84–5), and feeling threatened in competition for "*our* jobs (my emphasis) and apartments," (ll.87–9). By repeating the possessive adjective in "our jobs" (l.88), "our apartments" (l.89), the speaker begins a shift to the perspective of the addressee. The cliché that follows ("getting everything for free from our social welfare" (ll.89–90)), couched in terms of local bar talk, is in this same perspective. And again there comes the appeal, preceded by the reason: "a dictate of our self-respect to meet the weak without violence and to help them" (ll.96–8).

Descriptions of evil and appeals are repeated continuously, with added rhetorical elaboration. In contrast, it is remarkable that the prophecy of doom does not recur after it first appears precisely where it should – as if following the logic of an ecclesiastical morality sermon. In any case, even in its single occurrence, the prophecy is both unemotional and conditional. In this sense, our example of a public speech seems calm and composed, particularly in comparison with examples of Baroque church sermons or even with the apocalyptic visions in certain ecological milieus (Bergman et al. 1999).

The basic structure of the address is fairly simple. After the opening sequence come the three obligatory parts: first a firmly wedded pair consisting of a description of evil and the prophecy of doom, then the third part elicited and motivated by that pair, a call for repentance. Using both simple and complex rhetorical devices,[7] the descriptions of disaster and appeals, but not the prophecy of doom, are repeated several times. In the style of the *sermo humilis*, the address has the internal structure of a morality sermon.

The text is drafted in advance. One knows of course that such addresses are not improvised. One can also hear it: the speech contains hardly any grammatical errors, slips of the tongue, repairs. Even though the text is not "read out" in a monotone, the course of the speech is not spontaneous as a speech arising from a concrete event would be. It is retroactively "animated" as it were (see Goffman 1981). The style is earnest yet avoids being ponderous, The tempo is solemn and regular.

It was shown that the internal structure of the address (the pair consisting of *description* and *prophecy of doom* followed by a *call for repentance*) is that of a morality sermon. It is somewhat different than the exuberant baroque prototype, however. There is little similarity between the latter's threats of eternal damnation and exhortations being roared at the sinful congregation from the pulpit, and the subdued manner of our Christmas homily being broadcast through the mass media.

Not only the internal structure resembles that of a morality sermon, however; several elements of the external structure also show a similarity. What we have is also a one-sided, preplanned communicative act presented in the form of a monologue.[8] The social relationship between speaker and addressees is asymmetrical. Although the speaker cannot rely, as the preacher in church can, upon an institutionally secured religious charisma, he does possess an analogous, if much weaker, state-derived official charisma. This permits him to speak in the name of democratic civic ethics, perhaps not as an authorized mediator beyond doubt, in the way that preachers in traditional church homilies can present themselves, but still as *primus inter pares.* And finally, the address recurs on a regular basis, not in the calendar of weekly church events, but as a special event of state symbolism for the New Year. The canon of civic virtue is presented unambiguously: tolerance towards and care for (weaker, foreign, etc.) fellow humans, and a condemnation of intolerance.[9]

In sum, there is good reason for considering this address a secular specimen of the oral genre of the morality sermon. However, it differs from the traditional church variety in several respects. The prophecy of doom is, as was to be seen, in a minor key and – in contrast to the numerous repetitions of the other two basic elements – it is introduced only once. In addition, behind the nonecclesiastic variant there is no institution that can enforce the moral message that it preaches. And finally, the ecclesiastical morality sermon is an independent genre (or rather, an independent subtype of the genre). The Christmas address by the president, however, contains more than the sermon.

We have so far shown only the first part of the address. The following passage introduces a different part of the address:

100   It is the task of
politics to discern long-term
German interests and to
pursue them unflaggingly. That includes
the question concerning the large
105   refugee movements in Europe and
around the world; and the
foreigners living in our country.

"Foreigners" and "refugee movements" serve as a thematic bridge to a second part, which no longer bears the hallmarks of an homily. It represents a kind of statesmanlike accounting, with an eye to the tasks which the future will bring.[10] It is of no further interest to us here. It may foreshadow a new hybrid communicative genre that fuses moralizing homilies and "statesmanlike reflections."[11]

Although my associates and I did not investigate the entire repertoire of moralizing public speech, we did look closely at several solemn speeches made by various public personages at various historic occasions (50 years after World War II, after the liberation of the concentration camps at Auschwitz, Bergen-Belsen, etc.). The majority contain a core which is very close to a moralizing sermon in form, a message of tolerance such as that found in our Christmas address.

One may conclude that at the core of many solemn public speeches there is a moralizing sermon which varies according to such factors as its chronological or commemorative framework. Just as the moralizing ecclesiastic homily draws upon older components (prophecy of doom, prophetic warning and appeal) which in turn builds upon universal and elementary forms of moral communication, so does its secular counterpart. But whether it is a recent or an older and indirect heir of the ecclesiastical morality sermon is a question which can only be answered in investigations of cultural and social history.[12]

It is still another question to what extent it may have been partly an "independent invention" drawing directly upon the universal moralizing functions of communication. Preaching a moral is a communicative activity found in public speeches at political events that need not contain either the fundamental structural elements of a morality sermon nor represent an accepted moral authority. It frequently takes the form of reproach and counterreproach. The inherent risks of such moral communication become particularly apparent there. (Bergmann et al. 1999, Bergmann 1993).

Domestic Moral Preaching

Throughout the centuries moralizing sermons have reached a broad circle of addressees in the Western world, both as they were delivered from the pulpit and in widely circulated printed collections whose readership was not limited to the clergy. Therefore, it does not seem farfetched to assume that the basic pattern of this religious genre has influenced numerous informal kinds of moralizing and that this tradition entered into the patterns of less formal oral communicative acts. Evidently, there is no direct way to support this assumption by historical investigations. Past oral communication is available to us only indirectly.

Nonetheless, one may be able to support or weaken the credibility of the assumption by casting about to see whether the related components of morality sermons have taken root in everyday moralizing today. A likely place to begin looking for them might be the domestic arena. The family in which parents and children live together is structurally marked by an asymmetry of social relationships, a feature which probably favors this form of moralizing. An example from our data follows.[13]

(The situation: Mother and adult daughter are sitting in the living room, the daughter near the fireplace because that is the only place she is permitted to smoke in her parents' apartment. The mother (M) is sitting on the sofa reading. Mother sees and hears that the daughter (D) is lighting a cigarette. The episode commences with an appeal. It is instigated by the perceived "act of doom": the disaster to be expected is wafting through the air.)

M:	Now *do* stop smoking Katja.	1
D:	Oh Mamma	

The daughter wards off the appeal. The initially high, then falling intonation of "Mamma" marks the despairing resignation of someone being put upon – but in a slightly jocose modulation of voice. The thought suggests itself that the daughter is not only trying to ward off the present appeal concerning this one cigarette, but that she sees it as the beginning of something else with which she is overfamiliar and which she considers anything but desirable. What this might be becomes immediately evident.

M:	That's at least the *third* cigarette now	5
D:	So what?	
M:	Even Fritz has quit smoking. d'you hear?	
D:	Yes but he never really smoked	10
M:	He smoked much more – at least as much as you.	
D:	Oh come on he only – he never really –	
M:	*How silly you girls are* You're going to *regret* it bitterly in 10 or 20 years.	15
D:	Why "we girls"?	

M: *Ha. wherever you look*
      the young men aren't smoking, but the girls   20
      smoke. like chimneys!
D: Aha.

The daughter cockily tries to repudiate the reproach (l.6) that is pointedly implied in the enumeration of the cigarettes smoked (l.4) (in classical rhetoric, an *enumeratio* for the purpose of *vituperatio*. cf. Lausberg 1990). The mother ignores the attempt and introduces "Fritz" to demonstrate by his example that the daughter also could stop smoking (l.7). The daughter now "seriously" begins to argue by denying the validity of the example ("never really smoked," ll.9–10). Mother sticks to her guns, daughter ditto (ll.13–14). At this point, we already see a difference between this episode and moral homilies in church and secular addresses that have the structure of a morality sermon: the speaker doesn't own the speech monopoly; the addressee joins in, repudiates, argues. Even when the mother, in a loud and decisive voice, introduces the classic structural pair that is coconstitutive of moralizing sermons, description of doom ("how silly you girls are," l.15) and prophecy of doom ("regret it bitterly in 10 or 20 years," ll.16–17), the daughter doesn't meekly accept it but argues by picking up a weak detail ("why 'we girls'?" l.18). Mother counters with "empirical" support for her position (ll.19–21). Even then the daughter refuses to concede the point. The "aha" (l.22) doesn't sound like acquiescence.

Yet, as we shall see, mother continues her description of present evil (ll.23–4) and prophecy of future doom (ll.25–6):

M: You look *gray and thin*, you're   23
      ruining your stomach, you don't eat,
      just wait, in 10 years you're going to
      think *if only I'd listened.*

But then it is the mother herself, not the daughter, who manages to subvert, or at least weaken the further development of what was to be a moral homily.

M: And particularly not here in the house.   27
D: It goes straight up the chimney anyway.
M: It doesn't go straight up the chimney at
      all.

The moral authority necessary for preaching (which might have lain in the assumption that a mother worries about her daughter's health), is undermined by a shift to the worries of a meticulous housewife. The daughter immediately presents a counterargument. Mother can only think of a simple, reinforcing repetition. A similar "*si, si . . . no, no*" sequence also marks the subsequent passage in which "Erwin" is introduced as another example of pretended virtue by the daughter (ll.30–4). It is concluded with mother repeating her appeal (ll.40–1):

D: . . . and Erwin, when he creeps away   30
      to me to the car
M: *Erwin* has quit
      smoking!
D: Oh, that's what you think
M: Lisa told me   35
      that was only a little relapse on the
      week-end. Basically
      he has quit.
D: Then I'd like to . . .
M: Katja, *do stop*   40
      smoking.

The volume and the first high and then falling intonation, and the lengthening of words give the appeal an imploring, urgent note. The words themselves are almost identical to those of the appeal at the outset of the episode (the "now" is missing, and the naming, "Katja," now precedes the appeal as if to lend the subsequent words more drama). Almost the same, but the two appeals don't mean the same thing. The first appeal referred directly to the one-time action, the cigarette that was just lit. The second appeal refers to her smoking habit in general. The devil nicotine is a present evil which threatens future evil. The appeal is a call for repentance. The daughter, however, does not react to it. Instead she continues in an informal and jocular manner, evidently trying to undermine the solemnity of the (potential) elaboration of the moral homily.

D: Then I'd like to know how many little   42
      relapses he has every time he
      gets together with someone
      who also smokes (laughing).   45
M: It's not a laughing matter.
D: Oh dear.

But mother repudiates (1.46) her daughter's attempt to lend the episode a lighter note and leads it back to a "normal" conversation. Undaunted, she takes up the prophecy of doom again with solemn urgency:

M: You're ruining your health, in 10   47
      years you'll have a stomach ache
      after every meal. And then you'll think,
      if only I'd quit back then.   50
D: [unintelligible on the tape]
M: [unintelligible] as for other things thrombosis
      and who knows what you will get,
      lung cancer and you know yourself
      I won't even speak of . . .   55

Unlike the Christmas address, where the prophecy of doom consisted of one (potential) future disaster, mother's prophecy of doom consists of a hyperbolic five-part *enumeratio* ("stomach ache after every meal," ll.48–9; "thrombosis," l.52; "who knows what," l.53; "lung cancer," l.54; and "you know yourself," l.54). According to the structural "logic" of moralizing sermons, this impressive prophecy of coming retribution for present sins is followed by an appeal. It is not a call for inner repentance, it urges redemptive action: a "program" at some institution (ll.56–7) to help the daughter "quit smoking" (l.59) by certain methods ("a bunch of those kinds of things", ll.57–8). This appeal, too, is brusquely rejected:

M: Go to the health insurance   56
     and join their program. They have a bunch
     of those kind of things. They'll help you
     quit smoking.
D: That's all rubbish.

Although the argument continues, mother introducing another example of virtue, daughter mocking the antismoking propaganda to which mother refers, and so forth, the point is clear and there is no need to describe further details of the conversation. The point is that mother has preached a sermon with an anti-smoking moral, adhering to the canonical structure of such sermons, unde-terred by the attempts of her daughter to shift the conversation into a lighter key. Seriousness on the part of the preaching mother and irony as the defense on the part of the unwilling recipient of the sermon did not destroy each other. On the contrary, one gets the impression from this one conversational sequence that it contains elements of past performances, and that this is not the end of it. The episode shows that in the domestic arena, too, in the interaction of parents and children, even if the latter are already grown up, the "monological" religious genre of the moral homily can be a communicative resource in conversation.

Preaching Virtue in Modern Society

Morality sermons belong, in numerous variants, to the communicative stock of knowledge in our society. After two millennia, they are, although much dimin-ished and generally softened in tone, and adapted to "modern" mentality, still preserved as a genre of religious talk in church. But the frequent occurrence of a secular, more precisely nonecclesiastic counterpart both in public speeches and in informal conversation indicates that today this is probably of greater importance than the morality sermon in church. Still both are probably far less important than were the regular moral homilies at Sunday services for the construction and maintenance of a moral order for many centuries in Western societies. But these are mere assumptions, based on whatever scattered evidence is available to date.

Moralizing sermons are a time-honored form of direct moralizing, but like the other forms of direct moralizing[14] it is rarely if ever welcome by the recipient. The commonly held negative view of moral homilies, moralizing lectures, self-appointed preachers, and apostles of morals is well known. This is true at least for their use in direct, interactive communication.

It is difficult to say whether, and to what degree, this disdain also applies to moral homilies in public speech. Probably it is the genre itself, taken as a paradigm of direct moralizing, which is unpopular, hence also in public speech. In many interactional contexts and milieus of contemporary society in which moralizing is practiced, we find a general tendency to opt for indirect forms of moralizing (Luckmann 1997). All this is found relatively independently of the moral "content" of the morality sermon, whether it refers to responsibility for one's own health, a highly moral issue in modernity, or to the pluralistic moral of tolerance by a state moral which must accommodate heterogeneous partial morals and serve as an umbrella for them (Luckmann et al. 1998).

Notes

1   Published in its original form in *Moral im Alltag*, with Jörg Bergmann et al., Sinn-vermittlung und moralische Kommunikation in intermediären Institutionen, Gütersloh, Verlag Bertelsmann Stiftung, 1988.

2   For an extended and detailed discussion of morals, moral communication, and communicative genres I refer to the publications of a research project on morals and moral communication in contemporary society. The project was supported by the German Science Foundation over several years and directed by Jörg Bergmann and myself. The results are published in Bergman and Luckmann 1999, vols 1 and 2, Cf. also Luckmann (1996a, 1996b, 1997, Luckmann et al. 1998).

3   In Europe, attendance at Protestant as well as Catholic churches has decreased greatly in the last few generations. A striking example: in the past 30 years, attendance at Mass declined in the Federal Republic of Germany from barely half to less than a fifth of all Catholics (IKSE 1996).

4   Grünberg (1973:11), for instance, writes in the first sentence of his treatise on the relationship between homiletics and rhetoric: "The sermon is in 'crisis'. This statement has become stereotypical and nearly old-fashioned."

5   I pursued this question within the frame of the project mentioned in note 1 above. The chapter on the moraliz(ing) sermon (Bergman and Luckmann 1999, vol 2) also contains an overview of its origins and ecclesiastic development which I could not include here.

6   The German transcript uses an adaptation of the standard "conversational analytic" notation, marking, among other things pauses, loudness, intonation. Obviously, these cannot be sensibly reproduced in a translation. The reader may refer to

Bergman and Luckmann 1999 for an analysis which among other things, includes prosodic aspects. In order to make this task somewhat easier, the translation keeps to the lines of the German transcript wherever that is possible without loss of intelligibility, even at the cost of an occasional awkwardness.

7   Among the simple rhetorical devices are lists, especially tripartite lists (for example, "unemployed," "alone in the world," "depressing confrontations with the past," ll.10–16), oppositions (simple oppositions, for example in ll.43–4, "not only find comfort and safety, but also . . . offer them"). Elaborate rhetorical devices (allegory) can be found, e.g., in the antonymic pair "familiar/strange-alien." Apart from these figures, which are also figures used in informal everyday conversations, the address is marked by the skillful inclusion of lesser genres (genres mineurs) (e.g., in minimal form: the owner of the pizzeria, ll.75–6; in more detail: the knight in armor, ll.53–6) and legend (e.g., the Christmas legend).

8   As in every monologue, there are (virtual) dialogical elements in this one, too: the manner in which the address is geared to its listeners, the manner in which the speaker occasionally adapts the perspective of the addressee, even the manner in which he speaks "for" the addressee (the "local bar parlance") etc.

9   If there indeed exists such a thing as a "civil religion" – this is not the place for a discussion of the pros and cons in the case – then this address illustrates its main content: the ethics of civic tolerance and helpfulness. A strong case for civil religion is made in the analysis of a speech by President Weizsaecker in a treatise on civil religion (Vögele 1994:24ff.).

10   It shows a vague similarity to the (somewhat more partisan) State of the Union addresses by American presidents at the beginning of the New Year.

11   The German president who succeeded the one whose address is presented here also makes speeches with homily-like components, albeit in a completely different ("drier") style than his predecessor. It is moot whether official charisma suffices in order to give official moralizing sermons. The last two, Weizsäcker and Herzog, quite different in their style, were successful in this respect; at least one of their predecessors most definitely was not.

12   For example, the speeches of the French Revolutionary "Religion of Reason" and the postrevolutionary laicistic state celebrations.

13   Concerning the data base of the project mentioned in note 1: it contains relatively few conversation sequences with any similarity to morality sermons. The family dinner-table conversations, mostly involving families with teenage and adult children, are no exception. We began with the assumption that morality sermons would be most likely to appear in asymmetrical social relationships. Consequently, we expected to find even fewer or none in informal conversations among friends and acquaintances. This expectation was not fulfilled, however, at least not primarily for the expected reason. Relevant communicative episodes were not infrequently registered during "fieldwork," but permission to use the tapes in question was often subsequently revoked. The diagnosis that they possessed characteristics of morality sermons – containing as its structural components the paired description of doom and prophecy of doom, along with a call for reform – is based on observations by those collaborators who had taped the conversations in their own circle of friends.

14   and also, incidentally, of self-initiated "lecturing" which, although not necessarily "moral", is just as "well-intentioned" as are moral homilies. (cf. Keppler and Luckmann (1991).

References

Bergmann, J. 1993. *Discreet Indiscretions: The Social Organization of Gossip*, Transl. J. Bednarz, Jr. New York: Aldine de Gruyter.

Bergmann, T. and Luckmann, T. 1999. *Kommunikative Konstruction von Moral*. Wiesbaden: Westdeutscher Verlag.

Ebertz, M.N. 1993. "Erosionen im Jenseits – Erosionen im Diesseits. Predigten über 'Himmel,' 'Hölle,' 'Fegefeuer' in soziologischer Sicht," in *Ende des Katholizismus oder Gestaltwandel der Kirche*, Ed. J. Horstmann. Schwerte: Katholische Akademie.

Goffman, E. 1981. *Forms of Talk*. Philadelphia: University of Pennsylvania Press.

Grünberg, W. 1973. *Homiletik und Rhetorik*. Gütersloh: Gütersloh Verlagshaus Mohn.

Institut für Kirchliche Sozialforschung des Bistums Essen (IKSE). 1996. *Deutsche Bistümer in Zeitreihen. Daten der Statistischen Jahreserhebungen ab 1960*, Essen: IKSE.

Kaufmann, F-X. 1989. *Religion und Modernität. Sozialwissenschaftliche Perspektiven*. Tübingen: J.C.B. Mohr.

Keppler, A. and Luckmann, T. 1991. "'Teaching': Conversational Transmission of Knowledge," in *Asymmetries in Dialogue*, Eds, I. Marková and K. Foppa. Savage, MD: Barnes and Noble, pp. 143–65.

Lausberg, H. 1990. *Handbuch der literarischen Rhetorik: eine Grundlegung der Literaturwissenschaft*, 3rd edn. Stuttgart: Franz Steiner.

Luckmann, T. 1991. *Die unsichtbare Religion*. Frankfurt: Suhrkampt. English translation, 1967. *The Invisible Religion*. New York: MacMillan.

Luckmann, T. 1996a. "The Privatization of Religion and Morality," in *Detraditionalization: Critical Reflections on Authority and Identity at a Time of Uncertainty*, Eds, P. Heelas, S. Lash, and P. Morris. Oxford and Cambridge, MA: Blackwell, pp. 72–86.

Luckmann, T. 1996b. "Über Moral und Moralische Kommunikation in der modernen Gesellschaft," *Sociologia Internationalis* 34(1):1–11.

Luckmann, T. 1997. *The Moral Order of Modern Societies, Moral Communication and Indirect Moralizing*. Collegium Budapest/Institute for Advanced Study, Public Lectures No. 17.

Luckmann, T. et al. 1998. *Moral im Alltag*. Gütersloh: Bertelsmann Foundation.

Vögele, W. 1994. *Zivilreligion in der Bundesrepublik Deutschland*. Gütersloh: Bertelsmann Foundation.

CHAPTER 22

Health, Morality, and Sacrifice: The Sociology of Disasters

Douglas J. Davies

Introduction

How is human well-being related to justice, to bereavement, and to sacrifice? These are crucial issues for the sociology of religion and are analyzed in this theoretically orientated chapter through the social significance of merit, justice, the body, and death, all within the contexts of personal loss and communal disaster. Two ideal types are offered to account for what will be called the moral-somatic dimension of loss at the microlevel of individual and family, and the social category of offending deaths at the macrolevel affecting thousands of people.

Loss and tragedy, whether at the personal, national, or international level, reflect a continuum of disaster, and furnish part of the historical background to individual and communal identity. Disaster is far from easy to define (cf. Bell 1974:3ff.), yet whether in the form of personal bereavement, natural catastrophes, accidents, crimes, terrorism, or warfare, certain events stir a range of emotional values including sadness, grief, despair, shock, and rage. Amidst such negative sentiments excitement and hope elicit social responses that rise to meet the challenge of survival. And, as though life itself was insufficiently problematic, myth, literature, film, and television conspire to foster echoes of these emotions in imaginative tales of disaster (Benthall 1993).

Focus and Method

Against an extensive background literature in the sociology, psychology, economics, politics, and developmental studies of disaster, only two elements have been selected as the means of exposing relatively ignored, yet crucial, features of socially grounded moral processes. The first represents an individual focus, interpreted through the notion of what will be called the moral-somatic dimension of human life: this raises the issue of the mental and physical well-being of wronged individuals in relation to justice. The second addresses more communal concerns and is approached through what will be called the social category of offending deaths. Each of these types discloses processes of morality underlying social protest and can be further illuminated by the theoretical concept of rebounding vitality, which naturally takes the analysis through the human venture of survival against strong risk and potential absurdity into a consideration of sacrificial phenomena.

This sets the chapter firmly in the sociological perspective of Durkheim's preoccupation with the relation between individual and group, morality and society, sacrifice and transcendence. And there is no reticence attached to this retrospective theoretical reflection because studies of disaster seek theoretical leads; indeed one recent author called "for a return to fundamental sociological questions answerable by . . . empirical studies" (Stallings 1998:144). While this chapter cannot offer extensive empirical data it will suggest some firm theoretical possibilities for analysis.

Some brief consideration will also be given to biological and psychological perspectives as complements to the excessively restrictive affirmation that social facts demand exclusively sociological explanation (cf. Barkow, Cosmides, and Tooby 1992:627ff., Moscovici 1993:1ff.). Even though a condition such as posttraumatic stress disorder may only have been officially defined by The American Psychiatric Association in 1978, we have known for some time that physiological conditions may be influenced by an individual's social environment. Darwin's study of the emotions made this clear ([1872] 1998:310ff.), as did Mauss's early work on death ([1924] 1979:35ff.) and Cannon's seminal 1942 work on voodoo, itself utilized by Lévi-Strauss in his discussion of the "psychophysiological" aspects of magic (1968:167ff.). Recent studies of bereavement related to illness show that social situations intimately infuse the totality of body and mind (Cleiren 1991:41ff.). Similarly, when it comes to issues of status and health we find that, for example, "less powerful people . . . face a structurally inbuilt handicap . . . contributing to existential fear" (Williams and Bendelow, 1996:41). It is quite apparent that the social actor is grounded in an embodied response to the social environment and its underlying moral base. Certainly, "many current psychological and physiological studies reinforce the fact that physiological states can be significantly influenced by social environment"(Frijda 1986:195), or even by the memory of former contexts as in post-traumatic stress disorder (LeDoux 1998:256).

At a more symbolic level of interpretation, even the long-established association between the human predisposition to right-handedness and the positive moral value ascribed to right-laterality directly reflects the deep link between body and society as a moral community (Needham 1973:xi.ff., Corballis 1991:86ff.). While, as Kemper argued in relation to gender relations, "biology and social justice have sometimes been set against each other," this chapter reverses the emphasis, as far as loss and disasters are concerned, to foster a more fruitful relation between "the interaction of biology and the social" (1990:221).

The Moral-somatic Relationship: Justice and Well-being

If the neologism may be permitted, the relationship between justice and human well-being will be analyzed as a "moral-somatic" dimension of life. The idea of justice involves a clear reification of the valuation of social behavior, just as "somatic" sharply describes the bodily basis of life. Very loosely speaking, one might even gloss the "moral" as representing the "social" and the "somatic" the affectively personal dimension of Durkheim's *Homo duplex*. While one could consider each in relation to their respective institutional processes, judicial on the one hand and medical on the other, this discussion will focus more upon the legal elements. In basic terms Bauman was right to say that "once the ideas of justice and self-assertion were invented, it is impossible to forget them," since they "will haunt and pester us to the end of the world" (1992:225).

Justice affords one formal expression of the values by which societies exist, with courts of law and the legal profession effecting their concrete manifestation. "Contempt of court" remains one of the most powerful verbal expressions of the significance, incontrovertibility, and power of society as such: it is a close partner of blasphemy. In fact the closeness of "contempt" and blasphemy echoes Fenn's analysis of the relationship between courts of law, their language, and the language of religious liturgy (1982:139). His discussion highlighted processes of secularization and is far from irrelevant in the present context. For example, when considering the social manifestation of justice one was tempted to add "the police" to the list of court and judiciary, but did not do so because of the potential ambivalence in some people's minds over the entire probity of police forces. In that sense a lack of trust involves a loss of the sense of society and, with Durkheim in mind, a loss of the sacred.

Indeed, trust has become a key topic as traditional values and hierarchies fall beneath the postmodern gaze (Giddens 1991:136, Fukuyama 1995). Still, the way the legal profession and the police are perceived does vary a great deal, not only between societies but also amongst social groups within any particular society. The hallmark of justice is not universally guaranteed. By contrast well-being is universally sought but remains an extremely complex notion, closely allied to that of "quality of life," itself open to many definitional perspectives (cf. Grimby 1995:14). Here the chosen emphasis is placed upon an awareness of being treated justly in contexts of adversity and of bodily based consequences (Skultans 1999:310ff.).

One classic expression of this legal process in relation to a more traditional society is found in the liturgy of The Church of England's *Book of Common Prayer* of 1662. The prayer for "Christ's Church militant here in earth" contained in the Holy Communion service asks for those "set in authority" under the monarch, "that they may truly and indifferently minister justice, to the punishment of wickedness and vice, and to the maintenance of thy true religion, and virtue." The overall linguistic framework reflects a strongly stratified society from, "Christian Kings, Princes, and Governors," through, "Bishops and Curates," down to "all thy people." It asks God to "comfort and succor all them, who in this transitory life are in trouble, sorrow, need, sickness, or any adversity," until they join with all who have, "departed this life in thy fear and faith," to partake in that final heavenly kingdom. This prayer unites the totality of life through liturgical formulae and pinpoints human well-being in relation to the dimensions of morality and health and the official power of the state.

Well-being remains as important an issue in the secular world of the twenty-first century as in the religious domain of sixteenth century England. In this context, then, we identify the moral-somatic relationship as a crucial factor in the overall shaping of identity. To describe the moral-somatic relationship is to account for a situation in which the healthful well-being of an individual is deleteriously affected by the immoral behavior of others. Human beings, as social animals, are physically influenced by changes in the social relations constituting their networks of significance. Law underpins the form of these relations and legal reparation ensures their integrity.

It is perfectly obvious that particular cultural contexts are of prime significance for what is argued here and that generalizations are hazardous. Still, in terms of Western, developed, societies in which institutions, both of law and medicine, are well established and differentiated, this moral-somatic model is worthy of theoretical consideration. It may even become more significant if, in postmodern terms, community life fragments leaving very small groups, or attenuated networks, as the medium of social existence.

The moral-somatic model grounds abstract issues in the available realm of experience. It is a notion constructed after the model of alignments of otherwise discrete aspects of life, as with psychosomatic phenomena or, for example, with Durkheim's notion that "the study of socio-psychological phenomena is ... not a mere appendix to sociology: it is its very substance" (Moscovici 1993:122). Here moral-somatic relations are, also, deemed to be potent as the very meeting place of human feeling, expressed as well-being, and of social morality, expressed as justice. The subject or subjects are, in some sense, definable as victims and the overall phenomenon may be described in the following ideal-typical way.

The moral-somatic ideal type

The moral-somatic nature of human beings involves a sense of malaise, grounded in a grievance arising from a personal tragedy, often the killing of a relative, perceived as unjust and as an affront to the rights of the survivors as of the deceased. The sense of well-being is impugned by the absence of justice with those in positions of authority being deemed responsible for bringing retribution to the offended parties. Only when justice is achieved can paths to personal integrity and physical well-being be pursued anew.

The moral-somatic situation is one in which a social event triggers a response grounded in the embodied person of the individual concerned; it reveals the moral sense of which individuals are aware in response to social contexts of injustice. The more psychological possibility explored by Parkes and Weiss (1983) when arguing that a "pledge never to forget until justice is done can become a pledge to refuse to recover," needs to be given due weight regarding bereavement, but its social context ought also not to be ignored (cited in Weinberg 1994:592). While the oppression felt when under a sense of social injustice can lead to any number of physical consequences, it is the social fact of injustice, as perceived by the victim, that is crucial here: it emphasizes the way people say they "feel" when they have been treated badly.

Reciprocity and Justice

Individuals are socialized into moral conventions and anticipate a degree of justice in their ongoing lives, even though the level of risk they may anticipate varies from group to group, not least in relation to death (Leaman 1995:8ff.). Fundamental notions of reciprocity enter into the dynamic structure of systems of values and morals that comprise the every-day life-world. One sociological perspective, that of "assumptive world theory" (Janoff-Bulman and Frieze 1983:1), depicts a benevolent and meaningful environment for the self viewed as worthy: a realm that can, however, be shattered by trauma producing a weak sense of self, "in a malevolent, meaningless world" (Murphy et al. 1998:211). And the shattering of a personal world is not so far removed from the larger scale tragedies that, occasionally, beset societies at large. It is on this assumption that these "kinds of suffering . . . do not differ qualitatively to a significant degree from that of people bereaved under more commonplace circumstances" that this chapter is content to address both together (Brooke 1990:21).

Catastrophes within people's personal lifeworld activate notions of reciprocity and fairness, most especially if their distress has originated in or been aggravated by the institutions of law and medicine: law, in that it is the demarcated domain of justice; medicine, in that it is the designated source of fostering well-being. Each of these institutions is invested with a powerful moral charge to care for citizens, a care that is deeply negated if justice is abused or medicine leads to a loss of life. Abuses become abundantly clear in the death of partners, children, or innocent individuals. The personal tragedy, as hard to bear as it usually is, is further aggravated when the moral sense is bruised. The unintelligibility of catastrophe is also of profound import, striking the discord of anomie.

Two situations are of particular interest: one in which there is no sense of apparent meaning in a death, and the other in which there is an ascribable cause, but one deemed unjust. Indeed, there is often a sense in which there is an element of injustice in each but its precise nature differs.

The death of a child, for example, or of young people in their prime, is often met with the question of why such a thing should have happened to them: a question of the apt-reciprocity type. By invoking ideas of due reward for the style of life lived, people try to make sense of a situation, and they may do this even when this form of question expects no answer. In other words, in the absence of any obvious reason for a death that is intrinsically random, whether by accident or sudden illness, the bereaved would rather have the framework of questioning the situation than having nothing at all to say. This sort of context involves a sense of injustice that is very broad and vague, it might even be called "cosmic injustice." It is possible that the bereaved may express anger towards the deity but, essentially, there is no obvious cause and certainly not one that can be responded to by taking recourse to the law. The sense of unfairness simply has to be borne in the ongoing process of grief. Though, even in such contexts, individuals sometimes set out to create a meaning out of the meaninglessness by, for example, collecting money for research into the illness from which their relative died. This is one example of what I have extensively discussed elsewhere as the rhetoric of "words against death," where cultural utterances or endeavors seek to ensure that death does not have the last word, which is to say that chaos is accepted (Davies 1997).

The second example is different; it does offer recourse to law and presents a clear focus of moral blame. Culpability is not simply thought to exist in some vague domain, but is focused on particular persons. There is, in fact, some research evidence to indicate that unnatural death through accident, murder, or suicide, leads to an increase in "all forms of blaming," and that additional desires for revenge tend to hinder recovery from or development beyond the initial bereavement (Weinberg 1994:591). While Weinberg tentatively interpreted this hindering function of revenge as due to both an overconcentration on the loss and a sense of duty to the dead to avenge their death, the moral-somatic element might also be regarded as a significant factor.

In the case of the 1993 racist murder of black British teenager Stephen Lawrence, the stress fell not on revenge but upon the desire for justice. His parents, along with some other black and white Britons, felt that the police had not treated the death seriously enough, and had not pursued the perpetrators of the crime as they ought to have done. The search for justice came to be a moral campaign, a goal to be achieved before life could resume anything like an ordinary pathway. This concern was shared by many, as attested in the way tabloid newspapers reported this case. Six years later the discussion focused on making a payment to the parents in respect to the way investigations had been conducted. The chairwoman of the local Race Equality Council is reported as saying that, while no compensation could match the loss of a son, "for six years the family has struggled to get some sort of understanding about their feeling that the police did not do enough" (*The Sun* 4/16/99:17).

The very same edition of the tabloid paper reporting the Lawrence case also documented the case of the Hillsborough football disaster at Sheffield where 96 fans were crushed to death in an overcrowded stadium. A special feature marked the 10-year anniversary memorial service held at Liverpool, whose fans had been so grievously affected at the intercity match. The leader of the Hillsborough Families' Support Group presented 96 red roses, one for each of the dead, including his own two daughters. "Mr. Hicks vowed to continue the support group's battle for justice for the victims" (*The Sun* 4/16/99:30–1). The Sheffield police, already reckoned to be at fault from the public inquiry held by Lord Justice Taylor, were also criticized for not observing the respectful minute's silence at the anniversary. Much more significant than that is the fact that this family support group currently seeks to bring a private prosecution of police officers for alleged dereliction of duty on the day of the tragedy. Relatives say they cannot carry on with their lives while reckoning that people in authority had not let all the facts be known. This not only reflects that "sense of betrayal by public institutions," that might lead people to think the authorities cannot manage risk, but it also pinpoints the deeper awareness of society as the ground of morality (Horlick-Jones, 1995:312).

Yet another, though different, case was that of the Boeing 747 crash at Lockerbie in Scotland. Here there was no blame attached to the police, whose work was extensive and who appreciated that the issue lay in bringing the guilty to trial (cf. Mitchell 1993:22f.). Terrorism was to blame. Indeed, it was not until 1999, just 10 years later, that an international agreement led to alleged criminals being extradited from Libya to be tried in a unique Scottish Court held in the Netherlands, on land deemed to be Scottish for the purpose of this very court. Once more, parents and relatives voiced their opinions that justice had to be done for their own well-being as much as for any other reason.

This offers a global example of the need for practical justice. Many dead USA citizens, a crime committed over Scotland, the accused coming from Libya, and the court held in the Netherlands. These and other cases reflect in Western societies "that widespread idea that infringement of the moral code or tribal custom may bring about immediate retribution in the form of sickness or other disaster," known in many traditional cultures (Fürer-Haimendorf 1969:192), except that it marks the negative power of crime in the absence of retribution. It seems that a sense of human well-being is not attainable while a sense of injustice exists, whether it comes from the ancestors or human courts. The social animal depends upon a consonance of value and sentiment for normal functioning and, while major doubt exists over legal cases, the individuals involved exist in a form of moral-social liminality.

Never happen again!

One aspect of tragedy involves quite the opposite situation, in which there is an immediate response on the part of the proper authorities, where high-level investigation seeks the causes of devastation, and produces a report whose consequences and implementation will ensure that "this will never happen again." Phrases of this sort, including, "so that this will never happen again," sit uneasily in a risk-filled world from which accident and misadventure can never be eliminated. But, as Mary Douglas has done so much to demonstrate, the idea of risk expresses dangers awaiting the individual within an increasingly global context, and affords, "a common forensic vocabulary with which to hold persons accountable," rather than being a neutral term of statistical probability (1994:22ff.). In fact these phrases serve more the purpose of a litany against tragedy than as an attempt at preventing it. They express the desire for a moral meaning amidst chaos, the triumph of hope over misfortune.

Social Category of Offending Deaths

Where the moral-somatic type dealt with well-being and justice at the individual and small-group level, we now turn to the social category of offending deaths, which focuses on the level of a mass, popular, response to death. This too reveals a concern with justice and will be presented as another ideal type, one bearing a strong family resemblance to its moral-somatic counterpart. The difference between the two is one of the extent of the tragedy and the fact that while the moral-somatic type stresses the physical and mental condition of the aggrieved, that of offending death lays weight upon the group response at the crowd level of behavior.

The ideal type of offending death

The ideal type of offending deaths comprises an unrehearsed mass public reaction to the death of an individual or individuals perceived not only as unjust or untimely but also as an affront to current social values, and as an offense against group moral identity. The death is of innocent persons who come to symbolize key values of the prevailing social order. The cause of death, if not actually ascribed to those in positions of authority, is deemed not to have been properly prosecuted by them. Formal authorities are deemed culpable and mass action seeks reparation and redress from that guilty leadership.

When considering phenomena in relation to this ideal type I adopt a polythetic and not a monothetic form of classification of events. Theoretically speaking there is a very close similarity between the notion of ideal type and of a polythetic class. In monothetic classification one shared feature determines membership of the class, while phenomena arranged together in a polythetic class all share in some features of the class without possessing each feature of the class. The class is, then, not defined by any one specific attribute "but by a preponderance of the defining features" (Needham 1981:3). Such an exercise assumes a strong comparative dimension to sociological analysis and the following examples are but briefly sketched and have been chosen to represent a diversity of types, locales, and times.

Cases of offending deaths

The Bogota March took place on May 19, 1998 in Colombia's capital city and followed only days after a massacre of some 25 young men aged between 16 and 23 at a town called Barramcabermeja. They had been taken hostage by right-wing death squads, part of a wider set of political harassment. In October of the previous year, concurrent with their parliamentary elections, some 10 million had voted for peace in a symbolic referendum organized by a large number of nongovernment organizations. Soon after, following a growing sense of injustice, focused in this massacre, a mass of people responded. As the President of the Institute for Development and Peace in Colombia expressed it, "the people have crossed the threshold of fear and are reacting. Civic society is mobilizing" (*Newsweek* 6/22/1998:26–7).

A somewhat similar case occurred in the context of a joint Irish Nationalist and Loyalist political context when, following the August bombing at Omagh in Ireland some 60,000 people gathered on August 22, 1998, drawn from all quarters of the political and religious map protesting at the deaths and in affirmation that terrorism could no longer be justified (Price 1998).

The White March in Belgium, in September 1996, also expressed a marked level of response within a country not noted for its mass popular activism. Though widely reported internationally, its direct action and effect were local. Wearing or carrying something white, some 200,000 to 300,000 citizens took to the capital's streets in a display of protest against the way public authorities had seemed to treat a series of paedophile murders, focused on the arrest and trial of Mark Dutroux, with less than the seriousness they deserved. Those at home displayed white symbols in solidarity with the marchers. There was a public sense of corruption amongst persons in positions of authority, perhaps even of conspiracy amongst police and politicians, leading to a relative inactivity in bringing the guilty to punishment. This was echoed two years later when, for a brief spell of no more than a day, Dutroux escaped from police custody. Here the death of children was related to the moral issues of paedophilia, murder, and political corruption. Response in terms of serious police and political action was the desired goal.

The Live Aid case of 1984 was also triggered by death, this time of many Ethiopians, especially children, due to famine. The lack of apparent action on the part of politicians in many countries was a paramount trigger. The pop music performer Bob Geldof not only took a leading part in bringing the famine disaster to public view, through filming his visit to the drought-stricken area, but also engaged in sharp words of protest with the then Prime Minister, Mrs. Thatcher. This, too, was televised and caught something of the spirit of unease amongst many people. The Live Aid concert was televised internationally and involved a host of the best known popular music stars of the day giving freely of their normally expensive time, and experiencing a deep sense of commonality in so doing. As Geldof reported the finale, "there was a tremendous feeling of oneness on that stage. There had been no bitching, no displays of temperament all day. Now everyone was singing. They had their arms around each other . . . everyone was crying . . . not the easy tears of showbiz but genuine emotion"

(1986:310). The international status of the stars made this the greatest live broadcast of the 1980s and, until then, of history. The significance of the global element is considerable for it speaks of a form of shared ethics that is, otherwise, hard to establish, and which also needs serious consideration by scholars who, too easily, assume a postmodern world of atomistic self-interest. Here pop musicians made an excellent vehicle for a political message that could not be ignored.

The death and funeral of the Princess of Wales in 1997 was, even more than the Live Aid concert, a television phenomenon linked to a massed event at a London venue. Unlike the Live Aid and White March contexts it was entirely a surprise event focused on one of the best known individuals in the world. It also elicited gatherings in towns and cities across the United Kingdom and beyond to sign books of remembrance. One of its distinctive features lay in its relatively uncertain cause and focus of blame. The certainty was that a particular person was dead, one who was a symbolic figure related to many worlds. As a condensed symbol Diana reflected stardom, media presence, motherhood, frustrated and romantic love, illness, deprivation, and care of marginal groups, as well as intimate involvement with royalty: that family in whose affairs hundreds of thousands of Britons take a lively interest.

This event was one in which the issue of culpability shifted rapidly. Initially aimed at the paparazzi it embraced the broader scene of the media before the issue of the potentially drunken driver arose. Finally, in a less culpably precise but more focused form, the readily identifiable British royal family was not left untouched. The picture that emerged in the press was of a largely loved public figure who had been badly treated both by the media and the royal family, while the massed popular response of memorial was linked with a groundswell of desire to foster the issues Diana had favored. The blame attached to the royal family was only a partial blame. But it emerged as a significant element precisely because it belonged to the overall media frame of Diana's life and to the reason why ordinary people were interested in it; from the earlier royal wedding, through the birth of the princes and reported strained relations with the core royals, to the ultimate divorce and then the liaison with the Egyptian Dodi al Fayed.

The symbolic richness of this event, as far as sociological analysis is concerned, includes the fact that the memorial-funeral service was framed in something of the panoply of state, even though it was not a state funeral. The royal family was needed, whilst it might also have been disliked, in a similar way that the television and press were needed for the reporting of it all, even though they might have been viewed as partially responsible. The ambivalently viewed parties were integral to covering this offending death and to ensuring that appropriate reparation ensued. The media accepted that a degree of less intrusive reporting ought to be adopted in the future. Political concerns with the issue of land mines – one of Diana's favourite causes – led to new legislation. Considerable press attention has also been given to popularly desired changes of attitude in the royal family, to reflect Diana's perceived style of engagement with people so that, for example, the *Sun* newspaper could recently run the headline "I must be more like Diana" in outlining the Queen's reflection on the significance of the Diana event for the monarchy (*Scottish Sun* 8/29/1998).

Death Conquest

Both the individual awareness of injustice of the moral-somatic type, and the public response to offending deaths, display the power of moral values, but they are not mere reflections of values. On the contrary, these responsive processes are generative of morality, seek a conquest of negativity, including the negativity of death, and also reveal the power inherent within cultures to establish a social domain over and against the mere occurrence of events.

One means of explaining this process lies in the notion of rebounding vitality (Davies 1995:205ff.). This notion combines Maurice Bloch's idea of rebounding violence (1992), with Tambiah's concept of ethical vitality (1968) to yield a notion slightly different from each. Bloch's thesis, beginning with the natural scheme of nature running from birth to death, moves to the realm of culture which, through ritual, begins with symbolic death and passes, via symbolic rebirth, into an affirmation of life. Culture adds a dimension to nature and transcends it. Tambiah's contribution lies in the analyses of ways in which the keeping of religious rules generates merit that, almost like a commodity, becomes beneficial to those possessing it. By combining these ideas into the notion of rebounding vitality we arrive at the force behind one form of conquest of natural processes. The moral commodity of merit drives the process by which culture transcends nature.

Almost by analogy one might exemplify this by the dramatic phenomenon of the myriad flowers laid in tribute following the death of the Princess of Wales. These were not thrown away but, as symbols, were so powerful they could not simply be discarded, rather like the bread and wine remaining after the Eucharist. Flowers placed in London were composted and turned into fertilizer to be used in a new garden of remembrance. In other words, even the flowers that marked this death would not simply die but become the basis for life.

Theoretically speaking, both the moral-somatic and offending death categories are closely related to processes of rebounding vitality, in that each is triggered by a perceived injustice related to the unmerited death of a person identified as a victim. Negativity prevails, justice is undone, because all notions of merit are confounded. Only when this imbalance is rectified can "ordinary" life proceed or social life be validated. But in reality, it is not just "ordinary" life that ensues: life does not simply carry on as usual. Rather, a higher order of existence emerges, one that has come through a trial and is the stronger for it, indeed, "many disaster victims report a sense of personal growth and maturity arising out of the experience" (Brooke 1990:14). One handbook for social workers and those assisted in disasters advises them that they, "may come out wiser and stronger" (Newburn 1993:142). Often this is expressed by people wanting "something good to come out from this terrible disaster," as it is often described through the media.

The offending death context works towards a transcendence of the tragedy in striving to make the post-tragic life of society one that is better informed, more morally astute, or more wisely governed. Through the rhetoric of death rites, by means of "words against death," human culture turns death and tragedy into a cultural support rather than accepting it as an existential enemy. Thompson has, philosophically, described something similar as a coming to terms with "contingency, absurdity, and the other ontological burdens we bear" (1995:510), while Stallings has emphasized "the importance of existential definitions of disasters" (1998:143).

Merit and Sacrifice

These power-engendering processes of achieving justice and reparation, in close relation with the death of highly charged symbolic bodies, bring our discussion to its final focus in the phenomenon of sacrifice, a fundamental element within the Durkheimian stream of the sociology of religion. In recent decades sacrifice has attracted more interest from philosophically and psychoanalytically informed scholars than from sociologists as such, and these have emphasized the realm of culpability (Ricoeur 1960) and of violence (Girard 1977), echoing the inescapable Durkheimian concern with society and morality.

Sacrifices are often related both to moral-somatic dynamics of life and to the category of offending deaths. Table 22.1 shows how sacrifices usually involve the intentional death or offering of an innocent victim to achieve some social benefit by a symbolic removal of evil. They are explicable whereas offending deaths are not. Christianity has presented humanity with one of the most successful formulations of a sacrifice in the death of Christ and its ritual extension through the eucharistic sacrifice and the doctrine of substitutionary atonement.

One attribute of sacrificial victims is that they are often bearers of or vehicles for merit. And merit is one of the most potent of all social values, not least in the way it unites embodied activity and social value. Merit is acquired by following social rules to an advanced degree. It is conceived of as a power that confers benefit upon those possessing it, either by their own endeavor or when received as a gift. Most established religions operate on a basis of merit, either in terms of a zealous striving that generates it, or through love unions with deities that, intentionally, reckon to transcend it. Both Hinduism and Buddhism generate merit under varied schemes of *karma*. Merit is also basic to Christianity's foundational beliefs as well as to those of its Reformation doctrine that sees Christ as making merit with God, or the church distributing it to people who are quite incapable of generating it themselves.

So it is that merit emerges from the very heart of the social and communal nature of human beings, having secular consequences in the generation of strong work ethics, while also coming to be invested with religious significance within religious systems of sin and salvation. The crucial factor is that the outcome of social rule keeping is valuable whether in religious or nonreligious frames of action. On the same principle rule breaking, as in offending deaths,

Table 22.1 Offending Death and Sacrifice

Offending Deaths	*Sacrifices*
1 Unrehearsed mass public reaction	Ritualized performance
2 Death perceived as unjust or untimely	Death is justified and timely
3 Event as affront to social values	Ritual restores moral balance
4 Event is an offense against group moral identity	Ritual affirms corporate identity
5 Death is of an innocent person who symbolizes key social values	A pure victim is rendered ritually impure
6 Cause of death ascribed to culpable authorities	The rite removes culpability from the group
7 The mass action seeks reparation and redress	The ritual effects reparation and redress

is likely to produce moral-somatic responses of a negative kind. So it is that sacrifice and offending deaths are polar types expressing the need for moral power to be properly controlled by authority.

References

Barkow, J.H., Cosmides, L., and Tooby, J. 1992. *The Adapted Mind: Evolutionary Psychology and the Generation of Culture.* New York: Oxford University Press.
Bauman, Z. 1992. *Intimations of Postmodernity.* London: Routledge.
Bell, N. 1979. "Some Notes on Defining Disaster: Suggestions for a Disaster Continuum," *Disasters* 3(1):3–7.
Benthall, J. 1993. *Disasters, Relief, and the Media.* London: I.B. Tauris.
Bloch, M. 1992. *Prey into Hunter: The Politics of Religious Experience.* Cambridge: Cambridge University Press.
Brooke, R. 1990. *An Introduction to Disaster Theory for Social Workers.* Social Work Monographs 33. Norwich: University of East Anglia.
Cannon, W.B. 1942. "Voodoo Death," *American Anthropologist.* XLIV:182–90.
Cleiren, M. 1991. *Adaptation after Bereavement.* Leiden: University of Leiden Press.
Corballis, M.C. 1991. *The Lopsided Ape, Evolution of the Generative Mind.* New York: Oxford University Press.
Darwin, C. 1998. *The Expression of the Emotions in Man and Animals.* London: Harper-Collins.
Davies, D.J. 1995. "Rebounding Vitality: Resurrection and Spirit in Luke–Acts," in *The Bible in Human Society,* Eds. M.D. Carroll R., D.J. A. Clines, and R.P. Davies, Sheffield: Academic Press, pp. 205–24.
Davies, D.J. 1997. *Death, Ritual and Belief.* London: Cassell.
Douglas, M. 1994. *Risk and Blame: Essays in Cultural Theory.* London: Routledge.

Fenn, R.K. 1982. *Liturgies and Trials: The Secularization of Religious Language*. Oxford: Blackwell.

Frijda, N.H. 1986. *The Emotions*. Cambridge: Cambridge University Press.

Fukuyama, F. 1995. *Trust: The Social Virtues and the Creation of Prosperity*. London: Penguin Books.

Fürer-Haimendorf, C. von. 1969. *Morals and Merit*. London: Weidenfeld and Nicolson.

Geldof, B. 1986. *Is That It?* London: Sidgwick and Jackson.

Giddens, A. 1991. *Modernity and Self-Identity: Self and Society in the Late Modern Age*. Cambridge: Polity Press.

Girard, R. 1977. *Violence and the Sacred*. London: Johns Hopkins University Press.

Grimby, A. (1995) *Aspects of Quality of Life in Old Age: Studies on Life Events, Bereavement and Health*. Department of Geriatric Medicine, Göteborg University, Sweden.

Horlick-Jones, T. 1995. "Modern Disasters as Outrage and Betrayal," *International Journal of Mass Emergencies and Disasters* 13:305–16.

Janoff-Bulman, R. and Frieze, I. 1983. "A Theoretical Perspective for Understanding Reactions to Victimization," *Journal of Social Issues* 39(2):1–17.

Kemper, T.D. 1990. *Social Structure and Testosterone*. New Brunswick, NJ and London: Rutgers University Press.

Leaman, O. 1995. *Death and Loss*. London, Cassell.

LeDoux, J. 1998. *The Emotional Brain*. London: Weidenfeld and Nicolson.

Lévi-Strauss, C. 1968. *Structural Anthropology*, Vol. 1. London: Allen Lane.

Mauss, M. 1979. *Sociology and Psychology*. London: Routledge and Kegan Paul.

Mitchell, M. 1993. "The Eye of the Storm: Police Control of the Lockerbie Disaster," in *Working with Disaster*, Ed. T. Newburn. London: Longman, pp. 22–37.

Moscovici, S. 1993. *The Invention of Society*. Cambridge: Polity Press.

Murphy, S.A. et al. 1998. "Broad-Spectrum Group Treatment for Parents Bereaved by the Violent Deaths of their 12–28 Year Old Children: A Randomized Controlled Trial," *Death Studies*, 22(3):209–36.

Needham, R. 1973. *Right and Left*. Chicago: University of Chicago Press.

Needham, R. 1981. *Circumstantial Deliveries*. Berkeley: University of California Press.

Newburn, T., Ed. 1993. *Working with Disaster*. London: Longman.

Parkes, C.M. and Weiss, R.S. 1983. *Recovery from Bereavement*. New York: Basic Books.

Price, P. 1998. "Thousands Gather to Pray in Omagh," *Church Times*, No. 7072, p. 1.

Ricoeur, P. 1960. *Finitude et culpabilité*. Paris: Aubier.

Skultans, V. 1999. "Narratives of the Body and History: Illness in Judgement on the Soviet Past," *Sociology of Health and Illness* 21(3):310–28.

Stallings, R.A. 1998. "Disaster and the Theory of Social Order," in *What is a Disaster?*, Ed. E.L. Quarantelli. London: Routledge.

Tambiah, S.J. 1968. "The Ideology of Merit and the Social Correlates of Buddhism in a Thai Village," in *Dialectic in Practical Religion*, Ed. E.R. Leach. Cambridge:Cambridge University Press, pp. 41–121.

Thompson, N. 1995. "The Ontology of Disasters," *Death Studies* 19(5):501–10.

Weinberg, N. 1994. "Self-Blame, Other-Blame, and Desire for Revenge: Factors in Recovery from Bereavement," *Death Studies* 18(6):583–94.

Williams, S.J. and Bendelow, G. 1996. "Emotions, Health and Illness," in *Health and the Sociology of Emotions*, Eds. V. James and J. Gabe. Oxford: Blackwell, pp. 25–54.

CHAPTER 23

Contemporary Social Theory as it Applies to the Understanding of Religion in Cross-cultural Perspective

Peter Beyer

Introduction: The Questions of Religion and Culture

At first glance, studying religion cross-culturally from a sociological perspective would seem to be a fairly straightforward undertaking: after careful study of the religions of different cultures, we would compare the results for similarities, differences, and what these might tell us about both religion and culture. Although that is to some extent how it is done, upon closer inspection matters are not nearly so simple. First, there are the questions of what sociological observers mean by "religion" and "culture." How do they understand these terms so as to allow controlled comparison? What counts as religion and what exactly are cultures so that we can "cross" them? At another level, there is the parallel question of what the people sociologists observe understand: do the people who belong to these cultures and religions make the same distinctions? Do they even have words that parallel the ideas of culture and religion? And if their ideas are different or they have no corresponding notions, do sociologists then have a proper basis of comparison? These questions become even sharper when we take into account that the sociologists also belong to particular cultures with their corresponding religious expressions. The observers are part of what they are observing and that, in all likelihood, is going to have an effect on what and how they observe.

To look at all the various ramifications of these questions would be too much for a short chapter such as this to undertake. In what follows, therefore, I limit myself to addressing the interplay of contemporary social theory and modern historical developments in the understanding of religion as a pluralistic and cross-cultural phenomenon. How has social theory viewed the task of the cross-cultural study of religion, and why? How should social theory approach the matter today, and why? To respond, the presentation has three main sections.

The first looks very briefly at the nature of sociology and anthropology as modern disciplines that have always had a strong cross-cultural component. Comparison has been at the heart of these enterprises and this feature has affected the dominant understandings of religion as well. The second section then examines some of the more important sociological conceptions of religion with a view to understanding their strengths and limitations for undertaking cross-cultural study and indeed how they have been formulated more or less explicitly with such work in mind. The final section takes up various themes introduced in the previous two to discuss in what directions social theory needs to go now if it is to respond most self-consciously to the situation of religion(s) and culture(s) in contemporary world society.

Sociology and Anthropology as Cross-cultural Disciplines in the Modern World

Modern sociology, and indeed the social sciences more generally, have arisen during the last 200 years in the context of monumental social changes, first in Western society and then around the rest of the world as well. Sociology is both a response to those changes and a part of them. More specifically, sociology emerged as the scientific discipline most concerned with seeking to understand the transformations, and in particular how the "new" situation, dubbed "modern," differed from the societies that had existed before. The time-distinction between "traditional" (before) and "modern" (now) is critical for understanding not only modern social theory, but also the conceptions of religion that we find in these.

By contrast, anthropology, a very closely related field, became the discipline more concerned with understanding those places and social groups that existed in modern times, but were seen by Western social-scientific observers as having the characteristics of the traditional societies that came before. Anthropology has until quite recently used what is in effect a place-distinction between "us" here (usually in the West) and "them" there (usually in the non-West). But this distinction has often implicitly overlapped that between modern and traditional societies, so that, for instance, many parts of the world – in Africa and Asia especially – were treated by these disciplines as in certain respects existing in the (modern) present, but somehow also belonging to the (traditional) past.

That having been said, it becomes clear how both sociology and anthropology have, in their different ways, been cross-cultural enterprises. The main comparison for sociology has been the temporal one between modern and traditional societies. In this respect, Max Weber's monumental work on the rise of capitalism in the West is a classic example. In order to support his contention that Western religion played a key role in this rise, Weber undertook comparative historical studies of China, India, and the ancient Middle East to show that the critical religiocultural factor was missing in these cases (for examples, see Weber

1946:267–359, 396–444). Beyond such comparisons of modern and traditional, however, sociologists have also concerned themselves with differences *within* that part of the world deemed modern, usually the West. For such study, modern territorial states have served as the most common units of analysis. Indeed, even today, when sociologists talk about a society or about societies, they usually mean a state or states, even if they are somewhat vague about straightforwardly identifying states and societies (see, for example, Parsons 1971, Stark 1994:41). Using states as proxies for what we mean by distinct societies or cultures does have the advantage of allowing a convenient and controlled comparison between different regions of the world, and in that sense aids cross-cultural work. Yet one ought to be suspicious of the way that so many sociologists have taken this rough equation of state and society – the root concept of the entire discipline after all – for granted. I return to this point below.

The cross-cultural nature of anthropology has been even more obvious. Anthropologists have generally carried out their studies of particular cultures around the world with an eye to comparing all the different ways that people have organized their social lives. Indeed, the corpus of classic anthropological literature cannot be understood as anything but a vast cross-cultural enterprise. One of the factors that, until relatively recently, made this work more or less unproblematic is that the "cultures" studied existed in comparative isolation from one another and from the cultural region of the researchers. The possibilities of "contamination" and ambiguity were low. That situation has not lasted, however.

The connection of these observations to the sociological and anthropological study of religion is fairly straightforward. In keeping with the fundamental orientations just discussed, a key question among social scientists has been whether or not religion belongs more clearly in the traditional past than the modern present, and therefore also more clearly with the non-Western "other" than the Western culture of the vast majority of social scientific observers. In this light, it is not surprising that anthropologists have habitually paid much more attention to religion than have sociologists, and that the study of religion has been solidly integrated into the discipline as a whole. By contrast, the sociology of religion has been, as Beckford (1989:1–18) puts it, an "isolated" and "insulated" enterprise within the larger discipline; and much sociology of religion has either adopted or worked in the shadow of the idea of secularization. This notion, in its various forms, sees the relation between religion and modernity to be ambiguous at best, contradictory at worst. That, in a nutshell, describes the situation until relatively recently.

In the latter half of the twentieth century, it became more and more difficult for either discipline to maintain the somewhat paradoxical distinctions of modern–traditional overlapping onto that between the West and the "others." The rise of independent states in all parts of the world, the seemingly irrevocable incorporation of these same regions into what has become a truly global capitalist economy, and the much increased density of worldwide communication networks have been among the factors convincing many social scientists of the need to reconsider some of their most basic orientations. Sociologists, one might say, can no longer treat society in the West as the self-evident standard of modernity, judging other places only by how well they conform to this model. And anthropologists have run out of "cultures" that still exist in anything like isolation, thus making the distinctiveness of cultures more difficult to discern and blurring the neat difference between "us" and "them." Among sociologists, such recasting had, toward the end of the twentieth century, led to explicitly worldwide theoretical perspectives under labels like world-system theory (Wallerstein 1987) or globalization theory (see Robertson 1992, Waters 1995). Anthropologists favor other terms, especially "transnationalism" (Bamyeh 1993, Hannerz 1996) to understand the reorientation. In both disciplines, debates that go under the heading of "postmodernism" and new subdisciplines such as cultural studies are in key ways also symptomatic of this reassessment.

The more recent turn in both disciplines toward a global perspective has also had the effect of moving each, so to speak, more clearly and consistently into the camp of the other. Sociologists are now faced with the need to treat the culturally "other" as true contemporaries and fellow travelers in a single modern world. If their theories are to hold, then they must do so for these "others" as well. Above all, they can no longer dismiss seeming anomalies as mere vestiges of a now surpassed stage of human evolution. Anthropologists, while still focusing more often on socioeconomically marginalized groups and cultures, are now increasingly doing their work in all parts of the world, not just in those geographically separate from the dominant West. The difference between "here" and "elsewhere" is no longer clear. In effect, many social scientists have come to the realization that a world society has been emerging for quite some time, and that in this context cross-cultural work takes on a new and somewhat different importance: it is an unavoidable task if we are to understand how the obvious social and cultural differences that exist around the world can still be part of a single social unit; and vice versa, how we are to understand and, indeed, maintain differences if there is now but one worldwide society.

The new situation – or perhaps better, the new realization – does not mean that the social sciences have been entirely wrong in their approaches, including their approach to religion. What it does imply is that an adequate social theory for understanding religion in the contemporary world has to revisit and in many cases seriously revise some of the most basic assumptions of the past. The cross-cultural study of religion, like cross-cultural work more generally, will undergo a corresponding transformation. That said, we can now turn to a closer look at how this broad context has manifested itself in social theories of religion.

Sociological and Anthropological Conceptions of Religion

Most introductory textbooks in the sociology of religion begin with a discussion of definitions, noting the lack of agreement and the many definitions, and generally dividing these into two types, substantive and functional. Briefly, substantive definitions focus on what religion *is*, whereas functional definitions try to say what religion *does*. Anthropologists and sociologists have each offered several of both varieties. Of the many features of this definitional debate, there is one that I mention at this point because it is so strategic. It concerns the assumed universality or near universality of religion. By no means all social theorists make this assumption, but a great many do, defenders of substantive definitions but especially those putting forth functional definitions of religion. Almost invariably, the latter describe these defining functions as so basic to any society that, by definition, no society can endure without religion. Thus, for example, if religion is that which holds a society together or provides ultimate meaning, then it becomes hard to imagine a society without one. Under the assumption of universality, therefore, functional conceptions fill an important role for those social theorists who assume at least a partial incompatibility between religion and modernity; or who are looking at societies where the "religious" is an undifferentiated aspect of the culture. Traditional religion can be absent, can weaken, become unclear, or even disappear without questioning that universality. The obvious question is, of course, why so many social scientists have made this assumption. What does it tell us about the way that cross-cultural sociology and anthropology of religion have been done?

By way of working towards answers to these questions, a closer look at a few modern and contemporary social theorists of religion will be instructive. We can begin by noting that Karl Marx and Sigmund Freud, two of the most ardent modern critics of religion, nevertheless felt that it was a regrettable constant of human existence, at least during that vast historical period between a mythic prehistorical past and the utopian future. Emile Durkheim, who has the distinction of being a "founding father" of both anthropology and sociology, was more positive. Religion was for Durkheim essentially integrative: it "unites into one single moral community" (Durkheim 1965:62). The essence of religion Durkheim found in an "anthropological" society, in the totemic beliefs and practices of the Australian aborigines (Durkheim 1965:106ff.). In modern society, where such traditional religion was necessarily losing its hold, it was to be replaced by a "modern religion" which, although still not fully formed, he deemed necessary lest that society sink into anomie and chaos. According to Durkheim, if religion in modern society seemed weak, that was only because we were in a period of transition and the new modern religion was not yet clearly recognizable (Durkheim 1969).

As concerns the cross-cultural study of religion, Durkheim thereby introduced a very important question into the debate, namely that religion, while in terms of function universal and fundamental to social life, nonetheless takes on different forms from one society to another, from one culture to another. A key part of the problem of understanding religion across societies and cultures may therefore be the *cultural habits* of observers, who when looking for religion in their own or another culture, look only for familiar forms of religion and discount or simply miss the rest.

Another classical thinker, Georg Simmel, located this question of form at the very core of his conception of religion. For him, "religiousness" referred to a fundamental, and ultimately individual, attitude that people had to have for society to function. He analyzed this orientation or sentiment under various terms, for example piety, faith, love, solidarity, and dependency. Such feelings in individuals made society possible, but were, however, not already by themselves religion. For them to become religion they had to be projected into particular forms, such as gods, spirits, rituals, and the religious institutions that perpetuated these. This concretization or institutionalization often happened, but was not necessary: religiousness was necessary for society, religion was optional (see Simmel 1959). For cross-cultural study, Simmel's distinction between "religiousness" and "religion" can be very useful. One can foresee the Durkheimian notion of a fundamental change in the form of religion from one society to another, from one historical period to another. There also exists the possibility of a secular society in which religion weakens, disappears, or is reduced in importance to an optional or occasional involvement; but religiousness remains. And nothing excludes a whole range of possibilities in which formed religion is more or less present, more or less dominant, more or less differentiated from other aspects or domains of culture.

Most contemporary social theorists have, in one way or another, taken up this distinction between religion as form and religious function in their attempts to understand religion, and to understand it cross-culturally. Usually, the function has provided the unity of what we are comparing, while differences in form supply the basis of the differences. Not surprisingly, most sociologists made the distinction in order to understand the modern situation; whereas anthropologists have been more concerned to explain the variety of religious manifestations across (traditional) cultures. As illustration of these tendencies and to move the discussion forward, I take a very brief look at aspects of the theories of sociologists Thomas Luckmann and Talcott Parsons, and of anthropologists Clifford Geertz and Melford Spiro.

Representing perhaps one extreme, Luckmann takes the Simmelian starting point and intensifies it. Religion for him is the process by which humans create a meaningful world for themselves: it is worldview construction (Luckmann 1967:53). Having defined religion thus broadly, it becomes necessary in its function, but any particular form of religion is entirely optional. In consequence, Luckmann allows for the severe weakening of various collective and institutional forms of religion in modern society, while maintaining that religion construction is still happening, above all at the level of the individual. Although this approach has proven suggestive for understanding some aspects of modern society, at least in certain regions of the globe, from the perspective of cross-cultural study, it provides very little purchase on situations in which less individualistic, and more collective, forms of religion are dominant. Luckmann not only identifies the modern too much with certain parts of the West, he also seeks too great a coordination of form and function for any given society.

Talcott Parsons, by contrast, takes a different and perhaps less radical direction. Again, his primary objective is to understand religion in a modern society. But rather than intensifying the Simmelian starting point and thus, in effect reducing religion to religiousness, form to function, Parsons takes his cue more from Durkheim, among others. Thus, corresponding to the latter's idea of a specifically modern religion, Parsons posits a form of religiousness that is peculiar to modern societies, and this is what he, with Bellah, calls "civil religion," or the religiousness of national solidarity (see Parsons 1966:134ff., 1974:203ff., cf. Bellah 1970). Civil religions serve the integrative function at the level of the "national society" (e.g., the United States) that Durkheim considered so essential. Of particular note in this regard is that such a thesis would be impossible without that common sociological understanding already mentioned: societies and states are more or less homologous. Yet, beside this new form, which comparatively speaking does not look much like traditional forms of religion and can even be seen as rather formless, Parsons saw an important role for religious forms that are institutionalized precisely as religions. These, like American denominations, are differentiated from other institutional domains and especially separate from the state, and are individualistic and hence voluntary, that is, optional. This domain of privatized, voluntary religion includes the highly individualistic form that Luckmann stresses (cf. Bellah et al. 1985). Their function is also in this more individualistic domain.

Although Parsons' approach does allow for more possibilities in the modern context than does Luckmann's, there is comparatively little material here for doing cross-cultural study, unless that study is along a temporal axis, that is, comparing modern and traditional. In particular, Parsons' approach does not allow for traditional or clearly institutional religion to remain obligatory and collective. The modern world, which from a global perspective is the only world left, contains more variation than the Parsonian model will allow. For more adequate cross-cultural study, therefore, his points of departure would have to be significantly enhanced.

The work of contemporary anthropologists, as one might expect, responds to some of these insufficiencies, but also introduces a different set of ambiguities. Clifford Geertz, for instance, conceives religion expressly as a "cultural system" (Geertz 1966), leaving room in one stroke for institutionalized religion that is to a greater or lesser extent separate from other domains, as well as for situations in which religious expression is little differentiated from other cultural domains. Thus, on this basis, one could analyze American civil religion as a cultural system fulfilling the functions that Geertz foresees for religion: essentially, generating the "conception of a general order of existence [that seems to its adherents] uniquely realistic" (1966:4). Similar analyses could be carried out for the Islamic cultural system in the Middle East, the Maoist cultural system of the People's Republic of China (at least for the period from 1948 to 1975), or for a Pentecostal Christian group in Ghana or Canada. Each of these, and many more, would be possible, but – and here lies the insufficiency – only separately and in analytical isolation from one another.

Where a sociological theory like that of Parsons or Luckmann tends to leave out of consideration important ways of forming religion in contemporary world society, an anthropological approach such as that of Geertz provides too little conceptual material for conceiving the ways that the different "cultural systems" relate to one another. The same could be said for other anthropological approaches such as that of Claude Lévi-Strauss or Victor Turner. For, under contemporary circumstances, what one religion or cultural system is or becomes depends to some extent on how the others have formed. Quite aside from other factors, the density of contemporary worldwide communication presents each of them with the question of how to relate to a world in which all the others exist. The old anthropological condition of effective mutual isolation is gone, just as is the sociological self-evidence of modernity and tradition when conceived geographically as "we here" and "the others there."

The work of Melford Spiro represents a somewhat different strategy and the beginnings of a way forward. Where the three thinkers I have just discussed address the question of religious form through that of function, Spiro takes the reverse approach. His frankly substantive definition of religion is both short and indicative: "an institution consisting of culturally patterned interaction with culturally postulated superhuman beings" (Spiro 1987:197). Spiro, in speaking only of institutions, is only interested in form; function depends on context and is therefore variable. He is also restrictive, allowing that quite a range of things that might qualify are not going to count as religion. For cross-cultural study of religion in the contemporary world, this tactic has the distinct advantage of not prejudging religion according to modern or traditional, of allowing varying degrees of differentiation of religion from other social domains and institutions, and of leaving the relation of a plurality of such religious institutions open. Spiro thereby clearly and deliberately sacrifices universality: like Simmel, he simply allows that religiousness is not the same as religion and that therefore religion is, theoretically speaking, optional and variable. The corresponding difficulty, if there is one, has to do with the reason why the others seem to insist so much on universality.

As the above selection exemplifies, most social scientific theories of religion try to address at least two features of the religious: its sense of being foundational, which is to say something in the order of the completely self-evident, absolute, and beyond question; and its consistent appeal to something that is in one fashion or another transcendent as the basis for the absoluteness, whether this be God, Tao, society, the nation, or other symbols. At root, probably the main reason that most of the classical thinkers paid so much attention to religion – even those who felt traditional religion was destined to fade from the scene – was precisely that they were preoccupied with, as Simmel's famous essay puts it, how social order was possible under modern conditions (Simmel 1971). As the nineteenth century German philosopher Friedrich Nietzsche put it, if God (or the religious absolute) is dead and it is we moderns that have killed him, must we not become gods to replace him? Or in the words of Dostoevsky's fictional character, Ivan Karamazov, "If there is no God, then everything is permitted." From this perspective, one can understand the preoccupation of so many social thinkers, in the first order, with religious function, form seeming to be relegated to a secondary concern. Spiro's position therefore introduces a difficulty to the extent that we associate the question of religion with this supposedly rudimentary "religious" function. If it is not religion, then what does make society possible in the contemporary era?

Rather than offer an answer to this admittedly important question, I wish to suggest that the attempt to do so on the basis of the concept of religion is itself problematic in that it blocks the development of an adequate social theory for understanding and studying religion cross-culturally. In effect, the question of function, focused as it always has been on the overall problem of what makes social worlds possible, tends to underexpose the question of form. And yet, for cross-cultural study, form and differences in form make all the difference. Focus on the forms religion takes is therefore critical. The concluding section of this chapter focuses specifically on this question and thereby on the directions that social theory should take if it is to become more adequate to the task of cross-cultural study of religion.

Social Theory for Cross-cultural Study of Religions in a World Society

If, as has been argued in this chapter, the classical social scientific distinctions between modern and traditional, and between this society and that, can no longer serve as an adequate basis for understanding contemporary world society, then the old foundations for cross-cultural study of religion have to change. This injunction concerns both the basis upon which the disciplines distinguish cultures to be crossed and religions to be compared. Accordingly, one can no longer rely on the division between states as proxy for the different cultures to be studied. Nor, as noted, can we assume geographical isolation. The whole question of what counts as cultures requires reexamination. Moreover, in separating the issue of the supposed function(s) of religion from that of the concrete social forms that people call religion, social theory must rethink the question of what constitutes religion and the religions. In both cases, for culture and for religion, the terms will lose some of their universality and self-evidence in favor of more historical notions. Culture and religion will not just *have* modern forms, they will *be* modern forms. This realization does not restrict cross-cultural study to the modern present, but it will condition historical comparative research as well.

Geography has ceased being a viable aid in telling us where the boundaries between cultures are. What other ways are then justified? In today's global society, there are no longer social boundaries that include everything that is important for the lives of any particular group of people. Yet most of us in the world are still convinced that the differences between people are very important.

Given the lack of "natural boundaries," the two most defensible strategies are therefore one or both of the following: either we accept those boundaries that social groups in their own self-descriptions consider to be definitive, or we use whatever boundaries are convenient for the analysis we have in mind. Thus, for example, if the Kurds believe they form a distinct and unified group with its own distinct culture, then researchers can accept this description and use it in their work. Or we can compare American and Nepalese culture because state boundaries are still convenient. In neither case, however, will it be possible to deny the relative arbitrariness of the distinctions, and social theory must incorporate the fluidity and the constructed or deliberate character of such differences into its structures and assumptions. Cross-cultural research thereby becomes a way of understanding social and cultural differences without assuming that the units of comparison are anything more than matters of convenience or accommodation to the conscious self-identifications of our subjects. From here we can consider the implications for studying religion.

To the extent that we treat religions, along with Geertz, as "cultural systems," the question in this domain would be susceptible of a similar answer: religion, like culture, refers to a somewhat arbitrary and strategic distinction. Indeed, Meredith McGuire, among others, has suggested that defining religion should be a matter of research strategy and nothing more fundamental (McGuire 1992:10). Nonetheless, in parallel with the idea that culture can and often does refer to social differences that people use to identify themselves, and which they insist are real, a look at what actually counts as religion in the world society we all inhabit can take the discussion a step further.

A complaint that one hears not infrequently from scholars of religion (see, for example, Smith 1964, Fitzgerald 1997) is that the term itself is of Western provenance and carries Western biases. To apply it to other places and therefore to other cultures brings the risk of using an inappropriate concept to understand the lives of people who are not Westerners. The most frequent examples that such critics cite are those of Hinduism (Fitzgerald 1990) and Confucianism (Paper 1995), two "religions" that for these authors are not religions in that Western sense. It is probably for similar reasons that a good number of the most well-known anthropological definitions are functional: to avoid imposing a Western "form" on other cultures where these forms are unfamiliar or do not make ready sense. The restrictive nature of a substantive definition like that of Spiro can be understood as having a similar motivation.

As already noted, such a criticism along with the reactions would go a long way to resolving the issue if it were not for the fact that, in contemporary world society, the "others," whether Westerners or non-Westerners, have a great deal of contact with each other and have been influencing one another for at least the last two centuries. In fact, the arrival of the so-called modern era coincides with the effective expansion of Western influence all around the world and with the gradual rise of non-Western regions to renewed prominence and significant reverse effect on Western areas. The situation undermines the approach that sees religious function as what we all have in common and religious form as the way of understanding how we are different. With increased "intercultural" contact, the role of form and function may in fact be reversed: a form may be globally spread but serve different functions in different areas (or, in different "cultures"). A brief narrative look at the history and spread of the Western notion of religion can serve to clarify this hypothesis.

Although the word religion has a long history in European languages (with sufficiently close parallels in especially Semitic languages), it was only in the seventeenth century that we see the emergence of the notion that the generic "religion" always and only manifests itself in the real social world as a plurality of discrete "religions" (see Smith 1964, Despland 1979, Harrison 1990). People before this time and elsewhere of course acknowledged the diversity in religion but saw this more as different groups or individuals doing the same thing in various (better or worse) ways. A classic example of this latter conception is the way Islam has traditionally conceived religious pluralism: a variety of different peoples have all been given the same Koran, but only the Arabic Koran is the pure one, the rest (especially the Christian and the Jewish) being comparative distortions. Religious behavior that cannot be subsumed in this way does not count as religion. It is polytheism and is to be suppressed as the antithesis of real religion. The early modern European conception changed this thinking not only in that Judaism, Christianity, and Islam were now different religions that could not be reduced to one another; but also in that it included a kind of residual category, a religion called paganism. Thereafter, as the Europeans spread their influence to other parts of the world and there encountered civilizations with entirely different religious traditions, they attempted to understand these as so many more religions: Hinduism, Buddhism, Confucianism, Taoism, and eventually the "tribal" religions of the many nonliterate peoples around the world.

This vision of "the religions" was of Western provenance and of course works best for Western religions such as Islam and Judaism. As a particular form of what religion might be, however, it has to some extent been taken up by many non-Westerners; but it has also been rejected by others, depending on what is being called religion. In the first category, for example, fall a sizeable group of Hindu elite since the beginning of the nineteenth century; into the latter we can put the corresponding modernizing intelligentsia of China. In spite of the variable responses, the idea that religion is a type of human activity that manifests itself in principle as a plurality of distinct and different religions or religious systems is a quite strong and widespread one in today's world, including those such as the Chinese who reject the term for aspects of their own cultural traditions (Beyer 1998). That particular "form" becomes thereby an almost unavoidable basis for cross-cultural comparison in contemporary world society, irrespective of the Western origins of the form. It does not, however, simply take over: the possibility of doing cross-cultural study on the basis of a more general functional or substantive notion of religion remains both possible and necessary. The idea of a globalized and systemic form of religion nonetheless provides a way of trying to understand how the "religions" of different "cultures," and the various religious traditions themselves are influencing one another and how their adherents might be (re)constructing them in the awareness of living in a religiously pluralistic world society. The historical rise of new forms of religions complexifies the issue rather than just reversing it.

The question of religious form as a basis of comparison in modern global society has to be taken one step further before we can consider the consequences of this changed situation for social theory. Isolating a peculiarly modern global model or form for religion is by itself not enough because we do not as yet have a basis for understanding interreligious and cross-cultural differences. Here a combination of form and function enters the picture. Religions and religious institutions can be compared according to what functions they fulfill, for instance whether they serve as general worldviews for an entire population, whether they are resources for structuring conflict and contestation, whether they are politicized or highly privatized, and so forth. On the other hand, these same social structures can be compared as to level of institutional differentiation, degree and type of organization, structures of authority, the extent to which the networks they inform are local, translocal, or global, and other possibilities beside. And perhaps just as importantly, even the basis of identification, the form of the religions, can also become a basis of comparative difference: to what degree religion has formed as religion in a given culture; however, the latter is delimited.

A principal upshot of these considerations that has significant consequences for social theory is that the category of religion becomes a relatively fluid and even contested one in principle (see Robertson 1991); the same statement applies to the idea of culture. That conclusion flows from the observation that we can no longer derive the identity of religion from function – and perhaps not even strictly from substance – but only from contingent, that is, variable, form. The latter can be one thing under modern, global circumstances and quite another in other historical contexts. From this consequence flow a number of others. Here are a few:

- a social theory of religion can neither base itself on the assumption of a single function (as does for instance Durkheim's theory) nor even on a single form (as does for instance that of Spiro or Rodney Stark, see Stark and Bainbridge 1987).
- The distinction between functional and substantive conceptions can no longer be a fundamental organizing distinction because religion, like culture, is an invented or constructed category that varies according to how its users conceive it. Both will apply, not just according to the research strategy of the observer, but because social actors use the word in either sense.
- Religion cannot occupy the position of a universal in social theory: there must be the possibility of a society or culture without religion.
- In reverse, religion must be theoretically possible in all societies and cultures. Above all, modern society cannot be theorized as inherently secular just because certain forms disappear or weaken; or because what counts as religion no longer responds to specific functions.

- Religions must be conceived as historical, both in form and in function. If there is no longer a theoretically necessary form or function, no essence of a religion, then this conclusion follows.

Other similar statements could be added. Yet it is only on the basis of these sorts of assumption that we can derive a social theory that does not *a priori* impose a certain historically and culturally determined (whether Western or not) manifestation of religion on the important differences that existed historically and that exist in today's global society; while at the same time taking into account that in this society, the manifestations of religion are themselves mutually influencing each other. This shift does not have the effect of making the term "religion" useless because one can still isolate variable religious forms or functions; but above all because religion (or cognate terms in other languages) is very often an operative social category that people use in their interaction and discourse. It does, however, require that social theory for the cross-cultural study of religion be much more aware of its own contingency and dependence on the social context to which it is applied and in which it is framed. It also necessitates taking much more seriously the notion of how religion actually gets used in society. This probably eliminates the possibility of a universal theory for all times and circumstances; and it certainly makes precise theoretical prediction of future states of religion virtually impossible. Admitting these limitations nevertheless gives social science a better chance of understanding differences in a world where we realize that the aims of our observations are to a large degree the variable products of our own making.

References

Bamyeh, M.A. 1993. "Transnationalism," *Current Sociology* 41(3):1–95.

Beckford, J.A. 1989. *Religion and Advanced Industrial Society.* London: Unwin Hyman.

Bellah, R.N. 1970. "Civil Religion in America," in *Beyond Belief: Essays on Religion in a Post-Industrial World*, Ed. R.N. Bellah. New York: Harper & Row, pp. 168–89.

Bellah, R.N., Madsen, R., Sullivan, W.M., Swidler, A., and Tipton, S.M. 1985. *Habits of the Heart: Individualism and Commitment in American Life.* San Francisco: Harper & Row.

Beyer, P. 1998. "The Modern Emergence of Religions and a Global Social System for Religion," *International Sociology* 13:151–72.

Despland, M. 1979. *La religion en occident: Evolution des idées et du vécu.* Montreal: Fides.

Durkheim, E. 1965. *The Elementary Forms of the Religious Life*, Transl. J.W. Swain. New York: Free Press.

Durkheim, E. 1969. "Le sentiment religieux à l'heure actuelle," *Archives de Sociologie des Religions* 27:73–7.

Fitzgerald, T. 1990. "Hinduism and the 'World Religion' Fallacy," *Religion* 20:101–18.

Fitzgerald, T. 1997. "A Critique of 'Religion' as a Cross-Cultural Category," *Method and Theory in the Study of Religion* 9:91–110.

Geertz, C. 1966. "Religion as a Cultural System," in *Anthropological Approaches to the Study of Religion*, Ed. M. Banton. London: Tavistock, pp. 1–46.

Hannerz, U. 1996. *Transnational Connections: Culture, People, Places.* London: Routledge.

Harrison, P. 1990. *"Religion" and the Religions in the English Enlightenment.* Cambridge: Cambridge University Press.

Luckmann, T. 1967. *The Invisible Religion: The Problem of Religion in Modern Society.* New York: Macmillan.

McGuire, M. 1992. *Religion: The Social Context*, 3rd edn. Belmont, CA: Wadsworth.

Paper, J. 1995. *The Spirits are Drunk: Comparative Approaches to Chinese Religion.* Albany, NY: SUNY Press.

Parsons, T. 1966. "Religion in a Modern Pluralistic Society," *Review of Religious Research* 7:125–46.

Parsons, T. 1971. *The System of Modern Societies.* Englewood Cliffs, NJ: Prentice-Hall.

Parsons, T. 1974. "Religion in Post-Industrial America: The Problem of Secularization," *Social Research* 41:193–225.

Robertson, R. 1991. "The Globalization Paradigm: Thinking Globally," in *New Developments in Theory and Research. Religion and the Social Order* vol. 1. Ed. D.G. Bromley. Greenwich, CT: JAI Press, pp. 207–24.

Robertson, R. 1992. *Globalization: Social Theory and Global Culture.* London: Sage.

Simmel, G. 1959. *Sociology of Religion*, Transl. C. Rosenthal. New York: Philosophical Library.

Simmel, G. 1971. "How is Society Possible?" in *G. Simmel, On Individuality and Social Forms*, Ed. D.N. Levine. Chicago: University of Chicago Press, pp. 6–22.

Smith, W.C. 1964. *The Meaning and End of Religion: A New Approach to the Religions of Mankind.* New York: Mentor.

Spiro, M.E. 1987. "Religion: Problems of Definition and Explanation," in *Culture and Human Nature: Theoretical Papers of Melford E. Spiro*, Eds. E. Kilborne and L.L. Langness. Chicago: University of Chicago Press, pp. 187–222.

Stark, R. 1994. *Sociology*, 5th edn. Belmont, CA: Wadsworth.

Stark, R. and Bainbridge, W.S. 1987. *A Theory of Religion.* New York: Peter Lang.

Wallerstein, I. 1987. "World-Systems Analysis," in *Social Theory Today*, Eds., A. Giddens and J. Turner. Stanford, CA: Stanford University Press, pp. 309–24.

Waters, M. 1995. *Globalization.* London and New York: Routledge.

Weber, M. 1946. *From Max Weber: Essays in Sociology*, Transl. and ed. H.H. Gerth and C. Wright Mills. New York: Oxford University Press.

CHAPTER 24

The Return of Theology: Sociology's Distant Relative

Kieran Flanagan

It is a rare sociological textbook, whether in sociology of religion or at the intro-ductory level, that will recognize a connection between sociology and theology. The phenomenon of religion as part of popular culture, or in its organizational form, as church or sect, or as part of other issues, such as those of race or gender, might well be recognized. Religion is treated as an institution amongst many, one supposedly fading, or marching out from cathedral to cult (Spickard 1994, Bruce 1996). Theology is still part of what the religion of sociology seeks to expel in its accounts of culture. Admittance is a matter of disciplinary resistance.

The notion of a theology conveys an image of something antiquarian whose traditional forms of authority render it unfit for viable life in an enlightened modernity. The sociology of religion presumes an unscrutinized assumption of thinking away from theology. Yet, oddly, the advent of New Age religions marks a reversal of this trend, a fledgling interest in theology. These efforts to retreat to times before the corrupting effects of secularization and modernity have revived interest in beliefs systems dealing with the spirit. These belief systems embody their own theologies of paganism, Mother Earth, naturalism, and feminism. If the issues of theology creep in the backdoor of the sociological study of religion, in its latest analytical adventures, the question cannot but arise as to which form, if any, could or should sociology endorse?

Those who can affirm a religious faith and an affiliation with sociology are likely to be treated with suspicion by all parties. There is a convention of distance in treating the social in sociological analysis, which a religious faith somehow breaches. It also violates the notion that sociologists should have a benign humanist orientation to all, for a theological affiliation implies a duty of judg-ment and exclusion incompatible with the liberal inclusive values which sociol-ogy is supposed to proclaim.

Sociology will admit kinship to philosophy, ethics, aesthetics, psychology, and history. It is catholic in its disciplinary pedigrees, but one relative it discounts is theology. All sorts of reasons exist for theology being structured out of socio-logical existence. One is that sociology desires to live life in posttheological lanes. The properties theology embodies, of myth, magic, and superstition, straddle the relationships of sociology with anthropology. If admitted to sociology, they belong to issues of ethnography and exotic cultures. Theology is not a matter of concern for sober sociological minds with disciplinary ambitions. In its Comtean period, sociology was placed on the Vatican index; contemporary practitioners reciprocate by leaving theology off any sociological index. This disjunction between theology and sociology forms part of its tradition and has been only recently and exceptionally recast. The terms of reference governing how the two disciplines should proceed relate to a rulebook as yet unwritten.

Theology offers an immensely rich terrain for sociological deliberations. Their use requires that sociology recognizes its limitations, that it cannot man-ufacture values and supply a telling basis for their authentication. In dealing with present dilemmas of identity, character, and culture, theology gives to sociology what it cannot supply: a meaning and purpose to life. As modes of life become rigidified, predictable, and unoriginal there is an erosion of the spirit, a sense of diminishment of humanity as conditions of trust become untrust-worthy. The social bond, the site of sociological deliberations, has become precarious, and no amount of self-help manuals seem able to improve the present human lot. There is an abiding incapacity to make definite relationships of commitment that signifies the crisis of living life in a spiritually impoverished culture.

In this chapter, I wish to argue that sociology is implicated in theology and that its detachment from religion is untenable. Theological elements were part of the concerns of the "founding fathers" of the discipline. These elements still exist, as is indicated by the incapacity of sociology to think about the social without reference to metaphors that have a definite theological location. Reflex-ivity, or disciplinary self-awareness, points to a melting down of the traditional boundaries between sociology and theology. In such a situation, sociology has become a form of theology. It too, can be about a faith seeking self-understanding of God, starting from the ground of culture.

The time has come to reexamine the relation of sociology to theology. As the sacred has dissolved in the realm of theology, it has been reappropriated as a crucial means of characterizing mass culture. The notion of the sacred has come to apply to anything taken seriously, from a rugby match, to a moment of time in the cinema, to an object that an aesthetics of culture sanctifies and renders treatable as an icon. What is deemed beautiful is endowed with a given aura of the sacred. Institutional religion might have diminished in value in modernity, but as Jervis suggests, it has not been banished. It has just been devalued and reduced to another form of consumerism (Jervis 1998:185–6). Compensations are still required for this displacement of the sacred from its ecclesial nexus, for deeper questions still hold. Dispersed and disguised, they are still posed. There is now the game of "hunt the sacred" in all facets of culture, and what these all have in common is "the theme of communion with otherness, the attempt to get beyond the boundaries of selfhood; the sacred emerges as transcendence plus transgression" (Jervis 1998:172).

The recent history of the sociology of religion works with conventions that treat the dispersal of institutional religion as definite and irreversible. If theology claims to occupy a center of culture, then the sociology of religion feels called to amplify the activities of the fringe. It has a set agenda of dealing with the peripheries to institutional religion. Thus cults and sects, even New Age religions, are its center of gravity. In so dealing with the religious fringes it grants them a concern with the credibility of their beliefs, which it entirely denies to the center. Its interests are in the effects of the collapse of theology and the dispersal of the bits into cults and sects. The one thing it is not concerned with is the beliefs theology embodies. Edification is not part of the agenda of sociology of religion. It hears the confessions of those in sects and cults, but theological tales are denied entrance to the box.

The Advent of Reflexivity

In his writings, Martin has explored the link between sociology and theology in terms of the creative tension between the two disciplines. In his view, sociology has a crucial role of making space for theological reflection. It has a qualifying, but hazardous, function of reflecting on what theology risks misappropriating from its surrounding culture (Martin 1997). Likewise, Gill's pioneering and highly debated working of the context of theology and sociology needs to be noted (Gill 1975, 1996). The most important, watershed, collection was the Blackfriars symposium on sociology and theology (Martin, Mills, and Pickering 1980). Other significant collections have emerged since, but these are small in number (Repstad 1997).

However, Richard Martin finds that sociology has its own procedures for the cultivation of proprieties that secure belief in its disciplinary utterances. These quasi-religious procedures invoke their own pieties, of what is proper to the making of its orientations that require a mystique to ensure its desired and identifiable legitimacy to speak of the social. In this setting, graduate training involves rituals of understanding of the defining protocols of sociology (Martin 1974). Now it could be said that Martin is just being clever. Certainly, the argument he makes has been pursued since in accounts of teaching sociology. Yet his exploitation of religious metaphors to understand the formation of sociological orientations takes on some peculiar contradictions when the subject matter is religion itself.

These contradictions arise from the unresolved issue of the personal values of the sociologist. They become all the more accentuated in the context of an acceptance of notions of reflexivity, a self-awareness of the relationship of the discipline to the subject matter. These relate not only to the duty of the sociologist to confront the responsibilities in analysis that emerge from scrutinizing a particular subject matter. They also relate to duties of articulating the local culture of a subject matter. The whole direction of qualitative methodology in sociology is geared to amplifying these local testimonies. If it is difficult to exclude the study of religion from these reflexive imperatives, it is also hazardous to absolve sociology from confronting the theological implications of testimonies of religious believers.

If empathy is a long held goal of sociological understanding, it contains a risk of being partial, of going native and of being overly subjective and unavailable in the accounts so rendered. Reflexivity adds a necessary, if not moral, dimension to this ambition for *verstehen*. It is about the moral implications and responsibilities of articulating another's story. More importantly, reflexivity is about the sociologist's part in the narrative, its construction and reception. In asking, on whose behalf does the sociologist speak, his or her tale has to be told too. What is the testimony of the sociologist who so wants to hear? This disclosure has become a disciplinary responsibility.

Such shifts in sociological expectations have clear implications for the custom of distinguishing between religion and theology. With the advent of reflexivity, and the recognition of self-awareness of sociology's own identity this entails, the question cannot but emerge, especially in dealings with religion, of what belief is it to identify with. This is not a perverse question that the believer throws at the sociologist. The discipline has become positively confessional of late and its positions in relation to life politics are commonly adversarial. The climate has changed so that nonconfessional positions have become incredible. The idea that religion can be studied from the outside is being increasingly contested (McCutcheon 1999). If religions are to be studied from within, then references to the theologies they might embody are inescapable.

As far back as 1977, Johnson was observing that "sociologists can no longer keep their personal position on religion in one closet and their professional position in another." Yet, if it so emerges, it does so in conditions where it is "no longer possible to maintain that social science is irrelevant to theology and hence to the rest of religion" (Johnson 1977:369). He goes on to argue that the possibility that scientific research can cast light on questions of religious truths "can no longer be ignored or dismissed as absurd" (Johnson 1977:385). What Johnson confronted was the inconvenient question of theological elements in the sociology of religion.

If it is accepted that value-free sociology was a myth, then what values of truth should sociology of religion deal with that are fully authentic to its subject matter? In all this is the worry that if sociology does engage with theology, it might make its own version, one with claims to superiority and authority over those of the assumptions of believers, and perhaps theologians. Inadvertently, in setting out to find the truths of theology, sociology might just produce its own set of deceptions. A sociology compartmentalized in the category of religion faces no such credible worries. Moved over into theology, sociological ideas change not only about the status of their knowledge, but also about their disciplinary relationship to religion.

At some point the generalized notion of religion, as a quest for the sacred, for ethical values, for a ritual order, for the mystery of existence, and for sensibilities of the transcendent, might involve the need to refer to an issue of theological affiliation. Such a need is seldom discussed in sociological efforts to define religion (Turner 1991:242–6, Bennett 1996:12–15). Taking matters from religion into theology overturns conventions of a methodological atheism, the requisite bracketing of belief. As argued above, reflexivity stipulates that such bracketing reflects an abdication of personal responsibility and an unwarranted absolution from the need to find a position credible to the subject matter. Thus, if theology is to be authentically scrutinized in terms of the expectations established by the notion of reflexivity, recalibrations are required of the relationship between sociology and religion.

In these recalibrations there is always the risk of sociology moving from outside religion, a safe disembodied occupation of the category, and traveling within to occupy a position that involves a faith seeking understanding, a searching that represents another vocation for the sociologist. Thus, reflexivity comes to enjoin that religion is embodied in theology, and for the believer they are as one. If this is so, what makes religion so falsely different from theology?

The question is not only of some relationship, some focal point to the pursuit of ultimate meanings, but also some experience of what it is to be in religion, to be in belief. This points to a notion of religiosity which was of central concern to Simmel. In this regard, religion as an apparatus of belief is subservient to the theology it embodies. To follow Simmel, religion is the form, the enabling mechanism, that realizes an inner yearning or desire for God, which theology seeks to elucidate.

The Fathers: Augustine and Aquinas in Sociology

Whereas theology is concerned with scrutiny of the deposit of faith, religion is about its realization, functioning, ordering, and enacting. To that degree it is a necessary adjunct of theology. It fulfills what faith promises. Religion realizes what it enjoins, the rendering of worship to God. Theology and religion are realizations of virtue, of knowing and doing, and both are linked in a common task of contemplation. For Aquinas, religion is about the repeating of something lost but rediscovered in worship. Hence, like theology, it involves a property of moral virtue. Indeed, for Aquinas, religion is a theological virtue. It involves a property of *habitus* or disposition, and as a form of virtue, it is to be understood in the context of justice, as the fulfillment of obligations and entitlements to give worth to God. This is realized in forms of prayer and adoration (Aquinas 1964:11–33). In McDermott's apt summary, "religion is a virtue by which we offer God things in service and worship" (McDermott 1989:460). Theology is more than a science of reasoning about God. It is about a disposition, a *habitus* of contemplation of what is beyond reason and sight.

It is easy to fail to realize that the Enlightenment notions of religion as a projection, a false and ultimately futile illusion, had their counterparts in theological critiques that operated long before the advent of an age of reason. Some of the most brilliant criticism of religion as a mere projection without an adequate theology appear in Augustine's *The City of God*. His criticism of Roman religion was centered on its polytheism, the bizarre illogicalities of what it deified as social projections and the illusory basis of what it attributed to the gods in terms of powers and properties of virtue and vice. In Augustine's critiques, one sees the antecedents of thinkers ranging from Feuerbach to Marx to Bellah.

The "theological" distinctions of Varro were particularly criticized. In a eulogy of appreciation, that could be a sociologist's rather than a Roman historian's, Cicero wrote of him as a man who enabled his readers, like strangers in their own city, to recognize their own identities. Cicero felt that Varro:

> revealed to us the age of our country, the sequence of events, the laws of religious ceremonies and of the priesthoods, the traditional customs of private and public life, the position of geographical areas and of particular places, and the terminology of all matters, human and divine, with their various kinds, and functions, and causes. (Augustine 1972:229)

It is as if Varro was doing the sociology of religion before its invention. He was asking sociological questions, but without a disciplinary remit, which was to come much later in time. Varro's notion of a civil theology reflects his treatment of human affairs before those of the divine. Augustine's criticism was focused on the confusions between the fabulous (the mythical, what was appropriate to spectacle, performance, and theater) and the civil, which related to the life of the city. It was the disedifying basis of the fabulous rites, which Augustine regarded as illogical projections and immoral transactions, that brought these divisions of theology into disrepute (Augustine 1972:229–51). Apart from his devastating critique of worshiping worthless gods through unworthy means, and catching the contradictions of the allocation of virtues to different gods, Augustine's writing on religion has two points of significance for sociology that mark the illogicality of detaching religion from theology.

First, the precarious and arbitrary division between civil and fabulous theologies points to contradictions in the functions of these religions. Their appeal to different constituencies cannot be reconciled, yet both fulfill necessary functions for particular sites. When these are analyzed, rampant contradictions emerge, and bring them into disrepute. These contradictions point to the limitations of treating religion in terms of functions, for questions are begged about their arbitration. The second point relates to the issue of projection and bears on some aspects of Simmel's approach to religion. Again, reflecting on the contradictions of fabulous and civil theologies, Augustine treats these as mental pictures that are projected on reality. Thus, Augustine argues that thinkers of these two theologies "could not conceive of anything beyond the fantasies suggested by imagination, circumscribed by the bodily senses" (Augustine 1972:306).

The idea of religion as a human projection is old. Augustine cites Hermes of Egypt who seemed to predict the advent of Christianity as he mourned the falseness of worshiping deceitful images. His critique of man-made gods addresses the miracle of the spark of the divine within man. Since his ancestors lacked faith and neglected divine worship and true religion, "they invented the art of creating gods." They married power to technique "and called up the souls of angels or demons and made them inhere in sacred images and in divine mysteries, so that by their means the idols could have the power of doing good or inflicting harm"(Augustine 1972:334).

The detachment of religion from an authentic theology, that of Christianity, forms a central concern of Augustine's, whose writing is a mission to secure an authentic integration of both, an endeavor which Aquinas also pursued. Milbank's account of the secularizing tenets of sociology, which reduce religion to an issue of its function, and which therefore deserved expulsion from his radically orthodox idea of a City of God, might suggest that little more can be said (Milbank 1990). It is not the purpose of this chapter to be paralyzed by his reductionist caricature of sociology. Sociologists can read Augustine without feeling a need to adhere to such a pretentiously cast notion of radical orthodoxy operating a sociological vacuum.

Georg Simmel

The recent translation of 11 essays by Georg Simmel on religion shows a deeply sensitive spiritual mind, closely read in theology and seeking sociological answers to questions that are riddled with theological implications. Simmel set sociology to understand spiritual states of religiosity, of sanctity and prayer, that involved a yearning for God, a quest for faith that receives an incontestable sociological witness in his writings on religion (Simmel 1997). His question regarding the social forms of religiosity is both theological and sociological.

Hitherto, it might have been difficult to find any major sociologist who thought of religion and theology in an integrated manner. The translation of Simmel's essays on religion overcomes this difficulty. These essays permit a paradigm change in the way religion can be understood and point to a way in which sociology might think within a theology. They integrate religion into theology in a deliberate manner.

Simmel's interest in religion is as significant as it is unexpected. For many, Simmel's influence on sociology can only increase and his stature seems equivalent to that of Weber. Simmel can be regarded as the first sociological thinker on the culture of postmodernity, whose inception he foresaw almost a century ago. His concerns with the tragedy of culture, its fixation on social forms always exceeding the content they manifest, combined with a concern with the endless powers of commodification of money, point to a sense of exhaustion which has become more apparent with the advent of postmodernity. The disengaged, fatigued stranger venturing aimlessly in cosmopolitan culture is an enduring image of Simmel's writings. Within this wandering is a blasé attitude, a property which Bewes has explored in terms of a cynicism, a state of being alienated from one's own subjectivity. His notion of the "inner emigrant," intent on the preservation of self, is a process that involves strategies of disengagement. It is about cynicism as an enlightened false consciousness, a melancholy, that legitimizes a retreat from engagement. Thus, "postmodernity has in effect constituted a retreat from truth, rather than an annihilation of it" (Bewes 1997:24–5, 175–7, 201). These background comments make Simmel's writings on religion all the more interesting and significant.

Although Simmel was of Jewish background he belonged to a Protestant church. His writings on religion are deeply imbued with Christianity, although as his editor and translator Horst Helle observes (like Weber) his theological fate was to stand alone. Simmel traveled through many forms of religion. Even if his pilgrim's progress led him out of theological attachments, he passed through much of the territory of theology with a deepness of understanding perhaps unequaled by any sociologist since. Along his route, he did achieve some recognition, for Helle notes that many Catholic intellectuals approved of his writings (Simmel 1997:xvii). His writings, despite significant qualifications, are notably cited in the works of Hans Urs von Balthasar, the Swiss theologian.

The terms in which Simmel writes his sociology of religion operate from within theology. Thus, issues of sanctification, prayer, faith, and religiosity are central to his writings. Simmel's concern is with understanding what it is to believe, and in this regard, unlike Weber, he is profoundly musical in theological terms. His concern is with the way spiritual qualities of the soul need to use social forms to manifest a sensibility of religion. In curious contrast with the cynicism which Bewes invokes as the motif of postmodernity, Simmel's concerns are with the disposition, the capacity, and sympathy *for* religion. In his account religion has the power to transcend signs of contradiction within a culture that would otherwise fracture such a belief. Nicholas of Cusa emerges as a crucial resource for the characterization of the transcending power of religion. For a person who lays the contours down for what becomes apparent in a culture of postmodernity, Simmel's concern with the endeavor of belief rather than the fate of disbelief is significant. His concern is with sociological understandings of how religion operates between the pious dispositions of believers and their religious community, and what emerges in these transactions. In such a brief consideration of such a rich writer on the sociology of religion, it is not possible to encapsulate all the subtleties of his arguments. There are strands of Durkheim in Simmel's approach to religion, but its site of construction operates very much within theology. Projection is very much a factor in his account, but it is into a theological realm, cast in ways that enhance what is understood to be in religion.

Perhaps the most interesting facet of Simmel's writing is the way in which he captures a sociological property to belief. Whereas money is cast as powerful because of its colorlessness, its capacity to refract any transaction, religiosity, on the other hand, is about a quality, a sensibility for coloring, that refracts a distinct light. Its tone marks it out from pure egoism, for religiosity involves coping with a peculiar mixture of desire and surrender, of humility and exaltation. It is in harmonizing these contradictions that religiosity realizes what it seeks, an inclusion into an higher order, one which is felt inwardly and personally (Simmel 1997:104). These elements of color and light form significant aspects of his 1914 essay on Rembrandt's religious art (Simmel 1997:77–97). The issue of the desire, if not yearning, for belief, a faith that comes through prayer, is found in all these writings. It is about seeking to get past what is merely religion into the fullness of theology. Unfortunately, the human condition necessitates living rooted in the former, and seeking to escape into the latter.

Religiosity is the property of piety, of the inner life from which a content is developed. Thus, religiosity "is one of these formal and fundamental categories and thus brings its own tonality to the contents of certain mental images" (Simmel 1997:122–3). If this interior sensibility is not to be locked inside itself, it requires a factual content, a means of manifestation through the social. It requires the virtuous and humble use of a looking glass for the self to recognize itself in the social and to respond, otherwise it is difficult to understand how edification could be accomplished and a witness given. All this is part of a wider process, one which is far removed from reductionist sociological accounts of religion, yet very much within what sociology can strive to understand. The term that describes this process of seeking is embodied in Simmel's notion of sanctification. This is described as:

> the ultimate perfection of any moral endeavor, beyond attainment through individual actions and yet not a pale abstraction like so many purely moral ideals but rather arousing the soul in all its passion, like a call exhorting the prisoner to break his chains.

Salvation signifies the soul realizing its ultimate longing in "terms of its yearning for transcendence and fulfillment, stature and strength" (Simmel 1997:29).

Simmel reverses the direction sociological studies of religion usually take. They normally proceed from the structural, what is functional, social, and exterior, to the interior. This interior culture is seldom given sociological recognition in terms of the way it might come to mirror expectations of the exterior. The process of moving from the interior to the exterior is one of the hallmarks of symbolic interaction, so the form of argument is hardly new in sociology. When reset in Simmel's writing, however, the effect is novel as he is concerned with the impulses of religion, the spiritual state of religiosity, that causes the self to journey outwardly to the social to exploit its forms of manifestation and to utter what cannot be said, yet needs to be stated to make belief possible. Without these manifestations, faith has no means of self-recognition. Thus, in this venture outward, the social is a means through which the individual fulfills desires to find compass points upon which belief can be realized and recognized. The social is but the enabling facet of belief; and to that degree, it is kept subservient to what matters, that which is properly the province of theology, relationships with the divine, and their contemplation.

Simmel permits sociology an entry into theology, but in a way that complements and fulfills it. Sociology is made subservient to what is transcendent and in the scaffolding of analysis of religious belief, it gets the scaling and proportions right, of understanding what leads into theology. Rather than commence with objective manifestations of religion, Simmel is interested in their subjective basis and the way theology reconciles both. This permits sociology to think in terms of edification, the making of belief, rather than the obsessive scrutiny of its demolition under the rubrics of secularization. These are geared to scrutinizing the conditions of dispersal of belief, rather than its assembly.

Sociology in a Postmodern World

The above arguments might mark a crude requiem at the ruins of Comte's temples of positivism, whose metanarratives have also been secularized, but perniciously so in postmodernity. Theology is more geared to misreporting of its death than the science that replaced it. In this culture of postmodernity sociology faces a level field, where religion and science have both been destroyed. The divided loyalties between the hopes of scientific progress and the abiding unsettlements of the soul always existed in the genesis of sociology, and seeking the means of their reconciliation marked the lasting legacy of both Simmel and Weber. With postmodernity, these affiliations matter no more. What remains? As sociology runs out of concepts and imagination in the face of the fracturing burden of a culture of postmodernity, where all is possible and equally impossible, many return to more innocent times, to those of the early 1960s, to the beginnings when efforts to represent the fears and foibles of the marketplace began and the defining text was *The Sociological Imagination* (Mills 1959). Mills gave sociology the duty to articulate public anxieties. These are many, but what postmodern culture invokes is the sense of despiritualization of a generation that fears a looming and abiding emptiness, of being locked in an eternal present. Articulating this plight rehabilitates the duties which Weber laid on sociology.

The last part of Weber's tract for sociology, "Science as a Vocation", marks a shift from dalliances with the integrity of analysis science invoked, into a vision that returns to what is to be derived from theology. Weber castigated those who uncritically retired to the churches as rest homes. This did not mean that he was abdicating the duty to bring sociology to bear on theological matters. He did not criticize the notion that there had to be some affiliation to what is theological. Rather he was looking at the issue of the plain duty of intellectual integrity, of clarifying one's ultimate situation. His criticism was of the unethical basis of settling for "feeble relative judgments," now the lazy habit of those who live without belief in a culture of postmodernity. Weber concluded his essay in terms many neglect to note. His argument was about a return to a theological integrity, not about the escapism of a rest home. Thus, he stated unequivocally, that "in my eyes, such religious return stands higher than the academic prophecy," which does not recognize this duty of plain intellectual integrity. His criticism was addressed to those who delay for new prophets and saviors (the theological metaphors are notable) and who forget the Edomite watchman's song of the period of exile, which said "the morning cometh, and also the night: if ye will enquire, enquire ye: return, come" (Weber 1958:156). That return, that recoming, marks a calling of the sociologist as watchman, for its relative too long gone: theology. It is a call to gaze, not with the cold clarity of Foucault, classifying all and sundry, but to see with the possible eyes of faith, for in the vocation of sociology is a peculiar searching for God on the ground of culture, even amidst the fragments of postmodernity.

As the watchman of postmodernity, sociology gazes over a flattened field, whose stones stand up no more. In the gaze, one realizes an unusual naivety in Weber: the belief that the churches would welcome the return of the sociologist with open arms. The return to a theology implicated in religion betokens not the good news sociology might hope, for what is brought back from the battlements are tidings of great sorrow and perplexity. Theology has its own tales of prophets and messengers, but these are all unreflexive in sociology's terms. Piety has been accomplished for long without recourse to sociology. The making of sanctification has for long been realized without sociological attendances. The invocation of sociology is not what those seeking holiness have customarily used. Why should this watchman coming from the sociological field be heard? What grace has his prophecies? The message to return with is that theology has to confront its ground of sociology if it is to escape it.

Theology and the Watchman

Articles of faith might seem to be immune to sociological interventions. Yet, one finds teaching on the angels continually rearranged. In one generation, afflicted with a sophisticated scientific gaze, they believe too little, so angels were shelved, yet in another area, they are also kept in the closet, for too many wish to believe in all forms of the angelic, being so heavily influenced by New Age religions. Theology has its stratagems for what to display or what to shelve according to what representations the culture of the age might or not be able to affirm. In all this lies a sociology of reception, a task of recontextualizing religious messages, which when reset might qualify theological assumptions of what is credible and what is incredible. As it is, theologians steer into a culture of postmodernity with a remarkable sociological blindness. Assumptions of credibility relate to assumptions about what "works" in a culture, and in this regard sociologists and theologians are at odds, though the gap is lessening. For sociology, religions that strike against the grain of culture, that make demands, have structures that are "successful." For good sociological reasons, they make belief possible.

For some theologians, such assumptions are restrictive. The crucial dilemma between theology and sociology is whether the latter has any privileged position in terms of what it enunciates as good practice, as likely to "work." It is in this area – that of sociology moving to the intersection between religion and theology, to speak of what hitherto belonged to theological discourse, yet which is available to sociological scrutiny – that problems of authority, discernment, if not prophecy, are likely to emerge. Strategies of evangelization are laden with sociological assumptions. If these are misplaced and the results are disastrous, who is guilty of bad faith? Is it the sociologist for making presumptuous warnings blind to the issue of grace, that trespass into a theology of reception, or is it the theologian for not believing in sociological insights which only a presumption of grace can overturn?

Conclusion

All is about returns to grace, with endless restarts. The need to be apart still yields unexpected followers, and the religious impulse is felt deeply, even in a culture of postmodernity. The need to believe and to belong is part of the human condition as much as the need to marry a religion to theology, and sociology cannot but seek to articulate that endeavor. Simmel's notion of religion as a form of yearning returns. It pulsates in one's headphones, floating in the soaring voices of the men and boys of Ely cathedral singing the *Agnus Dei* of Tye's "Euge Bone" Mass. This platform of sound reminds us of that hauntingly beautiful cathedral, but also that all returns, especially those of theology, have images and memories. As the watchman turns away from the ruins of postmodernity, that cathedral might still stand for him to visit. If so, the choir might still sing and so again, there is the hope of invocation of the spiritual vision and the intellectual integrity to reconverse with sociology's forgotten relative. In such future conversations, sociology might feel impelled to boldly ask: who now fears to speak of theology?

References

Aquinas, T. St. 1964. *Summa Theologiae*, vol. 39. London: Eyre and Spottiswoode.
Augustine, St. 1972. *Concerning the City of God Against the Pagans*, Transl. H. Bettenson. Harmondsworth: Penguin.
Bennett, C. 1996. *In Search of the Sacred. Anthropology and the Study of Religions*. London: Cassell.
Bewes, T. 1997. *Cynicism and Postmodernity*. London: Verso.
Bruce, S. 1996. *Religion in the Modern World. From Cathedrals to Cults*. Oxford: Oxford University Press.
Gill, R. 1975. *The Social Context of Theology*. London: Mowbrays.
Gill, R., Ed. 1996. *Theology and Sociology: A Reader*. London: Cassell.
Jervis, J. 1998. *Exploring the Modern*. Oxford: Blackwell.

Johnson, B. 1977. "Sociological Theory and Religious Truth," *Sociological Analysis* 38(4):368–88.

McCutcheon, R.T. 1999. *The Insider/Outsider Problem in the Study of Religion. A Reader.* London: Cassell.

McDermott, T., Ed. 1991. *St. Thomas Aquinas. Summa Theologiae. A Concise Translation.* London: Methuen.

Martin, D. 1997. *Reflections on Sociology and Theology.* Oxford: Clarendon Press.

Martin, D., Mills, J.O., and Pickering, W.S.F. Eds. 1980. *Sociology and Theology: Alliance and Conflict.* Brighton: The Harvester Press.

Martin, R.J. 1974. "Cultic Aspects of Sociology: A Speculative Essay," *The British Journal of Sociology* 25(1):15–31.

Milbank, J. 1990. *Theology and Social Theory. Beyond Secular Reason.* Oxford: Blackwell.

Mills, C.W. 1959. *The Sociological Imagination.* New York: Grove Press.

Repstad, P., Ed. 1997. *Religion and Modernity: Modes of Co-existence.* Oslo: Scandinavian University Press.

Simmel, G. 1997. *Essays on Religion,* Ed. and transl. H.J. Helle with L. Nieder. New Haven, CT: Yale University Press.

Spickard, J.V. 1994. "Texts and Contexts: Recent Trends in the Sociology of Religion as Reflected in US Textbooks," *Social Compass* 41(3):313–28.

Turner, B.S. 1991. *Religion and Social Theory.* London: Sage.

Weber, M. 1958. *From Max Weber: Essays in Sociology.* New York: Oxford University Press.

CHAPTER 25

Epilogue: Toward a Secular View of the Individual

Richard K. Fenn
Princeton Theological Seminary

The Individual Beyond the Sociological Imagination

In the long run the sociology of religion will stand or fall on its conception of the individual. This is perhaps an awkward claim for someone in a field that defines itself as having to do with the social relationships rather than with individuals *per se*. The sociology of religion, as a part of sociology as a whole, focuses on the patterns of social life, on the way groups and communities, organizations, institutions, and even whole societies create and sustain themselves over time. It is understandable, given this focus, that sociologists would be at least agnostic about the interior life of the individual, except in so far as the individual comes, as it were, into play as a social actor. The existential, not to mention the unconscious, aspects of the individual are of interest only in so far as they show up on the screen of social observation.

As a result, the individual has suffered from a variety of sociological indifference and caricature. At one extreme, individuals are little more than unthinking animals adding their accretion to the solid deposit of previous generations. Or individuals, slightly enhanced in the sociological eye, may instead be those who unwittingly engage in more or less ritualized performances without realizing that they are being transformed in the process. Slightly more rounded out is the picture of individuals who are a mixture of social and psychological processes: torn, as it were, between living up to social expectations and having what passes for a life of their own. These views are largely Durkheimian, and they portray individuals who still reproduce social systems even when engaging in what they think is their very own, autonomous action. Properly understood, individuals are social artifacts: the result of processes of socialization without which they would be little more than feral children unable to communicate except in indecipherable grunts and whispers.

If this picture of the individual as a double agent, partly social, partly private, is at the midpoint of the sociological spectrum, there are other viewpoints that lead to a more enhanced notion of individuals as driven to pursue their own advantage over and against all others. From a Weberian viewpoint these interests may be material or cultural. That is, individuals may be better understood as seeking to own and control the means of production of goods and services, but they may also be best understood as seeking to enhance the value of their own social status and prestige, the authority of their communities and institutions, or the power of the societies to which they belong. Properly understood, societies are no more and no less than the result of the social actions of individuals who pursue their own interests in concert with – or at the expense of – others, as circumstances and other chances permit. On this view, society itself is an unwitting by-product of their actions and it is usually nothing that any one of them individually either wanted or intended.

What is lacking on this spectrum is a view of individuals who are capable of choosing their own ends without being limited to the possibilities offered by a particular social system. Such individuals are typically ecstatics, who are capable of standing outside their own society and facing a vast array of possibilities, both for life and death, without the guidance or protection of those who normally mediate the sacred. This is not a person easily recognizable by a Durkheim or a Bourdieu, because such an individual is capable of imagining social life in ways that owe relatively little to the collective past. Of course, as we have seen, even mystics imagine the life after death, and hell in particular, in ways that have been suggested by previous visionary literature, and their consciences have been infected by the authority of religious institutions. No ecstatic stands completely outside any social context. Nonetheless, there are vast areas of the psyche that are at best poorly socialized, and these lend themselves to an imagination that can be angelic or bestial, revolutionary or archaic. In that sense the primitive is generated in each society in every generation, and it is no wonder that so much social effort is designed to civilize or at least coopt it as far as possible.

To imagine the individual as capable of standing outside one social system is easier, of course, than imagining the individual as standing outside any and all social systems. Sociologists would agree that individuals may find sources of inspiration and authority in other cultures, in deviant traditions, and in literature that allows one access to a past that is less collective than it is merely collected in the archives of one institution or another. As Grace Davie has pointed out in her chapter for this volume, however, that collective memory is now largely held vicariously, and access to it is at best sporadic and tenuous. Individuals are increasingly finding the sacred in scattered times and places, or manufacturing their own forms of sanctity. However, these other forms of the sacred are gathered together from the remains of other cultures. The modern individual, as Flanagan has reminded us in his chapter, is very much like a traveler or primitive collector of this and that, who fashions together a patchwork form of the sacred.

None of these viewpoints, however, imagines the individual as standing outside any and all social systems to confront life and above all death without the benefit of relics, stones, shamans or clergy, creeds or formulae, institutional authority or national symbols. Few graves are so lonely as to lack a flag or an inscription, or to be empty of any possession that might help the individual mediate between this life and the world beyond all imagination. In fact, it is difficult from any of these sociological viewpoints to imagine an individual who would step wholly outside a social system; far enough at least to refuse all support, tacit or otherwise, to a particular system or regime. It is therefore difficult for sociologists of religion in particular, who have a vested interest in seeing the sacred even when it is hidden in, with, and under apparently secular forms of social life, to see an individual capable of facing death on its own terms. It is difficult from any of the sociological viewpoints I have mentioned above to find the basis for individuals to resist and refuse indirect or direct compliance with the authority of the social systems of which they are members. To put it bluntly, fascism is highly understandable. What is difficult for the sociologist to understand is not only the individual who says "No" to orders but the one who refuses to be enchanted by any form of the sacred.

In this chapter therefore, I will review some of the sources of the Western tradition in search of the ingredients for a sociological conception of human nature that will meet the following criteria. Individuals will be able to face uncertainty, ambiguity, and death itself without imagining themselves to enjoy privileged forms of insight or immunity. Nowhere will it be written, for such individuals, how they are to confront the full array of chances that life offers, including those that bring with them the risk of suffering and death. Individuals will therefore be exposed to the full range of dangers and opportunities that the future has to offer, but they will also have no protection from the memory of the past. Individuals will not be exempt from the burdens of past suffering, whether it was endured by their people or inflicted by them on others. The risks of this sort of engagement with both life and death are obvious: one can be excommunicated, damned, and killed without leaving a trace. No one will know or remember. On the other hand, the benefits could be immeasurable: the sort of benefit that the religious imagination has sometimes associated with beatitude. The price, I will argue, is a psychological confrontation with the irreversible passage of time: a secular descent into hell.

The Cloud of Unknowing: "Let it Go, I Beg You"

Toward the end of the fourteenth century a pastoral counselor wrote to one of his followers:

> So you must get down to the basic essentials of thought (some people, remember, consider it the most sophisticated!) and think of yourself in the simplest way

(again, some think it the wisest), not *what* you are, but *that* you are. Why, for you to be able to think *what* you are, you with all your characteristics and capacities, calls for a great deal of skill and knowledge and insight, and much shrewd inquiry into your natural intelligence. You have done this at some time already with the help of God's grace and now you know, at least in part and as much as is good for you, what you are: a human being by nature, and a filthy stinking wretch by sin. How well you know it! Perhaps, indeed, only too well all the filth that goes along with the wretch. Shame! Let go of it, I beg you. Don't keep stirring it up: the stench is frightful. But to know *that* one exists is possible for anyone, however ignorant or uncouth he may be; it does not call for any great knowledge or aptitude. (*The Epistle of Privy Counsel* 1978:163–4)

The author of this advice is no doubt a spiritual counselor, perhaps in East Anglia, writing to one of those under his (or her) spiritual direction. Earlier, in *The Cloud of Unknowing*, the spiritual master was writing his (or her) follower certain basic instructions on how to achieve the sense of the self apart from all its attachments and qualities, capacities, and skills. That is indeed what "the cloud of unknowing is": a psychological space in which one is wholly detached from what previously passed for self-knowledge: a place where "your natural mind can find nothing to feed on, for it thinks you are doing no thing" (*The Epistle of Privy Counsel* 1978:142). Therefore the mind – having nothing to feed on – will feed on itself and consume the follower's attention in an apparently endless regression to former states of mind. It was this regress, as we have seen, that now concerns the spiritual master and prompts him to urge his follower to terminate his chronic spiritual inquisition.

The apprentice in contemplation was indeed tempted to continue to wallow in the horrors of self-discovery. A contemporary analogy might be found in the case of a patient who, after years of psychoanalysis, still feels obligated to bring to his or her analyst fresh documentation of inner immaturity, turmoil, or even depravity, while the analyst is beginning to wonder whether the patient will ever be willing to terminate. Certainly Freud regarded the feeling of being a chronic apprentice as a sign of arrested development: a refusal to let go earlier parts of the self, or at the very least a longing to recover a prior – and only apparent – innocence. Thus the older contemplative says "Let it go, I beg you." This letting go is the final stage of the descent into hell. Without this final departure from one's own past, the descent can degenerate into a voyeuristic engagement with one's own life, a romantic interlude, a masochistic attachment to chronic struggle, or a fascist program for the restoration of the past.

Let us return to the author of *The Cloud of Unknowing* and of *The Epistle of Privy Counsel*. We are now in a better position to understand why the spiritual advisor of the person engaged in an exhaustive search of his own psyche should have been alarmed by this descent into hell. This is not to say that the spiritual advisor's earlier work in *The Cloud of Unknowing* had been unnecessary; on the contrary, for the true contemplative it is important at the outset to know "*what* you are," as the advisor put it in the later epistle. Just as one's free associations, metaphors, and imagination reveal the unconscious mind, so one's unconscious casts a shadow over what comes to the mind's inner eye in contemplation. No wonder that it takes "skill and knowledge and insight, and much shrewd inquiry" to be a contemplative, especially if, as Freud insisted, one has some resistance to discovering what lies beneath the surface of the mind. In the depths of one's own psyche one is likely to find a chamber of sad or frightening memory, illicit affection, and grandiose self-imagery: in the words of the master contemplative of *The Epistle of Privy Counsel*, one is "a filthy stinking wretch by sin."

At the outset "the cloud of unknowing" is like a perceptual vacuum that frees the soul to search for God without distraction. The "cloud" is thus a place in which God's absence foreshadows God's presence. First the soul removes itself from its earlier preoccupations: from its tendencies to confuse the life of the spirit with something more sensual or physical. Later, however, "the cloud of unknowing" becomes a psychological territory more like the outer circles of hell: a place, as Aquinas put it, where "only such things be dimly seen as are able to bring anguish to the heart" (quoted in Walls 1992:144). In fact, the author of *The Cloud of Unknowing* warned his pupil that this spiritual discipline might feel like a descent into hell:

> When a man is experiencing in his spirit this nothing in its nowhere, he will find that his outlook undergoes the most surprising changes. As the soul begins to look at it, he finds that all his past sins, spiritual and physical, which he has committed from the day he was born are secretly and sombrely depicted on it. They meet his gaze at every turn, until at last after much hard work, many heartfelt sighs and many bitter tears he has virtually washed them all away.
>
> At times in this spiritual struggle he thinks he might as well be looking at hell for the despair he feels of ever reaching perfection and peace out of all this suffering. (*The Cloud of Unknowing* 1978:143)

This "hell" into which the spiritual apprentice feels as if he has descended is very much like C.S. Lewis's notion of the damned person as "an isolated unit of misery" who lives in "his own individual world of self-inflicted suffering" (Walls 1992:145).

The essence of hell, as we have argued, is that it is too late to relieve or satisfy any of the longings that nonetheless persist unabated. In hell it is too late, as Augustine remarked, even for repentance (Walls 1992:141). Thus the soul remains in a continual struggle with its earlier self, remorseful, perhaps, but unable even to hope for the restoration of an earlier innocence. Whether it is longing and love that fill the soul with hopeless affection, or more violent and destructive emotions, these passions continue to demand a satisfaction or relief which the suffering spirit knows can never be achieved or given. It is no wonder, as the author of *The Cloud of Unknowing* pointed out, that many abandon their spiritual journey at this point and go back to the welcome distractions of everyday life.

Hell is, at least in this fourteenth century document, not only a place but a state of mind, and it is one into which one may descend voluntarily in pursuit of one's own sins and losses. It is also, however, a place from which one can ascend. It is not a permanent dwelling place for the soul. In this respect it resembles the earlier visions of hell as a place in this world that one can visit and where the soul, after death, can do time: not a permanent prison house of the soul but one from which one can hope eventually to be released. One is not at the mercy of an imperial dispenser of grace and punishment but on one's own, so to speak; it is individual merit and sin, perseverance and despair that count in the long run. One may find some of this earlier, less authoritarian and more laicized viewpoint in *The Cloud of Unknowing*. That is to open the door of the psyche to forgotten or repressed memory and emotion. Consider this advice from the spiritual advisor in *The Cloud of Unknowing*:

> For he that perseveres does at times feel comfort and have some hope of perfection, for he begins to feel, and indeed to see, that many of his past sins are by grace in process of being rubbed away. Though he still has to suffer, he now believes his suffering will one day come to an end, for it is all the time getting less and less. So he now begins to call it not "hell" but "purgatory." (*The Cloud of Unknowing* 1978:144)

As we have seen, the author was speaking to one whose perseverance eventually drove him further and further into an abyss of appalling self-revelation: further into his own solitary form of spiritual hell. That is why it was necessary, in the end, for the spiritual guide to give a specific directive: "Let go of it, I beg you."

There is also a secular remedy in the injunction to affirm merely *that* one is, as the spiritual director of *The Cloud of Unknowing* put it, as opposed to merely knowing *what* one is. Indeed, if this had been a psychoanalysis, we might find the analyst reminding the patient that he or she had waded through enough layers of pretense and ignorance to find an inner self that was real and sufficiently solid to withstand the shock of painful memory and intense passion. That is very much like the master contemplative saying to his follower, who knows "only too well the filth" that one harbors in one's soul, to stop "stirring it up" and simply acknowledge that he – or she – exists. The first spiritual fruit, then, is this: "the basic, plain fact is your awareness that you exist, even if you only perceive it vaguely" (*The Epistle of Privy Counsel* 1978:167–8). It is an awareness that one can have before learning how to contemplate and without being a contemplative, but it is also the first fruit of becoming a contemplative.

However, the impulse to complete the self by eliminating or submerging it in a higher being remains in the *The Cloud of Unknowing*'s emphasis on achieving "progress toward perfection in purity of spirit" (*The Epistle of Privy Counsel* 1978:168). To be sure, the author believes that there is a "perfect union which theoretically ought to exist between God and the soul" (p. 166). That union can only come from an act of surrender of "All-that-you-are-as-you-are" to "all-that-he-is-as-he-is." Such an act guarantees that one's acceptance of one's own being is not a mere whistling in the existential dark or a casual assessment such as "I'm OK, You're OK." The affirmation is won by the soul's discovery of its own inner sickness and depravity, just as the proximity to the divine was won by the death of Jesus on the cross.

Had the injunction been to achieve merely the basic affirmation of one's own being, without an elaborate recitation of one's own characteristics, the disciple would have been affirming merely the sheer hard fact that "I am," and the affirmation would not have been lost in a forest of predicates. What is needed is a descent into the hell of the psyche in order to reach a firm awareness of the substantial self, just as Dante discovered the weight of his own being when he was with shades in hell whose presence left no mark on the ground beneath them. Only then does one's being have sufficient *gravitas* to warrant the affirmation of a simple "I am." However, even this secular psychic self-awareness is lost in the simple act of self-surrender of the soul to God. It is that effort to mortify and surrender the self that keeps the religious quest from being fulfilled and makes it a perennial but hopeless pursuit. One does not have to be a psychoanalyst to detect a note of desperation in the following passage, in which the author of *The Epistle of Privy Counsel* urges his follower to avoid the temptation to go back into the abyss of self-inspection and analysis:

> So although your mind can find nothing to feed on, and therefore wants you to do something else, you are not to give up [the task of self-surrender to God] merely because it tells you to; you are to be its master. You are not to go back to feeding it, however cross it gets. Once you allow it to explore the various (and odd) theories about your faculties or your existence you are beginning to go backwards and feed it. Such meditations, good and helpful though they be, when they are preferred to this simple straightforward experience, this surrender of yourself, break up and destroy that perfect union which theoretically ought to exist between God and the soul. So keep a firm grip on this spiritual, fundamental principle, which is your own existence. On no account go back to the old ways, even when they seem good and holy and your mind is inclining thereto. (pp. 165–6)

Freud also knew that the journey to the center of the psyche could become not only perilous but seductive and interminable. Like his medieval predecessor he did become impatient with the perpetual spiritual journey, with daydreaming and fantasy, and with the waste of time that accompanies such arrested development. However, unlike the spiritual master of this epistle, he did not advocate a self-surrender to God as a means of terminating the trip backwards into the past of the psyche.

The origins of religion can thus be detected in a fascination with one's past that persists so long as one feels that there is still even a remote possibility for the recovery of the old self and the satisfaction of prior desire. The more mature self keeps reacting to earlier stages of the self, still present in the mind's eye, with various emotions ranging from longing to remorse and self-disgust. One can yearn to recover earlier enthusiasm and one's youthful illusions about one's place in the world; one can persist in being scandalized by one's youthful pretensions, or even persist in being fascinated by motives that are infantile and destructive. One can long for a self that one remembers as having been solid and

452 RICHARD K. FENN

taken-for-granted, at least when it was buttressed by a world as secure as the womb and by the embrace of parents in earliest infancy. The descent into hell is only complete, however, when one knows – and believes – that it is too late to fulfill these longings or fully to recover the infantile or youthful self.

> Many come as far as this on their spiritual journey, but because their suffering is great and they get no comfort, they go back to the consideration of worldly things. They look for physical and external comfort to compensate for the missing and so far undeserved, spiritual comfort, which as a matter of fact they would have got if they had persevered. (*The Epistle of Privy Counsel* 1978:143–4)

True, there are strong warnings in this passage about the rigors of the process, just as a psychoanalyst may argue that only those with strong selves are equipped for the rigors of analysis. Thus the novice is warned that he will find the emotional impact of reviewing his life similar to enduring hell; the emotions persist with their old intensity, but now one knows that it is too late to fulfill or relieve them. It is easier for some to look for other compensations or to give up the quest for the soul.

Certainly we cannot fault the author of *The Epistle of Privy Counsel* for not knowing that his follower would develop a taste for hell and that it would be necessary, years later, to write another letter in a plea to the follower to let go of the past. The descent into the hell of the psyche thus becomes itself a distraction and must be terminated if spiritual progress is to turn into the achievement of an unqualified apprehension of a sense of one's own being. The time comes for the disciple to acknowledge that it is too late to recover the self lost in the past, hidden in the unconscious, and disguised by illusion, but the disciple may still prefer to remain a follower for life: forever the apprentice or journeyman.

However, I would argue that even in the spiritual master's own directions we can see a suggestion that may well have contributed, quite unintentionally, to his follower's relentless and interminable fascination with emotional torment and remorse. As we have seen, the master of *The Cloud of Unknowing* warned that the one undertaking the search for the soul sometimes "thinks he might as well be looking at hell for the despair he feels of ever reaching perfection and peace out of all this suffering." Note the contradiction. Hell, I have argued, is a place where there is no hope for beatitude, no matter how severe one's penitence or heartfelt one's remorse. It is too late to feel anything but unmitigated desire or longing, remorse or grief. Therefore to offer the prospect of beatitude allows the seeker to experience hell only as a temporary spiritual possibility on the way to beatitude. It is a state of the soul that can therefore be imagined or entertained rather than experienced and endured. Indeed, to promise that there would be "perfection and peace out of all this suffering" is to place the follower in purgatory, where there is hope for the future state of the soul. In the purgatorial state penitence does indeed offer some relief in the long run, if one is willing to wait. The experience of the descent into hell, however, is without such hope; it is literally too late.

Ideally, the spiritual progress of the person being counselled by the author of *The Epistle of Privy Counsel* should have brought this seeker to a point at which there would be no further temptation "to go backwards and feed" the mind's insatiable curiosity about itself. However, the spiritual advisor's belief in one's continued access to God may have given a make-believe quality to the descent into hell. So long as grace is a prospect, it is literally never too late to recover the old self and to bask in the warmth of old flames. If one loves one's friends in God, as Augustine put it, one never truly loses them. If one's soul is held in a divine matrix, one never really runs out of time. If one is assured that, at the end of one's descent into hell, one will be restored to the vision or even the embrace of a divine mother or queen of heaven, one does not have to surrender old loves to the irretrievable past. If one was known from the womb by the mind of God, one need never believe that it will be impossible to recover the lost innocence or the certainty of one's own existence that was once provided by the tissues of the mother's body and the warmth of her presence. For those who believe themselves to have such access to the divine presence, their own descent into hell will never place them at the point of having to allow the past to pass away.

No wonder, then, that the author describes the experience of hell as having a certain "as if" quality: one feels as if he "might as well be looking at hell for the despair he feels" of reaching beatitude. Clearly the author is divided between describing the spiritual state of despair as a functional equivalent of hell, on the one hand, and, on the other, placing his follower in the position of a soul not in hell but only in purgatory, for in the latter there is indeed hope for eventual spiritual relief. Certainly the very assurance of spiritual beatitude at the end of the journey virtually assures that his follower will be only passing through hell, so to speak, rather than descending into it.

In the suggestion that divine grace will slowly eliminate the stain of the past and soften the anguish of memory of unfulfilled desire is planted the seed of an interminable spiritual journey. Thus even in a virtual hell one is not beyond the reach of divine grace; there is still time, as it were, for self-recovery and satisfaction. The sting of hell – that it is too late to make up for lost time and the lost self, for missed opportunity and for harm, real or imagined, done to others – has been drawn. Even for one who is supposed to engage in a spiritual experience of hell, the experience becomes a virtual reality rather than a dead end to hopeless desire. Given the promise that one will not be confronted with irreversible time and the irredeemable past, one can allow the descent into hell to be taken in the mode of "as if." One looks at one's past under the aspect, so to speak, of eternity.

No doubt the promised cure of union with the divine is well intended; the author reassures his follower that, in letting the past go, he will have a firm basis for a sense of his own being other than his own self-awareness. His "I am" will be linked with the divine "I am" who let his own being go for the sake of ours. The will of the follower to endure a spiritual hell is thus compromised by the promise that in the end he will be in the presence of the one who was there at the beginning. He is therefore not to drink the cup of despair, even in the middle of this "cloud of unknowing." That is why, years later, the follower is still enmeshed in what seems to his guide as the stench and filth of remorse for the past self. No wonder that the author of *The Epistle of Privy Counsel* is now eager to get the follower to give up once and for all his preoccupation and engagement with the past. Rather than expecting divine grace somehow to lift the burden of the past, it is now up to the follower through an act of the will to let it all go.

So long as one pretends to oneself that there will be a promised ecstasy or that one has wholly subsumed one's desire in a more sublime love or passion for justice, one builds one's psychic castle on the proverbial sand. The descent into hell requires one to suffer desire for which there is no hope of fulfillment. To endure a sense of loss for which there is no hope of recovery, while experiencing the desire for such restoration, does full justice, so to speak, both to the hard facts of reality and to the demands of the psyche. To pretend to oneself either that one's desire is less intense than it is, or that reality is less intransigent, is the beginning not of wisdom but of a chronic delusion either about the world or about oneself. Neither self-delusion nor romantic illusions about the world are conducive to the discovery of the innermost self, the soul; presumably they are no more serviceable in the search for God.

Beneath the grim determination of the masochist and the preference for extended stays in a psychological purgatory are often found dreams of theological glory. Like the spiritual master who advised his follower to enter into *The Cloud of Unknowing*, one can engage indefinitely in the contemplation of hell – even of one's own execrable past – so long as one is assured that the grace of God, being itself, will slowly erode this hell into the distant past. This is not a true descent since it retains a transcendent vantage-point.

There is no safe transcendence in a secular descent into hell, then, any more than there is a way to guarantee that all those who undertake a psychoanalytic descent into their unconscious will be able to endure what they discover and experience there. Some leave early; others temporize with the analyst in the search for a compromise with their illusions and desires; still others subvert the process of psychoanalysis into an interminable rumination on their own psyches, in order to keep open the door to the past and avoid facing their own limitations and death itself. That is why I have argued that from the disengaged and transcendent viewpoint of the poet or the philosopher absorbed in the romance with being, there is no way fully to engage in a descent into hell.

From the vantage point of the Thinker atop Auguste Rodin's monumental sculpture, "The Gates of Hell," the agonies of souls in hell are pitiable, perhaps, but their despair is not his own. From such an ecstatic vantage point, one form of suffering loses its distinct outline and blurs with others. That is how Heidegger could ". . . say that such incommensurables – motorization and murder, technology and the victim – are essentially the same . . ." (Caputo 1993b:133). From that elevated perspective human suffering appears to emerge temporarily from a vast miasma and then recedes into the background. Thus in arguing for the importance of the descent into hell as a spiritual discipline, I have tried also to make a point about the spiritual sources of a passion for justice. One is not, like Heidegger, to suggest that there is really no difference, at the level of being, between concentration camps and modern, mechanized agriculture, because they both rely on and express technological drive.

Like the figures on Rodin's "Gates of Hell," the tormented souls and bodies of the victims of the Holocaust seem like mere cases in a philosopher's point that – as Heidegger put it – "the essence of technology is nothing technological" (quoted in Marx 1997:3). Thus, in his discussion of Heidegger's "scandal," John Caputo quotes Heidegger as pointing out that "Agriculture is now a motorized food industry – in essence, the same as the manufacturing of corpses in gas chambers and the extermination camps" (Caputo 1993b:132).

There is thus a danger that the descent into hell will become more of a play: a performance in which one engages with the protection of an "as if" attitude that protects one from the anguish of hell itself. Like Dante, as we have seen, one learns to descend into hell while stifling one's native pity. In the secular descent into hell, there is no relief from the sting of time, no suspension of the limitations on one's ability to satisfy old longings, no way to rescue aspects of the self that are long outdated and outlived, and in the end a cessation of one's quarrel with one's more youthful self. Such a secular descent, not a continuing journey or spiritual pilgrimage, can yield a solid, simple, unqualified apprehension of one's own being. It is a prerequisite for more exalted perceptions, but the descent itself offers no guarantee of eventual exaltation.

Heidegger: The Prison House of Character

In the end the secular individual leaves hell very much as the spiritual advisor of *The Epistle of Privy Counsel* put it: by an act of the will in which one lets go of one's past self, renounces outdated states of mind, and refuses to be seduced into confusing progress with a persistent regression into the past. Heidegger himself appears to have been given such an opportunity and to have refused it. Caputo tells the following story of Heidegger's refusal to repudiate his complicity in the suffering of the Jews that he had legitimated by his ideological writing:

> When Bultmann suggested after the war that, like St. Augustine, Heidegger write his *Retractiones*, not waiting like the Saint until the end of his life, but now and for love of the truth of his thought, Heidegger's face froze over and he left Bultmann without saying a word. Indeed, even after his death what Heidegger left behind for us was no *Retractio* but the 1966 *Der Spiegel* interview, which, far from being a posthumous *retraction*, only perpetuated the cover-up, the protracted backpedaling. (Caputo 1993:132)

"Protracted backpedaling": the phrase reminds us of the person to whom the author of *The Epistle of Privy Counsel* addressed his plea to stop his interminable rehearsal of the past. To "let go of it" would involve a renunciation, a final retraction or confession: a true about-face, genuine *metanoia* or repentance, that consigns the past to a certain if eventual extinction. It is the opposite of a continued rehearsal, whether for the sake of lamentation or self-justification, in which one dwells in the past while dwelling on it. The would-be ecstatic thus remains in defiant rebellion against time, even while appearing to withstand the rigors of a descent into the hell of impossible longing and fruitless regret.

Thus Heidegger offers a highly anestheticized encounter with human suffering and the passage of time. In *The Concept of Time* Heidegger offers a form of ecstatic self-knowledge with antecedents in Western mysticism:

> *Dasein* as human life *is primarily being possible*, the Being of the possibility of its certain yet indeterminate past . . . This past, as that to which I run ahead, here makes a discovery in my running ahead to it: it is *my* past. As this past it uncovers my Dasein as suddenly no longer there; suddenly I am no longer there alongside such and such things, alongside such and such people, alongside these vanities, these tricks, this chattering. The past scatters all secretiveness and busyness, the past takes everything with it into the Nothing. (Heidegger 1992:12E)

The way to experience one's own being, then, is first to enter into the "Nothing," as Heidegger put it, or, in the the words of the author of *The Cloud of Unknowing*, "this nowhere and this nothing" (*The Cloud of Unknowing* 1978:143). Easier said than done of course; this is the same Heidegger who refused to take Bultmann's suggestion that, instead of waiting for the end of his life to write his *Retractiones*, Heidegger write them now. It would have required precisely an exercise of imagining oneself no longer there in order to pass judgment on his own previous "tricks" and "chattering."[1] The way to achieve this secular ecstasy is to look at oneself from the vantage point of the end, that is, from one's death, so that one can see that one is in fact no longer there. Only then can one experience oneself apart from the circumstances and conditions of daily life, where one is caught up in concern for others and knows oneself as a bundle of skills and capacities, emotions, and psychological strategies for pre-eminence or mere survival.

Like the author of *The Cloud of Unknowing*, Heidegger wishes to describe an experience in which one recovers a sense of one's own existence, one's very being. The difficulty in acquiring this sense of one's soul, as I would put it, is that one gets caught up in the everyday concerns of life: Heidegger's "vanities," "tricks," and "chattering," or – in the words of the author of *The Cloud of Unknowing* – the "what" of the self. The way out of this difficulty, for Heidegger, is to fast-forward to a full awareness of one's own ultimate possibilities: one's full potential, but of course, also one's inevitable death. It is only from this existential standpoint that one can then come back alongside the everyday concerns of life, enter into them fully, but this time with a sense of one's mortality, one's own being-in-time.

There is on the surface a brave secularity in Heidegger's search for an authentic sense of the self's being in time. To be sure, for Heidegger, as for the

Christian mystic of the fourteenth century, it was necessary to achieve this ecstatic sense of the basic self by being alongside one's self. However, the mystic may achieve this transcendence of the "whatness" or "busyness" of the self by looking at the soul under the aspect of eternity, whereas for Heidegger it is necessary to leave eternity to the theologian, "the legitimate expert on time," and to focus only on the temporal (Heidegger 1992:1E). For Heidegger the only way to be authentic as a being in time is to know oneself as immersed in time that is sure to end, although the time and the timing of one's end is wholly uncertain.

It might seem that this is a secular, existentialist version of the psychic hell described by the author of *The Cloud of Unknowing*. Certainly for the mystic, as for Heidegger, there is virtue to be acquired in not knowing when – for how long – one will have to endure the past in the present and into the future. In this patience – this capacity for suffering – the soul comes to a full knowledge of its own being in time. However, for the author of *The Cloud of Unknowing*, as we have seen, there comes a time when it is necessary to quit this chronic anguish and to say: enough, let it be, let it go. Not so for Heidegger, who prefers the exquisite masochism of not knowing the answer to the "question of the 'when' and 'how much longer' of the past." That is

> because inquiries about the past in the sense of "how much longer" and "when" are not at all alongside the past in the possibility we have characterized; they cling precisely to that which is not yet past and busy themselves with what possibly may remain for me. This questioning does not seize the indeterminacy of the certainty of the past, but precisely wishes to determine indeterminate time. (Heidegger 1992:14E)

To cling to "that which is not yet past" and to search for whatever possibilities may yet remain open for dealing with the past in the present is to live in a state of spiritual purgatory: of unfinished and unresolved engagement with the past in the present. One is therefore caught up in unending struggles and passions. Even if one knows that at some point it will be too late to fulfill and satisfy them, that point has been delayed. That is not a descent into hell.

Heidegger is making a case for living under no illusion that one has plenty of time and that one's time will not come to an end. Heidegger professes a belief in the necessity of fast-forwarding, so to speak, to the imagined time of one's death, but that encounter with nothingness has the paradoxical effect of freeing oneself from the tyranny of the present. One is immersed in the future, and in the repetition and reliving of the past; it is as if one bathes in a surfeit of time. In the meantime, then, one can live as if one has all the time in the world. Indeed, Heidegger says as much:

> Maintaining myself alongside my past in running ahead I have time. All idle talk, that in which such idle talk maintains itself, all restlessness, all busyness, all noise and all racing around breaks down. To have no time means to cast time into the

bad present of the everyday. Being futural gives time, cultivates the present and *allows the past to be repeated in how it is lived.* (Heidegger 1992:14E, emphasis added)

I emphasized the reference to the past to make it clear that Heidegger's apparent commitment to looking at life from the vantage point of the indeterminate end of one's life is really a strategy for avoiding the experience of running out of time. So long as the end is indeterminate one gives oneself time, and thus one need not terminate the past in order to have the present. *One lives in a secular version of the fullness of time: the future and the past spilling over into the present in such a way as to lift one above the mundane.*

This secular existentialist (Heidegger) thus gives a strange sort of privy counsel; instead of finally exhorting his followers to let go of the past and of its as yet unfulfilled desires, Heidegger promises a this-worldly ecstasy which gives one permanent access to the past: "The past – experienced as authentic historicity – is anything but what is past. It is something to which I can return again and again" (Heidegger 1978:19E). What Heidegger takes to be his own ecstatic achievement, I take to be the apparent conviction that one can indeed "return again and again" to the past, whether in a secular form of transcendence over time or as an apparently "authentic" way to become immersed, as Faust put it, in the "torrents of time."

For Freud, the problem was precisely that people did prefer to repeat the past, even to repeat unpleasant experiences, rather than to accept the fact that they are late in both the temporal and the mortal sense of the term. It is as if Heidegger decided that a flirtation with his own end (an imaginative running forward to the end) would allow him never to be late again. Freud, however, entertained no illusions about his ability to repeat the past, even while his unconscious kept reminding him of his abhorrence of being late in any sense of the word. Thus Freud takes it as a problem that the past remains in full force within the present. Those who, as Heidegger put it, return to the past "again and again" are for Freud like patients who are caught up in a compulsion to repeat the past – and especially to repeat unpleasant experiences. They live in a secular equivalent of purgatorial repetition.

Whereas Freud thought it a good thing to seize the moment, because the present is the only time that one has, for Heidegger those who are preoccupied with the present live in a temporal wasteland. Those who lack such access to the presence of the past, he thought, can only wonder about how long the present will go on. They live in the world of mundane time, the clock marking a succession of moments, each of which is for the time being all the time that one has: the "Now." These moments become lost in the past, which cannot be brought into the present because the past, like the present, is then filled with "an irretrievable busyness" (Heidegger 1978:19E). Such a present, devoid of the past, is dull and burdensome, and the soul that lives in it has no time for itself or time of its own; its only time is the time that is meted out impersonally in equal shares to everyone. Those who stand out from the mass, however, the truly ecstatic, can view the present from the vantage point of the end; they are therefore the ones – the only ones – who know time as their own and who thus alone can be said to have a history: a past which remains perennially at their disposal. There is clearly no spiritual counsel here to let the past go.

For the author of *The Cloud of Unknowing*, it is divine grace that allows one relief from the burden of the past, although the sufferer and seeker must eventually renounce old longings after a sufficient period of attempting to remain alongside the past. For Freud it is precisely the return of passions and fantasies that belong in the past that keeps one from coming into the possession of one's own soul and that makes one a perennial journeyman or arriviste. For Heidegger, however, by leaping forward imaginatively toward the hypothetical end-point of one's own time, all time, even the past, becomes accessible and can be "repeated in its 'how' – even if in its concrete circumstances it is gone forever" (1978:20E).

It is as if Heidegger had read *The Cloud of Unknowing* without going on to read *The Epistle of Privy Counsel*. Like the author of these epistles, Heidegger also relegates the knowledge of one's habits, skills, and dispositions to the "what" of one's own existence, that is, to what one is by virtue of being born in a certain time and place with a culture, associates, and experiences. Because all these circumstances and conditions of everyday life can get in the way of a truly anxious confrontation with one's own death as an ever-present possibility, and hence can interfere with an authentic experience of one's own being-in-time, individuals must run ahead in their imagination to the end, and to a radical confrontation with the possibility of death in the moment itself in order to grasp how very real and specific, as well as vulnerable and open to extinction is the self. As Piotr Hoffman puts it in his discussion of Heidegger's *Being and Time*: "my coming face to face with the (indefinite) possibility of death not only forces me to abandon the ordinary, everyday framework of intelligibility and truth, but at the same time leads me to discover the unshakeable certainty and truth of my *sum*" (Hoffman 1993:203). Similar advice was once given by the author of *The Cloud of Unknowing* to his follower: so to intensify the knowledge of his or her death that it becomes a lively possibility in the moment even of the most intense prayer.

On the other hand, as we have seen, the same author later, in *The Epistle of Privy Counsel*, literally begs his follower to return to a commonsensical view of time and history and to let the past go once and for all. Heidegger, however, rejects such a final dissolution of the tie of the self to the past. Here is Hoffman again, discussing Heidegger's notion (in *Being and Time*) of the repetition of the past:

> My past . . . is not something that has simply elapsed and is now left behind, something existing "no longer now – but earlier" [BT 375]. This is so because my past is nothing other than my "thrownness" – that is, my rootedness in a culture, my already established preferences, skills, habits, and so on – and it is precisely in terms of this thrownness that my present experiences get to be organized and endowed with a meaning. (Hoffman 1993:208)

It is this set of habits and skills that constitutes the prison house of character. It is a prison from which Heidegger shows no interest in escaping, and it may have allowed him to take a grandly metaphoric view of the other prison houses of Nazi Germany, from technology to concentration camps.

To be sure, for Heidegger one must get beyond these trappings of the self in order to encounter one's own being in time; on the other hand, these trappings are then restored as the only way to give one's present any meaning. Without the past, the present is nothing. An authentic self thus knows that it is constituted still by what happened earlier in life; thus its "earlier" life is never a past from which one dissociates oneself; there will be no advice from this counselor to "Let it go."

Heidegger would have rejected the advice in *The Epistle of Privy Counsel* to abandon the sense of chronic guilt and to let go of the past. For Heidegger, true authenticity in time is to recognize that "guilt" and "conscience" are just as basic to the self as "freedom," "finitude," and "death" itself (Hoffman 1993:210). His insistence on guilt is due to the discovery that one cannot be the source or condition of one's own being. One is constituted by what is in itself partial, fragmentary, and contingent: dependent on the relationships, on the circumstances, on the tradition, which constitute the past (Hoffman 1993:211). One has a "heritage," which becomes one's "fate." The saving grace is that this heritage no longer is merely part of the taken-for-granted world in which one lives without reflection, anxiety, or authenticity, but part of the world that one finally comes to own for oneself as an inevitable, ineluctable part of one's being-in-time (Hoffman 1993:212–13). The existentialist's private ecstasy allows him to accept the prison-house of his character as the only place to be. One takes on willingly and freely the world into which one is "thrown. These words would read differently within a ghetto or a concentration camp than in the professor's study.[2]

On the surface Heidegger's conscientious acceptance of the past as his future and as his fate would appear to be consistent with a sort of maturity that rejects an imaginary transcendence over the passage of time. Heidegger would appear to have moved beyond any rebellion against time and to have accepted what Freud called the reality principle. Heidegger knows that his "ordinary ties and attachments" offer no security, and he accepts the limitation that he can only find his own being-in-time in and through certain Western traditions, no matter how deeply he might steep himself in Eastern mysticism and philosophy (Hoffman 1993:212–13). Because he is no longer avoiding his anxiety about death, he no longer fills this life with anxious concern about schedules and deadlines. Instead of exercising a will to overcome the past, he lives ("resolutely") with his will directed toward the future certainty of his own death: a certainty that requires him to focus in the meantime on what matters for its own sake, as a way of being, rather than as a mere means to an end (Guignon 1993:229–30). Furthermore, because he sees life from the vantage point of the end, he is no longer attached to the traditions and contexts in which he has struggled to find his own existence. They are of *existentiell* rather than "existential" meaning to him. However, his experience of nothingness does not fill him with anguish, and he does not need to be released from the hell of the past. Rather, Heidegger insists that the past offers a reservoir of heroic models on the basis of which the individual can forge an authentic identity (cf. Hoffman 1993:213): a storehouse of character.

Heidegger thus claims to have produced a secular state of beatitude that releases one from the life of care and concern in a brief encounter with nothingness: all this with the apparent blessing of Western mysticism. Nonetheless, Heidegger refuses to part company with the past, just as he refused to write his own confessions and to renounce his own ideological complicity with fascism. There are indeed signs in Heidegger of the residues of grandiose and magical thinking: of a sense of having risen above the world of guilt and unfulfilled desire, of anguish and misfortune, all of which lack any truly "existential" significance. He is The Thinker: The Poet on top of The Gates of Hell.

It is as if Heidegger adapted the demythologizing project to his own life project. Just as he tried to mine the circumstances, speech, and contexts of the Gospels for their existential significance, he sought with a good conscience to slough off the chaff of his own traditions, to find in them ways of being-in-time that are truly heroic, and thus to rise above any preoccupation with the actual agonies and limitations in his own life and the life of others.[3]

His experience of Nothing was not really the equivalent of the courageous entry into the cloud of unknowing, since it lacked the painful marriage of incapacity with intense desire. Therefore, for Heidegger, there is no need to receive *The Epistle of Privy Counsel*: no need to be counseled by an act of the will to let go of the past and to move beyond an agonistic relationship to one's earlier self. Heidegger has sloughed off these aspects of the self as belonging to its mere "what"-ness, its "factic" nature, and is already writing from a secure knowledge of his own "that"-ness: a secular heaven, achieved without agony or genuine guilt, and without any acknowledgement of the hell that comes to inhabit the mind and body when one enters into the spiritual vacuum of the cloud of unknowing.[4] It is as if the young man who was not healthy enough to stand for the Catholic priesthood had managed to find in his own constant verbal stream the blessing of a secular, linguistic absolution and indeed to write his own scripture. Without a genuine experience of the hell of the past as it invades the thought and feeling of the moment, there is no need for the injunction to let go of it. Indeed, Heidegger stands the mystical command to "let go" on its head. Instead of an injunction to relinquish attachment to the past and to outmoded desire by an act of the will, Heidegger turns this command into an active renunciation of the will itself (Caputo 1993a:281–2).

Indeed, it would appear that Heidegger fundamentally misread what at least one mystic, Meister Eckhart, meant by letting-be and "unknowing." According to Heidegger, Eckhart considered the act of letting-be or letting go to be an act of the will. Indeed, for the author of *The Epistle of Privy Counsel*, as we have seen, it is just such an act of the will that is required if one is ever to relinquish the hell of preoccupation with the past and the anguish of longing. Only in this way could the follower of that mystical path ever enter into the sense of his or her own being and of the being of God. Heidegger attributes such an injunction to Meister Eckhart and criticizes him for it, because release and letting go ". . . in Meister Eckhart remains confined within the sphere of willing" (Caputo 1986:180).[5]

It would have been difficult for Heidegger, given his beliefs about the self, ever to undertake a descent into hell. As Michael Zimmerman puts it in his discussion of Heidegger's affair with Buddhism:

> So long as humans conceive of themselves as permanent things (such as egos), suffering ensues from the craving, aversion, and delusion associated with trying to make the impermanent permanent. Insight into the play of phenomena-arising-in-nothingness reveals that the ego, too, is impermanent and empty, merely a series of transient phenomena to which we assign the names "I" and "me." We suffer because we attempt to make the nothingness or emptiness that we "are" into a solid and enduring thing (an ego) that needs defending. (Zimmerman 1993:252)

Heidegger's version of this descent into hell, this entry into the experience of nothingness, "involves becoming the nothingness that we already are, such that we are open for and responsive to the phenomena that show up moment by moment in everyday life" (Zimmerman 1993:256). That sounds like the injunction of the author of *The Cloud of Unknowing* to allow anything – indeed everything – to come to mind: to free the self from defenses against forms of consciousness, states of mind, waves of feeling, and memories that might otherwise prove disturbing or even unbearable. Heidegger, in his later excursion into Soto Zen Buddhism, translates this injunction into a discovery that the self should be open to the "play of appearances" that include its own presence (Zimmerman 1993:259).

As we have seen, this reduction of the self to a mere appearance immunizes the self from the sort of suffering that comes from believing that the self truly is there, a substantial thing in itself, an irreducible – however perishable – core that constitutes one's own being-in-time. As a mere appearance among others, the self is relatively immune to the Hell that combines intense desire ("craving") with the knowledge that it is too late (i.e., consciousness of the futility of the attempt to make "the impermanent permanent"). It is never too late, for Heidegger, because the self is always impermanent, however much it is filled with the substance of the past. The Thinker–The Poet thus can have it both ways: *an imperishable past and a self that can never be more than moribund. That is a state of mind far closer to purgatory than to hell, and it is compatible with chronic injustice.*

I have been arguing that what appears to be a secular form of existential descent into hell nonetheless still relies on the covert religious reassurance that the past can be recovered and preserved, and that the self, shadowy as it is, can be made substantial by referring it to a higher being. Thus religious reassurances and secular quests both turn the descent into hell into an "as if" performance, in which there is no true renunciation of the past. That is why I have argued that one has to descend into hell without knowing that the past will be cleansed and removed by the grace of God or subsumed in being itself. One simply affirms and experiences the being of the innermost self without the guarantee of divine presence; one proceeds by faith, as it were, rather than by sight. There is nothing to hold on to, except a sense of one's own being, while letting go of the past. The danger is that one will be left with nothing, and it is therefore easier to hold on to a recollection of the past, from the safe distance of the thinker or the poet, than either to descend into hell or leave it behind forever without a trace of nostalgia.

The guide for such a journey, as I have argued, is therefore not the philosopher or the poet, nor even the one who speaks tellingly of life as a spiritual pilgrimage, but one who, like a psychoanalyst, not only knows the hellish aspects of the unconscious but when it is time to ignore them and let them go. Like the author of *The Epistle of Privy Counsel*, a good guide, like a good psychoanalyst, knows when followers have protracted far too long the journey into the mind's eye and urges them to leave the past, with all its unfulfilled longing, behind. Even psychoanalysts, however, cannot prevent their patients and pupils from substituting an endless regression into old longings for an uncompromising encounter with emotional suffering and reality: uncompromising either in its endurance or in its willingness finally to "let go of it." The preference for the past is often very difficult to cure, and there are various ways in which one can fall into the dilemma of a romanticized descent into hell: into Heideggerian "protracted backpedaling" and "cover-up." Like the follower of the author of *The Cloud of Unknowing* and of *The Epistle of Privy Counsel*, one can turn the search for the soul into a perennial journey and an unending psychological pilgrimage.

Finally, if I have spoken of that innermost self as the soul, it is not because I wish to use an antique expression or to import a covert theological or philosophical assumption into this discussion; it is because I wish to speak of the self as a center that is interior to the point of being presocial: a source of spontaneity, autonomy, orientation, and disposition that is not reducible to the products of early experience or later cultivation, and that is there even when the individual is apparently beyond the reach of communication. It is this center that can now be known only by faith, rather than by sight, although it may be discovered, I have argued, as that which conducts one from a descent into the hell of old longings and hatreds, old memories and injuries.

Conclusion

What, then, can be said of the process of secularization as the individual slowly is separated out from social systems? It is very difficult for sociologists to imagine a time when the individual and the larger society were part of a single system that was at once as psychological as it was social. Take, for example, Emile Durkheim's discussion of time. He fully intends to offer a description that would fit even the Australian aborigine, whose own mental state was apparently impoverished unless and until it was filled with what Durkheim called "collective representations." Speaking of the way time is constructed and construed in any society, Durkheim argues that it is virtually impossible for individuals to think of time without using the categories that societies have created: days and weeks, months and years. These categories, in turn, did not originate in the personal world of private experience but owe their origin to the round of sacred events commemorated in rituals and feast days. It is these that have given the shape and regularity to the "abstract and impersonal frame which surrounds, not only our individual existence, but that of all humanity":

> It is not *my time* that is thus arranged; it is time in general, such as it is objectively thought of by everybody in a single civilization. That alone is enough to give us a hint that such an arrangement ought to be collective. (Durkheim 1915:42, emphasis in the original)

Think for a moment how modern is this description of the experience of time. Durkheim emphasizes the distinction between the time of the larger society and his own personal time. The one is collective, the other private. Simply to be able to make this distinction is something of a feat of the social imagination, if we are to believe the accounts of earlier societies in which private and public times were overlapping, continuous, and mutually interactive. There, of course, in myth and ritual the community impresses its sense of time on the individual; however there is some evidence that even in these societies the individual was able to incorporate, reshape, and imagine myth and ritual in ways that produced changes in the ways these were understood and performed by the community. This is no doubt why Durkheim later argued not only that the psyche is a social phenomenon but that society is itself a psychic phenomenon. My point is simply that Durkheim's disclaimer that public time is not "my time" is in itself a sign of the times: that modernity has produced a degree of separation between public and private time that not even rituals have been successful in bridging.

What is held up as an icon of the individual, then, is a vast reduction of the complexity, vitality, and destructiveness of the individual psyche. It is therefore not surprising that Western societies have had to develop specialized techniques for recovering access to the dimensions and depths of the psyche that have been lost to view in most social performances. Neither is it any wonder that there is some public fascination for celebrities who act out these depths, make them visible in public performances, and seek to create roles in which these psychic dimensions can be portrayed and performed. As Wuthnow argues in his chapter for this volume, even the most creative and innovative spiritual practices of individuals are derived in part from institutional and cultural sources.

However, the development of these more privatized spiritual practices reflects a development in which the passions and longings that are permitted in most public and well-institutionalized roles are no longer an outward and visible sign of the inward and spiritual depths of the personal. The sacralization of the individual as a bearer of dignity, a possessor of inwardness, and the carrier of certain rights and responsibilities is a substitute for the loss of the sacramental sense of the person as a bearer of potent mystery or even of divinity.

The individual has been institutionalized as a bearer of constitutionally or legally guaranteed rights and duties that are at least quasi-sacred. The person of the individual is also sacred; its violation by unsolicited touch is harassment, and its exposure to public view carefully guarded by professional precautions. The persona of the individual is part of the person's charismatic endowment, and it can be spent or scattered in a variety of milieux from talk shows to memoirs and confessions. However, these public forms of the sacralization of the individual do not reveal the depths of the psyche, the individual's most carefully guarded passions and secrets, or the unconscious that is unavailable even to the individual. These continue to constitute a world that can only be imagined and, in many ways remains largely beyond the understanding, not to mention the control, even of the professions, the seers, and the psychics. Thus imaginary crimes, unconscious desires, and the necessary psychological punishment for them continue to form the stuff of violent and salacious entertainments on the media, much as visions of hell used to form popular entertainment in peepshows along the boardwalk or in carnivals.

These encounters with mortality and the other world of illicit and unfulfilled passion are the new rites of passage, I suggest, toward individuality. To contemplate one's individuality, over and above one's status in the community, one has to contemplate also one's death. This contemplation is the spiritual equivalent of a descent into hell.

There has been a vast democratization of hell. The earliest heroes to descend to its depths were usually exemplary and noble actors, often of regal stature: Gilgamesh, whose long journey to hell acquainted him with his own mortality, to which he finally became resigned; or Odysseus, whose journey to find his mother took him inevitably and sadly to the depths of the underworld. Later visions of hell also were taken under official or noble auspices: knights and monks whose early medieval journeys acquainted them with the agonies of damned souls. Their accounts were also authorized versions of the other world and came with caveats to monks to keep their disciplines and to donors to keep their promises. It is only after the turn of the first millennium that such accounts were given by a variety of more ordinary monks and lay persons, who reported their own experiences rather than make them conform to traditional models. Close encounters between the living and the dead became more accessible to the laity and to the lower orders of religious.

Not only have the mysteries of the other world, especially in its hellish dimensions, been opened to more ordinary mortals. That experience has also become more routinely attributed to the mundane and to everyday life. Hell has become this-worldly and a state of mind: a position taken by romantic poets as recently as the nineteenth century and in the last year by the Roman Catholic

Church itself. As Andrew Del Banco has noted, this is hardly a surprising development. Satan used to be the personification of self-interested desire and of self-gratification, especially when such pursuits would have disrupted the social fabric of traditional communities (Del Banco 1995). The elevation of the pursuit of individual happiness to a constitutional right, and the appeal to motives of self-enhancement by the occupational and commercial marketplace makes it difficult at the very least to imagine and comprehend what lies beyond the pale of legitimate or possible selfhood.

In chapter 19 we discussed the differentiation of one society from another, of social life from nature, and of the self from society. In each case it is a process of demystification that substitutes small mysteries for large ones by turning the unknown into forms of discourse, and yet much uncertainty remains unimagined and uncharted. It is also a process that undergoes partial and temporary reversals, such that it is difficult under some conditions to draw the line between one social system and another, or between what is human and what is natural, or between what is a legitimate and possible form of selfhood and what must remain forever demonic or angelic.

The self is defined by processes of differentiation that occur within any particular society. Not only do these, too, have their effects on the way the self is imagined and practiced; they have drawn the largest part of sociological attention over the last few decades. The separation of the state from the nation, for instance, has left the state scrambling for ideological justifications, many of which are derived either from folk or public religiosity or from more traditional forms of religious belief and practice. The resulting ideology has sometimes been called a civil religion or merely the religious "dimension" of political institutions; the terminology depends in part on the degree to which the religious beliefs and practices are supposed to have been differentiated out from the dominant political institutions of the society in question. Further, the ideology may lose its obvious religious symbols and become a relatively secular belief system that claims a place in history and among the nations for the nation-state.

The point is that each society not only reduces the ambiguity and mystery of the self into its own symbols, constitutions, rites, and monuments. Each state also generates its own forms of opposition, as other groups seek to claim a charismatic endowment for themselves. Thus sectarian opposition, both religious and political, sets up rival sources of inspiration and authority and offers a rival set of allegiances to those of the nation-state and the centralized temple. Galilee versus Jerusalem, Qumran versus the Temple, the Mormons versus the government of the United States, the Adventists versus the people of America: each suggests that the centralization of the sacred produces as though by sympathetic magic an opposition on the periphery. Thus the charismatic claims of the center are reduced and demystified by those on the margins of the nation-state who claim to represent the true Israel, so to speak.

Because of this dynamic, the differentiation of religion from politics or church from state can be diminished or reversed. The degree to which personal charisma is concentrated in the political center or dispersed among a wide range of constituencies and regions depends, of course, on the need of the state for individual support and participation. Further, the degree to which any charismatic endowment is not only dispersed but diffused in a wide range of circumstances and contexts determines whether the religious aspects of the political and the public are seen to be episodic or continuous, peripheral or basic to the nation-state's legitimacy and solidarity. Finally, in defense against the claims of the periphery the state itself or its constitution is credited with bearing a charismatic endowment, and politics becomes increasingly confessional. In this process the mystery of the sacred is further reduced, and those who claim to represent the society as a whole are seen to embody merely the strategies of partisan political conflict. The self remains the reservoir of unimaginable possibility and irreducible mystery and a perennial threat to the prevailing consensus on rights to compensation, comfort, and control.

Notes

1   Some may question the use of this earlier lecture, which was the origin of Heidegger's later, monumental work, *Being and Time*, especially since Heidegger's treatment of the themes of the First Division of *Being and Time* is "incomplete, diffuse, and even chaotic" (Kisiel 1993:319). There is a certain economy, however, in this lecture, and to one who is not a student of Heidegger it appears to be more accessible than the later, definitive work. The latter is more concerned with "the fundamental ontology of being, which comprehends Dasein," whereas this earlier lecture, however confused it may be, is focused on "the phenomenological ontology of Dasein" (Kisiel 1993:318).

2   In the end, the existentialist's ecstasy heals the division between "what" one is and "that" one is: just the opposite of the resolution required by *The Epistle of Privy Counsel*. After World War II Heidegger did appear to adopt a philosophy akin to the earlier mystics: to Meister Eckhart, however, rather than to the author of *The Cloud of Unknowing* and *The Epistle of Privy Counsel* (Caputo 1993a:281–2). Then Heidegger, too, would adopt the stance of "letting be," but it was not an act of the will, by which one renounces the past; rather, it was a form of open passivity that makes one receptive to "being's advent" (Caputo 1993a:282).

3   John D. Caputo (1993a:274) notes "a peculiar kind of ahistoricism in Heidegger": an attempt "to set forth universal *a priori* structures of existential life."

4   The notion of the "factic" and of the *existentiell* seem to have to do with "actual fact," which might include, for instance, the worldview and cosmology which informed the writing of the Gospels by the early church, but which now get in the way of an appropriation of the existential aspects of religion and of Christianity and would therefore interfere, for example, with "becoming authentic in the face of our finitude and guilt, a task that faces every human being" (Caputo 1993a:274–5).

5   Caputo (1986) points out that Eckhart's act of willed and willing renunciation is only the first "moment" in the process of letting-be or letting-go; later the soul turns to God in a selfless and open manner that is without will of any sort.

References

Caputo, J.D. 1986. *The Mystical Element in Heidegger's Thought*. New York: Fordham University Press.

Caputo, J.D. 1993a. "Heidegger and Theology," *in The Cambridge Companion to Heidegger*, Ed. C. Guignon. Cambridge: Cambridge University Press, pp. 270–88.

Caputo, J.D. 1993b. *Demythologizing Heidegger*. Bloomington and Indianapolis: Indiana University Press.

The Cloud of Unknowing 1978. Trans. C. Wolters. Harmondsworth, UK: Penguin.

Del Banco, A. 1995. *The Death of Satan*, New York: Columbia University Press.

Durkheim, E. 1915. *The Elementary Forms of the Religious Life*, Transl. J.M. Swain. George Allen & Unwin.

Guignon, C. 1993. "Authenticity, Moral Valves, and Psychotherapy," in *The Cambridge Companion to Heidegger*, Ed. C. Guignon. Cambridge: Cambridge University Press, pp. 215–39.

Hoffman, P. 1993. "Death, Time, and History: Division II of *Being and Time*," in *The Cambridge Companion to Heidegger*, Ed. C. Guignon. Cambridge: Cambridge University Press, pp. 195–214.

Heidegger, M. 1992. *The Concept of Time*, Transl. W. McNeill. Oxford: Basil Blackwell.

Kisiel, T. 1993. *The Genesis of Heidegger's Being and Time*. Berkeley: University of California Press.

Marx, L. 1997. "In the Driving Seat?," *The Times Literary Supplement*, No. 4926, August 29, p. 3.

Walls, J.L. 1992. *Hell. The Logic of Damnation*, Notre Dame, IN and London, University of Notre Dame Press.

The Epistle of Privy Counsel, 1978 in *The Cloud of Unknowing*, Trans. C. Wolters. Harmondsworth: Penguin.

Zimmerman, M.J. 1993. "Heidegger, Buddhism, and Deep Ecology," in *The Cambridge Companion to Heidegger*, Ed. C. Guignon. Cambridge: Cambridge University Press, pp. 240–69.

Index

Abbruzzese, S. 298, 299
Abelard, Peter 125
abortion 240, 241, 290, 297, 307, 310
Addison, Joseph 50
Adventists 214
advertising 49, 50, 232
Africa 71, 224
  Pentecostalism, evangelicalism 7, 16, 53, 56, 57, 197, 274
African-American churches 207–8, 209, 321–35
Afrocentrism 330
Agamben, Giorgio 116
agency 33
Ahmed, Leila 70
Aho, J. 239
Alexander, J.C. 140, 142–4, 150, 151, 152
alienation 105
  utopia as transcendence of 99
Alinsky, Saul 321
Allport, Gordon 310
altruism 287, 290, 333
ambiguity, individual and 447
American Journal of Sociology 106, 107
American Psychiatric Association 85, 405

Ammerman, Nancy 61, 62, 70, 78–9
amoral familism 208
ancestor rituals 372, 374, 376
angels 442
Anglicanism 241, 281, 282, 285, 286
  expression of legal process in liturgy 406–7
anomie 105, 126, 408
  "iron cage and anomie" paradigm 76–7, 79, 80
anthropology 359, 371
  conceptions of religion 421–6, 427
  cross-cultural discipline 419–21
  and Pentecostalism, evangelicalism 57, 60, 62–3
  relationship to sociology 363, 365–6, 367–8, 433
anti-Catholicism 24–5
anticult movement 60
anti-Semitism 107, 113, 269
apocalypse 349, 350, 352
Appleby, Scott 61–2, 71

Aquinas, Thomas 436, 449
arcadia, utopia as 95, 96
Argyle, M. 73
Aristotle 131, 315
Arminianism 42–3
Arnold, Matthew 220
Arweck, Elisabeth 60
Asad, Talal 376
asceticism 346–7
  decline 48–51
Asia, Pentecostalism 7
  see also individual countries
assumptive world theory 408
Attaturk, Kemal 222–3
Auerbach, Erich 185
Augustine, St 178, 179, 181–3, 186, 187, 190, 347, 437–8, 449, 453
Augustinianism 24, 32
Austin-Broos, Diane 64
Australia 261, 269, 283, 290
Australian aborigines 422, 464
authority 3, 4, 5, 13, 19, 149, 199, 206, 252
  China 379–80, 382
  doctrine of hell 344, 351
  theology 432

authority (*cont'd*)
  validation of faith in
    modern society
    14–15, 161–75
  see also charisma
autonomization of religion
  15, 148, 262

baby boomers 308, 310,
  311
Bailey, Edward 217
Bainbridge, W.S. 261, 275
Balkans 264–5
Balthasar, Hans Urs von
  439
Baltic states 260, 264
Banfield, Edward 208
Bann, S. 96, 97
base communities 7, 27, 63
Bastian, J.-P. 26, 57
Bauman, Z. 406
Baxter, Richard 356
Becker, H.S. 136
Beckford, J.A. 148, 154,
  202, 205, 229, 239,
  368, 420
Beijing massacres 4
being
  Heidegger's secular
    ecstasy of self-
    knowledge 456–62
  human search for Being
    111–12, 113
Beit-Hallahmi, B. 73
Belgium, offending deaths
  412
belief(s) 115, 126, 127–9,
  161, 165–7, 218, 219,
  291, 307, 439–41
  decline 282–4
  nontraditional 287, 289
Bell, Catherine 177,
  363–5, 367
Bell, Clive 31
Bell, Daniel 34, 213, 221
Bellah, Robert 68, 124,
  150, 213, 217, 424,
  437
Bendelow, G. 405
Berdyaev, N.A. 31
bereavement 319, 404,

  405, 408–10
Berger, Peter 23, 24, 76,
  213, 257, 270, 293
Bernstein, Alan 178, 351
Berry, W. 315
Besant, Annie 71
Bewes, T. 439
Beyer, Peter 367–8
Bible, concept of hell 351,
  355
Binski, Paul 344–5
birth control 290
birth place, longing for lost
  185–6
black churches 238, 310
  role in developing urban
    communities in USA
    207–8, 209, 321–35
Blackburn, J. 241
Blackfriars symposium on
  sociology and theology
  434
Blair, Tony 13
Bloch, Ernst 94, 99–101
Bloch, J.P. 242–3
Bloch, Maurice 414
Blumer, H. 292
body 404, 405
Bogota March (1998) 412
Book of Li (*Liji*) 383
Bosnia 224, 260
Boswell, James 87
boundaries xvii–xviii, 12,
  363
  convenience for social
    theory 426–7
  disciplinary 363–70, 433
  individual need for 115
  maintenance 230
Bourdieu, Pierre 356–7,
  359, 446
Bowen, Kurt 27, 56
bowing ritual 365, 377–8
Branch Davidians 4, 214
Brouwer, S. 62–3
Brown, Peter 352, 353
Bruce, Steve 22, 166, 199,
  200, 208, 209, 261,
  270, 275
Brusco, Elizabeth 26, 54,
  55, 57, 60, 63

Bryson, Norman 93–4
Buddhism 39, 172, 223,
  224, 233, 372, 379,
  415, 428, 462
Bulgaria 35–6
Bultmann, Rudolf 455, 456
Burdick, J. 27, 70
bureaucratic petitions 378,
  382–3
Burfield, D. 71
Burke, Edmund 50
Burton, Robert 86–7, 93,
  102
Bush administration 328

Calvaruso, C. 298, 299
Calvinism 162, 163, 164,
  255
Calvino, Italo 134
Campaign for Nuclear
  Disarmament (CND)
  34, 238
Campiche, R. 75
Canada 261, 269, 283,
  287, 290
Cannon, W.B. 405
capitalism 62–3, 162, 163,
  216, 217, 221, 358
Capps, Donald 20, 87, 205
Caputo, John 455, 467n3
cargo cults 225
Caribbean, Pentecostalism
  53, 64
caring 13, 73
Casanova, José 36, 270,
  274, 275
Castells, Manuel 231
categories 128–9, 130,
  131, 464
  hell as residual category
    336–60
Catherine of Genoa 356
causal explanation 48
Center for Community and
  Interfaith Partnerships
  325
Central Europe 229, 237,
  239, 264, 268–9
ceremonial practices *see*
  ritual and ceremonial
Chadwick, Owen 220

Chant, Sylvia 63
charisma 8, 14, 17, 19,
    395, 466–7
charismatics, charismatic
    Christianity 70, 79,
    274
    see also Pentecostal
    movement
Chavannes, Edouard 373
Chaves, Mark 213, 215
Chesnut, A. 27
China 212, 424, 428
    coercive secularization
        223
    Pentecostalism 53
    ritual 364, 365, 371–87
    sociology 372–6
    state and religion 3, 16
Christ, Carol 72
Christian Scientists 214
Christianity, Christian
    church 19, 428
    classical typology of
        groups 170–2
    decline 233, 280–4, 389
    and descent into hell
        178, 179, 180, 181–9
    feminist critique 68–71
    imperialist secularization
        224
    liturgy 272–3
    merit and sacrifice 415
    millenarianism and
        utopias 95, 96
    and moral order, values
        45, 48–9
    power and violence in
        19–20, 23, 33–4, 38,
        78
    and powerless 58
    rationalizing force 253–5
    role 37–8, 203
    and secularization 18,
        197–8, 199, 200,
        209–10, 224, 233
    signs 36
    Simmel and failure of
        114
    sociological reflections
        23–38
    and soul 338–59

and spiritual practices
    205
validation of faith
    168–73
women in 73–4, 80
church-based community
    organizing (CBCO)
    321–5
church/sect 148, 170–2
church/state separation
    257, 275
Cicero 437
Cioran, E.M. 98
Cipriani, Roberto 206–7,
    208, 293, 294, 295,
    296, 297, 298, 299,
    301, 302
Cisernos, Henry 325
city 8, 35, 37
    ideal, of utopias 95, 96
    see also urbanization
civil religion 124, 127,
    149, 150, 214, 217,
    402n8, 424, 466
civil rights movement 324
civil society 271, 276
civil theology of Varro 437
class 251–2, 255
    black African-American
        churches 333–4
classics 10, 11, 15–16, 20,
    33, 133–60
    and definitions of religion
        422–5
    humanities and 134,
        138
    role in sociology 135–44
    role in sociology of
        religion 145–53
    and theology 433
    typology of Christian
        groups 170–2
Cleary, E. 27
clergy
    role in CBCO and
        community economic
        development 323,
        324, 325–6, 329, 331,
        334
    see also professional elites;
        status groups

Clinton administration 328
Cloud of Unknowing, The
    178, 447–55, 456,
    457, 459, 462, 463
Cockaigne, utopia as 95,
    96, 97, 102
coercive secularization
    221–3
collective effervescence
    (Durkheim) 127, 210,
    242
collective memory, amnesia
    6–7, 203–4, 271–3,
    357, 359, 446
Colley, Linda 25
Columbia, offending deaths
    412
Comaroff, J. 71
commitment 13, 14
communal identity 173
communal validation of
    faith 167–70, 171,
    173, 174
communalization, religious
    161, 166–74
communication networks
    420
communicative interaction
    388
Communione e Liberazione
    274
community 73, 208, 255,
    256, 257, 260, 262,
    329
    and salvation 40, 41, 46,
        49
community economic
    development, role of
    African-American
    churches 207–8, 209,
    321–35
complex societies
    boundaries 363
    sacred/religion 16, 204,
        206
computers 13
Comte, A. 145, 151, 212,
    213, 216, 284, 441
Confucianism 376, 377,
    384, 427, 428
Connerton, P. 359

consciousness raising 200
Constable, G. 343
consumption, consumer
    societies 7, 49, 50
    influence on religion/
        spirituality 62, 319,
        433
contemplative, individual as
    447–63
content 292, 300, 301–4
    Simmel 108–9, 115
    see also form(s); religion,
        substantive/functional
        approach
contingencies 336, 369
contraception 290
convergence 173–4
conversion experiences
    318–19
Cornwall, M. 73
Cose, E. 330
cosmic ordering 378,
    380–1, 382
cosmology, Chinese
    374–84 passim
Council of Constantinople
    (AD 543) 354
critical theory 221
cross-cultural perspective
    on religion 418–31
Cucchiari, S. 55, 57, 63,
    64, 70
Cuddihy, J. 237
cults 172, 174, 214, 250,
    434
    China 374–5, 377, 379,
        380, 381
cultural defense, retarding
    tendency in
    secularization
    259–60
cultural diversity 255–8
cultural identity 334
cultural imperialism 62–3
cultural studies 421
cultural system, religion as
    424–5, 427
cultural transition,
    retarding tendency in
    secularization 258–9
culture 127, 230–1

cross-cultural perspective
    on religion 418–31
religion/sacred and
    216–18
secularization as cultural
    dynamic 219–26
culture war thesis 61–2,
    307–8, 310

Daly, Mary 69, 72
Dante, Alighieri 178, 180,
    183–7, 349, 451, 455
Darwinism 254, 405
Davidman, L. 70
Davie, Grace 6, 73, 75,
    203, 208, 264, 266,
    271, 350, 357, 446
Davies, Douglas 365–6,
    367
Day, Katherine 207–8,
    323, 324
Dean, Kenneth 375
death(s) and mortality 272
    hell as residual category
        340, 343–59 passim
    individual and
        development of self-
        knowledge 447, 456,
        457, 459, 460
    offending 366, 404,
        405, 408–16
    origins of religion
        177–92
    and utopias 99–100
dedifferentiation 12–13,
    207
deductive theory 152
deinstitutionalization of
    religion 172–4,
    199–200, 202, 206,
    208, 209, 232
    see also religion, decline of
        institutionalized
Del Banco, Andrew 466
Delaporte, Marianne 201
demagicalization (Weber)
    114
Demerath, N.J. 198, 213,
    219, 225, 239–40
democratization 136, 198,
    220, 221

de-moralization 7, 44, 45,
    46–8
    and hedonism 48–51
demystification of universe
    xix–xx, 11, 76, 199,
    254, 466
    see also disenchantment
denominations 33, 35,
    250, 257–8, 285, 289,
    290–1, 310
Derrida, Jacques 231
Descartes, René 131
desire see longing(s)
despair 186, 187
despiritualization 441
developing countries 251
    evangelical revival
        52–66
Diana, Princess of Wales 4,
    13, 79, 210, 232, 413,
    414
difference, sense of 23
differentiation 5, 11–12,
    35, 36, 79, 127, 202,
    220, 251–2, 257,
    274–5, 276, 368,
    466–7
diffused religion 206–7,
    208, 292–305
diffused secularization
    225–6
disasters, responses to 367,
    404–17
discourse 136, 142–4,
    150, 151, 152, 153
disenchantment of universe
    7, 11, 76, 120, 161,
    221
    see also demystification
dissidence, sociological 32
divine/human relationship
    79
divorce 297, 319
Dobbelaere, Karel 213
domestic moral preaching
    396–400
Dominicans 356
Dostoevsky, F.M. 425
doubling 344–6
Douglas, Ann 77
Douglas, Mary 411

dreams 20, 346, 353–4
   locus of utopia 100–2
dress, moral implications
   47
DuBois, W.E.B. 325
Dupront, A. 169
Durkheim, Emile 8, 9–10,
   12, 15, 46, 62, 76,
   107, 120–32, 200,
   201, 203, 210, 217,
   223, 292, 316, 356–7,
   369, 371, 384n1, 405,
   406, 407, 415, 422,
   423, 424, 429, 439,
   445, 446, 464
   as classic 11, 15, 16,
      135, 136, 138, 140,
      145, 146, 147, 149,
      150, 151, 152, 153
Dutroux, Mark 412
Dutton, P.E. 353–4
dystopias 20, 96

Easter uprising 4
Eastern Europe 224, 229,
   234, 239, 264, 268–9
   Pentecostalism,
      evangelicalism 7, 16,
      17, 18, 29–30, 53, 59,
      274
   secularization 35–6
Eckhart, Meister 461–2,
   467n2
ecology movement 242–3
economy
   decline of religious
      influence 308
   de-moralization 7
   see also capitalism
ecstatics, development of
   individual self-
      knowledge 446–63
education 220, 221, 253,
   272
   Locke's notion 339, 358
   personal reflections on
      evangelicalism 25, 28,
      30–1
egalitarianism 255–8
   Pentecostalism and
      54–7

Eliade, Mircea 217
Eliot, T.S. 134
emergent secularization
   219–21
empathy 112–13
   sociological 435
empiricism 146
England see United Kingdom
Enlightenment 34, 122,
   163, 212, 216, 220,
   223, 251, 437
Epistle of Privy Counsel, The
   448–55 passim, 459,
   460, 461, 463
Erickson, Victoria 8, 14,
   16, 17, 204, 365, 369
Erikson, E.H. 87, 93, 101
eschatologies 4, 17–18, 23
ethics 131, 253
   and individualism 162,
      163, 164
   see also moral
      communication; moral
      order; moral values;
      morality
Ethiopia, offending deaths
   412–13
ethnic groups 259–60
   and secularization 208,
      209
ethnic identity 259, 260,
   330
ethnic nationalism 265,
   274
ethology 363
Europe
   decline of collective
      memory 6–7, 203–4,
      271–3, 357
   decline of religious
      practice 283–4; see
      also religion, decline of
      institutionalized
   irreversible secularization
      208–9
   patterns of religion in
      264–78
   religious and moral
      pluralism 297, 303
   social process of
      secularization

   249–63; see also
      secularization
   see also Eastern Europe;
      individual countries
European Values Systems
   Study Group (EVSSG)
   265–9, 283–4
euthanasia 290
evangelicalism 17, 52, 70,
   79
   experience of 23–38
   moral order 42, 43
   responsible individualism
      16, 55
   see also Pentecostal
      movement
evil 32
   in moralizing sermon
      391–400 passim
existential version of
   descent into hell
      454–63

faith 463
   crises of 319
   and salvation 39–40
   Simmel 111, 112–13,
      440; see also
      faithfulness
   validation in modern
      societies 14–15,
      161–75
Faith-based Community
   Economic Development
   Program 322
faithfulness 107, 108,
   113–14
Falun Gong 3, 16
family 6, 70, 74, 75, 208,
   209, 251, 293, 302,
   329, 348
   Latin America 26
   and moral order 7, 44
   moralizing sermon
      396–400
   Pentecostalism and
      gender 8, 53, 54, 55
Family, The 60
fantasies 20, 205
Far East, evangelicalism 53,
   57

fascism 210, 447, 461
father religions 93
Fei Hsiao-t'ung 373
feminism 67–84, 311, 432
  critique/neglect of
    evangelicalism 7, 53,
    58, 63–4
feminization of religion
    77–80
Fenn, R.K. 154, 201, 213,
    356, 358, 359, 406
Ferenczi, S. 191
Feuchtwang, Stephan
    374–5
Feuerbach, Ludwig Andreas
    437
Fichter, Joseph 310
first wave feminism 67,
    68–9, 71, 72
Flake, Floyd 329
Flanagan, Kieran 16, 21,
    369, 446
Fogarty, M. 265, 266
folk Catholicism 26
Fontaine, Arturo 26
form(s) 368
  Simmel 108–9, 110,
    114–15, 116, 117,
    118, 436, 438
  versus function 422,
    423, 425–6, 427–30
Foucault, Michel 121, 142,
    442
founding fathers see classics
France
  religion as social
    movement 237
  religious patterns 270
  secularization 216–17,
    220–1
Francis, L. 73
Francis of Sales, St 313
Franklin, Robert 325,
    329–30
Freccero, John 186–7
Free Churches 281, 282,
    285–6
free will 33
Freedman, Maurice 371,
    374, 375
Freston, Paul 26

Freud, Sigmund 9, 20, 30,
    87–93, 100–2, 177,
    178, 179, 183,
    189–92, 346, 359,
    422, 448, 449, 451,
    458, 459, 460
Frijda, N.H. 405
function 41
  sociology's reduction of
    religion to 152, 438
  versus form and content
    292, 300, 301–4, 368,
    422, 423, 425–6,
    427–30
fundamentalism 70, 226,
    229, 273–4, 333
  confused with
    evangelicalism 61–3
Fundamentalism Project
    61–2, 71, 274

Geertz, Clifford 64, 72,
    218, 423, 424–5,
    427
Gehlen, Arnold 76
Geldof, Bob 412
Gellner, Ernest 35, 255
gender
  gender-blindness and
    gendered difference
    67–84
  paradox of
    Pentecostalism 7–8,
    52–66, 70
gender roles 8, 12
gender studies 67
Germany
  decline of belief and
    practice 284, 401n2
  moral communication
    366–7, 388–403
  religious patterns 270
Gifford, P. 62–3
Gilgamesh epic 178–9,
    465
Gill, Robin 21, 199, 250,
    434
globalization 26, 136, 225,
    363, 367, 420
globalization theory 421
Glock, Charles 310

God 79, 131
  belief in 283–4, 287,
    307
  and salvation 354
  transcendent 197, 209
  see also grace
Goffman, Erving 125–6
golden age, utopia as 95,
    96
Golden Rule Christians 79
good 32
good life 199
Gordon, Daniel 221
Gould, Julius 34
Gouldner, A. 136
government see state
grace 443
  divine 453, 454, 459,
    463
Gramsci, A. 64
grand narratives 68, 75–7,
    80, 289, 374, 441
Granet, Marcel 373, 374
Greece 35, 275
Greeks, and hell 350, 351
Greeley, Andrew 75
Gregory of Tours, Pope
    340–1, 343–4, 346
Greider, William 322
grieving see mourning
Griffith, R. Marie 70
Groot, J.J.M.de 373
groups 14, 22, 289
  identity 259–60, 262
  spirituality and spiritual
    practices 309, 311,
    313, 314
Groves, J.M. 242
Grünberg, W. 401n3
Gulbenkian Commission
    368
gypsies 53, 274

Habermas, Jürgen 142,
    221
Hackett, Rosalind 63
Hadaway, C.K. 215
Halévy, E. 26, 58
Hannigan, J.A. 239
Harding, S. 265, 266
Hare Krishna 214

Harrison, Jane Ellen 121
Harvard Divinity School
    325, 332
Haywood, C.L. 71
health 230
    and sociology of disasters
        404–17
hedonism 48–51, 95
Heelas, P. 68
Heidegger, Martin 178,
    454–63
hell 201–2
    belief in 350–1
    descent into 177–92
    development of individual
        self-knowledge
        446–66 passim
    as residual category
        336–60
Helle, Horst J. 108, 118,
    439
hermeneutics 368
Hermes of Egypt 438
Hertel, B.R. 75
Hervieu-Léger, Danièle 14,
    15, 271
hierophanies (Eliade) 217
Hillsborough disaster
    409–10
Hinduism 224, 226, 233,
    270, 286, 415, 427,
    428
Hoffman, Piotr 459
holidays 318
Holland 75, 261
Hollenweger, Walter 57
Homer 178, 180–1
homesickness, and utopia
    93–4, 99–100, 102
homily, moral
    communication likened
    to 366–7, 388–403
hope 17–18, 112, 242
    in utopian thinking 96,
        97
horoscopes, belief in 287
Hsu, Francis L.K. 373
Huber, E. 71
human nature, sociological
    conception 447
human well-being, personal

loss and disasters
    404–17
humanities
    and classics 134, 138
    and social sciences
        368–9
Hunter, James Davidson 61

Iannaccone, Laurence 212,
    260–1, 275
ideal city, utopia as 95, 96
identity
    formation 230
    see also ethnic identity;
        personal identity;
        religious identity; social
        identity
Ignatius, St 340, 344,
    347
illness 319
imagination xviii–xix
immigrant communities
    229, 270, 272
    Pentecostalism 53
    and religious practice and
        belief 199, 203–4,
        286, 288, 291
imperialist secularization
    223–5
implicit religion 59, 217
incense burning 378, 380,
    381, 382
India, imperialist
    secularization 224
individual 369–70,
    445–68
    and Durkheim 9–10,
        120, 122, 125, 126,
        128, 129–30
    and egalitarianism 255,
        256
    and pacifism 33
    and sacred 9–10, 12, 22,
        200–1
    and salvation 41
    and society 16, 125,
        128, 363, 368
    sociological view 445–7
individualism
    and modern religion
        14–15, 161–75,

199–200, 262, 302,
    307, 308, 423
    New Age 164–5, 166,
        167
    relationship between
        religious and modern
        15, 162–4
    responsible 16, 55
individuality
    hell as punishment for
        346
    religious and secular
        progress towards
        445–67
individualization of religion
    148, 162, 210
    see also individual;
        individualism
Industrial Areas Foundation
    (IAP) 208, 321, 322,
    324, 331
industrialization 42, 43,
    105, 136, 220, 255–6,
    259, 286
inspiration 3, 4, 13, 19,
    176, 344
institutional validation of
    faith 168–70, 171,
    173, 174
institutionalized religion see
    religion
Interdenominational
    Theological College
    (ITC) 325
International Conference of
    Sociology of Religion
    (1983) 294
international politics 32
International Society for
    Krishna Consciousness
    59, 60, 230
internationalism 33, 34
Internet 3, 13, 206, 232,
    363, 368
invisible religion 150, 294,
    296
Iran 202, 239
Ireland 259, 260
    religious imagination
        253
    see also Northern Ireland

Ireland, R. 27
"iron cage"
  and anomie, paradigm of
      76–7, 79, 80
  of capitalism 217, 221
ISKCON 59, 60, 230
Islam 58, 70, 172, 202,
      233, 239, 270, 286,
      288–9, 294, 424, 428
  revival 53, 223, 226
  transcendence 37
Italy 35
  diffused religion 206–7,
      208, 292–305
  fundamentalism 274
  see also Sicily

Jackson, Stanley W. 85, 93
Jacobs, Janet 72, 73
Jamaica 64
James, William 87, 309,
      315
Japan 286
  secularization 223, 224
Jefferson, 50
Jehovah's Witnesses 214,
      230, 289, 294
Jervis, J. 433–4
Jesuits 372
Jesus 125, 283, 284, 352
John of the Cross, St 313
Johnson, B. 435
Johnson, Samuel 87, 102
Joyce, James 347–8
Judaism, Jews 37, 53, 58,
      70, 110, 172, 199,
      233, 253, 254,
      269–70, 280, 286,
      288, 294, 428
  and hell 350–2
  transcendence 37
Jung, C.G. 87
justice, and disasters 366,
      404, 405, 406–16

Kaern, M. 108
Kant, I. 131
karma 415
Kaufman, D.R. 70
Kempe, Margery 341–3
Kemper, T.D. 405–6

Kensitites 24
Kermode, Frank 134
kinship ties 6
knowledge acquisition 313
Korea 57
Kosovo 13, 204, 224
Kristeva, Julia 85, 102n1
Kuhn, T. 142, 152
Kumar, Krishan 95–7

Laestadianism 259
Lancaster, Roger 63, 64
Latin America 239
  Pentecostalism,
      evangelicalism 7, 16,
      17, 18, 24, 26–8, 29,
      30, 53, 56, 57, 59, 62,
      63–4, 70, 197
  secularization 35
law, and personal loss
      406–11
Lawrence, Stephen, murder
      of 409
leftist views of development
      62
Lehmann, D. 27
leisure 49
Lenski, Gerhard 310
Lévi-Strauss, C. 126,
      384n2, 405, 425
Levine, Donald N. 105, 141
Levitas, Ruth 97, 99–100
Lewis, C.S. 449
li 376
liberation theology 7, 27,
      62, 63
limbo 116–18, 184, 365
Lincoln, C.E. 326
Lipset, Martin 34
Live Aid 412–13
Lloyd, Genevieve 182, 183
local community 6, 46, 79,
      208
local cults, China 374–5,
      379
local identity 375
Locke, John 339, 356, 358
Lockerbie plane crash 410
longing(s)
  melancholy and utopias
      20–1, 96–100, 205

religion as 443
and religious imagination
      20, 176–92, 340–1,
      342, 347, 355, 449,
      451–2, 454
sacred as product of 9
loss
  melancholy and utopias
      87–94, 95, 99–100,
      102
  personal 404, 405,
      408–11
  religious imagery as
      reflection of experience
      of 176–92
  sense of, in sacred 20
Louis the Pious 353
Lovejoy, Arthur 220
Lucifer 184, 341
  see also Satan
Luckmann, Thomas 76,
      150, 292, 293, 294,
      308, 309, 366–7, 423,
      424, 425
ludic sphere in modernity
      125
Lukes, S. 154
Lummis, A. 73
Luther, Martin 163, 164,
      255

McAdam, Doug 326–8
McCarthy, J.D. 234, 238
McDermott, T. 436
McDougall, Harold A. 324
McGuire, M. 72, 427
MacIntyre, Alasdair 312,
      317
McKinney, William 213
MacLeod, George 30
magic 197, 351, 352, 353
Malinowski, Bronislaw
      371, 375
Mamiya, L.H. 326
mana 8, 120–1
Manguel, Alberto 134
mania 89–90
manners 47–8, 50, 51
Mannheim, K. 33
Manuel, F.E. 85–6
Manuel, F.P. 85–6

Mao Zedong 223
Marabel, Manning 329
Marcuse, Herbert 221
market forces 260–1, 275
Marler, Penny Long 75,
    215
marriage 109
Marshall-Fratani, Ruth 63
Martin, Bernice 7–8, 17,
    52, 70, 364
Martin, David 8, 16,
    17–18, 19, 20, 21, 27,
    33, 34, 35, 36, 59, 70,
    78, 201, 213, 255,
    270, 364, 369, 434
Martin, Richard J. 434
Marty, Martin 61–2, 71
Marx, Karl 30, 76, 107,
    212, 213, 216, 217,
    221, 422, 437
  as classic 15, 135, 136,
    138, 146, 147–8, 151
Marxism 7, 35, 62, 63, 64
masochism 190–2
Mauss, Armand 234
Mauss, Marcel 123, 405
meaning
  religion as creation of
    423
  search for 291
  spiritual practices 310
media 272, 276
  and offending deaths
    366, 412–13
meditative practices 309,
    310, 312, 313
  China 3
mediums, China 379
melancholy 20, 85–104
merit 404, 414, 415–16
Merton, Robert 134, 135,
    139, 140, 144, 254
Methodism 52, 55, 58,
    259, 281, 285–6
  personal experience
    28–9, 31
microrituals 125–6
Middle East 424
migration, and religious
    participation 28,
    285–6, 288, 291

Milbank, J. 438
millenarianism 4, 27, 39
  utopia as millennium 95,
    96
Million Man March 329
Mills, C.W. 137, 147, 441
missiology 57
Model Cities program 328
modern/traditional
    distinction 363, 368,
    419–21, 426
modernity 215
  incompleteness of project
    of 356, 358–9
  religion in 274–5
  Simmel and crisis of 114
modernization 136, 220,
    251–2, 256, 258–9,
    262, 271
  evangelical revival and
    52, 54–7
  "iron cage" and anomie
    76
monks, social control
    343–4
Montgomery, Jill 192n3
moral communication 22,
    366–7, 388–403
moral order 6, 7, 287, 290,
    337, 341
  of Pentecostalism 55
  secularization as decline
    of 40, 43–8
  societies as 41–3
moral-somatic model of
    human well-being
    405, 406–11, 414,
    415–16
moral values 414
  changes in 48–51
morality 253
  moral effects of Chinese
    ritual 383, 384
  moral processes in
    response to offending
    deaths 405–16
  moral responsibility in
    spiritual practices 316
  see also ethics
More, Thomas 85, 97
Morgenthau, Hans 32

Mormons 214, 285, 290
mortality see death(s) and
    mortality
Mother Earth 432
mourning 341
  element in descent into
    hell 178–89
  and melancholy 87–8
multifaith societies,
    religious freedom
    237–8
music, and evangelicalism
    28–30
mutual validation of faith
    167, 168, 169, 170,
    171, 172, 173, 174
mysticism 21, 148, 149,
    162, 163, 164, 171
  individual and
    achievement of self-
    knowledge 446–63
    passim, 467n2
  see also Kempe, Margery
myth 149, 176–9, 351,
    353, 464

narcissism 15, 191
Nation of Islam 239
National Congress for
    Community Economic
    Development (NCCED)
    322
national culture 253, 256
nationalism 224–5, 275
Native Americans 222
natural sciences 368
  inappropriateness of
    models to sociology
    142, 144
naturalism 432
nature, and social order
    xvi–xviii, 337–8,
    354–5
nature mysticism 30
near-death experiences
    319, 343–4, 352–3
Neighborhood Reinvestment
    Training Institute 322,
    325
Neitz, M. 72
neoplatonism 163

neutrality, in social sciences 80
New Age spirituality 79, 149, 164–5, 166, 167, 233, 243, 258, 289, 432, 434, 442
New Guinea, secularization 225
new religious movements 35, 59–61, 72, 149, 172, 213, 214, 230, 233, 237, 270, 288, 289, 293, 311
New Zealand 269
Nicholas of Cusa 439
Niebuhr, Reinhold 31, 32, 148
Nielsen, Donald 9–10, 13, 15, 128, 130
Nietzsche, F. 114, 425
Nightingale, Florence 69
North Korea massacres 4
Northern Ireland 204, 259, 260, 274, 287
offending deaths 412
Norway 259, 261
nuclear family 55

objectivity, in social sciences 80
O'Connell, J. 265, 266
Odysseus 180–1, 185, 465
Oedipal emotions 21
Oedipal myth 90, 178–9, 181
Oklahoma City bombing 4
Omagh bombing 412
Operation Rescue 241
Opportunities Industrial Centers (OIC) 325, 326
Orthodox churches 229, 237
Osa, M. 241
O'Toole, Roger 10, 15–16
Otto, Rudolf 87
Ozorak, E.W. 73, 78, 79

Pacific Rim, Pentecostalism 53

pacifism 23, 24, 31–2, 33–4, 38
paganism 243, 428, 432
Pakistan 71
Palmer, S. 72
paradise, utopia as 95, 96
Parkes, C.M. 408
Parsons, Talcott 12, 34, 73, 135, 147, 151–2, 423, 424, 425
Pascal, Blaise 131
past 356–9
individual and development of self-knowledge 448–63
origins of religion 188–9
see also collective memory
patriarchal Christianity
feminist critique 7, 69, 70–1
women's adaptation 7, 53–7, 58
peace 4
and power and violence in religion 19–20, 33–4, 37–8, 78
peace movements 238, 240, 242
Pentecostal movement 3, 7–8, 16, 17, 18, 26, 27, 149, 197, 274, 289–90, 364, 424
gender paradox 7–8, 52–66, 70
personal identity 7, 289, 290, 291
Peru, Pentecostalism 56
Phillips, D. 265, 266
piety 440
Plato 131
pluralism 26, 35, 297, 303
cross-cultural perspective on religion 418, 428–9
Poggi, G. 139–40
Poland 36, 240–1, 259, 260, 268
politics

importance of religion 230, 231–4, 308
influence of religion in Italy 294, 297–8
response to offending deaths 366, 413
Polo, Marco 372
polytheism 428, 437
popular culture 13
Portugal 35
positivism 36, 216, 223, 441
postindustrial society 136, 289
and moral order 43–51
postmodernity, postmodernism 115, 136, 215, 231, 289, 438–9, 443
alienation in 105, 117
fragmentation 29, 406, 407
sociology in 421, 441–2
post-traumatic stress disorder 405
power 121
combined with caring 13
and violence 19–20, 23, 33–4, 38, 78
Powys, David 351–2
prayer 302, 304, 309, 310, 311, 313
premodernity 215, 249–50
primitive societies 363
sacred/profane in 123, 124
private/public 11, 76, 77, 79–80, 251
privatization
moral virtue 46
of religion 76–7, 79, 80, 148, 231, 307
profane see sacred, and profane
professional elites 9, 17, 210
and moral order 45
see also clergy; status groups

projection, sacred/religion
   as 9, 437–8, 439
prophecy 149
   of doom, in moralizing
      sermon 391–400
      passim
Protestant ethic 15, 42,
   126, 163–4, 216, 220,
   221, 254, 358
*Protestant Ethic and the Spirit
   of Capitalism, The* (M.
   Weber) 147, 153
Protestantism
   and apocalypticism 350
   and China 373
   Northern Ireland 274
   Romania 18
   and secularization 18,
      35, 199–200, 210,
      250, 252, 256, 261
   and social movements
      229, 240, 241
   and soul 338–9
   spirituality 163–4, 312
   validation of faith
      169–70
   work 42, 126
   see also Protestant ethic;
      Reformation; *and
      individual denominations*
Providence, reliance on 27
psyche 464, 465
psychoanalytic approach
   20, 359
   development of individual
      448, 450, 451, 452,
      454, 458, 459, 463
   to melancholy and
      utopias 20–1, 87–102
   religious imagination and
      177–8, 179, 183,
      189–92, 342–3
psychology 20–1, 35, 365
psychology of religion,
   applied to melancholy
      85–104
psychotherapeutic approach
   35, 48
public/private 11, 76, 77,
   79–80, 251

public response to death
   366, 411–16
public speech, analyzed as
   moralizing sermon
      389–96, 401
public sphere 252
   de-moralization 46–8
   see also public/private
public utilities, churches as
   203, 276
purgatory 184, 201, 352,
   356, 357–8, 359, 452,
   453, 454, 457, 458
Puritanism 42, 163, 221,
   254

Quakers *see* Religious
   Society of Friends
quality of life 406
quasi-religion 234, 244
quasi-sacred 203

race 202
   class interest in black
      churches 334
racism 222, 329, 333, 334
Rajneeshism 60
Rapture, the 349
rational-choice theory 148,
   152–3, 260–1, 275
rationalization 120
   of religion 253–5
Raven, Charles 30
Read, Herbert 31
Reagan administration
   326, 328
realized eschatology 342
reason 35, 161
rebounding vitality 405,
   414–15
reciprocity, and justice
   408–11
reflexivity, disciplinary 433,
   434–6
Reformation 42, 163, 168,
   169, 171, 172, 197,
   200, 252, 253, 254,
   255, 256, 415
regeneration, religious
   imagination 177

regression 342
reincarnation 39, 287
relationality 11, 13, 73,
   77–80
   Simmel and faith 111,
      112–13
relativism 210, 260, 307
Relf, Jan 103n1
religion
   collective memory
      203–4, 271–3
   contingency 206
   cross-cultural perspective
      418–31
   decline of
      institutionalized 3,
         21–2, 35, 161, 205,
         213, 214, 231–4, 243,
         250, 257, 280–4, 423,
         433–4; *see* also
         deinstitutionalization
   definitions in sociology
      and anthropology
         150, 243, 421–6, 436;
         see also below
         substantive/functional
         approach
   distinguished from
      spirituality 202–3,
         306–7, 312, 314
   Durkheim and 9, 13–14,
      120–32, 150
   future of, in the West
      199, 279–91
   individualism and
      validation of faith
         161–75
   origins xvi, 176–93, 451
   paradoxes 19–20, 37–8,
      202
   patterns in Western
      Europe 264–78
   and psychoanalysis 20
   and psychological loss 93
   rationalization of
      253–5
   redefinition needed 6,
      368, 426–30
   relationship with
      theology 436

religion (*cont'd*)
  and sacred 3, 9, 13–15,
    16, 18–22, 121, 208,
    210, 217
  Simmel and 107, 108,
    114–15, 118, 443
  and social movements
    202, 206, 229–48
  substantive/functional
    approach 292–3, 300,
    301–4, 368, 422, 423,
    425–6, 427–30
  Weber's refusal to define
    150
religions of difference 11,
  68–71, 76, 79
religions of humanity 68,
  74, 79
religiosity 231–2
  Simmel and 423, 424,
    425, 436, 438–41
  women 73–5, 80
religious freedom 237–8
religious identity 229,
  288–9
religious imagination
  and hell 177–92,
    337–55
  and melancholy 20
  mystics and development
    of self-knowledge
    446–63
  origins of religion
    176–89
religious individualism
  162–4
  New Age religion
    164–5
religious leadership 149
  see also clergy;
    professional elites;
    status groups
religious meanings 232,
  233
religious minorities 230,
  269–70
religious modernity 169
religious movements, and
  utopias 94–5, 96
religious reformers 21
  see also Reformation

Religious Society of Friends
  238, 252
religious symbols 232,
  233, 234, 244
religious values 232, 265–9
religious vision, parallels
  with sociological
  imagination 8, 23–38
religiousness *see* religiosity
re-moralization 7
Rendall, J. 71
reparation, for offending
  deaths 413, 415–16
repentance 348, 449, 452,
  456
  call for, in moralizing
    sermons/communica-
    tion 392–400 *passim*
resacralization of the world
  5
  see also sacralization
Resource Mobilization
  Theory 234, 238
revenge 409
revivalism 26, 259
  moral order 42
Rieff, Philip 102
right laterality 405
right, religious 209
risk 411
rites of passage 4, 465
ritual and ceremonial,
  ritualization 4, 177,
    293, 309, 359, 363–5,
    366
  China 365, 371–87
  Durkheim and 120, 121,
    122–9, 149, 464
  of everyday life 22, 366
  public sector 366
  see also sacrifice
Robbins, T. 237
Robertson-Smith, William
  371
roles 7, 12, 252
  gender 8, 12
  work order and de-
    moralization 42, 44,
    45–6
Roman Catholicism
  and Chinese ritual 372

  and diffused religion in
    Italy 206–7, 294–304
  and hell 338–9, 348–50,
    354, 355, 465–6
  and individualism 162–3
  and moral order 42
  reactionary movements
    274
  and secularization 35,
    261
  and Simmel 439
  and social movements
    238, 240
  and sociology 433
  spiritual practices 310,
    312
  trends 281, 283, 285,
    286, 288, 290
  validation of faith 169
  women and 75
Roman religion 437
Romania 18, 36
  evangelicalism 29–30
Roof, Wade Clark 105,
  213, 258
Rose, S.D. 62–3
Rousseau, Jean Jacques
  217
Rubin, Julius H. 85
Ruether, Rosemary Radford
  69, 72

sacralization 75, 123,
  126–8, 214–16, 217,
  225–6
  of everyday life 11–13
  of individual 126, 465
sacred xix, 3–22, 197,
  204, 357, 364, 365,
  369, 433–4, 446
  concept of hell 355
  and culture 198–9,
    216–18
  Durkheim 9–10,
    120–31, 150, 203
  loss of 406
  origins 8–9
  and profane 10, 12, 15,
    16, 59, 123–30 *passim*,
    199, 200, 207, 209,
    365, 367

social movements
    205–6, 241–3
and violence 366
sacred events, origin of
    categories in 464
sacred places 6, 272
sacred times 318
sacrifice, and offending
    deaths 366, 404, 405,
    415–16
sadism 190, 191
Saint Simon, Claude-Henri
    de Rouvroy, comte de
    145, 151
salvation 39–51, 131, 354
    communal 168–9
    and individualism 162,
        169
    and moral order 41–3,
        46, 48, 51
    New Age spirituality
        164, 165
    Pentecostalism 54–5
    Simmel and 112, 440
    society and 41–3, 112
Sanneh, Lamin 224
Satan 184, 338, 347, 466
    see also Lucifer
Scandinavia 253
Schipper, K. 376
Schmitt, T. 239–40
science 35, 111, 165, 220,
    221, 253–5, 368, 441
Scientology 39, 59, 230
second wave feminism 60,
    67, 69, 71, 72
secret societies, China 375
sects, sectarianism 149,
    163, 174, 199, 214,
    230, 250, 257, 258,
    285, 289, 358, 434
    and churches 148,
        170–2
secular address, analyzed as
    moralizing sermon
    389–96, 401
secular society 6, 9, 10,
    369, 423, 429
secularization xix–xx, 3, 4,
    5–6, 20, 22, 59, 76,
    161, 197–210, 231,

239, 249–63, 284,
    287, 308, 365, 367,
    406, 420
and Christianity 18, 35,
    197–8, 199, 200,
    209–10, 224, 233,
    261
coercive 221–3
as cultural dynamic
    219–26
as decline of moral order
    40, 43–8, 49
diffused 225–6
diffused religion and
    298–9
Durkheim 122
Eastern Europe 18,
    35–6, 199–200, 210,
    250, 252, 256, 261
emergent 219–21
and ethnic groups 208,
    209
extended to culture
    211–28
France 216–17, 220–1
ideological sources
    34–5
irreversibility 208–9,
    261–2, 291
Latin America 35
myth of myth of 212–14
personal reflections on
    evangelicalism and
    sociology 24, 27, 28,
    34–6
religion as cause of 18,
    197–8, 199–200,
    209–10
religious individualism
    162
retarding features
    258–60
of salvation 40–1
and separation of
    individual from social
    systems 463–7
and social systems 40–1
sociological classics and
    149, 150–3
theology and sociology
    438, 441

United States of America
    208, 216, 217, 220,
    222, 224, 250, 253,
    257
women and 11, 74–5, 80
self
    achievement of sense of
        447–63
    descent into hell 179,
        183, 188–92
    and melancholy 88–94
    religious individualism
        162, 164–5
    sacred and repressed
        aspects 205
    and society 16, 363,
        368, 466
self-control see self-restraint
self-denial 48, 49
self-destruction 190–2
self-discipline 8, 13
self-help 326
self-improvement 8
self-interest 47, 49
self-perfection 164, 165
self-regard 6
self-restraint 6, 46, 48,
    50
self-validation of faith
    14–15, 166–7, 169,
    170, 172
semiotics 363
Sephardic Jews 270, 288
sermons, moralizing
    366–7, 388–403
shamanism 9
    China 3, 379, 382
Shils, Edward 34
Shintoism, secularization
    223, 224
Sicily 63, 70, 297,
    299–301
Sikh faith 233, 270, 286
Simmel, Georg 8, 10, 14,
    15, 16, 17, 76,
    105–19, 135, 148,
    204–5, 369, 423, 425,
    436, 437, 438–41,
    443
skepticism 7, 250, 283,
    287, 288, 289

482 INDEX

Small, Albion W. 105–7,
    117–18
small groups see groups
Smith, Adam 148
sociability 17, 18–19, 106,
    112
social capital 79
social change
    Durkheim and 120–32
    longing for 20
    see also differentiation
social chaos, Simmel and
    106–8, 114
social cohesion 41, 49–50
    see also social unity
social conflict 6, 16, 19,
    47, 111, 127, 205
social consensus 41
social construction,
    spirituality as 318–19
social control 42, 46, 48
    Christian church as 198,
    337, 341–4, 348, 350
social crises 105–6
social cycles 121–7 passim
social differentiation 251–2
    see also differentiation
social forces 121
social identity 199, 258,
    280, 287–91
social immanence,
    Durkheim's theology of
    120, 127, 130, 131
social inclusion 230
social institutions 108–9,
    121
social interaction 262, 388
social movement theory,
    and African-American
    churches 326–32
social movements
    African-American
        churches as 323–6,
        332
    religion as 202, 206,
        229–48
    religious contributions
        towards 238–9
    religious/spiritual
        element in 239–43

sacred and 17
social obligations 6, 7
social order 46, 47, 425
social pantheism 126
social power 121
social protest 366, 405,
    412–13
social sciences
    critical reflection on
        spirituality 319
    and humanities 368–9
social system(s)
    hell as residual category
        for excluded
        possibilities 336–60
    individual and 445–7,
        463–4
    secularization and 40–1
social system theory 336
social theory, cross-cultural
    perspective on religion
    418–31
social unity 41
    China 373, 374, 383
    see also social cohesion
socialization 45, 51, 293,
    295, 373, 374, 377,
    378, 445
societalization 252–3,
    260
society
    Durkheim and
        transformations of
        120–32
    excluded possibilities
        336–60
    as moral order 41–3
    product of individuals
        446
    and sacred 8, 17, 18–19
    Simmel and 17, 111,
        112, 113–14
socioeconomic class 251–2,
    255, 333–4
sociolinguistics 363
sociology
    conception of religion
        421–6, 436
    as cross-cultural
        discipline 419–21

formation of American
    105–7, 117–18
neglect of Pentecostalism
    53, 57–9, 61
neglect of religion
    229–30, 275
tension between
    sociological
    imagination and
    religious vision 8,
    23–38
    see also classics and
    individual topics
sociology of occupations
    74
sociology of religion 229,
    420
    neglect of Pentecostalism
        53, 57–9, 61
    phases 68
    problematic of subject
        matter 10–11
    role of classics 145–53
Socrates 125
Soka Gakkai 214
Soper, Donald 30
Sorel, G. 33
Soto Zen Buddhism 462
soul 16
    contemplative 449–63
        passim, 465
    and descent into hell
        182–4, 188–9, 190
    and excluded possibilities
        of hell 338–48 passim,
        352–3, 358
    Simmel's sociology of
        8–9, 14, 110–12, 114,
        116–17, 205, 369, 440
South Africa 239, 326
South Korea 286
Soviet Union 202, 212,
    224, 229, 239
    Pentecostalism 7, 53
Spain 35
specialization 44, 45, 251
speech, moral implications
    47
Spencer, Herbert 30, 212
Spinoza, Baruch 128

spiritual practices 164,
    204–5, 309–17,
    464–5
spirituality(ies) 201, 202,
    204, 306–20
  individual interest 161,
    164
  inventive 3
  of life 11, 68, 71–2, 76,
    78, 79
  of social movements
    239–43
Spiro, Melford 423, 425,
    426, 427, 429
Stallings, R.A. 405, 415
standpoint methodology 80
Stanton, Elizabeth Cady 69
Stark, Rodney 212, 213,
    260, 261, 275, 429
state 252–3
  equated with society in
    sociology 420, 424
  and public/moral order
    7, 46, 50, 51
  and religion in China 3,
    16, 379–80
  and religion in Italy 294,
    297–8
  and sacred 466–7
  separation from church
    257, 275
  symbolism 395
state church 271, 275–6
statehood, and
    secularization 35
status groups 183
  and hell 336, 340, 341,
    342, 349, 350, 351
  see also clergy;
    professional elites
Steggarda, M. 75
Stewart-Gambino, H. 27
Stinchcombe, A.L. 140
Stokes, A. 73
Stoll, D. 27
stories
  Simmel 109, 111–12,
    118
  spiritual 313, 316, 317,
    319

Stout, Jeffrey 312
stranger 10, 110, 205, 439
structural differentiation
    251, 274–5, 276
Styron, William 85
subjectivity, research 368
sublime 231
suffering 48
suicide 89
Suicide (Durkheim) 122
Sullivan, Leon 325–6
supply-side model of
    religion 260–1, 275
surveillance 7, 46, 50
Swanson, G. 130
Swatos, W.H., Jr 74
symbolic interaction 368,
    440
symbolic realism 150
symbolism, symbols 9, 122,
    218, 219, 414

Tambiah, S.J. 414
Taoism 372, 375, 376,
    377, 379, 380, 381,
    382–3, 428
televangelism 272, 276
Teresa of Avila, St 313,
    339–40
terminology, in sociology 21
Thatcher, Margaret 412
thaumaturgy 39
Theobald of Etampes 243
theology 21
  of hell 337
  relationship to sociology
    36–8, 369, 432–44
Theravada Buddhism 39
third wave feminism, 53,
    67, 68, 70–1, 72, 80
third way 13
Thompson, E.H. 73
Thompson, E.P. 58
Thompson, Kenneth 153
Thompson, N. 415
time xvii, xviii, xx
  Durkheim and 464
  Heidegger's secular
    encounter with passage
    of 456–63

hell and loss of 177–89
    passim, 344–6, 348,
    349, 351, 355, 449,
    452
  sacred and 4, 203
  see also past
Tipton, Steven 68, 73
Tocqueville, Alexis de 26,
    148
Toennies, F. 76
Tolstoy, Leo 30
traditional faiths 225–6
traditional/modern
    distinction 363, 368,
    419–21, 426
traditional societies 13,
    199
trance 365, 378, 379–80,
    382
transcendence 19, 20, 131,
    231, 357, 425
  Christian 36, 37
  domesticated 115
transcendent God 197, 209
transference 359
transi tombs 344–5
transnationalism 421
tribal religions 39, 428
Troeltsch, Ernst 14, 15, 54,
    114, 148, 163, 170,
    171, 172, 309
trust 406
Turkey, coercive
    secularization 222–3
Turner, James 220
Turner, Victor 425
Tylor, E. 150

Ulster see Northern Ireland
uncanny, Freud and 90–2,
    100
uncertainty, individual and
    447
unconscious 465
Unification Church 59, 60,
    63, 214
United Kingdom
  decline of religion 75,
    232, 250, 257, 260,
    261, 280–4

United Kingdom (*cont'd*)
 future of religious
   participation and belief
   199, 279–91
 imperial secularization
   224
 personal experience of
   evangelicalism 24–38
 religious patterns 270
 secular education 253
 social movements 238,
   243
United States of America
 colonialism 7
 evangelicalism/
   fundamentalism 53,
   60, 61–3, 70
 Golden Rule Christians
   79
 melancholy 85
 religion 231, 260, 269,
   283, 284, 285, 287,
   288, 290, 389
 religion as social
   movement 202, 237,
   238–9, 240, 241,
   242
 religious and moral
   pluralism 297, 303
 role of African-American
   churches in developing
   urban communities
   207–8, 209,
   321–35
 sacralization 214–15
 secularization 208, 216,
   217, 220, 222, 224,
   250, 253, 257
 sociology 105–7,
   117–18
 spirituality and spiritual
   practice 307–19
 women and Catholicism
   75
universality of religion
   422, 425, 429
urbanization 259, 286
 see also city
USSR *see* Soviet Union
utopias 20, 21, 30, 85–7,
   90, 93–102

values 218, 219, 235, 236,
   406
 Europe 265–9
 of hedonism 48–51
 religion as diffusion of
   206, 292–305
 in sociology 434–6
 traditional 13, 48; *see
   also* moral order
 transmission in China
   374
van der Veer, P. 71
Varro 437
Vasquez, Manuel A. 62
Vatican II 26
Vattimo, Gianni 231
vicarious religion/
   spirituality 7, 271–3,
   276, 317, 446
Vico, Giambattista 304
Vietnam massacres 4
violence 19–20, 23, 33–6,
   38, 78, 366
Virgil, Pope 354
Virgil (Roman poet) 180,
   184, 185, 186
virtue
 preaching in modern
   society 388–403
 privatization 46
 religion as 436
Vision of Tundal, The 341,
   352–3
visions of hell 340–1,
   343–4, 346–7, 352–4,
   446
Voltaire 125, 212, 213,
   216, 372–3
voluntary organizations,
   churches as 271, 276

Wales, decline of religious
   participation 282
Wallace, Ruth 72–3
Wallis, Roy 61, 73
Walter, T. 73, 75
war 4
Warner, R.S. 79
Warner, Stephen 212
Watkins, Carl 353
Watson, James 374

Weber, Max 8, 14, 17, 18,
   26, 33, 36, 76, 107,
   120, 126, 161, 162,
   170, 172, 183, 201,
   216, 217, 220, 221,
   309, 324, 332, 333,
   349, 350, 351, 358,
   369, 382, 384n2,
   419, 438, 439, 441–2,
   446
 as classic 11, 15, 16,
   135, 136, 138, 145,
   146, 147, 149, 150,
   151, 153
Weinberg, N. 409
Weinstein, D. 115
Weinstein, M.A. 115
Weiss, R.S. 408
Wesley, John 26, 27, 43
West, Cornel 329
White March (Belgium
   1996) 412
Whitehead, Alfred North
   135, 136
Wicca 243
Williams, Preston 329
Williams, R.H. 241
Williams, S.J. 405
Wilson, Bryan 6, 7, 94, 96,
   154, 166, 213, 252,
   260, 270
Winter, M.T. 73–4
witchcraft 39
Wittgenstein, L. 86
Wolff, K.H. 108
women
 and Pentecostalism 7–8,
   52–66, 70
 religiosity 73–5, 80
 social control 341–3,
   344
 spiritualization of
   workplace 5, 11,
   78–80
Women Aglow movement
   70
women's movement,
   Pentecostalism as, in
   developing countries
   56
women's studies 67

Woodhead, Linda 11, 12, 13, 53, 60, 62, 68, 365
work
  moral texture 42, 43–6, 49, 163, 415
  spiritualization 5, 11, 78–80

world-system theory 421
Wuthnow, R. 79, 201, 204, 205, 213, 237, 464

X, Malcolm 4

Yang, C.K. 373
yi 376, 384

young men, social control 341, 343, 344
Youngblood, Johnnie Ray 331
Yugoslavia 224, 264–5

Zald, M.N. 234
Zimmerman, Michael 462